CONTRACT LAW

SIXTH EDITION

MINDY CHEN-WISHART

OXFORD

UNIVERSITY PRESS

OXFORD

UNIVERSITY PRESS

Great Clarendon Street, Oxford, OX2 6DP,
United Kingdom

Oxford University Press is a department of the University of Oxford.
It furthers the University's objective of excellence in research, scholarship,
and education by publishing worldwide. Oxford is a registered trade mark of
Oxford University Press in the UK and in certain other countries

Third edition 2010
Fourth edition 2012
Fifth edition 2015

Impression: 1

Published in the United States of America by Oxford University Press
198 Madison Avenue, New York, NY 10016, United States of America

British Library Cataloguing in Publication Data
Data available

Library of Congress Control Number: 2017959729

ISBN 978–0–19–880635–6

Printed in Great Britain by
Bell & Bain Ltd., Glasgow

To my parents, Peter and Jean Chen
Luodong—Taipei—Dunedin—Oxford

To my sons, James, Zachary, and Max—
You take my breath away.

PREFACE TO THE SIXTH EDITION

Students sometimes come to contract law with the preconception that it will be dry, rule-based, technical, and confusing, not to be understood but to be learnt by rote for the examination. I aim to counter any such impression by conveying the accessibility and practical importance of contract law, by provoking students to honest and critical engagement with the subject, and by imparting an appreciation of the interests, values, and concerns that must be balanced by the law and by the courts. Thus, this book seeks to:

- give a clear and accessible description of English contract law;
- give an overview of the interests, values, and concerns that arise in each area of contract law;
- encourage readers to critically assess the law; and
- assist readers to engage in the constructive process of law reform.

Over many years of teaching, I have evolved diagrams and tables to help explain concepts and give overviews to my students. I include some in this book. People learn in different ways; if these don't suit you, ignore them; the text can stand on its own. The law is updated to August 2017.

Other than general updating, the main new features of this edition includes are:

- A new Chapter 15 on Good faith.
- Chapter 3 on Enforceability: consideration, promissory estoppel, formalities discusses the significance of *MWB v Rock* (2016) on contract variations, including a new diagram. At the time of writing, the case has yet to be heard in the Supreme Court.
- Chapter 5 on Misrepresentation and non-disclosure has a new section on aggressive and misleading practices against consumers.
- Chapter 6 on Mistake includes a revised section on rectification and its relationship to interpretation of contract.
- Chapter 10 on Identifying and interpreting contractual terms includes:
  - a revised section on interpretation in the light of recent Supreme Court decisions in *Arnold v Britton* (2015), *Wood v Capita* (2017), and Lord Sumption's extrajudicial pronouncements; a new diagram here provides an overview;
  - a new trio of cases on *contra proferentem* construction;
  - a new decision of the Supreme Court on the relation between interpretation and implied terms (*Marks & Spencer Plc v BNP Paribas Securities Services Trust Co* (2016)); and
  - new decisions that illustrate the varying standards imposed by the law, depending on the nature of the contract, when a party exercises discretionary powers conferred by the contract (*Braganza v BP Shipping Ltd* (2015) and *Watson, Hersov and Moore v Watchfunder.co.uk Ltd* (2017)).

- Chapter 11 on Direct control over terms has been rewritten in the light of the enactment of the Consumer Rights Act 2015 and the changes made to the Unfair Contract Terms Act 1977.

- Chapters 12–14 now include a section on the remedies available to consumers in respect of their rights to reject, to price reduction and to repair or replacement, or repeat performance. In addition:

- Chapter 13 on Damages notes the contradictory answers given in respect of the measure of remoteness when concurrent liability in contract and tort (*Yapp v Foreign and Commonwealth Office* (2014) and *Wellesley Partners LLP v Withers LLP* (2015)); and

- Chapter 14 on Specific relief revises the law on agreed payments and forfeitures on breach on the light of the Supreme Court decision in *Cavendish Square v Makdessi*, and *Parkingeye Ltd v Beavis* (2015).

Additional Chapter 2 on Illegality, which is available in the online resources, is revised in the light of the Supreme Court decision in *Patel v Mirza* (2016).

Many people are owed thanks. My students past and present have taught me far more than I them. By asking the questions that prompt consideration and inquiry, and giving me repeated opportunities to explain the complexities and fascinations of contract law, they have deepened my understanding and provoked new lines of inquiry. I am extremely grateful to my colleagues at Oxford and elsewhere for stimulating discussions, to the OUP team for its expert handling of the production side, and for the dedicated, highly capable, and efficient research assistance of Victoria Dixon, who kept going with her DPhil, teaching, and assistance with this book right up until the late appearance of Sebastian, her first child. I also thank my sons for the insights that parenting them continues to give me into law-making, law-enforcement, and the doctrine of precedent ('because I am the Supreme Court and I said so!'). They have shown me the rough comparability of the roles of parent, teacher, and, by extension, perhaps also the state via contract law; that is, to enable those in its charge to live self-directed and worthwhile lives—be it as an artist, a physicist, or a musician cum quantum physics researcher. Thanks to James Chen-Wishart for the cover artwork.

Mindy Chen-Wishart
18 September 2017

Contract Law by Mindy Chen-Wishart is a resource rich in learning features. These pages will show you how to make the most of this textbook by illustrating each of the features used by the author to explain the key concepts of contract law.

In each chapter

Pause for reflection boxes

These boxes are ideally placed to help you stop, reflect on, and assess the law described. How the law works in practice, its consistency with other principles, its policy ramifications, possible alternatives, and other key issues are considered. References are given to related articles of interest to further your reading.

 Pause for reflection

The relevant factors point to concerns beyo representation distinction. They suggest th addressee's reasonable expectations induce the maker of the statement *should* fairly bea she has not actually agreed to bear it.

Counterpoint boxes

These boxes highlight criticisms of the law described and identify options for reform. Use these boxes to identify areas of controversy, problems with the current law, and possible alternatives.

 Counterpoint

The result in *Wales v Wadham* is objectiona only imply an honest reflection of the repre power of such statements to induce contra that they, like other statements of fact, hold

Diagrams

Overviews are given and key concepts are explained visually using clear and informative diagrams and tables. Read the relevant text in conjunction with each diagram for a clear explanation of even the most complex concepts.

Diagram 5A The remedial significance of classifying

MA Misrepresentation Act 1967		(3) Claimant's po	
		Damages	G
(1) Contract is made with the maker of statement. The statement	A term of the contract ↑ incorpo- ration ↓ s 1(a) MA	Expectation measure	Te

End of the chapter

Questions to consider

Use the exam-type questions to test your understanding of the topics covered. Hints on how to answer these questions appear on the online resources.

> **QUESTIONS**
>
> **1** How can you tell whether a pre-contra
> misrepresentation; or (c) a puff? Why doe
>
> **2** Explain (giving examples) the difference b
>   (a) damages for breach of contract;
>   (b) damages for misrepresentation; and

Further reading

Select titles from the further reading lists at the end of each chapter in order to broaden your knowledge of the individual topics covered.

> **KEY FURTHER READING**
>
> See generally Cartwright, J (2006), *Misrepre*
> Atiyah, P.S., and Treitel, G (1967), 'Misrepres
> Beale, H (1995), 'Damages in Lieu of Rescissi
> Brown, I, and Chandler, A (1992), 'Deceit, Da
>   s 2(1)', *LMCLQ* 40.

Outline Contents

TABLE OF CASES

TABLE OF STATUTES

Other Jurisdictions

France

Germany

India

New Zealand

United States of America

Abbreviations

Where the following authors' works are referred to, the relevant textbooks are:

P S Atiyah, *Introduction to the Law of Contract* (5th edn, Clarendon Press, 1995) ('Atiyah')
H Beale (ed), *Chitty on Contracts* (31st edn, Sweet & Maxwell, 2012) ('Chitty')
J Beatson, A Burrows, and J Cartwright, *Anson's Law of Contract* (29th edn, OUP, 2010) ('Anson's')
H Collins, *The Law of Contract* (4th edn, LexisNexis, UK, 2003) ('Collins')
E Peel, *Treitel on the Law of Contract* (13th edn, Sweet & Maxwell, 2011) ('Treitel')
C von Bar, H Beale, and others (eds), *Principles, Definitions and Model Rules of European Private Law—Draft Common Frame of Reference* (Sellier, 2009) ('European Draft Common Frame of Reference')
S M Waddams, *The Law of Contracts* (6th edn, Canada Law Books, 2010) ('Waddams')

PART I

Introduction

Making contracts is part of our everyday experience. We do it to buy, and sometimes to sell, all manner of goods, services, and digital products and we do so as part of our survival, our work or vocation, our recreation, our passion, and our thriving as human beings. Through contracting, we can determine the shape and direction of our lives. It is little wonder that contract is closely associated with the values of autonomy and welfare. Contract law supports the valuable activity of making contracts by conferring power on parties to create binding agreements enforceable in law. We can cooperate and do deals with our friends and family because we have trust in them and sanctions against them if they betray our trust. By filling the gap in trust and sanction in relation to strangers outside the inner circle of friends and family, contract law helps people to do things they could not otherwise do or do as easily; it is a form of state subsidisation. However, that subsidisation is not given in an unqualified way. Since contract is an activity that we engage in with others, the state must also regulate the basis on which we deal with others in order to preserve justice between parties, to differentiate trading from taking, and bargains from exploitation.

This chapter provides an introduction by putting contract law in a number of contexts that will give 'hinterland' to the doctrines that are recounted in the following chapters. It explores:

- the questions that may arise in the life cycle of a contract, from formation to performance or breach;
- the sources of contract law;
- the values reflected in contract law;
- the different theories about why contracts are enforced;
- the types of human interaction governed by contract law;
- the relationship between contract law and other branches of private law (ie governing the relationship between individuals); and
- how contract law fits in with European law, international commercial law, and human rights law.

1

Introduction

'What is contract law?'

1.1 **What is a contract?**

What is a 'contract' that contract law applies to? The common law offers no formal definition of a contract; textbooks generally define a contract as *an enforceable promise (or agreement)*.[1] We can derive three elements from this:

(i) **Promise**: the focus here is *one-sided*. The focus is on the *voluntariness* and *seriousness* of the undertaking given by the promisor.

(ii) **Agreement**: the focus here is *bilateral* or multi-lateral. We cannot make contracts by ourselves. It is something we do with others by reaching consensus as to our respective rights and liabilities.[2]

(iii) **Recognition by the law**: it is the *state* which provides the legal apparatus to enforce contracts; this enhances the reliability of voluntary exchanges and bridges any gap in trust and sanctions between parties by guaranteeing redress for breach, backed up by the coercive power of the state. While agreements would still be made without legal enforcement, parties would tend to regard each other with suspicion like participants of a hostage swap, and adopt a 'you first!' stance. They would have to devise alternative enforcement schemes (think of the Mafia) or bias exchanges towards those that take place instantly, with family or friends or towards persons with a reputation for keeping their promises. Thus, 'the supportive role of the law helps make contracts outside the framework of ongoing relations much more common',[3] and allows individuals to project their intentions into the future and plan actions that require concrete pre-commitments.

Moreover, whatever the parties intend, when disputes arise, it is ultimately contract *law* as applied by the courts that determines:

- whether, when and what the parties have agreed;
- whether one party can escape from the contract;
- how breach should be remedied; and
- what happens when the contract is silent or uncertain on a disputed matter.

1.2 **What is contract law?**

'Promises' or 'agreements' are not ' "things" that exist outside the law . . . [or] physical objects which can be perceived by the senses. They are themselves abstract concepts, just as much as the concept of contract itself' (Atiyah at 38). Yet, it is contract *law* as developed and applied by the courts that defines how the practice of making agreements should be conducted; how the contracting game should be played, eg the

---

[1] *Anson's* at 1 describes contract law 'as that branch of the law which determines the circumstances in which a promise shall be legally binding on the person making it'. Treitel at 1 states: 'a contract is an agreement giving rise to obligations which are enforced or recognised by law'. The US Second Restatement of Contracts states: 'a contract is a promise or a set of promises for the breach of which the law gives a remedy, or the performance of which the law in some way recognises as a duty'.

[2] However, deeds (see 3.3) are enforceable by beneficiaries even if they are ignorant of them when made; thus, agreement is unnecessary.

[3] J Raz, 'Promises in Morality and Law' (1981) *Harvard L Rev* 916, 934.

Diagram 1A What does contract law *do*?

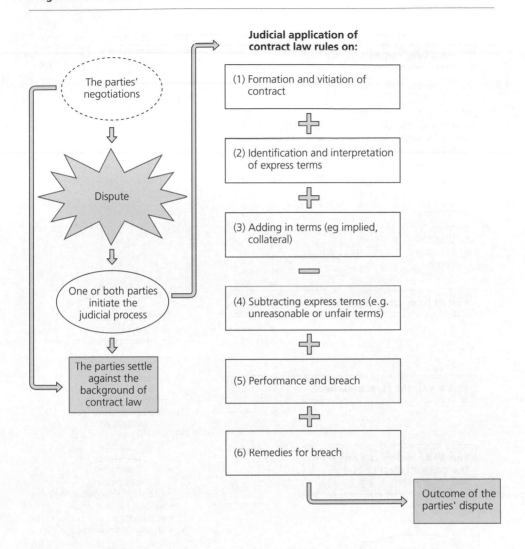

Judicial application of contract law rules on:

(1) Formation and vitiation of contract

(2) Identification and interpretation of express terms

(3) Adding in terms (eg implied, collateral)

(4) Subtracting express terms (e.g. unreasonable or unfair terms)

(5) Performance and breach

(6) Remedies for breach

Outcome of the parties' dispute

The parties' negotiations

Dispute

One or both parties initiate the judicial process

The parties settle against the background of contract law

law *deems* certain conduct, such as signing a document, as showing agreement to be bound by its contents, irrespective of the signer's knowledge, understanding, or intention in respect of it.

Diagram 1A shows that, although contract law rests on the foundation of the parties' voluntary assumption of obligations, that is only the starting point. The outcome of cases depends on the process of judicial application of contract law rules or on the parties' own bargaining in the shadow of the law.

1.2.1 **The questions which contract law addresses**

Diagram 1B gives an introductory overview of the questions addressed by contract law in the chronological sequence in which they arise in the life of the contract, and reflects the structure of this text. What follows is the briefest of overviews.

Diagram 1B Overview: legal questions arising in the life of a contract

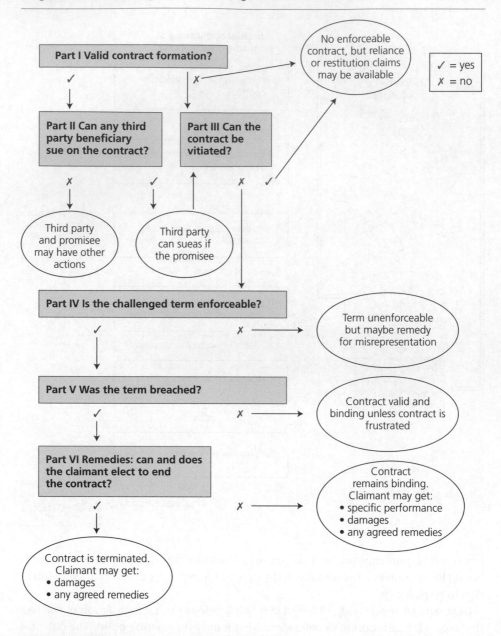

Part II of this text deals with contract formation: contract law determines the types of arrangements that will be recognised and supported *as contracts*. The court first looks for an **'agreement'** between the parties; contract law:

(i)   adopts an objective test of the parties' intentions;

(ii) adopts the mirror image approach to finding agreement: one party's offer must be mirrored by the other's acceptance;

(iii) requires sufficient certainty of agreement; and

(iv) presumes that commercial agreements have, but agreements made with family and friends do not have, the necessary 'intention to create legal relations'.

As well as agreement, a claimant must satisfy one of the following **tests of enforceability** to be able to sue on a promise:

(i) 'consideration': the claimant has given or promised something *in exchange* for the defendant's promise;

(ii) 'promissory estoppel': the claimant has relied on the defendant's promise and it is inequitable for the defendant to renege on it; or

(iii) 'formalities': the defendant's promise has complied with formalities requirements (eg has been signed and witnessed).

Part III deals with privity: *who* can *acquire rights* or *be subjected to liabilities* by a properly made contract (ie who can sue on or be sued under the contract)? The privity rule confines the legal impact of contracts to the contract parties. It seems right that contract parties should not be able to impose burdens on third parties. However, the traditional position that they cannot give third parties the right to enforce a contract made for their benefit is subject to a wide range of common law and statutory exceptions.

Part IV deals with **vitiation**: *when can a party be excused from (get out of) the contract?* Contract law contains *defeasibility rules* determining when arrangements that satisfy the requirements of contract formation will, nevertheless, not receive legal support. Namely, when there is: misrepresentation, mistake, frustration (ie radical change of circumstances), duress, undue influence, unconscionability, an improvident guarantee, incapacity, or illegality or contravention of public policy.

Part V deals with the **contents of the contract**: *what are each party's respective rights and liabilities under the contract?* Contract law breaks this question into smaller ones, namely:

(i) What are the express terms?

(ii) What do these terms mean?

(iii) Are there any implied terms or collateral terms that should be added?

(iv) Are any of the terms invalid and so should be subtracted?

(v) Is the whole contract unenforceable for being illegal or contrary to public policy?

Part VI deals with the **remedies for breach**; *when one party does not perform the contract, what can the law do?*

(i) If the parties have explicitly agreed on what should happen on breach, contract law decides whether the agreed remedies are enforceable.

(ii) If they are not or if the parties have not expressly agreed on the remedies, contract law provides a menu of default remedies to the aggrieved claimant who satisfies their requirements, so long as there is no double recovery:

• *termination*—the claimant may be allowed to discontinue her own contractual performance;

- *damages*—the claimant may be awarded a sum of money designed to put her in the position she would have been in had the contract been performed; and

- *actual performance*—the claimant may be able to compel the contract-breaker to perform the contract.

1.2.2 Sources of contract law

The sources of contract law are the common law and legislation. Legislation is readily understandable as statutes and regulations made by Parliament, but the expression 'common law' needs more explanation. Broadly, it means *judge-made law*, which has evolved from a pragmatic case-by-case analysis over time. Its line of reasoning is *inductive* (ie from the particular case to general principles, although courts are reluctant to give formal recognition to any overarching principles). It contrasts with the legal *codes* of European continental civilian systems of law, which adopt a *deductive* style of reasoning (applying general principles to specific cases). It can be said that common law is 'bottom up', while civil law is 'top down'. In 1965, the Law Commission of England, Wales and Scotland announced an ambitious plan to codify contract law. Eight years later, this was abandoned when many disagreements over substance proved irresolvable. The problem is that codes can be either too general (eg a rule that 'all agreements will be kept' is useless when applied to specific problems) or too specific (eg requiring all contracts to be evidenced by signed writing is apt to be inflexible and to give rise to many exceptions). As Waddams observes (at [5]):

> Human conduct is infinitely variable, and no codifier can foresee every problem that will arise, especially in an area covering so many different kinds of human interaction as contract law. The attempt to impose on a highly developed and developing common law system a code sufficiently specific to implement useful changes and yet not so specific as to set up inflexibilities and anomalies in unforeseen cases proves to be almost impossible.

The expression 'common law' *includes* but can also be used to *contrast* with **equity**. Before the late 19th century, there were two separate systems of courts: the courts of law ('common law courts'), and the courts of equity ('Chancery'). Every legal system must contain elements of certainty, predictability, and stability on the one hand, and elements of flexibility, fairness, and justice in the individual case, on the other. In English law, these competing sets of values were once institutionalised in these two separate systems of law. This separation remains important in understanding modern contract law. Law is fundamentally a reductionist system in that it selects what is considered relevant from the mass of facts of any particular dispute. In its original role of controlling the activation of proceedings in the (common law) courts, Chancery took increasing account of factors beyond those considered by the common law and so alleviated the rigidities of the common law. Moreover, someone dissatisfied with a result obtained from a court of law could appeal to the Chancellor, the king's deputy, for discretionary relief on the grounds of natural justice and fairness. Where the rules of common law and equity clash, equity prevails. It was said, disparagingly, of the early Chancery court, that 'justice varied according to the length of the Chancellor's foot'. But, just as elements of discretion crept into the common law, so, over time, rules grew up to govern the Chancellor's discretion, and equity itself became extremely rigid and inflexible.

Principles of fairness and good conscience have cut through the severity of some legal rules. Indeed, these rules may be utterly reversed by their equitable gloss. For example:

• it is irrelevant at common law that an agreement is harsh or unfair, but courts of equity can set aside *unconscionable bargains*; and

• an innocent misrepresentation inducing a contract attracts no relief at common law, but equity can set the contract aside.

The Judicature Act 1875 fused the two courts so that a *single court* now administers both common law and equity. However, this fusion of the courts did not result in a fusion of the laws; common law remedies were still tied to common law actions and equitable remedies to equitable actions. For example, even after fusion, no damages were available for non-fraudulent misrepresentation and statutory reform was needed to allow this (5.2.3 and 5.3). It seems anomalous for modern courts to restrict their own powers by reference to those of courts abolished over 100 years ago. Rather, modern courts should use the power inherited from *both* courts to develop appropriate and flexible responses to contractual problems.[4]

Legislation (or Parliament-made law) is the other source of contract law:

• Some statutes are codifying; they collect together and restate the common law (including equitable developments in a particular subject) (eg the Sale of Goods Act 1893).

• Other statutes are reforming; they remedy deficiencies in the common law.[5]

Reforming statutes free judges from adherence to previously decided cases ('precedents'), a self-imposed restriction which occasionally inhibits necessary judicial development in response to changing circumstances. Indeed, it is arguable that much legislation would be unnecessary if courts were more prepared to develop the law, rather than abdicate the task to the legislature. As Lord Wilberforce said:[6] 'The law on this topic is judge-made: it has been built up over the years from case to case. It is entirely within this House's duty, in the course of administering justice, to give the law a new direction in a particular case where, on principle and in reason, it appears right to do so. I cannot accept the suggestion that because a rule is long established only legislation can change it.' The danger of legislative reform is that it can stifle judicial development by hardening developing rules at an interim stage[7] or by curtailing judicial development in related areas.[8]

Judicial conservatism has necessitated legislation aimed at protecting certain vulnerable groups, such as consumers, employees, and tenants. Such legislation has broadly followed judicial leads and would have been unnecessary if judicial initiatives had

---

[4] See A S Burrows, 'We Do This at Common Law and That in Equity' (2002) 22 *OJLS* 1.

[5] Eg the Law Reform (Frustrated Contracts) Act 1943 (ch 7), Misrepresentation Act 1967 (ch 5), and Contracts (Rights of Third Parties) Act 1999 (ch 4).

[6] *Miliangos v George Frank (Textiles) Ltd* (1976) 443, 469.

[7] Eg Law Reform (Frustrated Contracts) Act 1943 on the calculation of restitution (7.6).

[8] Eg Contracts (Rights of Third Parties) Act 1999 on promisee actions (4.1.3).

been pushed further. Judicial conservatism is also evident in the tendency towards overly narrow interpretations of legislative innovations. Beatson argues persuasively that courts should treat legislative innovations as policy guidance on how to develop related areas of the law on rational and consistent lines.[9]

1.2.3 Understanding legal reasoning

Contract law is applied by the courts and courts have considerable latitude in determining the outcome of cases. At its most basic, legal rules take the following form:

Rule 1: $a + b + c = X$

Assuming:

Rule 2: $a + b + e = Z$

Rule 3: $a + b + f = Q$

Judicial latitude resides in:

(i)   determining the facts (whether a–f are present); and

(ii) selecting which rule to apply (1, 2, or 3); then

(iii) thereby determining the outcome (whether X, Y, Z, or Q).

For example, whether the parties have reached agreement is assessed *objectively*; it is for the *court* to say how a *reasonable* person would interpret the relevant conduct. A contract can be set aside when both parties enter it under a fundamentally mistaken assumption, but it is up to the *court* to decide whether:

• both parties were mistaken about a matter;

• the matter was of fundamental importance; and/or

• the mistake doctrine applies or a related doctrine such as misrepresentation (mistake induced by the other party's statement) or undue influence (mistake resulting from the claimant's unquestioning trust in or dependence on the other party).

The degree of *flexibility or indeterminacy* in the system is such that a range of fact-findings is possible and a range of rules can be applied without the courts being demonstrably 'wrong'.

Judicial discretion in the true sense is exercised when courts are required to apply broad standards such as reasonableness, eg courts once said that when circumstances change radically after the contract is made, they look for the parties' intention to decide whether the contract comes to an end. Absent express agreement, the courts ask what *reasonable* parties (not what the actual, perhaps unreasonable, parties) would have intended had they considered the matter. As Lord Radcliffe conceded in *Davis Contractors v Fareham UDC* (1956):

[I]t might seem that the parties have become so far disembodied spirits that their actual persons should be allowed to rest in peace. In their place there rises the figure of

---

[9] J Beatson, 'The Role of Statute in the Development of Common Law Doctrine' (2001) 117 *LQR* 247.

the fair and reasonable man. And the spokesman of the fair and reasonable man, who represents after all no more than the anthropomorphic conception of justice, is, and must be, the court itself.

Value judgments may, consciously or unconsciously and unavoidably, affect the particular facts found, the selection of applicable rules and the way in which discretionary standards are applied by the courts. Atiyah observes (at 58) that, although courts present themselves as reasoning *forwards* in resolving disputes (*from* the fact-findings and the relevant legal principles *to* the solution), they in fact often engage in *backward reasoning (from* the desirable solution *to* the selection of the most suitable legal principle and the finding of the necessary facts). Where courts reason backwards, the ostensible legal analysis merely *justifies*, rather than *explains*, the outcome.

This has led the *Critical Legal Studies* theorists (CLS)[10] to deny that the law is largely scientific and determinate: they point to the coexistence of contradictory norms (each principle can be countered by an opposing principle or numerous 'exceptions') and the imprecision of doctrines that fail to dictate a result, aside from the rare 'easy' case.[11] Mainstream theorists concede the latitude that courts have in 'hard' cases, but they regard the CLS view as exaggerated. Judges are not free to decide *whatever they like*; the answer does not vary according to the length of the Chancellor's foot or the contents of his breakfast. As Hart observes:[12] 'nothing can eliminate [the] duality of the core of certainty and a penumbra of doubt when we are engaged in bringing particular situations under general rules'. 'Hard' cases may often be decided either way and considerations of policy will often be determinative. However, to see legal questions as matters of pure policy, as if there were no authoritative legal context of judgments or statute, goes too far: it would destroy the essence of law and the point of legal education.

CLS theorists concede that legal outcomes *are* often predictable but only, they say, because the outcomes lean towards reinforcing the existing power structures (the 'legitimising thesis'). Whatever precise stance one takes on this, it is clear that law is not a value-free enterprise. Rules cannot be mechanically applied. Merely studying contract law *rules* does not tell us how they will be *applied* to particular disputes. To understand what is really going on, we must also appreciate the underlying and competing values which influence the courts' decision-making. This is the approach taken in this book.

1.3 **Values reflected in contract law**

The discussion here includes some details of substantive contract law rules. The purpose is just to give a sense of the direction of contract law, the issues in play, and the broader context within which contract law operates. You may wish to *reread this*

---

[10] See M Kelman, *A Guide to Critical Legal Studies* (Harvard University Press, 1987).

[11] J Feinman, 'Critical Approaches to Contract Law' [1983] *UCLA L Rev* 829; C Dalton, 'An Essay on the Deconstruction of Contract Doctrine' (1985) 94 *Yale LJ* 997, 1010–11.

[12] H L A Hart, *The Concept of Law* (3rd edn, OUP, 2012) 123.

section after studying the substantive law to help you to: pull together the strands; consider the big questions; and obtain a deeper understanding during revision.

Contract law reflects an uneasy mix of competing values or 'policies'. It supports the activity of contracting by making transactions legally enforceable to enhance individual freedom. At the same time, contract law places restraints on contracting behaviour, shapes the type of obligations that are created and limits the means by and extent to which parties may enforce their agreement. Thus, contract law both *facilitates* and *regulates* the practice of contracting. These functions of contract law can be understood by reference to the *classical* model of contract law (influential in the late 19th and early 20th centuries), which highlights the *facilitative* role of contract law, and the shift in emphasis as *modern* developments incorporate increasing elements of *regulation* into *neo-classical* contract law.

During the latter half of the 19th century, a concept of contract developed together with a body of legal doctrine which is now generally referred to as the '**classical law of contract**'. This was 'invented' in the sense that it was a synthesis and interpretation of case law into a coherent body of law by treatise writers such as Anson, whose *Law of Contract* (written for students) was first published in 1879. The major features of this classical model loomed large in the justificatory language (and reasoning) of the courts and were, paradoxically, reinforced by detractors who criticised them as unrealistic, unreflective of modern practices and stifling of desirable developments.[13] Classical contract law reflects the dominance of laissez-faire economic attitudes in the 19th century. Its assumption is that personal freedom and wealth creation go hand in hand. The corollaries of this emphasis on *freedom of contract* are that:

- the contract parties are sovereign: it is up to them to decide whether, when, and on what terms they wish to contract;

- the law should impose *minimal restrictions*: its primary function is simply to *give effect* to the parties' agreement;

- contract law rules should be *few, clear, consistent with commercial expectations* and apply to *all* contracts; and

- a contract should be *interpreted within its four corners*, without reference to the external context.

These ideals were reinforced by a particular *paradigm of contracting* in which:

- there is presumed *equality* between the parties (aside from infants, lunatics, and, for a time, married women);

- the contract is *negotiated, freely agreed*, and therefore *fair*;

- the contract is *discrete* in the sense that its boundaries are clear and performance more or less instantaneous (eg buying petrol or a coffee), and contract parties act only out of *self-interest* and adopt an *adversarial* stance.

While this 'story' did not hold absolute sway, in that it was minimally tempered by fairness and public policy (eg doctrines such as duress and the rules against penalties

---

[13] Eg M Horwitz, 'The Historical Foundations of Modern Contract Law' (1974) 87 *Harvard L Rev* 917; P S Atiyah, *The Rise and Fall of Freedom of Contract* (Clarendon Press, 1979); G Gilmore, *The Death of Contract* (Ohio State University Press, 1974).

and forfeitures could invalidate the whole contract or particular terms), it was the predominant model upon which cases were reasoned.

In very simplified terms, the story of modern or neo-classical contract law is characterised by a move away from these classical values towards doctrines and statutory provisions that *regulate* the practice of contracting in the interests of fairness and flexibility. The movement is masked because:

(i)   the classical law still casts a long shadow in the justificatory language of the courts. The doctrine of precedent means that courts tend to 'reinterpret' established legal concepts rather than abandon outmoded legal concepts or adopt new ones;

(ii)   particular types of contract that attract greater legal regulation (eg employment, tenancy, or consumer contracts) are usually ignored in discussions of the 'general' law of contract; and

(iii) the bulk of cases that actually reach the courts still mirrors those disputes that forged the classical model of contract law (ie large commercial disputes) and they, in turn, reinforce the rules derived from the classical model.

All of these paint a misleading picture of contract as a whole.

The following discussion gives a flavour of the values that must be integrated by contract law. It reveals the, albeit inconsistent and subtle, shift in the balance of values discernible in modern contract law. To assist understanding and exposition, the discussion is presented as pairs of competing ideas and methods of legal reasoning, broadly categorised as *classical* as opposed to *modern* (see **Diagram 1C**). However, contract law has never resided, and does not reside, only at one pole. Its complexity and interest result in large part from the simultaneous presence and interaction of *both* sets of values; the tension between the individualist and the interventionist strands

Diagram 1C Policy tensions shaping contract law

Values and emphasis identified with '**classical**' contract law: Freedom of contract.	Values and emphasis identified with '**modern**' contract law: Limits on freedom of contract.
1. Freedom and autonomy	**1. Limits on freedom and autonomy**
2. Minimal legal intervention	**2. Regulation and channelling of contracting**
3. Equality	**3. Responding to inequality**
4. Negotiated contracts	**4. Standard form contracts**
5. Assumed fairness of exchanges	**5. Unfairness of some exchanges**
6. Discrete contracts; self-interested individualism	**6. Relational contracts; cooperation, trust**
7. Literal interpretation	**7. Contextual interpretation**
8. Rules	**8. Discretionary standards**
9. General law	**9. Specialisation and differentiation**

is the constant theme of contract law; eg in 'The Ideologies of Contract Law' (1987) 7 *LS* 205, Adams and Brownsword argue that the rules and principles of contract law should be interpreted in the light of two 'ideologies'; 'Market-Individualism', which is aimed at facilitating competitive exchange, and 'Consumer-Welfarism', which leans towards consumer protection and principles of fairness and reasonableness. How the current law strikes the balance in different circumstances and why is the subject of contract law.

1.3.1 Freedom and limits on freedom

'Freedom of contract' demands that parties be free to choose whether, when, and to what they bind themselves via contracts. This enhances freedom by allowing individuals to achieve a wider range of desired outcomes through cooperation than by themselves, or only with their circle of friends and family. The idea that this freedom should not be restricted is characterised as 'negative' liberty. Even on this view, and paradoxically, some restrictions on freedom have long been recognised as necessary to *preserve* freedom. Thus, contract parties are protected from fraud, duress, and other conduct which inappropriately interferes with their exercise of choice. Courts also refuse to enforce agreements that permanently destroy freedom (eg contracts of slavery). But contract law does not support all free choices; it has always refused to enforce contracts that involve perceived gross immorality and criminality.[14] In addition, there is an increasing recognition that inequalities in resources, knowledge, and competence can result in oppressive or undesirable outcomes that should not be supported by the law. Thus, Collins (at 29) notes that choices to injure oneself, to sell one's property at gross undervalue, to enter into economic relations which give others oppressive power over major aspects of one's well-being and even to harm the environment, do not seem to be valuable choices which the law should support. Therefore, 'the law can tolerate a considerable range of economic transactions and give the benefit of the doubt to activities which seem of little worth to most people, but the law sets limits to freedom of contract when the choices made do not appear worthwhile on any reckoning'. On this view, the ability to make contracts is not unlimited but is a power to be exercised for *worthwhile* purposes. This is conceived as 'positive autonomy'. While the commitment to freedom means that the concept of 'positive autonomy' must have a large margin of tolerance, it nevertheless gives greater scope for legal regulation.

1.3.2 Minimal regulation of contracting

The classical model assigns contract law a non-interventionist role, confined to identifying and enforcing the parties' agreement. The argument runs that, once the rules of the contract 'game' (which should themselves be minimalist) have been observed, the courts should respect the outcome as the expression of the parties' exercise of freedom; if the procedure is fair, the outcome must logically be fair. Thus, contract law's legitimate sphere of control is traditionally confined to ensuring *procedural* fairness (in the negotiation process).

---

[14] See Additional Chapter 2 on illegality available on the online resources.

However, concern with *substantive* fairness (the outcomes of negotiation) may be justified in terms of ensuring a broadly acceptable 'pattern of welfare' in a liberal society; ready examples include minimum wage legislation and control of exorbitant interest rates in consumer credit contracts. While contract law adopts no systematic response to substantive unfairness, it has taken a piecemeal approach to trouble hotspots where the problem is serious and recurrent (eg in consumer or standard form contracts and with clauses which exclude liability or impose harsh remedies for breach). Moreover, procedural and substantive unfairness overlap: in setting the standard of fair *procedure*, the law is unavoidably influenced by the fairness of the *outcome* that is likely to result.

1.3.3 Equality and inequality

Classical contract law is strongly identified with the ideology of equality in the sense that it assumes that everyone is free to choose to enter any kind of transaction to improve her position in life. The corollary is that the distribution of wealth and power in society is said to depend upon one's merit (ie success in playing the contract game). This contrasts with traditional social orders which determine a person's welfare by reference to such factors as social status or rank, political power, religion, race, or physical force. This is the meaning of Sir Henry Maine's famous statement that 'the movement of the progressive societies has hitherto been a movement *from Status to Contract*'.[15]

The reality is that formal equality, in the sense of non-discrimination, does not guarantee substantive equality. Just because no one stops you using the Ritz Hotel does not mean that you can actually use it. *Initial* inequalities in the distribution of wealth, power, genetic inheritance, and luck will be reflected in the inequality of the *outcomes* of contracts. In this sense, the *same* treatment is not necessarily *equal* treatment, for there is no greater inequality than the equal treatment of unequals. Contract law has given increasing recognition to the need to protect weaker parties. But, since inequality of bargaining power is ubiquitous and a matter of degree, only the most vulnerable parties can be protected from the worst excesses of contractual exploitation.

1.3.4 Negotiated/standard form contracts

The classical paradigm of contract is the arm's-length individually *negotiated* exchange. But, the modern reality is the *standard form* contract, often online, pre-drafted by the stronger party to:

- maximise protection of its own interests;
- minimise its own liability to the other party; and
- avoid legal control.

The stronger party imposes its terms on a 'take-it-or-leave-it' basis, with such contracts attracting the label of 'adhesion contracts'. In combination with monopolies and cartels, there may be no meaningful freedom as to whom one contracts with and

---

[15] *Ancient Law, its Connection with the Early History of Society and its Relation to Modern Ideas* (John Murray, 1861; reprinted edn Tucson: University of Arizona Press, 1986) 141.

on what terms. A feature of the modern law is to restrict the advantages that can be obtained via standard form contracts, especially consumer contracts.

1.3.5 **Fairness of exchange**

Classical contract law emphasises the *subjectivity of values*; the idea is that since individuals value things differently, and we want people to be free to do this, it is impossible for courts to assess the fairness of exchanges. A contract freely entered into is fair by definition; courts should not second-guess the parties' preferences. Moreover, consistent with social Darwinism, the law should not protect parties from grossly unbalanced exchanges that result from foolishness and carelessness, lest it reduces their incentive to be more careful in future.

On the other hand, increasing recognition of contract parties' unequal bargaining power is coupled with the law's increasing, albeit piecemeal, legal control over the fairness of the exchange. While modern law tolerates considerable disparity of prices, it is increasingly sceptical of 'choices' that amount to extreme negative outcomes for one party.

1.3.6 **Discrete or relational contracts; self-interested individualism/ cooperation, trust, and altruism**

Where an exchange is practically simultaneous (eg buying groceries, petrol or a cup of coffee), parties rarely need the support of contract law. But legal support is necessary where parties enter non-simultaneous or deferred exchanges. Suppose that I commission you to paint a portrait of my father for his birthday:

• if I pay *in advance*, you may take the money and run, or demand a higher price once it is too late for me to obtain another in time; but

• if I only pay *on delivery*, you are vulnerable to my change of mind or my insistence on paying less since you cannot sell it elsewhere.

Contract law facilitates voluntary exchanges by ensuring the enforceability and security of the original deal.

The classical model of contracting pictures antagonistic individuals entering discrete transactions to further their self-interest. The emphasis is on *detachment,* self-interest, and the assertion of *rights* contained in the contract. In contrast, Macneil and others criticise this as unreflective of actual business practice, where more emphasis is given to the *relational* aspect of contracting,[16] in the sense that:

(i) *all* contracts must be interpreted in the context or 'social matrix' in which they are made; and

(ii) many contracts involve long-term or continuing relationships (eg employment and construction contracts, leases, franchises, and commercial agreements for the supply of goods or services over time) which affect the way they should be interpreted.

---

[16] I Macneil, 'Contracts: Adjustments of Long-Term Economic Relations under Classical, Neoclassical and Relational Contract Law' (1978) 72 *NWU L Rev* 854.

The longer the duration of the contract, the less likely it is that the parties can plan for future contingencies. Rather, they rely on *relational norms* to fill any gaps in their contract. These are characterised by cooperation, trust, flexibility, altruism, and a willingness to make adjustments in response to changing circumstances. This contrasts with the classical ideal that *all* the answers to contractual problems can and should be resolved by reference to the parties' intention *at formation*, as expressed in their contract. Relationalists argue that contract law should recognise or impose certain duties of cooperation or good faith which are implicit in the particular contractual relationship.

1.3.7 Literal or contextual meaning

Classical contract law focuses on the parties' intentions *as embodied in the contract*. Barring exceptional circumstances, factors external to the four corners of the contract are irrelevant (this is the 'parol evidence rule'). The apparent advantages of this approach are: increasing certainty and predictability; preventing courts from injecting moral or political values into contractual interpretation; and encouraging contract parties to spell out what should happen in future contingencies.

However, absolute certainty is unachievable; not every contingency is foreseeable. Predictability and fidelity to the parties' intentions are also undermined if courts ignore the social context that gives contractual behaviour meaning and purpose. Modern contract law has taken increasing account of the context in which the contract was made as well as considerations of fairness, for example, when interpreting what contracts mean, gap-filling by implying terms into contracts, and minimising or negating the impact of express terms that contradict the reasonable expectations of the parties.

1.3.8 Rules and discretionary standards

Classical contract law is identified with a preference for clear and certain rules rather than broad and uncertain discretionary standards:

- Rules ostensibly narrow the judicial inquiry by predetermining what is permissible and what is impermissible, leaving courts to determine factual issues on a finite set of questions.
- In contrast, standards leave both the specification of what is permissible and the determination of the facts to the court.

In practice, there is *no bright line* between rules and standards. The supposed gap between them is reduced by the judicial tendency to make standards more certain (more rule-like, by developing subsidiary principles) and as courts exercise more discretion in their interpretation and selection of rules. Rules that require judges to decide in a particular way on the basis of 'triggering facts', regardless of the context or equity of the case, are likely to lead to *backward reasoning*. Qualitative standards, such as reasonableness, fairness, good faith and unconscionability, and structured discretions play an increasing role in modern contract law.

1.3.9 **One law or many laws of contract**

Classical contract law was developed in an era when most litigation involved commercial transactions. This common fact situation nurtured the idea of a *unified* (and so more certain) law of contract applicable to *all* contracts, irrespective of their context, subject matter, or the nature of the parties. However, such a law was ill-suited to the fair and flexible resolution of non-commercial contractual disputes. The injection of broad standards into contract law opens the way for different types of contracts to be treated differently. Legislation embodies the most significant innovations of modern contract law by hiving off certain types of contracts for specialist treatment (eg consumers and traders, employees and employers, landlords and tenants). These specialist regimes shatter the unity of the law of contract. Their emphasis on avoiding domination and unfairness and encouraging cooperation 'demand a reconsideration of the fundamental assumptions of the classical model' (Collins at 38).

1.3.10 **Conclusion on the values reflected in contract law**

The story of the evolution of contract law is by no means straightforward. Although the tensions are presented as *rival clusters* of values, current contract law does not coalesce clearly around one cluster. There is much academic debate about whether contract law does or should facilitate individual *freedom* or defer to broad principles of *fairness*. However, it is misleading to highlight one at the expense of the other. Indeed, debating which side 'wins' or should do is a somewhat futile exercise. Individualist and interventionist principles must share the stage. Contract law is an evolving *integration* of ideals which is informed by, and which in turn informs, social views about contract's role in society.

1.4 **Why are contracts enforced?**

Why does the law recognise some agreements as legally binding but not others? Theories of contract law provide answers by explaining the basis of contractual obligations and, by implication, the main features of contract law. Thus, all contract theories are both *descriptive* and *normative*; they tell us what the law is and what it should be. There is an obvious overlap with the contract *values* or policies just discussed, but contract *theories* exist at a higher level of generality. A contract theory purports to give the 'big picture': it generates relatively open-ended propositions that do not necessarily dictate specific detailed *rules* or how such rules are *applied* in particular situations. Moreover, the detailed rules are often compatible with many different theories because ideally each theory offers a different explanation for them. A theory can 'run out' of predictive power at the level of practice where specific policies may prove more illuminating.

The limited aim of this section is to give a taste of the *range* of explanations for contractual obligations and to begin the task of evaluating them. Interested readers are directed to writings on each main theory and synthesis of different contract theories.[17] (See also **Diagram 1D**.)

---

[17] See S Smith, *Contract Theory* (Clarendon Press, 2004) for further sources.

Diagram 1D Contract theories: why enforce contracts?

1.4.1 Promissory and will theories	*'You should keep your promise.'* *'We agreed.'*
1.4.2 Reliance theory	*'You induced another to rely on your undertaking to his detriment.'*
1.4.3 Efficiency theory (wealth maximisation)	*'Everyone is better off if you keep your bargain.'*
1.4.4 Promoting distributive justice	*'Contract law does or should further wealth distribution.'*
1.4.5 Transfer theory	*'Your promised performance is my property.'*
1.4.6 Positive autonomy	*'Contract law does or should support worthwhile choices.'*
1.4.7 Mixed theories	*'Contracts are enforced for a variety of reasons including all of the above.'*

1.4.1 **Promise-keeping and will theories**

Broadly speaking, promissory and will theories explain contractual liability in terms of respect for *voluntarily* assumed obligations and the corresponding voluntarily created rights. Such *self-imposed* obligations are often contrasted with obligations (eg in tort or unjust enrichment) which are externally *imposed by the law*. Fried[18] famously relies on the morality *of promise-keeping to* explain contractual liability. The promisor creates a moral obligation by purposefully invoking 'the convention of promising' (ie conducting herself in a way that is generally understood as making a promise). Enforcement of such promises enables promisors to 'determine their own values'; 'If we declined to take seriously the assumption of an obligation . . . to that extent we do not take [the promisor] seriously as a person'.

On one level, the promissory and will theories **can explain** much of contract law, eg:

(i) They are consistent with the justificatory language of the law (the concepts and reasoning used by courts).

(ii) They explain who is affected by the contract. In general, a contract only generates *personal* rights and liabilities in the contracting parties and not third parties.

(iii) They explain when the parties become bound. Liability attaches from contract formation, even if the claimant has not yet relied on it and would suffer no harm if the contract were not enforced.

(iv) They explain why statements of fact ('this car runs well') or of intention ('I will fix your car') generate no contractual liability, while promises do ('I promise this car runs well'; 'I promise to fix your car').

---

[18] C Fried, *Contract as Promise: The Theory of Contractual Obligation* (Harvard University Press, 1981).

(v) They explain why the contents of the contract depend, at least in the first instance, on what the parties have expressly agreed.

(vi) They explain doctrines such as mistake, misrepresentation and duress in terms of a defect in one or both parties' consent to the contract.

(vii) They explain why courts can compel the performance of the contract.

On the other hand, promissory and will theories attract some **criticisms**, eg:

(i) They are inconsistent with the objective test of intention, which enforces promises that parties *appear* to have assumed rather than those that they have *actually* assumed.

(ii) They cannot explain why the promisee should benefit. Even if the promisor should keep her promise as a matter of self-consistency, they do not explain why the promisee is owed the *right* to sue for it as a matter of justice. The law could respond in other ways (eg by fining the promise-breaker). To enforce a promise is essentially to compel the promisor *to benefit* the promisee. Fuller and Perdue famously observed that expectation damages for breach of contract represent a 'queer kind of compensation' since they give the promisee something she never had.[19] As such, they seem to contradict the foundational principle of modern liberalism, the 'harm principle', according to which the state should only interfere with individual liberty to *prevent harm* to another; mere disappointment is not enough.

(iii) They cannot explain the requirement of consideration, ie why, in general, a party must give something in exchange for the promise to be entitled to enforce it.

(iv) They have difficulty explaining legal control of the contents of contracts. Contract law may render certain unfair terms or even entire contracts unenforceable, or may imply terms into contracts. These may owe more to conformity with an ideal of minimum justice in particular contracts than to the search for the parties' unexpressed intentions.

(v) They cannot explain why many rules on remedies do not reflect the morality of promise-keeping, eg breach is not punished, there is a distinct reluctance to compel performance, and various doctrines reduce the amount of damages payable on breach so that the claimant is not actually put in the position she would have been in had the contract been performed.

1.4.2 Reliance theory

The essence of the reliance theory[20] is that contractual liability arises (and should arise) where:

- *A* makes a *promise* to *B*, and
- *B* suffers loss by *relying* on it.

---

[19] L Fuller and W Perdue, 'The Reliance Interest in Contract Damages' (1936) 46 *Yale LJ* 52, 53.
[20] See P S Atiyah, *The Rise and Fall of the Freedom of Contract* (Clarendon Press, 1979); G Gilmore, *The Death of Contract* (Ohio State University Press, 1974); L Fuller and W Perdue 'The Reliance Interest in Contract Damages' (1936) 46 *Yale LJ* 52, 53.

Accordingly, contractual obligations are primarily aimed at ensuring that people are not made worse off by relying on others' reliance-inducing conduct. These are obligations *imposed by law* because of what people *do* and not because of what they *intend*. Accordingly, Atiyah argues that contracts are enforced as *admissions* of pre-existing obligations arising from reliance suffered or benefits conferred. Since contract law's primary aim is to negate the harm caused by induced reliance, much of it belongs in the law of tort and unjust enrichment, supplemented by principles of justice and public policy; contract is only treated as a distinct category for historical and pragmatic reasons.

Reliance theories have a number of **attractions**:

(i) Moral justification: reliance theories are consistent with the 'harm principle'; the state only interferes with individual liberty (by imposing obligations) to prevent harm to others. In their famous article, 'The Reliance Interest in Contract Damages' (1936) 46 *Yale LJ* 52, Fuller and Perdue compare the relative merits of a contract party's restitution, reliance, and expectation interests:

- the restitution interest has the strongest claim to protection because, where *A* causes *B* to lose one unit (–1) which is transferred to *A* (+1), there are two units of injustice to be remedied. On the Aristotelian ideal of *corrective justice*, aimed at maintaining the equilibrium among members of society, *B*'s restitution interest is twice as strong as her

- reliance interest (ie –1 without any corresponding enrichment to *A*, although reliance can also incorporate unjust enrichment where *B*'s –1 results in *A*'s +1),

- in turn, *B*'s reliance interest is stronger than her expectation interest; where *B*'s material position is unchanged (0), non-fulfilment of *B*'s expectation simply leaves her no 'worse off'.

Fuller and Perdue argue that fulfilling expectations passes from the realm of corrective justice to the realm of distributive justice; the law is not just responding to a disturbed status quo but bringing about a new situation.

(ii) Explain the objective test of intentions: the protection of reliance readily explains why courts are not concerned with what a contracting party *really* (actually or subjectively) intends, but with what a reasonable person would understand her conduct as intending. A party who acts as if she intends to contract when she actually does not is liable because she thereby induces the other party to rely on her apparent intention.

(iii) Explain restraints on unfair conduct: a reliance-based duty is broadly a *duty to take reasonable care of the interests of others*. This can explain the concept of good faith inherent in a number of contractual doctrines such as unconscionability, undue influence, misrepresentation, and promissory estoppel.

On the other hand, reliance theories are open to **criticisms**:

(i) Reliance is not of the essence of liability: since people also rely on statements, the reliance theory does not explain why a *promise* is necessary for contractual liability. The rationalisation that only reliance on a promise is worthy of protection free-rides on the voluntariness rationale, ie your reliance is not my problem, *unless* I have given a voluntary undertaking; but then the voluntary undertaking becomes the true source of my obligation.

(ii) Does not explain when obligations arise: contractual liability does not depend on reliance; it arises when an exchange is agreed *before* any acts of reliance on the contract. The exchange element ('consideration') can be met by simply *promising* to do something; the promisor need not *actually* have done it.

(iii) Failure in explaining remedies: the logical remedy for reliance-based obligations is to negate the loss suffered from relying. However, the remedies for breach of contract are expectation based. They go 'forwards' and not 'backwards'.

(iv) Judicial language: protecting reliance is not what judges say they are doing.

1.4.3 **Welfare maximisation**

Welfare maximisation theorists see contract law merely as the *means* to the proper *end* of maximising total welfare (alternatively 'happiness', 'utility', or 'efficiency'). Welfare is broadly defined as encompassing 'everything that an individual might value—goods and services that the individual can consume, social and environmental amenities, personally held notions of fulfilment, sympathetic feelings for others, and so forth'.[21] Contract law is said to promote wealth maximisation by giving parties the incentive to act efficiently and the disincentive to act inefficiently. Something is efficient if its *benefits* outweigh its *costs*. Since efficiency theories deploy economic analyses to defend their claims, they are also called 'economic' theories of contract law.

The core assumption is that voluntary exchanges in free markets should be supported because, by pursuing self-interest, people make themselves and, by extension, society in general better off. As 'rational maximisers' of their own welfare, parties will only give up resources in return for something they regard as more valuable. I will only offer you £10 for your book if I value the book more than the £10; your acceptance shows that you value the £10 over your book. Such exchanges tend to move resources to those who value them the most, and both parties are 'better off'.

The welfare maximisation or efficiency theory has a number of apparent **attractions**:

(i) Value neutrality: it offers a theory that claims to be largely objective, determinant, and divorced from politics. Efficiency theories are preferred by those who are fearful that law may be used to destroy autonomy and individuality.

(ii) Explains the value of voluntariness: only if exchanges are voluntary will resources move to higher value users.

(iii) Explains the consideration doctrine: in general, exchanges generate greater efficiency than gratuitous promises.

(iv) Explains vitiating factors: doctrines such as duress, misrepresentation, and mistake are explicable not only in terms of ensuring the voluntariness of consent, but also in terms of countering *market imperfections* such as imbalances of information which lead to inefficient outcomes.

---

[21] L Kaplow and S Shavell, 'Fairness v Welfare' (2001) 114 *Harvard L Rev* 961, 980.

(v) Explains the legal control of the contents of contracts: contract law implies terms and fills the gaps in the parties' agreements. This enhances efficiency by releasing parties from the time, cost, and practical impossibility of making a 'complete' contract to govern every eventuality. Furthermore, the *contents* of the gap-fillers are claimed to be efficient because they: express the parties' genuine but unexpressed intentions; mimic what parties would have agreed had they bargained over the matter with perfect information and without transaction costs; or put the risk of what has happened on the 'superior risk avoider' or the 'superior risk bearer'.

(vi) Explains remedies: one of the great strengths of the economic theory is its explanation of why specific performance is so rarely ordered. The theory of *efficient breach* says that it may be more efficient for parties not to perform the contract, but to breach it; eg where a third party would pay you more for your performance than I am contracted to do, it may maximise overall wealth to breach and perform for the third party, and pay damages to me so that I am left no worse off. Thus: deliberate breach is not punished; courts rarely compel performance, but instead award money as the primary response to breach; the measure of compensation is the value of the promised performance (this gives the promisor the incentive to perform unless breach is more profitable); and specific performance is only awarded if I cannot get performance elsewhere because it is unique.

Efficiency theories are open to trenchant **criticisms**:

(i) Difficulties in calculation: one commentator observes:[22]

> any serious pursuit of efficiency . . . will often require complex rules. After all, the goals and constraints relevant to a given policy are likely to be numerous, and the legal rules, in order to be efficient, must take account of, and be tailored to, each of them. Accomplishing this may necessitate a system of multi-factored rules, complex defences, complex party structures, sequential burden shifting, and so on.

Eric Posner famously (because his father, Richard Posner, is *the* father of law and economics, see Wikipedia) observes that:[23]

> Economics fails to explain contract law . . . And economics provides little normative guidance for reforming contract law. Models that have been proposed in the literature either focus on fine aspects of contractual behaviour or make optimal doctrine a function of variables that cannot realistically be observed, measured, or estimated. The models do give a sense of the factors that are at stake when the decisionmaker formulates doctrine, and might give that decisionmaker a sense of the trade-offs involved, but in the absence of information about the magnitude of these trade-offs—and the literature gives no sense of these magnitudes—the decisionmaker is left with little guidance.

---

[22] P Schuck, 'Legal Complexity: Some Causes, Consequences, and Cures' (1992) 42 *Duke LJ* 1, 37.
[23] E Posner, 'Economic Analysis of Contract Law after Three Decades: Success or Failure?' (2003) 112 *Yale LJ* 829, 880.

(ii) The 'efficient breach' theory is questionable:

- The cost of negotiating around the breach and of reselling the contractual subject matter to third parties is often ignored. As Macneil observes:[24]

  the whole thrust of the [efficient breach] analysis is breach first, talk afterwards . . . despite the fact that 'talking after a breach' may be one of the most expensive forms of conversation to be found, involving, as it so often does, engaging high-priced lawyers, and gambits like starting litigation, engaging in discovery, and even trying and appealing cases . . . [these are] uncooperative and—ironically enough—highly inefficient human behaviour.

- Specific performance is arguably the more efficient remedy since it avoids the costs of often difficult and uncertain calculations of damages.

- Even if specific performance were widely available, wasteful performance would not happen. *Rational parties would negotiate around the remedy* so that they share the profits (or savings) from breach rather than allow the contract-breaker total retention.

- Even if we can identify all the relevant factors in the efficiency equation, it is impossible to attach accurate figures to them.

(iii) Unrealistic assumptions: Efficiency theories are too simplistic in assuming, eg that parties act rationally with the single motivation of maximising their welfare, *measured by willingness to pay*. This ignores the complexities of human psychology, the irrational aspects of human behaviour and conduct which expresses preferences unrelated to wealth (broadly conceived) such as altruism, relational commitment, and integrity.

(iv) Moral objections:

- By accepting the starting point of pre-existing wealth distribution and measuring efficiency by reference to willingness to pay, critics argue that *such theory favours the rich*, eg it assumes that welfare is maximised by allocating a pair of shoes to someone willing to pay £100 for those shoes although she has thousands of other pairs, rather than to the poor person without shoes who can only pay £20.

- Efficiency theories do not take individual rights seriously,[25] eg they rest on the morally repugnant idea that one is free to take another's right (ie breach a legal duty) so long as one is willing to pay the 'price' for it.

- By refusing to engage with questions of whether preferences are good or bad in terms of the welfare of individuals and of society in general, and whether some ordering or hierarchy of an individual's preferences is possible or desirable, efficiency theories simply suppress the inescapable balancing between individual freedom, individual welfare, and the interests of society.

(v) Lack of transparency: judges rarely explain what they are doing in terms of promoting overall efficiency.

---

[24] I Macneil, 'Efficient Breach of Contract: Circles in the Sky' (1982) 68 *Virginia L Rev* 947, 968–9.
[25] R Dworkin, *Taking Rights Seriously* (Harvard University Press, 1978) 184–205.

1.4.4 **Promoting distributive justice**

Kronman argues[26] that 'distributive justice not only *ought* to be taken into account in designing rules for exchange, but *must* be taken into account if the law of contracts is to have even minimum moral acceptability'. In his view, contracting cannot be understood except as a distributional concept. The notion of individual autonomy, taken by itself, provides no guidance on which of the many forms of advantage-taking in exchange relations should be permitted. While it is generally thought that taxation and welfare are the primary tools for wealth distribution in a liberal society, contract law should also be used when alternatives may be more costly or intrusive.

This explanation of contract law has some **advantages**:

(i) Moral attractiveness: it places a robust emphasis on equality in liberal democratic societies in its concern with the distribution of resources and opportunities, if not equally, then at the level of some irreducible minimum.[27]

(ii) Explains vitiating factors such as misrepresentation and duress as legal restraints on the exercise of power, rather than the absence of 'real' consent.

(iii) Explains legal controls on substantive unfairness, such as implied terms, the invalidity of certain unfair terms, and the doctrine of unconscionable bargains.

However, a distributive theory of contract encounters enormous **criticisms**, eg:

(i) Contract law is a poor tool for distributing wealth. Indeed, contracting is a major *cause* of distributional inequalities.

(ii) Distributive contract law rules (eg increasing quality or reducing the price of goods or services) can be neutralised by the parties changing other contract terms (ie increasing price or reducing quality). Strongly distributive contract rules may make parties more reluctant to contract with the protected group.

1.4.5 **Transfer theory**

On this theory, contracts are like property.[28] The ability to *create* property rights (to obtain the exclusive use and possession of a *thing*) and to *transfer* property rights is a necessary precondition of individual autonomy. A contract right is the present ownership of the right to the promisor's future performance; it entails the right to *exclusive* possession of the goods or services promised and is proprietary in character. The wrong of breach of contract consists of depriving the promisee of the thing promised, including its value and use.

---

[26] A Kronman, 'Contract Law and Distributive Justice' (1980) 89 *Yale LJ* 472.

[27] J Rawls, *A Theory of Justice* (Belknap Press of Harvard University Press, 1971); R Dworkin, *Law's Empire* (Belknap Press of Harvard University Press, 1986).

[28] For a summary of this debate, see P Lee, 'Inducing Breach of Contract, Conversion and Contract as Property' (2009) 29 *OJLS* 511, 513–20. See also *OBG v Allan* [2007] UKHL 21, [2008] 1 AC 1, [309] (Baroness Hale). For criticism of this view, see eg A Goymour, 'Conversion of Contractual Rights' (2011) *LMCLQ* 67, 68–9.

This theory is **consistent with**:

(i)   the importance of voluntariness in contracting;

(ii) the 'harm principle', because breach is not just failure to benefit, but is interference with what already belongs to, the promisee; and

(iii) the remedies of specific performance and the expectation measure of damages.

The main **objections** are:

(i) Timing: contractual rights are transferred at formation prior to any later performance, while there is normally no such time lapse between the transfer of property ownership and performance. Benson replies that:[29] ' . . . most legal systems allow for ownership without physical possession, there can be no objection to contracts transferring ownership without transferring possession. The important issue in both contract and property is consent';

(ii) Contract rights are personal: they do not give the promisee rights of a proprietary character. Unlike property rights, contract rights confer no priority on the right-holder on the other's bankruptcy; she can only share in what is left along with the other creditors. Douglas argues that the label of property is not useful in determining the extent of legal protection that contractual rights should receive.[30] Instead, it is better to examine the specific characteristics of contractual rights to see whether they can fit within the framework of protection established for the core examples of property, such as physical objects. He concludes that they cannot.

1.4.6 **Positive autonomy**

Raz[31] sees the role of the state as *not* to hold people to their promises (which is mere legal moralism), but to create the conditions of 'positive autonomy': 'it is the goal of all political action to enable individuals to pursue valid conceptions of the good and to discourage evil or empty ones'. Hence, 'the autonomy principle . . . permits and even requires government [ie law] to create and support morally valuable opportunities, and to eliminate or discourage repugnant ones'. To support contract-making is to support people in making *worthwhile (positive) choices*. It facilitates special relationships with others; special, because contract provides a reason for one party to treat the other's interests as superior to all others' interests in relation to the contract's subject matter. This is distinct from freedom of contract in the *negative* sense of freedom *from* coercion or intervention which does not guarantee the exercise of *positive* autonomy.

Raz[32] regards the purpose of contract law as that of protecting 'both the practice of undertaking voluntary obligations and the individuals who rely on the practice'.

---

[29] P Benson, 'Abstract Right and the Possibility of a Nondistributive Conception of Contract: Hegel and Contemporary Contract Theory' (1989) 10 *Cardozo L Rev* 1077.

[30] S Douglas, 'The Scope of Conversion: Property and Contract' (2011) 74 *MLR* 329, 335–7.

[31] J Raz, *The Morality of Freedom* (OUP, 1986) 369; R Brownsword, 'Liberalism in the Law of Contract' (1988) 36 *Archives for Philosophy of Law and Social Philosophy* 86; S Smith 'Future Freedom and Freedom of Contract' (1996) 59 *MLR* 167.

[32] J Raz, 'Promises in Morality and Law' (1982) 95 *Harvard L Rev* 916.

Its role is *supportive* rather than initiating: it reinforces existing norms and practices, thereby increasing confidence in them and extending their use ('But for the support of the law, contracts between complete strangers would not be as numerous and common as they are').

Collins' transformation thesis takes this further, arguing that contract law does and should regulate the practice of contracting to ensure conformity with three ideals of social justice:

- the avoidance of unjustifiable domination;
- ensuring the substantive fairness of the exchange; and
- fostering cooperation.

This theory has the following main **attractions**:

(i) Consistency with the harm principle: unlike reliance theories which focus solely on harm to the *individual,* the relevant harm in question here includes *institutional* harm, ie preventing erosion in or debasement of the practice of contract.

(ii) Explains the objective test of intentions: people are prevented from abusing the *practice* of contracting by making it appear that they have agreed to obligations when they have not.

(iii) Consistency with contextual interpretation: it explains why courts do and should refer to the *social norms* which inform the practice of contracting when interpreting contracts, gap-filling incomplete contracts and formulating default rules.

(iv) Explains the vitiating factors: contracts resulting from duress, misrepresentation, undue influence, unconscionability, or fundamental mistake are not the sort of exercises of positive (worthwhile) autonomy that should be supported by the law. To enforce them would debase the practice of contracting.

On this view, the practice of contracting is a collective good that requires steering, channelling, and supplementation. Whilst the positive autonomy theory accords considerable respect to the parties' self-regulation, it also makes room for the law's role in regulating contractual practices with a view to *controlling the types of relationships established through contract and the distributive consequences.*

1.4.7 **Mixed theories**

Contract theorists do not generally claim total explanatory power for their favoured theory. Given the complexities and competing norms in contract law, they are prepared to concede some limited role to values highlighted by other theories, although not at the level of justifying first principles. The alternative is to say that no single theory can explain all of contract law but that *each contributes vital insights into the nature and basis of contract law.*[33] On this view, contract law does not need to fit

---

[33] See R Hillman, *The Richness of Contract Law: An Analysis and Critique of Contemporary Theories of Contract Law* (Kluwer, 1998); S M Waddams, *Dimensions of Private Law: Categories and Concepts in Anglo-American Legal Reasoning* (Cambridge University Press, 2003).

neatly or even largely into any slot. It recognises that contract law includes apparent contradictions, is subject to competing norms and various exceptions, and is fragmented by special rules applying to distinct kinds of contracts. This being so, contract law reflects the legal system's practical compromises over a multiplicity of methods, values, and goals. This should be unsurprising; it would be unrealistic to expect one unified theory to explain every aspect of a body of law which has evolved over hundreds of years in the hands of many individuals. We should be wary of theory's potential for excessive abstraction, reductionism, and oversimplification, however elegant.

The main **criticism** of a mixed theory view is that it is a largely ad hoc and unstable mix which is anti-theoretical.[34] One response is the 'vertical integration strategy' put forward by Kraus,[35] according to which different theories have a different role to play within one overall theory. Thus, he argues that while autonomy theories are normatively *foundational*, they are fundamentally vague, essentially contestable, and not sufficiently fine-grained to determine the many issues that fall within the grey area. They lack the resources to translate the value of autonomy into concrete analysis. Other theories, especially the efficiency theory, might then provide an *operational*, but subordinate, principle; useful for providing practical answers for questions raised in actual situations.

1.5 How far does contract law *reach*?

Three factors *limit* the impact of contract law:

(i)   contract law's reluctance to intervene in family or social arrangements;

(ii) specialist regimes that have replaced general contract law in many important areas; and

(iii) empirical studies which indicate the limited relevance of contract law in 'real' life.

1.5.1 Family and social arrangements

Contract law is largely concerned with *economic* exchange taking place in the *market* (eg buying and selling, leasing and hiring, employment and services, money-lending and borrowing). It is reluctant to get involved in *non-market* transactions which take place in a *family* or *social* context (eg 'You cook and I'll wash up', 'I will pay for your rent, car, or education'). This reluctance is expressed in the strong presumption that, even if all the other requirements of an enforceable contract are satisfied, there is no 'intention to create legal relations' in such agreements (2.7).

---

[34] J Feinman, 'The Significance of Contract Theory' (1990) 58 *U Cin L Rev* 1283.
[35] J S Kraus, 'Reconciling Autonomy and Efficiency in Contract Law: The Vertical Integration Strategy' (2001) 11 *Philosophical Issues* 420.

Pause for reflection

The question is how far the *state* should intervene in the private activities of individuals by state coercion. Two reasons weigh against the 'contractualisation of social life':

1. It may amount to an excessive intrusion into the private lives of citizens. Informal arrangements may be binding in morality or etiquette (to be settled by compromise or informal social sanctions), but they should not be the subject of state coercion.

2. It may subvert the values of the relationship, eg to see relationships such as those of husband–wife, parent–child, or friend–friend in contractual terms suggest that they can be reduced to measurable obligations. This can inhibit the open-ended and diffuse obligations characteristic of such relationships (eg trust, affection, commitment, and altruism).

1.5.2 Specialist areas: law of contract or law of contracts

In reality, the *general* law of contract is only applicable to a small portion of contracts actually made because enormous swathes of contracts are subject to specialist statutory regimes (eg contracts involving employment, land, hire purchase, consumer credit, financial services, companies, and sale of goods). Thus, it can be said that we do not have a *unified* law of contract but a *differentiated* law of contracts. Contract is not a monolithic phenomenon.

Atiyah questions the significance of general contract law rules which are 'general only by default, only because they are being superseded by detailed ad hoc rules lacking any principle or by new principles of narrow scope and application'.[36] There is truth in this. However, general contract principles remain important as the *foundation* on which specialist regimes are built. Moreover, specialist regimes emphasise certain values and policies which restrain the fundamental assumptions of classical contract law, eg statutory regimes identify categories of persons warranting special protection (eg consumers, employees, borrowers, and tenants) and aim to promote fairness (eg by specifying mandatory procedures or terms or by employing standards such as reasonableness, fairness, and good faith).

1.5.3 Empirical evidence: contract law in the real world

Studies[37] show that, in practice, people do not conform to the paradigm contract party. Even business people often do not:

- plan or draft agreements carefully;
- consult lawyers;
- think in terms of their legal rights;

[36] P S Atiyah, 'Contracts, Promises and the Law of Obligations' in P S Atiyah (ed), *Essays on Contract* (Clarendon Press, 1986) 19.
[37] Notably S Macaulay, 'Contract Law and Contract Research (Part II)' (1968) 20 *J Legal Educ* 460; H Beale and A Dugdale, 'Contracts between Businessmen: Planning and the Use of Contractual Remedies' (1975) 2 *Br JL & Soc* 45.

- understand the legal ramifications of their contracts; or
- resort to the law when something goes wrong.

Rather, the importance of establishing and preserving long-term business relationships and good reputations favours flexibility, compromise, and resort to customs or non-legal sanctions, rather than standing on one's legal rights.

Relational contract theorists argue that classical contract law is unsuitable for regulating most modern business arrangements as it ignores their *relational dimension*. However:

- business parties settle their disputes 'in the shadow of the law';
- numerous contract rules and standards *do* invite courts to analyse the implicit understandings and expectations of its participants;[38]
- contract law allows people to choose whether to enter a *binding* agreement rather than rely on purely informal arrangements, and provides a framework at the planning stage, especially where parties do not know each other or the contractual subject matter is unusual, important, or risky; and
- contract law helps to resolve *disputes* when flexibility and compromise run out or relationships break down irretrievably.

1.6 Contract law's relationship to other branches of private law

Seeing contract law in the context of neighbouring branches of private law:

(i)   gives another perspective on the nature and role of contract law; and

(ii) shows when other branches of private law may apply to resolve problems arising in the life of a contract. They may operate to fill perceived gaps in contract law, or take over where contract law naturally leaves off.

The subject is complex and controversial. *Again, don't worry about the details.* At this stage, it is enough to get a flavour of the issues that will be more fully explained in the text.

1.6.1 Contract law's place in private law

Public law is concerned with the relationship between the citizen and the state (eg constitutional, administrative, or criminal law). Private law is concerned with the rights and obligations *between citizens* generated by their interactions. Contract law is part of private law.

In **Diagram 1E**:

Row I shows that private law comprises the laws of contract, tort, unjust enrichment, and property.

---

[38] See generally D Campbell, H Collins, and J Wightman, *Implicit Dimensions of Contract: Discrete, Relational, and Network Contracts* (Hart Publishing, 2003).

Diagram 1E Comparing contract, tort, unjust enrichment and property law

I. PRIVATE LAW	CONTRACT	TORT	UNJUST ENRICHMENT	PROPERTY
II. Causative event	(a) Reciprocal undertakings (b) Deed	(c) Other's right to be free from harm	(d) Receipt of unjust or undue enrichment	Other's property rights
III. Source of the duty	'Self-imposed'	Imposed by the law		
IV. Nature of the duty	To perform one's undertaking	To avoid causing harm by the prescribed conduct with the specified state of mind	To return unjust enrichment	To respect property rights
V. Rights generated	'Law of obligations' generating *personal* rights			'Property law' generating *proprietary* rights
VI. Potentially enforceable against	Only the party owing the duty (*in personam*)			Everyone (*in rem*)
VII. Nature of the remedy	Actual performance or compensation for non-performance	Compensation for harm caused	Restitution of benefit gained	Return of property; and account for the fruits of the property (actionable as torts or equitable wrongs)

Row II denotes the *causative events* which generate the different types of liability. Whilst the matter is not free from controversy, the orthodox view is that:

- contractual obligations are generated by voluntarily undertaking obligations to another who gives a reciprocal voluntary undertaking or performance, or by deed;
- obligations in tort are generated by other people's right to be free from certain harms;
- obligations in unjust enrichment are generated by the receipt of an unjust enrichment at the expense of another; and
- obligations in property law arise on another's acquisition of property rights.[39]

Rows III to VI compare the source and nature of the duty, the rights generated and the nature of the remedy in each branch of private law.

---

[39] P Birks, *Unjust Enrichment* (2nd edn, Clarendon Press, 2005) 28–30.

Contract duties are traditionally seen as *self-imposed*. The duty is, broadly, to do what one has undertaken (ie perform the contract). It follows that the other party is entitled to the performance or its money equivalent (expectation damages).

In contrast, duties in tort, unjust enrichment, and property are generally said to be *imposed by the general law*. In **tort law**, the duty is not to cause harm, by engaging in the proscribed conduct with the specified state of mind (whether deliberately, carelessly, or even innocently (ie strict liability)), to another's physical well-being, property, economic position, or reputation. This points to remedies measured by the claimant's reliance and aimed at restoring her to the position she would have been in without the wrongful infliction of harm.

Unjust enrichment law rests on the corrective justice of reversing one party's unjust enrichment at the expense of another. The duty is to return the unjust enrichment and the corresponding remedy is the restitution of benefits received. The classic restitutionary claim arises where you pay me money by mistake. You can seek the return of the sum even if there is no contract between us and I have committed no tort against you.

Property rights include rights in the 'thing' itself and in the *fruits* (profits) of the thing. Correlatively, there is a duty to respect others' rights in property (eg land, tangible chattels or intangibles such as a debt, shares in a company, or a patent).[40] However, it is tort law (including equitable wrongs) which generates the wrongs arising from the infringement of property rights. A myriad of common law and equitable remedies aim to negate the infringement:

- by ordering return of the 'thing' itself;
- where this is impossible (eg the 'thing' has been used up, altered, or sold on) or inappropriate (eg the 'thing' has merely been used to generate profits or savings), or where the right was never 'to' the thing anyway (eg a right merely for its use), then by declaring trusts, or by awarding monetary relief in the form of damages measured by some combination of the value of the property, the value of the *use* of the property, or by an account of profits (such monetary awards may equally be said to belong in tort); or
- by ordering people to take action (or not to take action) calculated to protect the property right.[41]

Row VII shows that property rights (rights *in rem*) are potentially enforceable against the whole world.[42] In contrast, voluntary undertakings, wrongs, or unjust enrichment (collectively known as the 'law of obligations') give rise to personal rights (rights *in personam*): the right-holder can only enforce them against the specific party with whom their interaction generated the right. Voluntary undertakings, wrongs, and unjust enrichment can give rise to personal or sometimes property rights.

---

[40] See F Lawson and B Rudden, *The Law of Property* (2nd edn, Clarendon Press, 1982).

[41] Eg a *quia timet* injunction restraining a trespass or a breach of a restrictive covenant; an eviction order or a mandatory injunction correcting such wrongs *ex post*; an order replacing a corrupt trustee.

[42] But they do not generally bind everyone absolutely and always.

Pause for reflection

This brief overview is a useful starting point but it is, inevitably, an oversimplification. A few caveats should be lodged:

1. The contrast between 'self-imposed' duties (in contract) and duties 'imposed by the law' (in tort, unjust enrichment, and property) is false in the sense that all (legal) duties are imposed by the law. People can only impose duties on themselves (eg by making contracts) where that is what the *law* allows. In this sense, the real contrast is between the different kinds of reasons why the law imposes a duty.[43]

2. Tort and property law duties may also arise from voluntary undertakings (ie can be described as self-imposed), eg a tortious duty of care can arise from an 'assumption of responsibility' and property rights often arise from voluntary transfers.[44]

3. Conversely, contractual liability may arise other than from a voluntary undertaking (eg for breach of implied terms, especially where that liability cannot be excluded). Many features of modern contracting are not fixed by the parties but by the courts and the legislature. Some of these default rules may be modified by the parties to some extent (eg the remedies for breach); others may not be changed at all (eg when contracts are vitiated).

4. Damages for breach of contract are primarily aimed at fulfilling the expectation created by the contract, but they may, exceptionally, be measured by the claimant's reliance or restitution interest.

5. The contrast between contract and tort damages is blurred where reliance damages include loss of opportunity to make an alternative similar contract so that, in practice, they mimic expectation damages.

It is impossible to maintain the bright lines which ostensibly distinguish contract law from the other branches of private law. This is seized upon by those (eg Gilmore and Atiyah)[45] who call for the categories to be merged into a unitary law of obligations, reclassified according to the nature of the claimant's interest sought to be protected. This view is not generally accepted and it is questionable whether it would necessarily represent an improvement. Legal thinking demands some classifications, and a united law of obligations would need to include a category (whether called contract or not) which is concerned with the protection of expectations based on another's voluntary undertaking of obligations.

Property rights belong in the law of property and personal rights belong in the law of obligations.

---

[43] I am grateful to Simon Gardner for this point.

[44] It is true that, when property rights operate against third parties, they do so without a voluntary undertaking by the latter, but that is a facet of their legal quality as *in rem*, rather than their mode of creation.

[45] G Gilmore, *The Death of Contract* (Ohio State University Press, 1974); P S Atiyah, *The Rise and Fall of the Freedom of Contract* (Clarendon Press, 1979).

1.6.2 **Applying tort, unjust enrichment, and property law to contractual problems**

Disputes arising in the life of a contract are not the exclusive preserve of contract law. It is not 'contract law or nothing'. The laws of tort, unjust enrichment, and property law may also apply, eg:

- Conduct during contract negotiations which does not result in a contract may still transfer property rights or yield liability in tort or unjust enrichment.

- Although the general rule of privity is that contracts only create rights and duties between parties to the contract, third parties may have claims under, and be bound by, other branches of private law.

- While the contractual measure of damages is expectation, a claimant may, in certain circumstances, opt for the *reliance* measure, the restitutionary measure or even claim the profits made by the contract-breaker from her breach.

1.7 **External influences on English contract law**

English contract law operates in a world where markets are increasingly international in scope and interdependent in nature. International trade, the rise of instantaneous electronic communications, multinational enterprises, and the creation of free trade blocs such as the European Union, mean that sources of contract law external to domestic law can affect the legal significance of contracts. In fact, English contract law has been hugely influential internationally for three reasons:

- English law has been spread through its colonial history (hence it is the basis of the law in the United States, Canada, Australia, New Zealand, Hong Kong, and Singapore).

- England, and specifically the City of London, has historically been a great commercial centre.

- Parties in a position to dictate the choice of law may opt for English contract law, which is relatively more respectful of the agreement and so more certain, and apparently untrammelled by principles of disclosure, good faith, and fair dealing.

It is unsurprising that English lawyers are unenthusiastic about the creation of European or international contract law to supplement or replace English contract law.

1.7.1 **European law**

The UK's membership of the European Union has meant that European law may govern domestic contractual disputes. The Council of the European Union can adopt measures that have as their object 'the establishment and functioning of the internal market' (Art 100A Treaty of Rome) with the aim of facilitating the European internal market by reducing the deterrent effect on contracting resulting from variations between the contract laws of Member States. This aim of **harmonisation** has, to date, borne fruit primarily in the field of consumer protection, eg:[46]

- the Consumer Rights Directive (2011/83/EU; implemented by the Consumer Contracts (Information, Cancellation and Additional Charges) Regulations 2013 (SI 2013/3134));

- the Unfair Terms in Consumer Contracts Directive (1993/13/EEC; implemented by the Consumer Rights Act 2015, Part II);

- the Electronic Signatures Directive (1999/93/EC; implemented by the Electronic Communications Act 2000 and the Electronic Signatures Regulations 2002 (SI 2002/318));

- the E-Commerce Directive (2000/31/EC; implemented by the Electronic Commerce (EC Directive) Regulations 2002 (SI 2002/2013)); and

- the Unfair Commercial Practices Directive (2005/29/EC, implemented by the Consumer Protection from Unfair Trading Regulations 2008 (SI 2008/1277)).

Since 2001, the European Commission has taken steps towards a **European Contract Law**. The most recent are the European Draft Common Frame of Reference,[47] published in 2009; the European Commission's Green Paper (COM (2010) 348 final), and the *Expert Group Feasibility Study*, published in 2011. A range of options were debated; among them, from the least to the most assertive models, were:

- a **'non-binding instrument**, aimed at improving the consistency and quality of EU legislation'; this is a set of model rules that does not have the force of the law;

- a non-binding **'toolbox'**, which the Commission and Member States can draw from when drafting or reforming national or EU contract law;

- an **'optional instrument'** that would exist alongside the national laws of Member States and which contract parties could choose to govern their contract. This would add a layer of complexity to the contract law of any Member State;

- a Directive setting out the **'minimum common standards'** for Member States;

- a Directive setting out a **uniform set of rules** 'including mandatory rules affording a high level of protection for weaker parties' that could replace national laws; and

- a **'binding instrument'** setting out an alternative to the existing national law. This is highly unlikely to be accepted by the UK.

On 26 February 2014, the European Parliament voted in favour of introducing an optional **Common European Sales Law** (CESL). CESL would only apply to cross-border contracts (eg online or phone transactions) if both parties agreed. It covers both business-to-consumer (B2C) and business-to-business (B2B) contracts for the sale of goods and supply of digital content (eg video, audio and digital games), and related service contracts, such as installation, maintenance, and repair. In November 2012,

---

[46] See H Beale, 'The 'Europeanization' of Contract Law' in R Halson (ed), *Exploring the Boundaries of Contract* (Ashgate, 1996).

[47] Draft Common Frame of Reference. This is largely based on Lando and Beale's *Principles of European Contract Law*, published in 2000 under the auspices of the Commission.

the **UK government criticised the 'fundamental flaws in both the principle and practical operation'** of CESL. In particular, it said:

- 'The instrument is: too complex, incomplete in parts (some significant aspects of a contractual relationship are not covered), unworkable for certain types of contract, uncertain, both as to whether a contract is valid and as to the certainty of its terms, and unclear on its applicability, in particular how its provisions interact with other EU law.'

- The general duty to 'act in accordance with good faith and fair dealing' is 'likely to be abused or lead to protracted disputes'.

- CESL 'does not serve in resolving the specific problems that B2B, B2C and digital sectors may have'. In some situations, such as telephone sales, the regime would be 'unworkable'.

- Doubts surrounding various provisions and definitions in CESL undermine the certainty that businesses need.

The UK government opposes any form of comprehensive codification. The problems of codification, mentioned earlier (1.2.2), are multiplied when it comes to harmonisation at the European level. Significant differences exist not only at the level of *substance* but also at the level of *legal reasoning*. Recall the deductive style of reasoning of civil law systems (top down/general to particular), contrasted with common law's preference for inductive reasoning (bottom up/case-by-case analysis from which general principles may emerge). Adaptability is facilitated by the common law's ability to ignore or revive earlier lines of authority. The concern is that the pragmatic and inductive qualities of common law legal reasoning would be stifled by the influence of the formal deductive style of reasoning characteristic of legal systems governed by codes.

Brexit: A majority voted to leave the EU in a national referendum on 23 July 2016. What this means for contract law is still unclear. The question is whether, under any arrangement negotiated between the UK and the EU, the UK is required to retain any EU law (eg as a condition of access to the EU internal market):

- If so, then EU law and the jurisprudence of the European Court of Justice (ECJ) would continue to play a role in UK contract law.

- If not, then the UK would have to decide whether it wants to give continuing effect to Acts and Regulations that implement EU Directives, and also how to respond to ECJ jurisprudence and future changes in EU law.

1.7.2 International commercial law

The drive towards harmonisation of contract law goes beyond Europe. The primary mechanism is the production of **non-binding statements of principles or model contracts**. The UNIDROIT Principles of International Commercial Contracts were drawn up by a team of, mainly, legal academics from all over the world, published in 1994, expanded in 2004 to 185 Articles, and expanded again in 2010 to 211 Articles with accompanying commentary. Contract parties can incorporate these Principles as terms of their contract or as the law applicable to the contract. While the latter is not recognised in national courts, the UNIDROIT Principles play an important role in international commercial arbitration.

There is also a growing number of **international standard form contracts** on particular subjects that have been widely accepted by contract parties, eg the INCOTERMS (sponsored by the International Chamber of Commerce) on international sales, and the FIDIC (Fédération Internationale des Ingénieurs-Conseils) Conditions of Contract for Works of Civil Engineers for international construction contracts.

Mandatory schemes are more controversial, eg if a country ratifies the United Nations Convention on Contracts for the International Sale of Goods 1988 (also known as the 'Vienna Sales Convention' or 'CISG'), it is applicable to all international sale of goods contracts, unless the parties specifically opt out of it. The Convention has been ratified by over 60 countries including the United States, France, Germany, and China, but not the UK. Supporters of ratification argue that it will reduce the cost of negotiating international sales since parties can simply look to the Convention to govern their agreement. However, uniformity does not necessarily bring certainty: the Convention is the product of many compromises and is likely to receive varying interpretations in different national courts. Moreover, such a 'code' will be difficult to amend in response to the changing needs of international trade. The same could be said of any European contract code.

1.7.3 **Human rights law**

The **Human Rights Act 1998** (HRA) incorporates the European Convention for the Protection of Human Rights and Fundamental Freedoms 1950 by making Convention rights enforceable in UK domestic law. **Section 6(1)** makes it 'unlawful for a public authority to act in a way which is incompatible with a Convention right'. It is therefore clear that the Convention applies to a contract between a *public authority and a private party*. By virtue of **section 3**, the HRA also applies to contracts between private parties *when legislation must be interpreted*; it must be 'read and given effect in a way which is compatible with Convention rights'. If the legislation cannot be sufficiently 'read down', it must be declared to be incompatible with 'Convention rights'. Beyond that, it is arguable that the court, as a public authority, must act consistently with Convention rights, in the sense that it must observe Convention rights *in adjudication* between private parties. Thus, eg, enforcement of a contract of slavery would contravene **Article 4** of the Convention if it was not already invalid in English law. However, the precise impact of the HRA on domestic contract law is still unclear. Potentially relevant Articles include the following:

• **Article 1** of Protocol 1: the protection of the peaceful enjoyment of possessions—this could invalidate legislation which overrides traders' contractual rights or retention of property rights in pursuit of consumer protection.

• **Article 6**: the right to a fair trial—this may override the current refusal of courts to enforce contracts that are illegal or against public policy, or to grant restitution of benefits conferred under them (see Additional Chapter 2, available on the online

resources). The Law Commission recognises[48] that by denying enforcement and restitution, the courts are at risk of contravening a claimant's rights to a fair trial, to the
protection of her property (Art 1 of Protocol 1) and to not being punished without due
process (Art 7). If so, such contraventions must be justified by the public interest
exceptions of the Convention (*Shanshal v Al-Kishtaini* (2001)).

- **Article 9(2):** the right to manifest one's religion or belief, 'subject only to such
limitations as are prescribed by law and are necessary in a democratic society in the
interests of public safety, for the protection of public order, health or morals, or for the
protection of the rights and freedoms of others'. In *Bull v Hall & Anor* (2013), Christian
hoteliers refused to let a double-bedded room to two homosexual men in a civil partnership because of their policy to only let such rooms to heterosexual married couples. The Supreme Court held that they contravened regulation 3(1) of the Equality
Act (Sexual Orientation) Regulations 2007. The limitation on the hoteliers' right to
manifest their religion was a proportionate means of achieving a legitimate aim—the
protection of others' rights and freedoms.

- **Article 10:** the right to freedom of expression and information. In *Ashworth v
Royal National Theatre* (2014), the court refused to grant specific performance or a
mandatory injunction to musicians requiring the Royal National Theatre to re-engage
them in a production of a play (*War Horse*) because to do so would interfere with the
theatre's right of artistic freedom under Article 10 of the European Convention on
Human Rights 1950 and prevent it from continuing to stage a play in the form which
it judged to be artistically preferable.

- **Article 11:** the right to freedom of association. This may be used in support of the
ideal of freedom of contract and against rules which restrict that freedom.

- **Article 14:** prohibition against discrimination on any ground such as sex, race,
colour, language, religion, political or other opinion, national or social origin, association with a national minority, property, birth or other status. This and Article
8(1) (the right to respect for a person's home and private and family life) were used
to interpret provisions of the Rent Act 1977 granting a statutory tenancy to the 'sur-
viving spouse' of the original tenant to include a homosexual cohabitee (*Ghaidan v
Godin-Mendoza* (2004)).

Wilson v First County Trust Ltd (No 2) (2003) shows that courts will be slow to use
their powers under the Human Rights Act 1998 to undermine modern regulation
of contracts in the name of protecting property rights and freedom of contract (and
see *Jitesh Salat v Mindaugas Barutis* (2013)). The case relates to section 127(3) of the
Consumer Credit Act 1974, which aims to protect consumers by making a consumer
credit agreement unenforceable if the contract is not made in the prescribed form.
The Court of Appeal declared this a contravention of Article 1 of Protocol 1 (since the
creditor is barred from taking possession of any security in the event of the debtor's
default), and of Article 6 (since the more appropriate response is to give courts the
discretion to do justice between the parties in view of the seriousness of the breach

---

[48] *Illegal Transactions: The Effect of Illegality on Contracts and Trusts* (Law Com Consultation Paper
154, 1999).

and the degree of prejudice to the consumer). However, the House of Lords overturned this because the court had no jurisdiction (the events predated the operation of the Human Rights Act 1998)[49] and the relevant provision was not in any case incompatible with Convention rights.

- There was no breach of **Article 1** of Protocol 1 (protection of the peaceful enjoyment of possessions) because, in view of the social problems caused by money-lending transactions and the inequality of bargaining power between borrowers and lenders, Parliament was entitled to decide that the appropriate way of protecting borrowers was to deprive lenders of all rights under the agreement, including the rights to any security, unless the statutory requirements were strictly complied with. It was a *proportionate* means of achieving the legitimate aim of consumer protection.

- There was no breach of **Article 6** (right to a fair trial) since this is really aimed at *procedural* bars preventing *access* to the courts

THIS CHAPTER IN ESSENCE

The key areas and core topics in this chapter are summarised in an easy-to-use list, ideal for revision purposes, on the online resources at www.oup.com/uk/chenwishart6e/. Links to websites relevant to the topics covered and any updates to the chapter can also be found on the online resources.

QUESTIONS

1. 'Contract law probably works well enough in practice but its theory is in a mess.' Discuss.

2. To what extent does contract law enforce promises?

3. Does contract law interfere too much with contractual freedom?

4. What problems are caused by the prevalence of standard form contracts?

5. What values are, and what values should be, promoted by contract law? Illustrate with examples.

For hints on how to answer these questions, please see the online resources at www.oup.com/uk/chenwishart6e/

---

[49] However, in *PW & Co v Milton Gate Investments Ltd* (2003), Neuberger J held that the requirements of the Human Rights Act 1998 could be applied to a lease made before the Act came into force so long as it did not impair 'vested rights' or 'otherwise create unfairness' ([107]–[115]).

KEY FURTHER READING

Adams, J, and Brownsword, R (1987), 'The Ideologies of Contract Law', 7 *LS* 205.'

Atiyah, P S (1986), 'The Modern Role of Contract Law' in P S Atiyah (ed), *Essays on Contract* (OUP).

Beatson, J, and Friedmann, D (1995), 'Introduction: From "Classical" to Modern Contract Law' in J Beatson and D Friedmann (eds), *Good Faith and Fault in Contract Law* (Clarendon Press) 3.

Collins, H (2003), *The Law of Contract* (4th edn, Butterworths) chs 1–2.

McKendrick, E (1997), 'English Contract Law: A Rich Past, an Uncertain Future?', 50 *CLP* 25.

Simpson, A W B (1987), *A History of the Common Law of Contract* (OUP).

Smith, S (2004), *Contract Theory* (Clarendon Press).

Steyn, J (1997), 'Contract Law: Fulfilling the Reasonable Expectations of Honest Men', 113 *LQR* 433.

PART II

Contract formation

'I say there is a contract and you say there isn't'

INTRODUCTION

Contract law applies to contracts. But what arrangements are *recognised* as contracts and so attract the application of contract law rules? What are the 'entry requirements' to the game of contract? We saw in Chapter 1 that a contract is commonly defined as a *promise or agreement recognised* by the law. This yields three distinct areas of inquiry that will be examined in Chapters 2 and 3:

(i) Each party must *intend* to enter the contract: the voluntariness of the parties' consent to be bound by the contract they have made is *foundational* to most explanations of why contracts should be enforced (1.4). Chapter 2 addresses the following questions:

   - how is contractual intention assessed?

   - what happens when the parties disagree as to what terms they agreed?

(ii) The parties must be *in* agreement about the contents of their contract: the remainder of Chapter 2 examines what is required to find an *agreement*, namely:

   - offer;

   - corresponding acceptance;

   - certainty; and

   - intention to create legal relations.

(iii) The agreement must cross an *additional* hurdle to become a *contract* enforceable in law: Chapter 3 examines these hurdles, namely:

   - consideration ('the claimant paid for the promise');

   - promissory estoppel ('the claimant reasonably relied on the other's promise'); and

   - formalities ('the parties went through a ceremony').

2

Agreement

'Have the parties reached agreement?'

Disputes over contract formation usually arise when party *A* asserts that party *B* has failed to perform particular obligations owed to *A* under a binding contract. *B* may counter either that she owes *A* no contractual obligations *at all*, or that she does not owe the *particular* obligation *A* asserts. Three questions arise:

(i) The commitment question: *whether* the parties intended to bind themselves contractually?

(ii) The content question: *what* did the parties contract for?

(iii) The timing question: *when* were the parties locked into the contract?

These distinct questions are merged in the traditional 'mirror image' approach (also called the 'offer and acceptance' approach). Its deceptively simple proposition is that a contract results from an offer made by one party to another who accepts it. That is, at a definite point in time, one party intentionally makes an *offer* by words or conduct and the other party *accepts* this offer. At the precise moment of acceptance, the three formation questions (whether? when? and what?) are answered simultaneously. But, as will become evident, there are other requirements for a valid and enforceable contract beyond 'offer' and 'acceptance', namely 'certainty', 'intention to create legal relations', and 'consideration'.

Diagram 2A gives an overview of the rules of offer and acceptance. The diagram raises the issues in the chronological order in which they are likely to arise in practice. It should provide a useful summary for revision.

Diagram 2A Overview of contract formation

Look on the online resources to view this figure as a PowerPoint® presentation

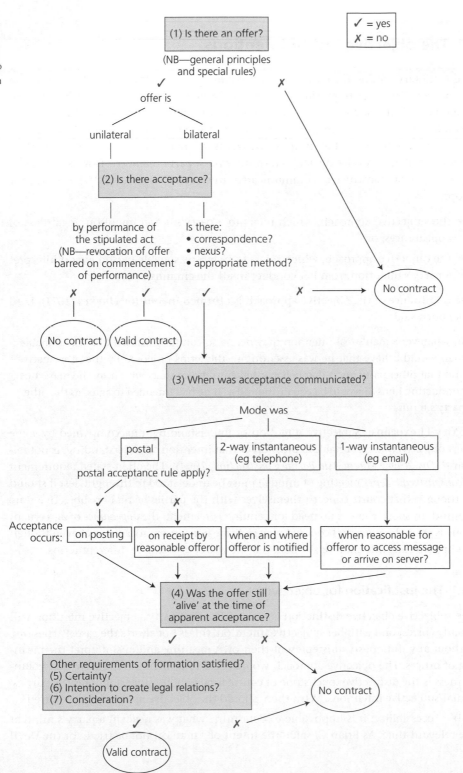

Before diving into the rules of offer and acceptance, we must first address the question of how contract law determines the intentions of the parties.

2.1 **The objective test of intentions**

The voluntary nature of contract parties' assumption of obligations is the foundation of contract law. It distinguishes contractual liability from liabilities arising in tort, property, and unjust enrichment law, which rest primarily on reasons other than the defendant's consent to them (1.6.2). Faced with various problems arising in the life of a contract, the traditional all-purpose answer is to say that it depends on the parties' intentions. But, how does the law determine what a party intended? How is the meaning of a person constructed, communicated, interpreted, or accessed? The court may adopt:

- the subjective approach, which refers to a party's *actual* intention, regardless of appearances; or

- the objective approach, which refers to how a reasonable person would interpret a party's intention from her conduct in all the circumstances.

The dominance of the objective approach is affirmed in *Smith v Hughes* (1871). Lord Blackburn said:

> If, whatever a man's real intention may be, he so conducts himself that a reasonable man would believe that he was assenting to the terms proposed by the other party, and that other party upon that belief enters into the contract with him, the man thus conducting himself would be equally bound as if he had intended to agree to the other party's terms.

As May LJ explains: 'Subjective intention or understanding, unaccompanied by some overt objectively ascertainable expression of that intention or understanding, is not relevant' (*Ove Arup v Mirant Asia Pacific Construction* (2004)). The often-stated requirement of *consensus ad idem* ('meeting of minds') must be understood in this light, lest it should be thought that courts concern themselves with the parties' actual or subjective state of mind. In short, there is no need for genuine agreement; the *appearance* of agreement alone is enough. A person's conduct may indicate her consent to a contract even though she had no such intention or she believed she was consenting to different terms.

2.1.1 **The justification for objectivity**

The subjective/objective distinction is real. Although a party's objective intention will usually correspond with her subjective intention, this is not always the case. Parties *can*, without any dishonesty, misrepresent their own meaning and misinterpret the meaning of others. The objective approach would seem to undermine the view that voluntariness is the distinctive touchstone of contractual liability since it ignores the parties' actual/subjective intentions. Why, then, should the objective approach be preferred?

(i) Accessibility: it is impossible to determine what was *really* in a party's mind at the relevant time. As Brian CJ said: 'the intent of a man cannot be tried, for the Devil himself knows not the intent of a man'.[1] An objective approach overcomes the eviden-tial difficulties in determining the parties' actual intentions.

(ii) Avoidance of fraud: to determine a person's intention simply by reference to her assertion of her subjective state of mind at the time is to invite dishonesty and chaos. Once a conflict between the parties has arisen, a person's incentive to distort the truth in favour of her self-interest (whether consciously or subconsciously) should disqualify such evidence.

(iii) Certainty and the protection of reasonable expectations: great disruption would ensue if one party could escape the liability she appeared to have assumed to the other party by simply asserting that she really meant something else. A vital func-tion of contract law is to facilitate the security of transactions: it should enable people to plan on the basis of an apparently enforceable contract. This function would be hopelessly undermined if a party could be heard to say (ie if legal significance attaches to the claim): 'When I said "white" I meant "black"'. The objective approach allows parties to know in advance how their conduct will be interpreted and how they are entitled to interpret the conduct of others.

 Pause for reflection

1. Objectivity is intrinsic to contracting and subjectivity simply irrelevant to it. Objectivity is indispensable when one seeks to relate to others in any way. Making a contract is essen-tially an exercise in the *communication* of choice, and communication is impossible without objectivity (ie the context of *conventions* gives meaning to conduct). Intention is wholly dependent on manifestations interpreted in a context of shared meaning, ie on the signs made, the moves in the language game being played. Any legal concern with undisclosed intention is senseless: it contradicts the very idea of contract as an agreement between parties who convey and receive meaning. Endicott argues that contract law takes the objective approach not for evidentiary or policy reasons, but because communication is objective by definition. The meaning of words is not determined by the speaker's intention, but by the *reasons* the speaker gives for another person to believe that she has one inten-tion or another ('Objectivity, Subjectivity, and Incomplete Agreements' in J Horder, *Oxford Essays in Jurisprudence* (OUP, 2000) 151).

2. *Voluntariness* can still be defended as the *distinctive feature of contractual liability*. Raz argues that contract law should protect the freedom-enhancing *practice* of undertaking voluntary obligations. Parties are held to the objective standard to protect the integrity of the *contracting process* and to prevent the abuse of a *cooperative practice* ('Promises in Morality and Law' (1982) 95 *Harvard L Rev* 916). The objective approach:

   ✓ prevents parties from reneging on their undertakings;

   ✓ gives parties a strong incentive to take care neither to misrepresent their own inten-tions (even innocently) nor to misinterpret the intentions of others; and

   ✓ extends the practice beyond pre-existing relationships to where it would otherwise not exist.

---

[1] *Anon* (1478) YB 17 Edw 4, Pasch. fo. 1, pl. 2.

2.1.2 **The meaning of objectivity**

While the case for objectivity is clear, compelling, and generally accepted, its precise meaning and scope are less so. The questions are as follows:

(i)   Objectivity from *whose* point of view?

(ii)   Objectivity on *what evidence*?

2.1.2.1 Detached, actor, or addressee objectivity?

In 'The Meaning of Objectivity in Contract' (1984) 100 *LQR* 265, Howarth sets out three perspectives from which courts have assessed objective meaning: 'detached', 'promisor', and 'promisee'.

Detached objectivity takes a viewpoint independent of that of either contract party. The main authority for this approach is *Upton on Severn UDC v Powell* (1942). P called for U's fire-fighting services, both parties mistakenly believing that P was within U's area and entitled to U's services free of charge. The court found a contract by P to pay for U's services although neither party intended the services to be paid for. This decision is inconsistent with the majority of English cases, has been discredited and is now generally regarded as an instance of restitution for failure of basis.[2] As Spencer observes, while '[i]t may be acceptable for the law occasionally to force upon *one* of the parties an agreement he did not want . . . surely there is something wrong with a theory which forces upon *both* of the parties an agreement which *neither* of them wants'.

Howarth says that 'promisor' objectivity adopts the interpretation of the honest and reasonable promisor, and 'promisee' objectivity adopts the interpretation of the honest and reasonable promisee. These labels are unnecessarily confusing since in a bilateral contract, each party is both a promisor and a promisee. It is preferable to distinguish between '*actor* objectivity' and '*addressee* objectivity'. On this terminology, each party's actions (the actor) should be interpreted as they would be reasonably understood by an honest and reasonable person in the *addressee*'s position. It is '*addressee objectivity*' that counts in determining which obligations each party has undertaken (*Smith v Hughes* (1871); *Freeman v Cooke* (1848)).

2.1.2.2 Conventional rules in attributing meaning: 'formal objectivity'

When determining a party's intention from the addressee's viewpoint, what evidence should be taken into account? Two versions can be contrasted: 'formal objectivity' and 'contextual objectivity'.

The traditional and narrower **formal objectivity** limits the kinds of conduct that count and prioritises them according to a fairly strict *hierarchy* of probative value as follows:

(i)   signed final writing contained in a contractual document is the best evidence of intention[3] and is superior to

(ii)   unsigned final writing contained in a contractual document, which is superior to

---

[2] P S Atiyah, *The Rise and Fall of the Freedom of Contract* (Clarendon Press, 1979), 663; J R Spencer, 'Signature, Consent, and the Rule in *L'Estrange v Graucob*' (1973) 32 *CLJ* 104, 110, 112 n 46; *TTMI v Statoil ASA* [2011] EWHC 1150 (Comm), [44].

[3] See the signature rule (10.3.3.1).

(iii) other writing or speech. This, in turn, is superior to

(iv) non-verbal conduct (a nod, a wink, contractual performance) and that, in turn, is superior to

(v)   silence or omissions.[4]

Examples of formal objectivity are the specific rules on which words or conduct are conventionally *deemed* to be 'offers' and which are 'invitations to treat' (2.2.1), and the signature rule as instanced by *L'Estrange v Graucob Ltd* (1934) (10.3.3.1). There, the court upheld a signed document excluding all the seller's liability for a defective slot machine, although the seller knew that the buyer did not read the 'regrettably small print'.

 Pause for reflection

This hierarchical scheme can yield results that do not conform with addressee objectivity, as *L'Estrange v Graucob Ltd* shows. To this extent, the rules must be explicable by reference to the needs of certainty and the administration of justice.

2.1.2.3 Attributing meaning in the whole context: 'contextual objectivity'

Whilst formal objectivity continues to influence some decisions, there has been a general move towards a more contextual approach to interpretation, culminating in Lord Hoffmann's restatement in *Investors Compensation Scheme Ltd v West Bromwich Building Society* (1998) (10.4). This approach exhorts the court to place itself in the same factual matrix that the parties were in at the time when the contract was made and to take account of *absolutely everything* reasonably available to the parties which would have affected the way in which the contractual documents (and logically, any other manifestations of intent) would have been reasonably understood. It adopts 'the common sense principles by which any serious utterances would be interpreted in ordinary life'. This yields the meaning *of the person*, and not merely of the disembodied conduct. It offers a more realistic and accurate approach to ascertaining intentions. The drawback in admitting a larger body of evidence is the potential problem of multiple and contradictory objective meanings,[5] but this is a question of weight for courts to assess. This contextual objective approach to the ascertainment of intentions is applied in the mirror image approach to determine the existence of agreement between the parties.

Diagram 2B gives an overview of the subjective-objective approach to determining a party's meaning or intention that will be discussed in this section and elsewhere. As with everything, the approach is not dichotomous, but rather a spectrum, ie a matter of degree. Thus, the arrow shows a spectrum from the subjective approach on the left to the more intensely objective going towards the right:

---

[4] Silence does not generally constitute acceptance even if clearly intended (2.3.3.2).
[5] C Staughton, 'How Do the Courts Interpret Commercial Contracts?' (1999) 58 *CLJ* 303.

Diagram 2B The subjective-objective approach to determining intention

The subjective - objective
approach to determining intention

✗ **The subjective approach** in the sense of a party's declaration of what she intended is not admissible to determine her intention in law.

The **objective approach** can be divided broadly into three sub-types:

✗ Actor objectivity is not generally accepted as legally relevant, even if it can be proved. The exceptions are:

✓ *non est factum*, and

✓ fundamental mistaken assumptions (discussed in Chapter 6).

✓ Addressee objectivity is generally accepted as legally relevant. This looks at the actor's conduct from the perspective of an honest and reasonable addressee against the background context, and is expressed in the following categories discussed here:

✓ contextual interpretation,

✓ knowledge of the other party's mistake as to terms,

✓ misleading offers, and

✓ latent ambiguity.

✗ Detached objectivity is not generally applied in contract formation. It has gone in and out of fashion in the interpretation of contracts (10.4), although its application can be seen in, eg:

✓ the literal meaning of words approach, and

✓ the signature rule.

At its simplest, the court, in determining contract formation, looks for an offer matched by a corresponding acceptance. A party may *deny* the existence of a valid contract by arguing that the alleged offer was invalid because it was:

(i)   mistakenly made (2.1.3);

(ii) not an offer at all (2.2.1); or

(iii) no longer 'live' at the time of the purported acceptance (2.2.3).

2.1.3 Objectivity and 'mistaken offers'

Since the reference point for fixing *whether* the parties intend to be bound, and *what* they intend to be bound by, is *objective*, this must trump a party's assertion of a different *subjective* intention. Yet a number of distinguished commentators[6] state that contract law recognises exceptional cases where the subjective approach trumps the objective approach to void the parties' agreement for so-called 'mistake as to terms'.

However, the authorities they rely on are entirely consistent with the objective approach on the more expansive contextual version of objectivity. However, this objectivity:

(i)   assumes the addressee's honesty in interpreting the actor's conduct;

(ii) is infused with the standard of reasonableness; and

(iii) can 'run out' in the case of latent ambiguity.

Each is discussed in what follows.

2.1.3.1 Knowledge of the other's 'mistake as to terms' and the objective interpretation of intention

In *Hartog v Colin & Shields* (1939), a seller offered to sell 3,000 Argentine hare skins at a fixed price 'per pound' when he really meant 'per piece'. Since there were three pieces to the pound, he mistakenly offered the hare skins at one-third of his intended asking price. The buyer purported to accept and sued for damages when the seller refused to deliver at that low price. The court found no contract since, in the context of the custom of the trade and the negotiations (verbal and written) between the parties, which always discussed the price 'per piece' and never 'per pound', the buyer 'must have realised, and did in fact know, that a mistake had occurred' in the seller's offer. The conventional interpretation of this case is that the seller's subjective intention trumps the buyer's objective interpretation when the buyer knows that the seller has made a mistake as to terms (ie knows of the seller's subjective intention); she is prevented from '*snatching a bargain*' known not to have been intended for her.

Smith v Hughes (1871) has been interpreted in the same way. There, a racehorse trainer agreed to buy oats from a farmer after inspecting a sample, which the trainer believed to be old oats. When the oats turned out to be *new* and useless to him, the trainer refused to pay. The jury found for the trainer but did not say which of the two possible reasons suggested by the trial judge applied, namely:

✗ that the parties had *agreed on old oats*, so the buyer was not obliged to pay for the new oats—the appeal court rejected this basis because the seller had given no such

---

[6] Treitel, at 8–048, refers to 'three exceptional situations, in which the objective principle does not apply, so that the mistake is '*operative*'. Atiyah, at 84, writes, 'In this case the law abandons the objective interpretation of the first party's intentions.' E McKendrick, *Contract Law: Text, Cases, and Materials* (7th edn, OUP, 2016) 21 discusses '[c]ases in which it has been argued that the courts have resorted to a subjective approach'.

undertaking, and the oats delivered corresponded with the sample inspected and agreed to by the buyer.

✓ that the *seller knew that the buyer 'believed . . . that he was contracting for old oats'*— the appeal court found this direction by the trial judge confusing; it failed to distinguish clearly between the seller's knowledge that the buyer believed:

   ✗ (i) the oats to be old (which does not void a contract); and

   ✓ (ii) that *the seller* was *promising* them to be old (which *does* void the contract).

The lack of evidence for (ii) suggested to the appeal court that the jury had errone-ously voided the contract on (i). The verdict being unsafe, a new trial was ordered.

 Counterpoint

We should reject the interpretation of both *Hartog v Shields* and *Smith v Hughes* as instances of a category of operative mistake (as to terms known to the other party) where subjectivity exceptionally trumps objectivity.

1. It *contradicts* the compelling case for objectivity to suddenly leap into subjectivity.

2. It is *unnecessary. Hartog* is entirely explicable in terms of the contextual objective approach to intentions; there were sufficient reasons for an honest and reasonable buyer to treat the seller's meaning as 'per piece', even though he said 'per pound'. In the context of the practice in the trade and the pre-contractual negotiations, the buyer 'could not reasonably have sup-posed' the seller intended to quote the price 'per pound'. There is no need to resort to talk of 'mistake' or 'knowledge of the mistake' or a subjective test of intention. Indeed, one could go further and argue that an honest and reasonable buyer knew that the seller meant to offer 'per piece', which the buyer purported to accept; this could be grounds for rectification of the contract to the price 'per piece', although the seller did not argue it (6.1.2.3).

3. It is *logically impossible*. A 'mistake as to terms' can only be defined as a deviation from the 'correct' contract terms, objectively determined. The latter is determined by finding that you and I gave each other reasonable grounds to believe we were each intending to contract on 'O' (the objective contract). But, once 'O' is stabilised, it is logically impossible for you to believe (know) that I intend to contract on different terms. Thus, it is impossible to find a 'mistake as to terms known to the other party' required to void the contract, eg:

   In *Smith v Hughes*, the objective agreement 'O' was for 'new oats' because this is what the buyer inspected and gave the seller reason to believe he was agreeing to. Therefore, it is logi-cally impossible to find that the buyer *also* gave the seller reason to believe that he thought he was contracting for something else, that is, 'old oats'. The court cannot find that the seller simultaneously believed that (i) the buyer was contracting for 'new oats', and also that (ii) the buyer was contracting for 'old oats'. The first belief makes the second logically inconsistent. In *Hartog*, despite the seller's mistaken use of the words 'per pound' when he meant 'per piece', the court found that an honest and reasonable buyer *had reason to know* that the seller reasonably meant 'per piece'. This makes 'per piece' the objective contract 'O'. The seller makes no *relevant* mistake because his intention is 'O'.

Smith v Hughes is weak authority for the doctrine of mistakes as to terms known to the other party. The case itself is not an example of it. The actual decision was only to order a new trial to determine whether the case was one of mistaken *assumption* about the subject matter of the contract, ie we make a contract for 'oats' which I simply believe to be 'old oats', (which does not void the contract unless it is shared and fundamental, Chapter 6).

Smith v Hughes should be regarded as a straightforward case of contextual objectivity. The court found that the parties' objective agreement was for the oats that were inspected (new oats). On retrial, the buyer could only void the contract if new evidence showed that: (a) there was actually a contract for 'old oats'; (b) the seller made an actionable misrepresentation that the oats were old (Chapter 5); or (c) there was no objective agreement at all because of latent ambiguity (2.1.3.3).

The same analysis can be applied to *Centrovincial Estates plc v Merchant Investors Assurance Co Ltd* (1983). During a rent review negotiation, the landlord mistakenly stated the figure of £65,000 (he meant to say *£126,000*), which the tenant immediately accepted. The previous rent was £68,320. The Court of Appeal held that the rent of £65,000 would stand *unless* the landlord could prove that the tenant knew or ought to have known (ie objectively had reason to know) that the landlord's offer was mistaken (ie he did not intend to offer £65,000).[7] An internet example is *Chwee v Digilandmall.com Pte Ltd* (2005). D's employee mistakenly advertised online a commercial laser printer for $66 (actual retail price $3,854). By the time the error was detected, 4,086 orders had been received and confirmation notes automatically dispatched within a few minutes. D refused to supply C's order for 1,606 printers. The Singapore Court of Appeal rejected C's contention that it was unaware of D's mistake. The Court required *actual* knowledge of the mistake to void the contract but held that it could be established by inference from circumstantial evidence: 'Phrases such as "must have known" or "could not reasonably have supposed" are really evidential factors or reasoning processes used by the court in finding that the non-mistaken party did, in fact, know of the error made by the mistaken party.' It also includes '"Nelsonian knowledge", namely, wilful blindness or shutting one's eyes to the obvious'.

If one party merely knows that the other party did not intend to contract on the literal terms, there is no contract. However, where that party *also* knows what terms the other party *does* intend, and she purports to accept that, then there is a contract on *that* basis (*Bashir v Ali* (2011) at [42]). On this basis, if, in *Hartog v Shields*, instead of the seller simply refusing to proceed with the sale, the seller had insisted on selling the hare skins at the price the seller must have known was intended, there should have been an enforceable contract on those terms (see further on rectification of contract, 6.1.2).

2.1.3.2 Misleading offers: fault

In *Scriven Brothers & Co v Hindley & Co* (1913), when the buyer bid for a lot he believed to contain hemp when it actually contained tow, a different and much cheaper

---

[7] The tenant was given leave to defend the landlord's action for a declaration that the tenant must have known of the landlord's mistake.

commodity, he refused to pay. In finding for the buyer, Lawrence J said there was no contract because 'the parties were never *ad idem* as to the subject-matter of the proposed sale', apparently a subjective test. However, the crux is that this non-coincidence of subjective meanings, unknown to either party, would have been irrelevant without the seller's misleading auction catalogue. This described the goods as so many bales in different lots all bearing the *same shipping marks*, which witnesses explained never happened for different commodities from the same ship. Thus, it was reasonable for the buyer not to have foreseen the potential for confusion: being only interested in buying hemp, he had only inspected the hemp on show and not the tow bearing the same shipping marks. Lawrence J found that, since the seller deliberately perpetrated the confusion in order to swindle the bank financing the shipment, 'it was peculiarly the duty of the auctioneer to make it clear to the bidder . . . which lots were hemp and which lots were tow'. Thus, while auctioneers are generally entitled to assume that bidders know what they are bidding for (making their mistakes legally irrelevant), they cannot do so if they have carelessly induced the bidder's mistake.

 Pause for reflection

The objective approach is not only contextual; it is also reasonable. It is infused with a *bias in favour of the just interpretation*, and against the unjust. It treats a contract party as an honest and reasonable person who will not take an unjust view of the other party's intentions, nor give a dishonest or misleading view of his or her own intentions. This aspect of justice is built into the identification of an agreement and its content on the objective approach.[8] The same idea underlies Collins' reference to the need for 'clean hands' and his identification of a 'duty to negotiate with care' and 'refrain from unconscionable conduct' (236–7).

2.1.3.3 Latent ambiguity

It can be particularly difficult to determine what the parties agreed where there is nothing in writing. In *South East Windscreens Ltd v Hamid Jamshidi* (2005), the court noted that 'the confused and informal way in which the deal was struck', attributable to the trust between the parties, gave 'enormous scope for confusion in what was discussed and agreed'. The court concluded that the parties were 'at cross purposes . . . [there was] no true agreement about the terms upon which the sale of the business was to take place'. Thus, '[n]either party has discharged the burden of proving, on the balance of probabilities, that their version of the agreement is correct'.

The same problem can arise even with written contracts if they lack sufficient specificity. In *Raffles v Wichelhaus* (1864), the parties contracted to buy and sell goods 'to

---

[8] T Endicott, 'Objectivity, Subjectivity, and Incomplete Agreements' in J Horder (ed), *Oxford Essays in Jurisprudence* (OUP, 2000) 151, 164–5.

arrive ex Peerless from Bombay', the buyer intending its delivery via the ship *Peerless* arriving in *October* while the seller delivered on a different ship, but also called *Peerless*, arriving in *December*. The court upheld the buyer's refusal to pay but without giving its reasons.

 Pause for reflection

Raffles v Wichelhaus has been explained on the basis of the non-coincidence of the parties' *subjective* intentions. This explanation is unnecessarily wide. Exact coincidence of intentions must be rare in contracting: non-coincidence is not generally a ground for voiding the contract. The case does not depart from the contextual objective approach if it is recognised that even this approach is not omniscient. It may not always be possible to choose between different, and each reasonable, versions of the contract by reference to the parties' conduct, even taking into account the full factual matrix of the case. In such exceptional cases where, moreover, the non-concurrence is over an *important* matter,[9] it is impossible to give sufficient content to the objective agreement to enforce it. The parties *were* objectively agreed, but the agreement suffered from *latent ambiguity* which was both important and impossible to resolve by reference to the context: objectivity simply 'ran out'. We may agree for a contract to buy my 'laptop', but not which of my five laptops that means.

2.2 **Offer**

An offer is an objective manifestation of intention (whether orally, in writing or by conduct) by the offeror of a willingness to be bound by the terms proposed to the offeree (the addressee), as soon as the offeree signifies acceptance of the terms. Thus, an offer contains:

(i)   a proposal of the terms of the exchange; and

(ii) an expression of willingness to be bound as soon as the offeree manifests acceptance.

An offer puts the offeror *on risk*: it confers a power on the offeree to bind the offeror at the precise moment of acceptance. Thereafter, the offeror loses her ability to withdraw from or further negotiate the arrangement.

2.2.1 **Offers and invitations to treat**

A party seeking to deny the existence of a contract may argue that what the other party purported to accept was not an offer, but something less. Whether a party's words or conduct amount to an offer can be difficult to determine because parties

---

[9] Existence of the seriousness threshold can be inferred from cases where ambiguity or vagueness does *not* invalidate the contract (2.6), and the suggestion that concurrence on the 'material terms' can overcome the problem of a battle of forms (2.3.1.3).

themselves are often ambivalent in the negotiation process. Each seeks the greatest commitment from the other whilst conceding the least possible commitment
herself.

 Pause for reflection

Parties should be able to spell out the terms on which they are willing to contract and to look
for the best deal without being locked into a contract before they are ready to commit. The
law must uphold not only the parties' freedom *to* contract, but also their freedom *from* contract. But the point will be reached when it would be unfair for one party to induce another
party's reliance while still remaining free to pull out. The law must strike a balance between
giving the parties adequate room to manoeuvre and protecting their reasonable expectation
and reliance.

2.2.1.1 General principles

Generally, no offer is made when a party communicates her proposed terms unless
she also communicates her commitment to be bound on the other's acceptance of the
terms. This is the substantive sense of 'intention to create legal relations'; not to be
confused with the presumption that agreements made in a social or domestic context
are not intended to be enforceable (2.7).

A communication may not be an offer, but merely a **request for or supply of information** that is not open to acceptance, eg in *Harvey v Facey* (1893), H sent a telegram
to F asking: 'Will you sell us Bumper Hall Pen? Telegraph lowest cash price.' F replied:
'Lowest price for Bumper Hall Pen, £900' and H purported to accept this 'offer'. The
Privy Council found no binding contract because F merely supplied information in
response to H's request. F evinced no intention to be bound by H's acceptance.

Alternatively, a party's communication may not amount to an offer because it is
only an **invitation to treat**, ie an expression of willingness to embark on negotiations with the other party to see whether agreement can be reached further down
the path. Even if serious terms are proposed, an offer is only made if the proposer
confers on the addressee the *power to bind* the proposer on the addressee's acceptance.
Two cases involving negotiation over the sale of council houses by the Conservative-
controlled Manchester City Council illustrate this distinction. In both, the sale was in
the process of being made when the local election returned a Labour majority and the
policy of selling off council houses was reversed. The issue was whether the particular
negotiation in each case had reached the point of a binding contract, making reversal
impossible.

✓ The answer was 'yes' in *Storer v Manchester CC* (1974). The council sent a brochure
advertising the details of a scheme for tenants to buy their council houses. S
ascertained the price and sent a formal application to buy. The council responded
by letter: 'I understand you wish to purchase your council house and enclose the
agreement for sale. If you will sign the agreement and return it to me I will send
you the agreement signed on behalf of the corporation in exchange'. S signed

and returned the agreement, but control of the council changed at that point. The Court of Appeal held that a contract *was* concluded because the council's letter evinced an intention to be bound by the terms of the agreement as soon as S accepted it (by signing and returning the agreement to the council). The new council could not halt the sale.

✗ In contrast, no concluded contract was found by the House of Lords in *Gibson v Manchester CC* (1979). In response to G's inquiry, the council wrote to G informing him of the price at which the 'council may be prepared to sell the house' and giving details of a mortgage proposal. The council expressly stated that its letter should *not* be 'regarded as a firm offer of a mortgage' and that G should complete a further form if he wished to make a 'formal application'. G applied and, after unsuccessful negotiation over the price and certain repairs, asked the council to proceed with his application. G then made the repairs himself and the council took the house off the list of tenant-occupied houses and put it on the house purchase list before the council changed hands. The House of Lords held that the council's letter did not confer power on G to bind the council to sell the house as soon as G manifested assent. On the contrary, the council warned against regarding their letter as a firm offer and invited G to make a 'formal application', the latter becoming the offer. The council's conduct indicated its *intention* to accept G's offer, but it had not yet completed the acceptance by *communicating* it to G. G had jumped the gun in his reliance and could not insist on the sale.

The *general* approach to making the distinction between offers and invitations to treat is superseded by some relatively specific rules or conventions applicable to particular common situations. These conventions have largely replaced the search for the parties' intentions in many common contracting situations. It is possible to displace these rules by evidence of contrary intention, but where the parties are silent, they will apply without reference to the intention of the maker of the statement.

2.2.1.2 Displays and advertisements

When goods are displayed in stores or advertised in newspapers or catalogues with clearly marked prices, the reasonable consumer or reader is likely to believe that the storekeeper or advertiser intends to offer the items for sale.

✗ However, the general rule is that displays or advertisement of goods for sale are *not offers* to sell those goods, but only invitations to treat. This is so even when the word 'offer' is used because the court may determine that it was not used in its legal sense (*Spencer v Harding* (1870)). Thus, the customer is generally regarded as making the offer when she presents the goods at the cash desk or otherwise evinces an intention to buy. This leaves traders with the all-important power to accept or reject the customer's offer.

This rule was established and reinforced in a line of cases on statutory offences relating to the sale of specific goods. The leading case is *Pharmaceutical Society of GB v Boots Cash Chemists* (1953). The Pharmacy and Poisons Act 1933 (PPA) required certain drugs to be sold under the supervision of a registered pharmacist. When Boots introduced self-service shopping, the pharmacist was positioned to supervise the sale at the cash desk. Whether or not Boots contravened the PPA was translated into the legal question of *when* offer and acceptance combined to complete the sale. *If* the display was an offer, and the customer's putting the item in her basket or presenting it for purchase was the acceptance, then Boots *would* have contravened the PPA since the pharmacist's supervision of the transaction only came later, at the cash desk.

The court held that Boots did not contravene the PPA since displays and advertisements are not offers (merely invitations to treat). It is the customer who makes the offer when she presents her selection for payment at the cash desk, where the pharmacist *could* stop the sale. None of the reasons given for this conclusion are very convincing:

(i) If displays were offers, then the customer's act of putting it into the basket amounts to acceptance, **preventing the customer from changing her mind** thereafter without breaching the contract; however, this problem is easily met by finding no acceptance until the customer presents the item for payment;[10] only then does the customer *communicate* her acceptance to the offeror. But then, the pharmacist's intervention thereafter would still come too late.

(ii) If displays or advertisements were offers, then vendors would be deprived of their **freedom not to deal** with particular customers and this would contradict the idea that a shop is a place for bargaining, not for compulsory sales. However, bargaining is not the reality in shops today where goods are presented on a 'take-it-or-leave-it' basis. Even if it is, the customer could be regarded as making a counter-offer, which the trader could reject. The crux is that traders should not be allowed to refuse to contract with any customers (consistent with legislation prohibiting discrimination),[11] or refuse to contract on the marked prices (in order to discourage deceptive trade practices).[12] The pharmacist's supervision could be the subject of an *implication* that the offer is 'subject to the pharmacist's approval in relation to restricted drugs'.

(iii) If displays or advertisements were offers, vendors would be obliged to supply goods to everyone who accepts, even if the vendor **runs out of stock**. However, this problem is easily met by implying a common-sense limit that the offer is 'subject to availability' or only applies 'while stocks last'.

The actual issue in *Boots* was not whether a vendor could refuse to sell an item to a particular customer: rather, it was whether a more efficient self-service pharmacy complied with legislation requiring supervised sales of restricted drugs. It is understandable that the court would not want to deter self-service pharmacies by convicting Boots of the offence. *To achieve this result*, the display had to be treated as an invitation to treat.

However, an inflexible application of the rule established in *Boots* could lead to errors in different contexts. In *Partridge v Crittenden* (1968), Bramble finch cocks and hens were advertised for sale at a stated price. The advertiser was charged with the offence of 'offering for sale' wild live birds contrary to the Protection of Birds Act

---

[10] This was held in the US decision of *Laskey v Economic Stores* (1946).

[11] See the Equality Act 2010.

[12] Criminal liability is imposed for misleading advertisements or indications as to the price of goods under the Consumer Protection Act 1987 and the Consumer Credit Act 1974.

1954. The advertiser was acquitted because the court rigidly applied the convention that an advertisement was only an invitation to treat and not an offer, citing some of the unconvincing reasons mentioned earlier, which were irrelevant to the case. Similarly, in *Fisher v Bell* (1961), it was held that a display of a flick-knife in a shop window was not an offer to sell the item in contravention of legislation restricting the sale of offensive weapons.

◆◆ Counterpoint

1. Such decisions bring the law into disrepute. Statutes prohibiting the offer of certain items for sale in *all* circumstances raise quite different issues (eg conservation or prevention of crime) from a statute prohibiting the offer of certain drugs for sale without pharmacist supervision (eg protection of consumers, as in *Boots*). The mischief behind the statutes in *Partridge* and *Bell* can only be met by preventing the display or advertisement of the prohibited items, if necessary by construing them as 'offers' in law, or by construing the statutes as impliedly prohibiting both offers and invitations to treat.

2. A rigid application of the decision in *Boots* can expose *consumers* to unfair trade practices (eg refusal to sell an item unless the customer pays more than the price displayed or advertised). The trader may be subject to criminal sanctions under the Consumer Protection from Unfair Trading Regulations 2008 for misleading customers, but the customer cannot insist on buying at the advertised price.[13] 'Bait advertising' (ie attracting customers by the prospect of heavily discounted items, when in fact there are few or no such items in the hope that disappointed customers will buy other, more profitable items) would also go unchecked. In the American case *Lefkowitz v Great Minneapolis Surplus Stores Inc* (1957), G placed a newspaper advertisement for the sale of three valuable fur coats and one lapin stole for $1 each, 'First Come, First Served'. L was first in the store on the dates advertised, but G refused to sell the goods to him, stating that the sale was intended only for women. The court held that the advertisement was an *offer* and not an invitation to treat: it was clearly defined and explicit in its terms, leaving nothing to negotiate between the parties.

Courts have exceptionally treated **displays and advertisements as offers** in order to reach just solutions.

✓ In *Chapelton v Barry UDC* (1940), it was held that the display of deckchairs for hire on a beach with a notice of the charges was an offer, which was accepted by a customer taking a chair. This meant that the ticket issued to the customer thereafter, which contained an exclusion of liability for injury, was not part of the contract. This cleared the way for the customer to claim compensation when the deckchair collapsed, injuring him. Treating the display as an offer allowed the court to *bring forward the time of contract formation* in order to keep out a harsh exclusion clause, which was introduced later.

---

[13] The Consumer Protection (Amendment) Regulations 2014 gives consumers the right to redress for eg misleading actions, in the form of unwinding the contract, discount on the price, or damages.

✓ An advertisement may also, exceptionally, be treated as an offer rather than an invitation to treat. In *Carlill v Carbolic Smoke Ball Co* (1893), the manufacturer advertised the 'carbolic smoke ball' and offered to pay £100 to anyone catching influenza after using it in the specified manner, adding that £1,000 had been deposited in the bank to show their 'sincerity in the matter'. C successfully sued for £100 when she caught influenza after proper use of the smoke ball. The court rejected the manufacturer's claim that the advertisement was too vague and not seriously made. The Court held that: (i) the advertisement was an offer to the whole world; and (ii) a unilateral contract (see 2.3.6) was made with those who met the condition 'on the faith of the advertisement'.

 Pause for reflection

These cases smack of 'backward reasoning' (1.2.3). Where a court concludes that it would be unfair to leave the claimant without a remedy (*Chapelton v Barry*) or to allow traders to make wild claims in support of quack remedies (*Carlill v Carbolic Smoke Ball*), it is prepared to treat the display or advertisement as an offer to reach the desired outcome. A different analysis was applied where the court concluded that it would be unfair to impose liability (here criminal) on Boots. This is illustrated in **Diagram 2C**.

Diagram 2C Inconsistent approaches to whether displays and advertisements are offers

	① Display or advertisement	② Customer selects	③ Trader agrees	Legal result
General legal rule	Invitation to treat	Offer	Acceptance	Contract at ③
Boots	Invitation to treat	Offer	Acceptance	No contract at ②. Boots has not contravened legislation
Chapelton	Offer	Acceptance		Contract at ②. Supplier cannot thereafter introduce term (here harsh)
Carlill	Offer	Acceptance		Contract at ②. Seller must pay up according to the contract

2.2.1.3 Timetables and automatic vending machines

• It has been held that railway and bus **timetables** are offers which are accepted by passengers buying railway tickets[14] or boarding buses.[15] However, most timetables

---

[14] *Denton v Great Northern Railway Co* (1856).
[15] *Wilkie v London Passenger Transport Board* (1947).

now contain express *disclaimers of any obligation* to provide the services contained in the timetable.[16]

- In *Thornton v Shoe Lane Parking Ltd* (1971), Lord Denning held that an **automatic machine** outside a car park stating charge rates makes an offer, which the motorist *accepts* by driving in and prompting the machine to issue a ticket. Thus, the exclusion of liability contained on a notice *inside* the car park is not part of the contract; it only comes to the motorist's notice after the contract is made and (like *Chapelton v Barry* in the 2.2.1.2) cannot bar the motorist's claim for his or her injury. Lord Denning explained that there is no expectation or opportunity for negotiation; once the consumer drives in, there is no scope for withdrawal since the product or service cannot be easily returned and the likely queue of cars behind will prevent the driver from backing out. These reasons would extend to analogous situations such as self-service petrol stations and vending machines, which dispense an ever-increasing range of goods.

2.2.1.4 Auctions

The law analyses a sale by auction in the following steps:

(i) the advertisement that an auction will take place on a certain day is merely an invitation to treat (*Harris v Nickerson* (1873));

(ii) putting up goods for sale is also an invitation to treat (*British Car Auctions Ltd v Wright* (1972));

(iii) a bid by the purchaser is the offer; and

(iv) the fall of the hammer indicates the **acceptance**.

This is codified in section 57(2) of the Sale of Goods Act 1979. On this analysis, the auctioneer can refuse to hold the auction at all (eg if it is poorly attended) or refuse to knock down to the highest bidder if the bid fails to reach the reserve (a minimum) price. Otherwise, an auctioneer could be exposed to a multiplicity of claims if the advertisement were to be construed as an offer, accepted by all those who turn up. It would be difficult, if not impossible, to quantify the loss of those disappointed (their wasted expenditure or loss of the chance to bid successfully?).

However, where the words 'without reserve' are added to the advertisement, this increases bidders' expectations that: (i) the auction will take place; (ii) no minimum price will be set; and (iii) the item will be sold to the highest bidder. Martin B stated obiter in *Warlow v Harrison* (1858) that the transaction should be analysed as **two separate contracts**:

(1) A unilateral collateral contract between the highest *bidder* and the *auctioneer* by which the auctioneer is obliged to accept the highest bid from the bidder making it. This can be understood as a *procedural contract* (to regulate the procedure for making the main contract).

---

[16] Moreover, regulations made under the Transport Act 1962 and the Railways Act 1993 effectively prevent contractual liability from arising.

(2) The main contract for sale of the main subject matter between the highest *bidder* and the *owner*.

This is confirmed by the Court of Appeal in *Barry v Davies (t/a Heathcote Ball & Co)* (2001), where two machines worth £28,000 were auctioned without reserve, but the auctioneer refused to accept B's bids of £200 each. B was awarded £27,600 in damages (the amount needed to buy replacements).

 Counterpoint

This analysis fits rather awkwardly with the offer and acceptance framework.[17]

1. It departs from the convention that an advertisement is merely an invitation to treat.

2. If the sale is not held or the item is withdrawn, it would still be impossible to identify the highest bidder to whom the obligation is owed since, until the hammer is brought down, a bid can always be withdrawn, or outbid.

Its justification is based on: (a) regulating the auctioneer's good faith conduct in contract negotiation; and (b) protecting the reasonable expectations of customers. The words 'without reserve' would be meaningless if the auction could be called off altogether or halted once bidding starts. This would allow the auctioneer to ignore its own statements about the auction and refuse to sell to the highest bidder (either by not giving a chance to make the highest bid or not accepting the highest bid).

2.2.1.5 Tenders

The same issues arise in contracts resulting from a tendering process. The traditional analysis is set out in *Harvela Investments Ltd v Royal Trust Co of Canada (CI) Ltd* (1986):

(i) an invitation to tender for a particular project is merely **an invitation to treat**;

(ii) the **offer** is made by those submitting the tenders; and

(iii) the **acceptance** is made when the person inviting the tenders accepts one of the tenders.

However, where justice has demanded, courts have invoked the **two-contract analysis** to impose liability for failure to consider, or to accept, the lowest or highest tender. In *Harvela Investments v Royal Trust Co of Canada* (1986), R decided to sell its shares by sealed competitive tender between two parties, stating that it would accept the highest complying 'offer'. H tendered a *fixed bid* of $2,175,000. X tendered a *referential bid* of '$2,100,000 or $101,000 in excess of any other offer . . . whichever is the higher'. R accepted X's bid as one for $2,276,000. But the House of Lords held that R was bound to accept H's bid. R's invitation to tender was held

---

[17] See the debate between C Slade, 'Auction Sales of Goods without Reserve' (1952) 68 *LQR* 238; criticised by L Gower (1952) 68 *LQR* 456; in reply, C Slade (1953) 69 *LQR* 21; C Cox, 'Auctions without Reserve—A Schematic Approach' (1982) 132 *New LJ* 719.

to be an offer of a unilateral contract to sell the shares to the highest bidder. X's bid was invalid because the object of the vendors' invitation was to ascertain the highest amount that each party was prepared to pay and this purpose would be frustrated by a referential bid.

 Pause for reflection

In *Harvela*, if *both* parties had bid referentially, it would have been impossible to determine which was the highest bid. The relevant policies are: (i) the encouragement of fair play; (ii) the protection of a tenderer's reasonable expectation that the process would be determined by fixed bids; and (iii) the tenderer's reliance on this by investing the resources in putting together the bid. These concerns are mirrored in other cases.

In *Blackpool and Fylde Aero Club Ltd v Blackpool BC* (1990), the council invited tenders for a concession to operate pleasure flights, but stipulated that 'the council do not bind themselves to accept all or any part of the tender. No tender which is received after the last date and time specified [noon, 17 March 1983] shall be admitted for consideration'. At 11 am that day, the Aero Club posted their tender in the town hall letterbox on which was a notice stating that it was emptied at noon each day. The letterbox was not duly processed and the council did not consider the Aero Club's 'late' bid, awarding the concession to another party with a lower tender. The court used the two-contract analysis:

(1) the main contract between the council and the party whose tender is actually accepted;

(2) the other procedural contract, comprising of the council's invitation to tender which constitutes a unilateral offer to 'consider' any conforming tender which was accepted by any party submitting such a tender. The council breached the contract to consider the Aero Club's tender.

Bingham LJ articulates the concern to protect the more vulnerable party in the tendering process:

A tendering procedure of this kind is, in many respects, heavily weighted in favour of the invitor. He can invite tenders from as many or as few parties as he chooses. He need not tell any of them who else, or how many others, he has invited. The invitee may often . . . be put to considerable labour and expense in preparing a tender, ordinarily without recompense if he is unsuccessful. The invitation to tender may itself, in a complex case . . . involve time and expense to prepare, but the invitor does not commit himself to proceed with the project, . . . he need not accept the highest tender; he need not accept any tender; he need not give reasons to justify his acceptance or rejection of any tender received . . . The invitee is in my judgement protected at least to this extent: if he submits a conforming tender before the deadline he is entitled, not as a matter of mere expectation but of contractual right, to be sure that his tender will after the deadline be opened and considered in conjunction with all other conforming tenders or at least that his tender will be considered if others are.

Pause for reflection

1. There will not always be a contract to consider. *When* will a court imply one? The Court of Appeal highlighted the following factors in *Blackpool*:

   • the invitation was made to a small number of parties;

   • the duty to consider was consistent with the parties' intentions; and

   • the tender process was 'clear, orderly and familiar', enabling the court to state the unilateral offer with reasonable precision.

   Other features of the case are also likely to have been persuasive:

   • as a local authority, the defendant owes a public law duty to act fairly and reasonably; and

   • the claimant was the existing concession holder and so had something akin to a legitimate *expectation* in public law that its bid would be considered.

2. *What* does the 'duty to consider' require? Bingham LJ stated that the duty would have been breached if the council had accepted the first tender received before the expiry of the deadline or if it had considered and accepted a tender received after the deadline. However, given that the council was *not* obliged 'to accept any tender or to award the concession, provided the decision was *bona fide* and honest, to any tenderer', breach of the duty to consider seems difficult to translate into remedies. The measure of damages was not in issue in the Court of Appeal; at most, the Aero Club could argue its 'loss of a chance' (13.2.5.4) of winning the tender.

2.2.2 Overview of considerations in determining the existence of an offer

Contractual consequences depend on finding an offer, which has been accepted. Thus, finding an *offer* is *pro-liability*, while finding a mere invitation to treat is *anti-liability*. The factors beyond the parties' intention, mentioned in the discussion in the previous section, which influence this determination are summarised in **Diagram 2D**.

2.2.3 Termination of offer

A party denying the existence of a contract may argue that, although a 'live' offer once existed, it was 'dead' (had ceased to exist) by the time the offeree attempted to accept it. Conceptually, the issue of termination of offer belongs with the topic of offer, but in practice the issue will not arise unless and until there is an alleged *acceptance* that has been communicated to the offeror. Thus, it makes sense to fix the point of acceptance first before asking whether its effect is negated by the termination of the offer (2.4).

Diagram 2D Overview of policies in determining existence of an offer

	Pro-liability: 'offer'	Anti-liability: 'invitation to treat'
Factors relating to the alleged offeror	Prevent exploitative trade practices, such as bait or misleading advertising, or failure to observe the offeror's own rules	Need for room to manoeuvre
Factor relating to the alleged offeree	Protection of reasonable expectation or reliance	
Other factors	Promote consumer protection (so bind trader); control of unfair exclusion clauses (so accelerate contract formation to exclude unfair term)	

2.3 **Acceptance**

An acceptance is an unequivocal expression of consent to the proposal contained in the offer and has the effect of immediately binding both parties to the contract. It locks the door on the contract 'room': neither party can get out of the contract or vary its contents. We noted that an apparent acceptance is not binding if the offeror knows that the offeree intended to agree to something else (2.1.3) In addition, a valid acceptance must:

(i)   correspond with the offer (2.3.1);

(ii) be made in response to the offer (there must be a *nexus* between the acceptance and the offer) (2.3.2);

(iii) be made by an appropriate method (2.3.3); and

(iv) be communicated to the offeror (this fixes the time of contract formation, crystallising the terms and making withdrawal impossible) (2.3.4).

A party can deny the existence of a contract by establishing the absence of *any* of these requirements. Again, the scope and operation of each requirement reveal the competing influence of considerations of certainty, fairness and respect for the parties' intentions.

2.3.1 Correspondence of acceptance with the offer

The mirror image approach to contract formation requires the acceptance to mirror the offer. The requirement of exact correspondence means that a purported acceptance that deviates in any way from the offered terms is unlikely to conclude a contract. Three situations warrant special mention.

2.3.1.1 Conditional acceptance

'Acceptances' that contemplate further conditions being satisfied or steps being taken, such as a more formal contract, generally render the agreement incomplete and not binding (2.6.1).

2.3.1.2 Counter-offer kills the original offer

An offeree whose response deviates from the terms of the offer will usually be regarded as having made a **counter-offer**. A counter-offer terminates the original offer. If the offer is rejected, it is no longer 'live' for acceptance. The offeror, on receiving the offeree's counter-offer (rejection of the original offer), should be immediately free to deal elsewhere and not be required to wait further. The practical effect is that the offeree loses the power to accept the original offer. In *Hyde v Wrench* (1840), W offered to sell his farm for £1,000. H said he would only pay £950; this was rejected by W. H then agreed to pay £1,000, which W also rejected. H's proposal of £950 was a counter-offer which terminated the original offer, making it incapable of subsequent acceptance.

The offeree can retain her power to accept the original offer if the court finds:

(i) that the original offeror's rejection of the counter-offer includes a **renewed offer** on the original terms; or

(ii) that the offeree's response was not a counter-offer but merely a **request for information** or clarification about the availability of better terms. In *Stevenson, Jacques & Co v McLean* (1880), M offered to sell S iron at '40s per ton net cash'. S asked whether M 'would accept forty for delivery over two months, or if not, longest limit you would give'. M then sold the iron to a third party. Hearing nothing, S accepted the original offer by telegram before M's revocation reached S. The court held that S merely made an inquiry, not a counter-offer extinguishing the offer, and so could bind M with his subsequent acceptance. The line between a counter-offer and a request for information can be a fine one. The lesson is that the offeree should be careful not to appear as if she is rejecting the original offer, so as to preserve (rather than destroy) her power to accept the original offer as a fall-back position.

2.3.1.3 Battle of forms

The offeree's counter-offer must itself be accepted before the parties are bound. If there is a signature or other clear manifestation of acceptance, all is fine. But, two common contracting practices lead to acute difficulties when parties dispute the content of the contract, although they have commenced performance. The issue is not *'whether there is a contract'*, but rather, *'on whose version of* the contract?' The first problematic situation is the so-called '**ticket cases**'. They concern the enforceability of terms in an unsigned standard form document which one party hands over to the other when making the contract. Essentially, the terms only bind if the recipient of the unsigned document has *reasonable notice* of the challenged term (10.3.3.2).

The second situation, the so-called 'battle of forms' cases, arises where the parties purport to conclude a contract by an *exchange of forms* containing incompatible terms (variously labelled 'offers', 'quotations', 'tenders', 'invoices', 'orders', 'delivery notes' and so on). For example, I offer to sell goods on my standard form terms X^{**} and you 'accept' by placing an order on your, different, terms Y^{**}. I then deliver the goods accompanied by my invoice X^{**} and you receive the goods without objection. There is an agreement of some sort, but on whose terms? The conventional answer is that it depends on which party *'fired the last shot'*: the party that presents its terms *last* without provoking objection from the recipient who acts on the 'contract', succeeds in binding the recipient on its terms (me in the above example). In *Brogden v Metropolitan Railway Co* (1877), M sent B a draft agreement for the supply of coal. B amended the agreement and returned it. Nothing further was done to formalise the agreement. M ordered coal from B, which B supplied and M paid for. When a dispute broke out, M denied any binding contract. It was held that B's amendment amounted to a counter-offer, which M accepted by conduct when M placed the order.

A more difficult case is ***Butler v Ex-Cell-O Corp (England) Ltd*** (1979). The manufacturer quoted the price for manufacturing a machine for the buyer on its standard terms B^{**} *with* a price variation clause. The buyer then placed an order on its standard form E^{**}, without any price variation. E^{**} contained a tear-off slip which invited the manufacturer's signature acknowledging the order to be on E^{**} terms. The manufacturer signed and returned this slip, *but also* attached a letter stating that they were supplying the machine on their original terms B^{**}. The manufacturer relied on B^{**} to claim an additional sum on delivery of the machine. The Court of Appeal held that manufacturer's original offer was met by the buyer's counter-offer, which the manufacturer accepted when it signed and returned the acknowledgement slip in E^{**}. The manufacturer's accompanying letter was not a counter-offer, but simply a means of identifying the order.

In *Tekdata Interconnectors Ltd v Amphenol Ltd* (2009), the Court of Appeal reaffirmed the 'last shot' rule, but held that the rule can be displaced where the parties' common intention is that some other terms were intended to prevail.

It is even possible for the court to conclude that there is a contract but on neither party's terms. In *GHSP Inc v AB Electronic Ltd* (2010), the issue was whether the contract was on the claimant's terms (which imposed unlimited liability on the seller), or on the defendant's terms (which effectively excluded liability for all consequential loss and damage). After reviewing the correspondence between the parties, Burton J concluded that they were in deadlock: 'both sides buttoned their lips, or fastened their seatbelts, and hoped that there would never be a problem'. Nevertheless, it was clear that a contract existed and had been performed. The court filled the gap by implying the term contained in section 14(2) of the Sale of Goods Act 1979 into the contract, namely, that the 'goods supplied under the contract are of satisfactory quality'.

➡️⬅️ **Counterpoint**

The 'last shot' approach set out in *Butler* is open to criticism:

1. It can hide the real basis for decisions: the court found a contract although, objectively interpreted, no agreement was ever reached. The letter accompanying B's signature on the tear-off slip plainly evinced B's intention to assert their terms and so was really a counter-offer. This was rejected by E when they refused to pay the extra sum. However, the parties had acted in reliance on their arrangement (B manufactured the machine to E's specification, and E made no alternative arrangements). To protect this reliance, the court *had* to find a contract: to do this, the court construed B's signed return of E's tear-off slip as an acceptance and discounted B's contradictory letter. Where contractual performance has begun or is completed (the contract is executed or partly executed), courts strive to impose liability even if this means constructing an agreement out of disagreement. In 'Contract Law: Fulfilling the Reasonable Expectations of Honest Men' (1997) 113 *LQR* 433, Lord Steyn, writing extrajudicially, explains:

> Each party insists on contracting only on his or her own standard conditions. In the meantime the work starts. Payments are made. Often it is a fiction to identify an offer and acceptance. Yet reason tells us that neither party should be able to withdraw unilaterally from the transaction. The reasonable expectations of the parties, albeit that they are still in disagreement about minor details of the transaction, often demand that the court must recognise that a contract has come into existence. The greater the evidence of reliance, and the further along the road towards implementation the transaction is, the greater the prospect that the court will find a contract made and do its best, in accordance with the reasonable expectations of the parties, to spell out the terms of the contract.

2. It creates a façade of agreement when there was none: contract parties tend to put forward their own standard terms for reasons of ease, efficiency, and self-interest, but may not insist on the other's overt acceptance of them for fear of aggravating the other party and losing the deal (1.5.3).[18] Each party proceeds on the optimistic expectation that no problems will arise and that, if they do, they will be able to sort them out. Indeed, it is conceded that '[c]ommerce could not be carried on, and no contract could ever be concluded if merchants were required to use the precision of solicitors in contracts with each other' (*Anglo-Newfoundland Fish Co v Smith & Co* (1902)). So, it is not surprising that, when disputes arise, courts may have the greatest difficulty in untangling the strands and fitting them into an offer and acceptance analysis.

3. It may produce unjust solutions: it may be a matter of chance which party gets the 'last shot' in and, although courts have some latitude in how they interpret the particular facts to decide which set of terms should prevail, the solution is still 'all or nothing'; the contract will be *entirely* on one party's terms. The solution in *Butler* in favour of the buyer was arguably just. Lord Denning MR noted that the manufacturer's performance

➡️

[18] H Beale and T Dugdale, 'Contracts between Businessmen: Planning and the Use of Contractual Remedies' (1975) 2 *BJLS* 45, 49–50.

➡

was five months late and the buyer could only take delivery two months after that. Since there was nothing that could be unequivocally construed as the buyer's acceptance of the manufacturer's terms, the latter's signature and return of the buyer's tear-off slip had to be construed as the acceptance, and the manufacturer's inconsistent letter discounted.

In *Butler v Ex-Cell-O Corp*, **Lord Denning** puts forward an alternative approach to battle of forms (see 2.5.3). He says: 'In many of these cases our traditional analysis of offer, counter-offer, rejection, acceptance and so forth is out of date.' The 'better way' is for the courts to determine reasonable compromises on the disputed terms if the parties are agreed on all material terms. This separates two hitherto merged questions:

(i)   the commitment question: the question is whether or not the parties 'have reached agreement on all material points, even though there may be differences between the forms and conditions'; and

(ii) the content question: '[i]f [the parties' terms] can be reconciled so as to give a harmonious result, all well and good. If differences are irreconcilable, so that they are mutually contradictory, then the conflicting terms may have to be scrapped and replaced by a reasonable implication.'

 Pause for reflection

Lord Denning's approach is criticised for uncertainty and for making the contract for the parties. In 'The Battle of the Forms' (1979) 42 *MLR* 715, Rawlings emphasises the difficulty and essential arbitrariness of distinguishing between 'material points', 'material differences', and residual terms. He concludes that the traditional analysis should be retained for its simplicity. On the other hand, Lord Denning's approach provides a more flexible framework for reconciling inconsistent terms and apparent lack of consensus. Indeed, it is broadly mirrored in:

• the US Uniform Commercial Code (§ 2-207);

• the Vienna Convention on Contracts for the International Sale of Goods (Art 19);

• the UNIDROIT Principles of International Commercial Contracts (Art 2.11); and

• the European Draft Common Frame of Reference (Arts II.-4:208–II.-4:209).

The basic idea is that only 'material' inconsistencies will prevent contract formation, while relatively minor ones will not. The Vienna Convention provides a non-exhaustive list of '*material*' terms, namely, those relating to 'price, payment, quality and quantity of the goods, place and time of delivery, extent of one party's liability to the other or the settlement of disputes'.

2.3.2 **Nexus between offer and acceptance**

A valid acceptance must be made in response to a known offer. This means that conduct purporting to be an acceptance is ineffective if it is done in ignorance of the offer, even if it matches the offer. The issue arises in cases of cross-offers and rewards.

2.3.2.1 Cross-offers

Two identical offers made in ignorance of each other do not amount to a contract, unless or until one is further accepted. In *Tinn v Hoffman* (1873), H wrote to T offering to *sell* him 800 tons of iron at 69s per ton. On the same day, T wrote to H offering to *buy* on the same terms. It was held obiter that these simultaneous offers, made in ignorance of each other, would not bind the parties.

 Pause for reflection

A shared intention or a meeting of minds does *not* create a contract. There must be a *causal nexus* between them. It is only when there is an offer on one side, and an acceptance *of that offer* on the other, that each party *knows when* she is contractually bound, when it is safe to act in *reliance* on there being a contract and when liability will be incurred for departure. In practice, no problems arise from cross-offers unless one party changes her mind.

2.3.2.2 Rewards

The offeree must not only *know* of the reward; she must also act *in response* to it. However, the cases show that these requirements are easily satisfied for meritorious claimants, perhaps because the offeror who receives the benefit she stipulated is thought to suffer no prejudice in paying what she promised for it. Moreover, public policy calls for claimants who perform beneficial acts (eg returning lost pets or providing useful information) to be rewarded for doing so. The cases are not entirely reconcilable and reveal some backward reasoning.

✗ In *R v Clarke* (1927), a reward was offered for information leading to the arrest of certain murderers. C was charged with the murders and gave the relevant information in order to absolve himself. C's claim for the reward was rejected because he admitted that, when giving the information, he had forgotten about the reward. C did not perform the act to get the reward.

✓ In *Gibbons v Proctor* (1891), a police officer could claim a reward because the court found that, although he was ignorant of the offer when he gave information to a fellow officer, he knew of it *by the time* the information reached the superintendent after passing through other hands.

✓ In *Williams v Carwardine* (1833), the informant acted because she believed she would not live long and wished to ease her conscience. The court held that she was entitled to the reward because she 'must have known' of the reward and interpreted the reward as payable even if the informant did not act from the desire to receive the reward.

2.3.3 **Method of acceptance**

An acceptance must be made in an appropriate way. The method of acceptance may be stipulated in the offer. Otherwise, any words or conduct that objectively evince the offeree's intention to accept are enough:

- a *signature* on a contractual document is a clear example of acceptance;
- acceptance can also be made by *conduct* in reliance on and consistent with the terms of the contract (eg *Brogden v Metropolitan Railway Co*, 2.3.1.3); or
- acceptance can be by *failing to object* (acquiescence) to the last shot fired by the other party in battle of forms cases.

2.3.3.1 Method of acceptance prescribed

If the offer *requires* the offeree to comply with a particular method of acceptance, a purported acceptance that deviates from this may not bind the offeror unless the offeror *waives* her right to insist on compliance. However, courts lean against treating the stipulated mode as *mandatory*: they are slow to conclude that the offeror *only* intends to be bound by the stated method of acceptance unless very clear words to the contrary are used. Rather, courts will treat the stipulated mode of acceptance as *permissive* so that the offeror will be bound if the actual method of acceptance did not disadvantage her (eg by occasioning delay) compared with the method prescribed. In *Manchester Diocesan Council for Education v Commercial and General Investments Ltd* (1970), M invited tenders (ie offers) on a particular form stating that the person whose bid was accepted would be informed by a letter sent to the address contained in the tender. However, M sent an acceptance of C's tender to C's surveyor rather than to the address in C's tender. C argued that there was no concluded contract. The court held that, as C was not disadvantaged by notification to its surveyor, M's acceptance was effective. Moreover, since it was really M who made the stipulation, M could waive strict compliance.

2.3.3.2 Acceptance by silence

The general rule is that acceptance cannot be inferred from the offeree's silence. In *Felthouse v Bindley* (1862),[19] F offered to buy his nephew's horse, adding that: 'If I hear no more about him, I consider the horse mine at £30 15s.' The nephew did not answer the letter, but told B, the auctioneer, that the horse had already been sold. B mistakenly sold the horse, and F sued B for conversion (ie for infringing F's ownership of the horse). The court held against F because his offer to buy the horse could not be accepted by his nephew's silence.

Three reasons support the rule that silence cannot constitute acceptance.

(i)   In general, silence is ambiguous: it will often be difficult to infer an intention to accept from it.

(ii) Acceptance must generally be communicated to the offeror so that she knows *when* a contract binds both parties.

---

[19] See C Miller, '*Felthouse v Bindley* Revisited' (1972) 35 *MLR* 489.

(iii) The rule prevents an offeror from exploiting an offeree's inertia (by imposing liability unless she actively rejects the offer). The Unsolicited Goods and
Services Act 1971 allows recipients of unsolicited goods to treat them as unconditional gifts in certain circumstances and prohibits suppliers from demanding
or threatening legal proceedings for payment.

 Pause for reflection

1. None of these reasons applied on the facts of *Felthouse v Bindley*:

   • the nephew (the offeree) *had* clearly manifested his acceptance by informing the auctioneer that the horse had been sold;

   • the uncle (the offeror) had waived the need for communication of the acceptance; and

   • the nephew did not need protection from unwanted contractual liability.

2. The rule against acceptance by silence cannot be absolute. If its justification is to protect
   offerees from unwanted contractual liability, it should not avail an *offeror* who has invited
   acceptance by silence when the offeree has relied on this invitation.

3. The context may make it reasonable to infer acceptance from silence, eg:

   • a householder would expect an insurer to give notice if an existing policy is not going
   to be renewed;

   • usual business practice for particular types of contract or the parties' previous course of
   dealing may make it reasonable to infer acceptance from silence (*Lucy v Mouflet* (1860));

   • in *The Hannah Blumenthal* (1983), the House of Lords held that the parties' silence
   over six years *could* constitute a contract to abandon their contract to arbitrate their
   disputes. The crucial features were: (i) the negative nature of the promise (ie *not* to arbitrate); (ii) the presence of a pre-existing contract; and (iii) the claimant's clear reliance
   on its belief that the contract had been abandoned.

2.3.4 Communication of acceptance

The general rule is that the offeree must communicate her acceptance to the offeror.
Only at that moment does the offeror know that the contract is binding, and each
party know that they can safely rely on the existence of the contract. Two practical
problems are posed by the communication requirement.

(i) **Timing**: when there is a delay between the sending and the receipt of the
acceptance, should the offeror's revocation or the offeree's quicker rejection of
the offer in the intervening period be effective to prevent contract formation?

(ii) **Failure of communication**: which party should bear the risk if the acceptance
does not reach the offeror without either party's fault?

The answers to these questions have traditionally depended on whether the method
used to communicate the acceptance is classified as postal or instantaneous:

- Where it is **postal**, acceptance takes effect when the letter is *sent*; the offer *cannot* be rejected or revoked thereafter.

- Where it is **instantaneous** (eg by telephone), acceptance takes effect *when* and *where* it comes to the offeror's attention; the offer *can* be rejected or revoked before then.

- But how should the law deal with recently developed methods of communication such as email and texts?

2.3.4.1 Acceptance by post

A letter of acceptance is posted, arrives some time later, and later again is read by the recipient. When does acceptance take effect? An offeror can only revoke the offer and prevent contract formation if her revocation takes effect before acceptance.

(i) The postal acceptance rule

If it is reasonable for the offeree to accept by post, acceptance takes place *when the offeree posts her acceptance* (*Adams v Lindsell* (1818)). Two consequences follow:

(i)   The offeror is bound before she knows of the acceptance, even if its arrival is delayed, and even if she never actually receives it (*Household Fire & Carriage Accident Insurance Co Ltd v Grant* (1879)). These risks lie firmly with the offeror.

(ii)   The offeror cannot revoke her offer after the offeree's acceptance is posted. In *Byrne v Van Tienhoven* (1880), V sent an offer to sell tin plates on 1 October. When it arrived on 11 October, B immediately sent an acceptance, concluding a contract on 11 October. However, on 8 October, V sent a letter revoking its offer; this reached B on 20 October. It was held that, since the *postal acceptance rule does not apply to revocations*, the revocation only took effect on 20 October, by which time a contract was already in existence.

(ii) Justifications for the postal acceptance rule

Many justifications have been ventured for the postal rule, none very convincingly. For example, the following have been suggested.

(i)   The Royal Mail is the agent of the offeror, so that communication to the agent is as good as communication to the offeror. *However*, if anything, it is the agent of the offeree who pays for its services. Moreover, the Royal Mail is an agent to transmit the message, not to receive its contents.

(ii)   The offeror who initiates negotiations through the post should assume the risk that the postal acceptance may be delayed or lost. *However*, the offeree may just as likely have initiated postal negotiations (by inviting the offeror to treat or to tender by post). Use of the postal system is not unusual and does not indicate that either party should particularly assume the risk of any delay or loss.

(iii) The offeree is less likely to detect that her acceptance letter has gone astray, because she expects her letter to arrive in the normal course and expects no further communication to conclude the contract. In contrast, the offeror, waiting for a response, is more likely to inquire if she does not hear from the offeree (ie the offeror is the best risk-avoider). *However*, the offeror may equally interpret the absence of a response as a rejection of her offer.

(iv) The offeror can always specify that acceptance must actually reach the offeror (ie that the postal rule does not apply). *However*, the fact that the parties can contract out of a rule does not explain the rule itself.

(v) Once the offeree posts her acceptance, she cannot know whether and when the offeror receives it, unless the offeror writes to tell her. The *offeree* would be disadvantaged since the offeror can safely rely on the existence of a contract while the offeree remains vulnerable to revocation until she knows that her acceptance has arrived. This leaves the timing to the offeror; she may not admit to receiving the acceptance and may try to revoke her offer if the contract turns out to be a bad one. *However*, the postal acceptance rule disadvantages the *offeror* by allowing the offeree to rely on the existence of a contract before the offeror can, and barring the offeror from revoking her offer before she can know of its acceptance.

 Pause for reflection

1. In truth, no really convincing reasons support the weight of the postal acceptance rule. The law cannot avoid preferring the offeror or the offeree and it must choose one in the interest of certainty, rather like the decision about which side of the road cars should be driven on. There is no particular reason to choose the left or the right, but making a decision is important for certainty.

2. Even so, a rigid application of the postal acceptance rule can yield perverse outcomes.

   • If you accept my offer by post, and then change your mind, you are bound even if you communicate your rejection to me by a quicker method, and your postal acceptance arrives after your rejection (2.4.2). This is absurd since you do not want to contract, and I know that any postal acceptance later received does not reflect your intention. Neither of us can reasonably rely on there being a contract, or is prejudiced if no contract is found.

   • The only reason for binding you to your postal acceptance is to prevent you from withdrawing from the contract if the market goes against you. However, it may not even do that. A rigid application of the postal acceptance rule has the bizarre result that if I rely on your apparent rejection and sell to a third party, I may find myself in breach of contract if you subsequently choose to rely on your postal acceptance.

3. Simon Gardner explains the rule by reference to the historical context in which the original cases were decided. The introduction of the uniform penny post in the 1840s brought great general enthusiasm for the post along with the idea that posting was as good as delivery. The second wave of cases in the 1870s and 1880s involved attempts to escape regretted applications to buy shares after posting and evince a preference in favour of companies. Gardner concludes that the postal acceptance rule is now 'something of a museum piece', and that we should be careful not to go down the same route with newer forms of communication, where delivery rather than mere transmission should be the rule with qualifications based on business practicality ('Trashing with Trollope: A Deconstruction of the Postal Rules in Contract' (1992) 12 *OJLS* 170).

Rather than abandoning the out-dated postal rule, the courts are more likely to distinguish it. Emphasis is placed on dicta in *Holwell Securities Ltd v Hughes* (1974) that the postal acceptance rule does *not* apply where:

✗ it is expressly or impliedly excluded in the offer. In *Holwell*, a contract stipulated that HS should accept an option to purchase certain property 'by notice in writing' to H within six months. HS's solicitor sent an acceptance by mail to H but it never arrived. The court held that the stipulation of 'notice in writing' required *actual* notice. Absent this, no contract was concluded between the parties.

✗ 'it would produce manifest inconvenience and absurdity'. With the abundance of new communication technologies, the postal acceptance rule will seem increasingly inappropriate and exceptional.

2.3.4.2 Two-way instantaneous

The assumption with instantaneous methods of communication is that *both parties are present*, there is no delay between the sending and receiving of the acceptance, and any failure of communication is usually immediately detectable and easily remediable. ***Brinkibon Ltd v Stahag Stahl und Stahlwarenhandelsgesellschaft mbH*** (1983) held that, in cases of instantaneous communication (specifically face-to-face dealing and telephone), acceptance takes effect when and where it is actually brought to the attention of the offeror, unless one of the parties should reasonably have detected and rectified the communication failure. Lord Denning gave the following examples in ***Entores v Miles Far East Corp*** (1955):

- if a face-to-face oral acceptance is drowned out by a noisy aircraft, the offeree must repeat his or her acceptance once the aircraft has passed;
- if the telephone goes 'dead' before the acceptance is completed, the offeree must telephone back to complete the acceptance;
- if the offeror does not catch the clear and audible words of an acceptance or the printer receiving a telex runs out of ink, but the offeror does not bother to ask for the message to be repeated, the offeror will be bound.

Where *neither* party is blameworthy, the general rule requiring actual communication of acceptance favours the offeror. Lord Denning said that if 'the offeror without any fault on his part does not receive the message of acceptance—yet the sender of it reasonably believes it has got home when it has not—then I think there is no contract'.

2.3.4.3 One-way instantaneous

Lord Wilberforce justified the rule on instantaneous communication 'where the condition of simultaneity is met' (in *Brinkibon v Stahag Stahl*). This allows us to draw a distinction between:

- *two-way* instantaneous communications 'where the condition of simultaneity is met' (the telephone, face-to-face conversation); and
- *one way* instantaneous communications where the condition of simultaneity is *not* met, eg with emails, text messaging, answerphone messages, faxes, or telexes,[20] the message arrives almost instantaneously, but the recipient does not necessarily access the message instantaneously.

---

[20] Although the *Brinkibon* case classifies the telex as an instantaneous method of communication, both parties are not necessarily present when the telex is used.

When does the acceptance take effect? A flexible approach is required. As Lord Wilberforce said, 'No universal rule can cover all such cases: they must be resolved by reference to the intentions of the parties, by sound business practice and in some cases by a judgement where the risks should lie.' Three possibilities can be mooted; acceptance can take place:

✗ when it is *sent*, following the postal rule; this prejudices the offeror who may not know of it at that time. *Entores v Miles Far East Corp* (1955) held that contracts, like those made by telex, that are 'virtually instantaneous' are not covered by the postal rule. Similar reasoning was endorsed by the House of Lords in *Brinkibon v Stahag Stahl mbH.*

✗ when it *actually comes to the offeror's notice*: this prejudices the offeree because it gives the offeror too much control over whether and when the contract is concluded. The offeror could revoke her offer without reading the acceptance or only read it after an unreasonable delay.

✓ when a reasonable offeror would access the message in all the circumstances. This allows a court to balance the parties' respective interests. *Tenax SS Co Ltd v The Brimnes* (1975) is instructive. In determining when a *revocation of offer* by telex (like a fax) was communicated, the Court of Appeal held that, if the telex was sent to *a place of business during ordinary business hours*, the revocation was effective when it was received on the telex machine, even if it remained unread. This implies a different result if the message was sent *out of office hours* or to *non-business premises*. If the mode of acceptance is permitted or invited by the offeror, she can be expected to act reasonably by checking the technology she puts into use in a timely manner (unless she indicates otherwise). This standard of reasonableness must also apply to acceptances made by post where the postal acceptance rule does *not* apply (2.3.4.1), ie the offeror is bound when the letter arrives, and cannot avoid contractual liability by refusing to actually read it.

2.3.5 Contract formation by electronic means

Contract formation involving email, websites, or instantaneous messaging has largely superseded previous methods of electronic contract formation, including facsimile and telex communications.

2.3.5.1 Offer

Existing common law principles point towards the conclusion that websites advertising goods and services and inviting customers to make an online purchase are not making contractual offers, but rather invitations to treat (*Pharmaceutical Society of Great Britain v Boots Cash Chemists (Southern)* (1953)). However, **traders** are required by the Electronic Commerce (EC Directive) Regulations 2002:

• to set out clearly for their customers the procedure for completion of a contract (reg 9); failure to comply renders the trader liable for breach of statutory duty (reg 13), and

• to offer the purchaser 'appropriate, effective and accessible means allowing him to identify and correct input errors prior to the placing of an order' (reg 11(1)(b)). Otherwise, the purchaser can rescind the contract (reg 15(b)).

Communication of an offer by email or electronic message will normally be presumed to have occurred when the message arrived in the server inbox of the recipient.

2.3.5.2 Acceptance

A valid acceptance must be successfully communicated to the offeror. In online purchases, an offer will be deemed to have been accepted either by the conduct of the trader (eg the delivery of goods) or upon communication of acceptance. Traders are required to acknowledge receipt of payment under regulation 11 of the Electronic Commerce (EC Directive) Regulations 2002. Whether or not this acknowledgement amounts to acceptance will depend on its precise wording.

The issue of the **timing of acceptance** has not been settled decisively in the English courts, but the problems arising from the postal acceptance rule point overwhelmingly against any extension of the rule to cover electronic contract formation. The previous discussion on one-way instantaneous acceptance expressed a preference for the view that the acceptance is operative when it ought reasonably to have come to the attention of the recipient (2.3.4.3). The alternative is that acceptance takes effect when the email or electronic message arrives in the server folder. This is supported by:

- Art 24 of the UN Convention on Contracts for the International Sale of Goods;
- § 68 of the US Second Restatement of Contracts (1981);
- the UN Model Law on Electronic Commerce (Art 15(2));
- the US Uniform Computer Information Transactions Act (§ 102(a)(52)(B)(II)); and
- the Law Commission's 'initial view' that emails should be deemed to be received when the message reaches the recipient's internet service provider (Law Commission, *Electronic Commerce: Formal Requirements in Commercial Transactions* (2001), para 3.56).

Who should bear the risk if there is a **failure of communication** (ie the offeree's acceptance fails to reach the offeror)? Fault or responsibility should be determinative. If the offeree has actual or constructive knowledge that the message has not got through, then no contract exists. Otherwise, the risk should lie with the party best placed to avoid the risk. Thus, if the mode of communication is within the offeror's control, such as an answerphone, it is arguable that she should bear the risk since she has invited reliance on it for acceptance. Otherwise, as with emails, which are processed via servers outside the control of the parties, failure which is neither party's fault or responsibility should leave the default position requiring actual communication. The risk lies with the offeree.

2.3.6 **Unilateral contracts**

Contracts may be:

- **bilateral**, involving an exchange of a promise for a promise, or
- **unilateral**, involving an exchange of a promise for a completed act (or refraining from an act).

The distinction matters in determining (i) what constitutes valid acceptance, and (ii) whether offers are revocable.

2.3.6.1 Acceptance

Bilateral contracts are concluded by *communication of the acceptance*, eg I promise to pay you £1,000 *to* complete the London marathon and you accept. You undertake to run and I can sue you if you do not. In contrast, unilateral contracts are only concluded by the *performance of the stipulated act*, eg I agree to pay you £1,000 *if* you complete the London Marathon (see reward cases, 2.3.2.2). The unilateral offer is only accepted when you perform the stipulated act. You need not run and need not communicate to me your intention to do so; any such communication is legally irrelevant. In *Carlill v Carbolic Smoke Ball*, C accepted the offer when she bought and used the smoke ball as instructed, although she was only entitled to the £100 when she satisfied the further condition of catching influenza. She did not need to communicate this to CSB to conclude the contract, although in practice she had to do so when she claimed the pay-out.

2.3.6.2 Revocation

In the marathon example in the previous section, it would be unjust to allow me to revoke my offer to pay when you have almost completed the marathon. The injustice lies in your induced reliance and, in some circumstances, my receipt of unpaid-for benefits (eg say you wore running gear advertising my products). Hence, courts can incline against allowing the offeror's revocation via two lines of reasoning:

- *Chitty* states that the unilateral offer can be accepted 'as soon as the offeree has unequivocally begun performance of the stipulated act or abstention . . . so that the offer can no longer be withdrawn' (at para 2-083). *However*, a contract is concluded on acceptance while a unilateral offeree cannot enforce the contract until she has actually *completed* the stipulated performance.

- Alternatively, the courts can imply an obligation on the offeror not to revoke the offer once the offeree has started performance. This requires a two-contract analysis. Aside from the main offer to pay on completed performance, the court implies a separate unilateral offer of a procedural nature; not to revoke the main offer once the offeree commences performance.

The clearest case in favour of **no revocation on commencement of performance** is *Errington v Errington* (1952). There, a father promised his son and daughter-in-law that if they paid off the mortgage, amounting to two-thirds of the value of the house that all three were living in, it would be theirs. The father died nine years later after a substantial part of the mortgage had been paid. As the couple had commenced payment, the Court of Appeal prevented the father's representatives from revoking the arrangement, provided that the couple's performance was not left 'incomplete and unperformed'. Aside from this family case, this position is only supported by Court of Appeal dicta in *Daulia Ltd v Four Millbank Nominees Ltd* (1978), involving an unenforceable oral agreement for property, and *Soulsbury v Soulsbury* (2007), where no question of revocation arose because the stipulated performance of a family arrangement was completed.

On the other side, *Luxor (Eastbourne) Ltd v Cooper* (1941) **denied an implied obligation barring revocation.** The House of Lords refused a real estate agent's claim for £10,000 in commission payable on completion of a sale; the agent found buyers but the owners refused to complete. The commission was the equivalent of a Lord Chancellor's annual payment, for work that had been done within eight or nine days. The court held that the common understanding was that estate agents take 'the risk in the hope of a substantial remuneration for comparatively small exertion'. Likewise, the Federal Court of Australia in *Mobil Oil Australia Ltd v Wellcome International Pty Ltd and Others* (1998) allowed Mobil to revoke its offer to give nine additional years of franchise free if the franchisee obtained at least 90% in the annual 'Circle of Excellence' judging for six years. The court rejected the suggestion 'that the attainment of 90% in the first year or even perfect operation of the service station for a day, a week or a month, albeit by reference to the offer, represents a commencement of attainment of 90% in all six years so it is immediately to bind Mobil not to revoke'.

> **Pause for reflection**
>
> A black and white rule on whether the offeror can revoke a unilateral offer once performance has commenced is tempting but may yield unintended and unjust results. In *Morrison Shipping Co v The Crown* (1924), the Lord Chancellor doubted: 'whether a conditional offer in general terms, whether made to the public (as in the *Carbolic Smoke Ball* case) or to a class of persons, is converted into a contract so soon as one of the persons to whom the offer is made takes some step towards performing the condition'. The Federal Court of Australia in *Mobil Oil Australia* declined to recognise a 'universal proposition that an offeror is not at liberty to revoke the offer once the offeree "commences" or "embarks upon" performance of the sought act of acceptance'. The issue is one of construction, but also of protecting a performing offeree from exploitation by the offeror. These features will vary greatly from case to case.

2.4 Termination of the offer

A party denying the existence of a contract may argue that, although a valid offer once existed, it had ceased to exist by the time of the offeree's attempted acceptance. An offer can be terminated by: (i) revocation by the offeror; (ii) rejection by the offeree; (iii) lapse of the offer; or (iv) death of either the offeror or the offeree.

2.4.1 Revocation by the offeror

An offeror can revoke her offer any time before the offeree communicates her acceptance. The **exception** is a unilateral offer, which *may* not be revocable once the offeree has commenced performance (2.3.6.2). The same need to protect the offeree's reliance may be present in options or firm offers (ie offers to keep an offer open for a specific period of time), but the rule is that they are revocable before the expiry of the specified time, even if the offeree has relied on the promise. To enforce this firm offer, it must be contained in a deed (3.3) or the offeree must have given consideration (3.1).

A revocation only becomes effective when it is communicated to the offeree before the latter's acceptance:

- A postal revocation is only effective when it is 'brought to the mind' of the offeree (*Henthorn v Fraser* (1892)), or when it would be reasonable to expect the offeree to acquire notice of it (eg when it arrives at business premises during office hours; if it arrives near or after closing hours, it takes effect at the next business opening; see *Tenax SS Co Ltd v The Brimnes* (1975) and 2.3.4.3).

- Revoking an offer in a newspaper advertisement can be effected by a similar advertisement even if unseen by the original offerees (*Shuey v US* (1875)).

- An offer can even be revoked by a reliable third party acting without the offeror's authority. In *Dickinson v Dodds* (1876), Mellish LJ said: 'once the person to whom the offer was made knows that the property has been sold to someone else, it is too late for him to accept the offer.' However, courts will be slow to conclude that the offeree should lose his or her power of acceptance on the say-so of a third party. The onus will be on the offeror to show that, in all the circumstances, it would be *unreasonable* for the offeree to doubt the accuracy of the information.

2.4.2 Rejection by the offeree

An offer is terminated as soon as the offeree communicates her rejection of it to the offeror. Recall that a counter-offer counts as a rejection and so 'kills' the offer, while a request for further information or clarification of the offer preserves the offeree's power to accept the original offer (2.3.1.2).

A rejection only takes effect when it is actually communicated to the offeror. This can logically lead to unpalatable conclusions when combined with the postal acceptance rule:

- Recall that where an offeree posts her acceptance, then changes her mind and notifies the offeror of her rejection by a speedier means (eg telephone), the parties are still contractually bound (2.3.4.1).

- An offeree who posts her rejection, then changes her mind and posts her acceptance before her rejection letter arrives, can bind the offeror, although her acceptance arrives after their rejection letter.

2.4.3 Lapse of the offer

An offer may lapse on:

(i)   the expiry of the stipulated period for which the offer is open;

(ii) the expiry of an express or implied condition, other than time, for the validity of the offer (eg 'while stocks last'); and

(iii) the passage of a reasonable period of time where no time limit or other condition is imposed. What is 'reasonable' depends on all the circumstances, including the urgency of the matter, the nature of the subject matter, the practice of the trade and the previous mode of communication used. In *Ramsgate Victoria Hotel Co Ltd v Montefiore* (1866), M offered to buy shares in a company. Although shares were allotted to him five months later, he was not bound since his offer had lapsed.

2.4.4 **Death of the offeror or offeree**

An offer is generally terminated by the death of the offeree (*Reynolds v Atherton* (1921), and *Re Irvine* (1928)) or of the offeror (*Coulthart v Clementson* (1879)). However, *Errington v Errington* shows that an offer remains open if the offeror could not have terminated the offer during his lifetime, and the performance of the contract does not depend on the offeror's personality but can be satisfied out of his estate (2.3.6.2).

 Counterpoint

Contracts other than those for personal services are usually enforceable against a party's executors and an option can be exercised by the option holder's estate. Analogously, an offer should be capable of acceptance by the offeree's estate. Unless the terms of the offer indicate that the offer is only valid during the offeror's lifetime, or is only addressed to the offeree personally, it should be possible for the offeree to accept (after the offeror's death) or the offeree's estate to accept (on the offeree's death), if performance can be satisfied out of the parties' estates and is independent of the parties' personalities.

2.4.5 **Change of circumstances**

Three approaches have been taken to deal with the situation when the subject matter of the offer deteriorates between offer and purported acceptance.

(i) The court can imply a condition into the offer that the offer will lapse if the subject matter of the contract is not, at the time of acceptance, in substantially the same condition as it was when the offer was made. In *Financings Ltd v Stimson* (1962), the court held that no valid contract was concluded when, after the buyer offered to buy a car from a finance company, the car was stolen, damaged, and subsequently recovered and sold for £224.

(ii) In *Dysart Timbers Ltd v Roderick William Nielsen* (2009), the New Zealand Supreme Court held that, as a rule of law, an offer can lapse if there has been a fundamental change in the basis of the offer (by analogy to the doctrine of frustration, Chapter 7).

(iii) The court can interpret the contract as being for the undeteriorated subject matter, eg in the Singaporean case of *Norwest Holdings Pte Ltd v Newport Mining* (2010), phosphate mines and production facilities in China sold for $10 million were damaged by an earthquake between the offer and the acceptance. The court found a contract to buy not only the company's shares, but also a *fully operational phosphate mining, processing, and production business*, which the seller could not deliver. This entitled the buyer to terminate the contract and get its deposit back.

2.5 Assessment of the mirror image approach

2.5.1 Criticisms of the mirror image approach

2.5.1.1 Unsuitability: cases that don't fit

Many common contracting situations 'do not fit easily into the normal analysis of contract being constituted by offer and acceptance' (*Gibson v Manchester CC*). In *New Zealand Shipping Co Ltd v AM Satterthwaite & Co Ltd (The Eurymedon)* (1975), Lord Wilberforce noted some awkward cases: sale at auction, supermarket purchases, boarding a bus, buying a train ticket, tenders for the supply of goods, offers of rewards, acceptance by post, warranties of authority by agents, manufacturers' guarantees, gratuitous bailments, and bankers' commercial credits. In his view: 'These are all examples which show that English law, having committed itself to a rather technical and schematic doctrine of contract, in application takes a practical approach, often at the cost of forcing the facts to fit uneasily into the marked slots of offer, acceptance and consideration.'

2.5.1.2 Misleading: concerns beyond consensus

While the mirror image approach points to a search for the parties' matching intentions, departures from this in the rules on contract formation reveal the influence of competing concerns (2.5.2).

(i)   The objective test of intention 'bites' precisely when a party's actual intention differs from her apparent intention, so that an enforceable contract may not reflect any genuine consensus.

(ii) The situation-specific rules may contradict the objective test as to whether there is an 'offer' or an 'acceptance' (eg displays do not generally constitute offers, and acceptance cannot be made by silence). Or the courts may find an agreement despite the evident lack of consensus (eg the 'last shot approach' to the 'battle of forms' or the two-contract analysis).

(iii) A contract may come into existence before both parties can know of it (eg the postal acceptance rule or the unilateral contract analysis).

(iv) Courts can cure agreements that are vague or incomplete by interpretation and gap-filling by reference to factors *external* to the parties' objective intentions (2.6).

2.5.1.3 Backward reasoning

Judges often give the impression that they reason deductively (ie *'forwards'*), assessing the facts of the case for compliance with the legal requirements and *thereby* arriving at the solution (ie offer + acceptance = agreement). This is reinforced by the long-standing fiction that judges merely *apply* settled rules without reference to the justice of the rules or the outcomes they yield. Indeed, Scrutton LJ describes concerns with justice as 'well-meaning sloppiness of thought' (*Holt v Markham* (1923)). However, any attempt to understand the formation cases as the product of a mechanical application of the rules is doomed to failure.

Judicial reasoning may sometimes be described as *'backwards'* in the sense that the judges *reason back* from their sense of the 'right' solution *to* 'find' the presence or absence of offer and acceptance necessary to *justify* it (1.2.3). On this view, findings on questions of 'offer' and 'acceptance' are less the outcome of an empirical examination of the parties' conduct than an expression of the court's *conclusion* of the labels that justice requires. The reasons must be sought elsewhere.

2.5.2 **The policy considerations**

Many factors enter the equation when courts have to decide whether contractual consequences should attach to the parties' dealings.

(i) Respecting the parties' intentions

- Courts are genuinely concerned to ascertain whether the parties have committed to a binding contract (2.2.1.1).

- Courts are also concerned to give parties some room to manoeuvre (to negotiate, compare alternatives, clarify details, and resolve differences) without the risk of making binding commitments. This can be done by finding a particular communication to be *less than* an offer (merely an invitation to treat) or *less than* an acceptance (merely a counter-offer or request for further information), or by concluding that the agreement was too uncertain or lacking in intention to create legal relations (2.6 and 2.7).

(ii) Certainty

- Sufficient certainty in the agreement is necessary in order to enforce it (2.6).

- The objective test of intentions and the rules on how specific and common conduct will normally be interpreted (eg display, advertisement, postal acceptance) allow parties to know where they stand.

(iii) Preventing unfairness

- Some rules discourage opportunism and encourage fair negotiating practices (eg the rule that silence is no acceptance).

- The use of the unilateral contract analysis (recall *Carlill v Carbolic Smoke Ball*) and the two-contract device (in auctions and tenders) prevents one party from acting inconsistently with the reasonable expectations or reliance induced in the other party.

- Courts are more ready to impose contractual liability to protect *reliance* where a party has commenced performance of an apparent or anticipated contract, 'even if it is impossible to identify the coincidence of offer and acceptance' (*Fitzpatrick Contracts Ltd v Tyco Fire and Integrated Solutions Ltd* (2008)) or a contract 'cannot be spelt out by a classic analysis of the sequence of offer and acceptance' (*RTS Flexible Systems Ltd v Molkerei Alois Müller* (2008)).

- Unfair terms (eg unfair exclusions of liability for breach) can be excluded by moving forward the time of contract formation to *before* the offending clause is introduced (recall *Chapelton v Barry*).

- Deterioration of the subject matter of the contract between offer and acceptance can be remedied in various ways (2.4.5).

2.5.3 **Alternative approaches to formation**

Despite its instability, lack of transparency, insufficiency, and, at times, unsuitability, the offer and acceptance model is still the dominant approach. In its favour are that:

(i)   Many contracts are naturally susceptible to this analysis.

(ii) It is *analytically convenient* and provides a degree of *certainty* (especially important in commercial transactions) about the general framework that courts will adopt in resolving questions about the existence or content of contracts.

(iii) Considerable *flexibility* is built in to take account of other policy concerns.

(iv) The offer and acceptance model is well established and has the weight of *authority*.

The flexible and discretionary elements of the mirror image approach are hidden behind the current formalistic facade. **Lord Denning advocated a more transparent approach** to resolving minor differences in the parties' intentions in battle of form cases (2.3.1.3). In *Gibson v Manchester CC*, he added: 'It is a mistake to think that all contracts can be analysed into the form of offer and acceptance . . . You should look at the correspondence as a whole and at the conduct of the parties . . . [to decide] *whether the parties have come to an agreement on everything that was material*' (emphasis added). Where the parties' terms are mutually contradictory, it should be possible for a court to 'scrap' the terms and replace them by a 'reasonable implication'.

In essence, a contract will be found if the parties are sufficiently committed to the *material* terms, leaving the court to iron out the differences on *immaterial* terms. The approach has not found favour with the House of Lords. In *Gibson v Manchester CC*, Lord Diplock viewed contracts that could not be analysed in the traditional way as 'exceptional'. English law remains firmly committed to the mirror image approach.

Pause for reflection

While Lord Denning's suggestion has been criticised for uncertainty and for judicial rewriting of the contract, a number of arguments can be put in its favour:

1. It is a more accurate reflection of business practice (1.5.3).

2. It is supported by European and international commercial law:

   - Article 2.1 of the UNIDROIT Principles of International Commercial Contracts states that: 'A contract may be concluded either by the acceptance of an offer *or by conduct of the parties that is sufficient to show agreement*' (emphasis added).

   - Article II.-4:211 of the European Draft Common Frame of Reference states that the rules relating to offer and acceptance 'apply with appropriate adaptations even though the process of conclusion of a contract cannot be analysed into offer and acceptance'.

3. Where the *commitment* question is answered affirmatively (especially where performance has begun), courts are very willing to resolve problems of uncertainty and incompleteness to uphold a contract (2.6).

2.6 **Certainty**

Even if there is valid offer and acceptance, there is no enforceable contract if the agreement:

- expressly anticipates the need for further agreement (the 'one more step' problem); or
- impliedly does so because it is too uncertain (the 'fuzziness' problem), or is silent or incomplete (the 'gap' problem) on material points.

Certainty as to the material contract terms is necessary in order to decide:

- whether a contract has been properly performed or not, and
- if not, the expectation position that the remedies for breach are aiming for.

Moreover, the nature and extent of the agreement's uncertainty may indicate that the parties have not yet committed to be bound. Maugham LJ said in *Foley v Classique Coaches Ltd* (1934) that 'unless all the material terms of the contract are agreed there is no binding obligation. An agreement to agree in the future is not a contract; nor is there a contract if a material term is neither settled nor implied by law and the document contains no machinery for ascertaining it.'

Note that only 'material' terms, not all terms, need to be agreed. The judicial task is to draw the line between uncertainties that are:

✓ *curable*, by a process of judicial construction of the parties' implied intentions (yielding an enforceable contract); and those that are

✗ *incurable*, being a mere 'agreement to agree' (where the agreement is unenforceable).

2.6.1 Conditional agreements

An agreement may stipulate that a further step should be taken (eg it may be made 'subject to contract'). The question is whether the stipulated step is:

• a *pre-condition* of the contract's *existence* so that, if one of the parties refuses to perform the stipulated step, there is no contract; or

• merely indicates the *manner of performance* of an *already enforceable* contract so that one party's refusal to take the next step does not prevent contract formation (*Von Hatzfeldt-Wildenburg v Alexander* (1912)).

In general, agreements that are expressed to be 'subject to contract' or 'subject to solicitor's advice' (or the like) indicate that there is no binding contract (*Winn v Bull* (1877); *Chillingworth v Esche* (1924)). That is one reason why agreements to buy land expressed in these terms may be worthless to buyers in a time of rising prices. They postpone formation until a formal document is drafted and signed. Even if a prospective buyer has invested in surveys and lawyers, and paid deposits, she can be jilted ('gazumped') for a more attractive offer.

However, the presumption of unenforceability attached to such expressions is **rebuttable by clear evidence to the contrary**. The court may enforce an agreement although it is expressed to be 'subject to the signing of a mutually agreeable contract' if:

✓ the expression is meaningless and can be severed because there is nothing left to be negotiated and no need for any further formal contract, and both parties had proceeded on this basis (*Michael Richards Properties Ltd v Corp of Wardens of St Saviour's Parish (Southwark)* (1975)). Recall *Storer v Manchester CC* (2.2.1.1) where the council stated: 'If you will sign the [agreement] and return it to me I will send you the agreement signed on behalf of the corporation in exchange.' A contract was formed on S's return of the signed agreement although the council never signed and returned the agreement.[21]

✓ there is a clear intention to be bound and the non-signing party's subsequent words and conduct amount to a waiver of the stipulated step, although the stipulated step has not been taken. In *RTS Flexible Systems Ltd v Molkerei Alois Muller GmbH* (2010), the parties entered into a contract formed by a 'letter of intent' to enable work to begin while the parties were negotiating the full formal contract. On 5 July, a draft final contract stipulated that it was ineffective until each party had executed and exchanged a counterpart. This was never done. However, substantial work was carried out and, on 25 August, the draft

---

[21] The Law of Property (Miscellaneous Provisions) Act 1989 now requires contracts for the sale of land to be in writing.

agreement was varied in important respects. R claimed payments for work done after the expiry of the letter of intent. The Supreme Court found an enforceable contract because:

- it made no commercial sense to say that the parties agreed to the work without any relevant contract terms;
- R had carried out substantial works, which M had paid for; and
- none of the issues outstanding after 25 August were regarded as essential matters requiring agreement before the contract could be binding.

The parties had impliedly waived the requirement of execution. In *Benourad v Compass Group plc* (2010), Beatson J set out the following guidance:

(a) The more complicated the subject matter, the more likely the parties are to want to enshrine their contract in a written document prepared by their solicitors. There is no binding contract unless a formal contract is duly executed, whether the parties provide for this expressly or impliedly.

(b) Nevertheless, if the parties' intentions have changed so that the need for an executed written agreement is expressly or impliedly waived or if a party is estopped from relying on her non-execution of the document, there is a valid contract. The courts are more likely to so find if all the essential or important terms have been agreed and substantial work has been done.

(c) Where certain terms of economic significance have not been agreed, the parties may be held to have agreed a separate preliminary contract to allow work to begin, although the more important the unagreed term, the less likely it is that the parties will have left it for future decision.

(d) Absent a binding contract, the work done may give rise to a restitutionary claim for recompense if the defendant has received an incontrovertible benefit (eg an immediate financial gain or saving of expense) from the claimant's services, where the defendant requested the claimant to provide services or accepted them when offered (having the ability to refuse them), knowing that the services were not being given freely.

(e) However, no award will be made if the claimant took the risk of doing the work in order to obtain and then perform the contract.

2.6.2 Vagueness and incompleteness

Vagueness overlaps with incompleteness since both may leave gaps in the contract that call into question the parties' intention to be bound. As Viscount Maugham said in *Scammell and Nephew Ltd v Ouston* (1941): 'In . . . a valid contract the parties must so express themselves that their meaning can be determined with a reasonable degree of certainty . . . [Otherwise] *consensus ad idem* would be a matter of mere conjecture.' The legal question is whether any vagueness can be resolved and any gaps filled *by the court* without further agreement between the parties.

Pause for reflection

The scope of the court's jurisdiction in this exercise is difficult to pin down. Indeed, Macneil describes the attempt to find 'coherent principles' in the uncertainty cases as 'a fool's errand'.[22] Two reasons may explain this situation:

1. Whilst the relevant principles can be stated, in practice the crucial distinction between the courts' legitimate interpretation and illegitimate imposition of terms can be a very fine one.

2. Judges vary in their views on the extent to which it is desirable or, indeed, possible to cure vagueness in contracts.

2.6.2.1 The bias towards cure

Whilst judges are keen to avoid any suggestion that they are making the contract for the parties, in practice they show a great willingness to *cure* uncertainty and uphold contracts. In *Hillas & Co v Arcos* (1932), Lord Tomlin said that: 'it is . . . necessary to exclude as impossible all reasonable meanings which would give certainty to the words' before enforcement would be denied. In *Brown v Gould* (1972), Megarry J said that this conclusion would only be reached 'if the court is driven to it'. Four reasons support this pro-enforcement stance:

(i)   Imprecision in business practice: many business people refrain from insisting on precise terms for fear of losing the deal or annoying the other party (1.5.3). They hope that no serious problems will arise and that, if they do, amicable and informal solutions can be reached. Lord Wright said: 'Businessmen often record the most important agreements in crude and summary fashion . . . It is . . . the duty of the Court to construe such documents fairly and broadly, without being too astute or subtle in finding defects' (*Hillas v Arcos*).

(ii)   The necessity and difficulty of building in flexibility: parties may try to agree terms that will allow some flexibility to accommodate market fluctuations and other future unknowns (eg in a contract to supply goods over a ten-year period). Building and civil engineering contracts often contain terms that allow variations in the work to be done, the time for performance or the price, in view of specific changes. However, it may be impossible to draft a workable and acceptable formula to meet *all* the contingencies that may eventuate and very expensive to try to do so. Courts will strive to fill the gaps and make the arrangement workable in such relational contracts.

(iii) Protecting expectation and reliance: courts are reluctant to deny the existence of a contract where the parties clearly act as if they have concluded a contract and have commenced its performance. Lord Denning said that 'when an agreement has

---

[22] 'Biographical Statement' in D Campbell (ed), *The Relational Theory of Contract: Selected Works of Ian Macneil* (Sweet & Maxwell, 2001).

been acted upon . . . we ought to imply all reasonable terms' (*F&G Sykes (Wessex) Ltd v Fine Fare Ltd* (1967); *G Percy Trentham Ltd v Archital Luxfer* (1993)).

(iv) Unmeritorious pleas of uncertainty: courts have little sympathy for parties who seek to escape from contracts for unmeritorious reasons (eg where market fluctuations have made the contract disadvantageous for them because they can sell for more or buy for less elsewhere), particularly if they have already received benefits under them.

 Pause for reflection

Endicott argues that where contract terms are vague or incomplete (and they *are* more often than not), the court is justified in imposing rights and duties that have not been agreed to because of the value to contracting parties of a regime in which disputed questions are answered, whether there is a reason for the answer or not. The job of giving an answer, even when reason does not support one answer over another, is an indispensable function of the courts ('Objectivity, Subjectivity, and Incomplete Agreements' in J Horder (ed), *Oxford Essays in Jurisprudence* (OUP, 2000) 151).

2.6.2.2 Overview of the techniques for overcoming uncertainty

Courts fill gaps and resolve vagueness by reference to:

(i)   any previous dealing, customs of the trade, and the standard of reasonableness;

(ii) the technique of severance;

(iii) the nature of the undertaking (to negotiate or not to negotiate); and

(iv) the workability or substitutability of any agreed, but defunct, method for ascertaining material terms.

This combination of techniques is reflected in the approach of the UNIDROIT Principles of International Commercial Contracts, the European Draft Common Frame of Reference, and the US Uniform Commercial Code.

The courts' stated task is to draw the line between:

• 'construing' a contract and 'making' a contract; or

• upholding a bargain and imposing a bargain on the parties.

The distinction is one of degree and not of kind.

2.6.2.3 Previous dealing, custom, and reasonableness

In *G Percy Trentham Ltd v Archital Luxfer Ltd* (1993), Steyn LJ said that where sufficient intention to be bound can be inferred from the reliance of the parties on the contract, it will be 'difficult to submit that the contract is void for vagueness or uncertainty. Specifically, the fact that the transaction is executed [performed] makes it easier to imply a term resolving any uncertainty, or, alternatively, it may make it possible to treat a matter not finalised in negotiations as inessential.' The following illustrate this liberal approach.

✓ In *Hillas v Arcos*, the parties agreed to buy and sell 22,000 standards of softwood goods 'of fair specification' in 1930. The agreement also gave the buyers an option to buy '100,000 standards for delivery during 1931'. The seller sought to escape the option by alleging that no enforceable meaning could be given to the agreed words. The court upheld the option by reference to the parties' previous dealing, the custom of the timber trade and the standard of reasonableness. The words 'of fair specification' were held to mean a reasonable assortment of timber on the basis of the seller's seasonal output, according to kinds, qualities, and sizes.

✓ In *Foley v Classique Coaches*, F sold some land adjoining his petrol station to C, a bus company, on the basis that C would enter another agreement to buy its petrol from F 'at a price to be agreed by the parties in writing and from time to time': an arbitration clause dealt with any disputes arising out of the pricing agreement. The court enforced the agreement as one to buy fuel at a reasonable price. Not only had C bought petrol from F for three years before denying the agreement, but refusal to enforce the petrol agreement would deprive F of part of the price of selling his land (the potential petrol sales).

✓ Where the parties are *silent* as to the price of goods or services supplied, the buyer must pay a reasonable price (Sale of Goods Act 1979, s 8; Supply of Goods and Services Act 1982, s 15(1); Consumer Rights Act 2015 s 51).

✓ In *Hughes v Pendragon Sabre Ltd (T/A Porche Centre Bolton)* (2016), the Court of Appeal found a binding contract by a consumer to buy a limited edition Porsche, even though the contract did not stipulate the price, specification, or delivery date of the vehicle. Under the Sale of Goods Act 1979, s 5, it was possible to enter into a contract for the sale of goods that had not yet been acquired by the seller, and even though the seller's acquisition of those goods depended on a contingency which might or might not happen.

✗ But these statutes do not apply where the parties are not silent but have stipulated that they will agree the price later. The question is then whether the parties have provided some formula or mechanism for determining the matter (2.6.2.6).

While courts adopt a pro-liability stance to uncertainty cases, sometimes they are driven to the conclusion that the uncertainty is *incurable*, eg:

✗ Agreements to sell goods 'on hire-purchase terms' (*Scammell and Nephew v Ouston*) or 'subject to war clause' (*Bishop & Baxter v Anglo-Eastern Trading and Industrial Co Ltd* (1944)) have been denied enforcement for vagueness. Similarly, a contract was denied in *Schweppe v Harper* (2008), where S agreed to seek 'reasonable finance' for H. The courts could not say which of the many different varieties of such terms the parties intended.

✗ *Raffles v Wichelhaus* (1864) is properly situated here. While the parties objectively agreed for goods to be delivered 'ex Peerless from Bombay', it was impossible to say which of the two ships fitting that description the contract referred to (2.1.3.3).

✗ In *Baird Textile Holdings Ltd v Marks & Spencer plc* (2002), M&S terminated its arrangement with B, its main supplier of clothing for 30 years. B's claim of an implied contract not to terminate except on reasonable notice of three years was denied because: (i) there were 'no objective criteria by which the court could assess what would be reasonable either as to quantity or price' of goods supplied during the notice period; and (ii) it would contradict M&S's deliberate abstention from committing itself to a long-term contract in order to maintain flexibility.

✗ In *Wells v Devani* (2016), an oral contract for an estate agent to find a buyer for a property was incomplete where the parties had failed to specify the event which would trigger the agent's entitlement to commission since such contracts do not follow a single pattern.

In the absence of a contract, the court may still impose *restitutionary* liability on the recipient of benefits conferred by the other's performance in anticipation of a contract, if the latter did not take the *risk* that the transaction might not eventuate (2.8).

2.6.2.4 Severance

If essential aspects of the transaction are agreed, vague words therein can be severed as meaningless and redundant, and the remaining agreement enforced. This was the conclusion in *Nicolene Ltd v Simmonds* (1953) in relation to the words 'I assume that we are in agreement that the usual conditions of acceptance apply'. Lord Denning drew a distinction between:

> a clause which is meaningless and a clause which is yet to be agreed . . . In the present case there was nothing yet to be agreed. There was nothing left to further negotiation . . . [The clause in question] was so vague and uncertain as to be incapable of any precise meaning . . . It can be rejected without impairing the sense or reasonableness of the contract as a whole.

If the parties clearly regard themselves as bound (eg by commencing or accepting performance), the law should honour this, lest defaulters search for 'some meaningless clause on which to free ride'.

2.6.2.5 Agreements to (or not to) negotiate

The parties may expressly agree *to* negotiate (a 'lock-in' agreement) on a particular matter with a view to reaching agreement, or they may agree *not to* negotiate with third parties over a particular matter (a 'lock-out' agreement).

Walford v Miles (1992) contained both. The parties agreed that if W provided an assurance from their bank confirming their financial resources to pay M's asking price for his business (a 'comfort letter'), M would:

(a) break off negotiations with any third party and would not consider any other alternative or accept a better offer; and

(b)   would deal exclusively with W with a view to concluding the deal as soon as possible.

M continued negotiations with, and eventually sold his business to, a third party. The court awarded damages for misrepresentation to compensate W for his wasted expenses, but held that:

✓ Agreements *not* to negotiate with third parties ('lock-out' agreements) are *enforceable* only if there is a *time limit* on their duration (*Pitt v PHH Asset Management Ltd* (1993)), for otherwise they may indirectly impose a duty to negotiate in good faith.[23]

✗ An agreement *to negotiate in good faith* (a 'lock-in' agreement) such as would put a party in breach if she walks away from negotiations without good reason, is unenforceable. Three reasons were given for this conclusion:

(i)   **A contract is about self-interest**: a duty to negotiate in good faith would be 'inherently repugnant to the adversarial position of the parties when involved in negotiations', who are entitled to act self-interestedly. So long as she makes no misrepresentations, a party can withdraw from the negotiations at any time and for any reason. *However*, if the parties have agreed to negotiate in good faith, they have chosen a cooperative, problem-solving mode of negotiation. Agreements to negotiate serve a useful commercial purpose. A party will have the incentive to take the (often considerable) trouble and expense of putting together a proposal if she knows that the other party will negotiate in good faith with her. To deny enforcement of the term contradicts the reasonable expectations of the parties. See further discussion of good faith in Chapter 15.

(ii)   **Uncertainty over whether breach has occurred**: 'How can a court be expected to decide whether, *subjectively*, a proper reason existed for the termination of negotiations?' *However*, this is inconsistent with the court's willingness to enforce an obligation to make 'best endeavours' (recognised in *Walford v Miles*, and applied in *Jet2.com Ltd v Blackpool Airport Ltd* (2012)) and to employ the reasonableness standard in other cases (2.6.2.3), when both are also uncertain. The Privy Council in an appeal from Australia *implied* an obligation to use 'reasonable endeavours' to reach agreement. In view of the parties' pre-existing and continuing relationship, Sir Robin Cooke said in *Queensland Electricity Generating Board v New Hope Collieries Pty Ltd* (1989):

> their Lordships have no doubt that here, by the agreement, the parties undertook implied primary obligations to make reasonable endeavours to agree on the terms of supply beyond the initial five-year period and, failing agreement and upon proper notice, to do everything reasonably necessary to procure the appointment of an arbitrator. Further, it is implicit in a commercial agreement of this kind that the terms of the new price structure are to be fair and reasonable as between the parties.

Berg (in 'Promises to Negotiate in Good Faith' (2003) 119 *LQR* 357) suggests that a duty to negotiate in good faith may require a party to:

---

[23] However, Bingham LJ dissenting in the Court of Appeal in *Walford v Miles* favoured the implication of reasonableness to fill any time limit gap.

- actively commence negotiations and participate in them;
- consider and put forward options;
- not take advantage of the other's known ignorance; and
- not withdraw from negotiations without giving a truthful reason, which should not be wholly unreasonable (in the *Wednesbury* sense (*Associated Provincial Picture Houses v Wednesbury Corp* (1948))), and without giving the other party a reasonable chance to respond.

(iii) **Damages for breach would be impossible to quantify**: Lord Denning said in *Courtney & Fairbairn Ltd v Tolaini Brothers (Hotels) Ltd* (1975): 'No court could estimate the damages because no one can tell whether the negotiations would be successful or would fall through: or if successful, what the result would be.' *However*, the courts can award damages for 'loss of a chance' (13.2.5.4).

 Pause for reflection

Article II.-3:301 of the European Draft Common Frame of Reference states:

(1) A person is free to negotiate and is not liable for failure to reach an agreement. A person who is engaged in negotiations has a duty to negotiate in accordance with good faith and fair dealing and not to break off negotiations contrary to good faith and fair dealing. This duty may not be excluded or limited by contract. A person who is in breach of the duty is liable for any loss caused to the other party by the breach. It is contrary to good faith and fair dealing, in particular, for a person to enter into or continue negotiations with no real intention of reaching an agreement with the other party.

In *Petromec Inc v Petroleo Brasileiro SA Petrobas* (2005), Longmore LJ said: 'I do not consider that *Walford v Miles* binds us to hold that the express obligation to negotiate is completely without legal substance.' He distinguished *Walford* from the present case because the parties' agreement to negotiate in good faith was:

(i) contained in an *otherwise legally enforceable agreement* (in *Walford*, there was no concluded agreement at all; everything was 'subject to contract');

(ii) *an express term* (not implied as in *Walford*);

(iii) 'which is part of a complex agreement drafted by City of London solicitors' and '[i]t would be a strong thing to declare unenforceable a clause into which the parties have deliberately and expressly entered . . . To decide that it has "no legal content" . . . would be for the law deliberately to defeat the reasonable expectations of honest men.'

(iv) related only to a particular cost, which was 'comparatively easy to ascertain . . . If there are any ascertainable losses which arise from a failure to negotiate in good faith, they will likewise be ascertainable with comparative ease'. Likewise, in *Tramtrack Croydon Ltd v London Bus Services Ltd* (2007), the good faith obligation was enforced since it was not abstract but linked to requirements of reasonableness and a mechanism for making the determination. Otherwise, it would have been 'intrinsically without objective criteria' and contradicted the principle in *Walford v Miles* (contrast *BBC Worldwide v Bee Load* (2007), where no machinery supported the assessment of good faith).

(v) breached by fraud: While Longmore LJ acknowledged that 'the concept of bringing negotiations to an end in bad faith is somewhat elusive', he said:

> If fraudulent representations as to the intention to continue negotiations were made, the obligation to negotiate in good faith is likely to fall away as a separate obligation; if there was no fraudulent representation, it is perhaps less likely that there will have been bad faith in terminating negotiations but it will not be particularly difficult to tell whether there was or not.

A requirement of fraud (which is actionable in its own right (Chapter 5)) would point to a much narrower duty to negotiate in good faith than Berg suggests.

In *Emirates Trading Agency v Prime Mineral Exports Private Ltd* (2014), Teare J held that a dispute resolution clause in an existing and enforceable contract which required the parties to seek to resolve a dispute by friendly discussions in good faith and within a limited period of time before the dispute may be referred to arbitration was enforceable because the agreement is:

- not incomplete or uncertain; it has an identifiable standard, namely fair, honest, and genuine discussions aimed at resolving a dispute; difficulty of proving a breach in some cases should not be confused with a suggestion that the clause lacks certainty;
- not inconsistent with the position of a negotiating party since the parties have voluntarily accepted a restriction upon their freedom not to negotiate;
- in the public interest, firstly, because the court should enforce freely agreed obligations and, second, because it may avoid expensive and time-consuming arbitration.

Lord Hope of Craighead has emphasised the **limited role of the principle of good faith in English private law** (*R (European Roma Rights Centre) v Immigration Officer at Prague Airport* (2004)):

> There are differences between the legal systems as to how extensive and how powerful the penetration of the principle [of good faith] has been. They range from systems in the civilian tradition where as a guideline for this contractual behaviour the principle is expressly recognised and acted upon, to those of the common law where a general obligation to conform to good faith is not recognised . . . The preferred approach in England is to avoid any commitment to over-arching principle, in favour of piecemeal solutions in response to demonstrated problems of unfairness . . . Good faith in Scottish law, as in South African law, is generally an underlying principle of an explanatory and legitimating rather than an active or creative nature . . . It is not a source of obligation in itself.

2.6.2.6 The workability of any agreed mechanism for ascertainment

✗ The standard of reasonableness *cannot* be used to fill gaps where the parties *expressly* **agree to agree** later. In *May and Butcher v R* (1934), R entered into a written agreement to sell M surplus tentage, explicitly leaving the price and date of payment to 'be agreed upon from time to time'. Lord Buckmaster said that 'an agreement between two parties to enter into an agreement in which some critical part of the contract matter is left undetermined is no contract at all'.

This broad exclusionary approach has been criticised. In *Fletcher Challenge Energy Ltd v Electricity Corp of New Zealand Ltd* (2002), Blanchard J of the New Zealand Court of Appeal confined *May and Butcher* to cases where an agreement omits an essential term *and* a means of determining such a term. He said: 'if the Court is satisfied that the parties intended to be bound, it will strive to find a means of giving effect to that intention by filling the gap'.

Courts are slow to invalidate a contract for uncertainty where *the parties* have agreed **workable criteria** (a formula, objective standard or machinery, eg arbitration) for resolving the matter left unresolved. If the parties fail to agree or if their designated machinery for ascertainment breaks down, *the court* can step in and apply the agreed formula or standard itself:

- ✓ *if* the agreed machinery is subsidiary, ie not 'essential';
- ✗ but not if the agreed machinery is essential, ie the parties only intend to be bound if their stipulated machinery fills the gap.
- ✓ In *Sudbrook Trading Estate Ltd v Eggleton* (1983), a lease granted the lessees an option to buy the premises at a price to be fixed by two valuers, one nominated by each party and, in the absence of agreement, by an umpire to be appointed by the valuers. When the lessees sought to exercise the option, the lessors refused to appoint a valuer and claimed that the option clause was void for uncertainty. The House of Lords held that the machinery for appointing the valuers was *subsidiary* (not essential) to the main purpose of ascertaining a fair and reasonable price. Its failure did not prevent the existence of a binding contract. The court could substitute its own machinery by ordering an inquiry into the fair value of the premises. Lord Diplock observed that it is the court's duty to administer justice and to overrule precedents not 'fit for survival in a civilised system of law'. The option clause should not be flouted by the lessor 'at his own sweet will'. It had induced the lessees' reliance (in entering the lease) and was contained in a long lease that had subsisted for many years.
- ✓ In *Queensland Electricity Generating Board v New Hope Collieries* (1989), the Privy Council enforced an agreement to supply coal beyond the first five years, although the agreement stated that the price 'shall be agreed by the parties thereto in accordance with clause 8' (setting out the broad criteria to be applied). The long-term agreement also contained a comprehensive arbitration clause. Sir Robin Cooke said that, in the presence of 'an arbitration or valuation clause in wide enough terms, the Courts accord full weight to their manifest intention to create continuing legal relations. Arguments invoking alleged uncertainty, or alleged inadequacy in the machinery available to the Courts for making contractual rights effective, exert minimal attraction.'

✓ In *MRI Trading AG v Erdenet Mining Corp LLC* (2013), a contract for the sale of goods that left matters, including certain charges and the shipping schedule, to be agreed, was held to be enforceable because, viewed in its wider context, it was one of three contracts entered into pursuant to a settlement agreement between the parties, and on which the parties had acted for over a year. A term was implied to the effect that the charges and the shipping schedule were to be reasonable and were to be determined by arbitration in the event of any dispute.

✗ But, if the stipulated machinery which fails is *essential* (eg if a particular valuer is named because of her special skill, knowledge, or personal judgment), there is no contract. In *Gillatt v Sky Television Ltd* (2000), the court held that the stipulation for payment of '55% of the open market value of such shares . . . as determined by an independent chartered accountant' in certain circumstances was essential and not merely a mechanism for determining the *quantum* of payment. There were several different ways of valuing shares in a private company and the parties intended an independent chartered accountant to do it. Since the machinery was only 'broken' because the parties had not bothered to appoint an independent chartered accountant, the court refused to substitute its own assessment.

2.7 Intention to create legal relations

2.7.1 The requirement and its justification

One 'innovation in 19th Century contract law' was to add the requirement of 'intention to create legal relations' to that of contract formation.[24] This translates into two strong presumptions that require clear evidence to rebut, namely, that:

✗ parties do *not* intend to create legal relations in *social* and *domestic* agreements; and

✓ parties *do* intend to create legal relations in *commercial* agreements.

On its face, this invites an inquiry into the *intention of the parties.*

 Counterpoint

The view that the 'intention to create legal relations' requirement requires investigation of whether the parties intend to be bound can be criticised as:

1. *superfluous*—an intention to be legally bound is already necessary to find: an offer, an acceptance, and for overcoming uncertainty or incompleteness;

2. *fictitious*—parties will often have given the matter no thought and will have no discernible (ie objective) intention on whether the arrangement entered should invoke legal sanctions; and

3. *inconclusive*—any intentions the parties have are likely to be inconsistent (one party intending the agreement to be legally binding, and the other intending it to be morally binding only).

[24] A W B Simpson, 'Innovations in Nineteenth Century Contract Law' (1975) 91 *LQR* 247, 263–5.

It is now widely accepted that the presumptions of intention to create legal relations are based on *public policy*:

(i)   Floodgates: the judicial system should not be swamped with social and domestic disputes. As Atkin LJ comments in *Balfour v Balfour* (1919): 'the small Courts of this country would have to be multiplied one hundredfold if these arrangements were held to result in legal obligations'.

(ii)   Facilitating market transactions: the presumption in *favour* of enforcing *commercial* contracts is consistent with the view that contract law's primary function is to facilitate transactions between people who may otherwise not deal with each other (see 1.3.6). It makes sense in *this* context to use state coercion (by awarding remedies for breach) to enforce agreements for which informal social sanctions are absent.

(iii) Freedom *from* contract: the concern is to limit state intrusion in the private lives of its citizens. Atkin LJ said of a wife's action to enforce her husband's promise in *Balfour*:

> Agreements such as these are outside the realm of contracts altogether. The common law does not regulate the form of agreements between spouses . . . The consideration that really obtains for them is that natural love and affection which counts for so little in these cold Courts. The terms may be repudiated, varied or renewed as performance proceeds or as disagreements develop, and the principles of common law . . . find no place in the domestic code . . . In respect of these promises each house is a domain into which the King's writ does not seek to run.

 Pause for reflection

1. Hedley argues that 'intention to create legal relations' is primarily designed to 'keep contract in its place', that is, 'in the commercial sphere and out of domestic cases, *except* where the judges think it has a useful role to play'; in practice, this means that agreements in domestic contexts will only be enforced if one party has already performed their side of the bargain. The real question is whether the contract is executed or executory ('Keeping Contract in its Place: *Balfour v Balfour* and the Enforceability of Informal Agreements' (1985) 5 *OJLS* 391).

2. Freeman criticises the presumption against the enforceability of family dealings as being out of step with modern developments. *Balfour v Balfour* concerns a Victorian marriage and emphasises status and obligation. This should now give way to autonomy and individual choice and contracts in the private domain should be enforced ('Contracting in the Haven: *Balfour v Balfour* Revisited' in R Halson (ed), *Exploring the Boundaries of Contract* (Dartmouth, 1996) 68).

3. But how far should family and social relationships be contractualised? When should agreements be binding in morality and subject to informal social sanctions, and when should they be binding in law and enforceable by state coercion? Contractual regulation of relationships risks reducing them to measurable obligations, shutting out the more open-ended

> ➜
>
> obligations arising from trust and friendship and subverting the values of the relationship, eg any suggestion that parent–child relationships can be defined by contracts and remedied for breach undermines the idea of unconditional love associated with the upbringing of children. Moreover, contract law should not become involved in private dealings just because the parties wish it to be (see 1.5.1). If two law students sharing a flat agree that their arrangement (for one to cook and the other to clean) should be legally enforceable, the courts are unlikely to award damages for breach. As the Scottish Law Commission has stated: 'it is, in general, right that courts should not enforce entirely social engagements, such as arrangements to play squash or to come to dinner, even though the parties themselves may intend to be legally bound thereby' (*Memorandum No 36 Constitution and Proof of Voluntary Obligations: Formation of Contract*, 10 March 1977, para 72).

2.7.2 Family and social agreements

2.7.2.1 Husband and wife

✗ In *Balfour v Balfour*, a husband and wife returned to England on leave from the husband's employment in Ceylon (now Sri Lanka). The wife remained in England on the doctor's advice and the husband agreed to pay her an allowance of £30 a month until she rejoined him. When the parties formally separated, she sued for the payments. The Court of Appeal denied her claim for lack of consideration (since her love and affection do not count, 3.1.3.5) and lack of intention to create legal relations because the agreement was made while they were living 'in amity'.

✓ The presumption against enforceability does not apply 'when the parties are not living in amity but are separated, or about to separate . . . [t]hey do not rely on honourable understandings. They want everything cut and dried. It may safely be presumed that they intend to create legal relations' (*Merritt v Merritt* (1970)).

2.7.2.2 Pre-nuptial agreements

Until relatively recently, pre-nuptial and post-nuptial agreements (agreements that determine the financial consequences of divorce where no divorce was actually planned) were void as a matter of contract law. They were deemed contrary to public policy, due to their potential to encourage or facilitate divorce. However, in *Radmacher v Granatino* (2010), the Supreme Court held by a majority of 8:1 that, in future, the court should give effect to a nuptial agreement that is freely entered into by each party with a full appreciation of its implications unless, in the circumstances prevailing, it would be unfair to hold the parties to their agreement.

This means that, once it is shown that the agreement was freely entered into, there is a rebuttable presumption that the agreement is enforceable. It will be up to the party seeking to avoid the agreement to prove that it would be unfair to give effect to it. The Supreme Court was keen to downplay this change since the 'fairness' of holding the parties to their agreement on divorce requires consideration of a far wider range of factors than those which would vitiate a contract (see Part IV); eg it would include the parties' emotional state at the time of their agreement, and also their age, maturity, and relationship history.

The Law Commission has recommended that couples should be able to decide in advance how they want to deal with their financial assets in the event of a divorce and therefore, where there is a 'qualifying nuptial agreement', this should be enforceable by the court (*Matrimonial Property Needs and Agreements* (Law Com No 343, 2014)).

Qualifying nuptial agreements must:

- meet the financial needs of the couple;
- meet any financial responsibilities to children;
- be informed by financial disclosure by both spouses; and
- be accompanied by independent legal advice for both parties.

 Counterpoint

In 'Ante-Nuptial Agreements: Fairness, Equality and Presumptions' (2011) 127 *LQR* 335, Herring, Harris, and George note that the Matrimonial Causes Act 1973 stipulates the factors a court should take into account in deciding on the parties' property distribution on divorce; the first consideration being the interests of any children. Until *Radmacher*, the courts had refused to allow the parties to restrict the exercise of their discretion. Yet, as Lady Hale (the only specialist family lawyer and only woman in the Supreme Court) points out in her strong dissenting judgment, the traditional view of marriage as a *status* means: 'First, the parties are not entirely free to determine all its legal consequences for themselves . . . Secondly, their marriage also has legal consequences for other people and for the state.' If couples can contract out of the court's redistributive powers on divorce then marriage ceases to have any particular legal meaning. Its legal effect depends substantially on the parties' agreement. Herring, Harris, and George comment:

> Does it really matter if marriage is now a contract? It does. Intimate relationships, especially those involving children, create inequalities in the parties' economic position. Through the obligations of support which marriage creates, the state has sought to provide some protection from the risks faced by those entering intimate relationships . . . [In general, they] combat gender discrimination and prevent exploitation of the wife's labour. Yet in Radmacher, the Supreme Court tells us that the couple can agree to bypass this protection. This is remarkable. There are few, if any, other areas of law where a person can engage in gender discrimination because the other person has consented to the treatment . . . Lady Hale was brave indeed to be explicit about the gendered nature of this decision.

2.7.2.3 Parents and children

✗ In *Jones v Padavatton* (1969), a mother bought a house for her daughter to live in and to maintain herself from the proceeds of letting the other rooms; the daughter agreed to give up her secretarial work in Washington to read for the

Bar in London. Six years later, the daughter had still not passed the course. The parties fell out; the daughter resisted the mother's claim for possession of the house by claiming a contractual entitlement to remain. The Court of Appeal found no enforceable contract because: (i) there was no intention to create legal relations since the parties were on good terms when the arrangement was made; and (ii) the terms of the arrangement were too vague, particularly as to its duration.

✗ Similarly, it was said in *Fleming v Beeves* (1994) that a parent's promise to pay an allowance while the child is at university normally creates a moral, but not a legal, obligation.

2.7.2.4 Social agreements

✗ The same presumption against enforcement applies to social arrangements. An agreement to meet for a movie, a walk, or a meal is unenforceable; likewise, arrangements to share petrol costs on a journey (*Coward v Motor Insurer's Bureau* (1963)) or to participate in a golf club competition (*Lens v Devonshire Club* (1914)).

✗ *Hadley v Kemp* (1999) involved the pop group Spandau Ballet. K, a member of the group, was credited with authorship of all the group's songs but he had shared the income from this with other members of the group and their manager. When K discontinued the payments, they claimed damages for breach of contract. The court found no enforceable contract. The evidence showed that the relationship between the members of the band was not simply one of business:

> The members of the band had known each other since their schooldays. They have all stressed how at the time they were a close-knit group of friends who were in company with each other constantly. They had formed themselves into a band not just for the business purpose of making money (though they certainly wanted to do that, and rightly so), but also because they loved what they were doing . . . I am not persuaded that the plaintiffs have established that [K's] decision to share his publishing income, and his statement to the band about it, were made with an intention to create legal relations.

2.7.2.5 Rebutting the presumption

The strong presumption *against* enforcement in family and social agreements is said to be rebuttable by clear evidence of contrary intention. Since the presumption is policy-based rather than intention-based, and since it will often be impossible to find a common intention, it is unsurprising that the courts usually refer to policy considerations in deciding whether the presumption is rebutted. Two stand out.

(i) Reliance: courts are more willing to find intention to be bound where one party has *detrimentally relied* upon the agreement.

> ✓ In *Parker v Clark* (1960), the Cs (an elderly couple) and the Ps (a couple 20 years their junior) agreed that if the Ps sold their cottage and came to live

with the Cs, sharing their household expenses, Mr C would leave them a portion of his estate. When the couples fell out, the Ps left on the Cs' demand and successfully claimed damages for breach of contract. Devlin J said that Mr C could not really have supposed 'that the law would leave him at liberty, if he so chose, to tell [the Ps] when they arrived that he had changed his mind, that they could take their furniture away, and that he was indifferent whether they found anywhere else to live or not'.

✓ In *John Sadler v George Reynolds* (2005), R agreed that S should ghostwrite R's autobiography. Slade QC dismissed R's argument that no contract emerged from his meetings with S, which were 'somewhere between an obviously commercial transaction and a social exchange'. R knew that S was an experienced journalist who made money from ghostwriting and met S in that context. Moreover, S had *relied* on an express term of the agreement by negotiating a publishing deal.

(ii) The agreement is only incidental to the parties' relationship or symbolic of its ending, rather than a manifestation of it.

✓ In *Snelling v Snelling* (1973), an agreement between three brothers in relation to the running of the family company, of which they were directors, was held to be enforceable. The same conclusion applies to agreements in respect of a husband and wife's separation.

2.7.3 **Commercial agreements**

✓ Commercial agreements attract a strong presumption that the parties *do* intend to create legal relations. In *Esso Petroleum Ltd v Commissioners of Customs and Excise* (1976), Esso offered to give away a World Cup coin for every minimum purchase of four gallons of petrol. In deciding whether the coins were subject to tax, the House of Lords concluded that an intention to create legal relations *did* attach to the supply of coins; the transaction took place in a business setting and *contemplated large commercial advantage to Esso from the scheme*.

✓ In *Edwards v Skyways Ltd* (1964), the court held that an employer's promise to pay a sum to employees made redundant was contractually enforceable, although it was described as 'ex gratia'.

The presumption of enforceability is **rebutted** in two notable instances.

(i) **Collective agreements between employers and trade unions** are conclusively presumed *not* to have been intended to create legal relations unless they are in writing and expressly provide to the contrary (*Ford Motor Co Ltd v AEF* (1969)). This is now embodied in section 179 of the Trade Union and Labour Relations (Consolidation) Act 1992. The policy is presumably to encourage consensus and discourage resort to courts when parties need to continue to work with each other.

(ii) **Agreements *expressed* to be without intention to create legal relations**, such as transactions made 'subject to contract' (2.6.1, especially *RTS Flexible Systems Ltd v*

Molkerei Alois Muller GMBH (2010)), letters of intent, letters of comfort, and honour clauses, are generally unenforceable.

✓ In *Rose and Frank Co v JR Crompton and Bros Ltd* (1925), R was appointed C's sole agents to finish in 1920, but C terminated without notice in 1919. The court of first instance found the presumption of enforceability rebutted by the clear 'honour clause' in the agreement, which stated that:

> This arrangement is not entered into . . . as a formal or legal agreement, and shall not be subject to legal jurisdiction in the Law Courts . . . but it is only a definite expression and record of the purpose and intention of the three parties concerned, to which they each honourably pledged themselves, with the fullest confidence—based on past business with each other—that it will be carried through by each of the three parties with mutual loyalty and friendly cooperation.

✗ In the Court of Appeal (1923), Scrutton LJ saw 'no reason why, even in business matters, the parties should not intend to rely on each other's good faith and honour, and to exclude all idea of settling disputes by any outside intervention', so long as this is clearly expressed.

✗ In *Kleinwort Benson Ltd v Malaysia Mining Corp Berhad* (1989), K agreed to provide a £10 million credit facility to M's subsidiary company. M refused to guarantee the debt but gave K a **comfort letter** stating that 'it is our policy to ensure that the business of [our subsidiary company] is at all times in a position to meet its liabilities to you under the above arrangements'. The subsidiary ceased to trade when its debts to K reached £10 million. K sued M for the sum, but the Court of Appeal held that the letter was simply an honest representation of M's policy at the time that the statement was made (5.1.2.3). M did not promise to stick by this policy in the future.

However, Lloyd QC warned in *ERDC Group v Brunel University* [2006] that:

> Letters of intent come in all sorts of forms. Some are merely expressions of hope; others are firmer but make it clear that no legal consequences ensue; others presage a contract and may be tantamount to an agreement 'subject to contract'; others are contracts falling short of the full-blown contract that is contemplated; others are in reality that contract in all but name . . . . The phrase 'letter of intent' is not a term of art. Its meaning and effect depend on the circumstances of each case.

The discussion at 2.6.1 is relevant here.

2.8 **Restitution for benefits conferred in anticipation of contracts that do not materialise**

Some cases that have been squeezed into an offer and acceptance format are instances of courts *imposing contracts* to achieve a just solution to what is essentially a non-contractual problem. Stretching the reach of contract law was understandable in a period when courts were slow to recognise induced reliance and unjust enrichment as a basis

of liability, but this approach should be abandoned now that courts are more willing to recognise such liability in the context of pre-contractual negotiations (1.6.2).
Thus, instead of, or in addition to, liberalising the rules on contract formation, it may
be more realistic to admit that sometimes no liability arises in *contract* but may arise
under other heads to reverse *unjust enrichment*. This would increase transparency and
yield more appropriate remedies.

A restitutionary analysis was adopted in **British Steel Corp v Cleveland Bridge
and Engineering Co Ltd** (1984). C sent B a *letter of intent* stating their intention to
place an order for the steel nodes on C's standard terms and requested B (the manufacturer) to commence work 'pending the preparation and issuing to you of the
official form of subcontract'. In the end, no formal contract was agreed; C refused
to pay after the final node was delivered. B argued that there was *no contract* and
sued for the reasonable value of its work (known as a *quantum meruit* claim). C
argued that there *was* a contract and counterclaimed for damages for breach by
B (late delivery and delivery out of sequence), which exceeded the contract price.
Goff J held that:

✗ There was *no contract* because there was no agreement on price and other essential matters; 'in the vast majority of business transactions, particularly those of
substantial size, the price will indeed be an essential term'. This denied C's substantial counterclaim for breach.

✓ B's claim in *unjust enrichment* was allowed. Goff J said:

> Both parties confidently expected a formal contract to eventuate. In these cir-
> cumstances, to expedite performance under that anticipated contract, one re-
> quested the other to commence the contract work, and the other complied with
> that request. If thereafter, as anticipated, a contract was entered into, the work
> done as requested will be treated as having been performed under that contract;
> if, contrary to the expectation, no contract was entered into, then the perfor-
> mance of the work is not referable to any contract the terms of which can be
> ascertained, and the law simply imposes an obligation on the party who made
> the request to pay a reasonable sum for such work as has been done pursuant to
> that request, such an obligation sounding . . . in restitution.

In *Yeoman's Row Management Ltd v James Cobbe* (2008), a property developer orally
agreed to buy property 'subject to contract'. The developer spent substantial time
and money in obtaining planning permission pursuant to the agreement, but the
owner subsequently refused to enter into a binding contract. The developer was
awarded a *quantum meruit* payment for his services in obtaining the planning
permission.

However, restitutionary awards are inappropriate if the court concludes that the
pre-contractual work was done *at the risk of* the performing party. This is likely to be
the case where the parties' agreement is expressly 'subject to contract' or where the
work done is of questionable value to the other party. Accordingly, no restitutionary
award was made in *Regalian Properties plc v London Docklands Development Corp* (1995),
where the work involved architectural and other professional fees paid in preparation
for a proposed land development, which was abandoned.

Pause for reflection

The unjust enrichment approach can be problematic when the benefit conferred deviates from that requested. While the performer is protected, the recipient may be left without redress for delayed or defective performance.[25] In *British Steel Corp v Cleveland Bridge and Engineering*, it was held that the delivery of the nodes out of sequence did not diminish the enrichment to the recipient. However, it should be open to a recipient to argue to the contrary.[26]

THIS CHAPTER IN ESSENCE

 The key areas and core topics in this chapter are summarised in an easy-to-use list, ideal for revision purposes, on the online resources at www.oup.com/uk/chenwishart6e/. Links to websites relevant to the topics covered and any updates to the chapter can also be found on the online resources.

QUESTIONS

1. Ada makes Bob a written offer to sell her house to Bob for £20,000. Ada in fact intended to sell for £200,000. Bob accepts immediately. Can he enforce the agreement? What further facts would you need to know?

2. 'The distinction between an offer and an invitation to treat is based on the intention of the party making the communication.' To what extent is this true?

3. How does, and how should, the law deal with problems arising from the 'battle of forms'?

4. Should the postal acceptance rule apply to modern methods of communication such as email?

5. 'The requirement of "intention to create legal relations" is a misnomer.' Discuss.

6. 'While the rules on contract formation purport to be an elaboration of the requirements of establishing consensus between the parties, an analysis of the rules themselves and their application suggests that other factors also play a role.' Discuss.

7. Conan offers to sell his computer for £300 'first come, first served, email me or text me'. Dan sends the first response by email. Eve texts her response a few hours later saying 'would you accept £250?' Conan sees the text first, then reads his emails but neglects to read Dan's email because the subject line was blank. Conan texts back to Eve 'Yours for £280 unless I hear otherwise within 24 hours'. A day later, he reads Dan's message. Advise Conan.

---

25 E McKendrick, 'The Battle of the Forms and the Law of Restitution' (1988) 8 *OJLS* 197, 212.

26 Either *objectively* (see *Crown House Engineering Ltd v Amec Projects Ltd* (1990)), or as a result of 'subjective devaluation' (ie that the value of the non-conforming performance is less than the objective value *to the recipient*). See P Birks, *An Introduction to the Law of Restitution* (Clarendon Press, 1985) 109–17.

For hints on how to answer these questions, please see the online resources at www.oup.com/uk/chenwishart6e/

KEY FURTHER READING

Chen-Wishart, M (2009), 'Objectivity and Mistake: The Oxymoron of *Smith v Hughes*' in J Neyers, R Bronough, and S G A Pitel (eds), *Exploring Contract Law* (Hart) 341.

Endicott, T (2000), 'Objectivity, Subjectivity, and Incomplete Agreements' in J Horder (ed), *Oxford Essays in Jurisprudence* (OUP) 151.

Gardner, S (1992), 'Trashing with Trollope: A Deconstruction of the Postal Rules in Contract', 12 *OJLS* 170.

Hedley, S (1985), 'Keeping Contract in its Place: *Balfour v Balfour* and the Enforceability of Informal Agreements', 5 *OJLS* 391.

Hill, S (2001), 'Flogging a Dead Horse—The Postal Acceptance Rule and E-mail', 17 *JCL* 151.

McLauchlan, D (1998), 'Rethinking Agreement to Agree', 18 *NZULR* 77.

Nolan, D (2010), 'Offer and Acceptance in the Electronic Age' in A Burrows and E Peel (eds), *Contract Formation and Parties* (OUP) 61.

Rawlings, R (1979), 'The Battle of the Forms', 42 *MLR* 715.

Simpson, AWB (1975), 'Innovation in Nineteenth Century Contract Law', 91 *LQR* 247.

Simpson, AWB (1995), 'Quackery and Contract Law: *Carlill v. Carbolic Smoke Ball Co* (1893)' in *Leading Cases in the Common Law* (Clarendon Press) 259.

3

Enforceability: consideration, promissory estoppel, formalities

'Will the law enforce the agreement?'

English law does not enforce all promises; it will not even enforce all agreements. While offer, acceptance, certainty, and intention to create legal relations (Chapter 2) are all necessary, they are not sufficient to make a contract legally enforceable; an additional element is required. This is most commonly satisfied by the presence of so-called 'consideration'. To be enforceable, an *informal* agreement (ie lacking the formalities that render it enforceable, 3.3) must comprise an exchange in which each party treats her own promise of (or actual) performance as the price of the other's promise of (or actual) performance. Consideration is the 'agreed equivalent and inducing cause of the promise'.[1] In qualifying circumstances, English law also permits some enforcement of promises that induce the promisee's *reliance* via the doctrine of promissory estoppel (3.2). If consideration is lacking, English law will enforce *formal* promises (as where the promise is contained in a deed (3.3)). Thus, *A*'s undertaking to *B* is enforceable by *B* if:

(i) *B* has 'paid for' it;

(ii) *B* has relied on *A*'s undertaking and it would be unconscionable for *A* to go back on it; or

(iii) it is embodied in the necessary formal instrument.

The questions to be considered in this chapter are:

(i) What are the requirements of consideration, promissory estoppel, and formalities?

(ii) What is the justification for each test of enforceability?

(iii) Are the rules and scope of each doctrine satisfactory? If not, how should each be developed?

Diagram 3A gives an overview of the enforceability of undertakings.

---

[1] K Llewellyn, 'What Price Contract?' (1930) 40 *Yale LJ* 704, 742.

Diagram 3A Overview: the enforceability of undertakings

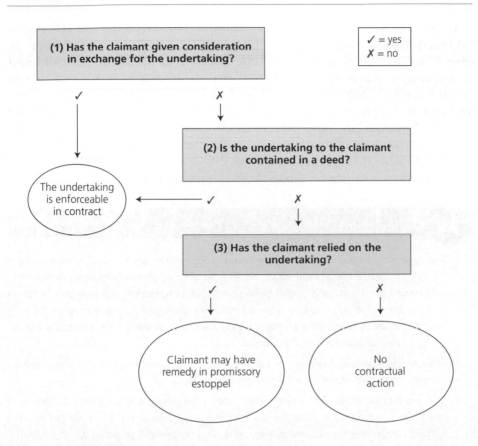

3.1 **Consideration**

'I paid for your promised performance'

3.1.1 **The basic idea and its justification**

The basic idea of the consideration requirement is that in order to *acquire the right* to enforce another's undertaking, a party must undertake (promise) to give, or actually give (perform), something stipulated by the other as the price for her undertaking. Thus, my undertaking X is enforceable by you if you have given:

- a reciprocal undertaking of Y (on a bilateral contract analysis), or
- actual performance of Y (on a unilateral contract analysis),

where Y is stipulated by me as the price for X, eg my promise of a laptop for your promise of £1,000 (or actual payment of £1,000) is enforceable by either of us; each promise is supported by consideration from the other.

The enforcement of agreements supported by consideration prioritises bargains over gifts. Why should this be so? The answer is important because it provides the basis for critically analysing the views expressed about the doctrine and suggestions for its reform.

(i) **Consideration is evidence of the existence and seriousness of the undertaking:** the most common view is that the consideration requirement performs an evidentiary, cautionary, and channelling function,[2] analogous to that performed by formality requirements (3.3). That is, its presence ensures that a promise was actually made (evidentiary), the promisor took care in making it (cautionary), and understood its consequences (channelling). Baragwanath J of the New Zealand Court of Appeal said in *Antons Trawling Co Ltd v Smith* (2003) that: 'The importance of consideration is as a valuable signal that the parties intend to be bound by their agreement, rather than an end in itself.' On this view, consideration is *unnecessary* if a party's serious intention to be bound can be proved in other ways.

 Counterpoint

1. Although consideration *may* perform an evidentiary function (eg nominal consideration, 3.1.3.4), its role cannot be reduced to this. The presence of consideration does not eliminate evidentiary, cautionary, or channelling problems; oral undertakings may be very difficult to prove, and an undertaking can be made impulsively without any intention to be bound. Conversely, even if the promisor clearly intends to be bound, her informal undertaking is unenforceable without consideration.

2. Moreover, just because keeping one's promise is a *moral* obligation, not all moral obligations are enforceable *legal* ones. Something more is needed.

3. Gratuitous promises are overwhelmingly made in the private domain where the promisee (as a friend, family member, or partner) may have a reciprocal moral obligation to forgive, compromise, or accommodate a repenting promisor. This would weigh against enforceability.

(ii) **Welfare maximisation:** the enforcement of bargains is consistent with efficiency theories that interpret contract law rules as being aimed at *welfare maximisation* (1.4.3). Since *exchanges* tend to transfer property or services to those who value them most highly, the consideration requirement (by ensuring an exchange) is the best indicator of value-maximising transactions. In contrast, donative promises (unsupported by a reciprocal promise or performance) are said to be 'sterile'.[3] However, this is easily challenged; donative promises *may* be efficient (eg a gift from rich grandparents to the needy student grandchild) and exchanges may *not* be (eg the buyer who

---

[2] L Fuller, 'Consideration and Form' (1941) 31 *Columbia L Rev* 799; *Williams v Roffey Brothers* (1991) at 18; R Flannigan, 'Privity—The End of an Era (Error)' (1987) 103 *LQR* 564, 586–7; S Smith, *Contract Theory* (OUP, 2004) 216–17; Law Commission, *Privity of Contract: Contracts for the Benefit of Third Parties* (Law Com Consultation Paper 121, 1991) para 2.9.

[3] Conversely, R Posner, *Economic Analysis of Law* (8th edn, Aspen, 2014) ch 4; R Posner, 'Gratuitous Promises in Economics and Law' (1977) 6 *JLS* 411; M Eisenberg, 'Donative Promises' (1979) 47 *U Chi L Rev* 1.

mistakenly overvalues the property). This only counts if one believes that contract law is aimed at maximising welfare.

(iii) **Reciprocity—the intuitive justice of exchange:** the enforcement of bargains expresses the idea of *reciprocity*. Reciprocation is the norm between equals in most social interactions. This is even clearer outside the social context; it symbolises an ideal of fairness, because it distinguishes *trading* from *taking*, and *bargains* from instances of *exploitation*. Popular sentiment favours the enforcement of promises involving some quid pro quo;[4] a promise ought to be enforced because it is the promisor's payment for getting something in return. Conversely, the promisee, having paid for the promise, has a more compelling reason to enforce the promise than one who has not paid. This is reinforced by the following:

- **The expectation measure of damages:** the bargain model explains the *extent* of liability for breach of contract. The expectation measure, the distinctive feature of a contractual action, gives the promisee the value of the promised performance (13.2), *because* she has given the agreed equivalence of that performance.

- It is often said that **other legal systems** do not require consideration. But this does not withstand closer scrutiny. In fact, they enforce substantially all agreements that would comply with our test of bargain and most legal systems treat gifts (gratuitous promises) differently.[5] While French and German law *appear* to enforce a much wider range of promises than English law, *in practice* they draw essentially the *same* line between gratuitous undertakings and reciprocal undertakings.[6] Thus, civil law enforces gratuitous promises, *but* subjects them to a stringent formality requirement unless they are 'synallagmatic' (ie bilateral reciprocal undertakings; these do not require formalities).[7] This is just a negative way of expressing what English law expresses positively in requiring consideration.[8]

- Stevens notes how widespread the idea of **reciprocity is in private law:**[9]

  That a party who has provided consideration is more deserving than one who has not is reflected in a number of rules of English law unrelated to contract formation. The force behind consideration is found in the equitable maxim that 'equity will not assist the volunteer'. Bare promises made by way of deed are therefore not susceptible to the equitable remedy of specific performance . . . a deed which has been mistakenly entered into is also much easier to set aside than a contract which has been made for good consideration. Similarly the protection

---

[4] E Patterson, 'An Apology for Consideration' (1958) 58 *Columbia L Rev* 929, 946–7.

[5] J Dawson, *Gifts and Promises: Continental and American Law Compared* (Yale University Press, 1980) 223; K Zweigert and H Kötz, *Introduction to Comparative Law* (3rd edn, Clarendon Press, 1998) 392, 395, and 397; O Lando and H Beale, *Principles of European Contract Law* (Kluwer, 2000) 130–3, 158.

[6] J Dawson, *Gifts and Promises: Continental and American Law Compared* (Yale University Press, 1980); A T von Mehren, 'Civil Law Analogous to Consideration: An Exercise in Comparative Analysis' (1959) 72 *Harvard L Rev* 1009.

[7] §§ 320–6 of the German Civil Code (BGB); Art 1102 of the French Civil Code (*Code civil*).

[8] R Zimmermann, *The Law of Obligations* (OUP, 1996) 504–5.

[9] R Stevens, 'The Contracts (Rights of Third Parties) Act 1999' (2004) 120 *LQR* 292, 322.

afforded to a *bona fide* purchaser for value without notice of a prior proprietary interest both at law and in equity is not extended to a party who is merely a donee. Further, whether consideration has been provided is relevant in deciding whether a transaction can be set aside upon one party's insolvency. In none of these areas is consideration fulfilling the role played by a requirement of form.

(iv) **Marking the boundary of appropriate legal involvement**: the consideration requirement draws the line between *public* enforceable transactions and *private* unenforceable agreements, a line further reinforced by the presumption against the enforcement of domestic and social agreements (2.7.2).

- Legal enforcement is unnecessary and inappropriate in the social domain within which we readily make arrangements with friends and family in whom we have a degree of trust, backed up by social or moral sanctions. They are private arrangements, which can be broken only on pain of moral, social, or non-legal sanctions. It is also the context in which gratuitous promises are most likely to occur. Gifts are expressions of the value of *altruism*: their intrinsic value is destroyed if the donor is compelled to give the gift. An enforced gift is an oxymoron.

- In contrast, we cannot readily 'do deals' with strangers; here, contract law bridges the gap in trust and provides sanctions to facilitate reciprocal undertakings that further the purposes of both parties.

3.1.2 **The requirement of nexus**

Where I undertake X in exchange for you undertaking Y:

(i)   there must be the necessary **nexus** (causal connection) between—

- the parties me and you; and
- the undertakings X and Y (each should be induced by and be the price for the other).

3.1.2.1 Consideration must move from the claimant

The traditional view is that the consideration doctrine deals with two questions, namely:

(i)   *Which* undertakings are enforceable? Answer: those which have been paid for.

(ii)   *Who* can enforce the undertaking? Answer: the party who has paid for it. This is often expressed as a requirement that 'consideration must move from the promisee'. You can enforce my undertaking to you because you have given me consideration for it.

- The corollary is that a party who has not provided consideration for a promise cannot enforce it. Thus, a third party cannot enforce my undertaking because you (not the third party) provided the consideration for it. This is the basis of the **privity rule** (4.1.1), which bars a third party from suing on a contract even where it was made for her benefit.

- The Contract (Rights of Third Parties) Act 1999 separates the two questions posed above (*'which* promises are enforceable?' and *'who* can enforce?'). Whilst promises continue to be enforceable only if they are supported by consideration, C(RTP)A dispenses with the requirement that consideration must move from the claimant. Hence, a third party can enforce a contract made for her benefit even if she gives no consideration for it (4.1.5). Thus, the consideration requirement is relaxed (or undermined).

3.1.2.2 Consideration must be requested by the promisor

✓ Consideration, broadly defined as conferring a benefit or obviating a disbenefit (or detriment), must be given *in return for* (ie in order to 'buy') the promise to be enforced.

✗ There is no consideration if the promisee incurs a detriment or confers a benefit merely in reliance on the promise. In *Combe v Combe* (1951), a husband promised to pay his wife £100 a year on their divorce. The wife sought to enforce the promise, arguing that she gave consideration for it by not applying for maintenance. The Court of Appeal rejected this because the husband did *not request* her to do this. Her forbearance *resulted from* his promise to pay but was not given *in return for it.*

However, the court can imply a request in finding consideration. In *Alliance Bank v Broom* (1864), B promised to provide some security for its debt to A. When A sued to enforce this, B argued that A gave no consideration for it. The court enforced B's undertaking because while B did not expressly ask A to forbear from suing B to recover the debt, the court implied such a request.

 Pause for reflection

Courts have considerable leeway in deciding whether to imply a request by the promisor and so treat the promisee's reliance or conferral of benefit as consideration. A request may have been more readily implied in *Alliance Bank v Broom* because a bank is much more likely to institute proceedings than a wife. Moreover, justice did not demand that a request be implied in *Combe* since the wife's income exceeded her husband's and she had delayed six years before initiating action.[10]

3.1.2.3 Past consideration is not good consideration

Since consideration must be given *in response to* (in return or as payment for) the promise, it cannot logically be given or done *before* the other's promise was made. If it is, the law regards the promise as a gratuitous and unenforceable response to the promisee's earlier gift.

---

[10] See 'Consideration: A Restatement' in P S Atiyah, *Essays on Contract* (Clarendon Press, 1986) 179, 232 and Atiyah, 147.

Consideration may be past because:

(i)   It has already been given for a reciprocal promise and cannot buy additional promises from the same promisor: if I promise to pay you £5 for one book, I cannot rely on the same £5 to enforce your later promise to give me an additional book. In *Roscorla v Thomas* (1842), R purchased a horse from T. T's *subsequent* assurance to R that the horse was sound and free from vice was unenforceable because the only possible consideration for it was the price already payable under the original contract and that consideration was past.

(ii)   Its performance predates the promise sought to be enforced: in *Eastwood v Kenyon* (1840), a young girl's guardian raised a loan to educate her and improve her marriage prospects. Although her husband promised to pay off the loan, the guardian was unable to enforce this promise because his consideration (in bringing up and financing the girl) was past. His actions were not requested by the husband and could not have been performed in response to his later promise. The husband's moral obligation to pay could not be converted into a legal obligation by his promise.

The courts look at the actual sequence of events, rather than the contractual words. Thus, in *Re McArdle* (1951), consideration was held to be past because, although the promise was made 'in consideration of your carrying out' certain work, the work was completed *before* the promise was made: it was not something yet to be performed.

However, the past consideration rule can operate harshly in some circumstances, and the exact order of events is not decisive if the court is satisfied that the promisor's promise and the promisee's past actions are, in fact, part of the *same overall transaction*. This is the gist of the major exception to the past consideration rule, the doctrine of implied assumpsit.

   ✓ In *Lampleigh v Brathwait* (1615), B (sentenced to death) asked L to obtain a pardon from King James I. L was successful. B's subsequent promise to pay L £1,000 was enforceable.

   ✓ In *Pao On v Lau Yiu Long* (1980), the Privy Council opined that a claimant must show that:

      (i)   she performed the act at the promisor's *request*;

      (ii)   it was clearly understood (implied) at the time of the request that she *would be rewarded* for the act; and

      (iii)   the eventual promise is one which *would have been enforceable* if it had been made at the time of the act.

In short, where I ask you to do something (Y) which you do, and I *thereafter* promise you X, the court could imply an understanding at the time of my request that you would be paid for doing Y. If so, my later promise of X can be 'backdated' to the time of my request as consideration for your performance of Y, which in turn becomes valid consideration for my 'backdated' promise. This reasoning was applied in *Pao On v Lau Yiu Long*. P sold shares to X company and was paid by shares in X company. L owned most of the shares in X Company and requested that P not sell 60% of the shares it received for a year to avoid triggering a fall in their value. To protect P from any fall in value in that period, L agreed to *buy back* those shares at $2.50 each at the end of the year. When P realised that this would deprive them of any increase in the value of the shares beyond $2.50, P refused to proceed with the main contract unless L agreed to give a *guarantee by way of indemnity* (ie L would only buy back *if* the shares fell below $2.50). When the shares fell well below $2.50, L refused to indemnify P, arguing lack of consideration from P and duress. The court found:

- ✗ no duress (8.4.2);
- ✓ valid consideration in P's promise to go ahead with the main contract, although it was already owed to a third party (ie X company, 3.1.4.2); and
- ✓ valid consideration in P's promise not to sell the shares for a year because it was given at L's request with the common intention that L should protect P against a drop in value. This intention survived through the cancellation of the buy-back agreement. L's subsequent promise may be regarded either as *evidence* of the amount payable (as in *In re Casey's Patents* (1892)), or as a new agreement in the nature of a *compromise* settling the amount payable (as in *Horton v Horton (No 2)* (1961)).

Parliament has also mitigated the rigours of the past consideration rule by providing that a pre-existing debt or liability is good consideration for a bill of exchange (Bills of Exchange Act 1882, s 27(1)(b)), and that a debt is deemed to have accrued on and not before the date of the debtor's acknowledgement of the debt (Limitation Act 1980, s 27(5)).

3.1.3 **The requirement of 'value'**

What *inclusionary* and *exclusionary* rules define the boundaries of valuable consideration? **Diagram 3B** gives an overview and summary of the discussion.

I the inner shaded circle provides the starting point: it shows the varied and unstable definitions of consideration.

II the area beyond the inner shaded circle represents the expansionist tendencies resulting from the principle that consideration *need not be adequate*. The left side of the diagram shows that valuable consideration includes: *nominal* benefits, *compromises* or *forbearances* of claim, and some *intangible* benefits.

III the outer broken circle shows how each of these expansionary tendency can be 'pushed back' (or contained) by the general qualification that consideration must be 'something which is of some value in the eye of the law' (*Thomas v Thomas* (1842)), and so disqualifying certain promises as good consideration.

The **right side** of the diagram at **II** addresses the troublesome issue of whether performance of, or promises to perform, a *pre-existing duty* amounts to valuable consideration. The answers are broadly:

- ✓ 'yes' if the pre-existing contractual duty is owed to a third party (3.1.4.2);
- ✗ 'no' if it is imposed by public law (3.1.4.1), *unless* it amounting to valuable consideration would not contravene public policy.
- ✓ 'yes' if the pre-existing duty is already owed to the other party in contract, and 'practical benefit' is conferred on the other party, whether the contract is of the 'same for more' (3.1.5.3) or 'less for the same' variety (3.1.5.4).

These are discussed in greater detail in what follows.

Diagram 3B What counts as valuable consideration?

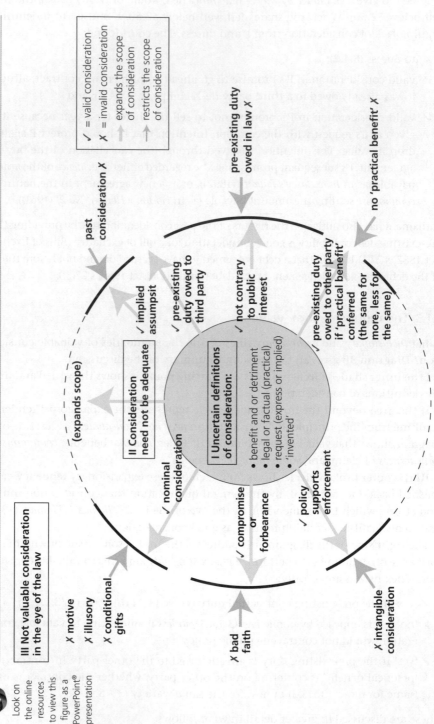

3.1.3.1 The definitions of valuable consideration

The idea that you have to *give* something to be able to *get* something in exchange is simple enough, but the devil is in the detail. What 'something' qualifies as consideration to enforce the reciprocal promise? Courts have considerable leeway in answering this question to reflect their assessment of the desirability of enforcing particular promises. This is facilitated by the unavoidable vagueness in the abstract concepts used to define consideration. *Currie v Misa* (1875) gives the classic definition: 'a valuable consideration, in the sense of the law, may consist either in some right, interest, profit, or benefit accruing to the one party, or some forbearance, detriment, loss, or responsibility given, suffered, or undertaken by the other' (at 162). A number of features complicate this apparently simple definition.

(i)   **Benefit or detriment**: usually, benefit *and* detriment are both present, eg, paying for something is a detriment to the buyer and a benefit to the seller; it renders the seller's promise to deliver goods or perform a service enforceable. Conversely, delivering or performing something is a detriment to the seller and a benefit to the buyer, and renders the buyer's promise to pay enforceable. *However,*

- there may be detriment to one party *without* apparent benefit to the other (eg a promise to pay a sum if the promisee gives up her job to retrain, as in *Jones v Padavatton* (1969) (2.7.2)); or
- there may be benefit to one party *without* detriment to the other (eg a promise to perform an existing duty to a third party, as in *Pao On v Lau Yiu Long* (3.1.4.2)); and
- while benefit or detriment may be apparent where consideration is *executed* (ie performed), where consideration is *executory* (ie yet to be performed), benefit or detriment can only be understood in terms of the *right to enforce* the promised performance.

(ii)   **Factual or legal**: *factual* benefit received or detriment suffered, as perceived by the *parties*, is usually sufficient for consideration. But courts sometimes insist on benefit or detriment in the 'eye of the *law*' and not just the eyes of the parties. Accordingly:

- consideration may be denied although there is factual benefit or detriment (eg the rule that the promisee confers no legal value by promising not to sue on an invalid claim, however much this may factually benefit the promisor, 3.1.3.6); and
- consideration may be found although there is no factual benefit or detriment, but only legal benefit or detriment (eg nominal consideration, 3.1.3.4).

(iii)   **Request**: *Value is subjective* and, if a party requests something, then she must value, and be factually benefited by, its receipt. However, this can blur the distinctions between the *value* question and the *nexus* question (ie whether consideration is past, 3.1.2), between consideration and motive (3.1.3.5), and between bargains and conditional gifts (3.1.3.5).

(iv) **Tangible and intangible value**: performance with economic value readily qualifies as consideration. But difficulty arises with non-monetary performance of doubtful economic value to the promisor (3.1.3.5). Thus, love and affection are not valid consideration (*Bret v JS* (1600)). On the other hand, valuable consideration has been found for an uncle's promise to pay a sum on the event of his nephew's marriage to a particular person (*Shadwell v Shadwell* (1860), 3.1.4.2), and for a man's promise to pay a sum to the mother of his child who promised that the child would be 'well looked after and happy' (*Ward v Byham* (1956)) (3.1.4.1).

(v) **'Invented' consideration**: in 'Consideration: A Critical Analysis of Professor Atiyah's Fundamental Restatement' (1976) 50 *Australian LJ* 439, **Treitel** argues for the traditional view of bargain consideration. However, he emphasises the flexibility of bargain consideration and the possibility of English courts 'inventing' consideration, by treating an act or forbearance as valid consideration, although it was not the promisor's purpose to obtain it (eg *Chappell v Nestlé* (1960), 3.1.3.4) and although there is no prejudice to the promisee (eg *Shadwell v Shadwell*, 3.1.4.2).

 Pause for reflection

The consideration doctrine is a moving target. The different definitions yield different pictures of the scope of valuable consideration (factual/legal; requested/impliedly requested; tangible/intangible). A set of facts may yield valid consideration on one conception but not on another. By moving between the different conceptions of value, courts have considerable latitude in determining whether to find consideration (or not), and hence whether to enforce a promise (or not). We need to go beyond bemoaning the instability at the heart of the consideration doctrine to identify and critically assess the factors which influence the finding of consideration.

3.1.3.2 The pros and cons of enforcement

This discussion presages and provides a context for understanding the detailed account of the rules. The **pro-enforcement factors** push out the boundaries of enforceable promises, as illustrated in **Diagram 3B II**. They include the desirability of:

(i) recognising the *subjectivity* of values and respecting the parties' *intention* (eg via nominal consideration (3.1.2.2 and 3.1.3.4) and 'practical benefit' in *Williams v Roffey Brothers* (3.1.5.3));

(ii) protecting the promisee's *reliance* (eg forbearance to sue (3.1.3.6));

(iii) preventing the promisor's enrichment at the promisee's expense (eg the exception to the past consideration rule (3.1.2.3));

(iv) encouraging *finality* in dispute resolution (eg compromises and forbearances (3.1.3.6)); and

(v)   imposing responsibility otherwise regarded as *just* (eg *Ward v Byham* (3.1.4.1)).

Anti-enforcement factors that restrain the scope of enforceable promises (**Diagram 3B III**) include the undesirability of enforcing:

(i)   *gifts* and other transactions in the *private* domain, because the law's involvement may do more harm than good (eg the invalidity of mere motive and intangible benefits (3.1.3.5));

(ii) *wholly one-sided* 'bargains' (eg illusory consideration (3.1.3.5)); and

(iii) prevention of *extortion or corruption* (eg the invalidity of promises to perform an existing duty (3.1.4.1)).

3.1.3.3 Consideration need not be adequate

A promise is enforceable as long as *something* valuable in the eye of the law is exchanged for it; the values exchanged need not be equivalent. In principle, there is valid consideration:

✓ in promising to pay £20 for a house in central London worth £3 million; or

✓ in exchanging your painting by Monet worth £10 million for a warm coat, even on a scorching day.

The central premise, that it is *for the parties* to determine what they value and how much they value it, fits closely with the free-market philosophy underlying efficiency theories of contract law (1.4.3). As Posner said:[11] 'Courts have no comparative advantage in determining at what price goods should be sold. On the contrary, in all but very exceptional cases, negotiation between buyer and seller is the more reliable method of determining a price at which exchange is mutually beneficial.'

 Counterpoint

The rule that consideration need not be adequate can be misleading. Although we can easily grasp the idea of subjective and idiosyncratic valuation of benefits (eg the rich paying vast sums for a trivial item on a whim), this cannot explain many cases involving a glaring disparity between the values exchanged. It is important to bear in mind that a contract supported by consideration can still:

• be **set aside** for a host of vitiating factors (eg misrepresentation, duress, or undue influence (Part IV)); or

• have its **contents added to** by *implied terms* or **subtracted from** because of unfairness (Part V).

In these cases, the presence of serious inadequacy of consideration will usually be a major, although not the sole, factor behind intervention.

---

[11] R Posner, *Economic Analysis of Law* (10th edn, Aspen, 2014) 100–1.

3.1.3.4 Trivial and nominal consideration

The most trifling benefit or detriment can constitute valid consideration. Lord Somervell said in *Chappell v Nestlé* (1960) that: 'A contracting party can stipulate for what consideration he chooses. A peppercorn does not cease to be good consideration if it is established that the promisee does not like pepper and will throw away the corn.' Thus, good consideration was found where:

- ✓ a promisee briefly lent two boilers to the promisor for weighing, in exchange for the promise to return the boilers in the same condition (*Bainbridge v Firmstone* (1838));

- ✓ a promisee surrendered a document that was thought to be a guarantee but was actually worthless, in exchange for a promise to pay certain bills (*Haigh v Brooks* (1839));

- ✓ a promisee supplied three wrappers from the promisor's chocolate bars, in exchange for a promised gramophone record (*Chappell v Nestlé*).

In these cases, *factual benefit* to the promisor and *factual detriment* to the promisee are doubtful. Atiyah argues that there was no consideration in *Nestlé* since: 'it would be ridiculous to assert that the sending or the receipt of the wrappers necessarily involved an actual detriment to the sender or a benefit to the defendants'. Indeed, the promisor insisted that the wrappers were worthless and thrown away on receipt. Treitel bridges the gap with his concept of 'invented' consideration and by emphasising that consideration need not be adequate; there is 'no doctrinal difficulty in holding that a piece of paper or some act of forbearance of very small value can constitute consideration'.

 Pause for reflection

1. *Chappell v Nestlé* makes better sense when seen in its broader context. The case arose *not* because a customer was trying to enforce the promise to give a gramophone record for the chocolate wrappers, but because the owners of the copyright sought an injunction to prevent the promisor's infringement of their copyright (by failing to pay them a percentage of the profits of the sales that the wrappers represented). The court's conclusion that the wrappers constituted valid consideration is understandable because of their value in Nestlé's marketing strategy. It makes sense, then, that Nestlé should not retain the whole benefit of their enhanced sales, without paying the owners of the copyright in the music. To recognise the bargain in *Chappell v Nestlé* (the gramophone record for the enhanced sales), the court used the *request* conception of value.

2. The converse is illustrated in *Lipkin Gorman v Karpnale Ltd* (1991), a case famous for recognising the principle of unjust enrichment in English law. It is of interest to us here for its *denial of consideration*. C (a solicitor) stole £150,000 from his firm's client account, which he then lost through gambling at the Playboy Club. When the firm claimed this sum from Playboy, the club argued that it was protected because it had given consideration for it in

➡

> the form of the *gaming chips* it gave to C in exchange for the money (since gaming and wagering contracts were void under the Gaming Act 1845). The House of Lords disagreed, saying that 'the chips themselves were worthless' (but then, why not also the wrappers in *Chappell v Nestlé*?) and were not regarded by the parties as valuable in themselves, but merely as a 'convenient mechanism for facilitating gambling' (but the wrappers were an equally convenient mechanism for facilitating marketing). The concern to protect the victims of the solicitor's theft led the House of Lords to deny that the gambling chips constituted consideration for the money, which the club was then required to return to the firm.
>
> 3. The rule that consideration need not be adequate can allow form to triumph over substance. Gratuitous promises are enforceable if they are 'dressed up' as bargains (eg a peppercorn for £5,000). Here, the doctrine of consideration does not serve its main purpose of distinguishing gratuitous promises from bargains. As Atiyah observes: 'a promise for nominal consideration is just about the clearest possible indication that the promisor intended his promise seriously and intended to give the promisee a legally enforceable right'.[12] Since compliance with *formalities* (eg deeds) also makes a promise enforceable (3.3), the law clearly has no objection to the enforceability of gratuitous promises per se. It is only *informal* gratuitous promises that are not enforceable; the nominal consideration device is thus analogous to invoking formalities to make gratuitous promises binding.

There are **two limits to the nominal consideration device:**

(i) The promise is unenforceable if the consideration alleged is incontrovertibly less than the promise sought to be enforced, as a matter of arithmetic, eg I cannot enforce your promise to pay £500 in exchange for my paying you £1. However, the exchange of *specific* money (bearing a certain date or in a certain currency), or payment at an *earlier time* in exchange for a sum of greater face value, is enforceable.

(ii) The right obtained by giving nominal consideration is less secure, if not negated, in certain circumstances, eg, specific performance of the promise will not be ordered, and the promise will not be enforced if it would prejudice third party interests (Law of Property Act 1925, s 205(1)(xxi)).

3.1.3.5 Motive and other consideration valueless in law

Although consideration need not be adequate, it must have some *minimum content*. A promisor will always have a motive (reason) for making a promise, but her promise is only enforceable if her motive can be construed as that of *obtaining something* valuable in the eye of the law from the promisee.

(i) Motive

Consideration requires at least the *form* of a present or future *exchange*. The promisor's mere wish to confer a benefit is unenforceable, since nothing comes back the other way *in exchange* for it. Thus, *mere motive* is not good consideration. This is another reason why past consideration is not good consideration (3.1.2.3); it is merely the

---

[12] P S Atiyah, 'Consideration: A Restatement' in *Atiyah's Essays on Contract* (Clarendon Press, 1986) 194.

motive for the promise. In *Thomas v Thomas* (1842), a testator expressed his intention to let his widow have his house for the rest of her life. After his death, his executors promised to carry out the testator's desire if the widow paid £1 per annum towards the ground rent and kept the house in repair. The court held that, while the testator's wish was merely the *motive* for the transaction, the widow's promise to pay rent and make repairs were of value in the eye of the law as consideration for the executor's promise.

(ii) Conditional gifts

The promisee's satisfaction of the qualifying *condition* for a promise is not good consideration, unless that condition was requested as the *price* for the promise. If the promise is to confer a benefit on the happening of an event that is *independent* of the promisee's action, there is only an unenforceable conditional gift (eg 'I'll pay you £20 if it rains tomorrow'). But conditions that consist of some action by the promisee are likely to be regarded as good consideration, eg:

- ✓ sending in chocolate wrappers in *Chappell v Nestlé*;
- ✓ purchasing four gallons of petrol to get a coin depicting a World Cup footballer in *Esso Petroleum Co Ltd v Customs and Excise Commissioners* (1976); and
- ✓ buying a smoke ball, using it as directed and catching influenza in *Carlill v Carbolic Smoke Ball* (1893).

(iii) Intangible benefits

The line between gratuitous promises and bargains is reinforced by the rule that intangible benefits are not consideration in the 'eye of the law'. Thus, the following were held to be unenforceable:

- ✗ a father's promise made in consideration of a son's 'natural love and affection' (*Bret v JS* (1600));
- ✗ a father's promise in consideration of his son's promise not to annoy the father with complaints (*White v Bluett* (1853)); and
- ✗ a customer's promise to pay the builder's demand 'in order to maintain an amicable relationship' (*North Ocean Shipping Co v Hyundai Construction Co (The Atlantic Baron)* (1979)).

However, the intangibility of the benefit promised poses no insurmountable obstacle if the courts think it just to enforce the reciprocal promise:

- ✓ a woman's promise to behave 'with sobriety, and in a respectable, orderly, and virtuous manner' and not to act in such a way as to bring on herself or her former husband 'hate, contempt, or ridicule' in exchange for an allowance from him (*Dunton v Dunton* (1892)); and
- ✓ a mother's promise to see that her child is 'well looked after and happy' in exchange for the father's promise to pay towards her upkeep (*Ward v Byham* (1956), 3.1.4.1).

The intangible benefit may arise from the promise to *refrain* from some activity.

- ✓ In the controversial American case of *Hamer v Sidaway* (1891), a promise to pay a nephew a sum of money if he refrained from 'drinking liquor, using tobacco, swearing and playing cards or billiards for money' until he was 21 was enforced. The court reasoned that the nephew gave consideration by forgoing his legal right to engage in such activities. However, it could equally be said that the son in *White v Bluett* refrained from perfectly lawful conduct, yet Pollock CB said that the son had 'no right to complain' to his father (it was the father's decision how he wanted to distribute his property). It may be relevant that the conduct forgone in *White v Bluett* (not to complain) is less deserving of reward than that in *Hamer* (not to drink, smoke, or gamble). But this cannot explain the next case.

✓ In *Pitt v PHH Asset Management Ltd* (1993), PHH accepted P's bid of £200,000 for a cottage 'subject to contract', but withdrew the next day when B (a third party) made a higher offer. PHH's subsequent promise to sell the cottage to P for £200,000 and not to consider other offers for the property (a 'lock-out' agreement, 2.6.2.5) was held to be enforceable because P gave good consideration by promising to:

(i)   exchange contracts within two weeks of receiving the draft contract;

(ii) refrain from telling B that he was no longer interested in the property to induce B to lower her offer to PHH; and

(iii) withdraw his threat to seek an injunction restraining the sale to B.

Whilst (i) is clearly good consideration, (ii) and (iii) are questionable since they amount to recognising value in being free from nuisance. Peter Gibson LJ held that P's threat to claim an injunction lacked substance; therefore, accepting (iii) as valid consideration contradicts the rule that no consideration is provided by compromising a claim that is made in bad faith (3.1.3.6).

 Pause for reflection

1. In *Pitt v PHH*, Peter Gibson LJ said: 'I accept that the threat of an injunction only had a nuisance value in that I cannot see how the plaintiff could have succeeded in any claim. Nevertheless, that nuisance was something which the defendant was freed from.' *However*, it is arguable that the promisee's conduct amounted to exploitation by abuse of the legal process and should have been denied recognition as consideration. If you pay me not to harm you, your not being harmed is clearly a benefit to you, but this should not constitute value in the eye of the law.

2. The general rule that intangible benefits are not valid consideration is justifiable because of their uncertainty and the impossibility of *enforcement* (how do you compel someone to give 'love and affection', or quantify its monetary worth in damages?).

However, courts may find consideration in intangible benefits resulting from *measurable* conduct via the concept of:

• request (although this may be practically indistinguishable from desire or mere motive); or

• forbearance from lawful action.

(iv) Illusory consideration

Although the law will tolerate a considerable variation between the values exchanged in deference to individual choice, it draws the line where the recipient will *inevitably* get nothing, nothing which is enforceable, or nothing more than she would have received anyway. Consideration may be illusory and of no value in the eye of the law in the following cases:

✗ Performance is impossible: if the promisee's performance is *known* by both parties to be physically or legally impossible at *formation*, 'the parties could not be supposed to have so contracted' (*Clifford (Lord) v Watts* (1870)); if the impossibility of performance is *unknown* to the parties, the contract may be void for mistake (6.3.4).

✗ Discretionary promises, eg where a party promises to do something 'if I feel like it', are not valid consideration. Whilst promises are *effectively* discretionary if they are accompanied by a clause excluding all liability for breach (eg where the promise 'to do X' is cancelled out by the term 'but I am not liable if I don't do X'), these are treated as raising issues not of consideration, but rather of incorporation, interpretation (Chapter 10) and invalidity (Chapter 11).

✗ Un-induced performance by the promisee: 'it is no consideration to refrain from a course of action which it was never intended to pursue' (*Arrale v Costain Civil Engineering Ltd* (1976)); if the promisor could show that the nephew in *Hamer v Sidaway* never intended to drink, smoke, or gamble, the nephew could not have enforced his uncle's promise to pay him for refraining.

3.1.3.6 Compromise and forbearance to sue

Where you have a legal claim against me, you may provide consideration for my promise if you:

- **forbear from suing** on your claim, ie I concede your claim and you agree not to enforce it for a specified time, or at all (eg a creditor gives a debtor extra time to pay or extinguishes the debt); or

- **compromise** your claim—here, I do not concede your claim but you agree to abandon your claim (eg where the parties agree to settle their differences).

✓ **Where your claim is valid in law,** your compromise or forbearance is clearly good consideration for my reciprocal promise. Where the *duration* of forbearance is unspecified, an implication of reasonable time will be made (*Payne v Wilson* (1827)). Forbearance is only consideration if it is *requested* by the promisor. However, a court may *imply a request* where the promisee's actual forbearance (ie detriment) is not merely in reliance on, but also *in return for*, the other party's promise (3.1.2.2).

✓ **Where your claim is *doubtful* in law,** your compromise or forbearance is still good consideration (*Haigh v Brooks* (1839)).

✗ **If you *know* that your claim is *invalid*,** your compromise or forbearance is not valid consideration. As Tindal CJ said in *Wade v Simeon* (1846): 'It is almost *contra bonos mores* [against good conscience], and certainly contrary to all the principles of natural justice, that a man should institute proceedings against another, when he is conscious that he has no good cause of action.' In practice, the more unreasonable a person's claim, the more likely it is to be inferred that she has no honest belief in its validity.

✓ If your claim is *invalid* in law, but made in *good faith and on reasonable grounds*, you give good consideration (*Cook v Wright* (1861)). Cockburn CJ explains in *Callisher v Bischoffsheim* (1870):

> Every day a compromise is effected on the ground that the party making it has a chance of succeeding in it, and if he *bona fide* believes he has a fair chance of success, he has a reasonable ground for suing, and his forbearance to sue will constitute a good consideration. When such a person forbears to sue he gives up what he believes to be a right of action, and the other party gets an advantage, and, instead of being annoyed with an action, he escapes from the vexations incident to it . . . It would be another matter if a person made a claim which he knew to be unfounded, and, by a compromise, derived an advantage under it: in that case his conduct would be fraudulent.

As long as a party forbears or compromises a claim which is not 'vexatious or frivolous, he gives up something of value. It is a mistake to suppose it is not an advantage . . . to be able to litigate his claim even if it turns out to be wrong' (*Miles v New Zealand Alford Estates Co* (1886)).

Pause for reflection

If a party's claim is *in fact* invalid, compromising or forbearing from suing on it entails no factual detriment to that party and confers no factual benefit on the other party. However, recognising legal value in *X*'s forbearance or compromise of an honest but mistaken claim is supportable as: (i) encouraging settlements (or 'finality in disputes'), and (ii) conferring factual benefit on the promisor in being rid of the nuisance of litigation.

3.1.4 Pre-existing duties

The most controversial aspect of the consideration doctrine relates to the question whether *X* gives good consideration where *X* does or promises to do something that *X* was already legally bound to do (ie it is the subject of *X*'s pre-existing duty). The traditional answer depends on whether *X*'s pre-existing duty was imposed:

   (i) by the general law;

  (ii) by a contract with a third party; or

 (iii) by an existing contract with the promisor.

Diagram 3C summarises the pro-enforcement and anti-enforcement policies in each category, and the legal techniques used to implement them.

Diagram 3C Consideration and pre-existing duties

Pre-existing duty:	*(i) In law*	*(ii) To a third party*	*(iii) In contract to the other party*
Pro-enforcement policies	1. Promisor undertakes new liability. 2. Promisee receives factual and legal benefit.	1. Promisor undertakes new liability. 2. Promisee receives factual and legal benefit.	1. Practical benefit to promisor of avoiding worse alternatives. 2. Promote cooperation. 3. Economic efficiency. 4. Quasi-frustration: prevent harshness to promisee.
Legal basis for enforcement	• Promisor receives and promisee undertakes something 'extra', ie *legal benefit*.	• *Presence of legal benefit*.	• Finding legal benefit. • Finding 'practical benefit'. • Replacement with *new contract*. • *Compromise* of claim.
Anti-enforcement policies	1. Risk of bribery, extortion, corruption in public life.	1. Merely gratuitous promise.	1. Risk of extortion, duress. 2. Promisee undertakes no new liability. 3. Promisor obtaining no new benefit. 4. Protect the sanctity of original contract.
Legal basis for non-enforcement	• *Finding no legal benefit or detriment*.	• *Mere motive*.	• *Finding no legal benefit or detriment*. • *Precedent against enforcement*.

3.1.4.1 Pre-existing duties imposed by public law

The general rule is that a promise to perform (or the performance of) an existing public duty is no consideration for a reciprocal promise. There is no value in the eye of the law even if there is undoubted factual value to the recipient. The concern is to prevent opportunistic exploitation; it would be undesirable to allow public officials to extract benefits in return for the performance of their existing legal duties (eg requesting payment for the attendance of an ambulance or fire brigade). It may also taint impartiality and probity in the administration of justice and in government (eg judges or politicians receiving payments to take certain actions).

✗ In *Collins v Godefroy* (1831), G's promise to pay if C gave evidence at G's trial was unenforceable, since C had already been subpoenaed to give evidence at the trial.

✓ However, where enforcement would *not* undermine public policy, courts can circumvent the general bar by 'finding' that *more* was promised than was strictly owed under the pre-existing legal duty. In *Glasbrook Bros v Glamorgan CC* (1925), mine owners, fearful of violence during a strike, agreed to pay the police £2,200 for protection. The court enforced the payment because the police had provided stronger protection than they had judged necessary. Section 25(1) of the Police Act 1996 now allows payments for 'special police services'. In *West Yorkshire Police Authority v Reading Festival Ltd* (2006), Scott Baker LJ said that the services to be paid for will either 'have been asked for but will be beyond what the police consider necessary to meet their public duty obligations, or they are services which, if the police do not provide them, the asker will have to provide them from his own or other resources.'

✓ In *Ward v Byham*, the father of an illegitimate child promised to pay the child's mother £1 per week provided that the child was 'well looked after and happy'. The father then refused to pay, arguing that the mother provided no consideration since she was simply performing her existing legal duty to look after her child (at the time, fathers of illegitimate children had no corresponding legal duty of support). The majority of the Court of Appeal found that the mother had promised to do *more* than was required under her legal duty. The fact that natural love and affection are not generally sufficient consideration (3.1.3.5(iii)) did not prevent the court from enforcing what was, otherwise, regarded as an appropriate payment. Lord Denning attacked the general rule head-on. He found that although there was no *legal* detriment to the mother, there was *factual benefit to the promisor.* The father was benefited by the mother's promise just as if a third party without a legal duty had promised to look after the child for payment.

Pause for reflection

The bar against recognising the promise or performance of pre-existing public duties as valid consideration is over-inclusive. The promisee receives not only practical benefit, but also *legal benefit* (she acquires a new right). The promisor suffers a corresponding *legal detriment* (she is now liable to the promisee, aside from any liability for breaching the public duty). In *Williams v Williams* (1957), Lord Denning said that 'a promise to perform an existing duty is . . . sufficient consideration to support a promise, so long as there is nothing in the transaction which is contrary to the public interest'.

3.1.4.2 Pre-existing contractual duties owed to a third party

The performance of (or promise to perform) an existing contractual duty owed to a third party is generally regarded as good consideration. The promisee obtains the desired performance or a directly enforceable obligation, and the promisor undertake a new liability that is quite independent from that owed to the third party. The policies therefore support enforcement.

✓ In *Shadwell v Shadwell* (1860), an uncle promised £150 yearly to his nephew until the nephew's income as a Chancery barrister reached 600 guineas (1 guinea being £1.05). This was held to be enforceable because the nephew provided consideration by marrying Ellen Nicholl, which he was already contractually bound to her to do.

This conclusion is not obvious; the value of the marriage to the uncle is, at most, intangible or sentimental, and unlikely to be accompanied by contractual intent. At most, it is a conditional gift. While the decision is easier to understand as a desirable family arrangement in 1860, it was treated as authority for the enforceability of promises supported by performance of a pre-existing duty to a third party in:

✓ *Scotson v Pegg* (1861), where P's promise for S's delivery of coal was held to be enforceable, although S was already contractually obliged to do so for a third party; and

✓ *Pao On v Lau Yiu Long,* where the House of Lords affirmed that the *mere promise* of performing the duty owed to a third party is good consideration (3.1.4.2).

• In *New Zealand Shipping v Satterthwaite, The Eurymedon* (1975), S (stevedores) unloaded goods from X's ship. S damaged some goods belonging to NZ who sued S. The Court held that NZ had agreed not to sue S for damage and S had provided consideration by unloading NZ's goods, although S already owed X a duty to do so.

3.1.4.3 Pre-existing duties owed to the other party

The most common modern-day consideration problem involves the performance of (or promise to perform) a pre-existing duty already contractually owed to the other party, eg you agree to pay me £3,000 to paint your house; subsequently, you agrees to pay me an additional £1,000 for the same job. In contrast to the previous categories, you (the promisor) obtain no new enforceable right over and above your existing entitlement (for me to paint your house). The traditional position was that my promise of 'the same' was not good consideration for your promise to pay more. This was overturned by *Williams v Roffey* (1990), where the promise to perform a pre-existing contractual duty was recognised as conferring 'practical benefit' on the party promising to pay more for it (3.1.5.3). The far-reaching implications of this case must, first, be put in the wider context of the role of consideration in contract modifications generally.

3.1.5 **Contract modifications**

In general, contract parties can make an enforceable agreement to end ('rescind', 'terminate', or 'discharge') or vary their contract, so long as this is supported by *consideration*.

3.1.5.1 Agreements to end the contract

✓ Where *both parties* owe outstanding obligations to (and so have outstanding rights against) each other, each party provides consideration for the release from her own obligation by releasing the other party from theirs.

✗ If *only one party* promises to give up her contractual rights, this is 'entirely unilateral and unsupported by any consideration' (*Collin v Duke of Westminster* (1985)). Thus, if I *have outstanding obligations* to you but you have no outstanding obligation to me (you have completed your performance), your promise to release me from my obligations is unsupported by consideration; I must give you something extra to enforce your promise.

3.1.5.2 Agreements to modify the contract

These may take a number of forms:

(i) **End the existing contract and make a new contract**: the existing contract can be ended by satisfying the requirements of consideration, followed by a *new contract* on different terms in relation to the same subject matter. In the American case of *Watkins & Sons Inc v Carrig* (1941), the parties entered a contract for W to excavate a cellar for C at a fixed price. After discovering solid rock, C agreed to pay eight times the original contract price, but then refused to pay. The judge held that the original contract was abandoned (when each party gave up their rights to sue the other) and replaced by a new agreement.

(ii) **Modification supported by consideration on both sides**: a modification is enforceable if *each* party gives consideration by conferring a new benefit or assuming a new burden. The mere possibility that either party *may* benefit or be prejudiced by the new arrangement is enough (*WJ Alan & Co Ltd v El Nasr Export & Import Co* (1972)), eg a change in the currency of future contractual payments may benefit or prejudice either party depending on currency fluctuations.

(iii) **Modifications that can only benefit one contracting party:**

- The promisor may agree to *pay more for the same* performance originally contracted for (the promisee gives 'the same for more').

- The promisor may agree to pay *the same for less* performance in satisfaction of the performance originally contracted for (the promisee gives 'less for the same').

3.1.5.3 *'The same for more'*: pre-existing contractual duty owed to the other party

(i) The traditional *Stilk v Myrick* **rule—no consideration**

Whether a promise of 'more for the same' is enforceable depends on whether the promisee's reciprocal promise of 'the same for more' is valid consideration. The traditional answer given by **Stilk v Myrick** (1809) is 'no'. There, two of the 11 seamen deserted during a voyage and the master agreed to share the deserters' wages with the remainder of the crew if they would work the ship back to London. S could not enforce the master's promise. Two reports give different reasons, giving rise to competing interpretations of the case by those who support and oppose the doctrine of consideration.

- In Campbell's report, S's claim failed because he gave **no consideration** for the master's promise: he was already contractually obliged to sail the ship home. This reasoning would bar *all* claims for additional payments supported by the performance or a promise to perform a pre-existing contract. This version was accepted as English law in *North Ocean Shipping Co v Hyundai Construction Co (The Atlantic Baron)*.

- In the Espinasse report, S's claim failed on the narrower ground of policy: namely, the concern to **prevent duress**—the possibility of sailors on the high seas making *extortionate demands* upon their masters as the price for bringing the ship safely back to the home port. On this rationale, absence of consideration does not necessarily bar enforcement of promises to pay more. The question is one of duress. The focus on this version was renewed in *Williams v Roffey*.

(ii) Traditional 'exceptions' to the traditional rule

A promise to pay more *is* enforceable if one of the following occurs:

✓ The promisee gives *something 'more'* than she was obliged to under the original contract, as in *Hartley v Ponsonby* (1857). The desertion of 17 out of 36 crew, leaving only four or five able seamen, was held to entitle the remaining crew to refuse to continue with the original contract. Thus, in agreeing to continue with the voyage, the remaining crew did *more* than they were obliged to do and so gave consideration for the promise of more pay. This would explain the *outcome* in the American case of *Watkins & Sons Inc v Carrig* (3.1.5.2(i)).

✓ *The parties agree to end the existing contract and make a new contract* on different terms relating to the same subject matter (3.1.5.2). In *Williams v Roffey*, Purchas LJ rejected 'the attractive invitation' to follow this reasoning.

✓ A *compromise of a dispute* between the parties (3.1.3.6).

(iii) *Williams v Roffey Brothers*—practical benefit is valid consideration

RB contracted to refurbish 27 flats, subcontracting the carpentry work to W for £20,000. W finished nine flats, but was at risk of not finishing the rest because of financial problems, arising (a) partly from underpricing the original job, and (b) partly from W's deficient supervision of his workers. Realising this and mindful of its potential liability to its main employer, RB promised to pay W an additional £575 on the timely completion of each of the remaining 18 flats (totalling £10,300). W substantially completed eight more flats, but RB did not pay the sums promised, so W discontinued work and sued for £10,847. RB engaged other carpenters to complete the job and incurred a week's time penalty under the main contract. RB argued that W gave no consideration for the additional sums promised. The Court of Appeal affirmed the lower court's decision in W's favour, but only awarded W £3,500 (see the next Pause for reflection).

Glidewell LJ concluded that:

(i) if A has entered into a contract with B to do work for, or to supply goods or services to, B in return for payment by B; and (ii) at some stage before A has completely performed his obligations under the contract, B has reason to doubt whether A will, or will be able to, complete his side of the bargain; and (iii) B thereupon promises A an additional payment in return for A's promise to perform his contractual obligations on time; and (iv) *as a result of giving his promise, B obtains in practice a benefit, or obviates a disbenefit*; and (v) *B's promise is not given as a result of economic duress or fraud on the part of A*; then (vi) the benefit to B is capable of being consideration for B's promise, so that the promise will be legally binding (emphasis added).

Pause for reflection

1. On the orthodox view that a contractual *right* is the right to *performance*, A's mere re-promise to perform its existing contractual duty confers no additional benefit to which B is not already *entitled*:

   - At most, it gives B reassurance, but that is intangible and is generally regarded as insufficient consideration (3.1.3.5).
   - It confers no additional enforceable benefit, and thus is illusory ('Consideration: Practical Benefit and the Emperor's New Clothes' in J Beatson and D Friedmann (eds), *Good Faith and Fault in Contract Law* (OUP, 1995) 123).

2. The unpalatable truth is that having a contractual right is not the same as getting actual contractual performance. Contract law does not take such an elevated view of contractual obligations. Many rules are inconsistent with the protection of a claimant's performance interest, in particular, the rarity of enforcing actual performance (Chapters 12–14). We bargain for performance, but we usually get a more fragile right in remedial terms, namely, money which is itself subject to many deductions. Consistently, Purchas LJ said in *Williams v Roffey* that it was open to W to be in deliberate breach of the contract in order to 'cut his losses' commercially.

3. Therefore, we should acknowledge that getting actual performance would be an additional benefit over and above having the mere right to sue. If we accept that a bird in the hand is worth two in the bush, then the idea that the *receipt* of (even part-) performance confers a benefit over and above the *right* to performance, and can be exchanged for something from the recipient, is consistent with the core idea of consideration as bargain. In 'A Bird in the Hand: Consideration and Promissory Estoppel' in A Burrows and E Peel (eds), *Contract Formation and Parties* (OUP, 2010) 89, I argue that this can be implemented by:

   ✗ replacing the bilateral contract analysis in *Williams v Roffey* with

   ✓ a collateral unilateral contract analysis (the collateral offer, which sits alongside the original contract, is that the promisor will pay an additional sum *if and only if* the stipulated performance is actually received).

   This was expressly approved and adopted by Arden LJ in *MWB Business Exchange Centres Ltd v Rock Advertising Ltd* (2016) in the context of part payment of a debt or 'promises to accept less for the same' (3.1.5.4). While McCombe LJ preferred not to base his concurrence with the outcome on this reasoning, and Kitchin LJ preferred to express no view on it, their decisions are consistent with a unilateral analysis and inconsistent with a bilateral analysis. At the time of writing, the Supreme Court has yet to hear the appeal on this case.

4. Despite Glidewell LJ's formal ratio adopting a bilateral contract view whereby a mere re-promise is sufficient to confer a practical benefit, many features of the reasoning in *Williams v Roffey* itself are more consistent with a unilateral contract analysis. First, the court identified four practical benefits to RB:

   (a) W's continued performance;

   →

➡

(b) avoiding the trouble and expense of obtaining a substitute;

(c) avoiding the penalty payment for late performance under the main contract; and

(d) RB's promise to pay more only as each flat was completed gave W the incentive to perform in a more orderly manner; this allowed RB to coordinate its other subcontractors more effectively and efficiently towards timely completion of the main contract.

Yet (a)–(c) will only be realised if W *actually performs*. That cannot be guaranteed from W's mere re-promise to perform. RB will only get actual performance in exchange for its additional promise of payment on a unilateral contract approach.

As for **(d)**, the description of this benefit is none other than that of a unilateral contract.

Second, the trial judge and the Court of Appeal accepted that the terms of the variation were: 'The [additional] sum of £10,300 was to be paid at a rate of £575 per flat to be paid on the completion of each flat.' This is a unilateral contract.

Third, it is often overlooked that the ultimate award in *Williams v Roffey* tallies with a unilateral contract analysis:

✗ The practical benefit did *not* buy W an *expectation* interest in RB's promise to pay more. It was RB's breach (by failing to make due payment) that entitled W to terminate his performance before completion. On a bilateral contract analysis, W *should* have got his full expectation (around £10,300). Indeed, that is what W claimed and was denied.

✓ Instead, the court awarded £3,500, based *explicitly* on the fact that W had substantially completed eight further flats up to the point of RB's breach, ie '(8 x £575) 'less some small deduction for defective and incomplete items'. This assumes a unilateral contract analysis.

5. The fairness of the unilateral contract analysis and the unfairness of the bilateral contract analysis is reinforced by a variation of the facts. If W simply failed to complete despite re-promising to do so, RB's expectation would derive no *more* protection from having been purchased twice. Indeed, on a bilateral contract analysis, RB would be worse off than before! **Diagram 3D** illustrates this. Let's say that, you promise to pay me £50,000 for a job and later promise an additional £10,000 (total £60,000); despite this, I still do not do the job, and the cost of substitute performance is £70,000. Your contract damages should be calculated as: the cost of substitute performance *minus* your saved costs from not having to pay me. Is your saved cost £50,000 or £60,000? If your *promise* to pay more is contractually enforceable (on the bilateral contract analysis, see (1) in Diagram 3D), then the answer is £60,000, yielding damages of £10,000. That would make you *worse off* than if you had not tried to salvage the situation. If you had not promised more, the calculation would have been £70,000 minus £50,000, yielding £20,000.

This is perverse. The proper analysis (see (2) in **Diagram 3D**), consistent with the intention of the parties, is that your promise to pay more is a unilateral offer to do so if, and only if, I complete the job. If I do not, this unilateral contract never comes into being and you are left with an action under the original contract. This is a unilateral contract analysis (on the revocation of such unilateral offers, 2.3.6.2). The justice of this was recognised by the Ontario Law Reform Commission which concluded that, in such an instance, the appropriate deduction

➡

➡ is the *original sum* promised and not the greater sum of the variation, because 'it would be an implicit understanding between the parties that failure to comply with the terms of the new agreement would revive the old one'.[13] The additional promise is only enforceable *on the promisee's performance.*

Diagram 3D 'More for the same': contrasting the bilateral and unilateral contract analysis

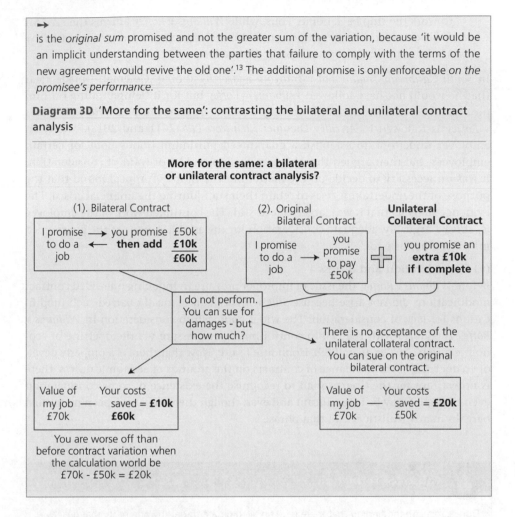

More for the same: a bilateral or unilateral contract analysis?

(1). Bilateral Contract

I promise → you promise £50k
to do a ← **then add** **£10k**
job ─────── **£60k**

(2). Original Bilateral Contract

Unilateral Collateral Contract

I promise → you promise to pay £50k ➕ you promise an **extra £10k if I complete**
to do a job

I do not perform. You can sue for damages - but how much?

There is no acceptance of the unilateral collateral contract. You can sue on the original bilateral contract.

Value of my job £70k ─── Your costs saved = **£10k** £60k

Value of my job £70k ─── Your costs saved = **£20k** £50k

You are worse off than before contract variation when the calculation world be £70k - £50k = £20k

(iv) The current status of *Stilk*

In essence, *Williams v Roffey* stands for two propositions:

(a) Consideration, in the bargain sense, is still necessary to enforce promises of more for the same. *Stilk v Myrick* has not been overruled, but only 'refined' and 'limited'. The scope of consideration is enlarged to include *practical* benefit moving to the promisor.

(b) Any concerns about the promisee applying improper pressure to induce the promisor's agreement to pay more should be dealt with by the doctrine of *economic duress.* Preventing even the chance of duress is how *Williams v Roffey* explains the outcome in *Stilk v Myrick.* However, the two cases are obviously analogous: if RB received practical benefit from W's promise to complete performance, so must the master of the ship have received benefit from S's promise

---

[13] Ontario Law Reform Commission, 'Report on the Amendment of the Law of Contract' (No 82, 1987) 12–13, discussing the promise to accept part-performance.

to work the ship back home. Thus, while *Williams v Roffey* affirms the *need* for fresh consideration to enforce an additional promise, it *has* overruled *Stilk v Myrick* as to what *counts* as fresh consideration.

In *South Caribbean Trading Ltd v Trafigura Beheer BV* (2005), Coleman J made clear that he would not have followed *Williams v Roffey* but for it being binding on him (not having 'yet' been declared 'wrongly decided' by the House of Lords). *Williams v Roffey* is followed in *Attrill v Dresdner Kleinwort Ltd* (2011 and 2013). There, an employer undertook to establish a guaranteed minimum bonus pool for certain employees, but then argued that this was unenforceable for want of consideration. It was unnecessary to decide on the matter but the Court of Appeal found that the purpose of the undertaking 'was to retain their staff [during the financial crisis]. The evidence suggests that it was largely successful. The continued work of the employee is, at least arguably, adequate consideration for the establishment of the guaranteed minimum bonus pool.'

(v) Consideration and duress

Before *Williams v Roffey*, the issue of improper pressure in inducing one-sided contract modifications did not arise because *Stilk v Myrick* automatically barred such modifi-cations for lack of consideration. The wider approach to consideration in *Williams v Roffey* is coupled with the call to control improper pressure via the doctrine of eco-nomic duress. In *The Alev* (1989), Hobhouse J said: 'Now that there is a properly devel-oped doctrine of the avoidance of contracts on the grounds of economic duress, there is no warrant for the Court to fail to recognise the existence of some consideration even though it may be insignificant and even though there may have been no mutual bargain in any realistic use of that phrase.'

 Pause for reflection

Duress rests on the finding that there is: (i) an 'illegitimate threat' by one party that (ii) leaves the other party with 'no practicable alternative' but to submit (8.4.3). There is debate over the proper scope of economic duress, but its potential for invalidating one-sided modifications is obvious. What is given by recognising 'practical benefit' seems liable to be taken away by the economic duress doctrine. The question is just shifted between consideration and duress.

1. Illegitimate pressure can include a threatened breach of contract, which can be *implied*; this could cover facts analogous to *Williams v Roffey*. A promisee who is aware of the promisor's need for completion can make known the unlikelihood of her timely completion and passively wait for, rather than actively demand, extra payment.

2. The doctrines of consideration and of economic duress are likely to operate on the *same facts* to yield *different conclusions* on the question of enforceability. The reasons for find-ing 'practical benefit' to the promisor (eg to avoid the problems consequent on breach) are the *very same* reasons for finding duress, because the promisor had 'no practicable alternative' but to agree (ie to avoid the problems consequent on breach).

→

➡

3. Coming from the direction of duress, Coleman J's approach in *South Caribbean Trading v Trafigura* (2005) could totally negate the effect of recognising practical benefit. He held that the promisee who threatens not to perform an existing duty *cannot* rely on the benefit that her performance would confer on the promisor, because her threat is 'analogous to economic duress' if the threat is unjustified. That is, *any unjustified* express or implied threat of non-performance disqualifies the promisee from relying on 'practical benefit'. Any promise to pay more pursuant to a *justified* threat not to perform is enforceable anyway as a legitimate compromise of claim.

3.1.5.4 'Less for the same': part-performance

(i) The rule in *Foakes v Beer*

Instead of you promising to *pay more* for the contractual performance I already owe you, you may promise to *accept less* than is already due from me, eg you lend me £1,000 but, when I plead poverty, you agree to accept £700 instead. Does my promise to pay less constitute 'practical benefit' enabling me to enforce your promise to accept less in discharge of my entire debt? And, if I do not pay the £700, can you claim the original £1,000 I owe, or only the £700 you agreed to accept? If I can enforce your new promise, you could only claim £700. The **general rule** is that a promise to accept part-payment of a debt in discharge of the whole debt is unenforceable for want of consideration. This is traceable to *Pinnel's Case* (1602), and was upheld by the House of Lords in *Foakes v Beer* (1884), where B's promise to give F extra time to repay his debt was interpreted as a promise to abandon her claim to interest. When B brought a claim for the interest incurred after F had paid the debt, F claimed that his payment of the debt was consideration for B's promise to forgo the interest. This was rejected. The promise was unenforceable for want of consideration. B could claim the interest.

(ii) Traditional exceptions to the rule in *Foakes*

Your promise to accept less than is due from me is enforceable if:

✓ I give something additional for the dispensation granted by you (eg I agree to pay earlier, at a different place or in a different currency). Part-payment cannot discharge the whole debt 'but the gift of a horse, hawk, or robe, &c., in satisfaction is good, for . . . [they] might be more beneficial to the plaintiff than the money . . . or otherwise the plaintiff would not have accepted it in satisfaction' (*Pinnel's Case*). The odd result is that my debt of £1,000 can be discharged for a peppercorn, but not for £700.

✓ I dispute your claim and the modification amounts to a compromise of your claim.

✓ The promise is made to third parties. This exception is necessary to support a composition among creditors, for where a composition has been agreed, it would be a fraud on other creditors for you, having promised to take less and received it, then to sue me for the balance. Moreover, I (the debtor) will have rearranged my affairs in reliance on such compositions. I may now be able to enforce such a composition under the Contracts (Rights of Third Parties) Act 1999 (4.1.3).

(iii) Practical benefit as consideration for a promise to accept less?
Although a *promise* of part-performance confers no *legal* benefit, the creditor may obtain practical benefit by the actual receipt of the part-performance. Again, a bird in the hand is worth two in the bush.

- In *Foakes v Beer*, Lord Blackburn acknowledged the:

  > conviction that all men of business, whether merchants or tradesmen, do every day recognise and act on the ground that prompt payment of a part of their demand may be more beneficial to them than it would be to insist on their rights and enforce payment of the whole. Even where the debtor is perfectly solvent, and sure to pay at last, this is often so. Where the credit of the debtor is doubtful it must be more so.

- In *Collier v P & M J Wright (Holdings) Ltd* (2008), Arden LJ said that, while the rule in *Pinnel's Case* 'may sound like a good result in terms of creditor protection, the consequence is . . . [that it] makes it difficult to enter into compromises of claims, which it can often be commercially beneficial for both parties to do'. The Supreme Court of New South Wales, Australia, in *Musumeci v Winadell Pty Ltd* (1995), applied *Williams v Roffey* to enforce 'less for the same' modifications. Santow J found no distinction between 'the same for more' modifications and 'less for the same' modifications.

- ✗ This logic was rejected in in *Re Selectmove Ltd* (1995). The Revenue applied for an order for the compulsory winding up of a company that owed arrears in taxes. The company argued that the debt was not yet due since the Revenue had agreed to give the company more time to pay. In exchange, the Revenue would receive the practical benefit of 'recover[ing] more from not enforcing its debt against the company which was known to be in financial difficulties, than from putting the company into liquidation'. Peter Gibson LJ acknowledged this, but refused to recognise it as valid consideration because the House of Lords in *Foakes v Beer* had declined to do so after expressly considering this argument. To treat 'practical benefit' as consideration here would leave *Foakes v Beer* without any application. This could only be done by the House of Lords, 'or more appropriately, by Parliament after consideration by the Law Commission'. It cannot be done by reference to the Court of Appeal decision in *Williams v Roffey* which did not expressly consider this issue.

- ✓ Yet, that step was taken by the Court of Appeal in *MWB Business Exchange Centres Ltd v Rock Advertising Ltd* (2016). MWB operated and managed office space where Rock was a licensee. Rock incurred arrears of licence fees and other charges, whereupon the parties agreed an oral variation to re-schedule the debt. Rock paid £3,500 on the same day in accordance with the re-schedule. MWB's argument that the variation lacked consideration was rejected. The Court of Appeal held that *Williams v Roffey*'s acceptance of 'practical benefit' as good consideration for promises to pay more logically applies to promises to accept less, as in this case. All the judges accepted that there were practical benefits flowing to MWB from its agreement to accept less from Rock, namely:

(i)   MWB would retain Rock as a licensee beyond the contractual term. This clearly amounts to *legal* benefit to support the contract variation.

(ii) More significantly, MWB would recover £3,500 immediately and have a greater chance of recovering the rest of the arrears.

 Pause for reflection

1. If (ii) above (the £3,500 part payment of debt plus the greater chance of recovering the balance of the debt) counts as practical benefit, then it must be sufficient *on its own* to support MWB's promise to accept lesser repayment.

2. This is difficult to square with the Court's insistence that the case is distinguishable from *Foakes v Beer* and *In re Selectmove*. In all three cases, there is the practical benefit of a greater chance of recovering the whole debt.

3. The cases may be reconcilable:

   • *Foakes v Beer* is a case where, in truth, no promise to forego the interest was made. Treitel points out that, when B promised F more time to pay the principal debt, the issue of interest was not discussed and B was probably 'tricked into making a promise which, on its true construction, had an effect not intended by her' (ie she only intended to give extra time to pay, but *not* to forgo interest on late payments). Whatever the faults of *Foakes*, the actual outcome 'does not seem to be unjust. What seems to have happened was that Dr Foakes' solicitor dug a technical trap for Mrs Beer and the House of Lords arranged an equally technical rescue' by relying on the rule that part-payment is not good consideration to discharge the whole (*Some Landmarks of 20th Century Contract Law* (OUP, 2002)). Alternatively, *Foakes v Beer* can be refined by acceptance of practical benefit in the same way that *Stilk v Myrick* was. Practical benefit means the *actual* performance of the stipulated pre-existing duty (the bird in the hand).

   • The outcome in *Re Selectmove* is explicable because, even if there had been a valid promise to give extra time to pay, there was no consideration because the company had not performed the stipulated obligations of the variation. On a unilateral contract analysis, the company had not 'accepted' the Revenue's offer, which could therefore be revoked.

   • In contrast, in *MWB v Rock*, MWB had actually paid £3,500 according to the agreed schedule. Therefore, it had commenced performance of the unilateral offer which could not be revoked while MWB continued performance. In the view of Arden LJ:[14]

   . . . Rock's acceptance of MWB's promise gave rise to a 'collateral unilateral contract,' meaning that, collaterally to the licence, for so long as Rock was entitled to and did

   ➔

---

[14] Citing M Chen-Wishart, 'Reform of Consideration: No Greener Grass' in S Degeling, J Edelman, and J Goudkamp (eds), *Contract in Commercial Law* (Thomson, 2017) and '*A Bird in the Hand: Consideration and Contract Modifications*' in A S Burrows and E Peel (eds), *Contract Formation and parties* (OUP, 2010) 89–113.

→   occupy the unit and paid the licence fee as renegotiated, MWB would be bound on payment of the initial £3,500 to accept the deferral of the arrears in accordance with the variation agreement. . . . [I]t was not suggested by either party that Rock could take the benefit of the variation agreement without performing its side of the bargain, or that MWB could withdraw from the variation agreement so long as Rock was complying with it.

While McCombe LJ preferred not to base his concurrence with the outcome on this reasoning, and Kitchin LJ preferred to express no view on it, the latter added that the 'variation agreement thereupon became binding upon MWB and it would remain binding for so long as Rock continued to make payments in accordance with the revised payment schedule.'

4. This unilateral collateral contract analysis is, again, reinforced by a consideration of the remedies. If a mere *promise* of 'less for the same' on a bilateral contract analysis were *contractually* enforceable, then, when the other party fails to pay the lesser sum agreed, the creditor's claim would logically be *reduced* to the lesser sum agreed. Thus, if you promise to accept £700 in discharge of my debt of £1,000 in the hope of *actually getting* £700, but *I still do not pay*, and your claim is now confined to £700, you are worse off than if you had not bothered to salvage the situation at all. This is patently absurd. The *Sixth Interim Report on the Statute of Frauds and the Doctrine of Consideration*[15] recommends (para 35) that 'the greater obligation can be discharged either by a promise to pay a lesser sum or by actual payment of it, but that if the new agreement is not performed then the original obligation shall revive'.[16] This is a unilateral contract analysis.

(v) The problem of pressure

The traditional rules in *Stilk v Myrick* and *Foakes v Beer* can counter a promisee's use of pressure to 'get more' or 'do less'. If *Williams v Roffey* were extended to counteract *Foakes v Beer*, the focus for controlling the enforceability of such modifications would again shift to economic duress. However, Treitel[17] warns that economic duress 'may not go far enough'. The justice of the outcome in *Foakes v Beer* (because the creditor was tricked) may not be achievable even by an expanded concept of duress.

3.1.5.5 The roles of consideration and promissory estoppel in modifications

In the absence of consideration, contract parties may seek to enforce promises on other grounds. The doctrine of promissory estoppel allows the limited enforcement of relieving (ie 'less for the same') promises that induce reliance, in qualifying circumstances (3.2). The doctrine undoubtedly undermines the rule in *Foakes v Beer*. However, it does so by reference to a wide-ranging assessment of events leading up to, and even after, the modification, and allows flexibility in the remedial response.

---

[15] Law Revision Committee (Cmd 5449, 1937).
[16] The Ontario Law Reform Commission (n 13; 10, 12–13) favours the actual performance option.
[17] G Treitel, *Some Landmarks of Twentieth Century Contract Law* (OUP, 2002) 24–6, 45–6.

To a significant extent, the doctrines of consideration, promissory estoppel, and duress operate in the same territory. The scope of each is uncertain at its margins. Yet, each affects the others, eg:

* Expanding the scope of consideration, eg accepting a mere re-promise as practical benefit (which should confer *full* enforcement of promises) would reduce the need to invoke promissory estoppel (which only confers enforcement 'as justice requires').

* Conversely, if the scope of promissory estoppel was expanded (3.2.3), there would be less need to develop consideration.

* Expanding the scope of duress undermines the effect of expanding the scope of consideration.

3.1.6 Consideration: an assessment

The **consideration doctrine has been criticised** for being:

   (i)   inconsistent with the intention of the parties;

  (ii)   over-inclusive, in enforcing some non-bargains as bargains (eg *Ward v Byham*);

 (iii)   under-inclusive, in failing to enforce some undertakings that deserve enforcement; and

 (iv)   overly technical, artificial, and internally incoherent.

This yields a picture of a doctrine plagued by uncertainty and inconsistency, flowing from the court's ability to manipulate the abstract concept of 'value' in response to the perceived intention, reliance, pressure, and fairness factors of the particular case. Lord Goff observed in *White v Jones* (1995) that: 'our law of contract is widely seen as deficient in the sense that it is perceived to be hampered by the presence of an unnecessary doctrine of consideration'. The Law Commission has identified the consideration doctrine as a suitable topic for a future separate review.[18] Some possibilities for reform can be identified and assessed (see **Diagram 3E**). In assessing these, we must bear in mind the justifications for the consideration doctrine discussed above (3.1.1).

3.1.6.1 Abolish consideration (Diagram 3E.1)

Williams v Roffey signals a shift away from the bargain view of contract towards one based on the *intention of the parties*. Russell LJ said in *Williams v Roffey*: 'consideration there must still be but, in my judgment, the courts nowadays should be more ready to find its existence so as to reflect the intention of the parties to the contract where the bargaining powers are not unequal.' On this view, consideration is simply *evidence* of the primary question about the intention of the parties (3.1.1(i)). This is reinforced by the new emphasis on duress. Indeed, in *Gay Choon Ing v Loh Sze Ti Terence Peter* (2009),

---

[18] Law Commission, *Privity of Contract: Contracts for the Benefit of Third Parties* (Law Com No 242, Cm 3329, 1996).

Diagram 3E Consideration: reform suggestions

3E.1 Abolish consideration

3E.2 Abolish consideration for contract modifications

3E.3 Abolish consideration for certain promises

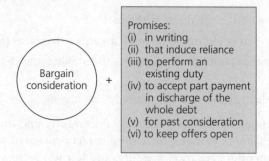

3E.4 Consideration means any 'good reason for enforcement'

'consideration'
But questionable that contract remedies are appropriate

3E.5 Retain bargain consideration but due recongnition to non-contractual sources of liability. Remedies as appropriate

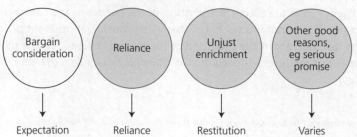

the Singapore Court of Appeal raised the spectre of replacing consideration with the doctrines of economic duress, undue influence, unconscionability, and promissory estoppel.

 Counterpoint

This reform proposal amounts to the abolition of the consideration doctrine. The following objections can be made:

1. *Lack of 'fit'*: the consideration doctrine is not reducible to its evidentiary and caution-ary functions, as supporters of its abolition assert (3.1.1(i)). An informal undertaking is unenforceable even if the promisor's intention to be bound is indisputable, if there is no consideration.

2. I have argued that the functions of consideration cannot be replaced by the *vitiating fac-tors* (discussed in Part IV, 'Consideration and Serious Intention' [2009] *SJLS* 434).

3. *Authority*: the abolition of consideration is unlikely to be judicially sanctioned anytime soon. Lord Steyn expresses the prevailing attitude: 'I have no radical proposals for the wholesale review of the doctrine of consideration. I am not persuaded that it is necessary. And great legal changes should only be embarked on when they are truly necessary . . . On balance it seems to me that in modern practice the restrictive influence of consideration has markedly receded in importance' ('Contract Law: Fulfilling the Reasonable Expectations of Honest Men' (1997) 113 *LQR* 433, 437).

4. *Normatively questionable:* the idea that the law should enforce all seriously intended prom-ises is normatively questionable. It is doubtful that many would choose to live in a world in which they were 'bound by every promise, no matter how foolish, without any chance of letting increased wisdom undo past foolishness. Certainly, some freedom to change one's mind is necessary for free intercourse between those who lack omniscience' (Morris R. Cohen, 'The Basis of Contract' (1933) 46 *Harvard L Rev* 553, 572). If we are concerned to uphold the autonomous intention of a party, why should we not take equally seriously that party's subsequent abandonment of her initial choice? Why privilege the latter when both are equally serious expressions of her will?

5. Is the requirement of *intention to create legal relations* enough?

   (i) We have seen that the requirement under that name is more about limiting legal involvement in private affairs than about any genuine or systematic search for the par-ties' intentions to be legally bound, of which there will rarely be direct evidence (2.7).

   (ii) It is not obvious that such an elastic criterion as the parties' intentions will be any easier to apply, or any less susceptible to judicial manipulation, than bargain consideration itself.

   (iii) Even if an intention to be bound can be proved, this simply begs the follow-on ques-tion: bound to *what* legal effect? What rights or liabilities were intended to be trans-ferred, created, waived, or suspended by the promisor? Was the transfer intended to be absolute or conditional?

3.1.6.2 Abolish consideration in contract *modifications* (Diagram 3E.2)

A more modest reform is to abolish the consideration requirement in contract *modifications*, while retaining it at the formation of the original contract.[19] Reiter argues against 'the illogicality of equating modifying with originating promises' because:[20]

> insofar as consideration serves to exclude gratuitous promise, it is of little assistance in the context of on-going, arms-length, commercial transactions where it is utterly fictional to describe what has been conceded as a gift, and in which there ought to be a strong presumption that good commercial 'considerations' underlie any seemingly detrimental modification.

§ 2-209(1) of the US *Uniform Commercial Code* dispenses with the consideration requirement for contract modifications. In *Antons Trawling Co Ltd v Smith* (2003), the New Zealand Court of Appeal said that promises of more for the same should be enforceable *in the absence of contrary 'policy reasons'*. This was applied in *Teat v Willcocks* (2013).

▶◀ Counterpoint

1. Insofar as the justification is based on the centrality of the *parties' intentions*, the same counterpoints as discussed at 3.1.6.1 apply.

2. Insofar as the consideration doctrine supports the distinction between gifts and bargains, there is a *lack of internal coherence* in making the distinction vital at formation, but not at modification. Why should one have to give consideration to enforce a reciprocal promise to pay £100, but not to enforce a promise to pay £100 *more*?

3. The scope of 'policy reasons' that would render modifications unenforceable is uncertain.

3.1.6.3 Abolish consideration for certain promises (Diagram 3E.3)

The report of the **1937 Law Revision Committee** ('LRC') (*Sixth Interim Report (Statute of Frauds and the Doctrine of Consideration)* (1937, Cmd 5449) [26]–[40], [50]) regards the abolition of consideration as unrealistic because it is 'too entrenched', but recommends that we 'prune away from the doctrine those aspects of it which can create hardship or cause unnecessary inconvenience'. In particular, the LRC recommended that six types of promises should be binding without consideration, namely:

(i)   promises in writing;

(ii) promises that induce foreseeable reliance;

(iii) promising to do what one is already bound to do;

(iv) promises to accept part payments in discharge of the whole debt;

(v)   promises for past consideration; and

(vi) promises to keep offers open for a definite period ('firm offers').

---

[19] B Coote, 'Consideration and Benefit in Fact and in Law' (1990) 2 *JCL* 23; F M B Reynolds and G Treitel, 'Consideration for the Modification of Contract' (1965) 7 *Malaysian L Rev* 1.
[20] B Reiter, 'Courts, Consideration and Common Sense' (1977) 27 *UTLJ* 439, 507.

Counterpoint

I argued against each of these 'exceptions' in 'Reform of Consideration: No Greener Grass' in S Degeling, J Edelman, and J Goudkamp (eds), *Contract in Commercial Law* (Sydney, Thomson, 2016) 77. In sum:

1. While a *seriously intended* promise is necessary, it has (for very good reasons) never been sufficient for contractual liability at common law; the LRC's recommendation that a writing requirement be added does not adequately protect the parties' freedom *from* contract; it is too easily (perhaps unintentionally) satisfied with the all-pervasiveness of electronic communications. Hence recommendation (i) from the LRC report should be rejected and the currently higher threshold of the deed retained (3.3).

2. One party's foreseeable reliance on another's promise cannot justify imposing *contractual* liability on the promisor; moreover, recommendation (ii) fails to give sufficient weight to the promisor's interests as the existing promissory estoppel doctrine (3.2) currently does through the inequitability requirement; it should also be rejected.

3. The enforceability of seriously intended *exchanges* was not questioned by the LRC. Rather, it is the *implementation* of the consideration doctrine that is rightly criticised for being too rigid and for failing to track common sense or business expediency. This logically points to the adjustment of the scope of valuable consideration and not its dispensation as recommendations (iii)–(vi) suggest. They should, therefore, also be rejected.

3.1.6.4 Consideration means *any* 'good reason for enforcement' (Diagram 3E.4)

In 'Consideration in Contract: A Fundamental Restatement' (1971) in P S Atiyah, *Essays in Contract* (Clarendon Press, 1986) 179, **Atiyah** argues for a fundamental restatement of the consideration doctrine based on an analysis of the law as actually enforced in the courts. He concludes that 'consideration' is used in a wider sense than simply bargain:

> When the courts found a sufficient reason for enforcing a promise they enforced it; and when they found that for one reason or another it was undesirable to enforce a promise, they did not enforce it. It seems highly probable that when the courts first used the word 'consideration' they meant no more than that there was a 'reason' for the enforcement of a promise.

This *pluralistic interpretation* of consideration relies on evidence that the courts have always, though inconsistently, adopted a functional approach to the finding of bargain consideration (ie they manipulate the rules or resort to avoidance devices to achieve just results). Better to openly admit that a finding of consideration merely signifies the conclusion rather than explains why a promise is enforceable. Consistently, Atiyah regards promissory estoppel (3.2), which protects reasonable reliance on a promise, not as an exception to consideration but as another 'consideration' supporting enforcement.

Counterpoint

An expansion into *non-bargain criteria for enforcement* necessitates enormous compromises of the fundamentals of contract law, which will weaken rather than strengthen its internal coherence. There is a vast difference between exceptional deviations because of countervailing policies, and an approach that invites all-comers. At its most basic, contract orthodoxy sets a threshold of enforceability based on bargain consideration, is restrictive of the scope of excuses for non-performance (see Part IV), and normally enforces to the full extent the promisee's expectations. Expanding the basis for enforcement will require appropriate adjustments. The demands of justice will vary with: (i) the particular *context* (whether commercial, consumer, charitable, family, and so on); (ii) the particular *reason* for enforcement (whether bargain, reliance suffered, benefit received, fulfilment of family responsibilities, and so on); and (iii) any excuses pleaded (eg non-disclosure, subsequent conduct, or change of circumstances). Moreover, if enforcement is to be divorced from exchange, it is not obvious what the proper **remedial response** should be. As Waddams observes (at [22]): 'There seems little point in arguing strenuously for the use of a single word [consideration] for all enforceable promises if an immediate division is to be required between fully enforceable promises and promises that are only partially enforceable.'

3.1.6.5 Retain bargain consideration whilst recognising other good reasons for non-contractual enforcement (Diagram 3.5)

To support the retention of bargain enforcement is not to deny that non-bargain promises may also be legally relevant. As Treitel points out, 'contract does not exhaust the category of statements which are actionable or otherwise capable of having legal effects'.[21] Consistently, Waddams (at [22]) supports 'continuing the present usage of reserving "consideration" for bargains leading to fully enforceable contracts and to recognise that though some promises may be enforceable without consideration, the full "normal" panoply of contract remedies, in particular damages measured by the value of the promised performance, may not always be appropriate'.

Pause for reflection

Consideration in the bargain sense requires that something which counts in law should be given in exchange for a promise in order to make that promise enforceable in a *contractual* action. Whilst there have always been exceptional examples of non-bargain enforcement via contract, bargain provides the overwhelming, and commercially most important, explanation of contractual liability. Moreover, preserving a distinct category for bargain transactions serves two important functions:

➔

---

[21] G Treitel, 'Consideration: A Critical Analysis of Professor Atiyah's Fundamental Restatement' (1976) 50 *Australian LJ* 439, 441.

➔
- it gives the promisee a compelling **justification for enforcing the promise**, because she has given an enforceable agreed exchange for that promise; and

- at the **remedial** end, it provides the basis for determining the *extent* of liability on the promise. The distinctive feature of a contractual action, the expectation measure, gives the promisee the value of the promised performance because he or she has given the agreed equivalence of that performance.

Other reasons set out at 3.1.1 about the centrality of reciprocity, and the appropriate limits of state involvement in citizens' affairs, reinforce the importance of bargain consideration.

While non-bargain policies have also influenced the development of the consideration doctrine (3.1.3.2), to sweep them all under the label of 'consideration' sacrifices too much in the orderly development and understanding of the law of enforceable promises. To open consideration to 'all-comers' dilutes the distinctiveness of a contractual action.

3.2 **Promissory estoppel**

'Your promise induced my reliance'

In a contractual setting, one party can say or do something that induces the other to act to her detriment. Undertakings that induce *reliance* may be enforceable via the doctrine of promissory estoppel (also known as 'equitable estoppel' and 'forbearance in equity'), *even absent consideration*. Promissory estoppel is one application of the broader principle of estoppel which is 'a principle of justice and of equity' (*Moorgate Mercantile Co Ltd v Twitchings* (1976)), one which is 'perhaps the most powerful and flexible instrument to be found in any system of court jurisprudence' (*Canada and Dominion Sugar Co Ltd v Canadian National (West Indies) Steamships Ltd* (1947)). Cooke (*The Modern Law of Estoppel*, OUP, 2000) gives a taste of the varieties of estoppel:

- **Estoppel by representation**: 'If your bank pays money into your account by mistake, it may be estopped from telling you later that it is not yours and demanding repayment—but only if it has assured you that the money is yours, and you have relied on that by spending the money.'

- **Estoppel by convention**: 'The parties to a commercial deal might agree: "we'll treat clause 2 as meaning such-and-such"; if they go ahead with the deal on that basis, they have to abide by that agreement if the construction of the document is disputed later'.

- **Proprietary estoppel**: A son who invites his elderly mother to build and live in a 'granny flat' on his land may be prevented from ejecting her when relations sour.

- **Promissory estoppel**: 'A landlord might reassure his or her tenant: "I will not insist that you pay for the roof repairs, even though your lease obliges you to do so"; he or she may then be estopped from going back on that promise and demanding payment.'

Although liability under this doctrine arises in a contractual context, it is a matter of debate whether the liability generated is *contractual* or *tortious* in nature:

- The contractual view: Birks says:[22] 'The word "stop" in the middle [of estoppel] gives a clue. The French original means 'bung' or 'stopper' . . . As a wine bottle is corked, so one is restricted or shut up. In short, one is bound . . . In most estoppels the thing in question is an undertaking, and in equitable [or promissory] estoppel it is an undertaking as to the future or, in short, a promise.' Likewise, Cooke explains that: 'Estoppel is a mechanism for enforcing consistency; when I have said or done something that leads you to believe in a particular state of affairs, I may be obliged to stand by what I have said or done, even though I am not contractually bound to do so.' On this view, estoppel is an *alternative* (to consideration) method of *contractual* enforcement of undertakings. In 'Estoppel and the Protection of Expectation' (1997) 17 *LS* 258, Cooke further argues that proprietary and promissory estoppel are and should be aimed at fulfilling expectation unless this would be inappropriate or there is unjust enrichment. Only protecting reliance would confuse and emasculate the law of estoppel, conflict with the law of contract, and be an inappropriate way to supplement the doctrine of consideration. Indeed, while promissory estoppel is based on the protection of *reliance*, its effect is often to hold the promisor to her promise, thus protecting the promisee's expectation. The contractual view is consistent with the abolition of consideration based on the promise-keeping view of contract. *However*, this view cannot explain the additional requirements of promissory estoppel beyond the promise, namely, reliance and inequitability, or its suspensory effect and defensive nature.

- The competing view is that estoppel is reliance-based (tortious) because of: (i) the basic rationale of induced reliance; (ii) the nature of its requirements; and (iii) its *potential* for less than contractual enforcement. These are discussed below.

3.2.1 **The requirements of promissory estoppel**

The foundation for the modern development of promissory estoppel was laid by the House of Lords in *Hughes v Metropolitan Railway Co* (1877). H, the landlord, gave notice to M, the tenant, requiring M to carry out certain repairs within six months. H then entered into negotiations to purchase M's interest in the premises. When negotiations broke down, H claimed to forfeit the lease because M failed to make the repairs within the original time frame. The House of Lords gave M relief against forfeiture because H's conduct had induced M to believe that the time period would stop 'running' during the negotiations. Thus, H had to give M a reasonable amount of time to make the repairs after the negotiations broke down. To allow H to enforce his original rights would be 'inequitable', although their Lordships found that H had 'no intention here to take advantage of, to lay a trap for, or to lull into false security those with whom he was dealing' (ie there was no bad faith).

Hughes was applied by Denning J in *Central London Property Ltd v High Trees House Ltd* (1947). C let a block of flats in London to H on a 99-year lease for £2,500 per year. In 1940, the outbreak of war and the evacuation of people from London meant that H could not sublet enough of the flats to cover the rent. C agreed to accept

---

[22] P Birks, 'Equity in the Modern Law: An Exercise in Taxonomy' (1996) 26 *UWALR* 1, 21–2.

half the rent. In 1945, when the war ended, the property market returned to normal and the flats were fully let. C requested H to resume paying the original rent, but H refused. Denning J held that C was entitled to demand the entire rent *from the date of its notice* in 1945. That is, had C sought it, C would have been estopped (prevented) from claiming *back payment* of the rent forgone between 1940 and 1945.

The **requirements** of promissory estoppel are that:

(i)   *A* makes a clear promise to *B* that she will not enforce her strict legal rights against B;

(ii) *B* acts in reliance on it; and

(iii) it would be inequitable for *A* to resile from the promise.

The **effect** of promissory estoppel is:

(iv) generally suspensory and not extinctive (ie it only extinguishes B's liability up to the point at which *A* gives reasonable notice of *A*'s intention to resume her rights, but not *B*'s future liability unless justice demands); and

(v)   generally restricted to relieving promises in its application. It can only prevent *A* from fully enforcing her existing rights against *B*; it cannot confer new or additional rights on *B*. Thus, the doctrine is said to act defensively, not offensively; it is a 'shield, but not a sword'.

Diagram 3F compares promissory estoppel with consideration. In contrast to promissory estoppel, the presence of consideration makes the promise *fully* enforceable,

Diagram 3F Comparison of promissory estoppel and consideration

A. Promissory estoppel	B. Consideration
(1) Clear promise	**Clear promise**
(2) Reliance (or change of position) by promisee; need not be requested but must be foreseeable by or known to promisor.	Promisee must have given **consideration** which may consist of requested reliance. Promise enforceable **without reliance.**
(3) Inequitable to resile: by reference to (1), (2) above and subsequent events.	**Irrelevant** short of vitiating factors (see Part III) with high thresholds.
(4) Suspensory and not extinctive: ie promise may not be awarded full expectation; the promisor can resume her original rights on giving reasonable notice to the extent that the promisee can resume her original position.	Enforcement of **full expectation** (ie can be extinctive).
(5) Shield not sword: only operates as a defence to enforce promises to accept less. Cannot create or add new rights. ***Is reform desirable to allow the creation or addition of new rights?***	**Shield and sword:** can operate as defence to enforce promises to accept less and to create or add new rights.

irrespective of reliance, the justice of enforcement, and whether the promise relieves from some pre-existing obligation or confers new or additional rights.

How do the consideration and promissory estoppel doctrines interact?

Since both doctrines broadly answer the same question (ie the enforceability of promises), their relationship depends on their relative *scope*. In particular, the wider the scope and effect of promissory estoppel, the more likely it is to challenge consideration as the key determinant of enforcement. The key lies in the answer to two questions, namely:

- Is and should be the *effect* of promissory estoppel to:
  - enforce the promise (ie give the *full* expectation, as consideration does; if so, promissory estoppel directly undermines consideration); or
  - merely avoid detrimental reliance (ie give relief on the reliance measure, so it would not directly undermine consideration, 3.2.2.4)?
- To which *types of promises* can promissory estoppel apply?
  - Only relieving promises (as currently prescribed); or
  - should it be extended to promises that create or add new rights (which would impinge more directly on consideration, 3.2.2.3)?

3.2.1.1 A clear relieving promise

The first requirement is that there must be a clear and unequivocal promise or representation that the promisor does not intend to insist on her strict legal rights against the promisee (*Woodhouse v Nigerian Produce Marketing Co Ltd* (1974)). As the *Hughes* case demonstrates, the promise need not be express but may be *implied* from the circumstances.

- ✗ No estoppel arises if the language is qualified or imprecise (eg a statement made 'without prejudice': *IMT Shipping v Chansung Shipping Co* (2009)).
- ✗ Silence or inaction in the face of a breach will not normally estop a party from suing on the breach. A party does not lose her rights simply because she has failed throughout to insist upon strict performance (*Société Italo-Belge pour le Commerce et l'Industrie SA v Palm & Vegetable Oils (Malaysia) Sdn Bhd (The Post Chaser)* (1982)).
- ✗ In *Legione v Hately* (1982), the statement: 'I think that'll be alright, but I'll have to get instructions' did not amount to a promise that an extension would be given.

3.2.1.2 Reliance: change of position

Second, the promisee must have *relied* on the promise or representation. This is conventionally understood as requiring *detrimental* reliance in the sense that, if the promise is revoked, the promisee will be *worse off* than she was before the promise was made (*United Overseas Bank Ltd v Jiwani* (1976)). Harm to the promisee is the main reason why it may be inequitable for the promisor to resile (3.2.1.3). In the *Hughes* case, we saw that the tenant relied on the landlord's implied promise to 'stop the clock' during negotiations by not carrying out timely repairs. If the landlord could renege on his promise, the tenant's reliance in failing to make timely repairs would have resulted in the forfeiture of its lease.

It is rather more difficult to find detrimental reliance in *High Trees*, where the landlord simply promised to accept half the rent; indeed, none was identified in the decision. Nevertheless, analogous to the defence of change of position in the law of unjust enrichment, where a promisee has, or can be presumed to have, committed herself to a course of action which she would not otherwise have adopted, such that she would be prejudiced if the promisor were to resile from the promise, this is sufficient for reliance (*The Post Chaser* (1982)). The lessee's reliance in *High Trees* can be understood in terms of its 'loss of opportunity' to rearrange its financial affairs by renegotiating the lease, seeking alternative finance or declaring itself bankrupt. Reliance can also take the form of dissipating the money saved by paying other expenses. In a very real sense, the lessee is worse off in having to find five years of back rent immediately (£7,910) than if it had budgeted on the basis of paying the full rent from the start. The nub is the promisee's *inability to resume her original position* due to the reliance.

The corollary is that, if she *can* resume her original position, or can do so on reasonable notice (as in *High Trees*), there is no inequity in resiling from the promise either completely or for the future, as the case may be. Notice serves to halt reliance. In *The Post Chaser*, the sellers of palm-oil delayed in handing over certain documents in breach of contract. The buyer waived this breach, but then rejected the oil when its sub-buyer rejected it. The seller's claim for damages against the buyer failed because it was not inequitable for the buyer to enforce its original right since the seller was not prejudiced by it.

A radical departure is signalled by *Collier v P & M J Wright (Holdings) Ltd* (2008). There, C, along with two former business partners, was jointly liable for a debt to W (ie each was fully liable to W). W told C to pay his one-third and said he would pursue the other debtors for their share. On the partners' bankruptcy, W sued C for the whole sum. C claimed that W was barred by promissory estoppel. The Court of Appeal found this a triable issue. Arden LJ relied on Lord Denning's dicta in *D & C Builders v Rees* (1966) that: 'Where there has been a true accord, under which the creditor voluntarily agrees to accept a lesser sum in satisfaction, and the debtor acts upon that accord by paying the lesser sum and the creditor accepts it, then it is inequitable for the creditor afterwards to insist on the balance.' Arden LJ concluded that if:

(1) a debtor offers to pay part only of the amount he owes; (2) the creditor voluntarily accepts that offer, and (3) in reliance on the creditor's acceptance the debtor pays that part of the amount he owes in full, the creditor will, by virtue of the doctrine of promissory estoppel, be bound to accept that sum in full and final satisfaction of the whole debt. For him to resile will of itself be inequitable. In addition, in these circumstances, the promissory estoppel has the effect of extinguishing the creditor's right to the balance of the debt.

In **MWB Business Exchange Centres Ltd v Rock Advertising** (2016), the Court of Appeal reset promissory estoppel on its original path, rejecting Arden LJ's digression.

Pause for reflection

1. Arden LJ's judgement denatures promissory estoppel; it is in truth a unilateral collateral contract analysis in holding that:

   - C's *'reliance'* is satisfied by making part-payment of his debt;
   - *that* reliance makes it automatically *'inequitable'* for W to resile from his promise; and
   - the effect is to *extinguish* W's rights to two-thirds of the debt.

2. There was no reliance—Arden LJ found reliance, although she noted that the lower court found it 'difficult to see any sufficient relevant alteration of position on the part of Mr Collier, rendering it inequitable for the creditor now to resile from its alleged promise'. Neither C's continuing to make the payments that he was already making, nor his 'wild speculation' that he could otherwise have pursued the other creditors amounted 'to anything rendering it unconscionable on the part of the creditor now to pursue Mr Collier for the full amount of the debt'. Indeed, her Ladyship agreed that 'there is no evidence that Mr Collier's position now is in any material respect different from that immediately before the agreement was made'.

3. Longmore LJ was less than enthusiastic in his endorsement of this position. He said that if this position is sustained, courts should be slow to find a promise to forgo rights in the first place.

4. *D&C Builders Ltd v Rees* (1966) does not support the proposition in *Collier v Wright*. Promissory estoppel did *not* apply on the facts. All three judges applied *Foakes v Beer*. Even Lord Denning, who applied promissory estoppel, held that the promisee's behaviour did not make it inequitable for the promisor to resile. The fact that part-payment was actually made did not, on the facts, make the modification enforceable.

Kitchin LJ reinstated the traditional understanding of the requirements of reliance and inequitability, and the suspensory effect of promissory estoppel. Recall that Rock incurred arrears of licence fees and other charges to MWB, whereupon the parties agreed an oral variation to re-schedule the debt. Kitchin LJ held that:

- When Rock paid £3,500 on the same day in accordance with the re-schedule, this did not amount to relevant reliance since it was payable in any event.

- Since MWB gave notice two days later of its intention to reassert its original rights and Rock suffered no prejudice in reliance on the promise, it was not inequitable for MWB to renege.

- MWB's original rights were only suspended and could be revived on giving reasonable notice, which it did.

3.2.1.3 Inequitable to go back on the promise

The third requirement of promissory estoppel is that it must be 'inequitable' for the promisor to go back on her promise. This is usually, but not always, satisfied by the promisee's reliance (change of position). Inequity is an *independent* requirement of reliance and considers other factors such as:

(i) The *time lag* before the promisor asserts her original right and the degree of *prejudice to the promisee*: there was no inequity in resiling in *The Post Chaser*, where the promisor reasserted its legal right just two days later and the promisee could be restored to its original position.

(ii) The *circumstances surrounding the relieving promise*: In **D&C Builders v Rees** (1966), R owed D&C £482 for building works but, knowing D&C were in 'desperate financial straits', R offered £300 in full settlement or 'nothing'. D&C eventually accepted this but later sued for the balance. The majority of the Court of Appeal refused to recognise the alleged settlement for lack of consideration. The court also rejected the plea of promissory estoppel because it was not inequitable for D&C to go back on its promise to accept less since R 'really behaved very badly'. R misled D&C as to her own financial position and used D&C's financial difficulties to intimidate D&C into accepting a lower sum in discharge of the entire debt.

(iii) Events *subsequent to the making of the promise*:

- in *Williams v Stern* (1879), a creditor promised a debtor extra time to pay before he exercised his right to seize the debtor's furniture, but he reneged when he heard that the debtor's landlord was about to seize the same assets for unpaid rent. The creditor's conduct was not inequitable.

- Similarly, if *A* excuses *B* from part of her obligations for a particular reason (eg because of labour shortages or price rises of raw materials), it may not be inequitable for *A* to renege if a subsequent change of circumstances eliminates the reason for the promise, at least if *A* gives sufficient notice.

- Recall **Re Selectmove**, where a company challenged an order for its compulsory winding up on the petition of the Revenue, to which the company owed arrears and taxes. The company argued that the Revenue had given it extra time to pay. Peter Gibson LJ rejected the claim of promissory estoppel because 'it was not inequitable or unfair' to go back on that agreement since 'the company failed to honour its [lesser] promise'. That is, since the promisee failed to actually perform its reduced obligations, the promisor could revert to its original rights.

3.2.1.4 The extent of enforcement: suspensory or extinctive?

The effect of promissory estoppel is generally said to be suspensory and not extinctive of the promisor's original rights; the promisor may, on giving due notice, assert her original rights (*Tool Metal Manufacturing Co Ltd v Tungsten Electric Co Ltd* (1955)), ie the relief contained in the relieving promise may be *temporary* or may be terminated by notice, *if* the promisee can resume her original position. The corollary is that promissory estoppel can *extinguish* part or all of the promisor's existing rights if the promisee cannot resume her position (*Ajayi v RT Briscoe (Nigeria) Ltd* (1964)).

The real issue is what is necessary to ensure that the promisee is not prejudiced by her reliance on the promise. This may require:

- total extinction of the original right—in *Hughes v Metropolitan Railway Co*, the landlord's implied promise was merely to suspend his right to *timely* repairs (ie stop time running) during their negotiations, and *this* right *was* extinguished because it was impossible for the tenant to wind the clock back;

- partial extinction of the original right—in *High Trees*, the lessors were permitted to revert to the full rent on giving reasonable notice, but would not have been entitled to demand the rent waived up to that point; the right to those payments *was* extinguished; or

- no effect to be given to the promise—in *MWB v Rock*, the promisee could resume its original position.

The potential for the promisor to reassert her original rights under promissory estoppel shows that it is:

✗ not primarily an instrument for the enforcement of a promise, but

✓ one for preventing injustice to the promisee by protecting reasonable reliance.

3.2.2 The types of promise subject to promissory estoppel

English law treats promissory estoppel as a 'shield but not a sword'. It only applies where there is *a pre-existing contractual or other legal relationship* between the parties, and one party promises to give up some of her rights under that relationship. Promissory estoppel operates *defensively* (to prevent the promisor from enforcing the original rights she has relinquished); it cannot operate *offensively* (to give the promisee an action for more than her original rights as in the *Williams v Roffey* situation, or a *new* cause of action where the parties have no pre-existing legal relationship). In short, promissory estoppel:

✓ *can enforce promises of 'the same for less'*;

✗ *cannot enforce promises of 'more for the same'*; and

✗ *cannot create new* legal rights independent of the parties' pre-existing legal relationship.

Although courts have permitted *claimants* to appeal to promissory estoppel, so that it can be said to operate as a sword,[23] it only does so to prevent the defendant *promisor* from relying on a defence which (but for her promise not to rely on it) would have defeated the promisee's claim, eg if I promise not to raise the defence that your claim is time-barred, you can appeal to promissory estoppel to prevent me from raising the defence, and thereby succeed in your claim against me (*Nippon Yusen Kaisha v Pacifica Navegacion SA (The Ion)* (1980)). The crucial point is that the claimant promisee's cause of action arises *independently* of the promise being enforced by promissory estoppel.

The reason for these restrictions is to *avoid undermining consideration as the primary test of contractual liability*. If a promise could be enforced simply because of the promisee's reliance, this would blow a great hole in the boundary of contractual liability put up by the doctrine of consideration. Lord Denning said in *Combe v Combe* that 'the doctrine of consideration is too firmly fixed to be overthrown by a side wind'.

Diagram 3G maps the roles of consideration and promissory estoppel in the enforcement of contract modifications.

---

[23] See R Halson, 'The Offensive Limits of Promissory Estoppel' [1999] *LMCLQ* 256, 259–61.

Diagram 3G Contract modifications: the role of consideration and promissory estoppel

		✓ is operative ✗ is inoperative
Enforceability of	**Via consideration?**	**Via promissory estoppel?**
(1) Promises to accept less	(1a) ✓ Legal benefit Practical benefit: ✗ *In Re Selectmove* ✓ *MWB v Rock*	(1b) ✓
(2) Promises to give more	(2a) ✓ Legal benefit ✓ Practical benefit *Williams v Roffey*	(2b) ✗

3.2.2.1 Promises to accept less

A agrees to build ten shelves for *B* by a certain date for £5,000. Subsequently, *A* says that she will have difficulty performing on time, and *B* allows *A* to deliver only seven shelves for the same price (this relieving promise is represented by **(1)** in Diagram 3F). Can *A* insist on only delivering seven?

- Relieving or 'subtracting' promises are enforceable if supported by **consideration (1a)**. *Legal* benefit or detriment certainly qualifies, but, at the time of writing, there are inconsistent Court of Appeal decisions on whether practical benefit qualifies with *In re Selectmove* saying 'no' and *MWB v Rock* saying 'yes'.

- Absent consideration, a relieving promise may, via **promissory estoppel (1b)**, operate as a *defence* against the promisor's enforcement of her original rights. Here, promissory estoppel *cuts back* the promisor's original rights. *Hughes v Metropolitan Railway Co* and *High Trees* are ready examples of the defensive function of promissory estoppel.

Promissory estoppel appears to contradict the rule in *Foakes v Beer* that promises to accept the same for less are unenforceable for want of legal consideration. However, the apparent contradiction disappears if it is understood that:

- **consideration** yields the *full* enforcement of the subtracting promise (*permanently extinguishing* the promisor's original rights),

- while **promissory estoppel** only reduces the promisor's original rights when it would be inequitable for the promisor to renege and only *to the extent necessary to protect the promisee's reliance.*

The defensive function of promissory estoppel is mirrored in two related doctrines:

(i)   Someone who makes a representation of an *existing fact* which induces another's *detrimental reliance* is permanently prevented from proving facts contrary to her representation, by the doctrine of **estoppel by representation**. In *Avon CC v Howlett* (1983), A could not recover a mistaken payment made to an employee H because A represented to H that he was entitled to the money and H had spent the money in reliance upon the representation. The estoppel operated as a 'shield' to defeat a claim which would otherwise have succeeded.

(ii)   The doctrine of **waiver** applies to statements of *intention* to forgo the speaker's strict legal rights against the addressee. Waiver is practically indistinguishable from promissory estoppel. Lord Denning said in *Charles Rickards Ltd v Oppenheim* (1950) that: 'Whether it be called waiver or forbearance on his part, or an agreed variation or substituted performance, does not matter . . . It is a particular application of the principle . . . in' the *High Trees* case. In *Brikom Investments Ltd v Carr* (1979), Lord Denning applied promissory estoppel, whilst Roskill and Cumming-Bruce LJJ treated the case as one of waiver; all agreed that the promise not to enforce certain terms of the lease should be enforced.

- In *WJ Alan & Co Ltd v El Nasr Export and Import Co* (1972), a contract for the sale of coffee required payment by irrevocable letter of credit. A non-conforming letter of credit was provided but the seller did not complain and drew on the credit. The Court of Appeal held that the seller had waived its strict legal rights.

- Waiver also operates as a shield and not a sword, but its effect (like promissory estoppel) could enable an independent claim to succeed which would otherwise fail, eg in *Hickman v Haynes* (1875), the buyer of goods asked the seller to delay delivery but then refused to accept the goods, claiming that the seller had breached by late delivery. The court allowed the seller's damages claim against the buyer because the buyer had waived his right to demand timely delivery and could not subsequently reassert it without giving reasonable notice.

3.2.2.2 Promises to give more

A agrees to build ten shelves for *B* by a certain date for £5,000. Subsequently, *A* says she cannot complete the job for the agreed price and *B* agrees to pay her an extra £1,000. Is that extra enforceable?

Diagram 3F row **(2)** reveals the law's inconsistent approach as between adding and subtracting promises:

- adding promises are enforceable if supported by **consideration**, in the sense of legal or *practical* benefit (*Williams v Roffey*). Recall that there is uncertainty over whether practical benefit is sufficient to enforce subtracting promises (compare **(1a)** with **(2a)** in **Diagram 3F**);

- adding promises *cannot* be enforced via **promissory estoppel** (*Williams v Roffey*), while subtracting promises *can* (compare **(1b)** with **(2b)** in **Diagram 3F**).

In short, while promissory estoppel can enforce *subtracting promises*, practical benefit cannot and, while practical benefit can enforce *adding promises*, promissory estoppel cannot.

Counterpoint

1. *Consistency and justice*: there is no logical justification for the law's inconsistent approach. There is no functional difference between a promise to 'pay more' or to 'accept less' than under the pre-existing contract. In both cases, the promisor is getting *proportionately* 'less' than her original entitlement, and the promisee is getting 'more'. If the promisee's reliance on subtracting promises is worthy of protection, so should her reliance on adding promises. It should not matter whether the promisee is the claimant or the defendant. In *Williams v Roffey*, Russell LJ said that he 'would have welcomed' an estoppel argument to the effect that it would be unconscionable to allow the defendants to renege on their promise. However, the expansion of consideration to include practical benefit removes the incentive to extend promissory estoppel in this way.

2. *Transparency, flexibility, and accuracy*: promissory estoppel permits greater transparency, flexibility, and accuracy in balancing the competing policies than the notion of practical benefit as consideration. It can do so in determining:

   - *whether a* modifying promise should be enforced:
     - by reference to the circumstances prompting the parties' renegotiation, the promisee's conduct in inducing the modification, the reasonableness of the modification, and any subsequent change in the circumstances of the parties.
     - In contrast, the consideration doctrine asks whether the promisor obtained a practical benefit and, if so, whether duress avoids the transaction.

   - and, the *extent* of appropriate enforcement of the modifying promise:
     - to protect the promisee's change of position in reliance on the promise.
     - In contrast, consideration and duress yield an all-or-nothing response—once consideration is found, adding promises are *fully* enforceable (at least in theory). But, if duress is found, the promise is totally unenforceable.

3.2.2.3 Promises that create or add more rights

If promissory estoppel can extend its application from subtracting promises to adding promises, should promissory estoppel also be able to enforce an entirely new cause of action in the absence of a pre-existing legal relationship between the parties? The answer is 'no'.

✗ Recall *Combe v Combe* (1951), where a husband promised, but did not pay, his wife £100 a year upon divorce. She claimed the arrears after six years, pointing to her reliance on the promise by not applying for maintenance payments. The court held that: (i) the wife's reliance was not requested by the husband and so was not good consideration (3.1.2.2); and (ii) promissory estoppel did not apply because it could not create new causes of action where none existed before. This avoids undermining consideration as the primary test of contractual liability.

However, if the nub of promissory estoppel is the promisor's unconscionability (in inducing the promisee's reliance on her promise and then reneging on it), it should not matter whether or not the parties are in a pre-existing legal relationship. Three reasons support the expansion of promissory estoppel to *create* new causes of action:

(i) Other estoppels can create new causes of action

Where the parties to a transaction have acted upon a common assumption (of fact or of law, whether resulting from mistake or misrepresentation), estoppel by convention prevents either party from denying that common assumption.

✓ In *Amalgamated Investment and Property Co v Texas Commerce International Bank Ltd* (1982), T's subsidiary made loans to A's subsidiary. T and A contracted on the common assumption that A was guaranteeing *that* loan; in fact, the wording of the guarantee only covered loans made *by* T itself (of which there were none). A's liquidators unsuccessfully sought a declaration that A had no such liability. A was estopped from denying that the guarantee was for the loan by T's subsidiary to A's subsidiary. On the facts, T used the estoppel as a shield to A's claim for a declaration; however, Lord Denning (and arguably Brandon LJ) held that T could have *sued on the guarantee* to recover the sum (ie created a cause of action). Anyway, since the guarantee did not literally cover the relevant loan, in substance T's right to the sum (whether claiming or keeping it) was founded on estoppel. Brandon LJ stated that while no one can 'found a cause of action on an estoppel, he may, as a result of being able to rely on an estoppel, succeed on a cause of action on which, without being able to rely on that estoppel, he would necessarily have failed'. The qualification can swallow the rule.

Proprietary estoppel can also found a cause of action. The typical scenario is that *A*, the landowner, 'stands by' ('acquiescence'), while *B* incurs detriment in reliance on *A*'s promise that she has, or will get, an interest in *A*'s land.

✓ In *Pascoe v Turner* (1979), P and T lived together for some years. When P left T for another woman, P told T that the house and everything in it was hers. After T spent £230 on repairs, P sued for possession of the house. T successfully counterclaimed for a declaration that the house and its contents were hers. Although T gave no consideration for P's promise, she had acted to her detriment in reliance on his promise and this created a *new* cause of action. The promisee's claim was not limited to the value of her work (a *quantum meruit*). She received the whole promise.

✓ In *Inwards v Baker* (1965), the promisee was induced by his father's invitation to build a bungalow on his father's land, but the land was left to another on the father's death. The promisee was allowed to stay on the property for as long as he wished.

✓ In *Crabb v Arun DC* (1976), A promised C, an adjoining landowner, a second right of way from a portion of A's land and erected gates for two access points. In reliance on this, C sold the portion of his land with the existing access, but A closed off the second access point, thereby locking in the land that C retained. A demanded £3,000 from C for the access. The Court of Appeal held that it would be inequitable to allow A to renege on its promise when this had induced C's detrimental reliance. Since A's conduct had 'sterilised' C's land for several years, the court granted the right of way without payment but said that, in an appropriate case, the promisee would be required to pay its fair value.

(ii) Differences in restriction unprincipled

- There have been calls to unify the various estoppels (eg Lord Denning in *Amalgamated Investment & Property Co v Texas Commerce International Bank Ltd*). In *Taylor Fashions Ltd v Liverpool Victoria Trustees*, Oliver J said that the question is: 'whether . . . it would be unconscionable for a party to be permitted to deny that which, knowingly or unknowingly, he has allowed or encouraged another to assume to his detriment'.

- However, it has also been cautioned that the differences are established (a) as a matter of authority, and (b) reflect the different contexts in which they are applied.

  - Lord Steyn said that: 'to restate the law in terms of an overarching principle might tend to blur the necessarily separate requirements, and distinct terrain of application' (*Republic of India v Indian Steamship Co Ltd (No 2)* (1997)).

  - Mance LJ said that: 'not only are we bound in this court by previous authority on the scope of particular types of estoppel, but it seems to me inherent in the doctrine's very flexibility that it may take different shapes to fit the context of different fields' (*Baird Textile Holdings v Marks & Spencer*).

  - Lord Goff was 'inclined to think that the many circumstances capable of giving rise to an estoppel cannot be accommodated within a single formula'. Nevertheless, he acknowledged that 'it is unconscionability which provides the link between them' (*Johnson v Gore Wood & Co (A Firm)* (2001)).

 Pause for reflection

If there is an overarching principle linking different estoppels, then a piecemeal approach seems difficult to justify. The appeal to *precedent* is an assertion that the differences 'just *are*'. The appeal to *contextual* differences does not explain why reliance on promises conferring interests in *land* can create a cause of action, but reliance on *other* promises cannot. Whilst the promisee's reliance on promises relating to land may enrich the promisor, it does not invariably do so. Moreover, although it is arguable that land warrants special treatment because of its historical importance as a form of wealth, this would tend to point to the need for very strict guidelines to transfer rights in land (recall the formalities requirements) which do not rest merely on reliance. Different manifestations of a common principle should not be allowed to ossify into different rules detached from the principle from which they were derived.

In 'The Offensive Limits of Promissory Estoppel' [1999] LMCLQ 256, Halson argues that promissory estoppel should *not* create a new cause of action because:

(i) it would create uncertainty and conflict with contractual actions;

> ➡
>
> (ii) it wrongly assumes that the disparate estoppel doctrines share a common purpose; in fact, they have distinct policy objectives; and
>
> (iii) promissory estoppel has been developed particularly in the context of contract modifications, and this expertise and experience will be wasted if promissory estoppel is merged in a wider doctrine of estoppel.

(iii) Promissory estoppel and consideration rest on different bases

The most convincing reason for preventing promissory estoppel from creating a new cause of action is to avoid a direct clash with the consideration requirement. However, there is no clash if we recognise that consideration and promissory estoppel are two distinct types of liability:

- **Consideration** yields a contractual cause of action for the enforcement of the promisee's *full expectation*.

- **Promissory estoppel** seeks to *avoid the detriment* arising from the promisee's reliance on the promise, if it would be inequitable for the promisor to renege.

(iv) Other jurisdictions have recognised promissory estoppel as a cause of action.

- The US 2nd Restatement on Contracts, §90 states:

  (1) A promise which the promisor should reasonably expect to induce action or forbearance on the part of the promisee or a third person and which does induce such action or forbearance is binding if injustice can be avoided only by enforcement of the promise. The remedy granted for breach may be limited as justice requires.

- In the High Court of Australia in ***Waltons Stores (Interstate) Ltd v Maher*** (1988), M entered into negotiations to lease land to W for a major construction project which required M to demolish the existing building on the site and erect a new building to W's specifications. Solicitors were instructed to prepare the formal documents. W's solicitors told M's solicitors that 'we believe that approval will be forthcoming. We shall let you know tomorrow if any amendments are not agreed to.' M signed the requisite documents, which were forwarded to W's solicitors for execution and exchange (to satisfy the formality requirements). Because W's timetable required urgent action, M began demolishing the building on his land. Meanwhile, W had second thoughts and instructed their solicitors to 'go slow', although it knew that M had commenced work on the site. After two months, when M had completed a substantial amount of the work, W informed M of their intention to withdraw from the project. The court held that W was estopped from denying the existence of a contract. It rejected W's argument that, since the parties had *no pre-existing legal relationship*, there was nothing for promissory estoppel to relieve from.

- In *Commonwealth of Australia v Verwayen* (1990), V was injured in a collision at sea while serving in the Navy. He sued C for negligence, but substantially out of time. C had repeatedly admitted liability and said it would not plead the time limit as a defence. The High Court of Australia decided by a majority of four to three that C was not entitled to rely on the defence and, since liability was not in issue, the action could proceed immediately to quantification of damages.

3.2.2.4 The nature of any action created by promissory estoppel

If promissory estoppel could *create new actions*, the liability it generates should *not* be classified as contractual.

- *Waltons Stores v Maher* stresses that the *aim* is not to enforce the promise but, rather, to *avoid the detriment* occasioned by the promisee's reliance on the promise.

- The focus is on the promisor's reprehensible conduct which causes *harm* to the promisee. This view is consistent with the references to 'unconscionability' in the cases and the academic literature.

- Promissory estoppel is analogous to misrepresentation, which attracts reliance damages. Even an innocent misrepresentation puts the representor under a duty to correct the representee if she becomes aware of its falsity before contract formation. She cannot stand by while the representee detrimentally relies on their misrepresentation (5.1.3.2).

- How do we explain the cases that seem to enforce the promisee's *expectations*? In *Waltons Stores v Maher*, damages were awarded on the basis that the promisor was estopped from going back on the promise that the contract would be completed (in effect, the expectation measure). In 'Reliance and Expectation in the Estoppel Remedies' (1998) 18 *LS* 360, Robertson argues that the expectation will be awarded if that is the only way of fully protecting the promisee's *reliance* interest (which includes the loss of opportunity to make other contracts). Thus, the expectation measure is sometimes the best proxy for the reliance measure. This is readily understandable in *Waltons Stores*, when reliance comprises demolishing one's own building and erecting another to the promisor's specifications.

- The crucial point is that, on the wrong-doing-hence-reliance-damages view, if the expectation greatly exceeds the reliance, there is scope to award *less than the expectation* (see the Australian decision in *Giumelli v Giumelli* (1990)). This very possibility distinguishes promissory estoppel from consideration. Acceptance of the wrongdoing view of promissory estoppel eliminates any necessary conflict with the doctrine of consideration. The source of liability and the remedial response are different.

3.2.3 Future development of promissory estoppel

Currently, promissory estoppel can only relieve a party from her pre-existing obligations. Its operation can be extended in three ways.

3.2.3.1 Extension to promises to comply with formalities

The narrowest extension of promissory estoppel is to promises to comply with *formalities* requirements in respect of an agreement *supported by consideration*. *Waltons Stores v Maher* made clear that enforcement via promissory estoppel rests on the 'creation or encouragement by the party estopped in the other party of an assumption that a contract will come into existence or a promise will be performed and that the other party relied on that assumption to his detriment to the knowledge of the first party'. The italicised words show the more limited interpretation of the case offered by Mance LJ in *Baird Textile Holdings v Marks & Spencer* (2002), as one involving:

> complete agreement on the terms of the lease. The agreement was *merely unenforceable for want of compliance with the statute*. It may be arguable that recognition of an estoppel here would not be to use estoppel 'as giving a cause of action in itself', and it would certainly not be to undermine the necessity of consideration. Rather, it would preclude the potential lessee from raising a collateral objection to the binding nature of the agreed lease.

On this view, promissory estoppel only bridges the gap in formalities and not in consideration, which remains necessary.

3.2.3.2 Extension to promises to give more

A wider extension of promissory estoppel is to cover contract modifications that *add* to the promisee's rights. On this view, promissory estoppel *can* fill a consideration gap, but only in contract modifications. The latter qualification can be criticised: the underlying problem of unconscionability may be present whether the promise relates to the formation or the modification of a contract, and whether it relates to rights in land or other subject matter.

3.2.3.3 Extension to the creation of new actions

The widest option is to allow promissory estoppel to create new causes of action (in addition to enforcing the promises referred to at 3.2.3.1 and 3.2.3.2). Spence[24] persuasively argues in favour of a 'duty to ensure the reliability of induced assumptions'. To recognise such a duty would be a radical departure from the current law. It would take an unusually bold House of Lords to sweep aside *Combe v Combe* in favour of *Waltons Stores v Maher*. If it is minded to do so, the concern not to undermine consideration can be met by emphasising the reliance basis of enforcement:

- consideration buys the full enforcement of the expectation; but
- promissory estoppel only negates detrimental reliance; the promisee's expectation should only be protected when, exceptionally, it is the only or most practical way of protecting her reliance (as in *Crabb v Arun*).

If this is accepted, the extension of promissory estoppel to create new actions that yield a fundamentally different remedy, will merely *supplement* and not usurp consideration. Promissory estoppel is only contractual in the sense that it can arise in the

---

[24] M Spence, *Protecting Reliance: The Emergent Doctrine of Equitable Estoppel* (Hart Publishing, 1999) 2–3.

context of contract formation or modification, but it is *non-contractual* in nature; it does not, and should not, automatically lead to the full enforcement of promises. This is reinforced by the suspensory effect of promissory estoppel. Promissory estoppel and consideration give effect to promises for different reasons, and so to different extents.

3.3 **Formalities**

'You went through the ceremony'

The law may require certain contracts be made in a stipulated way, in *addition to*, or *instead of*, the requirement of consideration. Failure to comply with these require-ments renders the contract unenforceable.

3.3.1 **The requirement of formalities *instead of* consideration**

Gratuitous promises are enforceable *without consideration* if they are contained in a deed. The deed is the common mechanism for making charitable donations because its enforceability enables the charities to claim the income tax paid on the promised sum by the donor. For a document to constitute a deed, section 1(2)–(3) of the Law of Property (Miscellaneous Provisions) Act 1989 requires that it:

(i)   is clear on its face that it is intended to be a deed by the person making it; and

(ii)   is validly executed as a deed by that person; ie the document must be:

- signed either by her (attested by one witness) or at her direction (requiring two witnesses); *and*

- delivered as a deed by her or an authorised person on her behalf.

A deed is enforceable without consideration, but specific performance will not be awarded.

 Pause for reflection

1. Insofar as we see deeds as part of contract law, it shows that contract law is not exclusively concerned with the enforcement of bargains. Deeds allow people to commit themselves *formally* to gratuitous promises. Parties who want to make gratuitous promises enforceable informally can cast them in the *form* of bargains for nominal consideration (3.1.3.4).

2. The specified formality performs an evidentiary and a cautionary function. Requiring someone to go through a 'ceremony' impresses on her the significance of what she is doing, giving a final opportunity to reflect on its wisdom, and operates as a check against impulsive action. The law is not against gifts; it just refuses to enforce *informal* gifts.

3. Absent formalities and consideration, a gratuitous promise, if executed (carried out), will not be reversed unless it is tainted by some vitiating factor.

3.3.2 **The requirement of formalities** *in addition* **to consideration**

The general rule is that contracts supported by consideration can be made in any form and evidenced by any means. However, some contracts require compliance with formalities, in addition to consideration. They are generally contracts that are particularly important or potentially one-sided, or where one party belongs to a vulnerable group warranting special protection.

The **stipulated formalities** may require that a particular type of contract be made:

(i)   by deed: eg a lease for more than three years (Law of Property Act 1925, s 52(1));

(ii)   in a particular documentary format: eg:

- most contracts for the sale or disposition of an interest in land must, among other things, be made in writing (Law of Property (Miscellaneous Provisions) Act 1989, s 2);

- regulated consumer credit contracts, such as hire purchases, must be made in the form prescribed by government regulations, setting out all the express terms, and giving notice of the debtor's right to cancel during the 'cooling off' period and other specified information; the contract must be signed by both parties and a copy given to the debtor (Consumer Credit Act 1974, ss 60–4; see also 1.7.3 and *Wilson v First County Trust Ltd (No 2)* (2003)); or

(iii)   evidenced in writing: for example, contracts of *guarantee* (Statute of Frauds Act 1677, s 4).

3.3.3 **The functions of formalities requirements**

(i) **The cautionary function**: this is particularly important in one-sided (eg guarantee) or traditionally important (eg land) transactions. In *Ruddick v Ormston* (2005), R sought specific performance of an alleged contract to buy O's flat. O offered to sell his house directly to R without valuation for £25,000. R realised that this was significantly under-priced, so he immediately signed, and got O to sign a hastily drawn up agreement on two diary pages (one stating that O would sell to R and the other that R would buy O's flat for £25,000). O refused to proceed with the sale when he realised that his flat was worth £65,000. The court refused specific performance because these signed pages did not comply with section 2(1) of the Law of Property (Miscellaneous Provisions) Act 1989. The contract was unenforceable without the need to consider whether it was also unconscionable (9.4).

(ii) **The evidentiary function**: formalities provide evidence of, and minimise disputes over, the existence and content of the alleged contract. Thus, commercial contracts are often reduced to writing, even though it is unnecessary to do so. Formalities also provide a marker for the parties engaged in lengthy negotiations to signify the point at which negotiations turn into a binding contract.

(iii) **The protective function**: Parliament affords protection in certain types of contracts to the party which typically has the weaker bargaining power (eg the tenant, employee, consumer borrower, and guarantor) by ensuring that she receives a written record of the agreement in clear language, and, in certain cases (eg consumer credit, timeshare, and package holidays), allowing her to escape the contract within the 'cooling off' period.

3.3.4 **Common problems raised by formalities requirements**

(i) Formalities requirements can be inconvenient, mysterious, and inaccessible to ordinary people.

(ii) **Inconsistency as to the types of contracts affected**: the evidentiary, cautionary, and protective functions of formalities are performed in a piecemeal and unsystematic way. It is impossible to explain why certain contracts require formalities while other similar contracts do not. This leads to the next difficulty.

(iii) Formalities can generate much litigation over the **jurisdictional question**; ie whether the disputed contract comes within the class of contracts which must comply with the formalities, eg:

✓ contracts of guarantee must be evidenced in writing,

✗ but not the functionally similar contracts of indemnity.

The difficulty in distinguishing them has 'raised many hair-splitting distinctions of exactly that kind which brings the law into hatred, ridicule and contempt by the public' (*Yeoman Credit Ltd v Latter* (1961)).

(iv) **Inconsistency in the formalities required**: it is not apparent why some contracts must be in the form of a deed, some must actually be in writing and others need only be evidenced in writing.

(v) **Dispute over how to satisfy the formalities requirements**: eg the simple requirement of a signature has required much judicial elucidation over, eg whether initials will do; whether the signature may be printed; whether it may be in any part of the document, not necessarily at the bottom; whether a signature page from an earlier draft can be substituted to a later draft agreement with substantially different terms; and whether it can be put on the document before the contract is made.

(vi) **Non-compliance** with formality requirements renders the contract void or unenforceable; this can cause hardship. In *Actionstrength Ltd v International Glass Engineering* (2003), the House of Lords denied enforcement to an oral contract of guarantee, but with regret because of the harsh consequences, particularly since this 'was not a bargain struck between inexperienced people, liable to misunderstand what they were doing . . . These were not small men in need of paternalist protection.' Moreover, it was doubtful that the parties appreciated that their agreement would be construed as a guarantee requiring formalities. In *Pitt v Jones* (2007), an unmeritorious party escaped his obligations because he gave a guarantee to minority shareholders which he refused to put in writing. Smith LJ concluded that the guarantee was unenforceable 'with some reluctance' since the defendant's stance was 'most unattractive'.

- This potential injustice caused to a party who has detrimentally relied on the validity of an unenforceable contract was historically mitigated by the doctrine of part-performance. It made a non-complying contract enforceable if one party had induced or knowingly allowed the other party to alter her position on the faith of the contract; it was considered a fraud to rely on the formalities requirements (*Wakeham v MacKenzie* (1968)). Unsurprisingly, the doctrine was perceived to undermine the formalities requirements.

- The Law of Property (Miscellaneous Provisions) Act 1989 (LP(MP)A) swung the pendulum firmly the other way. It requires contracts for the sale or other disposition of an interest in land to be *'made* in writing' and not merely *'evidenced* in writing'. Non-compliance with the LP(MP)A means that *no contract comes into existence* to be partly performed; the doctrine of part performance has nothing to apply to. In *Yaxley v Gotts* (2000), Robert Walker LJ said that the 1989 Act:

  > [c]an be seen as embodying Parliament's conclusion, in the general public interest, that the need for certainty as to the formation of contracts of this type must in general outweigh the disappointment of those who make informal bargains in ignorance of the statutory requirement. If an estoppel would have the effect of enforcing a void contract and subverting Parliament's purpose it may have to yield to the statutory law which confronts it, except so far as the statute's saving for a constructive trust provides a means of reconciliation of the apparent conflict.

- Thus, section 2(5) of the LP(MP)A specifically preserves 'the creation or operation of resulting, implied or constructive trusts' (ie proprietary solutions) to mitigate the potential injustice of the formalities requirements. As Beldam LJ stated in *Yaxley v Gotts*, the 'social policy of simplifying conveyancing by requiring the certainty of a written document' does not mean 'that unconscionable conduct or equitable fraud should be allowed to prevail'.

3.3.5 **Online contracts**

In response to the increasing prevalence of online contracting there have been several developments, including:

- Article 9 of the EC Directive on Electronic Commerce (2000/31/EC) requires Member States not to create obstacles to the creation of contracts by electronic means.

- Section 8 of the Electronic Communications Act 2000 empowers the relevant minister to modify existing legislation to authorise the use of electronic communications to comply with formalities requirements.

- The Law Commission regards changing the law as unnecessary since electronic communications will generally satisfy the requirements of 'writing' and 'signature' (*Electronic Commerce: Formal Requirements in Commercial Contracts* (2001), para 3.43). Indeed, in *Golden Ocean Group v Salgaocar Mining Industries* (2011), Christopher Clarke J held that an agreement concluded by a long sequence of emails satisfied the writing requirements of section 4 of the Statute of Frauds Act 1677.

However, given the cautionary and protective functions of formalities, it would be undesirable to allow electronic contracts to be made too easily. In *Caton v Caton* (1867), the House of Lords held that, to constitute a signature, a name must be inserted 'in such a manner as to have the effect of "authenticating the instrument" or "so as to govern the whole agreement"'. In *Pereira Fernandes SA v Mehta* (2006), Judge Pelling QC held that an email sent by M's staff (at M's request) offering to guarantee his company's debt and accepted orally by the creditor satisfied the memorandum, but not the signature, requirement of section 4 of the Statute of Frauds 1677. M's email address was automatically inserted by the Internet Service Provider and his name did not appear in the body of the email. It is 'a clear example of the inclusion of a name which is incidental . . . Its appearance divorced from the main body of the text of the message emphasises this to be so . . . To conclude . . . [otherwise would] have widespread and wholly unintended legal and commercial effects.' Thus:

> a party can sign a document . . . by using his full name or his last name prefixed by some or all of his initials or using his initials, and possibly by using a pseudonym or a combination of letters and numbers . . . providing always that whatever was used was inserted into the document in order to give, and with the intention of giving, authenticity to it. Its inclusion must have been intended as a signature for these purposes.

THIS CHAPTER IN ESSENCE

The key areas and core topics in this chapter are summarised in an easy-to-use list, ideal for revision purposes, on the online resources at www.oup.com/uk/chenwishart6e/. Links to websites relevant to the topics covered and any updates to the chapter can also be found on the online resources.

QUESTIONS

1 Ivan agrees to build an elaborate stage and 20 kiosks for Jo's concert on 1 January for £25,000. Progress is worryingly slow. Ivan informs Jo that this is due to a severe labour shortage. Jo agrees to (a) increase her payment to £30,000 to enable Ivan to attract workers; and (b) reduce the number of kiosks to 15. For extraneous reasons, the labour supply improves rapidly; Ivan attracts enough workers without paying more. Jo decides that she really will need all 20 kiosks. Is Jo entitled to 20 kiosks? How much must Jo pay?

2 'The presence of consideration is a sufficient but not a necessary reason for treating a promise as binding. The outer boundaries of consideration are uncertain.' Is this true? What other good reasons, if any, might there be?

3 Advise the Law Commission whether reform of the consideration doctrine is necessary or desirable, outlining any suggestions you have for reform.

4 'It is vital that promissory estoppel remains a shield and not a sword to prevent it from outflanking the requirement of consideration.' Discuss.

5 What is the relationship between the doctrines of promissory estoppel and of consideration? What should it be?

 For hints on how to answer these questions, please see the online resources at www.oup.com/uk/chenwishart6e/

KEY FURTHER READING

Atiyah, P S (1986), 'Consideration: A Restatement' in P S Atiyah, *Essays in Contract* (Clarendon Press) 179.

Barnes, M (2011), 'Estoppels as Swords', *LMCLQ* 372.

Chen-Wishart, M (1995), 'Consideration: Practical Benefit and the Emperor's New Clothes' in J Beatson and D Friedmann (eds), *Good Faith and Fault in Contract Law* (OUP) 123.

Chen-Wishart, M (2010), 'A Bird in the Hand: Consideration and Promissory Estoppel' in A Burrows and E Peel (eds), *Contract Formation and Parties* (OUP) 89.

Chen-Wishart, M (2013), 'In Defence of Consideration', 13 *OUCLJ* 209.

Chen-Wishart, M 'Reform of Consideration: No Greener Grass' in S Degeling, J Edelman, and J Goudkamp (eds), *Contract in Commercial Law* (Sydney, Thomson, 2016) 77.

Cooke, E (1997), 'Estoppel and the Protection of Expectations', 17 *LS* 258.

Halson, R (1999), 'The Offensive Limits of Promissory Estoppel', *LMCLQ* 256.

Kötz, H and Flessner, A (1997), *European Contract Law Volume One: Formation, Validity and Contents of Contracts; Contracts and Third Parties* (OUP) chs 4–5.

Treitel, G (1976), 'Consideration: A Critical Analysis of Professor Atiyah's Fundamental Restatement', 50 *Australian LJ* 439.

PART III

Privity

'Who can enforce and who is bound by the contract?'

INTRODUCTION

In Chapters 2 and 3, we examined how a contract is formed. Here we ask: whose legal position can be affected by a contract? A contract clearly alters the rights and liabilities of the contract parties: they are said to be privy to the contract. But what about someone who is not a contract party, a so-called 'third party' to the contract (hereafter 'TP')?

(i) Can a TP have *obligations* imposed on her by other people's contracts?

(II) Can a TP *acquire enforceable rights* under other people's contracts?

At common law, the answer to both questions is 'no': only the contract parties can be entitled or bound by the contract; only they can sue and be sued on it. This is known as **'privity of contract'**.

- The rule that contract parties *cannot impose obligations* on TPs is relatively obvious and uncontroversial, although not without exceptions (4.2). Such liability as there is focuses on the *wrongfulness* of a TP who knowingly interferes with a contract party's *proprietary* rights acquired by a contract; such rights 'run with the property' and so are enforceable in kind and against everyone.

- The rule against conferring *enforceable benefits* or immunities on TPs is more controversial since it seems to: (i) contradict the contract parties' freedom to confer such benefits, and (ii) defeat the TP's reasonable expectation of such a right. The rule was always subject to numerous exceptions and avoidance devices, making this area of the law complicated and technical prior to the Contracts (Rights of Third Parties) Act 1999 (hereafter 'C(RTP)A'). This added a 'general and wide-ranging exception',[1] conferring enforceable rights on TPs. This has brought its own practical and conceptual difficulties so that it cannot be said to have simplified the law on this topic. For example, C(RTP)A contradicts some fundamental tenets of contract law, such as that:

  - claimants in contract actions must be *promisees*,

---

[1] Law Commission, Privity of Contract: Contracts for the Benefit of Third Parties (Law Com No 242, Cm 3329, 1996) paras 5.16, 13.2.

- who have given *consideration*, and that
- damages compensate for the *promisee's loss*.

C(RTP)A also creates uncertainty as to:

- the scope of the qualifying test for TP enforcement, and
- when contract parties are barred from changing their contract.

It also raises the question about *the relative priority of rights* where the interests of the TP and either (or both) of the contract parties conflict.

The key question is **'whose loss is it?'** when a contract conferring a benefit on a TP is breached by the promisor? Is it the promisee who has given consideration, or the TP? The tensions in this area of the law arise out of our ambivalence over the answer to this question.

4

Privity

'Who can enforce and who is bound by the contract?'

This chapter addresses the following questions:

(i) What are the arguments *for*, and *against*, the general rule that only contract parties can (and hence TPs cannot) sue on a contract?

(ii) When can a TP sue on a contract under C(RTP)A, and for what remedies?

(iii) What is the relationship between C(RTP)A conferring the right to sue on TPs and the requirement that a contract claimant must have given *consideration*?

(iv) To what extent can *a promisee* enforce a contract for the benefit of a TP?

(v) Aside from C(RTP)A, what legal avenues exist for *TPs to enforce* promises made for their benefit?

(vi) When and how does a contract *bind TPs*?

4.1 Conferring benefits on third parties

4.1.1 The general rule

The orthodox rule is that a party seeking to enforce a contractual promise must:

(i) be the promisee (ie the offeree who accepted the promise contained in the offer); *and*

(ii) have provided consideration for that promise.

Thus, in a contract where *A* promises *B* to pay *C* £500 in exchange for *B*'s promise to paint *A*'s car, *C* cannot enforce *A*'s promise to pay her £500; *C* is not the promisee, nor has she given any consideration (see **Diagram 4A.1**).

The rule was established in *Tweddle v Atkinson* (1861). The fathers of an engaged couple contracted to pay a sum to the husband after the marriage. The husband could not enforce the contract against his wife's father although the contract expressly stated that he could because 'in general no action can be maintained upon a promise, unless the consideration moves from the party to whom it is made' (see **Diagram 4A.2**).

The House of Lords in *Dunlop Pneumatic Tyre Co Ltd v Selfridge* (1915) agreed. Dunlop operated a price-fixing ring by selling tyres to a dealer (Dew) on terms that Dew: (i) would not sell below Dunlop's list price; and (ii) would obtain a written undertaking from anyone to whom they sold Dunlop products that they would also not sell below Dunlop's list price. S bought Dunlop products from Dew, but sold them below Dunlop's list price. The court denied Dunlop's claim for an injunction and damages against S to enforce the price-fixing contract. Dew, and not Dunlop, had provided consideration for S's promise (see **Diagram 4A.3**). Viscount Haldane LC said that 'only a person who is a party to a contract can sue on it'. Dunlop could not enforce the promise for two separate reasons:

(i) Dunlop was not a party to the contract between Dew and S; and

(ii) Dunlop gave no consideration for S's promise as to selling price.

The case is authority for the independence of the two requirements: that a contract claimant must: (i) be the promisee; *and* (ii) have given consideration for the promise.

Diagram 4A Contracts for the benefit of third parties: illustrations

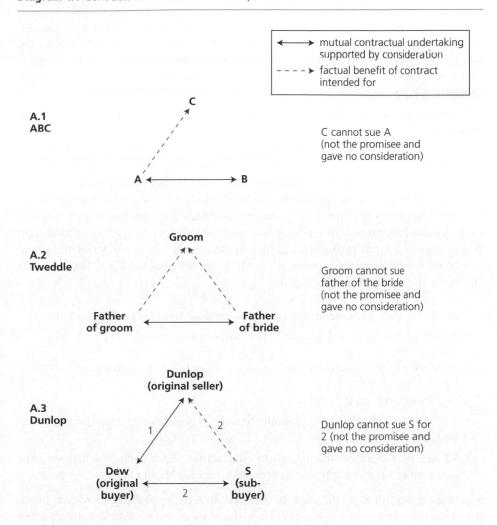

⟷	mutual contractual undertaking supported by consideration
----▸	factual benefit of contract intended for

A.1
ABC

C cannot sue A
(not the promisee and
gave no consideration)

A.2
Tweddle

Groom cannot sue
father of the bride
(not the promisee and
gave no consideration)

A.3
Dunlop

Dunlop cannot sue S for
2 (not the promisee and
gave no consideration)

4.1.2 Justifications for the privity rule

The privity rule follows logically from the definition of, and reasons for enforcing, a contract.

(i) **Exclusivity**: if contractual liability derives from a voluntary undertaking (1.4.1), it follows that only a person to whom the undertaking is addressed (the promisee) can enforce it. Contractual rights and duties *are personal* to those who create them. Collins (at 314) analogises it to a marriage in which the associated rights and duties remain personal to those who create them: TPs cannot claim the right to share in them. Smith argues that a promisor's only obligation is to the promisee to whom the promise is made ('Contracts for the Benefit of Third Parties: In Defence of the Third Party Rule' (1997) *OJLS* 645).

(ii) **The priority of buyers**: English law prioritises undertakings that are part of *bargains* over those that are given without reciprocal payment (eg gifts). A promisee who has provided consideration is more deserving than a TP who has not. Stevens, refuting the Law Commission's reasons for C(RTP)A (4.1.4), argues that there is no justification for giving TPs the right to enforce contracts because they are not promisees and have given no consideration ('The Contracts (Rights of Third Parties) Act 1999' (2004) 120 *LQR* 292).

(iii) **Floodgates**: any suggestion that the privity rule can be abolished is absurd. Without it, *anyone* could potentially enforce *any* contract, a position that no legal system or commentator would support. The problem remains even if we limit enforcement to TPs who *rely on* or *would benefit from* a contract, eg if a contract to build a motorway beside a village is not performed, should all those living in the village or buying houses there in anticipation of a rise in property values be able to sue the builder? The privity rule limits both liability for others' disappointment and responsibility for the fulfilment of others' *expectations*. Traditionally, contractual enforcement is restricted to: (a) parties to a bargain; (b) beneficiaries of a deed; and (c) relying promisees who sue on promissory estoppel, as **Diagram 4B** shows at **I**. C(RTP)A expands the range of liability from **I** to include:

- **II** TPs *expressly given the right to sue* in the contract under section 1(1)(a); and
- **III** TPs on whom *the contract purports to confer a benefit* under section 1(1)(b).

However, the range of potential liability can be stretched further to include:

- **IV** TPs who *rely* on the contract;
- **V** TPs who would benefit incidentally or indirectly from contractual performance; and
- **VI** TPs who merely want to enforce contractual performance, each raising the question of what the appropriate remedial response should be.

Kincaid argues that C(RTP)A departs from the underlying philosophy of civil liability. Hitherto, '[i]f P is to single out D from the mass of the population and seek the coercive power of the state to force D to realise P's interests, the state (the law) has required P to show that they have both participated in a relationship which justifies making D responsible to P.' In contrast, C(RTP)A amounts to an 'abdication of the law's duty to define justice between parties'. The new law is equivalent to the law's saying 'Justice is whatever you, the parties, say it is' ('Privity Reform in England' (2000) 15 *LQR* 43).

4.1.3 **Contracts (Rights of Third Parties) Act 1999**

C(RTP)A, introduced following criticism of the privity rule including in a Law Commission report, *Privity of Contract: Contracts for the Benefit of Third Parties* **(Law Com No 242, Cm 3329, 1996), hereafter 'Report 242'** (4.1.4), sets out a wide-ranging exception to the privity rule.

Diagram 4B Who can sue on a promise? What for?

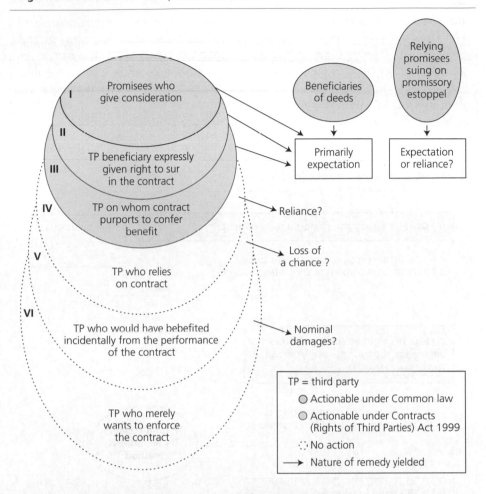

4.1.3.1 The test of enforceability by a third party

C(RTP)A sets out the qualifying conditions for a TP to enforce a contractual term as if she were the promisee (see **Diagram 4C**). A deed is treated as a contract for the purposes of C(RTP)A (*Prudential Assurance Company Ltd v Ayres* (2007)).

Section 1(1)(a) allows a TP to enforce a contractual term where the contract '*expressly provides that he may*'. Under section 1(6), the term enforced may be an exclusion or limitation of the TP's liability.

 Pause for reflection

Section 1(1)(a) arguably gives effect to the intention of the contract parties (meeting the Law Commission's first criticism of privity rule, 4.1.4). The outcome in *Tweddle v Atkinson* would now be reversed. As Collins states (at 314): 'The purpose of entering contracts is to restrict

➡

→
the freedom of the parties in certain ways for their mutual advantage, and if they choose to give a legal right to a third person this is no greater interference with their autonomy than any other term of the contract.' We could regard the promisor's liability to the TP as *part of the promisor's consideration* for the promisee's reciprocal promise, eg where *A* promises *B* that if *B* paints *A*'s house, she will give *C* an enforceable right to £100, *A*'s consideration for *B*'s painting is to pay *C* £100 *and* to allow *C* to sue on it.

Diagram 4C Third party action under C(RTP)A

Look on the online resources to view this figure as a PowerPoint® presentation

(1) Does TP satisfy the standing requirements?

TP = third party
✓ = yes
✗ = no

s 1(1)(a) contract confers express right to sue?
s 1(1)(b) contract purports to confer benefit on TP?

✓   ✗

(2) Has TP's right to sue crystallised before the contract parties' attempt to vary or rescind it?

s 2 Has TP assented to contract?
    Is TP's reliance on contract known to
    or reasonably foreseeable by promisor?

✓   ✗

TP cannot claim. Try an indirect method

(3) Is TP's claim weakened or negated?

by:
• promisor's defences, set-offs, counterclaims against TP (s 3)
• promisee's claim for TP's loss (s 5)
• exemption clause (s 7(2))
• exclusion from other contract legislation (s 7(4))
• exclusion from scope of the C(RTP)A (s 6)

✗   ✓

TP can claim as if the promisee

TP claim reduced or negated accordingly

Section 1(1)(b) is quite different. It allows a TP to enforce a contractual term where the contract merely *'purports to confer a benefit on him'*. Burrows[1] offers three reasons for section 1(1)(b):

- section 1(1)(b) recognises the contract parties' *implied* conferral of rights on the TP;

- section 1(1)(a) would not cover many situations where TP actions are desirable; and

- section 1(1)(a) will only be invoked in well-drafted contracts and TP action should be recognised beyond these.

The presumption in favour of TP enforcement is said to be a 'strong one'.[2] The promisor has the burden of proving that 'the parties did not intend the term to be enforceable by the third party' (**s 1(2)**), as where, eg:

✗ the contract expressly says so; or

✗ it expressly prohibits assignment without the promisor's consent (as in *Linden Gardens Trust Ltd v Lenesta Sludge Disposals Ltd* (1994)).

Decided cases have confirmed the wide scope, and relative ease of satisfying, section 1(1)(b):

✓ *Nisshin Shipping Co Ltd v Cleaves & Co Ltd* (2003);

✓ *The Laemthong Glory* (2005); and

✓ *Dolphin Maritime & Aviation Services Ltd v Sveriges Angfartygs Assurans Forening* (2009).

Section 1(1)(b) may apply even if:

- benefiting the TP is not the contract's predominant purpose;
- other parties are also benefited (*Prudential Insurance v Ayres* (2007)); or
- the TP has an existing, alternative right of action (*Nisshin Shipping*).

However, it must be *a* purpose of the contract to benefit the TP. It is not enough that the TP's position will be incidentally benefited by performance of the contract (*Dolphin Maritime & Aviation Services Ltd v Sveriges Angfartygs Assurans Forening* (2009)).

Under both tests in section 1(1), **section 1(3)** requires the TP to be *expressly* identified in the contract 'by name, as a member of a class or as answering a particular description, but need not be in existence when the contract is entered into'. In *Avraamides v Colwill* (2006), B (a contractor refurbishing bathrooms) transferred its liabilities to C but the contract did not 'identify any third party or class of third parties'. Waller LJ said that 'section 1(3), by use of the word 'express', simply does not allow a process of construction or implication.' Accordingly, TP customers who had rights against B could not enforce them directly against C. However, the scope of

---

[1] A S Burrows, 'The Contracts (Rights of Third Parties) Act 1999 and Its Implications for Commercial Contracts' [2000] *LMCLQ* 540, 542–6.

[2] A S Burrows, 'Reforming Privity of Contract: Law Commission Report No 242' [1996] *LMCLQ* 467, 473.

section 1(3) is unclear in the light of *The Alexandros T* (2014), where Flaux J seemed to interpret 'underwriters' as 'encompassing the servants or agents of insurers'.

The TP's claim can only be made 'subject to and in accordance with any other relevant terms of the contract' (**section 1(4)**, eg requirement of arbitration).

➡◀ Counterpoint

Section 1(1)(b) goes too far in permitting TP enforcement:

1. Uncertain: when does a contract, which 'purports to confer a benefit' on a TP, raise a rebuttable presumption that the contract parties intend the TP to sue for the benefit?

   ✓ *Beswick v Beswick* (1968, see 4.1.6.1) clearly comes within section 1(1)(b); the widow would now be able to sue in her own right.

   ✗ Incidental benefits to the TP from the promisor's performance clearly fall outside section 1(1)(b), as where *A* contracts with *B* to cut down a tree obstructing *B*'s light and view; the fact that *A*'s performance would also benefit *B*'s neighbour, *C*, is irrelevant; the contract does not purport to confer a benefit on *C*.

   ? However, the Law Commission viewed *White v Jones* (1995) as also falling outside section 1(1)(b), which is puzzling (4.1.4). What is the difference between:

   ✗ a father who employs a *solicitor* to change his will in favour of his daughter (which the Law Commission regards as outside section 1(1)(b), barring the daughter's enforcement), and

   ✓ a father who employs a *builder* to add an extension to his daughter's house (which the Law Commission regards as entitling the daughter to sue under section 1(1)(b))?

   The Law Commission's answer is that drafting the will only enables the *father* to confer the benefit; the solicitor does not *directly* confer the benefit itself. But, it can equally be said that the builder is simply enabling the *father* to confer the benefit, whilst the solicitor, by amending the will, is conferring a benefit on the daughter.

2. Over-inclusive: TP enforcement under section 1(1)(b) entails three leaps from the original rationale of giving effect to the parties' *express* intention to allow TP action.

   • First, the view that such intentions may be *implied* is unobjectionable.

   • But, second, C(RTP)A *presuming* this implied intention when the contract 'purports to confer a benefit on a third party' *is* objectionable. It replaces the tighter earlier formulations of an 'intention to create a legally enforceable obligation on the third party', *in addition* to an intention to benefit the TP (Consultation Paper 121, 1991, para 5.10). The two formulations are not interchangeable. Purporting to confer a benefit on someone does not equate with intending that they be able to sue for it. Just because a mother contracts for her son to receive drug rehabilitation treatment does not automatically imply that she wants him to be able to sue on the contract, and to keep the damages without accounting to her!

   • Third, where a contract is *silent* on whether the parties intend to allow the TP to sue (as will often be the case), the *default position* is that there will be a strong presumption

→

that they so intend, rebuttable only by positive evidence to the contrary (s 1(2)). In practice, this reverses the burden of proof: once the TP shows that the contract purports to benefit her, it is over to the promisor to positively show that the parties did *not* intend to empower the TP to sue.

The argument has been made that this still respects the contract parties' intention since they can 'contract out' (ie state in the contract that the TP should not be able to sue). But it is no justification *for* a default position to say that the parties can say they *don't* want it, *if* they know the law. Many, perhaps most, parties not legally advised would be ignorant of it.

3. Wrong solution? It is arguable that contract law should uphold the parties' intentions *not* by empowering TPs to sue, but rather, by ensuring effective remedies for promisees (an important theme of Chapters 13 and 14). Where the promisor fails to perform, only the promisee's expectation is defeated. As Stevens observes, if 'the promisor wishes to comply with his original promise all he needs to do is keep it'.[3] Traditionally, upholding 'the intention of the parties' translates, on breach, into protection of the *promisee*'s expectation. Insofar as the promisee's remedies against the promisor are inadequate (4.1.6), the logical response is to strengthen the promisee's remedies, rather than allow TPs to sue the promisor. The Law Commission prefers the latter course because the promisee: (i) may be *unable to sue*, being dead, sick, away, or unable to finance the claim; or (ii) may *not want to sue* (Report 242, para 3.4). However, circumstances in (i) can affect *any* right-holder, yet rights are not thereby standardly transferred to others. And, giving TPs the right to sue in circumstance (ii) contradicts the concern to protect the promisee's intention. Atiyah points out (at 360) that promisees will usually be closely related to TPs; promisees' reasons for conferring the benefit in the first place will usually prompt them to sue on their own initiative, or at least lend their name to the TPs' actions (as the insured do to their insurers). If promisees choose not to do so, it contradicts their intention to allow TPs to sue.

4. Creating the potential for double liability: C(RTP)A assumes that loss from breach resides solely with the TP and makes *no provision for the promisee's recovery for her own loss*. Thus, **section 5**:

   ✓ reduces a TP's claim only if the promisee has already recovered a sum *in respect of the* TP's *loss* (although it does not explicitly require the promisee to account for this sum to the TP) or for her own expense in making good *that* loss; but

   • does not reduce the claim if the promisee recovers in respect of her *own* loss (see 4.1.6.3).

Say you contract for me to make a particularly meaningful ring for your friend that you have designed. I breach by making a different and less valuable ring, which your friend nevertheless likes and keeps. Your friend can sue me for the difference in value between the ring ordered and the one delivered, but it is arguable on the basis of the 'broad ground' in *Alfred McAlpine Construction Ltd v Panatown Ltd* (2001) (13.2.4.6) that *you* can also claim damages for your *own loss*, namely your inability to give the gift you intended and paid for. C(RTP)A exposes the promisor to liability to both the promisee and the TP.

---

[3] R Stevens, 'The Contracts (Rights of Third Parties) Act 1999' (2004) 120 *LQR* 292, 293.

4.1.3.2 Variation and rescission by the contract parties

Section 2 of C(RTP)A attempts to reconcile the potential conflict between:

- the *contract parties'* ability to modify their contract; and
- *the TP's* reliance on or expectation from the original contract.

It does so by setting out when contract parties are barred from extinguishing or altering the rights of a TP qualifying under section 1 without her consent. Namely, where **(s 2(1))**:

(i)   the TP has communicated her *assent* to the promisor (by words or conduct; communications sent by post or other means take effect when *received*);

(ii)   the promisor *knows* of the TP's actual *reliance* on the term; or

(iii)   the promisor can *reasonably foresee* the TP's actual *reliance*;

unless the contract parties *expressly* state **(s 2(3))**:

(i)   that they can rescind or vary the contract without the TP's consent; or

(ii)   the specific circumstances (other than those spelt out in s 2(1)) in which the TP's consent is required.

Courts have limited residual discretion to authorise variation or discharge (on such terms as seems appropriate, including payment of *compensation* to the TP, s 2(6)) where:

- the parties cannot contact the TP to get her consent (s 2(4)(a));
- the TP is mentally incapable of consenting (s 2(4)(b)); or
- the parties are uncertain whether the TP has relied and so whether the latter's consent is required (s 2(5)).

 Counterpoint

The *default presumption* that the contract parties intend to forgo their usual right to vary or rescind their contract, *unless* they *expressly* say otherwise, is open to criticism:

1. Inadequate respect for the parties' intention: the cumulative effect of presuming that the contract parties intend to allow TP action under section 1(1)(b), and do *not* intend to retain their power to vary or rescind the contract tilts the balance too far in favour of protecting the TP. To permit TP rights (which may be *imputed* by operation of a strong legal presumption) to outweigh the contract parties' *express* agreement to vary or rescind their contract undermines the Law Commission's stated primary aim of giving effect to the contract parties' intentions (4.1.4). Why should the parties' usual sovereignty over their contract (including the power to waive or alter it) be so constrained? Again, it is no answer to say that parties who know of the presumption can 'contract out' of it.

2. Weakness of the TP's claim: why should TPs be protected? Contract law is not generally concerned to prevent disappointment. Even promises that generate foreseeable

→

→

expectations in (or reliance by) *promisees* are not enforceable without consideration, formalities or promissory estoppel (Chapter 3). There is no justification for treating TPs who are *not promisees* more favourably than gratuitous promisees. As Coote[4] observes: 'The fact that a gift is less or other than what was hoped for by the recipient does not by itself constitute loss or damages in the legal sense of those words. Even expenditure on repairing the defect is merely by way of augmentation or improvement of the benefit as received.' Likewise, there is no justification for treating the TP who has relied on the contract more favourably than promissory estoppel claimants. Recall that the latter must be promisees, only get such remedy 'as justice requires' (usually the reliance measure), and are vulnerable to the promisor reneging if that would not be inequitable. In contrast, the TP need not be the promisee, can obtain the expectation, and is generally protected from the promisor reneging.

3. Remedy is too generous to TP: why should the TP's expectations be protected, as opposed to her reliance? Say I contract for you to landscape *X*'s garden, but then change my mind (I have fallen on hard times or fallen out with *X*). You are busy and therefore happy to call the deal off. C(RTP)A prevents us from rescinding or varying the benefit to *X* once she communicates 'I accept' or has relied on the gift (eg bought new plants) where we know of or can reasonably foresee that reliance. *X*'s remedy against you under C(RTP)A is the expectation measure, even if her reliance falls far short of this. Recall that even civil law jurisdictions that enforce gratuitous contracts allow a defence of ingratitude of the donee or hardship to the donor. Yet TPs who are not promisees are in an even stronger position under C(RTP)A.

4.1.3.3 **The third party's claim**

C(RTP)A only treats the TP *as if she were a party to the contract* for the specified purposes outlined therein:

- **Section 1(5)** allows a qualifying TP to claim 'any remedy that would have been available to him in an action for breach of contract if he had been a party to the contract (the rules relating to damages, injunctions, specific performance and other relief shall apply accordingly)'. The remedy of termination is excluded on the basis that it is not a judicial remedy and because it 'may be contrary to the promisee's wishes or interests' (Report 242, para 3.33). Since the TP's rights are *derivative* from the promisee's, the starting point is that her claim replicates the promisee's; the promisor is liable to the same extent as if she were sued by the promisee.

- Subject to *express* agreement to the *contrary*, **section 3(2)** allows the promisor to rely on any defences or set-offs against the TP that would have been available against the promisee (eg misrepresentation, or repudiation by the promisee).

---

[4] B Coote, 'The Performance Interest, *Panatown*, and the Problem of Loss' (2001) 117 *LQR* 81, 93.

However, **the TP may be in a better position than the promisee** in two respects:

(i) The promisor can only rely on an otherwise effective defence or set-off where it arises 'from or in connection with the contract *and is relevant to the term*' sought to be enforced by the TP (s 3(2)(a)).

(ii) The promisor cannot bring any counterclaim against the promisee into the calculation where the TP claims. This is superficially justifiable on the basis that no 'burden' can be imposed on TPs (they should not end up being potentially liable to the promisor). However, it is inconsistent with the derivative nature of the TP's claim. The simple solution should have been to allow a counterclaim to reduce the TP's claim to zero.

The **TP may be in weaker position than the promisee** in four respects:

(i) The promisor can rely on any defences, set-offs, or counterclaims (not arising from the contract) that would have been available had the TP been a party to the contract (eg if the TP had induced the contract by misrepresentation or owes the promisor money) (**s 3(4)**).

(ii) The TP is not treated as a contract party 'for the purposes of any other Act' (**s 7(4)**). Thus, the TP cannot appeal to, eg, the Law Reform (Frustrated Contracts) Act 1943 (Chapter 7) or the Misrepresentation Act 1967 (Chapter 5).

(iii) The TP only receives very limited protection from the Unfair Contract Terms Act 1977 (UCTA) (and the Consumer Rights Act 1015 (CRA)) (Chapter 11) since it only applies to *parties* to the contract. Therefore, unfair exemptions of liability and other unfair non-core terms are effective against the TP apart from exemptions for negligently caused death or personal injury, which would be actionable anyway in tort (Report 242, para 13.12).

 Pause for reflection

On the one hand, this can be criticised because the unreasonableness and unfairness targeted by UCTA and CRA respectively may equally arise in the context of contracts for the benefit of TPs. Conversely, it can be supported for respecting the parties' intentions. Moreover, it is unclear how the 'reasonableness' or 'fairness' tests, designed to apply to the contract parties, should be applied to TP beneficiaries. The Law Commission saw it as raising complex policy issues going beyond those involved in reforming the doctrine of privity (Report 242, para 13.10(vii) and (viii)).

(iv) Certain types of contract are excluded from the scope of C(RTP)A, barring TPs from suing on them (eg bills of exchange, promissory notes, or other negotiable instruments, carriage of goods contracts, bills of lading, company and partnership agreements, and employment contracts).

4.1.4 **Assessment of C(RTP)A**

In *Privity of Contract: Contracts for the Benefit of Third Parties* (Law Com No 242, Cm 3329, 1996) ('Report 242'), paras 3.1–3.28, the Law Commission sets out its criticisms of the privity rule as the basis for its recommendation for reform:

(i) It **defeats the intentions of the contract parties** by preventing TPs from suing when the contract parties want them to be able to sue.

However, we have seen that C(RTP)A, intended to uphold the parties' intentions, may actually contradict them since:

- section 1(1)(b) will confer a right to sue on the TP when the parties merely 'purport to confer a benefit' on the TP;
- section 2 will bar the parties from rescinding or varying the contract if the TP has accepted, relied to the parties' knowledge, or foreseeably relied without the parties' knowledge; and
- under section 1(5), the TP will usually recover damages and this will often change the form of the benefit in kind that the parties intended to confer on the TP by monetising it. That is, where the parties intended to confer some non-money benefit on the TP under the contract, the TP will now receive money.

(ii) It is **unjust to TPs** because it defeats their: (a) expectation interest; and (b) reliance interest.

However, giving TPs the right to sue is inconsistent with:

- the treatment of gratuitous donees whose expectations are not regarded as worthy of protection in law because they have not given consideration; it seems odd that if I promise to give you a car, you cannot enforce it as a donee, but if I make a contract with someone else to give you a car, you *can* enforce as a TP; and
- the treatment of promisees who are promissory estoppel claimants; their rights are more narrowly circumscribed than those of TPs under C(RTP)A. It seems odd that if you rely on my promise, I may still be able to renege (if it would not be inequitable), but not if you rely on my contract with someone else.

(iii) It creates **difficulty in commercial life**:[5] for example, in *insurance* (*A* takes out insurance from *B* for *C*'s benefit); in *construction* (*A* employs *B* to do work for *C*); and where contract parties try to exempt the liability of their subcontractor (*A* agrees that *B*'s subcontractor *C* can exclude or limit liability to *A*).

However, insurance is dealt with by statute, and standard form construction contracts have routinely excluded the operation of C(RTP)A.

---

[5] See A S Burrows, 'The Contracts (Rights of Third Parties) Act 1999 and Its Implications for Commercial Contracts' [2000] *LMCLQ* 540, 553.

(iv) It creates a **legal 'black hole'**[6] into which contractual rights and liabilities simply disappear because:

(a) the contract party (the promisee) can sue but can obtain no effective remedy for breach since she suffers no loss (the factual benefit being directed to the TP);

(b) the TP who suffers the 'loss' cannot sue;

(c) moreover, the promisor may be unjustly enriched if she has been paid but has not performed; and

(d) the sanctity of contract is undermined without an effective remedy.

However:

(a) the obvious response is to give the promisee more adequate remedies; section 4 preserves the right of the promisee to sue, so that if the common law were more willing to recognise the genuine loss of the promisee (and award eg specific performance, the *Albazero* exception, the cost of cure, loss of amenity, or even the *Panatown* broad ground for the loss of performance), then the legal blackhole would be filled and the need for a TP right of action correspondingly reduced;

(b) here, the question is why TP's loss is legally relevant where she is neither the promisee nor has given consideration; moreover, concern with reasonable and foreseeable reliance can be met by a reliance award;

(c) here, the promisor can be required to make restitution to the promisee; and

(d) here, again, the problem would disappear if the promisee's remedies were made 'adequate'.

(v) The **'exceptions'** to the privity rule (4.1.6 and 4.1.7) are piecemeal, complex, and uncertain. However, these are preserved under C(RTP)A and cannot realistically be streamlined, although the availability of TP action under C(RTP)A reduces the importance of some of the 'exceptions'.

(vi) The **'rule has been abrogated throughout much of the common law world**, including the United States, New Zealand, and parts of Australia'. Moreover, 'the legal systems of most of the **Member States of the European Union** recognise and enforce the rights of TP beneficiaries under contracts' (see Arts II.-9:301–II.-303 of the European Draft Common Frame of Reference).

 Pause for reflection

To what extent does C(RTP)A address the Law Commission's criticisms of the privity rule?

The privity reform receives **support** from:

• N Andrews, 'Strangers to Justice No Longer: The Reversal of the Privity Rule under the Contracts (Rights of Third Parties) Act 1999' (2001) 60 *CLJ* 353;

➡

---

[6] D Wallace, 'Third Party Damage: No Legal Black Hole?' (1999) 115 *LQR* 394; *McAlpine v Panatown* at 534 (Lord Clyde).

→
- R Flannigan, 'Privity—the End of an Era (Error)' (1987) 103 *LQR* 564; and

- C MacMillan, 'A Birthday Present for Lord Denning: the Contracts (Rights of Third Parties) Act 1999' (2000) 63 *MLR* 721.

The reform is **criticised** in:

- P Kincaid, 'Privity Reform in England' (2000) 15 *LQR* 43;

- S Smith, 'Contracts for the Benefit of Third Parties: In Defence of the Third-Party Rule' (1997) 7 *OJLS* 643; and

- R Stevens, 'The Contracts (Rights of Third Parties) Act 1999' (2004) 120 *LQR* 292.

4.1.5 **Consideration, privity, and C(RTP)A**

The *impact* of C(RTP)A on the doctrine of consideration depends on how we see the *relationship* between it and the privity rule.

The **traditional analysis** is that the consideration doctrine answers two questions:

(i)   *'Which* promises are enforceable?' Answer: those that have been paid for.

(ii) *'Who* can enforce the promise?' Answer: the promisee who paid for it.

A party can only enforce a promise if she: (1) has given consideration for the promise, and (2) is the promisee. On this view, the privity rule is merely the flipside of the consideration doctrine and cannot be reformed without reforming ('undermining', 'creating an exception to', or 'distorting') the consideration doctrine. C(RTP)A does not expressly dispense with (1) or (2) but, by allowing a party to sue who conforms with neither requirement, it implicitly recognises an *exception to each requirement*; otherwise, the reform would be rendered pointless.

The **alternative view** is that the consideration doctrine *only* addresses question (1), not question (2).[7] It is only concerned with *which* promises are potentially enforceable; it serves *notice to the promisor* that the law will only hold her liable if she has been paid for the promise. The question of *who* can enforce promises supported by consideration is a separate issue. Authorities supporting this are:

- Viscount Haldane's judgment in ***Dunlop Pneumatic Tyre Co***; and

- the joint promisee doctrine suggested by the High Court of Australia in ***Coulls v Bagot's Executor & Trustee Co Ltd*** (1967). There, in exchange for the right to quarry from B's property, A promised to pay £5 and royalties to B and C (B's wife). When B died, the majority barred C's claim against A, but said, obiter, that if the contract had been by A to pay B and C as joint promisees, C would be entitled to sue although she provided no consideration.

Accordingly, as long as consideration has been provided by *someone*, a third party beneficiary can sue without herself giving consideration. In this way, *exchange* can be maintained as a pre-condition of enforceability, while not limiting enforcement to those

---

[7] Collins (at 308); R Flannigan, 'Privity—The End of an Era (Error)' (1987) 103 *LQR* 564.

providing the exchange. On this view, while C(RTP)A clearly contradicts (2) (that the claimant be the promisee), it does not contradict (1) since consideration is still provided by the promisee. *C(RTP)A merely adds to the categories of persons who can sue*, being:

- ✓ promisees who provide consideration;
- ✓ joint promisees; and
- ✓ TPs qualifying under C(RTP)A.

C(RTP)A undermines the importance of the consideration requirement. Indeed, the Law Commission suggests that the doctrine of consideration may be a 'suitable topic for a future separate review' (Report 242, para 6.17).

 Counterpoint

1. *Questionable authorities*: All the judges in *Dunlop Pneumatic Tyre Co* (except Lord Parmoor) based their decisions on the absence of consideration, as did the court in *Tweddle*, so that these two leading cases can be seen as straightforward applications of the traditional view of consideration (fusing the *which* and *who* questions). In 'Consideration and the Joint Promisee' (1978) 37 *CLJ* 301, Coote strongly supports Windeyer J's dissenting view in *Coulls v Bagot* that C was not merely a promisee as a signatory, but also gave consideration, not by actually providing the quarry but by her 'accountability in law should her husband have defaulted'. Providing consideration means *being liable for it* as opposed to *actually performing it*. Windeyer J said that where A makes a promise to B and C jointly, the requirement of consideration does not require consideration to be 'furnished by them separately. It means a consideration given on behalf of them all, and therefore moving from all of them . . . as between [the promisor and the promisees] it matters not how they [the promisees] were able to provide the price of his promise to them.'

2. Promisee and consideration are inextricably linked: Merely being a promisee confers no right to sue on a promise; it is the provision of consideration that entitles the provider to sue on an informal contract. Since consideration is by definition something given *in return for* the promise (usually *at the promisor's request*), the provider of good consideration will therefore *be* the promisee. To say that a person is not a party to the contract is just to say that she is not one of the reciprocating promisors. This explains the rule that 'consideration must move *from the promisee*' (3.1.2.1).

3. Justice: A party who has 'paid for' a promise is more deserving of the law's assistance (3.1.1) than a TP who has not 'paid for' nor promised anything.

4.1.6 **Enforcement by the promisee**

The claims available to the promisee and the TP aside from C(RTP)A are set out in **Diagram 4D**. They are significant because they:

- continue to be available;
- undermine the criticism of the privity rule based on the piecemeal, complex, and uncertain nature of the exceptions, since C(RTP)A leaves them intact; and

- undermine the legal 'black hole' argument in support of C(RTP)A, since the promisee can sue.

Diagram 4D Overview of actions available to the promisee and the third party beneficiary

Where A undertakes a contractual obligation to B to perform for C's benefit:

B (promisee) can claim:	C (third party) can claim:
1. *Specific performance* 2. *Damages for C's loss via action in:* • Trust • Agency • Social or domestic contexts • The *Albazera* exception 3. ***Damages for B's own loss?*** • Direct pecuniary loss • Broad ground?	1. As a *principal* in a *contract* with A via: • Agency • Collateral contract 2. As a victim of A's *tort* 3. As a beneficiary of a *trust* of the promise 4. As an *assignee* from B 5. Via the rules on *negotiable instruments* 6. Via *statutory exceptions* (other than 7.) 7. Via the **Contracts (Rights of Third Parties) Act 1999**

4.1.6.1 Specific performance

The promisee can ask the court to compel the promisor to perform her promise (via claims for specific performance, an injunction, or a stay of proceedings, 14.2). These remedies compel the promisor to benefit the TP as she contracted to do, so that the interests of the promisee and the TP are satisfied simultaneously. In *Beswick v Beswick* (1968), an elderly man sold his business to his nephew in exchange for the nephew's agreement, inter alia, to pay an annuity of £5 a week to his wife after his death. The House of Lords awarded specific performance to compel the nephew to pay. However, the widow could only sue because she was the *administratrix* (representative) *of her husband's estate*; she could not have sued simply as a beneficiary. The court rejected the nephew's argument that she could only obtain nominal damages because the breach caused no loss to his uncle's estate. Such a result 'would be grossly unjust', particularly since the nephew had 'received the whole benefit of the contract and it is a matter of conscience for the court to see that he now performs his part of it'.

 Pause for reflection

1. The wife in *Beswick* would now be able to sue in her own right as a TP under C(RTP)A. However, C(RTP)A preserves the promisee's right to also claim specific performance, whether or not the TP has acquired the right to sue.

2. Specific performance is the most obvious and efficient way to meet the interests of the promisee and the TP while simultaneously preventing the unjust enrichment of the promisor. The remedy avoids the problems of locating and quantifying the loss, particularly as the promisee's own loss is traditionally regarded as nominal (although Lord Pearce casts

➡

> ➜
>
> doubt on this in *Beswick*) and she is barred from suing for another's loss. Moreover, award-ing specific performance in these contracts is consistent with the main qualification for the remedy: that damages are inadequate to compensate for the loss (14.2.1.2). If specific performance were awarded more often in third party benefit cases, there would be less need for TP actions.
>
> 3. However, the standard bars against the award of specific performance apply (14.2.1.1).

If the relevant promise was to *refrain from suing* the TP, the promisee could ask the court to exercise its discretion to stay the proceedings against the TP, where the promisee has a *sufficient interest* in doing so. In *Snelling v Snelling* (1973), a family company was indebted to three brothers who were directors of the company. The brothers agreed that any of them resigning from the company would forfeit his debt (so benefiting the company). When the claimant resigned, his brothers could prevent him from suing the company to recover his money because of their interest in the family company.

4.1.6.2 Damages for the loss of the third party

The House of Lords in *Alfred McAlpine Construction Ltd v Panatown Ltd* (2001) affirms the orthodox position that a promisee cannot sue for a TP's loss of expecta-tion. Lord Millett said:

> It is inherent in the concept of compensation that only the person who has suffered the loss is entitled to have it made good by compensation. Compensation for a TP's loss is a contradiction in terms. It is impossible on any logical basis to justify the re-covery of compensatory damages by a person who has not suffered the loss in respect of which they are awarded unless he is accountable for them to the person who has.

Lord Goff highlights the difficulty with this position:

> A wealthy man who lives in a village decides to carry out at his own expense major repairs to, or renovation or even construction of, the village hall, and himself enters into a contract with a local builder to carry out the work to the existing building which belongs to another, for example to trustees, or to the parish council.

What can the wealthy man do if the builder breaches?

A number of avenues exist for a **promisee to sue on behalf of the TP**, *handing over any damages to the TP*. The first two commercially important avenues involve technical qualifying conditions and require an understanding of the relationships of trust and agency. They are merely listed here.

(i) A promisee who is also a **trustee** in respect of the subject matter of the promise can recover damages for the beneficiary's loss flowing from breach (the beneficiary can also sue in her own right, 4.1.6.3).

(ii) A promisee who is also an **agent** in respect of the subject matter of the promise can recover damages for the loss suffered by her principal (the principal can also sue in her own right, 4.1.7.1).

(iii) **Quasi-agency in domestic and social situations** may also entitle the promisee to sue on behalf of TP beneficiaries. In *Jackson v Horizon Holidays Ltd* (1975), J booked a holiday for himself, his wife, and their sons for £1,200. The substandard accommodation, food, amenities, and facilities were in breach of contract and caused distress and inconvenience for the whole family. The Court of Appeal upheld the award of £1,100 in damages to J. James LJ regarded the sum as damages *solely for J's loss* and not that of his family. But Lord Denning MR felt that this would make the award excessive and explained it in terms of compensation for the loss suffered by *the whole family*. Lord Denning's interpretation was disapproved by the House of Lords in *Woodar Investment Development Ltd v Wimpey Construction UK Ltd* (1980); their Lordships, in obiter dicta, preferred James LJ's explanation of *Jackson v Horizon Holidays* 'as a broad decision on the measure of damages' or as 'an example of a type of contract—examples of which are persons contracting for family holidays, ordering meals in restaurants for a party, hiring a taxi for a group—calling for special treatment'.

The most important exception for our purposes is '**The Albazero exception**' (*Albacruz v Albazero* (1977)) which allows the promisee to recover damages for the TP's loss, *held in trust for* the TP. Originally, the claim applied to *loss or damage* to goods in contracts of carriage by sea where the parties contemplated that the promisee would *transfer* the *ownership* of the goods, carried by the promisor, to the TP after the contract's formation but before its performance. From this narrow beginning, the scope of the exception has broadened considerably:

(a) to allow claims for incomplete or defective performance (ie from claims of being 'worse off' in respect of the cargo being transported by sea to not being 'better off' in respect of contracts generally) in building contracts (*Linden Gardens* (1994));

(b) to allow recovery in respect of building works without any transfer of ownership (see *Darlington BC v Wiltshire Northern Ltd* (1995), where the promisee never owned the property in question, but contracted for work to be done on the TP's property).

As Lord Millett observes in *McAlpine v Panatown*, the second step (b) 'uncouples the rule from . . . the grounds which originally sustained it'. Nevertheless, it continues to be necessary to show that the TP:

• is *identifiable* at the time of contract formation as *likely to suffer damage* on breach (*Rolls-Royce Power Engineering plc v Ricardo Consulting Engineers Ltd* (2003)); and

• has no claim of its own against the promisor (the TP in *Panatown could* claim against the promisor under their 'duty of care deed' so did not come within the *Albazero* exception, 13.2.4.6).

In *McAlpine v Panatown*, two contracts were made:

(i) The main contract under which Panatown (the promisee) engaged McAlpine (the promisor) to construct a new building on land owned by UIPL (the third party). Panatown and UIPL belonged to the same corporate group and the building contract was so structured to avoid payment of VAT.

(ii) The duty of care deed agreed between McAlpine (the promisor) and UIPL (the third party) which UIPL could assign to its successors in title.

Panatown claimed £40 million under the main contract for the cost of repairing McAlpine's defective work. A majority of the House of Lords (Lords Clyde, Jauncey, and Browne-Wilkinson) **denied the claim** as falling *outside* the *Albazero* exception, the so-called 'narrow ground', because:

- Panatown (the promisee) suffered *no* loss; and

- Panatown had no claim under the *Albazero* exception because, although UIPL *had* suffered loss, the duty of care deed gave UIPL a *direct contractual right* against McAlpine (the promisor); there was no 'legal black hole'.

 Counterpoint

The duty of care deed conferred significantly fewer rights on UIPL (only to McAlpine's exercise of reasonable care) than the main contract intended for it to have (eg strict liability in building, provisions on arbitration, and liquidated damages). Thus, the decision renders illusory the rights conferred by the main contract which exceeded those contained in the duty of care deed; *these* rights did indeed disappear down a 'legal black hole'.

 Pause for reflection

1. The promisee may recover loss on behalf of a TP where: (i) the contract parties intend to benefit an identifiable TP; and (ii) the TP acquires no contractual rights against the promisor. Thus, the *Albazero* exception is available in a wide range of circumstances. If that is so, no legal 'black hole' exists in Lord Goff's example. The philanthropist can sue on behalf of the TP beneficiary. There is little need for direct TP action.

2. However, the width of *The Albazero* exception is of questionable legitimacy. As Lord Millett observes in *Panatown*, to apply the exception in the absence of an anticipated transfer of ownership 'uncouples the rule from . . . the grounds which originally sustained it'.

3. Moreover, the promisee's duty to account to the TP may be objectionable if it changes the type of the benefit conferred on the TP. A promisee who intends to give a specific non-monetary benefit should not be compelled to hand over money instead. In Lord Goff's example, if the philanthropist is accountable to the parish council, there is nothing to stop the latter spending the money in some way unintended by the donor. This objection applies equally to TP claims under C(RTP)A.

4.1.6.3 Damages for the promisee's own loss

Can the promisee recover for her own loss so that she need not hand over any damages awarded to the TP? The traditional approach is to deny any compensable loss on the promisee's part in contracts to benefit TPs.

Four claims are arguable (13.2.4.6):

(i) The promisee can claim if it suffers **direct pecuniary loss**, as where breach results in its own obligation to the TP not being discharged or brings it under a legal or factual obligation to the TP. In Lord Goff's example, the philanthropist could claim if he cured the breach or was likely to do so (see also *Radford v de Froberville* (1977), where the promisee landlord built the fence himself for the benefit of his tenants).

(ii) Absent direct pecuniary loss, the promisee *may* have a claim *in its own right* for substantial damages under the '**broad ground**' in *Panatown* for not receiving the promised performance. Although the claim on this ground in *Panatown* failed on the facts, controversy surrounds the precise *ratio* of the case (13.2.4.6).

 Pause for reflection

1. It is strongly arguable that the loss belongs to the promisee, even in contracts made for the benefit of a TP (although supporters of TP actions are highly critical of such an approach).[8] Allowing the promisee to recover substantial damages in her own right eliminates the 'black hole' and the need for direct TP action.

2. The possibility of a TP claim creates the risk of double liability for the promisor if she is sued by both parties for their own loss, since section 5 of C(RTP)A only reduces the TP's claim if the promisee has already claimed for the TP's loss.

3. If the promisee and the TP both sue on their own behalf for the same breach, how should their claims be prioritised? C(RTP)A is silent.

   • In *Panatown*, Lord Millett suggests that payment to either will *pro tanto* discharge the liability to both, but also that the promisee's action should be stayed until the court is assured that the TP is content for it to proceed (ie either 'first come, first served' or the TP should have the 'first bite').

   • In contrast, Lord Goff saw the promisee's claim as principal and the TP's claim as derivative so that satisfaction of the former eliminates the TP's loss. This interpretation is preferable since it allows the promisee to retain control over whether and what benefit is conferred on the TP.

4. Although section 4 of C(RTP)A states that the availability of TP actions does 'not affect any right of the promisee to enforce any term of the contract', in practice it will stifle the promisee's claim whether in her own right or on behalf of the TP.

(iii) The promisee may claim for her own **loss of amenity**; ie her loss of satisfaction (enjoyment, peace of mind, or freedom from distress, 13.2.4.2) from the promisor's failure to confer the benefit on the TP. This is consistent with James LJ's judgment in *Jackson v Horizon Holidays* and supported by the House of Lords in *Woodar*. If the law is willing to compensate a promisee for the loss of satisfaction in knowing that the pool he is safely diving into is 7 feet 6 inches deep whereas it is really only 6 feet deep (*Ruxley v Forsyth* (1996)), the law should also be willing to compensate a promisee for the loss of satisfaction in failing to confer a specific benefit on the TP (eg a new

---

[8] A S Burrows, 'No Damages for a Third Party's Loss' (2001) 1 *OUCLJ* 107, 112; N Andrews, 'Strangers to Justice No Longer: The Reversal of the Privity Rule under the Contracts (Rights of Third Parties) Act 1999' (2001) 60 *CLJ* 353, 377.

roof for her elderly parents' house). The first requirement for loss of amenity claims, namely that the promisee's non-pecuniary purpose should be distinct, important, and communicated to the promisor, will be relatively easy to meet where the contract is for a TP's benefit. The second requirement, that damages should take account of 'reasonableness', requires courts to determine *why* the promisee wants performance, *whether* and *how much* she still wants it, and the proportionality between the cost of cure on the one hand, and the contractual price, the benefits already conferred, and the additional benefit to be derived from cure, on the other. However, loss of amenity will not be available in commercial cases.

(iv) **Restitution** of money paid is available if there is total failure of consideration from the promisor (13.4.2).

4.1.7 Third party enforcement aside from C(RTP)A

Numerous common law techniques allow TPs to circumvent the privity rule and sue the promisor. They are retained by C(RTP)A. Some are not true exceptions to the privity rule, although they are often labelled as such (refer back to **Diagram 4D**). The first three operate by **promoting the TP into a 'first' party** with a direct right to sue as:

(i) a promisee in a separate *contract* with the promisor (via agency or a collateral contract (10.3.2));

(ii) a party to whom the promisor owes a duty of care in *tort*; or

(iii) a beneficiary of a *trust* of the promise.

Other devices are **genuine exceptions**, namely:

(iv) assignment;

(v) negotiable instruments; and

(vi) statutory exceptions.

4.1.7.1 Contractual devices

(i) Agency

An agent is someone who acts on behalf of her principal. Where *A* makes a contract with *B* who acts on behalf of *C*, *C* is not really a TP but is a contract party in her own right. *C* can therefore sue on the contract without contravening the privity rule. Where *C* is a *disclosed* principal, *A* knows that *C* is really the other party to the contract. The difficulty arises where *C* is an *undisclosed* principal. In that case, both *B* and *C* can sue *A* and be sued by *A*, and *A* can appeal to any defences she may have against *B* in an action with *C*. Reynolds observes that: 'it is difficult to deny that the undisclosed principal is really a TP intervening on a contract which he or she did not make'.[9] See **Diagram 4E.1**.

---

[9] F M B Reynolds, M Graziadei, and W Bowstead, *Bowstead and Reynolds on Agency* (19th edn, Sweet & Maxwell, 2012) para 8–071.

Diagram 4E.1–9 Indirect third party enforcement
Diagram 4E.1 Agency

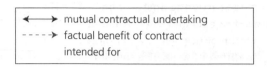

C can sue A as a principal.

(ii) Collateral contract

A party can also enforce the benefit of a promise if the court is prepared to find (or create) a collateral contract between her and the promisor. For example, in *Shanklin Pier Ltd v Detel Products Ltd* (1951), D told S that its paint was suitable for painting S's pier and would last for seven to ten years. S then instructed its contractor to buy and use D's paint, which turned out to be less durable than stated. S successfully sued D on the basis of a collateral contract between them; D's promise on the paint's durability was supported by S's consideration in directing its contractor to buy paint from D. See **Diagram 4E.2**.

Diagram 4E.2 Collateral contract: *Shanklin*

S can sue D under 3.

(iii) Exemption of third parties from liability
See **Diagram 4E.3**.

Diagram 4E.3 Exemption clause: *Eurymedon*

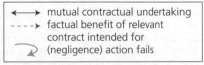

S can enforce benefit of exemption clause in 1 to defeat CO's negligence action by relying on 3 (made by CC as S's agent) by which CO exempts S from liability in exchange for S performing 2.

Section 1(6) of C(RTP)A allows qualifying TPs to benefit from exclusion or limitation clauses. Prior to this, courts combined the agency and collateral contract devices to do the same job, typically protecting a TP *S* (the stevedore) working for *CC* (the cargo carrier) against a claim by *CO* (the cargo owner or shipper), where *CO* had promised to exempt *CC* from liability. The task of balancing the protection of *CO* as the victim of negligence and holding *CO* to the agreed contractual risk allocation is struck in different ways. The solution is a complicated **agency–collateral contract analysis**.

The template (known as a *Himalaya clause*, after the name of a ship in *Adler v Dixon* (1955)) was set out by Lord Reid in **Midland Silicones Ltd v Scrutton's Ltd** (1962) (see also *The Starsin* (2003) and *The Mahkutai* (1996)) Accordingly, the contract (a 'bill of lading'[10] in carriage of goods by sea) must stipulate that:

- *CC* acts as *S's agent*,

- in concluding a *collateral* contract with *CO*,

- in which *CO* exempts *S* from liability in exchange for *S's consideration* of (i) performing (on a *unilateral* contractual analysis),[11] or (ii) agreeing to perform (on a *bilateral* contractual analysis), services in relation to the cargo which *S* already owes under a contract with *CC*.

However, this collateral contract may still fall short, eg:

- if *S* damages goods *before* he starts unloading (ie performing the act which constitutes acceptance of the unilateral contract and triggers the protection of the exemption clause); or

- where *S* is unaware of the exemption on commencing performance (one cannot accept an offer of which one is ignorant).

Lord Wilberforce urged a relaxed approach: 'their Lordships would not encourage, a search for fine distinctions which would diminish the general applicability, in the light of established commercial practice, of the principle' (*The New York Star* (1980)).

 Pause for reflection

The common law could have avoided these contortions and achieved the same result as section 1(6) of C(RTP)A via the doctrine of vicarious immunity.[12] Despite its rejection (*New Zealand Shipping Co Ltd v A M Satterthwaite & Co Ltd (The Eurymedon)* (1975); *Port Jackson Stevedoring Pty Ltd v Salmond & Spraggon (Australia) Pty Ltd (The New York Star)* (1981)), the doctrine has substantive force. If we accept the doctrine of vicarious liability (making the employer liable for her employee's tort), why should we not also accept the idea of vicarious immunity (allowing the employee to enjoy the same immunity in tort as her employer contracts for)?[13]

---

[10] A list of a ship's cargo in the form of a receipt given by the master of the ship (*CC*) to the Cargo owner (*CO*).

[11] This avoids *S* being in breach if he validly terminates his contract with *CO*.

[12] In *London Drugs Ltd v Kuehne & Nagel International* (1993).

[13] H Beale, W Bishop, and M Furmston, *Contract: Cases and Materials* (5th edn, Butterworths, 2007) 1157.

4.1.7.2 Tort of negligence

Can a contract confer on a TP the benefit of:

(1) *a tortious action* against a contract party?

(2) an exemption of liability that negates *the TP's* tortious liability to a contract party?

(1) Might *A*'s breach of her contractual duty owed to *B* also amount to a breach of *A*'s tortious duty of care owed to *C* (the TP), entitling *C* to sue *A* in negligence? (see **Diagram 4E.4**). *C*'s claim is relatively straightforward where the loss involves physical injury or property damage.

However, courts are far more reluctant to impose negligence liability for *purely economic loss*. This is reflected in the very narrow scope of the promisor's duty of care in such cases.

✓ A controversial decision *allowing* a TP claim for pure economic loss is *Junior Books v Veitchi Co Ltd* (1983), represented in **Diagram 4E.5**. J employed a main contractor (MC) to build a factory. MC subcontracted the flooring to V (J became the TP to the latter contract). When the floor was laid defectively, J did not sue his main contractor but sued V directly. The House of Lords allowed the claim on the questionable assumption that V *assumed a responsibility* towards J, despite the contractual structure, which made V directly responsible to MC, and MC to J. *Junior Books* is now regarded as an anomalous case on negligence liability for pure economic loss and has been confined to its own facts.

Diagram 4E.4 Negligence causing physical injury or property damage

Look on the online resources to view this figure as a PowerPoint® presentation

Diagram 4E.5 Exceptional negligence claim for pure economic loss: *Junior Books*

Look on the online resources to view this figure as a PowerPoint® presentation

✓ *White v Jones* (see **Diagram 4E.6**) is a more widely accepted decision allowing a TP indirect enforcement of a contract via a negligence action. A solicitor's negligent preparation of a will deprived each of the intended beneficiaries of £9,000. By a bare majority of 3:2, the House of Lords allowed the beneficiaries to claim the intended legacies from the solicitor. Their Lordships recognised that this contradicted the privity rule, but thought it necessary to do 'practical justice' and avoid a legal 'black hole'. Since the testator's estate could not seek specific performance (it was too late), nor claim more than nominal damages, the solicitor would get away with it unless he was held liable to the beneficiaries in tort. The case is confined to wills and does not apply to gifts made during the donor's lifetime since the donor can choose whether to rectify the solicitor's negligence.

Diagram 4E.6 Exceptional negligence claim for pure economic loss: *White v Jones*

Look on the online resources to view this figure as a PowerPoint® presentation

✓ Where a TP can sue in negligence, this is distinctive from (and usually *more restrictive* than) any available contractual action (eg via agency, collateral contract, or C(RTP)A):

  (i) The TP must be owed a *duty of care* in respect of: (a) the conduct representing the contractual performance; and (b) the nature of the loss incurred.

  (ii) The promisor must *breach this duty*, and the *standard* of liability in negligence (carelessness) is usually lower than that in contract (usually strict).

  (iii) The *measure of damages* differs in principle; a *contract* action protects the claimant's expectation while a *tort* action protects the claimant's reliance. In *Muirhead v Industrial Tank Specialties Ltd* (1986), M sued I, suppliers of a defective motor in a pump which was used to run M's lobster farm. Although M had no contractual relationship with I, M succeeded in his claim for: (a) physical loss (the dead lobsters); and (b) economic loss consequential on this (the loss of profits on these lobsters); but *not* in respect of (c) his pure economic loss (the general loss of profits from the installation of the pump) which is normally considered the subject of contract actions. In *White v Jones*, the damages awarded in tort were indistinguishable from those in contract because, in the will-making context, the only measure of damages which imposes meaningful liability on the negligent solicitor is

Diagram 4E.7 Exemption clause: *Norwich*

Look on
the online
resources
to view this
figure as a
PowerPoint®
presentation

1 main contract
2 subcontract

N ⟶ 1 ⟶ contractor

H can enforce benefit of exemption clause in 1
by negating duty of care in negligence to N,
ie subject matter of exemption.

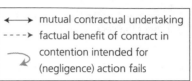

⟵⟶ mutual contractual undertaking
----➤ factual benefit of contract in
        contention intended for
        (negligence) action fails

the value of the benefit not received (strictly speaking, the legatees suffered no reliance loss).

(2) Can *A*'s contract with *B* negate *C*'s tortious liability to *A*? This revisits, *via tort reasoning*, the question of whether *C* can benefit from an exemption of liability contained in the contract of others (see 4.1.7.1(iii)). The short answer is 'yes', whether the loss involved is physical (*Norwich CC v Harvey* (1989)) or purely economic (*Hedley Byrne v Heller* (1964)). Where *A* agrees with *B* to exempt *B*'s subcontractor *C* from tortious liability, this may negate any duty of care that *C* would otherwise owe *A*.

Thus, in *Norwich CC v Harvey*, represented by **Diagram 4E.7**, N contracted with X for an extension to a swimming pool, accepting the risk (ie exempting liability) for loss or damage by fire and agreeing to maintain adequate insurance cover. The same exemption was contained in X's contract with H to provide the roofing. When the property was extensively damaged due to the negligence of H's employee, the Court of Appeal denied N's claim against H for negligence because H owed N no duty of care. May LJ observed that the mere absence of privity between N (the employer) and H (the subcontractor) should not prevent H from relying on the clear basis on which all the parties contracted in relation to fire damage, even if it was caused by negligence.

4.1.7.3 Trust of the contractual right

A TP has a direct action against the promisor if the court construes the promisee as holding her contractual right to sue the promisor on *trust* for the TP. As the beneficiary of the trust, the TP acquires *a property* right enforceable against the promisor. Thus, if *A* promises a sum to *C* in exchange for *B*'s transfer of a benefit to *A*, *C* can sue *A* for the sum if the trust device can be invoked (*Les Affreteurs Reunis v Walford* (1919)). Once a trust is recognised, it is irrevocable; the TP's rights crystallise and the contract parties cannot change their minds. The utility of this device in circumventing the privity rule is restricted by the courts' insistence on robust evidence of the parties' intention to create a trust. The Court of Appeal refused to adopt a liberal approach in *Re Schebsman* (1944). Where S agreed to the termination of his contract in exchange for six instalments payable to himself and, on his death, to his wife and daughter, the court found no evidence that the parties intended to create a trust in favour of the widow and daughter. Lord Greene MR said: 'To interpret this contract as creating a

Diagram 4E.8 Trust of a contractual right

trust would, in my judgement, be to disregard the dividing line between the case of a trust and the simple case of contract made between two persons for the benefit of a third.' See **Diagram 4E.8**.

4.1.7.4 Assignment

Although contract parties cannot confer a directly enforceable benefit on the TP, the promisee can subsequently *assign* her contractual rights to the TP (see **Diagram 4E.9**). Thus, if *A* makes an enforceable promise to *B* to pay *B* a sum of money, *B* can assign the benefit of that promise to *C*, enabling *C* to enforce the promise against *A*. The assignee takes the benefit 'subject to equities' and is therefore vulnerable to all the promisor's defences against the promisee/assignor. A party can assign her right without the other party's consent *unless*:

✗ the contract forbids such assignment;

✗ the assignee has no genuine or commercial interest in taking the assignment;

✗ the relationship between the contract parties is personal (eg where contractual performance involves personal skill); or

✗ the promisor *reasonably* prefers to perform for the promisee (*Tolhurst v Associated Portland Cement Manufacturers Ltd* (1902)).

The courts are keen to ensure that 'there should if at all possible be a real remedy which directs recovery from the defendant towards the party which has suffered the loss' (*Technotrade Ltd v Larkstore Ltd* (2006)).

Diagram 4E.9 Assignment

4.1.7.5 Negotiable instruments

The best-known example of a negotiable instrument is the cheque (though many cheques are no longer negotiable instruments since they cannot be transferred by the payee any longer). The writer of the cheque (the drawer) instructs the bank (the drawee) to pay a specified sum to the named TP (the payee). The TP is better off than the assignee because she takes free from any defects in the title of the prior parties: the cheque gives her the secure right to demand payment.

4.1.7.6 Statutory exceptions

Legislation has made inroads into the privity doctrine to regulate three important TP relationships. The most obvious is that of insurance, where policies often confer benefits on someone other than the insured. TP beneficiaries can sue directly for the contractual benefit under the:

- Married Women's Property Act 1882: under section 11, a husband or wife (or children) can sue in respect of the spouse's (or parent's) life insurance policy;
- Marine Insurance Act 1906: under section 14(2), a party with an interest in the subject matter (eg mortgagee or consignee) may insure it on behalf of another interested party; and
- Road Traffic Act 1988: under section 148(7), a TP can sue the insurer directly in respect of the insured's liability to the TP covered by the policy.

4.2 Imposing burdens on third parties

C(RTP)A does not change the rule that contract parties cannot, via their contract:

(i) impose positive burdens (eg obligations, liabilities) on TPs (ie to do something); or

(ii) deprive TPs of some right or restrict their freedom of action (ie *not* to do something).

These rules are subject to a small number of exceptions to which we turn.

4.2.1 Inducing breach of contract

Tort law imposes an obligation on TPs not to intentionally or recklessly induce one party to breach her contract (eg a publisher should not induce *A* to disclose confidential information in breach of *A*'s contract with *B*). In *OBG v Allan* (2007), Lord Hoffmann said that there must be:

- an actual breach of the relevant contract (it is not enough to have merely 'interfered' with the performance of the contract); and
- the TP must know that it is inducing a breach of contract (it is not enough that the act procured by the TP does in fact amount to a breach).

If so, the TP would incur liability to the innocent contract party for the tort of inducing or procuring breach of contract.

   ✓ In *Lumley v Gye* (1853), L (a theatre owner) engaged a famous singer W to sing only at his theatre for a set time. G, a rival theatre owner, persuaded W to break her contract with L by promising more pay. L successfully claimed damages against G for causing him loss by inducing W to break her contract.

 Pause for reflection

This conclusion is not obvious. After all, it was W who chose to break her contract and L could equally have sued her for his loss. However, in the context of rival 'bidders' for a particular skill, the court seems to have attributed greater mischief to the TP's enticement than the contract party's succumbing to the enticement.

✓ Likewise, a TP can be liable if she acquires property with knowledge of a contract affecting it and her acquisition or use of the property is inconsistent with that contract. In *BMTA v Salvadori* (1949), B bought a car and undertook to A not to resell it for a year without first offering it to A. When C bought the car from B with notice of the undertaking, C was liable to A for wrongful interference with A's contractual right.

4.2.2 Sub-bailment contracts

Where *C* (the bailor) entrusts property to *A* (the bailee) for *A* to hold for or at the direction of *C*, and *A* then entrusts the property to *B* (the sub-bailee), *C* is bound by the terms of the sub-bailment between *A* and *B* to which she has consented, whether expressly or impliedly. Thus:

✓ where *C* entrusts a mink stole to *A* (a furrier) for cleaning and, with *C's* consent, *A* sends the mink to *B* (a specialist cleaner), *C* is bound by the exemption clause in the sub-bailment contract (*Morris v Martin & Sons Ltd* (1965)).

✓ Where owners of goods (*C*) contract with freight carriers (*A*) on terms that the latter could subcontract 'on any terms' the handling, storage, and carriage of the goods, *C* are bound by the exclusive jurisdiction clause in *A's* contract with subcontractors *B* whereby *B* carried the goods (*The Pioneer Container* (1994)).

4.2.3 Restrictions on property acquired

Where *A* makes a contract (1) with *B* regarding the use of *B's* property, and *B* then transfers the property to *C* via transaction (2), is *C* bound by the terms of contract (1)? The policy arguments are those of:

• free trade (buyers (*C*) should be free from strings which might be attached to their purchases); versus

• the security of *A's* proprietary rights (which should be enforceable against anyone).

4.2.3.1 Respect for proprietary rights

Where *A* has acquired *a proprietary interest* from contract (1) with *B* (eg the contract may create a lien, a lease, an equitable proprietary interest, or a constructive trust which 'runs with' the property in favour of *A*), *A*'s proprietary rights attach to the property (which may physically remain with *B*) and can prejudice the rights of TPs *C* who later acquire the property from *B*. Thus, covenants contained in leases bind the successors in title of both the landlord and the tenant, and contractual rights which are specifically enforceable vest an equitable proprietary right in *A*. Thereafter, in the eyes of equity, *C* can only take the property from *B* subject to *A*'s proprietary interest.

4.2.3.2 A wider principle?

Is there a wider principle that operates in the absence of recognised proprietary interests—simply on the basis of the TP's *knowledge* of the vendor's contractual obligations towards the claimant in respect of the property acquired (ie *C* has notice of *B*'s contract with *A*)? The answer that has evolved is: 'no, but not always'.

The first step was taken in a case on **restrictive covenants attached to *land*.** In *Tulk v Moxhay* (1848), T sold land subject to a restrictive covenant that the land should be preserved in its existing condition and not be built upon. A number of conveyances later, M acquired the land with notice of the restrictive covenant but sought to build on the land. T was awarded an injunction to restrain the proposed building. The basis for the decision was M's *notice of the covenant at the time of purchase*.

But subsequent cases have narrowed the interpretation of *Tulk* by emphasising the *additional* requirement that the covenant must have been for the benefit of neighbouring land owned by the party enforcing the restrictive covenant (*London CC v Allen* (1914)). That is, *C* is only bound by a restrictive covenant in respect of land acquired from *B* if, at the time of the purchase:

- *C* knows of the restrictive covenant in favour of *A*; and
- *A* owns the adjoining land which could benefit from the covenant.

A's right to prevent *C*'s inconsistent use is described as an 'equitable interest' (*Re Nisbet and Potts' Contract* (1905)). Thus, the analysis is not so much that *C* is bound because of her *notice* of *A*'s right, but because the restrictive covenant agreed between *A* and *B* is promoted to the status of *a proprietary* right.

The proprietary analysis has also been used when *C* **undertakes to honour** *A*'s contractual rights against *B* in respect of *C*'s acquisition from *B*. *C* will be restrained from acting unconscionably by exercising her legal right to treat the property as hers regardless of *A*'s rights. The mechanism deployed is the *constructive trust* (*Binions v Evans* (1972); *Ashburn Anstalt v Arnold* (1989)).

Despite the narrowing of *Tulk* along proprietary lines, the case was relied upon in *De Mattos v Gibson* (1858) to introduce a **general principle** that equity will protect the original promisee's *contractual right* in respect of the property (including **chattels**) transferred by imposing restrictions on the TP who acquired the property with *knowledge* of those rights. Knight Bruce LJ said:

> Reason and justice seem to prescribe that, at least as a general rule, where a man, by gift
> or purchase, acquires property from another, with knowledge of a previous contract,

lawfully and for valuable consideration made by him with a third person, to use and employ the property for a particular purpose in a specified manner, the acquirer shall not to the material damage of the third person, in opposition to the contract and inconsistently with it, use and employ the property in a manner not allowable to the giver or seller.

This principle from *De Mattos* was applied by the Privy Council in *Lord Strathcona Co Ltd v Dominion Coal Co Ltd* (1926) to restrain S (the purchaser of a ship) from using the ship in a manner inconsistent with the time charter made by a previous owner with D and which S *knew of and agreed to respect*. S was said to be 'plainly in the position of a constructive trustee with obligations which a Court of equity will not allow him to violate'. The decision has attracted judicial **criticism** (*Clore v Theatrical Properties* (1936); *Greenhalgh v Mallard* (1943)):

(i)   While *De Mattos* in relied on *Tulk*, it ignored the emphasis (by the restrictive covenant cases subsequent to *Tulk*) on the *claimant's ownership of adjacent land* capable of benefiting from an injunction against the TP.

(ii)   A proprietary analysis along the line of *De Mattos* is *too wide*: The use of proprietary reasoning (the constructive trust) would suggest the expansion of TP liability:

- to cases of mere *constructive notice* (which, while normally enough to bar TPs from appeal to the bona fide purchaser for value defence in proprietary claims, is undesirable in commercial affairs); and

- beyond the mere award of an injunction to restrain TP actions which contradict the claimant's rights (eg to an award of account of profits or a reasonable user fee or equitable compensation).

This would substantially outflank the privity rule against imposing burdens on TPs.

✗   *Port Line Ltd v Ben Line Steamers Ltd* (1958) refused to follow *Lord Strathcona*, so far as it relates to contracts concerning chattels.

✓   However, the *De Mattos* principle was confirmed although narrowed by Browne-Wilkinson J in *Swiss Bank Corp v Lloyds Bank Ltd* (1979): *A* can obtain an injunction to prevent *C* from dealing with property in such a way as to cause *B* to breach its contract with *A* if:

(i)   *C* had *actual knowledge* of the contract between *A* and *B* when it acquired the property (constructive knowledge is insufficient); *and*

(ii)   it is still possible for *B* to perform the contract (if not, it is *B*'s conduct (not *C*'s) which undermines *A*'s right).

The cases can then be rationalised along the following lines:

- The actual decision in *De Mattos* to deny an injunction is explicable on point (ii). D chartered a ship from C who subsequently charged the ship to G; G knew of the D-C charterparty. G sought to sell the ship prior to the completion of the charterparty. D's application for an injunction against G was refused because, although G knew of the charterparty, C could not complete the charterparty due to its financial difficulties. Thus, it was not G's proposed action that interfered with D's contractual rights.

- *Lord Strathcona* is explicable in terms of the proprietary right generated by C's *undertaking* in its contract with B to *respect A's right* in relation to the property acquired.

- The refusal to grant an injunction in *Port Line* is explicable on point (i) (since C did not have sufficient knowledge of A's right), and because A was not merely seeking an injunction but claimed the compensation C received when the ship was requisitioned.

- Since the remedy is limited to an injunction, the TP cannot be compelled to perform the terms of the contract. Thus, in *Law Debenture Trust Corp v Ural Caspian Oil Corp* (1993), where A obtained shares from B, promising to pay B when certain events occurred, B could not enforce the payment against C (who acquired the shares from B) or D (who acquired the shares from C) when these events later eventuated, although C and D both had knowledge of the contract between A and B.

Although the *existence* of this exception to the rule against imposing restrictions on a TP's use of property acquired is established, the *basis of the exception* remains clouded by talk of constructive trusts. The equitable proprietary reasoning is insecure given the criticisms and qualifications mentioned previously. The preferable explanation is that *De Mattos* and *Lord Strathcona* represent the equitable counterpart to the tort of knowing interference with contractual rights (*Port Line Ltd* and *Swiss Bank*). Thus, a TP may, exceptionally, be bound by the contract of others where its conduct amounts to unconscionable conduct in exercising its legal right in respect of property acquired in a manner inconsistent with the claimant's right, where it had undertaken to honour the claimant's right when it acquired the property.

THIS CHAPTER IN ESSENCE

The key areas and core topics in this chapter are summarised in an easy-to-use list, ideal for revision purposes, on the online resources at www.oup.com/uk/chenwishart6e/. Links to websites relevant to the topics covered and any updates to the chapter can also be found on the online resources.

QUESTIONS

1 'The Contracts (Rights of Third Parties) Act 1999 was necessary to counter the legal 'black hole' created by the privity doctrine.' Discuss.

2 'The Contracts (Rights of Third Parties) Act 1999 has brought as many problems as it has solved.' Discuss.

3 What is the effect of the Contracts (Rights of Third Parties) Act 1999 on the requirement of consideration?

4 Pat and Quentin agree that they would each pay Rose half of the cost of a 'round the world' holiday when she finishes her law exams. Rose is delighted. Subsequently, Pat and Quentin refuse to pay because they disapprove of Rose's new lifestyle. Can Rose sue?

5 Sam pays Toby £5,000 to make alterations to his daughter Una's business premises to prepare it for a major marketing event. Toby limits his liability for breach to £500. Toby botches the job and parts of the ceiling fall down during Una's presentation, injuring Una. Una has also suffered: (a) damage to her premises; and (b) loss of profits she would have made from the event. Advise Sam and Una.

 For hints on how to answer these questions, please see the online resources at www.oup.com/uk/chenwishart6e/

KEY FURTHER READING

Andrews, N (2001), 'Strangers to Justice No Longer: The Reversal of the Privity Rule under the Contracts (Rights of Third Parties) Act 1999', 60 *CLJ* 353.

Burrows, A S (2000), 'The Contracts (Rights of Third Parties) Act 1999 and its Implications for Commercial Contracts', *LMCLQ* 540.

Flannigan, R (1987), 'Privity—The End of an Era (Error)', 103 *LQR* 564.

Kincaid, P (2000), 'Privity Reform in England', 15 *LQR* 43.

Law Commission (UK) (1996), *Privity of Contract: Contracts for the Benefit of Third Parties* (Law Com No 242, Cm 3329).

MacMillan, C (2000), 'A Birthday Present for Lord Denning: The Contracts (Rights of Third Parties) Act 1999', 63 *MLR* 721.

Roe, T (2000), 'Contractual Intention Under Section 1(1)(b) and Section 1(2) of the Contracts (Rights of Third Parties) Act 1999', 63 *MLR* 887.

Smith, S (1997), 'Contracts for the Benefit of Third Parties: In Defence of the Third Party Rule', 7 *OJLS* 643.

Stevens, R (2004), 'The Contracts (Rights of Third Parties) Act 1999', 120 *LQR* 292.

PART IV

'Vitiating' factors

'Can I get out of this contract?'

INTRODUCTION

Even if an agreement satisfies the test of formation discussed in Part II, its enforceability is not guaranteed. The contract may still be avoided if there is a good reason for releasing one party from it. This question is logically prior to that of ascertaining the *contents* of the contract (Part V) since that question only arises if an initially valid contract is not set aside.

Good reasons for releasing party *A* from the contract can broadly be described in terms of:

(i) *A*'s impaired consent due to deficiencies in *A*'s knowledge or judgment;

(ii) *B*'s improper behaviour in inducing *A*'s consent to the contract;

(iii) an unforeseeable change of circumstances that radically alters the significance (point) of the contract; or

(iv) the unfairness of the contract in the sense of a marked imbalance in the values exchanged.

On the classical model of contract law, the law's legitimate concern is confined to ensuring that the bargain was fairly negotiated, not with whether the outcome was fair (1.3.5). Policing *procedural* unfairness is permitted, while policing *substantive* unfairness is not.

Procedural fairness has two aspects:

• it looks to the quality of the claimant's consent, which may be adversely affected by her incapacity or a less serious 'bargaining disability' that makes her more vulnerable to exploitation or serious mistakes ((i) in the list of good reasons); and

• it looks to the *blameworthiness of the defendant* (the party seeking to enforce the contract): has she lied to, coerced or otherwise taken advantage of the claimant ((ii) in the list)?

In addition, despite judicial insistence that **substantive unfairness** is irrelevant to the validity of a contract, it can play an important, if often covert, role in vitiating contracts ((iv) in the list). Lastly, a contract may be brought to an end ('frustrated') by a **radical change of circumstances** after formation ((iii) in the list).

These situations are regulated to different degrees by the doctrines to be discussed in this part as follows:

Chapter 5 Misrepresentation and non-disclosure

Chapter 6 Mistaken assumptions

Chapter 7   Frustration—the *reason* for allowing the claimant to escape closely resembles the mistake doctrine, although its *effect* is to discharge an initially valid contract, rather than to wipe away the contract from the beginning.

Chapter 8   Duress

Chapter 9   Undue influence, non-commercial guarantees, unconscionable bargains, and the desirability of a general doctrine on unfairness. This chapter also contains a brief introduction to the incapacity doctrine, which is more fully discussed in Additional Chapter 1 (available on the online resources).

These doctrines are collectively described as 'vitiating factors', but they affect the status of contracts in different ways. As we will see, they may render the affected contract void, voidable, unenforceable, or discharged, as the Introductory Diagram shows. It is enough to note for now that:

- most vitiating factors render a contract voidable at the option of the claimant (she can elect to 'rescind' or 'affirm');

- but the mistake doctrine may render the contract void from the beginning (there is no choice); and

- the frustration doctrine automatically discharges both parties from performance irrespective of their wishes, but only from the time of the radical change of circumstances.

The questions for consideration are the following.

(i)   What must a claimant prove under each of these doctrines to escape the contract?

(ii) To what extent do the burdens of proof relate to the defendant's blameworthy behaviour, the claimant's defective consent, or the fairness of the outcome?

(iii) On the *theoretical* level, what do the answers to the second question tell us about the *reasons* for judicial intervention in respect of each vitiation doctrine?

(iv) What is the law's role in controlling procedural and substantive unfairness?

(v)   Is the current law satisfactory? If not, how might it be reformed?

Part IV Introductory Diagram: The effect of 'vitiating' factors

	valid	void	voidable	discharge	unenforceable
Misrepresentation			✓		
Mistake		✓	✓ (?)		
Frustration				✓	
Duress			✓		
Incapacity	✓	✓	✓		✓
Undue influence			✓		
Improvident guarantees			✓		
Unconscionable bargains			✓		
Illegal contracts	✓	✓			✓

5

Misrepresentation and non-disclosure

'You misled me'

Consistent with an adversarial model of contract negotiation, English law recognises no general duty of good faith (see further discussion on good faith in Chapter 15). The parties have no duty to disclose important matters about the transaction to each other. However, a contract party should not make false statements to induce the other party's consent to the contract. This is regulated by the law on misrepresentation, which is complicated by two factors:

- its rules are a patchwork of common law, equity, and statute; and
- it must be put in the context of related doctrines that deal with the same general problem (of disappointed expectations), but yield different legal responses, eg proof of misrepresentation allows the claimant to get out of a contract and even claim money, but other causes of action (eg mistake or breach of contract) may also be available on the facts and may give, perhaps, better remedies; thus, the claimant must navigate these related doctrines to find the most advantageous cause of action.

The questions addressed in this chapter are:

(i)   What is a misrepresentation?

(ii) What liability is there, if any, for non-disclosure?

(iii) When can the claimant get out of the contract for misrepresentation?

(iv) When can the claimant get money for misrepresentation? How is any compensation to the claimant measured?

(v) To what extent can a party exclude or limit her liability for making a misrepresentation?

(vi) What justifications underlie the remedies for misrepresentation?

(vii) Is the current law on misrepresentation satisfactory? If not, how might it be developed in the future?

5.1 **What is an actionable misrepresentation?**

In brief, a misrepresentation is:

(i) an unambiguous false statement of existing fact,

(ii) made to the claimant,

(iii) which induces her to enter the contract.

If these requirements are satisfied, the claimant can rescind the contract subject to the bars (5.2.2). But, if she *also* (or *instead*) wants to claim damages to compensate her for the loss suffered from entering the contract, an *additional* element is required:

(iv) the misrepresentation must have been made with *the requisite state of mind*. A misrepresentation that the defendant can prove was made honestly and on reasonable grounds will yield no damages (except perhaps in lieu of rescission, 5.2.3).

Before examining these requirements in more detail, we need to mention two preliminary issues with important analytical and remedial consequences. **Diagram 5A** shows how different **classifications of the statements** made yield different *remedies* if the statements turn out to be false.

Starting at the left side, the first question is: 'Did the statement complained of induce the claimant into a contract with the misrepresentor?'

✗ If the answer is 'no' **(2)** (eg where *A*'s misrepresentation induces *B* to contract with *C*, as in *Hedley Byrne v Heller* (1964)), the claimant must rely on the common law tort actions of fraudulent or negligent misrepresentation and the equitable action for innocent misrepresentation.

✓ This being a text on contract law, our discussion will focus on the scenario where the statement *does* induce a contract between the parties **(1)**. The next question relates to the *status* of the false statement, for this determines **(3)** the remedies available, and **(4)** the law applicable to any exemptions of liability.

• If the statement is a **term** inside the contract, its falsity gives the claimant an action for breach of contract (Part VI), and any term exempting liability is subject to particular legislative control (Chapter 11; in B2B contracts (business-to-business), the claimant must look to the Unfair Contract Terms Act 1977 (UCTA); in B2C contracts (business-to-consumer), the consumer must look to the Consumer Rights Act 2015 (CRA)).

• If it is a **representation** outside the contract, the claimant has access to the advantageous action for damages under the Misrepresentation Act 1967 (MA). Any terms exempting liability in B2B contracts are subject to control by the MA itself, and in B2C contracts are subject to CRA (5.4). Although the pre-existing tort and equity actions continue to be available, the claimant will have no incentive to resort to them.

• If it is a mere '**puff**', it has no legal effect; the claimant has no action.

Diagram 5A The remedial significance of classifying statements

MA Misrepresentation Act 1967		**(3) Claimant's potential remedies**			**(4) Effect of exclusion or limitation of liability**
		Damages	**Get out of contract**	**Performance**	
(1) Contract is made with the maker of statement. The statement is:	**A term of the contract** incorpo-ration ↑ ↓ s 1(a) MA	Expectation measure	Termination	Specific performance	(1) B2B : UCTA 1977 B2C : CRA 2015
	A representation	Fraud measure s 2(1) MA	Rescission	No	(2) B2B : MA 1967 B2C : CRA 2015
	A mere 'puff' without legal effect	No	No	No	
(2) No contract is made with the maker of the statement. The statement is made:	Fraudulently	Fraud measure	No contract to escape	No contract to escape	(3) B2B : UCTA 1977 B2C : CRA 2015
	Negligently	Negligence measure			
	Innocently	No			

5.1.1 **Representations and terms**

5.1.1.1 The remedial importance of the distinction

If an untrue statement induces a contract with the maker of the statement, the remedies available depend on whether the statement is classified as a term *inside* the contract or a representation *outside* the contract:

- A **term** is an enforceable contractual undertaking to do (or refrain from doing) something, or to guarantee the truth of something. Where a term is breached, the remedies are, broadly speaking, 'forward looking'. The aggrieved party can claim damages aimed at putting her in the position she would have been in if the contract had been performed. She may also have a claim to compel the contract-breaker's performance or be able to end (terminate) the contract for a sufficiently serious breach (see Part VI).

- A **representation** is a statement which asserts the truth of a given state of affairs and invites reliance upon it, but does not *give an enforceable guarantee of its truth*. If it is actionable, the remedial response is, broadly speaking, 'backward looking'. The claimant may be able to get out of (rescind) the contract and/or claim damages aimed at putting her in the position she would have been in had she not relied on the representation, ie not entered the contract,[1] (see the three columns beneath **(3)** on **Diagram 5A** (and also see **Diagram 10A**)).

---

[1] The distinction between contractual damages for loss of bargain and tortious damages for reliance losses is blurred if reliance damages include the '*loss of opportunity*' to make another similar contract, 5.3.1.2.

Diagram 5B Good bargain, bad bargain, and measure of damages

	Contract measure	Tort measure
Good bargain: C pays £50,000 for value of £70,000	£ 40,000 = £70,000 – £30,000	£20,000 = £50,000 – £30,000
Bad bargain: C pays £80,000 for value of £70,000	£ 40,000 = £70,000 – £30,000	£50,000 = £80,000 – £30,000

A party may be able to prove that the statement made to her is *both* a misrepresentation and a contractual term, for a statement that induces the contract *may* also be incorporated as a, usually written, term of the contract:

- The claimant will prefer to rely on the statement's contractual status if her remedies for breach are superior to her remedies for misrepresentation (eg if her preference is for specific performance, expectation damages, or termination) or if her remedy of rescission for misrepresentation is barred (5.2.2).

- Exceptionally, a party will prefer the remedies for misrepresentation (eg where she cannot meet the high threshold for terminating the contract for breach (12.2.2), but *can* meet the lower threshold for rescission for misrepresentation (5.2)).

- **Diagram 5B** compares the measure of damages yielded by the different actions depending on whether the claimant made a good bargain or a bad bargain. Here, C pays £50,000 for goods that turn out to be worth only £30,000 because D's statement was untrue.

If C has made a good bargain (eg the goods would be worth £70,000 *if the statement had been true*):

- ✓ C will prefer the contractual measure of damages, and so rely on the statement being a contractual term to claim expectation damages, being the value expected minus the value received, yielding £30,000.

- ✗ On an action for misrepresentation, C will only receive the sum paid minus the sum received, yielding £20,000.

Conversely, if C has made a bad bargain (eg if C paid £80,000 for goods which would only be worth £70,000 *if the statement was true*):

- ✗ Contract damages would yield the same as above, being £40,000.

- ✓ However, C would get more in a misrepresentation claim, being the sum paid (£80,000) minus the value received (£30,000), yielding £50,000.[2]

---

[2] Although it is arguable that the claimant's over-payment is not caused by the misrepresentation, the 'fiction of fraud' (5.3.1.2) allows the court to assume that the claimant would not have contracted at all without the misrepresentation, and so should be fully restored by damages. The claimant would certainly recover the sum on rescission.

The term-or-representation distinction is also important if the claimant wants to get out of the contract. Ironically, it is easier to end the contract for misrepresentation than for breach; *any* misrepresentation entitles the claimant to rescind the contract, yet only a *serious* breach (12.2.2) allows the claimant to terminate the contract. Before the MA, if a statement was both a misrepresentation and a contract term, the latter status took priority so that the claimant lost her right to rescind the contract for misrepresentation. She could only get out of the contract if the breach was a serious one. This anomaly is remedied by section 1(a) of the MA, which gives the representee the *option* of treating the statement as a misrepresentation. This means that she can claim the remedies for misrepresentation (including rescission) *even* if the statement was incorporated into the contract as a term. However, this solution would generate its own problem: it would allow the representee to escape a bad bargain (by rescinding it) for a relatively trivial breach. This problem is dealt with by section 2(2) of the MA, which empowers courts to *deny rescission* by reference to equitable considerations (5.2.2.6). The reforms of the MA to the remedies for misrepresentation (narrowing the right to rescission and expanding the right to damages) have reduced the practical importance of the term–representation distinction, although the distinction remains fundamental in principle.

5.1.1.2 How is the representation–term distinction made?

The distinction is said to be based on the intention of the parties as objectively manifested by their words and conduct (*Heilbut, Symons & Co v Buckleton* (1913); *Oscar Chess Ltd v Williams* (1957)). However, the parties will often, in truth, have no intention at all on the matter, for, as Atiyah observes (at 180), such intention would virtually require the parties to appreciate the legal distinction between a term and a representation. Moreover, even if the parties thought about the matter, their intentions are likely to differ. The real question is not whether the maker of the statement *has* agreed to *bear contractual* responsibility for the truth of the statement, but whether she *should*. The courts are guided by the following criteria, although none is said to be decisive (*Heilbut, Symons & Co v Buckleton*):

(i) **Importance of the truth of the statement**: the more important the statement to the representee, the more likely it is to be a term. In *Bannerman v White* (1861), W was expressly assured that the hops on sale had not been treated with sulphur, after saying that he would not even bother asking the price if they had. In fact, sulphur was used on a small portion of the hops. The statement was held to be a *term* of the contract. In *Couchman v Hill* (1947), the seller's reply to the buyer's question that the heifer being auctioned was 'not in calf' was held to be a *term* of the contract because the seller knew that the buyer would not have been interested otherwise. The heifer suffered a miscarriage and died within two months of its purchase.

(ii) **Special knowledge**: a court is more likely to find a term if the maker of the statement has special skill or knowledge in the subject matter of the statement, is in a better position to ascertain, or bears more responsibility for ascertaining, the accuracy of the statement than the other party. Accordingly:

✓ a *term* was found in *Dick Bentley Productions Ltd v Harold Smith (Motors) Ltd* (1965) where a car dealer made a false statement to a private buyer about the mileage of the car since its engine replacement ('20,000 miles', when actually it was 100,000 miles). The dealer, being 'in a position to know, or at least find out the history of the car . . . stated a fact that should be within his own knowledge'; but

✗ only a *misrepresentation* was found in *Oscar Chess Ltd v Williams* (1957) where a private seller (without special knowledge) stated the model of the car he was selling to a car dealer as '1948' (relying on the car's log book which had been altered by the previous owner) when it was actually a 1939 model. It was held that the car dealer was in at least as good a position to discover the car's true age as the private seller.

(iii) **Request to verify**: a statement is unlikely to be a term if the maker of the statement tells the other party not to rely solely on the statement but to verify its truth:

✗ A representation was found in *Ecay v Godfrey* (1947), where a seller stated that the boat was sound but advised the buyer to have it surveyed.

✓ However, a *term* was found in *Schawel v Reade* (1913), where the seller said to the buyer: 'You need not look for anything; the horse is perfectly sound. If there was anything wrong with this horse, I should tell you.'

(iv) **Initiation or merely passing on**: *Routledge v McKay* (1954) indicates that, *where* a motor car is sold second-hand from one person to another in succession and each seller in the chain is passing on information about the year the car was made by relying on a false entry in the registration book by some remote seller, the statement would be treated as a representation and not a term. The seller, unless the person who altered the registration book, is not the originator of the false statement, but a mere innocent passer-on (as in *Oscar Chess*).

(v) **Formal recording**: if a contract is recorded in writing, the presumption is that the document records the complete terms (*Heilbut Symons v Buckleton*; this is the 'parol evidence rule' (10.3.1)); anything not included therein is a representation. Nevertheless, the court may, although it will be slow to, find a statement outside the document to be a binding *collateral* term or contract (10.3.2).

 Pause for reflection

The relevant factors point to concerns beyond the parties' intentions in making the term–representation distinction. They suggest that courts are also concerned to protect the addressee's reasonable expectations induced by the statement, and to determine whether the maker of the statement *should* fairly bear the responsibility for that expectation, even if she has not actually agreed to bear it.

5.1.2 **Statements of fact and other statements**

A representation, to be actionable, must be an unambiguous, false statement of existing *fact* or *law*. **Diagram 5C** gives an overview of actionable statements and non-disclosures. Express statements of fact and law are clearly included. Statements of *intention*, *opinion*, or '*puffs*', although not prima facie statements of fact, may contain

Diagram 5C Identifying actionable statements and omissions

The objectionable conduct:	Legal category:	Test of actionability:	Actionable as :
ACTS words or conduct amounting to statements of:	**Fact or law**	Statement is false, or statement is true but: • misleading, or • falsified before contract formation	Misrepresentation
	Intention	There is a false implied statement of fact that the representor: • is honest, or • has a reasonable basis for the statement	
	Opinion		
	'Puffs'	Not actionable	
OMISSIONS	**Contract uberrimae fidei**	There is a duty to disclose the fact withheld	Actionable non-disclosure
	Fiduciary relationship		Breach of fiduciary duty
	Doctrines indirectly relieving non-disclosure	Different tests according to the doctrine invoked	Different remedies according to the doctrine invoked

implied statements of fact. Even *omissions* (silence) are actionable if there was an independent duty to disclose the omitted information.

5.1.2.1 Statements of fact

Statements of fact can be made by words or by conduct. In *Walters v Morgan* (1861), Campbell LC said that, whilst simple reticence is not actionable, 'a nod or a wink, or a shake of the head, or a smile from the purchaser intended to induce the vendor to believe the existence of a non-existing fact, which might influence the price of the subject to be sold' is actionable. Statements of fact may also be implied. In *Spice Girls Ltd v Aprilia World Service BV* (2002), the band, the Spice Girls, made a contract to promote the defendant's motorcycles on 6 May 1998. One member left the band three weeks later causing considerable loss to the defendant. Since all five members participated in a commercial photo shoot, and supplied logos, images, and designs, the Court of Appeal held that the Spice Girls had made an implied misrepresentation by conduct that they did not know and had no grounds to believe that any of the Spice Girls were intending to leave when they knew this was untrue.

5.1.2.2 Statements of law

Even a statement as to the law may be a misrepresentation if it was reasonable, in all the circumstances, for the representee to rely upon it (*Pankhania v Hackney LBC* (2002)).

5.1.2.3 Statements of intention

A statement about the speaker's intention is not *in itself* a statement of fact, but it is *actionable* if:

(i)   it is a **term** of the contract (5.1.1 and 10.2); or

(ii) it is **dishonest**: a statement of intention *always* implies a statement of fact to the effect that it reflects the speaker's state of mind.

   ✗ If it is honest, there is no misrepresentation. The representor can change her mind; her failure to carry out her stated intention is not actionable (*Wales v Wadham* (1977)).

   ✗ In *Kleinwort Benson Ltd v Malaysia Mining Corp Berhad* (1989), M refused to guarantee the debt of its subsidiary company to K, but gave K a 'letter of comfort' stating 'it is our policy to ensure that the business of [our subsidiary company] is at all times in a position to meet its liabilities to you under the above arrangements'. When K sued M for the loan, the court held that the letter was simply an honest *representation* of M's policy at the time. M did not promise to stick by this policy in the future (2.7.3).

   ✓ A statement is actionable if the representor was dishonest. In *Edgington v Fitzmaurice* (1885), company directors issued a prospectus inviting subscriptions for debentures which said that it was raising money to develop and expand the business; in fact, the money was used to repay existing company debts. Denman J held the directors liable for deceit, explaining that:

   > the state of a man's mind is as much a fact as the state of his digestion. It is true that it is very difficult to prove what the state of a man's mind at a particular time is, but if it can be ascertained it is as much a fact as anything else. A misrepresentation as to the state of a man's mind is, therefore, a misstatement of fact.

5.1.2.4 Statements of opinion

Statements of opinion or belief are not statements of fact and are not actionable just because they turn out to be wrong. However, such statements may be *actionable* if:

(i) They are **dishonest**: like statements of intention, dishonesty in asserting an opinion not genuinely held is *always* a misstatement of fact (regarding the state of one's mind). The same applies if the speaker could not honestly hold the opinion she asserts, given the facts known to her. This shades into the second exception.

(ii) There is **no reasonable ground**: *if* the representor is in a better position than the representee to know the truth, the court may *imply* a statement of fact that the representor has reasonable ground for her opinion, making her liable if she does not (*Brown v Raphael* (1958)). In *Smith v Land and House Property Corp* (1884), Bowen LJ said:

> where the facts are equally well known to both parties, what one of them says to the other is frequently nothing but an expression of opinion . . . But if the facts are not equally known to both sides, then a statement of opinion by the one who knows the facts best involves very often a statement of a material fact, for he impliedly states that he knows facts which justify his opinion.

However, a speaker *without* greater knowledge than the representee who offers an honest opinion makes no actionable misrepresentation. In *Bisset v Wilkinson* (1927), the vendor of a farm in New Zealand told the prospective buyer that he thought the land could carry 2,000 sheep. Both parties knew that the land was untried as a sheep farm and so were in the same position to form an opinion on the matter. The court held the vendor's statement to be an honest opinion that did not imply he knew facts justifying it.

(iii) They are contractual terms: an opinion made by one having superior knowledge and experience may amount to a contractual *term* to the effect that care and skill had been exercised in giving the opinion. But, in practice, the damages available for breach of such a term confer no remedial advantages over a claim for misrepresentation; in both cases, damages are measured by reference to the addressee's loss flowing from the speaker's lack of skill and care in making the statement. In **Esso Petroleum Ltd v Mardon** (1976), M was induced to lease a petrol station then under construction by E's statement that the estimated future annual turnover was 200,000 gallons per year. E reaffirmed this estimate although the local authority refused planning permission for the original layout. In fact, the necessary changes reduced the annual turnover to 78,000 gallons. M incurred considerable losses from operating the station and successfully claimed for damages for negligent misrepresentation and breach of contract.

5.1.2.5 'Puffs'

Vague and exaggerated laudatory statements about the subject matter of the contract may amount to neither terms nor representations because it would be *unreasonable to rely* on them. Advertising slogans which claim, eg, that a brand of petrol will put 'a tiger in your tank' or that a deodorant will make you totally irresistible to the opposite sex, are not statements that a reasonable person would take literally. In *Dimmock v Hallett* (1866), it was held that a statement that land was 'fertile and improvable' would only exceptionally be considered an actionable misrepresentation.

However, the more resemblance the statement bears to a statement of opinion, the more likely it will be found to contain an implied statement of fact. It is a matter of degree. In *Smith v Land and House Property Corp*, a purchaser was allowed to rescind the contract for misrepresentation where the vendor of property told him that it was 'let to a most desirable tenant', when the vendor knew that rent had been hard to extract and was in arrears. The vendor's dishonest and unreasonable statement was vague, but the buyer was entitled to rely on it because the vendor had knowledge not available to the buyer. In addition, the context and specificity of the statement may also elevate a statement to the status of a term. In *Carlill v Carbolic Smoke Ball Co* (1893), the court rejected the seller's claim that its advertisement was a mere puff (2.2.1.2). It stated that £100 would be paid to anyone 'who contracts the increasing epidemic influenza, colds, or any disease by taking cold, after having used the ball three times daily for two weeks according to the printed directions', adding that £1,000 had been deposited with the Alliance Bank 'showing our sincerity in the matter'.

Pause for reflection

To summarise: the key question is whether, having regard to all the circumstances, it is reasonable for *the representee to rely* on the statement made and, on the other side, for the misrepresentor to be answerable for the representee's loss incurred by such reliance. The simple answer that it is only reasonable to rely on statements of *fact* is subject to qualifications. Not only is the old bar against actions for misrepresentations of law now dissolved, courts can construct *implied* statements of fact out of statements of intention and opinions taking into account:

- the importance of the statement;
- the context in which it is made (social, professional, or commercial); and
- the relative expertise and knowledge of the parties.

The last factor is also important in distinguishing: (i) an actionable misrepresentation from an unactionable one; *and* (ii) terms from representations (5.1.1.2). This is unsurprising when the questions are essentially the same, ie whether and to what extent the maker of the statement should take responsibility for its accuracy.

5.1.3 **Silence**

5.1.3.1 No general duty of disclosure

During contractual negotiations, a party need not say anything, but anything she *does* say should at least be honest. Contract law responds to *active* misrepresentations; at common law, there is no general liability for omissions. Silence or non-disclosure, even if it relates to important facts of which the other party is ignorant or mistaken, generate no liability (*Keates v Cadogan* (1851)). Blackburn J said in *Smith v Hughes* (1871):

> if the vendor was aware that the purchaser thought that the article possessed that quality, and would not have entered into the contract unless he had so thought, still the purchaser is bound, . . . a mere abstinence from disabusing the purchaser of that impression is not fraud or deceit; for, whatever may be the case in a court of morals, there is no legal obligation on the vendor to inform the purchaser that he is under a mistake, not induced by the act of the vendor.

Consistently, the MA only applies where the defendant *makes* a positive representation, and not where she is completely silent on the matter (*Banque Keyser Ullman SA v Skandia (UK) Insurance Co Ltd* (1990)).

Pause for reflection

Non-disclosure raises the problem of *informational asymmetry* between the parties; the party with less information will undoubtedly come off worse in the contract. Four arguments support the general **denial of liability for non-disclosure:**

1. Incentive to invest: since accurate information enhances the efficiency of the market system, the law should give parties the incentive to acquire such information. This means that

→ a knowledgeable party must generally be allowed to take advantage of a less knowledge-able party. If an oil company has invested heavily in research to identify land holding pos-sible oil reserves, it should not have to share its information in negotiations to buy this land. To require disclosure would discourage investment in the acquisition of such information.

2. Permissible self-interest: parties are under no obligation to help others; there is no general duty to rescue (1.3.6).

3. No liability for omissions: the common law does not generally impose liability for mere non-feasance or pure omissions (*Smith v Littlewoods* (1987)).

4. Uncertainty and floodgates: if a duty of disclosure were recognised, it would be very dif-ficult to determine when the duty arises and what its precise contents are (no one can be expected to disclose everything that may influence the other party's judgment).

On the other hand, blanket immunity for non-disclosure could result in sharp practice and unacceptable advantage-taking. The need for economic investment in skill and knowledge will only justify so much and the picture of robust self-interest is not always appropriate. Where one party knows that the other is relying on her skill, knowledge, and judgment, economic arguments carry less weight and uncertainty (or floodgates) arguments are less compelling, especially when the representee cannot discover the truth or can only do so with great difficulty or expense.

English law contrasts sharply with the position in the **European Draft Common Frame of Reference**. Article II.-3:101 recognises a general duty of disclosure which applies to *all* business and consumer contracts, with the latter attracting a higher duty. The business is liable for any loss caused to the other party by its failure to dis-close, even if no contract is concluded (Art II.-3:109(3)).

Nevertheless, **English law can protect the less knowledgeable party by**:

(i) extending the scope of actionable misrepresentations;

(ii) imposing a duty to disclose where the parties are in special relationships; and

(iii) invoking other doctrines that indirectly address the problem of non-disclosure.

5.1.3.2 Extending the scope of actionable misrepresentation

The court can imply, from what the defendant has said, *other* statements that, if false, may be actionable.

(i) Change of facts: *falsification by later events*

A statement of fact is deemed to be continuing, so that a change of circumstances *prior to the conclusion of the contract* can convert what was a true statement into an actionable misrepresentation, *unless* the representor corrects it (ie makes disclosure: *Shankland & Co v Robinson and Co* (1920)). In *With v O'Flanagan* (1936), the vendor of a medical practice correctly represented its value as £2,000 at the start of negotiations. However, the practice was almost worthless by the time the sale was concluded five months later because of the vendor's supervening ill health. The sale was rescinded for misrepresentation. The decision effectively imposes on the vendor a duty to correct (ie to disclose the change of circumstances), which would almost certainly put off the purchaser, either completely or on the original terms.

Must the representor know of the change of circumstances? It seems only reasonable to expect the representor to disclose known changes and Romer LJ in *With v O'Flanagan* suggests that the rule is so confined (see also *Shankland v Robinson* (1920)). However, to require knowledge amounts to imposing liability only for fraud and this contradicts the general position that even non-fraudulent misrepresentations are actionable. Lord Wright MR did not specifically require knowledge. Unhelpfully, Clauson J agreed with both his brethren.

Does the continuing representation rule apply to statements of intention? Here, the representor will invariably know of the falsifying change of circumstances (ie her own change of mind), unless she has forgotten her original statement.

✓ *Trail v Baring* (1864) requires the representor to disclose her change of intentions before the conclusion of the contract.

✗ However, *Wales v Wadham* does not. Here, the wife told her husband that she had religious objections to remarriage after divorce, resulting in her obtaining a more generous divorce settlement on the basis that she would remain single. The court upheld the settlement, although the wife had secretly agreed to marry another prior to the conclusion of the settlement. *Wales v Wadham* has been approved in *Livesey v Jenkins* (1985).[3]

 Counterpoint

The result in *Wales v Wadham* is objectionable. While it is arguable that intention statements only imply an honest reflection of the representor's state of mind *at the time of speaking*, the power of such statements to induce contracts clearly rests on the representee's assumption that they, like other statements of fact, hold good, at least up to the formation of the contract.

(ii) 'Half-truths': *representations that only give part of the picture*

A party who chooses to say something may be liable although what she says is literally true, if she omits important qualifications that *distort* the representee's assessment of the proper *weight* to be attached to the statement. The representor fails to make clear that implications that are likely to be drawn, cannot in fact be drawn. She is 'economical with the truth', 'paints a misleading picture', tells a 'half-truth', or implies that the material facts omitted do not exist, eg:

✓ in *Nottingham Patent Brick and Tile Co v Butler* (1886), the vendor's solicitor said that he did not know of any restrictive covenants affecting the land under negotiation, but failed to add that this was because he had not bothered to check. The purchaser was entitled to rescind the contract;

---

[3] Although it was held that a duty of disclosure was owed *to the court* making a family settlement order, breach of which entitled the other party to set the agreement aside.

✓ in *Clinicare Ltd v Orchard Homes & Developments Ltd* (2004), the prospective land-lord (O) stated, in response to the prospective tenant's (C) inquiry, that it was unaware of the property being affected by dry rot. In fact, O's surveyor had advised further investigation to determine the true extent of the dry rot that had been discovered. O dealt with the obvious dry rot but made no further investigation. O was liable for misrepresentation because its better position to discover the dry rot (which was hidden by O's refurbishment) implied that reasonable steps had been taken to see whether dry rot existed; and

✓ regulation 5 of the Consumer Protection from Unfair Trading Regulations 2008 (SI 2008/1277) and section 20 of the Consumer Protection Act 1987 make it an offence for a business party to give misleading information about the subject matter of the contract even if what is said is strictly true.

5.1.3.3 Disclosure requirement based on special relationships

(i) Contracts *uberrimae fidei*: contracts of utmost good faith
In these cases, the material facts lie within the exclusive knowledge of one party and failure to disclose them makes the contract voidable. The *content* of the duty of disclosure varies with the type of contract in question.

- Historically, in contracts of insurance, the insured has a duty to disclose[4] all facts which a reasonable or prudent insurer would regard as material to the risk assessment (*Pan Atlantic Insurance Co Ltd v Pine Top Insurance Co* (1995); Marine Insurance Act 1906, s 18(2)). Failure to disclose will entitle the insurer to avoid the contract and deny claims under it. This duty can operate oppressively since it assumes that the insured knows what information affects the insurer's estimation of risk.

  (i) The Consumer Insurance (Disclosure and Representations) Act 2012 has abolished the consumer's duty to volunteer material facts. Instead, consumers must take reasonable care to answer their insurer's questions fully and accurately.

    - If the consumer's misrepresentation was honest and reasonable, the insurer must pay the claim;

    - if it was careless, the insurer has a compensatory remedy based upon what the insurer would have done had the consumer taken care to answer the question accurately; and

    - if it was deliberate or reckless, the insurer can decline all claims and retain the premiums, unless there is a good reason why they should be returned.

  (ii) Under the Insurance Act 2015, the non-consumer insured's duty of disclosure will be replaced by a duty to make a fair presentation of the risk to the insurer.

- Other types of contracts call for some measure of disclosure, although they may not all be *uberrimae fidei* in the strict sense. These include contracts of partnership,

---

[4] The insurer also has duty to disclose: *Banque Financière de la Cité v Westgate Insurance Co Ltd* (1990).

contracts to subscribe to company shares, family settlements, and contracts of guarantee.

It is arguable that these instances can be generalised into a duty of disclosure whenever one party has knowledge that is inaccessible to the other.

(ii) Fiduciary relationships

Broadly speaking, fiduciary relationships arise where *A* entrusts *B* to perform a specific job, or to hold or control *A*'s property, or *A* trusts in or depends on *B* (see undue influence at 9.2). Where *B* abuses *A*'s trust to obtain an advantage at *A*'s expense, *B* 'will not be permitted to retain the advantage, although the transaction could not have been impeached if no such confidential relation had existed' (*Tate v Williamson* (1866)). The usual objections to a disclosure duty based on the need to give incentives to acquire knowledge, to allow self-interested behaviour and the concern about floodgates largely disappear in such cases. The *scope* of fiduciary relationships is potentially very broad.[5] The *content* of the duty (eg to make particular disclosures, to avoid a conflict of interests, to give disinterested advice or to suggest independent advice) and the appropriate *remedies* for breach (eg rescission, account of profits made, or liability for equitable compensation) will vary with the precise nature of the fiduciary relationship.

5.1.3.4 Indirect techniques of giving relief for non-disclosure

Other contract rules and doctrines can, in practice, impose a duty of disclosure on the knowing party seeking to enforce the contract or particular terms. The law protects ignorant parties by giving the knowing party incentives to disclose (mainly the *terms* of the contract) in a number of situations:

(i) Where *A* knows of *B*'s mistake as to the *terms* of the contract, the contract is void. Thus, to enforce the contract on *A*'s terms, *A* must correct *B*'s mistake (2.1.3.1).

(ii) If *A* has exploited *B*'s disability (including ignorance of the value of the contract's subject matter) to extract a grossly unfair exchange, it may be set aside as an unconscionable bargain (eg *Ayres v Hazelgrove* (1984) and 9.4).

(iii) Non-commercial guarantees are only enforceable if lenders ensure that guarantors are independently advised of the material features of the contract (9.3).

(iv) Onerous or unusual terms in an unsigned document can only bind a party who had reasonable notice of them before the conclusion of the contract (10.3.3.2).

(v) There are numerous statutory duties of disclosure designed to mitigate the effects of inequality of bargaining power between consumers (generally less knowledgeable, expert and experienced about the subject matter of the contract) and traders (eg the Consumer Contracts (Information, Cancellation and Additional Charges) Regulations 2013, and the Package Travel, Package Holidays and Package Tours Regulations 1992 (SI 1992/3288)). Traders may commit an offence or be unable to enforce particular

---

[5] P Finn describes a fiduciary as 'simply, someone who undertakes to act for or on behalf of another in some particular matter' whether requested or not, whether gratuitously or for payment (*Fiduciary Obligations* (Law Book Co, 1977) 201). Similar descriptions have been used judicially.

terms unless they present the terms in legible, plain English, follow a particular set of words (eg in consumer credit), or highlight them by colour, size, or position on the page. Consumers may have to be provided with copies of the contract or 'cooling off' periods during which they can cancel.

(vi) While there is no general duty to rescue others from harm (*Yuen Kun-Yeu v AG of Hong Kong* (1988)), a duty of care arising between parties in a 'special relationship' may impose a tortious duty to disclose information relevant to the contract (*Banque Keyser Ullman SA v Skandia (UK) Insurance Co Ltd* (1990)).

(vii) The use of implied terms (10.6) is arguably the most effective technique for protecting the parties' reasonable expectations. Rather than requiring A to disclose *deviations* from B's reasonable expectation, implied terms make these expectations contractually enforceable unless A discloses deviations. Moreover, A may be barred from excluding these implied terms (eg under CRA (10.6.2.1 and) and UCTA (11.5.2)). While the categories of contracts requiring disclosure are regarded as *closed*, and generally arise only where relevant facts are *known*, implied terms are not so confined. Moreover, implied terms are ostensibly justified by the parties' implied intentions, whereas disclosure obligations are derived from less easily justified factors external to the parties' intentions.

 Pause for reflection

These apparently isolated and discrete common law and statutory rules are unified by the policy of protecting contract parties from informational asymmetry (especially when the information is only accessible to one party) and inequality of bargaining power. This policy could guide the courts when they are considering possible extensions of disclosure requirements in the common law. Still, duties of disclosure can only do so much. There is no guarantee that weaker parties such as consumers will understand or even read the often vast amount of information provided; nor, if they did, that they could negotiate any change in their favour. This explains the statutory controls of contractual fairness discussed in Chapter 11.

5.1.4 **Made to the claimant**

Statements can travel along a chain as they are repeated (from A to B to C to D and so on). It would be unfair to impose liability on the original representor for every subsequent representee's reliance on her statement. Thus, an actionable misrepresentation must have been addressed either to the claimant *directly*, or to a third party with the *intention* that it be passed on to the claimant (*Smith v Eric S Bush* (1990)), who may be a member of the public at large (*Andrews v Mockford* (1896)). Beyond these, the misrepresentation is regarded as 'spent' (*Gross v Lewis Hillman Ltd* (1970)). In cases of indirect communication, the MA only applies to A's misrepresentation communicated via B to C if it induces C to contract with A; otherwise, C's actions lie in the common law torts of deceit or negligent misrepresentation.

5.1.5 Inducement and materiality

5.1.5.1 Inducement

The claimant must prove that the misrepresentation *induced* (caused) her to enter into the contract. The claimant must show that she would not have entered the contract 'but for' the misrepresentation (*Assicurazioni Generali v Arab Insurance* (2003)).

However, the standard of *causation* required is lowered in the case of fraud; the claimant need only show that the misrepresentation 'materially influenced' her, or 'was actively present' in her mind. It need only be *'one of' her reasons* for entering into the contract (*Edgington v Fitzmaurice*). Thus, it is no bar that the claimant had other reasons for entering into the contract or that she might have entered into the contract anyway without the misrepresentation (*Re Leeds Bank* (1887)). Inducement is strongly inferable from the *materiality* (or importance) of the misrepresentation (5.1.5.2). Jessel MR said: 'if a man has a material misstatement made to him which may, from its nature, induce him to enter into the contract, it is an inference that he is induced to enter into the contract by it. You need not prove it affirmatively' (*Mathias v Yetts* (1882)). Indeed, it will be for the representor to show that the representee was *not* induced by it to enter the transaction (*Vahey v Kenyon* (2013)).

The fact that the claimant could have, but did not, verify the accuracy of the representation will not ordinarily bar her claim. In *Redgrave v Hurd* (1881), the prospective buyer queried the seller's statement about the turnover of the business, but he declined an invitation to examine further documents. Baggallay LJ said that the seller should not blame the buyer for trusting him: '[t]he representation once made relieves the party from an investigation . . . [Ordinarily], the mere fact that he does not avail himself of the opportunity of testing the accuracy of the representation made to him will not enable the opposing party to succeed.'

However, the scope of *Redgrave v Hurd* has been confined by *Smith v Bush* so that, if it would be *reasonable* for a representee to take an opportunity to discover the truth (or unreasonable for her not to or her reliance was unforeseeable to the non-fraudulent misrepresentor), her claim in *negligent* misrepresentation will fail; the position should, *a fortiori*, be the same where the misrepresentation is *wholly innocent*. Aside from this, a failure to verify may reduce a representee's damages for *contributory negligence* (5.3.1.2).

✗ In *Peekay Intermark Ltd v ANZ Banking Group Ltd* (2006), the Court of Appeal found that P was not induced to invest by ANZ's misrepresentation as to the nature of the investment. ANZ's agent gave only a 'rough and ready' description and P's agent was an experienced investor who must have appreciated the need for a definitive and detailed description of the 'product' from the contract documents. Indeed, P's agent had agreed 'as per the attached document' to ANZ and had signed a Risk Disclosure Statement stating that he had read and understood the document. Thus, P was induced to sign the documents, not by ANZ's misrepresentation, but by its own assumption that the contractual document corresponded with ANZ's representation.

✗ In *Kyle Bay Ltd v Underwriters* (2007), K, the insured, carelessly relied on U's erroneous statement about the basis for calculating an insurance claim without checking the policy itself. The Court of Appeal held that U only gave its opinion and did not make a representation of fact. K's agent was professionally qualified and experienced and must be taken to have a copy of the policy. It was open to the trial judge to find that K's agent was not induced to enter the contract by U's statement, but simply proceeded on its own assumption that U's contention was correct.

There will not be the requisite inducement if the claimant:

✗ is *unaware* of the representation (*Horsfall v Thomas* (1862));[6]

✗ is *unaffected* by the representation because she relies on other information (*Atwood v Small* (1863));

✗ regards it as *unimportant* (*Smith v Chadwick* (1884)), although the line between this and the rule that the representation need only be *one* of the reasons inducing the contract will be a fine one. In *JEB Fasteners v Marks Bloom and Co* (1983), the court denied J's claim for damages for M's negligent preparation of the accounts of a company J was taking over; J did not rely on these accounts but proceeded with the takeover because it wished to secure the services of two of its directors; or *knows* that the representation is untrue (*Cooper v Tamms* (1988)).

✓ However, in a case of fraudulent misrepresentation, courts are particularly ready to find inducement even if the representee did not believe in the truth of the misrepresentation at the time of the contract. In ***Zurich Insurance Co plc v Hayward***, (2016) the defendant brought a claim against his employers for a back injury suffered at work. The employer's insurers suspected that the defendant had exaggerated his claim but would not have been able to prove it in court and so agreed to settle the claim for £135,000. Thereafter, the defendant's neighbours provided the evidence to substantiate the insurer's suspicion and the insurer sought to rescind the settlement agreement. Reversing the Court of Appeal, the Supreme Court held that insurers did not have to prove that they settled because they believed that the defendant's misrepresentations were true; they merely had to show that they had been *influenced* by those misrepresentations.

◆◀ Counterpoint

1. Misrepresentations are *induced* mistakes; hence inducement should be fundamental to the burden of proof. A claimant must be shut out from rescission for misrepresentation if she has not been misled or mistaken because she knew the statement was false. Yet, Lord Clark said that: 'there may be circumstances in which a representee may know that the representation is false but nevertheless may be held to rely upon the misrepresentation as a matter of fact.' His Lordship cites an example of a staged road traffic 'accident' 'where the representee may actually be certain from his own direct knowledge that the statement

➡

---

[6] Where the seller tried to conceal a defect in the cannon to be sold by inserting the metal plug into a weak spot but the buyer never examined it.

➡️

is a deliberate lie. But even then he and his advisers cannot choose to ignore it; they must still take into account the risk that it will be believed by the judge at trial.'

2. Loi argues that this is not a case of misrepresentation in the sense of an induced mistake, but rather one of economic duress and lawful act duress analogous to *Borrelli v Ting* (2010) (8.6, 'Pre-Contractual Misrepresentations: Mistaken Belief Induced by Mis-statements' [2017] JBL 597).

3. Other factors weigh against a finding of misrepresentation: (i) the insurer consciously took the risk that they were settling a suspicious claim; and (ii) the public policy in favour of encouraging the compromise of claims disputed in litigation by upholding settlement agreements.

5.1.5.2 Materiality

The immateriality (ie unimportance of the matter stated) of the misrepresentation will not defeat a claim if the representor was fraudulent (*Smith v Kay* (1859)), or knows or ought to know that her statement will influence the claimant (*Nicholas v Thompson* (1924); *Goff v Gauthier* (1991)). Even absent fraud, *Chitty* observes that: 'There is no clear authority denying relief to a representee who has in fact been influenced by a misrepresentation which would not have does influenced a reasonable person' (para 7-041). Such cases may be dealt with:

- as *evidence of inducement*; if the misrepresentation is material (ie would induce a reasonable person to enter the contract), inducement is presumed and the onus is on the misrepresentor to show no reliance by the claimant; if it is *not* material, the claimant must prove affirmatively that she *was* induced into the contract (*Museprime Properties Ltd v Adhill Properties Ltd* (1991)); or
- as 'mere puffs' which are non-actionable.

5.2 Rescission for misrepresentation

Rescission of the contract is available to the misrepresentee for all types of misrepresentations: fraudulent, negligent, or innocent. However, there are certain bars to rescission.

5.2.1 What is rescission?

Students sometimes confuse the *rescission* of voidable contracts (eg those induced by misrepresentation and other vitiating factors in Part IV) with the *termination* of valid but breached contracts (Chapter 12). This is unsurprising since some courts and texts refer to both as 'rescission' (as recognised in *Photo Production Ltd v Securicor Transport Ltd* (1980)). Both bring a contract to an end but they are quite distinct (*Johnson v Agnew* (1979)).

- **Rescission** of contracts for misrepresentation (and other vitiating factors such as duress and undue influence) is often described as 'rescission *ab initio*' (the contract is set aside *from the beginning*). Although property rights *can* pass under a voidable contract up to the time of rescission, *as against the other contract party* (here, the misrepresentor), rescission nullifies the contract prospectively *and* retrospectively. Any obligations yet to be performed are cancelled and any benefits transferred are treated as if they were never due and so must be *returned*. This includes indemnifying the representee for any costs assumed under the contract (5.3.3). Rescission is backwards looking. The representee can elect to rescind or affirm; there can be no partial rescission (*Potter v Dyer* (2011), 9.2.5.3).

- **Termination** of contracts for *breach* recognises the existence of a valid contract between the parties, but that, in limited circumstances (12.2.2), the contract may be terminated by the innocent party, thereby dispensing both parties from *further* performance of their primary obligations. In their place is substituted the contract-breaker's liability to remedy the breach. Termination is therefore only prospective; it is 'rescission *de futuro*' (for the future). Anything transferred under the contract up to the point of termination is generally not recoverable by the claimant (she cannot go 'backwards', but see 13.4) but is taken into account in calculating her damages, which are designed to take her 'forwards' to her expectation position (*Photo Production v Securicor Transport* (1980)).

Rescission is only effective once it is communicated to the other party. The timing of rescission is important if the representee wants to recover property transferred under the voidable contract. If *A* transfers property to *B* under a contract induced by *B*'s misrepresentation, and *B* then sells that property to *C*, *A* can only recover the property from *C* if:

✓ she rescinds her contract with *B* before *B* passes the property to *C* (6.2.1); or

✓ C is not a good faith purchaser from B.

Rescission is a self-help remedy (effected by the representee's *own action*) and is generally communicated when the representee notifies the representor. Exceptionally, a representee need not actually notify the representor if she has otherwise taken all possible steps to recover the goods. In ***Car and Universal Finance Co Ltd v Caldwell*** (1965), C was fraudulently induced to sell his car in return for a bad cheque. The buyer disappeared and C immediately sought assistance from the police and the Automobile Association, but was obviously unable to communicate his rescission to the fraudster. *Subsequently*, the fraudster sold the car to CUF. It was held that C had effectively rescinded the contract by his actions, thereby re-vesting title to the car in himself and preventing CUF from acquiring effective title thereafter. C could recover the car from CUF. This outcome is harsh for the third party buying property from the fraudster in good faith, and the Law Reform Committee has recommended that such a purchaser should acquire a good title (*Transfer of Title to Chattels* (12th Report (Cmnd 2958, 1966) at para 16)).

5.2.2 The 'bars' to rescission

Misrepresentation makes a contract voidable. Unlike void contracts, the right to set aside voidable contracts is not absolute: it can be lost or 'barred'. The MA:

✗ removes two pre-existing bars to rescission; and

✓ adds one, making the final list: (i) impossibility of mutual restitution; (ii) affirmation; (iii) lapse of time; (iv) third party rights; and (v) inequity. **Diagram 5D** gives an overview of their effect on the different types of misrepresentation. It shows that the bars may be lowered or removed where there is fraud.

5.2.2.1 Removal of bars by section 1 MA

We saw that **section 1(a)** of the MA preserves the representee's right to rescission even if the representation becomes incorporated as a term of the contract (5.1.1.1). She can elect.

Pause for reflection

1. Where the claimant refuses to continue with the contract, the court must decide whether this amounts to rescission (limiting her to reliance damages) or termination (preserving her right to expectation damages).

2. Since the threshold for termination is very high (it is only available for 'serious' breaches (12.2.2)), a claimant may find that she has unwittingly rescinded the contract (eg by returning defective items), thereby extinguishing her right to potentially superior contractual damages.

Diagram 5D How the bars to rescission apply to different types of misrepresentation

✓ = yes
✗ = no

'Bars'	Fraudulent	Negligent	Innocent
1. Affirmation	✓	✓	✓
2. Lapse of time prejudicing representor	✗	✓	✓
3. Third party rights	✓	✓	✓
4. Impossibility of mutual rescission	✓ but less stringent	✓	✓
5. Inequity under s 2(2) Misrepresentation Act	✗	✓	✓

Section 1(b) removes the former bar to rescission where contracts for the sale of property induced by non-fraudulent misrepresentations have been performed (*Angel v Jay* (1911)), so that rescission is now available even if the contract has been executed.

5.2.2.2 Impossibility of mutual restitution

Rescission involves the 'giving back and taking back of the obligations which the contract has created, as well as the giving back and the taking back of the advantages' (*Newbigging v Adam* (1886)). Executory (unperformed) contracts pose no problems since rescission just cancels both parties' contractual obligations. But where the contract is partially or wholly executed (performed), rescission is barred if it is impossible to return the benefits transferred under the contract. In practice, this is the *main bar to rescission* because English law treats rescission as a *proprietary* rather than a personal remedy. This means that, money aside, what must be restored is the *exact* thing received. So, rescission has been barred where return in kind:

- ✗ to the *representee* was never possible, as with services (*Boyd & Forrest v Glasgow & South Western Railway* (1915)); or has become impossible, as where the property is substantially dissipated through use, consumption or selling on to a third party (*White v Garden* (1851)); and

- ✗ to the *representor* is not substantially possible, as where the claimant bought a mine and sought to rescind after it had been worked out (*Vigers v Pike* (1842)).

This bar has shown signs of relaxation by allowing monetary substitution for benefits that cannot be physically returned. The crux is that the representee should not be unjustly enriched at the representor's expense; that the representor should not be prejudiced is a secondary. It is for the representor to prove the extent of the representee's enrichment that must be returned.

- ✓ In *O'Sullivan v Management Agency & Music Ltd* (1985), a pop singer rescinded the contract with his manager. The latter had to account for their profits, but were given credit for their skill and labour in promoting the singer and significantly contributing to his success (9.2.5.1).

- ✓ In *Erlanger v New Sombrero Phosphate Co* (1878), the court emphasised its *equitable* jurisdiction to give rescission 'whenever, by the exercise of its powers, it can do what is practically just [eg by giving an *account of profits* made from use of the property and making *allowances* for deterioration of the property] though it cannot restore the parties precisely to the state they were in before the contract'.

- ✓ In *Salt v Stratstone Specialist Ltd* (2015), the Court of Appeal allowed rescission of a contract to sell a 'brand new' Cadillac that turned out not to be so, although the car had become registered, had depreciated in the meantime and had been driven 15,000 miles. 'Practical justice' could be achieved by compensating the representor who could prove depreciation or use.

- ✓ *Fraud* increases the courts' willingness to make adjustments to allow rescission. In *Spence v Crawford* (1939), Lord Wright said:

The court will be less ready to pull a transaction to pieces where the defendant is innocent, whereas in the case of fraud the Court will exercise its jurisdiction to the full in order, if possible, to prevent the defendant from enjoying the benefit of his fraud at the expense of the innocent plaintiff. But restoration is essential to the idea of restitution . . . the court can go a long way in ordering restitution if the *substantial identity of the subject-matter of the contract remains* (emphasis added).

However, by requiring 'substantial' (even if not precise) restitution, the bar retains much of its force. Thus, even in a fraud case, Lord Browne-Wilkinson thought it necessary to say that shares, which had been sold on to third parties, could be 'returned' *if* the representee could buy and return 'other, identical, shares' on the market (*Smith New Court Securities Ltd v Scrimgeour Vickers*). By implication, the shares could not simply be returned in money's worth.

 Counterpoint

Impossibility of precise return in kind by either party should not bar rescission. If English law is prepared to make small money adjustments to *supplement* a representee's return of substantially subsisting property, then it should be prepared to make big money adjustments, even to the extent of wholly *substituting* for benefits which could never, or can no longer, be returned in kind. The same applies to the representor's restitutionary liability. The current insistence on substantial restitution can give rise to unfair results. If rescission is barred, the admittedly unfair contract remains enforceable (even by a party guilty of fraud or duress). The representee has no claim for damages if the misrepresentation is purely innocent, and may become liable in damages for breach of this unfair contract (even if specific performance can be resisted). The requirement of substantial mutual restitution is further discredited when we consider that the object of rescission is not, strictly speaking, to restore the parties to their pre-contractual position (*MacKenzie v Royal Bank of Canada* (1934)). Rather, it is to prevent the claimant from being unjustly enriched at the other's expense by keeping the benefits received while getting back their own 'payment' for that benefit (*Bouygues Offshore v Owner of the M/T Tigr Ultisol Transport Contractors* (1996)). A fairer solution is to recognise that benefits received can *always* be given back, by money substitution if not in kind.

5.2.2.3 Affirmation

Misrepresentation only makes a contract voidable, and not absolutely void. The claimant can elect to rescind or affirm the contract.

(i) Affirmation requires knowledge of the facts giving rise to the right to rescind. However, a representee without the relevant knowledge may be *estopped* from denying affirmation if the representor has detrimentally relied on the representee's unequivocal conduct indicating her intention to affirm (*Peyman v Lanjani* (1985)).

(ii) Affirmation can be express or implied from conduct. Thus, rescission has been barred where, after discovering the misrepresentation, the claimant continues using the goods bought (*United Shoe Machinery Co of Canada v Brunet* (1909)), accepts dividends, votes at meetings, attempts to sell the shares bought (*Scholey v Central Rly Co of Venezuela* (1867)), or continues to reside and pay rent on premises leased (*Kennard v Ashman* (1894)). However, the mere use of property, or delay in rescinding, in order to verify the suspicion of misrepresentation does not amount to an affirmation (*Long v Lloyd* (1958)). The court will take into account the nature of the contract, any lapse of time, any change of position by the representor in reliance on the absence of protest by the representee, and whether third parties have been affected (*Clough v London & NW Rly* (1871); *BCCI (In Liquidation) v Ali (No 1)* (1999)).

(iii) Affirmation is closely related to estoppel. The claimant may be estopped from rescinding the contract, even where she does not know the facts or her rights, where she has led the defendant, by unequivocal statements or actions, to believe that she intends to affirm the contract, and the defendant has acted on this to its prejudice. It is 'inequitable' for the claimant to rely on her right because of the defendant's detrimental reliance (*Habib Bank Ltd v Nasira Tufail* (2006)).

5.2.2.4 Lapse of time

Lapse of time can amount to affirmation of the contract, barring rescission. Where the misrepresentation is **fraudulent**, lapse of time *cannot* bar rescission whilst the representee remains ignorant of the misrepresentation (*Armstrong v Jackson* (1917)). With **non-fraudulent** misrepresentations, a representee who fails to rescind the contract within a *reasonable* time of discovering the truth may be held to have affirmed the contract (*Clough v London & NW Rly* (1871)). But even if the representee remains ignorant of the non-fraudulent misrepresentation, it was once thought that a substantial passage of time *may* itself bar rescission. In *Leaf v International Galleries* (1950), L was induced to buy a picture of Salisbury Cathedral by I's innocent misrepresentation that it was painted by the famous artist Constable. L only discovered this was false when he tried to sell the picture some five years later. Nevertheless, L's claim to rescind the contract was denied due to lapse of time. Jenkins LJ said that contracts 'cannot be kept open and subject to the possibility of rescission indefinitely'. In addition, the representor should not be worse off than if the statement had become a term, when the representee would be barred from termination if she had 'accepted' the goods under the Sale of Goods Act 1893. This was questioned by the Court of Appeal in *Salt v Stratstone Specialist Ltd* (2015), since section 1 MA allows a representee to treat a term as a representation (5.2.2.1). Moreover, the Court of Appeal held that the bars to rescission must rest on an equitable basis: 'It is only the lapse of a reasonable time such that it would be inequitable in all the circumstances to grant rescission which constitutes a bar to the remedy', eg because the delay amounted to affirmation of the contract or otherwise put the other party in a prejudicial situation if rescission were thereafter asserted. This is in essence the principle of laches. Longmore LJ also said that it did not seem to him that 'lapse of time on its own can be a bar to rescission . . .'.

5.2.2.5 Third party rights

Rescission will be barred if an innocent third party has given consideration to acquire an interest in the subject matter of the contract (*White v Garden* (1851)), eg rescission of a contract for shares is barred once the company goes into liquidation, since this fixes the creditors' rights to share in the company's assets. This bar promotes the general interest in the security of transactions. The *voidable* status of contracts tainted by misrepresentations (and most other vitiating factors) means that the contract's ability to transfer rights is effective until the contract is rescinded. It follows that a bona fide third party who acquires property rights for value before the contract is rescinded is protected (5.2.1 and 6.2.1). Moreover, if a third party has acquired property rights in the subject matter of the contract, it is obviously impossible for the *representor* to return the precise property to the representee as part of rescission; the representee can only include the value of the property in her reliance claim against the representor.

5.2.2.6 Inequity: section 2(2) MA

Where the misrepresentation is non-fraudulent (ie negligent, innocent, or purely innocent), section 2(2) empowers courts to deny rescission (or reinstate an already rescinded contract), awarding the claimant damages in lieu (5.2.3), where 'it would be equitable to do so, having regard to the nature of the misrepresentation and the loss that would be caused by it if the contract were upheld, as well as to the loss that rescission would cause to the other party'. Section 2(2) is *pro-misrepresentor*.[7] Recall that, while termination is only available for a *serious* breach of contract, rescission is available for *any* and even trivial misrepresentation (subject to the bars). The MA irons out this anomaly in two moves:

(i) section 1(a) *liberalises* access to rescission (preserving the representee's right to rescind even if the representation is incorporated only as a warranty (a less 'serious' term that would not permit termination for its breach) of the contract, 5.2.2.1); but

(ii) **section 2(2)** *restricts* access to rescission by giving courts the discretion to protect a non-fraudulent representor from being deprived of her entire bargain for a relatively trivial misrepresentation and to prevent the representee from escaping a bad bargain. In return (or in consolation), the representee is awarded damages.

In *William Sindall plc v Cambridgeshire CC* (1994), W bought land for development from C for over £5 million in 1988. In 1990, W discovered that a sewer buried under the land would prevent its proposed development unless the sewer could be rerouted. W's claim of misrepresentation failed, but Hoffmann LJ expressed the view that, even if it had succeeded, the court would have barred rescission under section 2(2) because of:

- the relatively *minor impact* on the buyer if rescission was denied—it would only cost £18,000 to rectify the problem, and was unlikely to interfere seriously with the development or resale value of the property;
- the relative *unimportance of the representation* in the *context* of a £5 million sale; and

---

[7] Law Reform Committee, *Innocent Misrepresentation* (10th Report, Cmnd 1782, 1952) paras 11, 12; A Fairest, 'Misrepresentation and the Act of 1967' (1967) 25 *CLJ* 239, 245.

- the colossal loss to the seller if rescission was allowed—the seller would have recovered land now worth less than £2 million due to a general fall in land values while having to repay the buyer about £8 million (purchase price plus interest).

5.2.3 Section 2(2) MA: damages in lieu of rescission

5.2.3.1 Availability of section 2(2) damages

(i) The representee must have a good (not barred) claim for rescission to be eligible for damages 'in lieu of' rescission; the claimant must have something of value to 'trade in' for the damages, which are 'in lieu' of rescission. If rescission is barred, so is resort to section 2(2) (*Salt v Stratstone Specialist Ltd* (2015)).

(ii) Section 2(2) is not an independent route to previously unavailable damages (eg for purely innocent misrepresentation); the representee can only obtain damages 'in lieu' where she has *sought* but been *denied rescission* by the court. A rational representee will only seek rescission (ie to go backwards) if that will make her better off than affirming the contract (ie when she has made a bad bargain). This was the case in *William Sindall* where the purchased property dramatically plunged in value. But, bearing in mind the *pro-representor thrust* of section 2(2), this is precisely the situation when rescission will be barred and a *less advantageous* award of damages in lieu substituted. True, the representee will get a previously unavailable *monetary* award, but only by trading in a *more valuable* remedy which would have yielded more money or money's worth.

To press the point, if the property in *William Sindall* had increased in value, say to £10 million, W would not have wanted rescission (for that would mean returning the land and getting back only £5 million), yet that is what W would have to plead to get into section 2(2). The court would grant rescission unless the misrepresentor argues for the exercise of the discretion to refuse rescission, which the latter has no incentive to do.

5.2.3.2 Damages under section 2(2)

If rescission is barred under section 2(2), how are 'damages in lieu' measured?

✗ Section 2(2) damages cannot simply replicate section 2(1) reliance damages; that would deprive section 2(2) of any effect, and would make nonsense of section 2(3), which recognises the possibility of concurrent claims under both and requires section 2(1) awards to take account of any section 2(2) awards.

✗ Although the words 'in lieu of rescission' suggest that the measure should be the *money's worth of actual rescission* of the contract, this cannot be right. In *William Sindall*, it would undermine the reason for denying rescission (ie to prevent the hardship to the representor of being deprived of the whole bargain because of some minor misrepresentation) if the representor were then required to pay £6 million in lieu to compensate the representee for not getting rescission.

The move is towards measuring damages in lieu of rescission on the basis that the misrepresentation is a term of the contract that has been breached, although the representor has not promised the truth of the statement. In the Court of Appeal, Evans

LJ in *William Sindall* held that the correct measure is the difference in value between what the representee believed they were acquiring and what they in fact acquired. Likewise, Hoffmann LJ said that section 2(2) is 'concerned with damage caused by the property not being what it was represented to be'.

Pause for reflection

1. The measure under section 2(2) may be: (i) the difference between the contract price and the actual value of the property, without taking account of the general fall in the value of the property (this would reverse any unjust enrichment of the misrepresentor). Alternatively, the court can award (ii) the cost of correcting the defect (Evans LJ in *William Sindall*).

2. Section 2(2) damages should not cover consequential reliance losses (which belong under s 2(1)), or consequential losses of expectation (which belong properly in a breach of contract claim).

3. Beale argues that it is undesirable and unprincipled to measure section 2(2) damages by the contract measure because no promise has been given in respect of the statement ('Damages in Lieu of Rescission for Misrepresentation' (1995) 111 *LQR* 60). However, section 6(1)(a) of the New Zealand Contractual Remedies Act 1979 entitles a misrepresentee to damages 'in the same manner and to the same extent as if the representation were a term of the contract that has been broken'.

5.3 **Money awards for misrepresentation**

In addition to rescission, the misrepresentee may be able to claim *damages* compensating her for loss incurred by entering the contract. She succeeds under section 2(1) of the MA *unless* the *misrepresentor* can show that she honestly believed, *and* had reasonable grounds to believe, in the accuracy of her statement (if the misrepresentor *can*, no damages are available). This is represented by **column I** in **Diagram 5E**. The diagram gives an overview of the *types* of money claims available for a false statement.

The relatively simple picture presented by section 2(1) is complicated by two factors:

(i) **Section 2(1) MA** widens the test for actionable misrepresentations (**column I**), but links the *measure* of damages to the common law action for *deceit*, necessitating reference to the common law actions of deceit and negligent misrepresentation (**column II**).

(ii) **Other money claims** may be available for the misrepresentation instead of (or in addition to) any section 2(1) claim:

   • **column III**: Expectation damages for breach where the statement is classified as a contractual term (irrespective of the defendant's state of mind);

   • **column IV**: Restitution and indemnity which implement rescission (also available irrespective of the speaker's state of mind); and

   • **column V**: Damages in lieu of rescission under section 2(2) (only available for non-fraudulent misrepresentation).

Look on the online resources to view this figure as a PowerPoint® presentation

Diagram 5E Money claims for misrepresentation

✓ = actionable
✗ = not actionable

I. S 2 (1) Misrepresentation Act (reliance damages 'fiction of fraud')	II. Misrepresentation at Common law (reliance damages)	III. Breach of term (expectation damages)	IV. Restitution & indemnity (getting back)	V. S 2(2) Misrepresentation Act (damages in lieu of rescission for non-fraudulent misrepresentation)
✓ If the representor cannot prove **honest and reasonable belief.** Damages as for fraud (but, may be reduced for contributory negligence if action for negligent misrepresentation co-exists)	✓ **Fraudulent** problems of proof but 'fraud' measure (no remoteness limit, no reduction for contributory negligence)	✓ If the false statement is classified as a term, irrespective of maker's state of mind	✓ For all types of misrepresentations if rescission is allowed	✗ Fraudulent misrepresentation
	✓ **Negligent** problems of proof, more 'limited' reliance measure (remoteness limit, reduction for contributory negligence)			✓ Non-fraudulent misrepresentation if rescission is denied
✓ The representee cannot show he is honest and reasonable but neither can the representee prove fraud or negligence	✗ **Innocent** if representee cannot show fraud or negligence*			
✗ **'Purely' innocent** if representor can prove honest and reasonable belief*	✗			

* The distinction between an 'innocent misrepresentation' at common law and an unactionable misrepresentation under section 2(1) Misrepresentation Act, called a 'purely' innocent misrepresentation, is further explained at 5.3.1.1(iv).

5.3.1 **Damages under section 2(1) MA**

Since the MA does not define misrepresentation, the common law applies on what constitutes a misrepresentation that has induced the claimant to enter a contract with the representor. However, the common law claims for misrepresentation (ie fraudulent, negligent, and innocent misrepresentation), while they continue to be available, have all been 'out-gunned' by a claim under section 2(1) MA where the misrepresentation induced a contract between *A* the representee and *B* the representor. Section 2(1):

- lowers the qualifying threshold; and
- yields the most generous measure of damages via the so-called 'fiction of fraud' (5.3.1.2).

The common law actions are only needed where no contract results between *A* and *B*. In the contractual context, this can occur where:

- *A*'s misrepresentation induces *B* into a contract with *C*; or
- *A*'s misrepresentation induces *B* into a contract with *A*, but the contract is void, as for mistake (eg mistake of identity or *non est factum*, 6.2 and 6.1.3) or illegality (see Additional Chapter 2 available on the online resources).

5.3.1.1 Lowering the qualifying threshold: comparing fraudulent, negligent, and section 2(1) misrepresentation

(i) Section 2(1) of the Misrepresentation Act 1967
This prescribes:

(i) the measure of damages: a misrepresentor is liable *as if* he had made a fraudulent misrepresentation *even though* his 'misrepresentation was *not* made fraudulently' (this is known as the 'fiction of fraud' (5.3.1.2)); and,

(ii) the qualifying threshold: the misrepresentor is liable *unless* 'he proves that he had reasonable ground to believe and did believe up to the time the contract was made that the facts represented were true'.

Thus, in order to *qualify* for the (most generous) fraud measure of damages, a claimant under section 2(1) need not show fraud, or even negligence; she only needs to show that:

✓ the other party made a false statement of fact or law (express or implied) which

✓ induced her into the contract with the representor.

It is then for the *representor* to show that she *honestly* believed on *reasonable* grounds that her statement was true when she made it. In *Howard Marine and Dredging Co v A Ogden & Sons* (1978), H's manager misrepresented the carrying capacity of two barges being hired out to O as 1,600 tonnes. O refused to pay on discovering, six months later, that they could only carry 1,055 tonnes. H sued for the hire charges and O counterclaimed for £600,000 lost due to the lower carrying capacity. The Court of Appeal accepted H's honesty in making the statement and two of the three judges thought there was probably no liability even for common law negligent misrepresentation. But H was liable (as for fraud) under section 2(1) because H did not have reasonable grounds for its belief. H could not explain why it was reasonable to disregard the ships' documents containing the accurate figures, in favour of the figures in the Lloyd's register.

This reversal of the burden of proof regarding the representor's state of mind is a radical departure from the common law actions. This *pro-representee* move is aimed at eliminating the obstacles of proof in the common law actions for fraudulent and negligent misrepresentations to which we turn.

(ii) Fraudulent misrepresentation (deceit)

To succeed in common law deceit, the *representee* must prove that the representor made the false statement (*Derry v Peek* (1889)):

(i) knowingly;

(ii) without belief in its truth (including knowing that she is ignorant of its truth); or

(iii) recklessly; careless of whether it be true or false, even if her motive is worthy (*Polhill v Walter* (1832)). Acting unreasonably is not enough; what is required is gross carelessness justifying an inference of fraud (*Angus v Clifford* (1891)).

✗ Fraud was rejected in *Derry v Peek* where the representee bought shares in a company, relying on claims in its prospectus that the company was entitled to use steam power to run its trams. The company honestly believed this, although it had still to obtain permission, which was later denied. The House of Lords held that the directors were *not* liable merely because they had acted unreasonably in failing to check the truth of the statement.

Under section 2(1), a representee can access the generous deceit measure of damages (5.3.1.2) unless the *representor* proves her honesty and reasonable basis in making the statement.

(iii) Negligent misrepresentation

Until 1964, *Derry v Peek* was thought to rule out liability for negligent misrepresentations (statements made carelessly or without reasonable grounds for believing their truth), apart from when the parties were in a fiduciary relationship (*Nocton v Lord Ashburton* (1914)). *Hedley Byrne v Heller* recognised other 'special relationships' that can trigger a duty to take care in making statements. In that case, HB sought assurances from H bank about the financial health of a third party with whom HB proposed to contract. H gave a negligent assurance that the third party was 'considered good for its ordinary business transactions', and HB proceeded with the contract, suffering loss when the third party breached its obligations. HB's claim for negligent misrepresentation would have succeeded but for H's stipulation that its assurance was given 'without responsibility'.

Hedley Byrne v Heller widened the scope of damages-yielding misrepresentations, but is still subject to uncertain limits. The uncertainty arises, in large part, from the concern to restrain liability in an already overstretched legal system. After all, carelessness is less blameworthy than deliberate falsehood, and careless *words* can travel far and trigger widespread and purely economic losses, the latter being considered less worthy of protection than physical injuries or damage to property. Thus, liability is confined by the requirement that the claimant be in a *'special relationship'* with the representor such that the latter owes her a duty to take reasonable care in making the statement. However, the instability of the notion of 'special relationship' is reflected in the vagueness, and variety of the formulations put forward in *Hedley Byrne v Heller* itself ('reliance', 'assumption of responsibility', 'undertaking').

A section 2(1) claim dispenses with the need to prove a special relationship where a misrepresentation *induces the representee to contract* with the representor.

The measure of damages for negligence is *less generous* than for deceit because it is vulnerable to *two reductions* from which deceit claims are immune:

- The rule on *remoteness of damages* limits damages to losses that the representor could reasonably foresee as flowing from the misrepresentation (*Overseas Tankship (UK) Ltd v Morts Dock & Engineering Co Ltd (The Wagon Mound (No 1))* (1961)).

- Damages are further reducible by reference to the representee's *contributory negligence* (Law Reform (Contributory Negligence) Act 1945 (LR(CN)A), s 1; *Gran Gelato Ltd v Richcliff (Group) Ltd*).

Since section 2(1) invokes the 'fiction of fraud', it would seem to be immune from these reductions (5.3.1.2).

(iv) Innocent misrepresentation

At common law, *no damages* are available for 'innocent misrepresentation' because no tort (wrong) is committed. The only remedies were rescission and indemnity (5.2 and 5.3.3). The court could circumvent this by classifying the false statement as a *term* of the contract (5.1.1 and 10.3.2) and awarding expectation damages for breach (eg *De Lassalle v Guildford* (1901)). However, there is less need to do this as the category of 'innocent misrepresentation' has dwindled.

- **Prior to** *Hedley Byrne v Heller*, the category described all non-fraudulent misrepresentations.

- **After** *Hedley Byrne v Heller*, its scope narrowed to misrepresentations that were not fraudulent or negligent.

- **The MA** reduces the category further. The reversal of the burden of proof means that a misrepresentation that would have been 'innocent' at common law (because the *representee* cannot prove fraud or negligence) may still attract liability under section 2(1) if the *representor* cannot show her honesty and reasonable basis in making the statement. Thus, it is only if the representor *can* prove her representation to be honest and on a reasonable basis that the misrepresentation is *'innocent'*. We can call this 'purely innocent' misrepresentation to signal its different scope from common law 'innocent' misrepresentation law.

(v) Non-disclosure

Section 2(1) does not apply to *pure non-disclosures* (5.1.3) since an *active misrepresentation* is required under the MA (*Banque Financière de la Cité SA v Westgate Insurance Co* (1989)).

 Pause for reflection

The scope of section 2(1) includes: (i) common law fraud; (ii) common law negligent misrepresentations; and (iii) some misrepresentations which would be regarded as 'innocent' under the common law. Only *'purely innocent'* misrepresentations and non-disclosure cases fall outside the scope of section 2(1).

5.3.1.2 The remedial advantages of a section 2(1) claim: the 'fiction of fraud'

A complex body of law governs the award of damages for misrepresentation. It is now settled that:

(i) **The basic measure of damages** under the MA (as with fraudulent or negligent misrepresentations at common law) is the tortious or reliance measure (*Doyle v Olby* (1969), *Royscot Trust Ltd v Rogerson* (1991)) and not the contractual measure as some initially suggested (eg Lord Denning in *Gosling v Anderson* (1972)). The reliance measure aims to protect the representee's *status quo interest* by putting her, as far as money can do, in the position she would have been in had the misrepresentation *not been made* (ie the contract not entered).

(ii) **The starting point** is that the representee can recover for:

- reduction in property value at the time of contracting: where the representee is induced to buy some property, she is entitled to the difference between the price paid and the actual market value of the property at the time the contract was entered; and

- consequential losses: the representee can recover damages for other 'out of pocket' losses such as personal injury, loss of or damage to property, and wasted expenses.

(iii) **The 'fiction of fraud'**: the generous common law measure for fraud applies to claims under section 2(1); the representor is liable for damages *as if* she was fraudulent *even though* she was not (*Royscot Trust v Rogerson*). This has been criticised for yielding an unjustifiably favourable measure of damages where the representor was merely negligent or simply unable to prove that she was not negligent. We will first examine the remedial advantages conferred by the fiction of fraud and then assess the criticisms of the fiction. **Diagram 5F** gives an overview of the advantages of the fraud measure over the negligence measure at common law and the extent to which the section 2(1) claims mimic the fraud measure.

Doyle v Olby (Ironmongers) Ltd (1969) and *Smith New Court Securities Ltd v Scrimgeour Vickers (Asset Management) Ltd* (1997) set out the main principles in assessing damages for fraud.

1. **Causation**: in cases of fraud, damages are calculated on the *assumption* that the representee would not have entered the contract 'but for' the misrepresentation, hence she can claim *all* her losses from *entering* the contract. This position is mimicked by section 2(1) claims.[8] It is only if the representor can show that the representee would have entered the contract anyway (without the fraud) that the claim for damages will fail. In contrast, in cases of negligent misrepresentation, it *is* relevant that the representee might have entered the contract anyway, even if on different terms, since this affects the causal connection between the misrepresentation and the loss claimed (*South Australia Asset Management Corp v York Montague Ltd* (1997)).

2. **No remoteness limit**: whilst damages for negligent misrepresentation are limited to losses which were reasonably foreseeable by the other party (ie not too remote),

---

[8] *Downs v Chappell* (1997); *Smith New Court Securities v Scrimgeour Vicker; Avon Insurance plc v Swire Fraser* (2001).

Diagram 5F The remedial advantages of the 'fiction of fraud'

	Fraud	s 2(1)	Negligence
✓ = yes ✗ = no			
1. 'But for' causation	✗	✗	✓
2. Remoteness limit	✗	✗	✓
3. Claim for devaluation of property *after* contract formation	✓	✓	✗
4. Claim for loss of opportunity	✓	✓	✗
5. Reduction of claim for contributory negligence	✗	✗ ✓ if concurrent action in negligence	✓
6. Exemplary damages	✓	✓	✗
7. Limitation of claim	6 years from *discovery*	may not mimic fraud (?)	6 years from *making of statement*

damages for deceit are not so limited; the claimant can recover *all* losses flowing from the fraud, even if they were unforeseeable by the representor.

3. 'Existing flaw' and being 'locked into the property': we noted that the representee is entitled to the difference between the price paid and the market value of the property *at the time the purchase was made*. In cases of fraud, the representee must mitigate her loss on discovery of the fraud, but she can claim for falls in the value of the property *after* contract formation, even if unforeseeable, if: 'either (a) the misrepresentation has continued to operate after the date of the acquisition of the asset so as to induce the plaintiff to retain the asset or (b) the circumstances of the case are such that the plaintiff is, by reason of the fraud, locked into the property' (**Smith New Court v Scrimgeour Vickers**). In this case, SV's fraudulent misrepresentation about the presence of rival bidders induced SNC to buy shares for £23 million when the market price at the time was £21.8 million (on the true facts). The House of Lords allowed SNC's claim for:

✓ the difference between these figures;

✓ SNC's loss due to *'existing flaws'* in the property: the subsequent discovery of an unconnected and unknown fraud in the company meant that the value of the shares at the time of the contract (had the fraud been known) was only £12.25 million. The House of Lords drew an analogy with someone who is fraudulently induced to buy an already diseased racehorse which later dies; he can recover the entire price paid;[9] and

[9] *Naughten v O'Callaghan* (1990).

✓ SNC's loss due to being *'locked into' the property*: since it was not commercially feasible for SNC to resell the shares immediately on discovering the fraud, it suffered further losses from a general fall in the share market. The shares were eventually sold for £11.75 million.

In short:

£23.00 million = Price paid

£21.80 million = Devaluation due to fraud

£12.25 million = Further devaluation due to existing flaw

£11.75 million = Further devaluation due to being locked into property; price received.

Damages = £23 million – £11.75 million = **£11.25 million**

4. **Loss of opportunity**: in principle, reliance damages for fraud are different from expectation damages for breach of contract but, in practice, the two measures can yield the same sum where reliance damages includes 'loss of opportunity' to make another similarly profitable contract.[10]

The idea is that, *if* the representee had not been induced into the contract with the representor, she would have invested it in *another* similar profit-making contract. Therefore, to restore her to the position that she would have been in had she not entered *this* contract, damages must include the loss of profits that she would have made from entering *another* similar contract not tainted by misrepresentation. The representee can even recover loss to reflect the fact that, but for the misrepresentation, she would have made a more profitable contract (ie on better terms) with the representor (*Clef Aquitaine SARL v Laporte Materials Ltd* (2001)). In theory, this is distinct from the contract measure (which puts the representee in the position she would be in if the statement was *true*) but, in practice, the difference is invisible because the contract measure is used to *quantify* the measure of the loss of opportunity. Sedley J conceded that 'loss of opportunity' 'mimic[s] reasoning more familiar in contract' (*Clef Aquitaine*). *In East v Maurer* (1991), E was induced to buy a hairdressing business for £20,000 by M's fraudulent misrepresentation that he had no intention of working regularly in another hairdressing salon in the same town. In fact, M did so and many of his clients followed him, resulting in significant trading losses to E, who eventually sold the business for £5,000. The court awarded E:

✓ the difference between what E paid and what was received;

✓ E's wasted expenditure, eg in trying to improve the business; *and*

✓ £10,000, representing the loss of profits which E would have made from buying another similar hairdressing business. In quantifying this, the court referred to the profit that the salon actually purchased would have made *if the representation had been true*.

In *4Eng Ltd v Harper* (2007), H sold 4Eng, a company with fraudulent practices which subsequently went into liquidation. 4Eng's damages included its loss of opportunity to acquire another company, T, in which it was seriously considering investing at the

---

[10] This reasoning led Fuller and Perdue, in 'The Reliance Interest in Contract Damages' (1936) 46 *Yale LJ* 52, 60 to argue that contract damages are in fact merely a surrogate for the more justifiable reliance (tortious) damages (1.4.2).

time it acquired H's company. David Richards J held that, in a deceit claim, 'a loss is too remote only if it is not in the eyes of the law directly caused by a defendant's deceit'. On the balance of probabilities, the judge found that 4Eng would have bought T had it not been for H's fraud, and awarded substantial damages to reflect lost capital value and profits, discounted for any uncertainties.

5. **Contributory negligence:** while damages for *negligent* misrepresentation can be reduced if the loss was partly the representee's fault (LR(CN)A, s 1), damages for fraud are immune from this reduction (*Alliance & Leicester BS v Edgestop Ltd* (1993)). The 'fiction of fraud' points to section 2(1) claims being likewise immune. However, in *Gran Gelato v Richcliff (Group)*, Nicholls VC held that contributory negligence *can* bite 'where there are concurrent claims . . . in negligence in tort and under the Act of 1967'. Ironically, it would be the *representor* who would have the incentive to argue that she owes and has breached a tortious duty of care against the representee, in order to bring the latter's contributory negligence into account.

6. **Damages for non-pecuniary loss:** damages for worry and inconvenience (*Jones v Emerton-Court* (1983)), and for mental and physical suffering (*Shelley v Paddock* (1980)), can be awarded for fraud.

7. **Exemplary damages:** it is arguable that exemplary damages may now be available for fraudulent misrepresentation (13.2.1).

Although the fraud measure of damages is supported by the literal wording of section 2(1) and by the Law Reform Committee Report,[11] the 'fiction of fraud' measure of damages has attracted the criticism that 'fools should not be treated as if they were rogues'.[12]

- It is widely thought to be undesirable and unjustifiable to treat non-fraudulent misrepresentors as if they were fraudulent, since the rules on fraud are justified by considerations of morality and deterrence. SNC's full compensation for all its losses is justified by 'considerations of morality and deterrence', which do not apply where the misrepresentation is negligent (*Smith New Court v Scrimgeour Vickers*).

- It is unlikely that the legislature really intended unintentional misrepresentation to attract the same moral opprobrium as deceit, and section 2(2) signals the legislature's intention to differentiate between them.[13]

- The House of Lords in *Smith New Court Securities v Scrimgeour Vickers* notes the 'trenchant academic criticisms' of the fiction of fraud. It declined to comment on the correctness of *Royscot Trust v Rogerson* while questioning whether 'the rather loose wording of the statute compels the court to treat a person who was morally innocent as if he was guilty of fraud when it comes to the measure of damages' (see also *Avon Insurance v Swire* (2001) and *Yam Seng v International Trade* (2013)).

---

[11] Law Reform Committee, *Innocent Misrepresentation* (10th Report, Cmnd 1782, 1962); and see *F&B Entertainments Ltd v Leisure Enterprises Ltd* (1976) 461, where Walton J, a member of the Law Reform Committee, indicates that the deceit measure was intended by the Committee.

[12] *Anson's* at 350; A Fairest, 'Misrepresentation and the Act of 1967' (1967) 25 *CLJ* 239, 244; R Hooley, 'Damages and the Misrepresentation Act 1967' (1991) 107 *LQR* 547, 549–51; cf P S Atiyah and G Treitel, 'The Misrepresentation Act 1967' (1967) 30 *MLR* 369, 373; J Cartwright, *Unequal Bargaining: A Study of Vitiating Factors in the Formation of Contracts* (Clarendon Press, 1991) 131–2.

[13] I Brown and A Chandler, 'Deceit, Damages and the Misrepresentation Act 1967, s2(1)' (1992) *LMCLQ* 40.

- Section 2(1) is said to be out of step with modern developments. It is the product of the Law Reform Committee's report, published in 1962 when it was not thought to be the 'general function of the civil law to grade the damages which an injured person may recover in accordance with the moral guilt of the defendant'.[14] Since 1962, the law *has* come to reflect the relative degree of moral fault in damages awards (eg *The Wagon Mound (No 1)*, tying liability to foreseeability, and *Hedley Byrne v Heller*, recognising lesser liability for negligent misrepresentation than for deceit). Section 2(1) is out of line with this approach.

 Counterpoint

The arguments do not all go one way. The *representee's* position must also be weighed in the balance. The aim of the MA was to *simplify and enhance protection* for the victims of contract-inducing misrepresentations by lowering the qualifying conditions for damages *in tandem with* awarding the most advantageous measure of damages.[15] Dispensing the representee from proving fraud or negligence but still awarding fraud damages straightforwardly achieves simplification and greater protection for the representee. If the default measure for section 2(1) claims is the negligence measure, the representee would revert to the position of having to prove fraud to access the fraud damages, so undermining the aims of the MA. Moreover, the fraud measure merely compensates the representee for her *provable* losses (it does not give her a windfall) and this does not seem inherently unjust.

5.3.2 Advantages to claiming fraud over section 2(1)

Despite the advantages of a section 2(1) damages claim, including the 'fiction of fraud', there are still some advantages in claiming fraud over section 2(1) that may make fraud the preferable route:[16]

(i)   Fraud makes statements of opinion, law, or intention actionable.

(ii)   Reliance or inducement is easier to establish:

- there is no need to show materiality;
- the claimant need not believe the misrepresentation (*Zurich Insurance v Hayward*);
- 'but for' causation is not required for *rescission* for fraud; and
- the representor cannot argue that the claimant might still have entered into the contract absent the misrepresentation.

(iii) Time only runs, in respect of the bar of rescission based on lapse of time, from the representee's discovery of fraud (not from time of contract).

---

[14] Law Reform Committee, *Innocent Misrepresentation* (10th Report, Cmnd 1782, 1962) para 22.

[15] A Fairest, 'Misrepresentation and the Act of 1967' (1967) 25 *CLJ* 239, 243–4; Law Reform Committee, *Innocent Misrepresentation* (10th Report, Cmnd 1782, 1962) para 22; J Cartwright, *Unequal Bargaining: A Study of Vitiating Factors in the Formation of Contracts* (Clarendon Press, 1991) 131–2.

[16] J Cartwright, *Misrepresentation, Mistake and Non-Disclosure* (4th edn, Sweet & Maxwell, 2016) 101, 155 et seq.

(iv)   The bar to rescission of mutual restitution operates less stringently for fraud.

(v)   Fraud relaxes the requirement that the representee must communicate her election to rescind to the representor (*Car & Universal Finance v Caldwell*).

(vi)   Under section 2(2) MA, rescission cannot be barred and damages awarded in lieu of rescission in fraud cases.

(vii)   Contributory negligence (at common law or under the LR(CN)A) is no defence against fraud damages.

(viii)   The limitation period for fraud is six years after it was or could have been discovered (rather than six years after the cause of action accrues, when the statement is made). *Garden Neptune Shipping Ltd v Occidental World Wide Investment Corp* (1990) suggests that the fraud limitation period of six years may *not* apply under section 2(1).

(ix)   Exclusion clauses are ineffective against fraud (5.4).

5.3.3 **Other money claims: expectation damages, restitution, and indemnity**

Facts supporting an actionable misrepresentation under section 2(1) may also yield other money claims in addition to or instead of a section 2(1) claim, as **Diagram 5E**, columns III–V show. An understanding that they rest on different bases and yield potentially different measures of damages will enable a claimant to decide which claim, or combination of claims, is most advantageous in her circumstances. The possible claims are the following:

(i) **Damages on the contract** where the representation is incorporated as a term of the contract.

The following all aim to restore the representee to the position she would be in had she not entered the contract:

(ii) **Restitution on rescission** (5.2.1): where the contract is rescinded for misrepresentation, the representor must return any benefit (money or non-money) received under the contract.

(iii) **Indemnity on rescission** of any costs incurred in discharging legal obligations necessitated by the (now rescinded) contract must be paid by the representor since they would not have been incurred by her had there been no contract. In *Whittington v Seale-Hayne* (1900), W was induced to lease premises for breeding prize poultry by S's innocent misrepresentation that the premises were in good sanitary condition. In fact, the water supply was contaminated. W's manager became sick and the poultry died. The court allowed rescission of the lease and indemnity-based recovery for what was spent on rent, rates, and the replacement of drains which had been ordered by the local authority, since these expenses were incurred in meeting 'obligations created by the contract' (the seller would have been liable for them had he kept the property). However, W could not recover for the lost stock, the manager's medical expenses, or the loss from being required to remove the poultry shed W built. These reliance losses would now be available under section 2(1) MA unless S could prove its honesty and reasonable basis in making the statement.

(iv) **Damages in lieu of rescission** under section 2(2) of the 1967 Act if the court exercises its discretion to bar rescission (5.2.3).

5.3.4 Combination of claims

Any item of loss can only be claimed once (*Archer v Brown* (1984)). The rule of thumb is that a claimant must choose between going 'forwards' and 'backwards'; she cannot do both at the same time. Thus, claimants *can*:

- go 'backwards' and claim (a) restitution and indemnity on rescission (or damages in lieu of rescission), plus (b) reliance damages, (c) loss of opportunity to make profits from another contract, and (d) exemplary damages; or
- go 'forwards' and claim remedies for breach of contract.

Claimants *cannot*:

✗ simultaneously go *forwards* and *backwards* by claiming expectation damages and either reliance damages or rescission; or

✗ go *backwards in money and in kind* by claiming rescission *and* either damages in lieu of rescission or devaluation of the property acquired under the contract.

5.4 Exemption of liability for misrepresentation

At common law, a party **cannot exclude or restrict liability for fraud** (*S Pearson & Son v Dublin Corp* (1907)). A party may attempt to limit or exclude liability for **non-fraudulent** misrepresentations via:

(i) Terms that overtly exempt liability for misrepresentation.

(ii) 'No representation' or 'no reliance' clauses: these seek to prevent the claimant from establishing one of the requirements of an actionable misrepresentation by agreement to a state of affairs that may not actually be true, ie that the defendant did make any representations or the claimant did rely upon them.

(iii) Entire agreement clauses: these clauses state that the written contract constitutes the 'entire agreement' between them. They prevent the claimant from arguing that the defendant's statement amounted to a collateral term or contract, which the defendant has breached, but they do not exempt liability for misrepresentation.

The effectiveness of such clauses depends on their construction and on statutory provisions.

5.4.1 Construction

To avoid liability for misrepresentation, the relevant clause must be interpreted (or 'construed') according to the ordinary principles applicable to exemptions of liability (10.5). In *AXA Sun Life v Campbell Martin* (2011), a term, referred to as an 'Entire Agreement' clause, stated: 'This Agreement . . . constitute the entire agreement and understanding between you and us in relation to the subject matter thereof . . . [It] shall supersede any prior promises, agreements, representations, undertakings or implications whether made orally or in writing . . .' This clearly excluded any collateral terms. But does it also operate as a no-representation clause?

Rix LJ held that an exclusion of liability for misrepresentation must be *clearly* stated either by express exclusions of liability, or by no-representation or no-reliance clauses; otherwise, talk of the contract superseding prior 'representations' will not by itself absolve the defendant of misrepresentation. On the facts, the clause was *ineffective* as a no-representation clause because, inter alia the word 'representations' was 'completely sandwiched between words of contractual import'; that is, the surrounding clauses were concerned with the scope of the contractual agreement, whereas the effect of misrepresentations is quite distinct.

5.4.2 **Evidential and contractual estoppel**

Until recently, courts have held that a 'no-reliance' clause may raise an 'evidential estoppel' to prevent the representee from claiming for misrepresentation, but only if the representor satisfies the court that she believed the representee did not rely on the representation (*Watford Electronics v Sanderson* (2001)).

However, *Springwell Navigation Corp v JP Morgan* (2010) held that the representor can rely on the clause even if she knew the representee *did* rely on the representation. The Court of Appeal held that there is nothing in principle to prevent parties from *contractually* agreeing upon the existence of a fictitious state of affairs; such clauses give rise to a 'contractual estoppel' which *prevents* the claimant in a misrepresentation action from alleging facts inconsistent with the contractual agreement. This approach is affirmed by the Court of Appeal in *AXA Sun Life Services v Campbell Martin* (2011).

The label 'contractual estoppel' seems misleading since the ground bears very little family resemblance to the other doctrines of estoppel (3.2); in particular, the defendant need not show that it would be unconscionable for the other party to resile from the agreed state of affairs. In truth, these are simply contractual terms.

5.4.3 **Statutory controls**

Even if a term seeking to exempt liability is properly incorporated (10.3.3) and construed to cover the situation (5.4.1), it is still subject to various statutory tests of validity.

5.4.3.1 **Section 3 MA 1967**

This section provides that a term which excludes or restricts *liability* or the available *remedies* for misrepresentation 'shall be of no effect except insofar as it satisfies the requirement of **reasonableness** as stated in section 11(1) of the Unfair Contract Terms Act 1977' (11.5.5.2); the onus is on a person claiming to rely upon the exemption to show that it is reasonable. Section 3 has been amended to remove the control of exemptions of misrepresentation liability in consumer contracts and transfer their control to CRA 2015 (5.4.3, 11.6).

Two questions arise in respect of non-consumer contracts:

- Does the clause come within the scope of section 3; ie does it exclude or restrict liability or the available remedies for misrepresentation?
- If so, does it satisfy the requirement of reasonableness?

The scope of section 3 terms includes:

✓ *excluding liability* for damages for misrepresentation, and

✓ presumably terms excluding the right to rescind or set up misrepresentation as a defence.

✗ It does not cover terms that limit the agent's authority, even though the effect is to exempt liability.

Section 3 does not expressly cover terms that prevent any liability from arising in the first place, eg a 'no reliance' clause. Do these come within section 3? The authorities are inconsistent:

✗ In *Springwell Navigation*, the Court of Appeal held that a party's agreement that it had made its decision to contract independently, without relying on the other party, and that it was fully familiar with the risks, created a contractual estoppel to the effect that any statement by the other would amount to merely one of opinion and was not within section 3.

✓ However, a sentence in the same paragraph stating that the other party would not be liable for any loss unless it was caused by gross negligence or wilful misconduct was within section 3.

✓ Aikens LJ said that a statement that ' . . . no representation or warranty, express or implied, is or will be made' by the relevant party 'is more difficult to classify', but he was inclined to treat it as falling within section 3. In *AXA Sun Life v Campbell Martin*, Stanley Burnton LJ held (obiter) that any contrary view would be 'too formalistic', adding that the matter should be looked at 'sensibly and practically'.

 Pause for reflection

In favour of the enforceability of 'no-representation' and 'no-reliance' clauses (and so exclusion from section 3's control) are the following:

✓ *Freedom of contract:* parties are entitled to agree what they like.

✓ *Certainty:* it may be desirable to settle a disagreement as to an existing state of affairs in order to establish a clear basis for the contract itself and its subsequent performance.

✗ Against the enforceability of 'no-representation' and 'no-reliance' clauses, the concerns are that of *unfairness and lack of consent:* here, the parties' bargaining power is important. In *Raiffeisen Zentralbank Osterreich AG v Royal Bank of Scotland* (2010), Christopher Clarke J said that:

> . . . If sophisticated commercial parties agree, in terms of which they are both aware, to regulate their future relationship by prescribing the basis on which they will be dealing

→

→

with each other and what representations they are or are not making, a suitably drafted clause may properly be regarded as establishing that no representations (or none other than honest belief) are being made or are intended to be relied on . . ..

Per contra, to tell the man in the street that the car you are selling him is perfect and then agree that the basis of your contract is that no representations have been made or relied on, may be nothing more than an attempt retrospectively to alter the character and effect of what has gone before, and in substance an attempt to exclude or restrict liability.

Ultimately, the question is whether a misrepresentation was made:

✗ if the evidence, including the clause, shows that the representee did not, or was not entitled to, rely on a misrepresentation, then section 3 does not apply; but

✓ if the contract *was* induced by misrepresentation, section 3 applies, and its effect cannot be excluded (*Cremdean v Nash* (1977)).

As Toulson J said in *IFE Fund SA v Goldman Sachs International* (2006):

✓ If a seller of a car said to a buyer 'I have serviced the car since it was new, it has had only one owner and the clock reading is accurate', those statements would be representations, and they would still have that character even if the seller added the words 'but those statements are not representations on which you can rely' . . .

✗ If, however, the seller of the car said 'The clock reading is 20,000 miles, but I have no knowledge whether the reading is true or false', the position would be different, because the qualifying words could not fairly be regarded as an attempt to exclude liability for a false representation arising from the first half of the sentence.

In sum:

✓ **exclusions of liability or of an otherwise available remedy for misrepresentation** are within the scope of section 3 (*Walker v Boyle* (1982));

? **no-representation' or 'no-reliance' clauses** may be within the scope of section 3;

✗ **entire agreement clauses** which merely prevent the finding of any collateral term or contract relating to the subject matter of the main agreement are *outside* the scope of section 3 (*Watford Electronics v Sanderson* (2001)); but

✗ they may come within section 3(2)(b)(i) of UCTA, which controls for unreasonableness terms that entitle a business to render performance that is substantially different from that reasonably expected of it.

The reasonableness requirement is determined in accordance with section 11 of UCTA (11.5.5.2 for a full explanation of this test). In contrast to exemptions for breach, courts seem relatively willing to uphold exemptions for misrepresentation, eg in *Cleaver v Schyde Investments* (2011) Etherton LJ said:

. . . there is nothing self-evidently offensive, in terms of reasonableness and fairness, in a contractual term which restricts a purchaser's right to rescind the contract in the event of the vendor's misrepresentation to cases of fraud or recklessness or where the property differs substantially in quantity, quality or tenure from what the purchaser had been led to expect, and to confine the purchaser to damages in all other cases. That is a perfectly rational and commercially justifiable apportionment of risk in the interests of certainty and the avoidance of litigation. While each case turns on its own particular facts, the argument in favour of upholding such a provision as a matter of the commercial autonomy of the contracting parties is particularly strong where, as here, (1) the term has a long history, (2) it is a well established feature of property transactions, (3) it is endorsed by the leading professional body for qualified conveyancers, (4) both sides are represented by solicitors, and (5) the parties (through their solicitors) have negotiated variations of other provisions in the standard form.

Likewise, in *Lloyd v Browning* (2013), liability was excluded where the seller had misrepresented the extent of planning permission, which reduced the value of the farmland sold by £55,000. A clause in the contract stipulated that the buyer had entered the agreement solely on the basis of his inspection, and had not been induced by any statement made by the seller except for written responses to pre-contractual inquiries. The Court of Appeal approved such clauses as facilitating certainty and forestalling disputes. It endorsed the approach of *FoodCo UK LLP (t/a Muffin Break) v Henry Boot Developments Ltd* (2010) to the reasonableness assessment of such clauses. In this case, the term was reasonable since: (1) each side was legally advised and the buyer had also instructed architects and planning consultants; (2) the law required sale of land contracts to be in a signed contractual document; (3) the clause was not of the 'take-it-or-leave-it' type sometimes imposed in small print; it was a special condition agreed by both parties' lawyers, with equal negotiating positions; (4) the term was used by the regional law society and in common use; and (5) had the buyers wished to rely on an oral statement, they could have made a written pre-contractual inquiry and relied upon the written response.

Similar considerations were decisive in upholding the term in *AXA* (5.4.1).

Ironically, once exemptions are interpreted as not covering fraud, more exemptions are likely to satisfy the reasonableness requirement and be effective against claimants (*Govt of Zanzibar v British Aerospace*).

However, a clause in the lease which purported to exclude liability for reliance on any statement made by the landlord failed the test of reasonableness in *First Tower Trustees Ltd v CDS (Superstores International) Ltd* (2017). A landlord was liable for the cost of remedial works to remove asbestos and of alternative warehouse accommodation whilst those works were carried out where it had misrepresented to the tenant, in its replies to pre-contract enquiries, that it had no knowledge of any environmental problems affecting the property. The non-reliance clause was an attempt retrospectively to alter the character and effect of what had gone before and was therefore in substance an attempt to exclude or restrict liability, engaging section 3 MA. The burden was on the landlord to prove its reasonableness. Given the well-recognised importance of pre-contractual enquiries, it was highly unreasonable for the landlord to withhold, in its replies to those enquiries, knowledge of a serious problem.

5.5 **The regime governing consumers**

5.5.1 **Misleading and aggressive practices against consumers**

In consumer transactions, the European Unfair Commercial Practices Directive[17] requires Member States to prohibit, and to provide 'adequate and effective' means to combat, unfair commercial practices; these include misleading and aggressive practices. The Directive and the Regulations passed to implement it[18] criminalise such unfair commercial practices. In addition, a 2014 amendment inserted in Part 4A of the **Consumer Protection from Unfair Trading Regulations 2008** allows consumers to seek redress where misleading[19] or aggressive practices by businesses have caused them to enter the contract or to make payments for goods or services (including digital content).

Regulation 5 defines **'misleading actions'** as:

✓ any false information in relation to the contract;

✓ if the overall presentation in any way deceives or is likely to deceive the average consumer, even if the information is factually correct;

✓ any marketing of a product (including comparative advertising) which creates confusion with any products, trade marks, trade names, or other distinguishing marks of a competitor; and

✓ any failure by a trader to comply with a commitment contained in a code of conduct with which the trader has undertaken to comply.

This must cause or be likely to cause the average consumer to take a transactional decision she would not have taken otherwise.

Regulation 7 defines **'aggressive commercial practices'** as conduct that significantly impairs or is likely significantly to impair the average consumer's freedom of choice or conduct in relation to the product concerned through the use of:

✓ harassment;

✓ coercion (including the use of physical force); or

✓ undue influence (ie exploiting a position of power so as to apply pressure, even without using or threatening to use physical force, in a way which significantly limits the consumer's ability to make an informed decision);

and it thereby causes or is likely to cause the consumer to take a transactional decision she would not have taken otherwise.

In determining whether a commercial practice uses harassment, coercion, or undue influence, account should be taken of:

(a) its timing, location, nature, or persistence;

(b) the use of threatening or abusive language or behaviour;

---

[17] Directive 2005/29 on unfair commercial practices [2005] OJ L149/22.

[18] The Consumer Protection from Unfair Trading Regulations 2008 (SI 2008/1277), reg 29; Business Protection from Misleading Marketing Regulations 2008 (SI 2008/1276), reg 29.

[19] There is no right to bring a claim for a misleading omission.

(c)   the exploitation by the trader of any specific misfortune or circumstance of such gravity as to impair the consumer's judgment, of which the trader is aware, to influence the consumer's decision with regard to the product;

(d)   any onerous or disproportionate non-contractual barrier imposed by the trader where a consumer wishes to exercise rights under the contract, including rights to terminate a contract or to switch to another product or another trader; and

(e)   any threat to take any action which cannot legally be taken.

A good example is *R v Waters (Oliver Frederic)* (2016), where a company sold reclining armchairs in an aggressive and intimidating manner to vulnerable elderly (or very elderly) customers. They used high pressure sales techniques, refusing to leave the customers' homes until large deposits had been paid, attempting to prevent customers from withdrawing from unfair transactions, attempting to retain as much money as they could in the event of cancellation by their approach to settlements, and requiring consumers to keep the original offer and the settlement confidential to prevent the customers seeking advice. The company and its director were convicted of engaging in unfair commercial practice contrary to the 2008 Regulations.

The remedies available to a consumer are:

*   a right to unwind the contract and receive a full refund;[20] or
*   a right to a discount of 25, 50, 75, or 100% in respect of past or future payments due, depending on the seriousness of the incident;
*   in either case, the consumer can also claim damages for:

    (i)   consequential financial loss; and/or

    (ii)   alarm, distress, or physical inconvenience or discomfort,

    unless the trader can show that it used due diligence.

The right to claim such statutory remedies now exists alongside common law actions in misrepresentation, duress (Chapter 8), undue influence, and unconscionable bargains (Chapter 9), which are expensive and complex, and therefore little used by consumers. To avoid duplication of claims, consumers who can claim under the Consumer Protection from Unfair Trading Regulations 2008 in respect of the misrepresentation cannot claim under the MA.

5.6   The justification for remedying misrepresentations

Rescission and damages for **fraudulent or negligent** misrepresentations are readily explicable in terms of preventing the representor from profiting from her own *wrong* and ensuring that she compensates for the loss she has caused. The wider scope of liability under **section 2(1)** MA can be explained by the concern to raise the *standard of care* in pre-contractual negotiations: someone who makes statements to induce

---

[20] Assuming the product has not been fully consumed, and the consumer rejects it within 90 days of the later of the date of the contract or of its delivery or supply, and any goods supplied are made available for collection by the trader.

another to contract with her should take care to ensure that she does so honestly and on reasonable grounds, *and* can show that she has done so.

Something beyond the representor's wrongdoing or lack of care is required to explain *rescission for* purely **innocent** misrepresentations. Although Jessel MR (*Redgrave v Hurd* at 13) refers to the innocent misrepresentor's 'moral delinquency' in enforcing a beneficial contract obtained by a statement 'which he knows *now* to be false', this sort of constructive unconscientiousness (after the fact) is unhelpful in pinpointing the exact reason for invalidating the contract. Why, otherwise, does it not apply equally to widen the very narrow scope of operative mistake and frustration?

 Pause for reflection

It is helpful to understand misrepresentations as induced mistakes, invoking the rationale of the claimant's defective consent (6.3.7.3), rather than the misrepresentor's unconscientiousness. Nevertheless, the analogy with mistake is not exact. The explanation for the significantly wider scope of relief for misrepresentation than for mistake may lie in the parties' respective degrees of responsibility for the mistakes and in the seriousness of the mistake. Thus, while spontaneous un-induced mistakes only operate if they are catastrophic (but then trigger the very serious consequence of voidness), a party's mistake induced by the other's misrepresentation is always operative (but only renders the contract voidable subject to various bars and adjustments). But, this suggests that a very serious misrepresentation should also be able to void the contract, for the defendant who has induced the claimant's mistake should not be better off than one who has not.

THIS CHAPTER IN ESSENCE

The key areas and core topics in this chapter are summarised in an easy-to-use list, ideal for revision purposes, on the online resources at www.oup.com/uk/chenwishart6e/. Links to websites relevant to the topics covered and any updates to the chapter can also be found on the online resources.

QUESTIONS

1 How can you tell whether a pre-contractual statement is: (a) a term; (b) an actionable misrepresentation; or (c) a puff? Why does it matter?

2 Explain (giving examples) the difference between:
   (a) damages for breach of contract;
   (b) damages for misrepresentation; and
   (c) money claims related to rescission.

3 When is, and when should, rescission be available for misrepresentation?

4 To what extent can a party exclude or restrict liability for misrepresentation?

5 Did the Misrepresentation Act 1967 improve the law on misrepresentation?

6 Katie wants to set up an ostrich farm and discusses with Leo the possibility of buying Leo's flock. Leo says:

You take them as they are. Get them checked if you like, but I'm an old hand and I say they're in the peak of health. I saw an article yesterday that said you'll get a 500% return. If you go ahead, my restaurant chain will be your best customer.

Katie buys Leo's ostriches. Advise Katie on the following facts:

(i) no orders were ever placed by Leo's restaurants;

(ii) 25% of the birds were sick at the time of purchase and died shortly after;

(iii) the article Leo mentioned is two years old; more recent and available market research shows declining consumer demand for ostrich meat; Katie can only sell the remaining flock at a loss.

 For hints on how to answer these questions, please see the online resources at www.oup.com/uk/chenwishart6e/

KEY FURTHER READING

See generally Cartwright, J (2006), *Misrepresentation* (2nd edn, Sweet & Maxwell).

Atiyah, P.S., and Treitel, G (1967), 'Misrepresentation Act 1967', 30 *MLR* 369.

Beale, H (1995), 'Damages in Lieu of Rescission for Misrepresentation', 111 *LQR* 60.

Brown, I, and Chandler, A (1992), 'Deceit, Damages and the Misrepresentation Act 1967, s 2(1)', *LMCLQ* 40.

Hooley, R (1991), 'Damages and the Misrepresentation Act 1967', 107 *LQR* 547.

6

Mistake

'I should not be bound as things really are'

Situations where parties enter contracts under mistake can trigger the application of many doctrines other than that of mistake. Thus, the mistake may be resolvable by other doctrines as **Diagram 6A** shows.

The law of mistake is riddled with very difficult distinctions, some of which have only superficial logic and can cut across each other to yield contradictory results, eg:

- *Mistakes as to **terms**/mistaken **assumptions** as to background fact*: this fundamental distinction lies in the difference between saying:

- 'I did not mean to buy that guitar' (this raises problems of contract formation (2.1.3) and mistake as to terms (6.1)); and

- 'I *did* mean to buy it, but only because I (mistakenly) thought it once belonged to Elvis' (this mistaken assumption may invalidate a prima facie valid contract).

However, the difference can reduce to vanishing point when the mistaken assumption relates to some *quality of the contract's subject matter*. It will be very difficult, in practice, to distinguish between the claims:

✗ 'I thought the guitar belonged to Elvis' (no relief unless mistake is judged to be 'fundamental'); and

✓ 'I thought you were *promising* that the guitar belonged to Elvis' (relief if mistake known by the other party)?

- *Common **law** and **equity*** impose different thresholds, and grant different forms of relief.

Diagram 6A Mistake and applicable legal doctrines

Nature of mistake	Applicable law
'I didn't mean to agree to *that*'	Objectivity and mistake as to terms (2.1.3)
	Uncertainty (2.6)
	Rectification (6.1.2)
	Non est factum (6.1.3)
	Incorporation (10.3.3)
	Interpretation (10.4)
	Implied terms (10.6)
'You *induced* my mistaken assumption'	Misrepresentation (Ch 5)
'You took *unfair advantage* of my mistake'	Unconscionable bargains (9.4)
	Rectification (6.1.2)
'I didn't *anticipate* the *change of circumstances*'	Frustration (Ch 7)
'I thought our agreement was *allowed*'	Illegality (Additional Chapter 2 available on the online resources)

- *Recognised categories* of *mistaken assumptions* attract different presumptions about their invalidity (6.3), eg:

✓ common mistakes as to the *existence or ownership* of the contractual subject matter will *void* the contract; but

✗ but common mistakes as to the *quality* of the subject matter will *not*.

However, the same mistake may be described in different ways to attract inconsistent assumptions.

The main questions to be addressed in this chapter are:

(i) *When* can a claimant obtain relief from her contractual obligations on the ground of mistake as to:

- the nature or contents of the contract?
- the other party's identity?
- the background facts or law surrounding the contract?

(ii) • *What* types of *relief* are available for such mistakes?

- What is the *justification* for any relief?

(iii) Is the current law *satisfactory*? How might it be *developed*?

The most fundamental distinction is between:

- Mistake as to **terms**: what is *in* the contract or what the contract is *for*.

- Mistake as to **background assumptions**: some fact or law that affects a party's reasons for entering the contract.

Diagram 6B gives an overview of the law on mistake.

Diagram 6B Overview of the law on mistake

	Unilateral	Common (shared)
Mistake as to TERM Contractual obligations (Formation)	• **Common law** if: (i) no objective offer and acceptance (2.1.3) (ii) unilateral mistake about nature of the document (*non est factum*) (6.1.3) • **Equity** if: (i) Mistake about recording of contract; rectification, 6.1.2.3) (ii) fundamental mistaken identity (6.2)	• Equity: rectification of written contract (6.1.2)
Mistaken assumptions Inducing the contract (Vitiation)	Action in misrepresentation if mistake is induced by the other party (Chapter 5)	• **Common Law** if: mistake is fundamental (6.3.1–6.3.5) ? **Equity** if less fundamental but still serious (6.3.6)

6.1 **Mistake as to terms**

6.1.1 **Unilateral mistake**

6.1.1.1 Invalidity of contracts at common law

When a party complains of a mistake as to what was agreed, the starting point must be the objective test of what was agreed (2.1). There is no contract if:

✗ the defendant knows of the complainant's 'mistake as to terms' so there is no mirror image offer and acceptance (2.1.3.1);

✗ the defendant made a misleading offer so that it is unreasonable for the defendant to bind the complainant (2.1.3.2); or

✗ the contract is tainted by latent ambiguity so that it is impossible to say objectively what the contract is for (2.1.3.3).

The invalidity of contracts in these circumstances has been presented as instances of exceptional resort to the subjective test of intentions (eg Chitty, para 3-022), but the preferable interpretation is that the law is simply applying the objective test, but that test is:

(i)   contextual, so that the question is what a reasonable defendant would believe the complainant was intending to agree to, given all the background context;

(ii) infused with the standard of reasonableness; and

(iii) can 'run out' in the case of latent ambiguity.

6.1.1.2 Denying specific performance at equity

Even if a unilateral mistake has no effect at common law (eg because the other party had no reason to know of it), the court may refuse specific performance against the mistaken party, although she may still be liable for damages at law (*Tamplin v James* (1880)). In *Barrow v Scammell* (1881), Bacon VC said:

. . . courts of equity have at all times relieved against honest mistakes and contracts, where the literal effect and the specific performance of them would be to impose a burden not contemplated, and which it would be against all reason and justice to fix, upon the person who, without the imputation of fraud, has inadvertently committed an accidental mistake; and also where not to correct the mistake would be to give an unconscionable advantage to the other party.

Most cases have involved mistakes as to terms, where, moreover, the other party contributed to the mistake (eg *Denny v Hancock* (1870)), but, in principle, it may also apply to mistaken assumptions (see *Chitty*, para 3-014).

6.1.2 **Common mistake in recording the contract: rectification**

Parties who wrongly record their agreement (eg the amount of the rent or the area of land to be sold) can apply for rectification to make the contract accurately reflect their agreement.

6.1.2.1 What must be proved?

Lord Hoffmann approved the following conditions for allowing rectification (*Chartbrook Ltd v Persimmon Homes Ltd* (2009)):

(i) The parties had a common **continuing** intention up to the execution of the instrument to be rectified, whether or not amounting to a concluded contract, in respect of a particular matter in the instrument.

(ii) There was an **outward expression** of accord: the test is objective. This requirement is not absolute; what is needed is evidence that the parties shared a common intention even if not put into words. It would include the party resisting rectification admitting the same understanding as the claimant (*Munt v Beasely* (2006)) or understandings that were so obvious that they were not spelt out (*JSL Ltd v MCP Investment Nominees Ltd* (2003)). *Chitty* (at para 3-067) states that: 'when A submits to B a draft which differs from the parties' earlier agreement, the correct approach in principle is to ask whether B realised or should reasonably have realised that the draft agreement was intended to differ from the prior agreement rather than to implement the prior accord.' Rectification is only available in the latter case. In *Joscelyne v Nissen* (1970), the daughter's agreement to purchase her father's business was rectified in line with the parties' continuing common intention that the daughter should pay all his household expenses, although the written agreement was silent on it and no prior contract existed on this issue.

(iii) The parties' common intention was not accurately reflected in the instrument by **mistake**, even if it is glaringly obvious (*Milton Keyes BC v Viridor (Community Recycling MK) Ltd* (2017)). The mistake must be in the *recording* of the contract and not in the *making* of it.

There is **no** *rectification* if there is:

(i) any confusion over what was agreed (*Cambro Contractors Ltd v John Kennelly Sales* (1994));

(ii) merely an *omission* to deal with some matter (*Kemp v Neptune Concrete* (1989));

(iii) an intention to vary the earlier agreement (*PT Berlian Laju Tanker v Nuse Shipping Ltd (The Aktor)*);

(iv) *no literal disparity* between the terms used in the parties' agreement and the document purporting to record it. Thus, rectification was denied in *Frederick E Rose v William H Pim Junior* (1953), where the parties entered an oral agreement for 'horse beans', later recorded in a written agreement, although both parties mistook them for 'feveroles' (the seller's innocent misrepresentation would have allowed rescission but the buyer wanted rectification so that he could claim expectation damages). In contrast, Megaw J held in *London Weekend Television v Paris and Griffith* (1969) that rectification is available where the parties *expressly* agreed the meaning of particular words used in the written contract; or

(v) *no shared mistake*, only unilateral mistake; a party is not mistaken if she is indifferent to the relevant matter (*Riverlate Properties v Paul* (1975)).

6.1.2.2 Rectification and interpretation

The court always had some power to correct mistakes in written contracts where: (i) the error is patent (ie obvious on the face of the instrument), and (ii) it is clear what correction should be made (*East v Pantiles Plant Hire Ltd* (1982)). Lord Hoffmann's more liberal approach to the interpretation of contract (10.4) would dispense with (i) above; it would be sufficient if the error emerges from a consideration of the background context. Recall that Lord Hoffmann said that if the court concludes that 'the parties must . . . have used the wrong words or syntax' or 'that something must have gone wrong with the language, the law does not require judges to attribute to the parties an intention which they plainly could not have had'. In *Cherry Tree Investments Ltd v Landmain Ltd* (2012), Arden LJ described this as a process of 'corrective interpretation'. Burrows has argued that this renders the rectification doctrine largely superfluous ('Construction and Rectification' in A Burrows and E Peel (eds), *Contract Terms* (OUP, 2007) 77).

However, Lewison LJ said that 'there is still a useful role for rectification to play' (*Cherry Tree*). In particular, he said that the court cannot, by the process of interpretation, insert whole clauses that the parties have mistakenly failed to include. This is especially so when it relates to a legal charge, which is a public document on a public register upon which third parties are expected to rely for an accurate picture of the state of the title to the land. In *Daventry DC v Daventry & District Housing Ltd* (2011), Lord Neuberger MR observed **three differences between interpretation and rectification:**

(i)   prior negotiations are admissible in a rectification claim (*Murray v Parker* (1854) 19 Beav 305), but not generally for interpretation (10.4.4);

(ii) the claimant for rectification must provide evidence of the parties' prior intention or understanding that deviates from the written contract; and

(iii) rectification is an equitable remedy and, therefore, subject to somewhat different rules from interpretation (eg no rectification if it would affect third party rights).

In *LSREF III Wight Limited v Millvalley Limited* (2016), a swap agreement had mistakenly referred to the wrong version of the master agreement. Cooke J refused to correct the mistake via interpretation; on the face of the documents, there was no ambiguity, no syntactical error, and no lack of commercial sense as to make it absurd. However, the agreement would be rectified.

6.1.2.3 Rectification for unilateral mistake

Rectification may be allowed for a unilateral mistake in recording the contract if it would be **inequitable** for the other party to object because the mistake results in benefit to the unmistaken party or detriment to the mistaken party, *and*:

(i)   she *actually*[1] knew of the mistake and of the mistaken party's real intentions (*Thomas Bates & Sons Ltd v Wyndhams Ltd* (1981); *Commission for the New Towns v Cooper* (1995)); or

(ii) she failed to draw the mistaken party's attention to the mistake, or made 'false and misleading statements' to divert the other from discovering the mistake (*Commission for the New Towns v Cooper*).

---

[1] Actual knowledge includes wilfully shutting one's eyes to the obvious, or wilfully and recklessly failing to make such inquiries as an honest and reasonable person would have made.

The contract may be enforced on the mistaken party's understanding.

 Pause for reflection

McLauchlan argues that rectification for unilateral mistake is simply the objective test of contract formation in action ('The "Drastic" Remedy of Rectification for Unilateral Mistake' (2008) 124 *LQR* 608). Rectification is allowed where *A* leads *B* into believing that *A* is agreeing to *B*'s terms (2.1.3.1). This also overlaps with the principles of contextual interpretation when something is thought to have 'gone wrong with the language' (10.4.2).

6.1.2.4 The *Chartbrook* extension

In *Chartbrook v Persimmon Homes* (2009), Lord Hoffmann said that rectification for common mistake only requires the document to differ from the parties' prior *objective* agreement; the parties need not be subjectively agreed. Thus, where *A* and *B* had different understandings of the prior agreement, which is then reduced to writing in accordance with *A*'s understanding, both parties can be said to be mistaken that the final written contract reflected their previous agreement and rectification is available.

 Counterpoint

1. The parties made *different* mistakes: *B* is mistaken as to the terms of the contract but *A*'s only 'mistake' is in thinking that *B* actually agrees to the contract.

2. It is odd to say that *A*'s mistake is legally relevant since *A* makes no mistake about the contract.

6.1.3 Unilateral mistake about the nature of the document: *non est factum*

6.1.3.1 The problem

The importance of ensuring the certainty and security of transactions means that a person is normally bound by her signature to a contractual document irrespective of her knowledge or understanding of its contents (10.3.3.1). The doctrine of *non est factum* ('this is not my deed') is an exception that can void a contract and any transfers of rights under it. It recognises that, in wholly exceptional circumstances (eg where the signer is blind or illiterate, and the nature or effect of the document is misrepresented to her), the interest of certainty may be outweighed by the concern for justice and the importance of ensuring a minimum of meaningful consent to the contract. However, in deference to certainty and security, the thresholds of the seriousness of the mistake made and the claimant's impairment are set very high.

In two-party cases, where *A* signs or executes a document under mistake as to its real nature and effect, relief may be available even without resort to *non est factum*:

- as a *misrepresentation*, if *B*'s misrepresentation has induced *A*'s mistake (*Lloyds Bank plc v Waterhouse* (1991)); or

- there is no contract, if *B* knows of *A*'s mistake as to terms or has negligently induced *A*'s mistake (2.1.3.1 and 2.1.3.2).

B's unconscientious conduct or knowledge entitles *A* to some remedy, even if *A* has been careless.

The case for *A*'s relief is much weaker in **three-party cases**. The situation may arise where *B*'s misrepresentation:

- induces *A* into a contract under which *A* transfers rights to *B*, which *B* then transfers to *D*; or

- induces *A* to contract with *D* who is ignorant of *B*'s misrepresentation (eg *United Dominion's Trust v Western* (1976)).

B disappears or is not worth suing; can *A* sue *D*? *A*'s catastrophic mistake as to the nature of the signed document must be balanced against protection of *D*, the third party good faith purchaser who relies on the document. The law resolves such cases by reference to the void–voidable distinction (see **Diagram 6C** (6.2)):

- If the mistake is sufficiently fundamental (6.1.3.2), the contract is void and the third party is not protected even as a bone fide purchaser (who has given consideration in ignorance of *A*'s rights).

- If the mistake is not sufficiently fundamental, the contract may be voidable if the original mistake was induced by *B*'s misrepresentation; *D* is only protected if *D* is a bona fide purchaser.

6.1.3.2 How serious must the mistake be?

There must be a *'fundamental'*, *'essential'*, *'radical'*, *'very substantial'*, or *'serious'* difference between the nature of the actual document and the document as it is believed to be (*Saunders v Anglia Building Society*, affirming *Gaillie v Lee* (1969)). The difference is one of *degree* rather than of kind: it must be determined by the 'difference in practical result', rather than 'difference in legal character'.

Instances of operative *non est factum* are rare:

✓ In *Foster v Mackinnon* (1869), M was induced to endorse a bill of exchange by a misrepresentation that it was a guarantee like one he had previously signed.

✗ *Non est factum* is rejected where the purpose of the contract is not fundamentally undermined. In *Saunders v Anglia Building Society*, S (a 78-year-old widow) wanted to help her nephew raise money on the security of her house, provided she could remain there for life. She signed a document without reading it, having broken her glasses and having been told that it was a deed of gift to her nephew. She actually signed a sale of her house to *L*, her nephew's friend (who had agreed with the nephew to raise money in his own name for the nephew because the latter wanted to avoid his wife's maintenance claim). *L* mortgaged the house to *A* but kept the money it raised. Although a gift to her nephew seems fundamentally different from a sale to his friend, the court held that it was not: her purpose of assisting her nephew by raising money on her house would have been achieved by the actual sale, had the nephew's friend paid up.

✗ No relief is available if *there is no positive mistake but mere ignorance*. In *Gillman v Gillman* (1946), a woman signed a separation deed in ignorance of its true nature, but without any positive idea of what she was signing. One should not sign something if one has no idea of its contents.

6.1.3.3 Who qualifies for relief?

Saunders v Anglia Building Society held that *non est factum* cannot normally be relied upon by literate persons of full capacity, but only to 'those who are permanently or temporarily unable through no fault of their own to have without explanation any real understanding of the purport of a particular document, whether that be from defective education, illness or innate incapacity', or from being tricked. A qualifying complainant must still take such care as could be expected of them. This was an alternative basis for denying relief to the widow in *Saunders v Anglia Building Society*. It was held that, while she might not have understood all the document's complexities, she could at least have checked the identity of the transferee. This carelessness may explain why she also failed to void the contract for mistaken identity. The requirement of care disqualifies a complainant who signs a document in blank leaving another to fill in the details (*United Dominion's Trust Ltd v Western*).

In **two-party cases,** the claimant's carelessness is irrelevant (*Peterlin v Cullen* (1975); *Bradley West Solicitors Nominee Co Ltd v Keenen* (1994)): it cannot lie in the fraudster's mouth to say that the complainant should not have been taken in, and the fraudster should not profit from her wrong.

In **three-party cases** where the contest is between two innocent parties, the complainant's carelessness is directly relevant to the question of who should bear the loss. The policies encouraging responsibility in contractual formation and protecting reasonable reliance on signatures would allocate the risk to the complainant whose mistake and careless signature initiated the disastrous train of events, rather than the innocent third party who has merely acted in reliance on the signed document.

6.2 **Mistake as to identity**

6.2.1 **The nature of the problem**

The typical problem arises where *A* makes an apparent contract with *B* believing *B* to be *C; A* passes property to *B* under this contract, but *B* fails to pay. *B* then passes the property to *D* in a subsequent transaction before *B* disappears or is not worth suing. Can *A* sue *D* for the return of the property?

$$A \rightarrow B(C) \rightarrow D$$

The legal response to this question is beset by 'illogical and sometimes barely perceptible distinctions' (*Shogun Finance Ltd v Hudson* (2002) and (2003)). Two factors have contributed to this:

(i) Several different doctrines with distinct lines of reasoning that can yield different results are inconsistently applied to the problem.

(ii) There is a failure to respond transparently to the relevant issues:

- In *two-party cases*, *B*'s fraud or knowledge that *A* only intends to contract with someone else is usually enough to deny *B* the contract.

- However, *three-party cases* raise different issues. The law must allocate the risk of *B*'s fraud between *A* and *D*.

The public interest in protecting the security of transactions is largely suppressed by the law's overly technical approach in deciding whether *B*'s transaction with *A* is void or voidable as illustrated in **Diagram 6C**.

Diagram 6C.1: where the *A*–*B* transaction is *void*, no legal title passes with the physical transfer of the property to *B*; *B* then cannot pass title to *D* (since *B* can give no better title than she has). Since the *legal title* to the property remains with *A*, *A* can recover the property from *D*, who is left unprotected.

Diagram 6C.2: where the *A*–*B* transaction is *voidable*, the contract is valid *until A rescinds it*. Until then, *B* obtains good legal title from *A* and can validly pass the property on to *D*. *D* is protected if *A* rescinds *after B* transfers title to *D*, and *D* is a 'bona fide purchaser for value' (ie *D* gave consideration for the property in ignorance of the defect in *B*'s title). *A* cannot recover the property from *D*; *A*'s only action is against *B* for reliance damages, if *B* can be found and is worth suing.

Diagram 6C.3: if *A* rescinds the **voidable** contract *before B* transfers the property to *D* as a bona fide purchaser, this revests title to the property in *A* from that point in time. *D* cannot subsequently obtain legal title from *B*, even if she obtains physical possession of it. *A* can then recover the property from *D*.

Look on the online resources to view this figure as a PowerPoint® presentation

Diagram 6C Void and voidable contracts in three-party cases

⟶ physical transfer of property
⇢ transfer of title to the property

1 If contract between A and B is void, A can recover property from D

2 If contract between A and B is voidable and A rescinds after B transfers to D, A cannot recover property from D if D is a good faith purchaser

3 If contract between A and B is voidable and A rescinds before B transfers to D, A can recover property from D even if D is a good faith purchaser

6.2.2 **Identity vs attributes**

The general rule is that a mistake as to the identity of the other party will only void a contract if it goes to the other party's 'identity' as opposed to merely her 'attributes' (eg as to solvency, character, or social position). The problems are that:

- the identity of a person is an accumulation of her respective attributes;
- a particular attribute of a person may be so *essential* that its absence voids the contract; and
- four sometimes *contradictory* 'rules' guide the courts in making the identity–attribute distinction: (i) objectivity; (ii) written contracts; (iii) non-existence of the identity assumed; and (iv) face-to-face dealings.

6.2.3 **Objectivity: you cannot accept someone else's offer**

The objective test of formation prevents a party from accepting an offer that she knows was not intended to be made to her. In *Bolton v Jones* (1857), J sent a written order for some goods to Brocklehurst, with whom J had previously dealt and against whom he could set-off (deduct) sums that Brocklehurst owed him. Bolton took over Brocklehurst's business and filled out J's order without disclosing the change of ownership. The court held that J need not pay since Bolton could not accept an offer that he *must have known* was not addressed to him. Likewise, there would be no valid contract if the offeror knows that the offeree has accepted an offer reasonably believing it came from another party. All of this assumes that the identity of the other contract party is *vital* to the complainant (*Ingram v Little* (1961); *Lewis v Averay* (1972)). If it is not, mistake as to identity does not bar formation. For example, retailers are not generally concerned about the identity of the shopper, or the auctioneer with the identity of the bidder (*Dennant v Skinner* (1948)).

6.2.4 **Written contracts**

Where a contract is reduced to writing, it can only be between the persons *named in a written contract as the parties* to the contract. In *Cundy v Lindsay* (1878), L received an order for goods from Blenkarn of '37 Wood Street, Cheapside', who had forged the signature of Blenkiron & Co of 123 Wood Street, with whom L had previously dealt. L sent the goods to Blenkarn, who sold them on to C. The House of Lords voided the contract for L's mistake of identity: L only made a contract with Blenkiron & Co, the party identified in the writing. C had to return the goods to L. The decision was applied by the House of Lords in *Shogun Finance v Hudson* (2003). S sold a car on hire purchase to R, a fraudster posing as 'Mr Patel', after checking the credit rating of Mr Patel, whose driver's licence R produced. R then sold on to H. The House of Lords allowed S to recover the car from H because the buyer's identity named in the agreement was crucially important to S; therefore, there was no valid contract between S and R. H could not rely on section 27 of the Hire Purchase Act 1964 (which protects a good faith third party who buys a car from the 'debtor' under a 'hire purchase agreement' before the debtor has acquired legal title to the car) because R was not such a 'debtor'.

Pause for reflection

1. The decision in *Shogun* can cut across other rules, eg that a contract is only voidable (not void) for mistaken identity where: (i) the mistaken identity is non-existent; and (ii) the contract is concluded by face-to-face dealings (6.2.5 and 6.2.6).

2. Lord Millett, dissenting, reasoned that the contract should only be voidable for misrepresentation (rather than void for mistake) because of the presumption that a party intends to deal with the person with whom she is *physically dealing*. Moreover, whether the parties deal face-to-face or *in writing*, a contract should come into being if there is a *sufficient correlation* between the offer and the acceptance. A good faith third party should be protected if she buys the property before the original owner rescinds the contract. Accordingly, the minority regarded *Cundy v Lindsay* as wrongly decided.

3. MacMillan explains *Cundy v Lindsay* as the result of 19th-century criminal law. It was assumed that 'convictions of the rogue for obtaining goods by false pretences necessarily meant that the contract was void', and the Larceny Act 1861 allowed the original owner to recover their goods from innocent third party buyers as long as they prosecuted the felon to conviction. Since this no longer applies, there is no sound basis for the decision in *Cundy* ('Rogues, Swindlers and Cheats: The Development of Mistake of Identity in English Contract Law' (2005) 63 *CLJ* 711).

6.2.5 **Non-existence of the identity assumed**

According to this rule, *A*'s mistake as to *B*'s identity will only void their contract if *A* mistook *B* for another existing and identifiable party, *C*. If *A* merely believes that *B* is *C* who is *non-existent* or unidentifiable, the contract is only voidable. In *King's Norton Metal Co Ltd v Edridge, Merrett & Co Ltd* (1897), K sent goods in response to an order from the fictitious 'Hallam & Co', written on headed stationery with a picture of a large factory and a list of overseas depots. The fraudster then sold the goods to E. Although the contract was in writing, the contract was only *voidable* for fraud because K intended to contract with the writer of the letter, being mistaken only as to his attributes; namely, solvency and respectability. The contract was not *void* for K's mistake that it was contracting with 'Hallam & Co' because 'Hallam & Co' was non-existent. 'If it could have been shown that there was a separate entity called Hallam & Co . . . then the case might have come within the decision in *Cundy v Lindsay*.'

It is difficult to see why *A* and *D*'s rights should depend on whether *A* mistook *B* for another *real* entity or not. Furthermore, why was it not enough in *King's Norton* that K believed that 'Hallam & Co' existed, when it did not?

This supposed rule is subject to two exceptions, which require impossible distinctions to be drawn:

(i) A contract may be voided if *A* makes the additional mistake that *C* exists, even if *C* does not exist. But is there a meaningful difference between *A* believing '*B* to be not *B*', and by implication someone else (contract not void); and *A* believing '*B* to be *C*, mistakenly believing that *C* exists' (contract is void)? After all, in *Lake v Simmons*

(1927), the mistress of a wealthy customer, a widower, purchased some items from L, and then persuaded L to let her take away valuable pearl necklaces for her 'husband's approval'. L's loss was only insured if no valid contract was made with the mistress. The court so found, although she was posing as a non-existent wife.

(ii) A contract is void when *A* believes that *B* who pretends to be *C* is not *B* (whether *C* exists or not), as long as there is an *implied term* that *B* is not *B* (*Said v Butt* (1920)), as where:

- an offer is made only to persons fitting particular descriptions which excludes *B* (eg 'current students of a particular university', or being 'over 18 years' to buy alcohol); or

- *B* may know from previous dealings that *A* is unwilling to contract with them (eg *B* is barred from a pub or a soccer match).

If the rationale is merely that *B* cannot accept an offer known not to be meant for her, then why did this not apply in *King's Norton Metal* when the fraudster must have known that K had no intention of contracting with him?

6.2.6 **Face-to-face dealings**

Where the parties deal with each other face to face (*inter praesentes*), the law presumes that each intends to deal with the 'person present, and identified by sight and hearing'. The contract is only voidable and bona fide third party purchasers who obtain title before the mistaken party rescinds the contract are protected. In *Phillips v Brooks Ltd* (1919), a fraudster selected some jewellery in P's shop and wrote a cheque for £3,000 saying 'I am Sir George Bullough', a person of good credit known by reputation to P. P used a directory to check the address the fraudster had given and accepted the cheque. The fraudster then pledged the jewellery to B for £350. P's mistake did not prevent the property passing to B. It was held that P *intended to sell to the person present in the shop*, even though P believed that person was Sir George Bullough, an identifiable and existing third party. The contract was only voidable for fraud.

The decision is difficult to reconcile with *Lake v Simmons* and *Ingram v Little*. In both cases, it could equally be said that the claimant intended to contract with the party before them. In *Ingram v Little* (1961), a fraudster calling himself 'Hutchinson' offered to buy the Ingram sisters' car, offering payment by cheque. On their insistence for cash, he gave his initials and address and described himself as a respectable businessman. The sisters did not know of this person, but ascertained his existence and address from the telephone directory. They then accepted the cheque, which was dishonoured. Meanwhile, the fraudster sold the car to L. The Court of Appeal held the original sale to be void, allowing the sisters to recover their car from L. Their checking of the telephone directory *rebutted the presumption* that they intended to deal with the person in front of them: they only intended to deal with Hutchinson.

Ingram was criticised in *Lewis v Averay* (1972), where structurally identical facts only made the contract voidable. A fraudster posing as a well-known actor Richard Green offered to buy L's car with a cheque. When L refused to let the car go until the cheque cleared, the fraudster produced an officially stamped pass to Pinewood Studios bearing the fraudster's photograph but the name 'Richard Green'. L then let the fraudster take the car which was sold on to A. The cheque was dishonoured. The court held that L intended to contract with the person before him, so that property validly passed to A via the fraudster; L could not recover his car.

The different results reached in *Phillips v Brooks* and *Lewis v Averay* on one side (contracts only voidable) and in *Lake v Simmons* and *Ingram v Little* on the other (contracts void) are impossible to reconcile. All the sellers (other than in *Lake*) took steps to check the alleged identity of the buyers: there is no difference between the merits of the respective sellers' claims. The conflict seems now to have been resolved in favour of **voidability** *unless the contract is in writing*. The House of Lords held in *Shogun Finance v Hudson* that the presumption against a contract being void for mistaken identity in face-to-face dealings is a strong one. Indeed, two of their Lordships even doubted the possibility of rebutting this presumption, although Lord Walker was prepared to accept it in wholly exceptional cases (eg where the fraudster impersonates a person known to the mistaken party whose senses are impaired). Nevertheless, despite the *face-to-face dealing* on the facts of *Shogun*, the majority of their Lordships sidestepped this presumption. The fact that S's written contract was with 'Mr Patel' trumped S's face-to-face dealing with R to void the contract.

 Counterpoint

The law's approach in asking whether the original contract is void or voidable does not address the real problem before the court in three-party cases; that is, how to balance the interests of innocent purchasers (*D*) who deal with the apparent owners of goods (*B*), with the interests of (*A*) innocent sellers who are duped into parting with their goods. Why should *D*'s rights depend on the particular way that *B* defrauds *A* (ie making *A* think *B* was '*C*' or just 'not *B*'; in person or in writing)? If such irrelevant criteria are adopted, it is unsurprising that the law becomes complex and incoherent. The crucial point is that it is *A* who assesses the risk and decides whether to sell on credit. This makes *A* better able to self-protect than *D* and so *A* should take the risk of mistake. The increase in identity theft (eg credit card fraud) underlines the importance of reform. Three alternative approaches can be suggested:

1. Good faith third party purchasers fully protected if they obtain title before rescission: the Law Reform Committee recommends that mistaken identity in sale of goods contracts should only be regarded as rendering the contract voidable ('Transfer of Title to Chattels' (12th Report (Cmnd 2958, 1966) at para 15)).

2. Loss sharing: Devlin LJ, dissenting in *Ingram v Little*, suggested loss sharing between the two innocent parties according to the *comparative negligence* of each. This mitigates the 'all-or-nothing' result of the void-voidable approach, but substitutes it with the uncertainty of assessing what counts as loss and how it should be apportioned. Loss apportionment on the basis of fault (contributory negligence) is still generally avoided by the common law.

3. Protection of third party change of position: the law of unjust enrichment allows recovery of mistaken transfers subject to the defence of change of position. This defence protects the recipient's innocent expenditure in reliance on the security of her receipt by offsetting that sum against that which must be returned. Accordingly, *A* should be able to recover

➡

the property (or its value) on condition that she compensates *D* for the price *D* paid for the property (or deducts this from the value returned). If, as will often happen, *D* acquired the goods at undervalue from *B*, *A* could recover the value of the goods exceeding the price *D* paid. In *Phillips v Brooks*, the third party would be compensated for the £350 paid, but the original seller would recover the jewellery worth almost ten times that. This solution balances the equities between two innocent parties.

6.3 **Mistaken assumptions: reasons for contracting**

A party may know *who* she has contracted with, and for *what*, but still be mistaken in her background assumptions as to facts or law that explain *why* she made the contract. If a party would not have entered the contract had she known the true state of facts or law, the law may, exceptionally, provide relief. This section on mistaken assumptions should be read in tandem with Chapter 7 on frustration of contracts. The two doctrines are closely related:

- if a contract party's assumption deviates from the state of things *at the time of formation* (eg you buy a ticket to a gig which has already been cancelled), this is a 'present' mistake and is regulated by the doctrine of **mistake**; but

- if a contract party's assumption deviates from the state of things *as they turn out to be* due to a subsequent and unexpected change of circumstances (eg you buy a ticket to a gig, but it is cancelled when the venue is later destroyed by fire), this can be called a 'future' mistake and is the subject of the doctrine of **frustration**.

Diagram 6D shows the mistake doctrine in the context of related doctrines.

Recent judicial recognition of the common ground between mistaken assumptions and frustration has reduced the importance of this *temporal* distinction (7.1.1), although it raises the question of why the consequences of mistake and frustration should differ (as they currently do), and whether they should be unified.

6.3.1 **General principles**

This doctrine is variously called '*mistaken assumption*', 'motivation mistake', 'mistake of fact' or more opaquely 'mutual mistake' or 'common mistake', since both parties must share the mistake. The mistake may be as to background fact or a relevant law (*Brennan v Bolt Burdon* (2004)). However, a compromise of claim (3.1.3.6) based on a view of the law which turns out to have been 'mistaken' because it is subsequently overruled does *not* amount to a mistake of law; each party *takes the risk* that their view of the law might turn out to be wrong (*Kleinwort Benson Ltd v Lincoln CC* (1999)).

In the two leading cases on the modern law, relief for mistaken assumption of fact was denied. In *Bell v Lever Brothers* (1932), L paid £50,000 to terminate the employment of two employees as part of its corporate reorganisation. Unknown to L, the employees had breached their contracts by speculating in cocoa on their own account, entitling L to dismiss them without compensation. On discovering this, L sought the

Diagram 6D Mistake and related doctrines

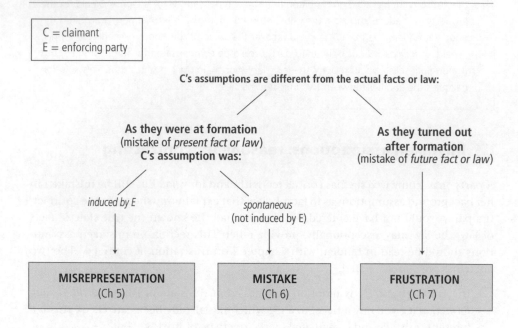

return of the £50,000 for fraud. When this failed, L relied on the alternative ground of mistake. The jury found that L would never have paid if they had known the truth, and that the employees did not have their breach in mind so that they were also 'mistaken' in believing that their employment contracts were only terminable by agreement. The House of Lords recognised the jurisdiction to void a contract for common mistaken assumption, but held by a 3:2 majority that the mistake here was *not* sufficiently fundamental to void the contract (6.3.4.4).

In *Great Peace v Tsavliris* (2002), T agreed to provide salvage services to the ship the *Cape Providence* (CP), which had suffered serious structural damage in the South Indian Ocean and was in imminent danger of going down with her crew and cargo. Since the tug that T proposed to use was some five days away, T looked for merchant vessels in the vicinity that could evacuate the crew of the CP in the meantime if necessary. Relying on information from a third party that one vessel, the *Great Peace* (GP), was about 35 miles away, T hired the GP for a minimum of five days to divert to the CP as back-up pending the tug's arrival. In fact, the GP was 400 miles away while another vessel was substantially closer to the CP. T refused to pay the hire, claiming that the contract was (i) void for common mistake (ie that the GP was 'in close proximity' to the CP) under *Bell v Lever Brothers*, or (ii) voidable for mistake in equity under *Solle v Butcher* (1950) (6.3.6). The Court of Appeal rejected both grounds. Phillips MR set out the conditions for voiding a contract for common mistake at common law:

(i) there must be a common assumption as to the existence of a state of affairs; (ii) there must be no warranty by either party that that state of affairs exists; (iii) the non-existence of the state of affairs must not be attributable to the fault of either party; (iv) the non-existence of the state of affairs must render performance of the contract

Diagram 6E Mistaken assumption: the three-step approach

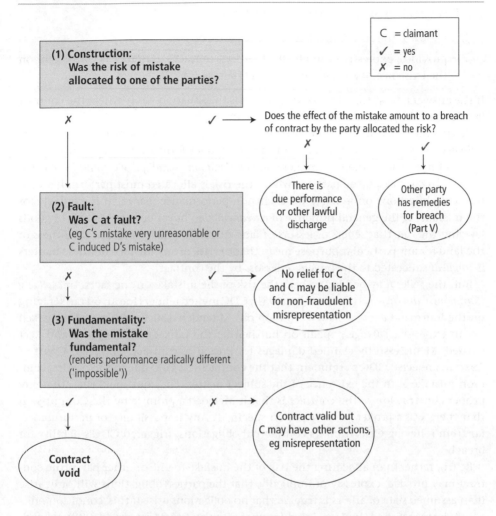

impossible; (v) the state of affairs may be the existence, or a vital attribute, of the consideration to be provided or circumstances which must subsist if performance of the contractual adventure is to be possible.

This can be summarised as a three-step inquiry represented by **Diagram 6E**. A complainant can only void a contract by showing that:

(1) **construction**: the risk of the mistake was not allocated to either party in the contract;

(2) **fault**: she was not at fault (eg by making a very unreasonable mistake or inducing the other party's mistake); and

(3) **fundamentality**: her mistaken assumption was shared by the other party and was so serious as to make performance 'impossible'.

This approach mirrors that adopted by Steyn J in *Associated Japanese Bank (International) Ltd v Crédit du Nord SA* (1989), which was generally approved in *Great Peace v Tsavliris*.

6.3.2 **The contractual allocation of risk: construction**

The first questions are whether the contract has:

(i)   allocated the risk of mistake to either party; or

(ii) provided, expressly or impliedly, that the contract's existence is contingent on the existence of an assumed state of affairs (12.2.2.1).

If the answer is 'yes', then the contract governs the situation. Only where the contract is 'silent on the point' can the mistake doctrine apply.

Re (i), courts will usually find that one or other party has assumed the risk of the *ordinary uncertainties* existing at the time of contract formation by reference to the contract itself and to the rules of general law (*William Sindall plc v Cambridgeshire CC* (1994)). In such cases, the party to whom the risk is allocated must perform her contractual obligations or be liable for their non-performance. No relief is available for the mistake, eg the general principle of *caveat emptor* ('buyer beware') in sale of goods law and the rule that sellers or lessors of land do not impliedly warrant the fitness of the land for any particular purpose mean that the risk of any mistake on these matters is *impliedly* allocated to the buyers or lessors by the contract.

But, the seller may be held to bear the risk of the mistake on the facts. In *McRae v Commonwealth Disposals Commission* (1951), CDC invited tenders for 'an oil tanker lying on the Jourmand Reef . . . said to contain oil'. M tendered successfully and embarked on an expensive salvage expedition but neither the tanker nor the Jourmand Reef existed. M successfully claimed damages for breach of contract. The High Court of Australia rejected CDC's argument that the contract was void due to the parties' common mistake as to the existence of the subject matter. The court held that 'the only proper construction of the contract is that it included a promise by the Commission that there was a tanker in the position specified'. Any impossibility of performance, far from relieving CDC from its contractual obligations, triggered CDC's liability for breach.

Re (ii), rather than allocating the risk of the mistake to one or other party, the contract may provide, expressly or impliedly, that the parties' obligations will only arise if an assumed state of affairs is true, so that no obligations arise if this 'condition precedent' is not satisfied. In *Associated Japanese Bank v Crédit du Nord* (1988), a fraudster purported to sell to, and then lease back from, AJB four machines, which did not actually exist. CN was sued as the fraudster's guarantor on the fraudster's bankruptcy. The Court of Appeal held that, since the guarantee stipulated that the machines could only be substituted with CN's consent, this amounted to an *express* condition precedent that the guarantee was for the lease of *existing* machines. Alternatively, the court was prepared to *imply* such a condition from all the facts (6.3.4.4).

6.3.3 **Fault**

In *Associated Japanese Bank v Crédit du Nord*, Steyn J stated (approved in *Great Peace v Tsavliris*) that: 'a party cannot be allowed to rely on a common mistake where the mistake consists of a belief which is entertained by him without any reasonable grounds for such belief' because 'policy and good sense dictate that the positive rules regarding common mistake should be so qualified'. Moreover, no relief is available if a party contracts 'with minimal knowledge of the facts to which the mistake relates but is content that it is a good speculative risk'. Thus, another reason for the decision in *McRae v Commonwealth Disposals Commission* is that a party cannot rely on a mistake which 'consists of a belief which is, on the one hand, entertained by him without any reasonable ground, and, on the other hand, deliberately induced by him in the mind of the other party'. Induced mistakes give the representee an action for misrepresentation.

6.3.4 **Fundamental common mistake at common law**

An actionable common mistake at common law must be: (i) shared; and (ii) of fundamental importance. The explanation for requiring a **shared mistake** is pragmatic. The concern to uphold contractual certainty and avoid giving contract parties an easy escape route necessitates a very narrow scope for operative mistakes. The requirement that both parties make the same mistake:

(i) serves an *evidentiary function* by corroborating:

  • the complainant's assertion of the *existence* of the mistake; and

  • the *importance* of the mistake; shared assumptions are more likely to relate to the essential substance of the contract;

(ii) shows that the other party's expectations are not reasonable since they are *also* tainted by catastrophic mistake. Voiding the contract in such circumstances deprives her of benefits (including unexpected windfalls) which are *unworthy of protection* because she could not reasonably have expected them at contract formation.

The **fundamentality requirement** asks whether there is a sufficient degree of *disparity* between performance of the contract on the *mistaken* state of affairs, and its performance on the *actual* state of affairs, that consent to the contract can be regarded as nullified.

Operative mistake must relate to 'the existence, or a vital attribute, of the consideration to be provided or circumstances which must subsist if performance of the contractual adventure is to be possible' (*Great Peace v Tsavliris*). This yields the traditional categories of common mistake:

(i)   mistake as to the *existence* of the subject matter;

(ii) mistakenly acquiring one's *own property*;

(iii) mistake as to the *essential quality* of the thing contracted for; and

(iv) mistake as to an *essential background assumption*.

It is important to emphasise that this is not a list of *qualifying* 'impossibilities', but merely *illustrations* of mistakes that *can* (but not necessarily will) so undermine the substance of the contract as to make the performance of the original contract 'impossible' and so negate the apparent consent given to it. Relief may not be granted on the facts just because a case seems to come within one of the categories.

6.3.4.1 Mistake as to the existence of the subject matter

The non-existence of the subject matter of the contract that is mistakenly thought to exist (*res extincta*) will normally negate the essential *purpose* of a contract or the *means* for achieving it. This is the most widely accepted example of operative common mistake. Lord Atkin said that: 'the agreement of A and B to purchase a specific article is void if in fact the article had perished before the date of sale . . . a consent to transfer or take delivery of something nonexistent is deemed useless, the consent is nullified' (*Bell v Lever Brothers*). The same should apply if the subject matter had never existed, as in *McRae v Commonwealth Disposals Commission,* unless the risk was allocated (which it was in *McRae*).

Subsequent cases have regarded *Couturier v Hastie* (1856) as the leading case of *res extincta*. It involved the sale of corn that was in transit to England. The cargo had deteriorated and had already been sold on *before* the date of the sale. The seller sued for the price, claiming that the buyer had bought not the corn itself but the rights derived from the shipping documents, so that the risk of the non-existence of the corn was allocated to the buyer. The House of Lords disagreed. Analogous to the *McRae* case, it held that, *as a matter of construction*, the contract was for the sale of *existing* cargo (the corn itself) and not for cargo whether existing or not (the buyer was not taking a gamble, in the nature of a 'lucky dip'). Thus, the risk of mistake as to existence of the corn was allocated to the seller; its non-existence meant that there was a '**total failure of consideration**' (complete non-performance, 13.4.2) by the seller, so that the buyer did not have to pay. The House of Lords never actually mentioned 'mistake' in its reasoning. However, the ground of 'total failure of consideration' can mask operative mistake. In *Strickland v Turner* (1852), S bought and paid for an annuity on the life of a man who, unknown to both parties, had already died. S recovered the purchase price for total failure of consideration. The ground only allows the complainant not to pay or to recover payments made, so the ground of mistake is only necessary where the *buyer* sues for the seller's non-delivery, and neither party is allocated the risk of non-existence.

Section 6 of the Sale of Goods Act 1979 stipulates that: 'Where there is a contract for the sale of specific goods, and the goods without the knowledge of the seller have perished at the time when the contract is made, the contract is void.' This differs in scope from the common law because: (i) it only applies to specific goods *that once existed* but then perished; and (ii) unlike many other sections of the SGA, section 6 is not expressly subject to contrary intention and therefore seems to apply irrespective of the parties' risk allocation. Section 6 should be reformed to cover goods that never existed and to allow parties to opt out of having their contract automatically voided.

6.3.4.2 Mistakenly acquiring one's own property

Where the parties' contract transfers some interest in property that, unknown to either, already belongs to the buyer (*res sua*), the contract is void. It is not only senseless to buy one's own property, but 'such a transfer is impossible' (*Bell v Lever Brothers*). In *Cooper v Phibbs* (1867), C agreed to lease a fishery from P but, unknown to both parties, P had no title while C was already tenant for life of the fishery; the lease was set aside. Although the proceedings were brought in equity (making the contract *voidable*) to allow an award for the improvements P made to the fishery, the House of Lords in

Bell said that 'the common law would have ruled the contract void for mistake' (*Great Peace*). This category is often called 'mistake as to title', but this is too broad since it would also cover mistakes as to the *seller*'s title. This risk is allocated to the seller by section 12 of the Sale of Goods Act 1979 by an implied term that the seller warrants (guarantees) her title to the property sold and is therefore liable for breach if this is untrue.

6.3.4.3 Mistake as to an *essential* quality of the subject matter

In both of the previous categories (*res extincta* and *res sua*), performance of the contract is physically impossible. This is not necessarily so with the next two categories (mistakes as to the quality and as to background assumptions). Here, 'impossibility' of performance is measured by the extent of deviation from the 'substance of the contract' which is, in turn, determined by the parties' common purpose (in the broadest sense of what they thought they were contracting about). What is required is a mistake about 'the existence of some quality which makes the thing without the quality *essentially different* from the thing as it was believed to be' (*Bell v Lever Brothers*). The enormity of the difference required is captured in the distinction between:

✗ mistakes as to 'quality' (or attributes), which will not void the contract; and

✓ mistakes as to 'substance' (or 'essence' or 'vital quality'), which will.

However, the application of the distinction has given rise to much *uncertainty* and *inconsistency*. **Diagram 6F** summarizes some cases.

(i)   Examples of inoperative mistakes as to *quality*
The courts have emphasised the narrow scope of mistakes void for mistake as to **quality** because of the 'paramount importance that contracts should be observed' (*Bell v Lever Brothers*). Relief will only be given in 'unexpected and wholly exceptional' situations (*Associated Japanese Bank v Crédit du Nord*). It is not enough that the mistake was causative (ie the complainant would not have entered this contract but for the mistake) or that it will result in unexpected hardship to one or advantage to the other. Hence, mistakes as to the quality of the subject matter will not generally void contracts of sale. The complainant is only protected if stipulations in the contract expressly (*Gompertz v Barlett* (1853)) or impliedly[2] warrant the *quality* to be as believed. The mistakes made were **not sufficiently fundamental** in the following:

✗ in *Kennedy v Panama, New Zealand, and Australian Royal Mail Co Ltd* (1867), the complainant purchased shares in a company in reliance on the company's prospectus saying that money was being raised to fulfil a lucrative contract which turned out to be ultra vires, triggering a plunge in the value of the shares (no damages were available for innocent misrepresentation at common law but equity would have allowed rescission in this case);

✗ in *Smith v Hughes* (1871), the complainant purchased oats believing them to be 'old' oats, only having use for such, when they were in fact 'new' oats (the mistake was neither fundamental nor shared, 2.1.3.1);

---

[2] Eg the Sales of Goods Act 1979, s 12 (title); s 13 (correspondence with description); s 14 (quality and fitness for purpose); s 15 (sale by sample).

Diagram 6F Mistakes as to quality: an overview of some cases

✗ (i) Inoperative mistakes as to quality	✗ (ii) Inoperative mistakes as to substance	✓ (iii) Operative mistakes as to substance
✗ shares in a company with a lucrative contract when contract ultra vires (*Kennedy v Panama*); ✗ old oats when new oats (*Smith v Hughes*); ✗ 1948 model of car when 1939 (*Oscar Chess v Williams*); ✗ pure kapok when inferior product (*Harrison v Bunten*); ✗ sound horse when unsound horse (example given in *Bell*).	✗ picture by Constable when not (*Leaf v International Galleries*); ✗ rental of 'new' dwelling house when not (*Solie v Butcher*); ✗ 'horse beans' when 'feveroles' (*Rose v Pim*).	✓ racehorse when carthorse (example given in *Bell*); ✓ table napkins of Charles I when Georgian (*Nicholson and Venn v Smith Marriott*); ✓ sterile cow when pregnant cow (*Sherwood v Walker, US*); ✓ building land when building permit was unobtainable (*Alessio v Jovica, Canada*); ✓ prefabricated cottage when not conforming with building regulations (*Frazer v Dalgety, NZ*). ✓ settlement on intestacy when a will existed (*British Red Cross v Werry*).

✗ in *Oscar Chess Ltd v Williams* (1957), the complainant purchased a car which both believed to be a 1948 model when it was in fact a less valuable 1939 model; and

✗ in *Bell v Lever Brothers*, Lord Atkin said that the purchase of an unsound horse believed to be sound still gives the buyer the substance of what was bargained for.

✓ On the other hand, Greer LJ, in the Court of Appeal said that the contract for the sale of a racehorse *would* be void if it turned out to be a carthorse.

(ii)   Examples of inoperative mistakes as to *substance*
Difficulty arises because relief has been denied in some cases although the mistake appears to go to the **substance** (or the identity) of the subject matter. However, it may be significant that, in all three cases, the complainant had alternative avenues of relief:

✗ In *Leaf v International Galleries*, the complainant bought a picture which both parties mistakenly believed was painted by the famous artist Constable (however, the court held that the complainant could have obtained damages for breach but he chose not to do so, hence the case was really decided on construction (risk allocation), analogous to *McRae v Commonwealth Disposals Commission*, 6.3.2).

✗ In *Solle v Butcher*, the parties entered a lease for £250 of rent per year mistakenly believing that the property had undergone sufficient renovations to qualify as a 'new' dwelling house, thus evading the £140 limit imposed by the Rent Acts (but equity allowed rescission on terms that the landlord give the tenant the option of staying on at the higher rent, 6.3.6).

✗ In *Frederick E Rose (London) Ltd v William H Pim Junior & Co Ltd* (1953), the parties contracted for 'horse beans' mistakenly believing these were 'feveroles', which the buyer needed to meet its customer's order. In fact, 'feveroles' were an entirely different sort of bean although they could also be described as 'horse beans' (however, rescission would have been allowed for innocent misrepresentation).

(iii) Examples of operative mistakes as to *quality*

The following contracts of sale *were* voided for fundamental mistake, although they seem to entail only mistakes as to quality:

✓ In the US case of *Sherwood v Walker* (1887), a cow ('Rose of Abalone the II'), believed to be sterile, was sold for beef for about $80 when it was actually in calf and worth at least $750.

✓ In the Canadian case of *Alessio v Jovica* (1974), land zoned as building land was bought but no building permit could be obtained because it lacked sewage facilities.

✓ In the New Zealand case of *Frazer v Dalgety & Co Ltd* (1953), a prefabricated 'cottage' was bought, but could never be erected because it did not conform to the building regulations.

✓ in the English case of *Nicholson and Venn v Smith Marriott* (1947), the buyer successfully sued for damages for breach when he purchased table napkins described as 'the authentic property of Charles I' for £787 10s, when they were in fact Georgian and worth only £105. The court suggested, somewhat inconsistently with awarding contract damages, that the contract could have been voided for mistake.

 Pause for reflection

1. These cases are unlikely to convince a modern court, three being from other jurisdictions and the last being decidedly unconvincing as well as internally inconsistent, since the contract must have been valid (not void) for it to be breached and contract damages awarded.

2. The supposed distinction between 'substance' and 'quality' (or 'identity' vs 'attribute') is quite illusory. The 'substance' or 'identity' of a thing must be comprised of its various qualities or attributes.

3. Treitel suggests (at 8-019) asking 'the parties, immediately after they made the contract, what its subject matter was. If, in spite of the mistake, they would give the right answer [eg 'horse' rather than 'racehorse'] the contract is valid at law.' The difficulty is that contract parties might reasonably describe the subject matter of their contract in various ways, and relief should not hang on the *degree of specificity* with which they happen to describe that subject matter: whether 'cow' or 'barren cow', 'table linen' or 'Charles I's table linen'. Moreover, it would not explain *Leaf v International Galleries*; the buyer would certainly have said he was buying 'a Constable' and not simply 'a picture'. Further, in *Bell v Lever Brothers*, Lord Thankerton emphasises the *objective* quality of the test: it must have 'either appeared *on the face of the contract* that the matter as to which the mistake existed was an essential and integral element of the subject matter of the contract, or it was an inevitable inference from the *nature of the contract* that all the parties so regarded it' (emphasis added). The parties' belief at a greater level of detail is irrelevant.

6.3.4.4 Other mistaken fundamental assumptions

Aside from the categories of mistake discussed earlier, the parties may make a mistake about other background assumptions fundamental to the essential point of the contract. They are 'circumstances which must subsist if performance of the contractual adventure is to be possible' (*Great Peace v Tsavliris*), eg:

✓ In *Gallaway v Gallaway* (1914), a separation deed was voided because the parties thought they were validly married but they were not; their mistake destroyed the very point of the deed.

✓ In *British Red Cross v Werry* (2017), a settlement following a supposed intestacy was void for common mistake when it was subsequently discovered that the deceased had left a will.

✓ In *Scott v Coulson* (1903), a life insurance policy was sold for £460 on the assumption that the insured was alive. In fact, the aptly named insured (Death) was dead, increasing the value of the policy to its full surrender value of £777.

✓ In *Sheikh Brothers Ltd v Ochsner* (1957), S granted O a licence to cut and manufacture all sisal grown on their estate in exchange for O's payment and delivery of 50 tons of sisal per month. However, the estate was incapable of yielding this quantity of sisal so performance of the contract was *physically impossible*. The Privy Council, relying on *Bell v Lever Brothers* to interpret and apply the Indian Contract Act 1872, voided the contract because 'both the parties to an agreement are under a mistake as to a matter of fact essential to the agreement'.

 Pause for reflection

Physical impossibility of performance does not, in itself, void contracts; people are normally responsible for the obligations they have undertaken and will be liable for breach if performance is impossible. The contract was only voided in *Sheikh Brothers v Ochsner* because it was held to be in the nature of a joint venture to exploit the sisal on the land and entered *on the basis* that the area was *capable* of producing an average of 50 tons a month throughout the term of the contract. That being so, the decision is really based on implied condition precedent and not mistake.

✓ In *Griffith v Brymer* (1903), a contract for 'hire of a room *to see the coronation procession of King Edward VII*' (and not just 'a room hire') was made when the procession was already cancelled. The contract was voided, although its performance was perfectly possible. The falsification of the parties' common and fundamental assumption that the event would take place made the *substance* of the contract impossible to achieve.

✗ In *Great Peace v Tsavliris*, mistaken assumption did not affect the contract's *purpose* but it undermined the *means* for achieving it. The question was whether the GP was actually so far away from T's distressed ship 'at the time of the contract as to defeat the contractual purpose [to provide escort and standby services for five days until the rescue tug arrived]'—or, in other words, to turn it into something essentially different from that for which the parties had bargained? This is a question of fact and degree. The court concluded that, although the parties believed that the GP was 35 miles (three hours' sailing) away, rather than actually 400 miles (39 hours' sailing) away, this did not defeat the parties' common assumption that it could still act as a backup. This was reinforced by T's failure to cancel the agreement on discovering the mistake until they found and hired a nearer vessel to assist. Significantly, Toulson J said that, if there was five days' sailing distance between the ships, the contract *would be void* since its purpose would be unachievable.

✗ In *Bell v Lever Brothers*, the court upheld the contract to terminate a *valid* employment contract when it was really *voidable*. Lord Atkin explained that: 'The contract released is the identical contract in both cases, and the party paying for release gets exactly what he bargains for.' Analogously, he said that there would be no remedy where a purchaser of a roadside garage was unaware that a decision had already been taken to construct a bypass road that would divert substantially all the traffic from passing his garage.

 Pause for reflection

1. *Inconsistency with other cases*: the denial of relief in *Bell v Lever Brothers* sits uneasily with the relief granted in *Associated Japanese Bank v Crédit du Nord*. There, a *guarantee* of a lease of machines was *voided* because the non-existence of the machines made the lease voidable for fraud. Since the subject matter of the guarantee contract was not the non-existent machinery but the *lease* which, while voidable, undoubtedly existed, Steyn J's analogy with the *res extincta* cases is questionable. The closer analogy is to *Bell v Lever Brothers* (which also involved a contract dealing with a voidable contract thought to be valid), but no relief was given there.

2. *Payment not unfair*: it was judicially noted in *Bell v Lever Brothers* that the employers were anxious to facilitate smooth and urgent corporate reorganisation and might have agreed the severance package even knowing the truth (*Bell v Lever Brothers*, and *Associated Japanese Bank*). In 'How Temptation Led to Mistake: An Explanation of *Bell v Lever Bros Ltd*' (2003) 119 *LQR* 625, MacMillan offers a different explanation for the outcome in terms of: (i) the absence of fraud; (ii) the outstanding service given by the employees who had been 'most efficient, devoted, strenuous, and successful' on behalf of the company; (iii) the fairly minor nature of their breaches of duty which had yielded relatively small gains; and (iv) the harshness of depriving them of £50,000 (*Bell v Lever Brothers*). It is arguable that relief was not denied *because* the mistake was insufficiently fundamental or causative; rather, the mistake was held to be insufficiently fundamental *so that* the employees could keep their severance payments, which were fair in the circumstances.

3. *Discretion in categorising the mistake made*: the mistake in *Bell v Lever Brothers* was treated as a mistake as to the quality of the subject matter, which does not generally void the contract. However, in 'Contracts—Mistake, Frustration and Implied Terms' (1994) *LQR*

➜

> ➡
>
> 400, Smith points out (at 414) that the mistake could also have been described as one which *is* generally regarded as voiding contracts, namely:
>
> ✓ *res sua* (the employer was buying the right to terminate an employment contract which it already had); or
>
> ✓ *res extincta* (the employees were selling their right to continued employment which was non-existent).

6.3.5 **The effect of common mistake**

Operative common mistake at common law voids the contract for all purposes. This means that property rights will not pass under it and good faith third parties who purchase the property are left unprotected when the original mistaken transferor claims recovery of the property. This contrasts with the more flexible *equitable* remedies of: (i) *rescission* which can protect third party bona fide purchasers; and (ii) *refusal of specific performance* for unilateral mistake.

The Court of Appeal in *Great Peace v Tsavliris* recognised the desirability of greater remedial flexibility in cases of common mistake at common law analogous to that available in cases of frustration (the Law Reform (Frustrated Contracts) Act 1943 allows courts more scope to fine-tune the effects of frustration (7.6.3 and 7.6.4)).

6.3.6 **Common mistake at equity**

6.3.6.1 Rescission (on terms)

Until recently, the judgment of Denning LJ in *Solle v Butcher* was authority for an *equitable* doctrine of common mistake that conferred a *wider scope* of relief and *greater remedial flexibility*. In *Associated Japanese Bank v Crédit du Nord*, Steyn J said: 'Equity will give relief against common mistake in cases where the common law will not, and it provides more flexible remedies including the power to set aside the contract on terms.'

✓ In *Solle v Butcher*, the parties agreed a £250 yearly rental when they were, in fact, subject to a £140 limit under the Rent Act unless a 'notice of increase' was served. This was not served due to a common mistake about the status of the property. The court granted the landlord rescission of the lease, but on the terms that he offer the tenant a new lease for £250.

✓ Similarly, in *Grist v Bailey* (1967), a house was sold for £850 on the common mistaken assumption that a protected tenant was still in occupation when in fact the tenant had died before the sale; this raised the value of the property to £2,250. Although the risk of such a mistake is generally allocated to the seller, the sale was rescinded in equity on the terms that the seller offer the buyer the option of buying it at the 'proper vacant possession price'.

6.3.6.2 Rejection of the equitable jurisdiction

The Court of Appeal in *Great Peace v Tsavliris*, agreeing with Toulson J at first instance, rejected an equitable jurisdiction that would render voidable contracts not void at common law. Four reasons can be identified:

(i) **Contradiction of *Bell v Lever Brothers***: *Solle v Butcher* represents 'a significant extension of any jurisdiction exercised up to that point and one that was not readily reconcilable with the result in *Bell v Lever*'. *Solle v Butcher* did not so much supplement or mitigate the common law, as outflank and contradict it.

(ii) **Lack of precedent**: there was no clear authority for a more expansive equitable jurisdiction either before or in the House of Lords decision in *Bell v Lever Brothers* itself. *Solle v Butcher* (a Court of Appeal decision) had relied heavily on *Cooper v Phibbs* (a House of Lords decision, 6.3.4.2), but the case is not authority for a lower threshold since it involved mistakenly acquiring one's own property, which would have voided the contract at common law. Neither is *Cooper v Phibbs* authority for greater remedial flexibility in setting aside contracts 'on such terms as the court thinks fit'. The restitutionary remedy ordered there (rescission subject to a lien in favour of the mistaken lessor) merely recognised the latter's improvements to the fishery in the mistaken belief that it was his and ensured that the party recovering the property was not unjustly enriched. Denning LJ's suggestion in *Solle v Butcher* that the House of Lords in *Bell v Lever Brothers* had overlooked existing equitable principles relieving mistakes was unrealistic.

(iii) **Uncertainty**: the scope of the more expansive equitable jurisdiction is also said to require 'fundamental' mistakes (*Solle v Butcher*), although they must logically be *less* 'fundamental' than those required at common law. Subsequent cases applying *Solle v Butcher* have not identified 'the test of mistake that gives rise to the equitable jurisdiction to rescind in a manner that distinguishes this from the test of a mistake that renders a contract void in law'.

(iv) **Illegitimacy**: the equitable jurisdiction is largely motivated by the desire to avoid unjust outcomes. In essence, Denning LJ in *Solle v Butcher* supported the landlord's claim 'that it is unfair' for the tenant to pay £140 for the remaining five years of the lease when the market rent is £250. The Court of Appeal in *Great Peace* affirmed Toulson J's view that it was not the court's role to dissolve or vary contracts thought to be harsh on the basis of so-called equitable principles. Such considerations were properly considered under other existing equitable doctrines such as fraud, misrepresentation, and undue influence. Some of the post-*Solle v Butcher* cases were dismissed as muddled, confused, and failing to take account of contractual allocations of risk (eg *Grist v Bailey* (1967) and *Laurence v Lexcourt Holdings* (1978)).

6.3.6.3 The future of equitable common mistake

In practice, the Court of Appeal's abolition of equitable common mistake seems secure since a litigant will now be reluctant to argue the point given the prohibitive cost of litigation. Further, as *Great Peace* noted, decisions in lower courts present no clear resistance to the demise of *Solle v Butcher*.

Counterpoint

1. Uncertainty: whilst the scope of equitable mistake is admittedly uncertain, the scope of common law mistake is itself highly unstable. In *Chwee Kin Keong v Digilandmall.com Pte Ltd* (2005), the Singapore Court of Appeal regards the view that equitable intervention would create unacceptable uncertainty as exaggerated and affirmed the continued existence of an equitable jurisdiction for mistake after *Great Peace*.

2. Authority: the existence of equitable common mistake is accepted by a number of decisions after *Solle v Butcher*, including Court of Appeal decisions.[3] Steyn J in *Associated Japanese Bank v Crédit du Nord* regards the interacting set of rules as 'an entirely satisfactory state of the law'. In '*Great Peace* and Precedent' (2003) 119 *LQR* 180, Midwinter points out that, since the mistake in *Great Peace* was insufficiently serious to qualify even for equitable relief, it was unnecessary to decide on the validity of the doctrine. As a matter of precedent, *Solle v Butcher* should have been regarded as binding on both the High Court and the Court of Appeal in *Great Peace*.

3. The relevance of fairness: considerations of fairness permeate contract law; they are present in common law mistake as instanced by the accounts of *Bell v Lever Brothers* itself. The denial of relief in *Great Peace* can also be regarded as fair in the context of a commercial contract which had been relied upon. Indeed, it is arguable that the owners of the *Great Peace* made no mistake at all. Reynolds observes that they merely believed, 'correctly, that the salvors had reason to believe that the *Great Peace* was the nearest ship'.[4] The case for relief is stronger in non-commercial or consumer cases. Deserving cases driven out of mistake are likely to find their way into other vitiating factors.

4. Proportionality of legal response: it would be perfectly rational to have a system where serious mistakes void contracts, and less serious mistakes merely render contracts voidable, whether the mistakes are induced or not.[5] Moreover, it seems odd that an innocent misrepresentation will only render contracts voidable whilst a common mistake induced by an innocent misrepresentation may render the contract void.

5. Judicial vs legislative development: the Court of Appeal's rejection of the equitable jurisdiction (evolved to introduce remedial flexibility) is accompanied by a simultaneous call for the introduction of legislation to give greater remedial flexibility, analogous to the Law Reform (Frustrated Contracts) Act 1943 (7.6.3 and 7.6.4). Reynolds observes: 'It is not clear why a statute (hardly an item of priority for law reformers) would do any better than a careful judicial interpretation of Lord Denning's doctrine, which is after all but a slight extension of lines of existing equity cases on misrepresentation and unconscionability in general.'[6]

6. Remedial flexibility: the Court of Appeal's call for greater flexibility is odd in the context of its denial of equitable mistake, because, if a mistake is not sufficiently fundamental to

➡

---

[3] *Rose v Pim* (1953); *Grist v Bailey* (1967); *Magee v Pennine Insurance* (1969); *Laurence v Lexcourt Holdings* (1978); *William Sindall v Cambridgeshire CC* (1994); *Nutt v Reed* (1999); *Clarion v National Provident Institution* (2000); *West Sussex Properties v Chichester DC* (2000).

[4] F M B Reynolds, 'Reconsider the Contract Textbook' (2003) 119 *LQR* 177, 178.

[5] See A S Burrows, 'We Do This at Common Law and That at Equity' (2002) 22 *OJLS* 1, 5–6.

[6] F M B Reynolds, 'Reconsider the Contract Textbook' (2003) 119 *LQR* 177, 179.

➜ void the contract, it is *valid* and cannot be the subject of '*remedial* flexibility'. The Court of Appeal must be read as supporting a wider *scope* (lowering the threshold) for relievable mistake *and* wider discretion to tailor appropriate remedies (beyond voiding contracts). While the law of frustration is held up as the example to follow, it is questionable that the Law Reform (Frustrated Contracts) Act 1943 permits sufficient remedial flexibility (it only allows restitution and limited loss apportionment, 7.6.3 and 7.6.4). In comparison:

- In German law, a party making a unilateral mistake can set aside the contract on compensating the other party who does not know of the mistake (§ 122 of the German Civil Code (BGB)).

- The New Zealand Contractual Mistakes Act 1977 confers on the court a wide discretion to grant relief including cancellation, validation, or variation of the contract, and the awarding of restitution or compensation.

6.3.7 **Justifications for the mistake doctrine**

Relief for mistaken assumptions undermines the enforceability of contracts. How can it be justified?

6.3.7.1 The implied terms analysis

Some distinguished commentators deny there is even a mistake jurisdiction at common law:

- Slade, 'The Myth of Mistake in the English Law of Contract' (1954) 70 *LS* 385;
- Atiyah and Bennion, 'Mistake in the Construction of Contracts' (1961) 24 *MLR* 421; and
- Smith, 'Contract—Mistake, Frustration and Implied Terms' (1994) 110 *LQR* 400.

These authors argue that all the problems of contractual mistake can be dealt with by:

✓ the law on contract formation (because there is no mirror image offer and acceptance); or

✓ implied terms (specifically, the 'implied condition precedent' that no contract comes into effect if the parties' common assumption is incorrect). Questions about 'mistake' are really questions about the *risk allocation* for mistake and the answers, they argue, can *always* be found in the contract, contextually interpreted. So, when contracts are voided, this is the result of something that the *parties themselves* have agreed, albeit impliedly; it is not *imposed* by the law. There is no room left for the operation of a distinct doctrine of mistake.

Moreover, these are the *right* approaches because of the **policies against relief for mistakes**. Namely:

- the concern that a mistake doctrine would provide an open-ended excuse to escape bad bargains and undermine the contractual risk allocation;
- the need to promote certainty by upholding the parties' objective intention; and

- the need to reward research and knowledge in a free-market system, so that knowledgeable parties must generally be allowed to take advantage of less knowledgeable (mistaken) parties.

 Counterpoint

The implied terms analysis is sometimes realistic, as in *Associated Japanese Bank*. But, the argument that it can provide a complete explanation for *all* cases where contracts are voided for mistake does not ring true:

1. Contradicted by weight of authority: Lord Atkins said in *Bell v Lever Brothers* that the 'implied condition precedent' reasoning is merely an 'alternative mode of expressing the result of a mutual [ie common][7] mistake'; it is only a synonym for common mistake. The general judicial consensus is that an independent mistake doctrine *does* exist and only operates *after* construction has exhausted the contract's ability to determine the consequences of the mistake. Mistake only kicks in to sort out the mess once the contract runs out (*Associated Japanese Bank (International) Ltd v Crédit du Nord SA*; *William Sindall v Cambridgeshire CC*; *Grains & Fourrages SA v Huyton* (1997); *Bank of Credit and Commerce International SA (in liquidation) v Ali* (1999)).

2. Odd reasoning: there is something distinctly odd in saying that a contract is void (a nullity *from the beginning*) because an implied term *inside* that void contract says so: the contract 'self-destructs' before coming into being.

3. Uncertain: the concept of an implied condition precedent tells us little about *when* such a condition (the 'self-destruct' instruction) will be implied.

4. Over-inclusive: an implied condition precedent need not be limited to very serious (fundamental) mistakes; it would be a matter of contract interpretation.

5. Unrealistic: the implied terms story of mistake necessitates the fiction that contract parties have agreed what should happen in a state of affairs that is completely *different* from the one they both believed existed at formation. In truth, it is usually impossible to say in any meaningful, non-attributive, way what *the parties* would have wanted in the event of catastrophic mistake. It is certainly unlikely that they would have been happy for the contract to simply fall away regardless of what gains and losses may have been accrued under it. The implied terms view of mistake was rejected in *Great Peace v Tsavliris* as 'unrealistic'. Rather, '[t]he avoidance of contract on the ground of common mistake results from a rule of law'; it is imposed by law.

6.3.7.2 Impossibility of performance

- In *Great Peace v Tsavliris*, mistake is said to operate 'if it transpires that one or both of the parties have agreed to do something which it is impossible to perform'.
- Lords Atkin and Thankerton in *Bell v Lever Brothers* support the impossibility justification by analogy to the frustration doctrine.

---

[7] Confusingly, the expression 'mutual mistake' is sometimes used to describe shared or common mistake.

- In *Great Peace*, the court agreed that 'consideration of the development of the law of frustration assists with the analysis of the law of common mistake'.

The frustration doctrine discharges a contract that has *become* impossible to perform. The basic idea is illustrated by *Taylor v Caldwell* (1863), in which a music hall hired for concerts for four nights was burnt down before the first concert. The court excused performance since it depended on the continued existence of the music hall. If the music hall was already, unknown to either party, destroyed *at the time* the contract was made, the impossibility of performance would be resolved by the mistake doctrine.
What does 'impossibility of performance' mean?

- Recall that impossibility of performance was insufficient in *McRae v Commonwealth Disposals Commission* and the risk of the impossibility was allocated to the seller.

- On the other hand, impossibility of performance was unnecessary in *Great Peace*. Performance may be perfectly possible, yet the contract may be void for mistake if the *'substance'* of the contract is deemed to be 'impossible' to achieve. That is, if the significance/meaning/point of the, even physically *possible*, performance in the *actual* state of affairs is radically different from that supposed by the parties at formation, then the contract is void.

In other words, mistake is operative if it results in the non-existence of a state of affairs assumed by both parties as going to the foundation (or the 'substance', 'root', 'essence', or 'basis') of the contract. In *Great Peace*, Lord Phillips MR approved Vaughan Williams LJ's view in *Krell v Henry* (1903) that:

> you first have to ascertain, not necessarily from the terms of the contract, but, if required, from necessary inferences, drawn from surrounding circumstances recognised by both contracting parties, what is *the substance of the contract*, and then to ask the question whether that substantial contract needs for its foundation the assumption of the existence of a particular state of things. If it does, this will limit the operation of the general words [ie qualify the obligation], and in such a case, if the contract becomes impossible of performance by reason of the *non-existence of the state of things assumed by both parties as the foundation of the contract*, there will be no breach of the contract thus limited (emphasis added).

Why should the law care about 'impossibility' of performance when the non-performing party can always be sued for breach? In the High Court, Toulson J (*Great Peace v Tsavliris*, affirmed by the Court of Appeal) rejected any suggestion that the mistake doctrine is aimed at avoiding the injustice resulting from mistake because this would put 'palm tree justice in place of party autonomy', when concerns to avoid injustice are adequately dealt with by other doctrines such as fraud, misrepresentation, and undue influence.

6.3.7.3 Consent nullified

The no consent rationale ultimately offers the best explanation for the mistake doctrine. As Lord Atkin said in *Bell v Lever Brothers*: 'If mistake operates at all it operates so as to negative or in some cases to nullify consent.' Four reasons support this:

(i) **Impossibility, essential context, and lack of consent:** The test of 'impossibility of performance' is just shorthand for saying that the parties' *consent* is absent where the falsification of their *essential assumption* about the context of the contract makes performance of the *substance* (its purpose and not just its literal terms) *impossible* (*Bell v Lever Brothers*).

(ii) **Meaningful consent**: while effective consent to a contract does not require knowing consent to every *detail* of the content (hence the objective test of intention), the parties must, minimally, consent to (be correct about) the 'gist', 'core', or 'substance' of what they have undertaken; they must at least be in the right 'ball park'. You need not have actually agreed every rule of the club to be bound by them, but you must at least have joined the right club. This explains why only mistakes that fatally undermine the 'root', 'substance', 'essence', 'basis', or 'foundation' of the contract void the contract. Only such mistakes negate commitment to the contract.

(iii) **Threshold of consent is fixed by the law**: the no consent view explains why the effect of fundamental mistake is rightly regarded as being imposed by the *law* rather than agreed by the *parties*. The law proceeds on the basis that the objective consent giving rise to prima facie contractual liability at formation can be negated by a catastrophic mistake going to the root or substance of the contract; it negates the justification for enforcement.

(iv) **Explains the effect of voidness**: the no consent view explains why contracts tainted by mistake are *void* (of no effect from the beginning), rather than voidable (good until the claimant rescinds) as with most vitiating factors.

 Pause for reflection

The stark effect of voidness has its drawbacks:

1. *Innocent third party purchasers are not protected* against claims by the mistaken party for the return of property transferred under the void contract (since ownership does not generally pass under a void contract (6.2.1)).

2. Benefits transferred under the void contract must be returned but there is no mechanism for taking account of losses sustained in the performance of the contract that do not end up as a benefit in the other's hands (in contrast, some allowance for loss apportionment is permitted where contracts are discharged for frustration (7.6)).

3. These problems prompted Lord Denning to develop the *equitable* doctrine of common mistake to access more flexible remedies, including rescission on terms (6.3.6), and the House of Lords' call for remedial flexibility whilst simultaneously abolishing Lord Denning's solution.

THIS CHAPTER IN ESSENCE

The key areas and core topics in this chapter are summarised in an easy-to-use list, ideal for revision purposes, on the online resources at www.oup.com/uk/chenwishart6e/. Links to websites relevant to the topics covered and any updates to the chapter can also be found on the online resources.

QUESTIONS

1 The law on mistaken identity is beset by 'illogical and sometimes barely perceptible distinctions'. Are matters clearer after *Shogun Finance Ltd v Hudson*?

2 Max, who bears a striking resemblance to a well-known pop star, walks into Nina's jewellery shop and selects an expensive diamond ring priced at £50,000. He says to Nina, 'I've forgotten my credit card, but you know who I am and that I'm good for it.' Nina is overawed and says 'yes, of course'. She allows Max to take the ring after Max signs a sale agreement. Max sells the ring to Otis for £2,000. Max cannot now be found. Advise Nina.

3 'There is no doctrine of mistake; there is only the parties' contractual risk allocation.' Discuss.

4 'It is impossible to explain a doctrine of mistaken assumptions whilst also insisting on an objective approach to contractual formation.' Discuss.

5 'It is irrational to recognise an equitable jurisdiction to relieve for common mistake co-existing with a common law jurisdiction to do the same. *Solle v Butcher* is inconsistent with *Bell v Lever Brothers*. One of them must go.' Discuss.

6 'There is scope for legislation to give greater flexibility to our law of mistake than the common law allows' (*Great Peace v Tsavliris*). Do you agree? How might greater flexibility be achieved?

 For hints on how to answer these questions, please see the online resources at www.oup.com/uk/chenwishart6e/

KEY FURTHER READING

Atiyah, P S, and Bennion, F (1961), 'Mistake in the Construction of Contracts', 24 *MLR* 421.

Chen-Wishart, M (2009), 'Objectivity and Mistake: The Oxymoron of *Smith v Hughes*' in J Neyers, R Bronough, and S G A Pitel (eds), *Exploring Contract Law* (Hart Publishing) 341.

Davies, P (2016), 'Rectification versus Interpretation: The Nature and Scope of the Equitable Jurisdiction' 75 *CLJ* 62.

McMeel, G (2006), 'Interpretation and Mistake in Contract Law: "The Fox Knows Many Things . . .", *LMCLQ* 49.

MacMillan, C (2003), 'How Temptation Led to Mistake: An Explanation of *Bell v Lever Bros. Ltd*', 119 *LQR* 625.

Slade, C (1954), 'The Myth of Mistake in the English Law of Contract', 70 *LQR* 385.

Smith, J (1994), 'Contract—Mistake, Frustration and Implied Terms', 110 *LQR* 400.

Stevens, R (2007), 'Objectivity, Mistake and the Parol Evidence Rule' in A Burrows and E Peel (eds), *Contract Terms* (OUP) 101.

7

Frustration

'I should not be bound as things have turned out'

7.1 **Introduction**

If an earthquake destroys a high-rise office block just before you complete its renovation, must the building owner still pay you? Can you be sued for failure to complete? The absurdity of a positive answer in either case is assumed by the doctrine of frustration. In *National Carriers Ltd v Panalpina (Northern) Ltd* (1981), Lord Simon said:

> Frustration of a contract takes place when there supervenes an event (without default of either party and for which the contract makes no sufficient provision) which so significantly changes the nature (not merely the expense or onerousness) of the outstanding contractual rights and/or obligations from what the parties could reasonably have contemplated at the time of its execution that it would be unjust to hold them to the literal sense of its stipulations in the new circumstances.

The doctrine excuses parties from further contractual performance when unforeseen events, *subsequent* to contract formation, make performance *illegal, impossible,* or *radically different* from the obligations the parties undertook at formation. Any obligations accruing before the frustrating event remain binding, but *neither party can be sued for failure to perform outstanding obligations* (they are extinguished). Thus, frustration is a defence to an action for breach of contract. As with the mistake doctrine (Chapter 6), the frustration doctrine is extremely narrow because of the concern to uphold contractual certainty and the parties' risk allocation. It is not enough that the change of circumstances makes performance more onerous or less advantageous for one of the parties. Contracts will only be discharged in the most exceptional circumstances. The main questions to be considered are the following:

(i)   What is the relationship between the doctrines of *frustration* and of *mistake*?

(ii) What is the *justification* for the frustration doctrine?

(iii) What must be *proved* to frustrate a contract?

(iv) What is the *effect* of frustration?

(v)   Is the current law on frustration *satisfactory*? If not, how might it be developed?

7.1.1 **Frustration and mistake**

The doctrines of frustration and common (ie shared) mistaken assumption (6.3) deal with essentially the *same* problem, namely how the law should respond when the parties' assumptions are, or turn out to be, radically different from those which the parties assumed when they entered the contract. Three points support this analysis:

(i) **Only difference in timing**: if the parties' common assumption is false *at* contract formation, the law treats this as a mistake; if their common assumption is falsified *after* contract formation, the law treats this as a case of frustration (Diagram 6D). This temporal difference determines *when* the contract loses its binding force. Mistake sets the contract aside from the beginning (*ab initio*, although voidable contracts can pass property to third parties before they are rescinded). In contrast, frustration *discharges* an otherwise valid contract (discharging future performance) on the occurrence of the frustrating event. Mistake and frustration are essentially similar doctrines:

- the parties' mistake concerns an *existing* or a *future* non-term assumption;
- the assumption *is* or *has become* different from that supposed at formation; and
- both doctrines have been justified in similar terms: risk allocation, implied terms, impossibility of performance, unfairness or deficiency of consent (7.2).

(ii) **Two coronation cases:**

- In *Krell v Henry* (1903), a flat overlooking Pall Mall was rented out for the purpose of watching the coronation procession pass by. The contract was **frustrated** when the king fell ill and the coronation was cancelled. The common assumption that the coronation would take place was falsified *after* formation; but
- In *Griffith v Brymer* (1903), a similar contract was made at 11 am but the decision to cancel the procession for the king's illness had already been made an hour earlier. The contract was voided for **mistake** as made upon a 'missupposition of the state of facts which went to the whole root of the matter'.

Any apparent difference between these cases disappears when it is realised that the mistake in *Krell v Henry* could easily be described in terms of the state of the king's health at the time of contract formation. The legal response should not depend on whether the parties made their contract five minutes before or five minutes after the first appearance of the symptoms, the diagnosis of the disease, the advice to postpone, the king's decision to accept the advice, or the announcement of the cancellation itself.

(iii) **Judicial recognition of similarity:** many cases have noted the similarity between frustration and common mistake.[1] The Court of Appeal has assimilated the two doctrines under the formulation of '*impossibility of performance*' (*Great Peace Shipping Ltd v Tsavliris Salvage (International) Ltd* (2002)). One doctrine can cater for both situations. **Diagram 7A** shows that the test for relief is reducible to a three-step inquiry (mirroring that for mistake):

(1) **Construction:** was the risk of the change of circumstances expressly or impliedly allocated to one of the parties?

(2) **Fault:** was the frustration self-induced?

(3) **Fundamentality:** do the new circumstances render the obligation to perform radically or fundamentally different from that originally undertaken?

Three main differences between mistake and frustration can be identified.

(i) Scope: the scope of frustration is wider than that for mistake; events amounting to frustration may not be sufficient to warrant relief for mistake.

---

[1] *Associated Japanese Bank (International) Ltd v Crédit du Nord SA* (1989) ('related areas'); *William Sindall plc v Cambridgeshire CC* (1994 ('same concept'); *Grains & Fourrages SA v Huyton* (1997) ('analogous concepts'); cf *Joseph Constantine Steamship Line v Imperial Smelting Corp Ltd* (1942) at 186 ('different juristic concepts').

Diagram 7A Frustration: the three-step approach

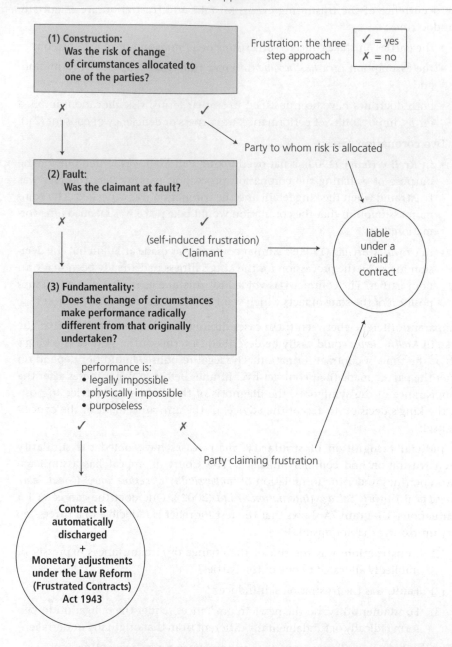

However, the difference is one of degree and not of kind, and rests on the intuition that present facts are more knowable or discoverable than future facts. Courts are understandably readier to allocate to promisors the risk that performance may prove more difficult, or even impossible, in the circumstances existing *at* contract formation, than to hold them to the *further* risk that they will perform 'come hell or high water'. Nevertheless, some future facts are readily knowable (eg when the sun will rise or set on a particular future date), while some present facts are not (eg the cure for AIDS, the whereabouts of a missing person).

(ii) Contract discharged, not void or voidable: both doctrines bring contracts to an end. However, mistake makes contracts *void* or *voidable*, while frustration *discharges* the contract from the time of frustration, automatically extinguishing both parties' obligations, irrespective of their wishes (7.6.1). This can affect the position of good faith third party buyers who acquire rights in the subject matter of the contract (6.2.1). Third parties are fully protected irrespective of frustration since the contract is fully valid at formation.

(iii) Monetary adjustments: the Law Reform (Frustrated Contracts) Act 1943 (LR(FC) A) allows courts to adjust the gains and losses under the contract up to the point of frustration (to reverse enrichment and allow limited loss apportionment, 7.6.3 and 7.6.4). No analogous statutory power exists to sort out the aftermath of operative mistake (although some restitution is available at common law).

However, this difference is fortuitous rather than principled. LR(FC)A was based on a Law Revision Committee report whose terms of reference were limited to considering the frustration problem arising from *Chandler v Webster* (1904) (7.6.2.2). The Court of Appeal in *Great Peace v Tsavliris* recognised that, just as LR(FC)A 'was needed to temper the effect of the common law doctrine of frustration, so there is scope for legislation to give greater flexibility to our law of mistake than the common law allows'.

7.1.2 Development of the frustration doctrine

Prior to 1863, *Paradine v Jane* (1647) was authority for the rule of absolute contractual liability (the *'no excuses'* rule). Accordingly, the court rejected J's plea for relief from paying rent when an enemy invasion drove him out of the premises. The court said: 'if the lessee covenants to repair a house, though it be burnt by lightning, or thrown down by enemies, yet he ought to repair it'.

This extreme position was overturned by *Taylor v Caldwell* (1863). There, C hired a music hall and gardens to T for concerts on four nights and was sued for breach when the music hall burnt down before the first night. Blackburn J found C not liable because the perishing of the person or thing upon which the performance depended excuses the performance. Subsequently, the doctrine was extended *beyond physical impossibility* to cases, like the coronation cases, where performance, although literally possible, 'had become something radically different from that which the parties contemplated when it was concluded' (*Great Peace v Tsavliris*); this has also been called 'failure of adventure', 'impracticability', or 'impossibility of purpose'. In *Jackson v The Union Marine Insurance Co Ltd* (1874), J's ship was chartered to proceed from Liverpool, load a cargo of iron rails and continue to San Francisco. The contract was frustrated when the voyage was delayed for over six months, because the ship was stranded before loading the cargo. The court held that 'a voyage undertaken after the ship was sufficiently repaired would have been a different voyage . . . different as a different adventure'; the delay was so substantial that it destroyed the *commercial sense* of the original transaction.

7.2 **Justification**

As with mistake, the basis for the frustration doctrine has been controversial. The main explanations put forward are:

(i)   implied terms;

(ii) just and reasonable solution; and

(iii) no consent to a radical change in the obligations assumed at formation.

Analogous to the mistake doctrine, explanation (iii), ultimately rooted in no consent, yields the best 'fit' with the three-step inquiry of frustration.

7.2.1 **Implied terms**

Taylor v Caldwell justified the doctrine on the basis of an implied term to the effect that the contract will come to an end on the occurrence of the event that actually occurred. In *FA Tamplin Steamship Co Ltd v Anglo-Mexican Petroleum Products Co Ltd* (1916), Earl Loreburn said the relevant question is: 'Were the altered conditions such that, had [the parties] thought of them, they would have taken their chance of them, or such that as sensible men they would have said, "if that happens, of course, it is all over between us"?' On this view, the contract is discharged because that is what *the parties* have provided for *in* the contract and not because the court has imposed a solution from *outside* the contract; 'the law is only doing what the parties really (though subconsciously) meant to do themselves' (*Hirji Mulji v Cheong Yue SS Co Ltd* (1926)).

 Counterpoint

The attraction of this theory is its consistency with freedom of contract and the will of the contract parties. However, it is open to strong criticisms:

1. Can agreement be implied about an unforeseeable event? Lord Radcliffe observes in *Davis Contractors Ltd v Fareham UDC* (1956) that: 'there is something of a logical difficulty in seeing how the parties could even impliedly have provided for something which *ex hypothesi they* neither expected nor foresaw'. As Lord Sands elaborates (in *James Scott & Sons Ltd v Del Sel* (1922)): 'A tiger has escaped from a travelling menagerie. The milk girl fails to deliver the milk. Possibly the milkman may be exonerated from any breach of contract; but, even so, it would seem hardly reasonable to base that exoneration on the ground that "tiger days excepted" must be held as if written into the milk contract.'

2. Would the parties have agreed to discharge? Even if the parties *had* contemplated the supervening event, they are unlikely to have agreed that the contract should simply cease to bind the parties, leaving losses and gains to lie where they fall as the common law ordains. Lord Wright observes: 'On the contrary, they would almost certainly on the one

→

→ side or the other have sought to introduce reservations or qualifications or compensa-
tions' (*Denny, Mott & Dickson Ltd v Fraser (James B) & Co Ltd* (1944)). This is confirmed by
the widespread use of *force majeure* clauses (7.4.1) where the *parties* (not the frustration
doctrine) stipulate the fate of the contract, and the gains made and losses suffered in its
performance, on the occurrence of various contingencies.

3. Courts can override the parties' attempt to continue the contract: the implied terms
rationale sits uncomfortably with cases where contracts are frustrated despite the parties
expressly *agreeing otherwise* (7.4.2). Thus, a contract was discharged for frustration on a
change of law, although the parties expressly provided that their obligations should only
be postponed (*Ertel Bieber & Co v Rio Tinto Co Ltd* (1918); and 7.3.1).

These difficulties led Lord Watson to say: 'the meaning of the contract must be taken to
be, not what the parties did intend (for they had neither thought nor intention regarding
it), but that which the parties, as fair and reasonable men, would presumably have agreed
upon' (*Dahl v Nelson, Donkin & Co Ltd* (1881)). As Lord Radcliffe famously observes in **Davis
Contractors v Fareham** (1956):

> By this time it might seem that the parties themselves have become so far disembodied
> spirits that their actual persons should be allowed to rest in peace. In their place there
> rises the figure of the fair and reasonable man. And the spokesman of the fair and rea-
> sonable man, who represents after all no more than the anthropomorphic conception
> of justice, is and must be the court itself.

In truth, the contract is discharged by *operation of the law*; the outcome is *imposed* on, rather
than intended by, the parties.

7.2.2 **Just and reasonable solution**

The frustration doctrine has also been explained as 'a device, by which the rules as
to absolute contracts are reconciled with a special exception which justice demands'
(eg, *Hirji Mulji v Cheong Yue SS* (1926)). This view acknowledges that discharge by frustration is imposed *by the courts*. Lord Wright said:[2] 'The truth is that the Court . . .
decides on the question in accordance with what seems just and reasonable in its
eyes.' Similarly, Bingham LJ in *J Lauritzen AS v Wijsmuller BV (The Super Servant Two)*
(1990) said that the frustration doctrine:

> was evolved to mitigate the rigour of the common law's insistence on literal perfor-
> mance of absolute promises. The object of the doctrine was to give effect to the de-
> mands of justice, to achieve a just and reasonable result, to do what is reasonable and
> fair, as an expedient to escape from injustice where such would result from enforce-
> ment of a contract in its literal terms after a significant change in circumstances.

[2] R Wright, *Legal Essays and Addresses* (CUP, 1939) 259; *Denny, Mott & Dickson Ltd v Fraser (James B) &
Co Ltd* (1944).

> ## ➡◀ Counterpoint
>
> 1. Inconsistent with other judicial statements: the House of Lords has denied any broad judi-
>   cial discretion to release parties from contracts whenever a change of circumstances makes
>   the contract significantly more onerous or less advantageous than first anticipated (*British
>   Movietonews Ltd v London and District Cinemas Ltd* (1952)). Nevertheless, it would be dif-
>   ficult to disagree with Rix LJ in *The Sea Angel* (2007) that justice 'is a relevant factor which
>   underlies all and provides the ultimate rationale of the doctrine'.
>
> 2. Inconsistent with drastic consequences: the concern with justice and reasonableness does
>   not explain why contracts are *automatically discharged* rather than, for example, modified
>   to make them more just and reasonable.

7.2.3 Radical change in the obligations: no consent

There is now general agreement[3] that the appropriate test for frustration is that of
'radical change in the obligations undertaken', as set out by Lord Radcliffe in *Davis
Contractors v Fareham*:

> Frustration occurs whenever the law recognises that without default of either party a
> contractual obligation has become incapable of being performed because the circum-
> stances in which performance is called for would render it a thing radically different
> from that which was undertaken by the contract. *Non haec in foedera veni*. It was not
> this that I promised to do.

No consent is the rationale. It is distinguishable from the 'just and reasonable' rationale, which presumes the parties' consent to the obligations from which *the court* gives
relief in the new circumstances. It is distinguishable from the 'implied terms' rationale,
which pretends that *the parties* themselves have consented to end the contract in the
new circumstances. The 'radical change' test assumes that the parties only consent to
perform in a limited (although wide) range of circumstances; when events radically
change the circumstances, taking them *outside* that range, the **consent runs out**:

- 'The question is whether the contract made is, on its true construction, wide
  enough to apply to the new situation: if not, the contract is at an end' (*Davis
  Contractors v Fareham*).

- The change of circumstances must be 'fundamental enough to transmute the job
  the contractors had undertaken into a job of a different kind, which the contract
  did not contemplate and to which it could not apply' (*Sir Lindsay Parkinson & Co
  Ltd v Commissioners of Works* (1949)).

- '[If] consideration of the terms of the contract, in the light of the circumstances existing when it was made, shows that they *never agreed to be bound in a*

---

[3] *Tsakiroglou & Co Ltd v Noblee Thorl GmbH* (1962); *Pioneer Shipping Ltd v BTP Tioxide* (1982); *Paal & Co A/S
v Partenreederei Hannah Blumenthal* (1983); *National Carriers Ltd v Panalpina (Northern) Ltd* (1981).

fundamentally different situation which has now unexpectedly emerged, the contract ceases to bind at that point—not because the court in its discretion thinks it just and reasonable to qualify the terms of the contract, but because *on its true construction it does not apply in that situation'* (*British Movietonews v London & District Cinemas*, emphasis added).

The no consent rationale, underlying the 'radical change of obligations' test, is consistent with *other judicial formulations* of frustration which 'shade into one another' (*National Carriers v Panalpina* (1981)):

(i) *The construction approach:* the range of circumstances to which the obligations attach must be construed from the contract (*Davis Contractors v Fareham*).

(ii) *Disappearance of the foundation of the contract:* in *Krell v Henry*, Vaughan Williams LJ defined the foundation as 'rooms to view the coronation procession' which was destroyed when the procession was cancelled (see also *FA Tamplin Steamship v Anglo-Mexican Petroleum Products*).

(iii) *Impossibility of performance:* in *Great Peace v Tsavliris*, Lord Phillips MR, while not objecting to the 'radical difference' formulation, preferred the *'impossibility of performance'* formulation. He approved Vaughan Williams LJ's statement in *Krell v Henry* which merges the 'construction', 'foundation', and 'impossibility' approaches:

> You first have to ascertain, not necessarily from the terms of contract, but, if required, from necessary inferences, drawn from surrounding circumstances recognised by both contracting parties, what is the substance of the contract, and then to ask the question whether that substantial contract needs for its foundation the assumption of the existence of a particular state of things. If it does, this will limit the operation of the general words, and in such a case, if the contract becomes impossible of performance by reason of the non-existence of the state of things assumed by both parties as the foundation of the contract, there will be no breach.

We will now examine the three stages of the frustration inquiry set out in **Diagram 7A**, but we will start with the changes of circumstances that are fundamental enough to trigger the frustration doctrine.

7.3 **Frustrating circumstances**

Diagram 7A shows that, subject to the risk allocation contained in the contract (7.4) and the complainant's 'fault' (7.5), frustration will only be found if literal performance in the changed circumstances would amount to the performance of a fundamentally or radically different obligation from that originally undertaken. So, a court must:

✓ **first,** construe the contract terms 'in the light of the nature of the contract and of the relevant surrounding circumstances when the contract was made' to determine *the scope of the original rights and obligations* (*Davis Contractors v Fareham*); and

✓ **second**, compare this with a literal enforcement of the obligations in the *new circumstances* to see whether it is *radically or fundamentally different* from the original rights and obligation (*Tsakiroglou & Co Ltd v Noblee Thorl GmbH*).

'[W]hether a supervening event is a frustrating event or not is, in a wide variety of cases, a question of degree' (*National Carriers v Panalpina*). A contract for the carriage of ice would be frustrated by a shorter delay than one for the carriage of iron rails (*Jackson v Union Marine Insurance Co* (1874)). Frustration is not lightly invoked to relieve parties from the consequences of bad bargains. Hardship, inconvenience, or material loss is insufficient. The question is whether the new circumstances make 'performance . . . fundamentally different in a commercial sense' (*Tsakiroglou v Noblee Thorl* (1962); *The Nema* (1982)). In *The Sea Angel* (2007), Rix LJ concedes that the circumstances of frustration 'can be so various as to defy rule making' and advocates a 'multi-factorial approach', taking into account:

- the terms of the contract itself;

- the matrix or context of the contract;

- the parties' knowledge, expectations, assumptions, and contemplations, in particular as to risk, as at the time of contracting, objectively determined;

- the nature of the supervening event; and

- the parties' reasonable and objectively ascertainable calculations as to the possibilities of future performance in the new circumstances.

The scope of frustrating circumstances can only be understood by reference to decided cases. The following overlapping categories give a sense of the shape and size of the doctrine:

(i)   legal impossibility;

(ii) physical impossibility; and

(iii) impossibility of purpose.

The catastrophic destruction of the Twin Towers in New York on 11 September 2001 would frustrate any contract to provide cleaning services on the premises; performance would be illegal (entry being barred), physically impossible, and purposeless.

7.3.1 Legal impossibility

Contractual performance is sometimes made legally impossible by a change in the *law*, or by a change of *circumstances* triggering the operation of pre-existing law. The law may:

(i)   **prohibit the performance undertaken in the contract**: eg,

- trading with the enemy (*Fibrosa Spolka Akcyjna v Fairbairn Lawson Combe Barbour Ltd* (1943)); or

- continuing with a project (*Metropolitan Water Board v Dick Kerr & Co Ltd* (1918)), a certain type of trading (*Denny, Mott & Dickson v Fraser* (1944)), or employment (*Reilly v R* (1934)).

(ii) **deprive a party of control over the subject matter of the contract**: as where the state compulsorily acquires land (*Baily v De Crespigny* (1869)), ships (*Bank Line Ltd v Arthur Capel & Co* (1919)), or oil fields (*BP Exploration Co (Libya) Ltd v Hunt (No 2)* (1979)).

In this category, the *public policy* underlying the illegality *trumps the parties' express provisions*. Thus, a prohibition against trading with enemy aliens will frustrate a contract between residents of warring countries even if their contract agrees to postpone their obligations until the cessation of hostilities (*Ertel Bieber v Rio Tinto* (1918)).

Aside from trading with the enemy, a supervening law (or fact, triggering the application of existing law) will only frustrate a contract if it makes a radical difference to the contractual obligations originally undertaken and not if it merely delays or hinder its operation in part. Again, it is a matter of degree:

✓ A contract to build a reservoir in six years was halted when the government ordered the builders to cease work and remove and sell their plant. Although the contract provided for extensions of time 'whatsoever and howsoever occasioned', this was held not to apply because the interruption was of such a character and likely to last so long as to fundamentally change the obligations undertaken; the builder 'is not bound to submit to an aleatory [ie random] bargain to which he has not agreed' (*Metropolitan Water Board v Dick Kerr*).

✗ A 99-year lease was not frustrated by government restrictions on building since the lease still had over 90 years to run and 'the length of the interruption so caused is presumably a small fraction of the whole term' (*Cricklewood Property and Investment Trust Ltd v Leighton's Investment Trust Ltd* (1945)).

✗ A ship chartered for five years was requisitioned by the government after two years and altered for use as a troopship. The ship-owner claimed substantial compensation from the Crown, arguing frustration of the charterparty. The House of Lords denied frustration since the charterparty expressly permitted the charterer to sublet the ship on Admiralty or other service and there remained many months when the ship might still be free for commercial use; thus, the compensation belonged to the charterer (*FA Tamplin Steamship v Anglo-Mexican Petroleum Products* (1916)).

7.3.2 Physical impossibility

The clearest case of frustration occurs when the supervening event makes performance physically impossible (usually only for one party, the other still being able to perform by paying money). However:

(i) Impossibility of performance is *insufficient*: even a wholly unforeseen catastrophe will not excuse a party if the construction (risk allocation) of the contract shows that she has undertaken to pay damages anyway. There is a difference between misjudgment and wholly unforeseen events; 'a man may undertake to do that which turns out to be impossible, and yet he may still be bound by his agreement' (*Taylor v Caldwell*).

(ii) Impossibility of performance is *unnecessary*: legal impossibility and impossibility of purpose (7.3.1 and 7.3.3) may frustrate contracts although they are still *physically* possible to perform. Moreover, supervening events may only result in *partial* impossibility or only make the contract more onerous or time-consuming to perform. Whether they frustrate the contract is a question of *degree*. Courts are particularly unwilling to allow *commercial* parties to escape bad bargains or risks against which they could reasonably be expected to provide for.

Physical impossibility cases can be divided into:

- death or incapacity in personal service contracts;
- destruction of the subject matter of the contract;
- failure of supplies; and
- delay and hardship.

7.3.2.1 Death or incapacity in personal service contracts

A contract of personal service is frustrated if the death or incapacitating illness of one party renders its performance impossible or radically different. Contracts have been frustrated where the performing party:

✓ dies (*Stubbs v Holywell Railway Co* (1867); *Condor v The Barron Knights Ltd* (1966); *Whincup v Hughes* (1871));

✓ is interned, conscripted, or imprisoned for all or the substantial remainder of the contract's duration; although only the employer can frustrate the contract for an employee's imprisonment. The employee is barred since it is her fault (ie the frustration is self-induced, 7.5) (*Horlock v Beal* (1916); *Morgan v Manser* (1948); *FC Shepherd & Co v Jerrom* (1987));

✓ is incapacitated by illness: in *Notcutt v Universal Equipment Co* (1986), an employment contract was frustrated when an employee suffered a heart attack and could never work again. Illness will not necessarily frustrate a contract of employment. The question is one of degree; namely, whether the employee's incapacity or likely incapacity is such that 'further performance of his obligations in the future would either be impossible or would be a thing radically different from that undertaken by him and accepted by the employer under the agreed terms of this employment' (*Marshall v Harland & Wolff Ltd* (1972)). Relevant considerations include: the *terms* of the contract; the *nature* and *duration* of the employment and of the *illness*; the period of past service; and the prospect of recovery.

The contract is not necessarily frustrated by death or incapacity if performance is not of a personal character:

✗ a contract between performers and music hall proprietors was not frustrated by the death of one of the proprietors (*Phillips v Alhambra Palace Co Ltd* (1901)).

7.3.2.2 Destruction of the subject matter

Destruction of something necessary for contractual performance may frustrate the contract. Destruction by fire is a ready example (eg *Taylor v Caldwell*, discussed earlier, and *Appleby v Myers* (1867), where the contract to supply and install machinery in a factory was frustrated when fire destroyed the factory including the machinery). The courts have suggested that *leases* (7.3.3.2) could, wholly exceptionally, be frustrated by the *literal disappearance of the premises*, as where 'some vast convulsion of nature swallowed up the property altogether, or buried it in the depths of the sea [eg a tsunami]' (*Cricklewood v Leightons*) or if an upper floor flat were totally destroyed by fire or earthquake (*National Carriers v Panalpina*).

Where the subject matter is only **partially destroyed**, frustration is a matter of degree.

✓ In *Asfar v Blundell* (1895), a cargo of dates was submerged for two days and so affected by water sewage as to become 'for business purposes something else', although it could still be distilled into spirit and sold for £2,400.

✓ In *Jackson v Union Marine Insurance Co*, a charterparty was frustrated when, on the first day, the ship ran aground and was not refloated and repaired for seven months. The damage occasioned such delay that it amounted to 'practical commercial destruction'; performance after such delay would be of no use to the charterer.

All this is subject to the *contractual allocation of risks* for the supervening destruction of the subject matter (7.4). After all, very little is physically impossible to replace today if one puts in enough money and effort; the music hall and the factory can be rebuilt. Thus, physical destruction cases overlap with cases of delay and increased costs discussed at 7.3.2.4.

7.3.2.3 Failure or disruption of supplies

✓ Section 7 of the Sale of Goods Act 1979 provides: 'Where there is an agreement to sell specific goods and subsequently the goods, without any fault on the part of the seller or buyer, perish before the risk passes to the buyer, the agreement is avoided.' '**Specific goods**' are goods identified and agreed on at the time the contract is made (otherwise it is impossible to tell whether 'they' have perished).

✗ Contracts for **unascertained goods** are rarely frustrated because, subject to physical or legal impossibility, the *source of supply is normally at the supplier's risk*. The supplier can always find an alternative source, albeit at greater cost and inconvenience. Consistently, where a particular source was only intended by *one* of the parties, failure of that source will not frustrate the contract (*Blackburn Bobbin Co Ltd v TW Allen Ltd* (1918)). For instance, in *CTI Group Inc v Transclear SA* (2008), C planned to export a cargo of cement to Mexico to try to break a cartel operated by Cemex. C contracted to buy from T, who would not perform because of Cemex's influence. There was no frustration because the source of the cement, which failed, was not agreed.

✓ But a contract may be frustrated if the source of supply was intended by *both* parties and it fails without the fault of either party, eg where:

- a potato crop grown on land specified in the contract fails through drought or disease (*Howell v Coupland* (1876)); or

- Importation of the goods from a particular place has become impossible due to war, natural disasters, or prohibition of export *(Re Badische Co Ltd* (1921)).

Where the commonly intended source **partially fails**, a term will be implied requiring the supplier to deliver the smaller quantity available. The supplier is relieved only to the extent of the deficiency (7.5.3 Pause for reflection). In *Sainsbury v Street* (1972), S agreed to sell Sainsbury's 275 tons of barley grown on S's farm, but the yield was only 140 tons, which S sold to a third party. The court held that Sainsbury's should have the option of requiring S to deliver the tonnage actually produced. Otherwise, in times of failing crops, the supplier could disregard its contracts and profit from rising prices by selling elsewhere.

 Pause for reflection

Although partial excuse for non-performance was justified by reference to *implied terms* in *Sainsbury v Street* (see also *Howell v Coupland*), the solution draws from the same well as frustration. It permits a more flexible response by, in effect, *varying the contract* (7.7), rather than automatically discharging it. By analogy, where a supplier makes a *number of contracts* intending to satisfy them from a supply which partly fails, a *pro rata division* is the fair response, but if partial performance is impossible because the supply cannot be sensibly divided (eg ships or hotel rooms) then allocation along the lines of '*first come, first served*' can be justified, frustrating the rest (7.5.3).

7.3.2.4 Delay and hardship

Few contracts are 'impossible' to perform; it all depends on the state of technology and the amount of trouble and expense a party can be expected to go to. At what point should frustration be found? The United States prefers the terminology of 'impracticality' (Uniform Commercial Code, § 2-615). The Second Restatement of the Law of Contracts, § 261, refers to 'extreme and unreasonable difficulty, expense, injury or loss' to one of the parties. These terms suggest a wider scope of frustrating circumstances than under English law where it is not enough that performance has become commercially unreasonable; a radical change in the obligations originally undertaken is required. However, in practice, the line is difficult to stabilise.

Delay and hardship have many potential causes. **Charterparties** may be affected by the ship being:

- stranded (*Jackson v Union Marine Insurance Co Ltd*);
- requisitioned (*FA Tamplin Steamship v Anglo-Mexican Petroleum Products*);
- seized (*WJ Tatem v Gamboa* (1939); *The Adelfa* (1988)); or
- detained (*Embiricos v Reid (Sydney) & Co* (1914)).

They may also be affected by strikes (*Budgett & Co v Binnington & Co* (1891)), or the closure of intended routes (*Tsakiroglou v Noblee Thorl; The Eugenia* (1962)).

Building contracts may be affected by:

- shortages of labour and materials (*Davis Contractors v Fareham*); or
- wartime restrictions (*Metropolitan Water Board v Dick Kerr*).

The focus is not the *cause* of the delay or hardship, but the *effect* it has on the *performance* of the obligations undertaken (*The Nema*). Do they fall outside what the parties could reasonably contemplate at the time of contracting? Three factors are particularly significant to a finding of frustration:

(i) The increased difficulty of performance must be caused by a new and unforeseeable event, and not merely be within the commercial risks undertaken

✗ In *Davis Contractors v Fareham*, D agreed to build 78 houses for F. The work took almost three times longer and cost £17,000 more than was planned because of serious labour shortages and difficulties in obtaining building supplies. D completed performance but argued that the contract was frustrated so that they were not confined to the contract price but could claim an extra £17,000 on a *quantum meruit* (a reasonable price in the absence of a contract). The House of Lords rejected this since:

(i) by agreeing a fixed price, D took the risk of increased costs and delay;

(ii) the difficulties were clearly foreseeable and D could have provided for them in the contract; and

(iii) although D's performance was significantly more onerous, it was *not radically different* from that originally undertaken.

Lord Radcliffe said: 'it is not hardship or inconvenience or material loss itself which calls the principle of frustration into play. There must be as well such a change in the significance of the obligation that the thing undertaken would, if performed, be a different thing from that contracted for.' Thus, frustration will not avail where building contracts encounter delays or disruptions in the supply of labour or materials, or where rising prices eat into the builder's expected profit. As Lord Reid said, although 'the delay was greater in degree than was to be expected . . . [i]t was not caused by any new and unforeseeable factor or event: the job proved to be more onerous but it never became a job of a different kind from that contemplated in the contract.'

✗ *Inflation* and *fluctuations in the value of currencies* will not normally frustrate the contract, although fluctuations of a wholly astronomical order may do so.[4]

✗ *Severe economic crises* will not normally frustrate the contract. In *Tandrin Aviation v Aero Toy Store* (2010), the court rejected the argument that the 'unanticipated, unforeseeable and cataclysmic downward spiral of the world's financial markets' was sufficient to constitute a *force majeure* event (7.4.1), nor would it amount to frustration.

✗ *Bad weather conditions* which delayed the unloading of cargo by four days did not frustrate the contract in *Thiis v Byers* (1876). Since the charterer was given a number of days for unloading, it must 'take the risk of any ordinary vicissitudes'; it was liable for demurrage.

[4] *Multiservice Bookbinding Ltd v Marden* (1979); *British Movietonews v London and District Cinemas* (1952); *Davis Contractors Ltd v Fareham*; *National Carriers v Panalpina*.

✗ The same generally applies where delays in loading or unloading are caused by *strikes* (*Budgett & Co v Binnington & Co* (1891)).

✓ However, a prolonged strike may exceptionally frustrate the charterparty because of the operation of the following two factors:

(i) Parties are entitled to know where they stand

A party can claim frustration through delay *before* the expiry of the time for performance, since parties should be able to rearrange their affairs in response to the event and not be left in suspense. In *The Nema*, Lord Roskill said (and see *National Carriers v Panalpina*; *Bank Line v Arthur Capel*):

> it is often necessary to wait upon events in order to see whether the delay already suffered and the prospects of further delay from that cause, will make any ultimate performance of the relevant contractual obligations 'radically different' . . . from that which was undertaken by the contract. But, as has often been said, businessmen must not be required to await events too long. They are entitled to know where they stand. Whether or not the delay is such as to bring about frustration must be a question to be determined by an informed judgment based upon all the evidence of what has occurred and what is likely thereafter to occur. Often it will be a question of degree whether the effect of delay suffered, and likely to be suffered, will be such as to bring about frustration of the particular adventure in question.

Lord Roskill recognised that judgments may differ on what is ultimately a question of law, and said that appeal courts should be slow to interfere with a lower tribunal's finding on this issue.

✓ In *The Nema*, a ship was chartered for seven consecutive voyages between April and December 1979. After the first voyage, strikes beginning on 6 June grounded *The Nema*. On 3 October, an arbitrator (later upheld by the House of Lords) decided that the contract was frustrated although the strike ended two days later.

✓ In *Embiricos v Reid*, a charterparty for a voyage through the Dardanelles was frustrated on the outbreak of war between Greece and Turkey when it was thought that the Dardanelles would be closed for the entire length of the charterparty, although it was actually opened for a period during which the contract could have been performed.

(iii) Performance in the new circumstances radically alters the original rights and obligations

Three categories can be isolated.

First, if it is clear from the terms or nature of the contract that it was to be performed only at a specified time or within a specified period, subsequent delayed performance may be of *no use to the recipient* and so frustrate the contract. Thus:

✓ in *Jackson v Union Marine Insurance Ltd*, a seven-month delay in a charterparty, according to which a ship was to sail 'with all possible despatch' to load a cargo at Newport for San Francisco, frustrated the contract. The court held that a voyage after the delay would be a 'different voyage' from the one undertaken, as it would be an autumn rather than a spring voyage which was crucial in the context of the contract.

Second, performance after the delay may be radically different because performance would occur in a radically altered market.

✓ In *Acetylene Corp of Great Britain v Canada Carbide Co* (1921), a shipment of goods sold was delayed for three years by wartime requisitioning. The contract was held to be frustrated because the market conditions had radically changed in that time.

✓ In *Metropolitan Water Board v Dick Kerr* (7.4.1), wartime restrictions delayed indefinitely the performance of a contract to build a reservoir two years into the six-year contract period. The House of Lords found frustration since the project was so disrupted that enforcement of performance would not be to maintain the original contract but to substitute a different contract: Lord Parmoor said:

> I agree that the probability of hardship to one side or the other is not a matter of material consideration, but it is quite a different matter when there is an indefinite and indeterminate liability which might impose on either party an unforeseen burden totally foreign to the ordinary incidents in a contract of this character ... [Performance] at some future period ... will be under a different contract based on changed considerations. All the prices will have to be fixed in reference to different conditions, and the time over which the work will be carried on will be wholly different.

✓ In *Bank Line Ltd v Arthur Capel & Co Ltd* (1919), a charterparty to start in April for 12 months was frustrated when the ship was requisitioned until September. Later performance would be, 'as a matter of business a totally different thing', mainly because the hire rates had increased enormously over the short period.

Third, a contract may be frustrated if the contemplated *means* of performance is made impossible by a supervening event when: (i) it is the *only* method of complying with the contract; or (ii) the alternative means radically alters the obligations undertaken.

✓ In *Nicholl & Knight v Ashton Etridge & Co* (1901), a contract for the sale of goods 'to be shipped per steamship Orlando from Alexandria during . . . January' was frustrated when the ship ran aground and could not reach Alexandria in January.

✓ In *Codelfa Construction Pty Ltd v SRA (NSW)* (1982), a contract to excavate tunnels within 130 weeks was frustrated when the means contemplated by both parties to enable timely completion was prohibited by an injunction preventing work from 10 pm to 6 am.

✗ In *The Eugenia* (1964), a charterparty between Genoa and India (normally through the Suez Canal) was not frustrated by the blocking of the canal during the Anglo-French invasion of Egypt in 1956, although the alternative route, via the Cape of Good Hope, increased the journey time from 108 to 138 days. The difference was not sufficiently radical since '[t]he cargo was such as not to be affected by this delay and there was no evidence that the early arrival of the cargo in India was of particular importance'.

✗ In *Tsakiroglou v Noblee Thorl*, no frustration was found although alternative performance via the Cape of Good Hope (rather than the stipulated one through the Suez Canal) was *three times* longer and far costlier. The House of Lords held that the contract was not commercially or fundamentally different because: the route of delivery is normally irrelevant to the buyer of goods; the goods were not perishable; there was no date fixed for delivery; and there was no shortage of available shipping carrying goods via the Cape. Thus, a contract is not frustrated if the alternative means of performance does not fundamentally differ from the intended means, even if that was *stipulated in the contract* (applied in *The Captain George K* (1970)).

7.3.3 Impossibility of purpose

A contract may be frustrated although performance of the contract is not illegal, impossible or more onerous. Rather, the recipient of the performance claims that the supervening event has so undermined the *purpose* of the contract for her that she should not be required to accept or pay for it. The obvious danger with such a category is its potential width and the danger of allowing complainants to escape bad bargains. Its existence has attracted criticism (eg *Blackburn Bobbin v TW Allen*). Two factors severely limit its scope:

(i) The purpose which has become impossible to achieve must be common to both parties and have, expressly or impliedly, 'been assumed by the parties to be the foundation or basis of the contract' (*Krell v Henry*); the frustrated purposes of only one party will not suffice. It will generally be difficult for a complainant to establish that her purpose, even if obvious, was shared by the other party.

(ii) The common purpose must be thwarted to a *very high degree*.

7.3.3.1 Non-occurrence of an event

Very exceptionally, the *non-occurrence of an event* which constitutes the basis of the contract can frustrate a contract:

✓ In *Krell v Henry*, a contract to hire rooms to see the passing coronation was frustrated when the coronation was cancelled, because the hire was 'for the purpose of seeing the Royal procession' and not simply 'an agreement to let and take the rooms'. This could be inferred from the position of the flat, the flat owner's advertisement for windows to view the royal coronation, and the unusual hire terms (an enhanced price charged for two days excluding nights). Clearly, *the more detailed the description of the common contractual purpose, the more likely that a supervening event will frustrate it.*

✗ *Krell v Henry* said that there would be no frustration if a contract to hire a cab to go to Epsom on Derby Day at an enhanced price was made pointless when the races are cancelled. The purpose is only that of the hirer; 'the cab had no special qualifications for the purpose which led to the selection of the cab for this particular occasion. Any other cab would have done as well.'

✗ Frustration was rejected in *Herne Bay Steamboat v Hutton* (1903), where HBS hired out a pleasure boat 'for the purpose of viewing the naval review and for a day's cruise around the fleet'. Although the naval review was cancelled along with the coronation, the Court of Appeal regarded H's venture to charge passengers for the cruise as his own and at his own risk. By analogy to a cab hire, 'although the object of the hirer might be stated, that statement would not make the object any the less a matter for the hirer alone, and would not directly affect the person who was letting out the vehicle for hire'. Moreover, H's purpose was not entirely thwarted; he could still 'cruise round the fleet. The fleet was there.'

7.3.3.2 Leases and sales of land

It was once thought that leases could not be frustrated since a lease is more than a contract and vests an estate in land (a proprietary interest) that remains even if a supervening event negates the purpose of the lease. However, the House of Lords in *National Carriers v Panalpina* accepted that leases can, in principle, be frustrated (eg *short-term leases* with a *closely prescribed purpose*), although 'hardly ever':

✗ In *National Carriers v Panalpina*, a ten-year lease of a warehouse covenanted for use only as a warehouse for the lessee's business was not frustrated although, five years into the lease, the local authority closed the street giving the only vehicular access to the warehouse for 20 months. The length of the unexpired term (more than three years) was a 'potent factor' in the court's decision, suggesting that the lease would have been frustrated had the prohibition been much longer or permanent.

✗ A 99-year building lease would not be frustrated by wartime building restrictions imposed when it still had 90 years to run and the war was likely to last for only a fraction of that term (*Cricklewood v Leightons*).

Frustration is more likely if commercial premises are let for a *short term*, for *one principal purpose known to the lessor*, that purpose gives the premises its substantial *value* and the supervening event defeats that purpose for a *substantial proportion* of the lease (*National Carriers v Panalpina*):

✓ In the US, leases restricting the use of premises to that of a drinking saloon were held to be frustrated when that use was outlawed.[5]

✓ In *Denny, Mott & Dickson v Fraser*, an agreement to lease a timber yard to allow the parties to perform their contract was frustrated when wartime regulations prohibited the performance.

✓ Leases may also be frustrated by catastrophic events that physically destroy the leased premises (7.3.2.2).

Frustration of **sales of land** is even more rare than frustration of leases, since the risk of destruction, damage, or changes to the land's uses is usually borne by the purchaser as the equitable owner in the period between the making and completion of the contract (when she becomes the legal owner):

✗ A contract is not frustrated if, between the formation and completion of the contract, the land is compulsorily purchased (*Hillingdon Estates Co v Stonefield Estates Ltd* (1952); *E Johnson & Co (Barbados) Ltd v NSR Ltd* (1997)).

---

[5] See G Treitel, *Frustration and Force Majeure* (Sweet & Maxwell, 1994) paras 7–021, 11–017.

✗ In *Amalgamated Investment & Property Ltd v John Walker & Sons Ltd* (1977), J advertised a site as suitable for redevelopment and A made clear that it was buying the property for this purpose. Shortly after the contract was made, the building was listed as a place of special architectural and historical interest. This inhibited redevelopment and reduced the property value £1.7 million to about £200,000. The Court of Appeal rejected A's claim of frustration because there was no warranty that the property could be redeveloped, and the risk that the property might be listed was one that all buyers of property assumed. Performance was not radically different from what was undertaken by the contract. This is something of a retreat from *Krell v Henry*, since the property seems to have been bought and sold *for redevelopment*.

7.4 Construction of the contract

Faced with a defence of frustration to a claim for breach, the court must decide whether the contract, on its proper construction, has *positively* allocated the risk of the supervening events. Only if the contract has *not* expressly or impliedly provided for what should happen in the new circumstances does the frustration doctrine step in to determine whether the parties are absolved from liability for non-performance.

7.4.1 Express provision: *force majeure* and hardship clauses

The uncertainties and rigidity of the frustration doctrine means that many contracting parties are wary of leaving it to the courts. Rather, *they* stipulate in the contract what should happen in certain eventualities (known as *force majeure, hardship*, or *intervener* clauses). Parties can frequently anticipate, in more or less general terms, occurrences that will disturb the equilibrium of their contract to an unacceptable degree. Inserting clauses to deal with such eventualities increases certainty; it lets parties know where they stand, and allows them to depart from the default rules provided by the frustration doctrine. Parties can specify:

(i) the **circumstances** excusing further performance of the contract (these may be wider or narrower than the scope of frustrating circumstances), eg acts of God or of war, strikes, riots, breakdown of machinery, currency fluctuation, or increased costs;

(ii) the **consequences** of the triggering circumstance, eg provision for delay or suspension of performance, conferring rights of cancellation on one or both parties, requiring submission to arbitration, disciplinary procedures, or good faith renegotiation between the parties,[6] or triggering a price-escalation clause.

The parties' express provision for a supervening event must still be **interpreted by the courts** to determine whether it actually covers the supervening event in a 'full and

---

[6] This is distinguishable from *Walford v Miles* (1992) where the *existence* of the contract depended on good faith negotiation (2.6.2.5), and is closer to *Petromec Inc v Petroleo Brasileiro SA Petrobas* (2005) where within an otherwise legally enforceable commercial agreement, the good faith negotiation related to certain specific costs which are 'ascertainable with comparative ease'.

complete' way. The courts have taken a restrictive approach to the interpretation of such clauses to avoid unfair outcomes, analogous to their *contra proferentem* interpretation of very wide clauses excluding or limiting liability for breach (10.5.3); likewise, this is done in the name of the parties' *presumed* intention, eg:

✓ Frustration was found in **Metropolitan Water Board v Dick Kerr** for prolonged delay, although a clause in the contract provided for an extension of time in the event of delay *'whatsoever and howsoever occasioned'*. This was held *not* to cover the situation when the government stopped the work and required the plant to be sold because the disruption and delay ensuing 'could not possibly have been in the contemplation of the parties to the contract when it was made'. Thus, although the clause patently covered the situation, it was very narrowly interpreted to exclude the situation and so absolve the builder from liability. Asquith LJ said (in *Sir Lindsay Parkinson v Commissioners of Works*) that a delay clause suspending the contract does *not* 'apply where the delay was so abnormal, so preemptive, as to fall outside what the parties could possibly have contemplated'. Thus, 'delay' 'has been read as limited to normal, moderate delay, and as not extending to an interruption so differing in degree and magnitude from anything which could have been contemplated as to differ from it in kind. Events will be excluded from the parties' provision if they render further performance of the contract 'unthinkable' (*The Playa Larga* (1983)).

✓ In *Staffordshire Area Health Authority v South Staffordshire Waterworks Co* (1978), a contract was made in 1929 for the supply of water for 7 pence per 1,000 gallons *'at all times hereafter'*. Lord Denning MR held that the contract ceased to bind the parties 50 years later when it cost 20 times more to supply the water. Although the Court of Appeal disagreed with this reasoning, it arrived at the same result by *implying a term* that the contract was terminable by the supplier on reasonable notice.

✗ On the other hand, the court adopted a more literal interpretation of the *force majeure* term in a charterparty, so that charterers were not allowed to frustrate the charter when the vessel was seized by pirates (*Cosco Bulk Carrier Co Ltd v Team-Up Owning Co Ltd (The Saldanha)* (2010)). This was justified by reference to the great importance of certainty in commercial law and the fact that, under a typical time charterparty, hire is payable continuously unless the charterers could bring themselves within any exceptions, the onus being on the charterers to do so.

7.4.2 Implied allocations of risk: foresight

The court may infer from the parties' silence that they have *impliedly* allocated the risk of the supervening event to the performing party (ie the latter remains liable for non-performance). Whether this is so depends on the *type of transaction* and the *particular risk*, eg:

- a long-term lease or a sale of property generally allocates almost all risks to the lessor/buyer; a short-term lease for a specific purpose allocates fewer risks (7.3.3.2);

- a building contract allocates to the builder the risk that the soil conditions and the cost and availability of labour and materials will make performance more onerous than anticipated (*Davis Contractors v Fareham*), but *not* that subsequent legislation will make it illegal; and

- fluctuations in prices or the value of currencies will not normally frustrate the contract (*Davis Contractors v Fareham*, but Lord Reid reserved his position on fluctuations of a wholly astronomical order).

7.4.2.1 How foreseeable must the supervening event be to oust the frustration doctrine?

The narrowness of the doctrine is often justified on the basis that it should only cover unforeseeable events for which the parties could not be expected to provide. However, this point should not be taken too far; foreseeability is a matter of degree. Anything is foreseeable if you are paranoid enough. Provision for every foreseeable contingency would be enormously costly and ultimately wasteful since most will never happen. Hence, parties should be able to rely on the law for a default solution. It is a question of construction whether the parties' silence, despite foreseeing the risk, should be taken to mean:

(i) that the fate of the contract should be *left to 'the lawyers to sort it out'*, by reference to the frustration doctrine (*The Eugenia*); or

(ii) that the contract *remains binding* irrespective of the change of circumstances (ousting the frustration doctrine, eg *Walton Harvey Ltd v Walker & Homfrays Ltd* (1931)). This inference should only be drawn where the *degree of foreseeability is very high*. The event or its consequences must be one which any person of ordinary intelligence would regard as likely to occur and, moreover, one which is foreseeable *in some detail*. The courts will not allow frustration to be ousted easily by silence. In *The Eugenia*, Lord Denning explains:

> It has frequently been said that the doctrine of frustration only applies when the new situation is 'unforeseen' or 'unexpected' or 'uncontemplated', as if that were an essential feature. But it is not so. The only thing that is essential is that the parties should have made no provision for it in their contract ... cases have occurred where the parties have foreseen the danger ahead, and yet made no provision for it in the contract.

✓ Thus, frustration was found in *WJ Tatem Ltd v Gamboa* (1939), where G chartered from T a steamship for 30 days to evacuate refugees from the Spanish Civil War. A daily rate of hire was payable until the ship's return and would only cease if the ship went 'missing'. Halfway through the charter period, the ship was seized and not returned for about two months. T's claim for the daily hire rate during that entire period was denied because the contract was frustrated on the ship's seizure. Although it was foreseeable that the ship might be seized (inferable from the very high rate of hire), it was not foreseeable that the ship would be detained for so long after the hire period.

7.5 **Fault: self-induced frustration**

Even if the supervening event is sufficiently fundamental and its risk not allocated by the contract to one of the parties, frustration is barred if the complainant's own deliberate or negligent conduct has brought about the alleged frustrating event. This is not 'something altogether outside the control of the parties' (*Denmark Productions Ltd v Boscabel Productions Ltd* (1969)); the complainant remains liable for breach. It is up to the party suing for breach to prove that the event was self-induced (*Joseph Constantine SS Line v Imperial Smelting Corp Ltd* (1942)). In *The Super Servant Two*, Hobhouse J set out three such categories: breach of contract, anticipatory breach of contract, and power to elect.

7.5.1 Breach of contract

A party cannot plead frustration if she has contributed to the alleged frustrating event by conduct amounting to a breach of the contract. Thus, there was no frustration where:

- ✗ a charterer ordered a ship into a war zone where it was then detained (*The Eugenia*); and

- ✗ a carrier's ship was unseaworthy, which caused delays which then made the journey impossible to complete because of the supervening outbreak of war (*Monarch SS Co v A/B Karlshamns Oljefabriker* (1949)).

7.5.2 Anticipatory breach of contract

A party is also disqualified from claiming frustration if her deliberate, voluntary or negligent conduct has the effect of disabling her from performance of the contract, analogous to anticipatory breach by the party's own act. The issue is one of *control*; the test is whether the complainant had the *means and opportunity to prevent* the alleged frustrating event from occurring, but nevertheless caused or permitted it to occur. As Lord Russell said: 'The possible varieties are infinite, and can range from the criminality of the scuttler who opens the sea-cocks and sinks his ship, to the thoughtlessness of the prima donna who sits in a draught and loses her voice.' However, not 'every destruction of corpus for which a contractor can be said, to some extent or in some sense, to be responsible, necessarily' excludes frustration for being self-induced (*Joseph Constantine v Imperial Smelting Corp* (1942)); it is a matter of degree. If one party is disqualified by her self-induced frustration, the other party can still rely on the otherwise frustrating event. In *FC Shepherd v Jerrom* (1987), J's detention in borstal for 39 weeks prevented his performance of his apprenticeship. However, his employer could rely upon this as frustrating the contract to counter J's claim for unfair dismissal.

7.5.3 Power to elect

Where a party enters into a number of contracts and an external event *partially* destroys her supplies so that she cannot satisfy all her contracts, she must *choose* which contracts to allocate remaining supplies to, and which to leave unperformed. The very fact that a party has *exercised a choice* not to perform a certain contract bars the frustration of that contract; her choice breaks the chain of causation between the external event and her inability to perform. In contrast, frustration is permitted if: (i) the outside event *completely* destroys a party's supplies; or (ii) she had specified only one mode of performance or allocated a specific supply to a particular contract, and that becomes impossible to perform due to the outside event.

✗ In *Maritime National Fish v Ocean Trawlers* (1935), M chartered from O a trawler for otter trawling. M applied for five licences but received only three, which they allocated to other trawlers (including two of their own), and unsuccessfully sought to frustrate the contract with O. The Privy Council held M liable to O for the hire because O's trawler was only not usable for otter trawling due to M's own election. The contract with O would have been possible to perform if M had allocated a licence to O's trawler.

✗ In *The Super Servant Two*, W agreed to transport L's drilling rig between 20 June and 20 August using, *at its option*, either *The Super Servant One* or *The Super Servant Two*. W internally allocated the latter to this contract and committed *The Super Servant One* to other contracts. Prior to performance, *The Super Servant Two* sank. The Court of Appeal rejected W's claim of frustration because it was W's own election not to use the remaining ship (*The Super Servant One*) that led to its non-performance, and not the sinking of *The Super Servant Two*. The court also justified allocating the risk of partial failure of supplies to the carrier because 'it is within the promisor's control how many contracts he enters into'. In the end, the carrier was excused under the *force majeure* clause in the contract, which covered certain events, including 'perils or dangers and accidents of the sea'.

Two objections can be raised:

(i) If frustration is barred because the complainant has chosen to enter a contract or could have provided for the frustrating event, then we are back to absolute liability because these will always be the case.

(ii) W's power to allocate *The Super Servant One* to its contract with L was entirely *theoretical* since the ship was already allocated to other jobs. Thus, a party can only *guard against the finding of self-induced frustration* by:

- eliminating any choice by expressly allocating specific supplies to particular contracts; or

- including a suitable *force majeure* clause.

 Pause for reflection

The Super Servant Two can be criticised for leaving a seller or supplier of goods in an impossible position where her source partially fails due to an unforeseen event. She cannot perform all of her contracts, but, because she can perform *some*, she will not be able to frustrate *any*; merely choosing *which* contract not to perform breaks the chain of causation with the supervening event. The rationale of the frustration doctrine should permit a party not at fault to frustrate only *some* of her contracts where a supervening event makes it impossible for her to perform them all. Four arguments support this contention:

→

➡

1. Conclusion unnecessary: the Court of Appeal in *The Super Servant Two* said that *Maritime National Fish v Ocean Trawlers* required it to find no frustration. However, while it was possible in *Maritime National Fish* for the complainant to perform *all* of its contracts despite the partial failure of supplies (by not allocating a license to its own boat), this was impossible in *The Super Servant Two*. Strictly speaking, *Maritime National Fish* only bars frustration where a party has a genuine choice *whether* to perform all her contracts and chooses not to; it does not apply where a party's only choice is as to *which* of her contracts will be left unperformed.

2. Existence of choice is not inconsistent with discharge: the presence of choice was also said to bar frustration because choice is inconsistent with the automatic discharge effected by frustration. However, *FC Shepherd v Jerrom* (7.5.2) shows that, in certain cases, only one of the parties can claim frustration; if that party does not, the contract remains valid.

3. The problem is not choice but favouritism: the complainant's choice as to which contracts to perform should not eclipse the greater causative potency of the external event which destroys the complainant's ability to perform all of her contracts, and forces her to choose in the first place. The real objection is the potential for her to give *preferential treatment* to her most profitable contract partners (whether present or prospective). The same objection may underlie the finding in *George Mitchell (Chesterhall) Ltd v Finney Lock Seeds Ltd* (1983) that the wide clause limiting damages for breach of contract to supply seeds was unreasonable under the Unfair Contract Terms Act 1977 because, inter alia, the evidence showed that, in practice, the seller, at its discretion, often negotiated settlements well beyond that stipulated in the limitation clause (11.5.5.2).

4. Other solution preferable: the solution is to eliminate the complainant's choice by requiring her to allocate her remaining supplies fairly. In relation to fungible (ie interchangeable) goods like potatoes or widgets, the supplier could be required to deliver her supplies *rateably* to each contract partner (ie reducing the amount to each in proportion to what was originally contracted for). This is consistent with the cases on partial failure of supply where *force majeure* or 'prohibition of export' clauses were in place[7] and where they were not[8] (7.3.2.3). Suppliers were excused from full performance if they acted fairly and reasonably in allocating their remaining supplies along the lines suggested. Of course, ships, unlike potatoes or widgets, are not capable of rateable division, but the principle is the same. The supplier should be required to perform her contracts in the order that the contracts were made or performance required: 'first come, first served'. The denial of frustration in *The Super Servant Two* is consistent with this approach. One of the two contracts which the complainant chose to perform instead of L's contract was made *after* the contract with L. Moreover, the complainant only finally allocated *The Super Servant One* to the other contracts after successfully extracting extra fees from them after the sinking of *The Super Servant Two*.

---

[7] *Intertradax SA v Lesieur-Tourteaux SARL* (1978); *Bremer Handelsgesellschaft v Continental Grain Co* (1983).
[8] *Howell v Coupland* (1876); *Sainsbury Ltd v Street* (1972).

7.6 **The effect of frustration**

7.6.1 **Automatic discharge**

A contract is automatically *discharged* for frustration. The consent that initially attaches to the contract at formation 'runs out' on the occurrence of the frustrating event, relieving both parties from further performance (or liability for non-performance). The contract cannot be kept alive or revived at the option of either party; neither can the court keep the contract on foot and adjust the terms to meet the new circumstances (subject to the discussion on partial failure of supply at 7.3.2.3). In *Hirji Mulji v Cheong Yue* (1926), a charterparty was frustrated although the complainant initially confirmed its willingness to continue with the charter after the ship was released from government requisitioning. However, a party responsible for the frustrating event cannot treat herself as automatically discharged from the contract, although her contract partner can do so (*FC Shepherd v Jerrom*, 7.5.2).

7.6.2 **Losses and gains under the contract**

7.6.2.1 Overview

Automatic discharge is straightforward where the contract is executory (yet to be performed), but problems arise where the contract is partly executed (performance has begun). Take the example in **Diagram 7B** of a contract where *A* contracts to pay £50,000 for ten performances by *B* in *A*'s theatre. At the point of frustration:

- *A* may have actually made some payment (*A$*) to B or the payment may be owing (*A$* due); *A* may also have incurred other costs in furtherance of its own contractual performance, eg maintaining the theatre and advertising the performances (*A* costs); and

- *B* may have given all or just some of the performances (*B* non-$ benefit) and may also have incurred costs in furtherance of its contractual performance by, eg hiring actors and making costumes (*B* costs).

'*A$*', '*A$* due', and '*B* non-$ benefit' represent the extent of contractual *performances actually conferred* on or owed to the other party under the contract. They are on the plus side of any restitutionary claim under LR(FC)A.

'*A* costs' and '*B* costs' represent the *cost* of performance (which may exceed the value of any benefit conferred on the other party); they are the minus side, which can be deducted from each party's restitutionary liability under LR(FC)A.

The law's response to the gains and losses before and after LR(FC)A is summarised in **Diagram 7B**.

7.6.2.2 The common law position

The common law position, although superseded by LR(FC)A, is important to an understanding of LR(FC)A itself.

(i) **Money paid or due:**
- originally, losses lay where they fell—any sums paid before the frustrating event were *unrecoverable* and any sums *due* before the frustrating event still

Diagram 7B The Law Reform (Frustrated Contracts) Act 1943

Look on the online resources to view this figure as a PowerPoint® presentation

B's s 1(3) claim =

B non-$ (value of benefit to A)

A's s 1(2) claim =

A$ (money paid to B)

+ A$ due (money due to B)

− B expenses (B's 'just expenses')

$A \xrightarrow{\quad £50,000 \quad} $

$ \xleftarrow{\quad} B$

10 performances

Taking account of:

- the evaluation in the contract
- the effect of the frustration
- whether A$ received is kept or returned
- A's other performance expenses

	Common law (superseded)	LR(FC)A 1943	Issues under LR(FC)A
1. Money paid : A$	A can only recover if total failure of consideration (TFC) from B (*Fibrosa*)	A can recover *without* TFC **(s 1(2))**	• *Calculation of B's 'just expenses'*
	If so, A can recover entire payment	A's recovery is subject to B's retention of 'just expenses' to reflect B expenses **(s 1(2))**	• B's 'just expenses' cannot exceed money paid and payable (ie no more than A$ + A$ due) (*Gamerco*)
2. Money due but unpaid : A$ due	A must still pay this (*Chandler*)	A is only *liable* to the extent that B's 'just expenses' (B expenses) exceed recovery of money paid (A$) **(s 1(2))**	
3. Non-money benefits conferred by B on A: B non-$	B can only recover sums that are 'due' (*Appleby*)	B can claim 'just sum' **(s 1(3))** = sum not exceeding the benefit conferred on A (B non-$) taking into account: • the effect of frustration on the value of B non-$; • the contract valuation of B's expenses and services (B expenses); • payments from A (A$) subject to s 1(2) claim by A; and • A's other expenses	• *Stage I:* Identification and valuation of benefit received (B non-$) • *Stage II:* Calculation of 'just sum' which cannot exceed B non-$ (*BP v Hunt*)

had to be paid. In *Chandler v Webster* (1904), C paid £100 immediately to hire a room to watch the coronation, £41 being payable later, but before the coronation was cancelled and the contract frustrated. C could not recover the £100 paid and was liable for the £41; however

- this position was softened by allowing recovery of money paid for *total failure of consideration* in **Fibrosa Spolka Ackcyjna v Fairbairn Lawson Combe Barbour Ltd** (1943). FSA prepaid £1,000 for the manufacture of machinery. When the contract was frustrated by the outbreak of war, FLCB refused to return the money because they had incurred considerable expenses under the contract. The court allowed recovery of the £1,000. Note that the 'consideration', which had totally failed, is not the consideration required for contract *formation* (this will often just be a *promise* of performance). It is the *performance* of the contract itself; the buyer had received nothing at all. This left the law in an *unsatisfactory* state: (a) the requirement of *total failure* barred recovery if the payer has received *any*, even trivial, performance (*Whincup v Hughes* (1871)); and (b) the payee cannot offset their wasted expenses in performance of the contract.

(ii) **Non-money benefits**: prior to LR(FC)A, the value of goods or services conferred under the contract was only recoverable if payment for them was 'due' under the contract *before* the frustrating event. Obligations to pay thereafter, as with all outstanding obligations, are discharged on frustration. In *Appleby v Myers* (1867), a contract to install machinery in M's factory and maintain it for two years, *payment on completion* of the work, was frustrated when an accidental fire destroyed the factory and machinery. M recovered nothing for the work already done since payment only fell due on completion. This is unjust where the benefit conferred survives the frustrating event.

7.6.2.3 The aims of LR(FC)A

The problems identified under the common law are addressed by LR(FC)A, which regulates the effects of frustrated contracts unless the parties have expressly provided otherwise (s 2(3)). Goff J said (in *BP Exploration Co (Libya) Ltd v Hunt* (1979)) that the 'fundamental principle underlying the Act . . . is prevention of unjust enrichment of either party to the contract at the other's expense' and *not* the apportionment of the loss caused by the frustration of the contract. More broadly, Lawton LJ said in the Court of Appeal that LR(FC)A was simply to 'make the operation of the law more fair' (*BP v Hunt* (1981)).

▶◀ Counterpoint

1. LR(FC)A is primarily aimed at reversing unjust enrichment, but this is tempered by *some loss apportionment* to take some account of the recipient's wasted expenses in performance of the contract.

2. Both are justifiable responses to the impact of catastrophic events on innocent parties engaged in a joint enterprise.

3. McKendrick criticises LR(FC)A as inadequately thought through but he regards the loss-sharing schemes in other jurisdictions as having gone too far ('Frustration, Restitution and Loss Apportionment' in A S Burrows (ed), *Essays on the Law of Restitution* (OUP, 1991)).

7.6.3 **Money paid or payable under LR(FC)A**

Section 1(2) of LR(FC)A:

- allows the payer's claim to recover *payments* made prior to the frustrating event (*A* can claim *A*$);
- relieves the payer from paying *sums due* prior to discharge; and
- empowers the court 'if it considers it just to do so having regard to all the circumstances' to allow the payee to set off against the sum to be returned, and claim against the sum payable by *A* but not paid, the whole or part of her *expenses* incurred, before the time of discharge, in or for the purpose of, the performance of the contract (ie (*A*$ + *A*$ due)—*B* expenses).

    - 'Expenses' include 'such sum as appears to be reasonable in respect of overhead expenses and in respect of any work or services performed personally by the said party' (s 1(4)), including *pre-contract expenses* incurred 'for the purpose of, the performance of the contract'.

(i) **How should the payee's 'just expenses' (*B*2) be calculated?** In *Gamerco SA v ICM/Fair Warning (Agency) Ltd* (1995), represented in **Diagram 7C**, $775,000 was payable by the promoters of a concert, of which $412,500 had been paid to the pop group (Guns N' Roses) by the time the concert venue was declared unsafe and the contract frustrated. Both sides had incurred wasted expenses in preparation for the concert (the group $50,000 and the promoters $450,000). How much should be deducted from the promoters' claim under section 1(2) for the sum paid, as 'just expenses', to reflect the group's wasted expenses? Garland J posits three possible approaches:

✗ **Total retention:** this would allow Guns N' Roses to offset *all* its wasted expenses, and reduce the promoter's recovery ($412,500 – $50,000). In *BP v Hunt*, Goff J

Diagram 7C Restitution of money paid: deduction of 'just expenses' in *Gamerco*

	Promoter = s 1(2) claimant	**Pop group**
Contractual obligation	Pay $775K	Give performance
Benefit received from the other party prior to frustration	Nothing	$412.5K
Expenses incurred under the contract prior to frustration	$450K	$50K

Promoter claims restitution of **$412.5K** paid. How much should be deducted as the pop group's 'just expenses' for its wasted expenses of $50K?
(a) Total: $412.5K – **$50K** = $362.5K
(b) Equal apportionment $412.5K – **$25K** = $387.5K
(c) **Broad discretion:** $412.5K – **$0**   = $412.5K

supports this on the basis that LR(FC)A gave statutory recognition to the defence of *change of position*; that is, the payee can deduct from the sum to be returned (or, claim it against the sum due) the amount spent in reliance on the security of its receipt.

✗ **Equal apportionment**: this offsets half of Guns N' Roses's wasted expenses, and the promoter would recover $412,500 – $25,000.

✓ **Broad discretion**: this is exercised by the court to 'do justice in a situation which the parties had neither contemplated nor provided for, and to mitigate the possible harshness of allowing all loss to lie where it has fallen'.

Garland J thought there was 'no indication in the Act, the authorities, or the relevant literature that the court is obliged to incline either towards total retention or equal division'. Moreover, neither of these approaches takes account of *the payer*'s wasted expenses. On the facts, Garland J exercised a broad discretion in allowing the promoters to recover the whole of the $412,500 paid *without deduction* to reflect the group's wasted expenses of $50,000. This seems eminently fair given the promoters' wasted expenses of $450,000.

 Pause for reflection

Full **loss apportionment** would require Guns N' Roses to pay the promoter £200,000 (ie (£450,000 – £50,000) ÷ 2). But the logic of this would extend to all cases where the contract fails without the fault of either party, as in common mistake (6.3.6). The problem is that the law would have to take into account the reasonableness of the parties' wasted expenses, raising obvious complexities, uncertainties and prolonging of litigation. The current approach of allowing just expenses to be deducted from the sum to be returned is a rough and ready, one-step, response to the aftermath of frustration.

(ii) **What is the ceiling of 'just expenses'?** The sums paid plus any sum due is the *ceiling* of the payee's allowance or claim for 'just expenses'; her wasted expenses in *excess* of that figure are not recoverable. Changing the facts of *Gamerco v ICM* a little:

- if the group's wasted expenses were $1,000,000, it would only have been able to offset up to $775,000 of that, being the total sum due from the promoters; and

- the group cannot recover any of its expenses if no sums were paid by or due from the promoter at the time of frustration.

It is obviously advantageous for a party to secure a large *pre-payment* from the other party against which it can offset its wasted expenses in the event of frustration. The party who has not done so is treated as if she had assumed the risk of loss from her performance prior to frustration, although this contradicts the idea that frustration is an unforeseeable event for which neither party has assumed the risk. The only alternative is for that party to make a section 1(3) *claim* if her expenditure has *benefited* the other party.

7.6.4 **Non-money benefits under LR(FC)A**

Diagram 7B shows that **section 1(3)** of LR(FC)A allows **B to claim a 'just sum'** where *B*'s contractual performance before discharge confers on *A* a 'valuable benefit' other than money. The 'just sum' cannot exceed the value of the benefit conferred *on A* (ie *B* non-$) and should be fixed having regard to all the circumstances of the case and, in particular:

(i) *A*'s expenses incurred before the time of discharge in, or for the purpose of, the performance of the contract, including any sums paid or payable by *A* to *B* under the contract and retained or recoverable by *A* under section 1(2); and

(ii) the effect of the frustrating circumstances on the benefit conferred.

In *BP v Hunt*, Goff J broke down such claims to two stages:

Stage I: identifying and valuing the benefit (ie *B* non-$); and

Stage II: assessing the 'just sum' to be awarded to *B*.

7.6.4.1 Stage I: identification and valuation of the benefits conferred

The starting point is to assess the objective (or market) value of the benefits conferred.

- Where *B* transfers goods to *A*, the benefit is easily identifiable.
- Where *B* performs services, this is more complicated. The services may be intended to yield an *end product* (eg a building or a manuscript) or not (eg transportation, surveying, entertainment, or a holiday). Goff J said that 'benefit' under LR(FC)A will usually denote the end product of services rather than the services themselves, although a small service may create a very valuable end product while lengthy service may create a worthless product.
- However, he acknowledged that in cases of 'pure' services, which are never intended to produce end products, the 'benefit' must be the value of the services themselves. There are no difficulties where *A* receives *completed* performance with an *objective value* from *B*'s services whether they produce an end product or not. Where such services have *no objective value* (such as *B*'s redecoration of a room already in good decorative order to *A*'s appalling taste), its value to *A* must lie in *A*'s request and preparedness to pay the contract price. Two situations present more difficulties:

(i) **Partial performance:** where *B* has only partially performed before the frustrating event, its precise value to *A* may be problematic. What is *part* of a building, a painting, a play, a haircut, or a voyage worth to the recipient? Even if part performance of services can be objectively valued, the recipient should still be entitled to say 'but it isn't worth that *to me*. I only promised to pay for completed performance'. The point is underscored where the contract is 'entire' (ie payment is only due on completion, 12.2.2.1). This problem, called 'subjective devaluation',[9] is exacerbated in pure services cases. The better course is to accord any objective value of the partial performance at Stage I, leaving the problem of determining the just sum to be paid to Stage II.

(ii) **Reduction of the benefit by the frustrating event**: the frustrating event may reduce or completely destroy the value of the end product of B's goods or services.

- Goff J interprets this as belonging in **Stage I** to reduce or eliminate the benefit transferred so that there is a lower ceiling for *B*'s 'just sum' claim at Stage II.

 Counterpoint

On this approach, the harshness of *Appleby v Myers*, where the benefit conferred was destroyed by fire (7.6.2.2(ii)), remains under LR(FC)A; the claimant would still get nothing. The preferable approach is to consider, at **Stage II**:

- the 'subjective devaluation' of the claimant's partial performance; and
- the effect of the frustrating event on the benefit conferred, in the court's discretionary assessment of the 'just sum'.

This approach is supported by:

- the wording of section 1(3), which defines valuable benefit (at Stage I) as that obtained '*before* the time of discharge'; and
- the reference to the effect of the frustrating circumstance in section 1(3)(b) as *one of the factors* to be considered in fixing the 'just sum' (at Stage II).

7.6.4.2 Stage II: assessment of the 'just sum'

There is little guidance yet on how the court will calculate the 'just sum'. Whilst Goff J confined the aim of LR(FC)A to the prevention of unjust enrichment, the Court of Appeal in *BP v Hunt* (1981) preferred a broader discretionary approach. Lawton LJ said: 'what is just is what the trial judge thinks is just' and an appellate court should not interfere with that assessment 'unless it is so plainly wrong that it cannot be just'. This discretion is confined by five factors:

(i) **Ceiling**: the value of the benefit fixed at Stage I is the maximum for the 'just sum'.

(ii) **The effect of the frustrating event on the benefit conferred**: section 1(3)(b) requires this to be taken into account here (contrary to Goff J's view, 7.6.4.1(ii)).

(iii) **Contractual risk allocation**: Goff J said:

- that the assessment should be undertaken in a similar way to a *quantum meruit* or a *quantum valebat* claim (ie by reference to the objective value of the claimant's goods or services in the absence of a contract);

---

[9] P Birks, *An Introduction to the Law of Restitution* (Clarendon Press, 1989) 109–14.

- but he also said that the *contractual* allocation of risk is an important consideration; he thought it 'likely' that most section 1(3) claims will be limited to a rateable portion of the contract price. Where the market price exceeds the contract price, it makes sense that a claimant should not profit from the frustration (and escape a bad bargain) by being able to claim *more* than she would have earned if the contract had run its course.

(iv) **The date of valuation:** this is generally the date of frustration. However, under section 1(2) and (3), even if money and services were conferred long before that date, no allowance can be made for their time value (ie the recipient's *use* of the benefit conferred before the frustrating event).

(v) **Recipient's expenses:** section 1(3)(a) directs the court to take account of the *recipient's expenses* in, or for the purpose of, the performance of the contract, including sums paid or payable by the recipient under the contract which are retained or recoverable by her under section 1(2).

In *BP v Hunt* (1979), BP entered an agreement to explore and develop H's oil concession in Libya. BP was also to make initial 'farm-in' payments of cash and oil to H in exchange for a 50% share in the concession and a portion of the oil discovered until BP had recouped 125% of its initial expenditure. An oil field was discovered and worked from 1967 to 1971 before the contract was frustrated by the Libyan government's expropriation of the concession. BP had only received part of the oil to which it would ultimately be entitled and made a section 1(3) claim. **Diagram 7D** summarises the basis of the award made.

Stage I: the benefit to Hunt conferred by BP—Goff J measured this by the *end product* of BP's work in exploring and working the oil field (ie the enhancement of the value of H's share of the concession), rather than the cost to BP of its work. The value of this end product was substantially reduced by the expropriation. H's benefit was identified as half the value of:

(a) H's receipt of oil from the concession; and

(b) the compensation from the Libyan government.

This amounted to $85 million (ie 50% of $170 million). This is the ceiling of any section 1(3) award. The other half of the value to H was attributable to H's ownership of the concession.

Stage II: the just sum due to BP—Goff J held that the restitutionary award of the just sum is the *reasonable value* of BP's work and expenses conferred on H. He regarded the best evidence of this value as that which the parties themselves fixed, namely, the consideration due to BP (the contract valuation). Thus, the just sum was the value of the contractual performance *due* to BP from H ($98 million) *minus* that already *received* by BP from H ($63 million), being $35 million. This was awarded in full since it came well under the ceiling of $85 million calculated at Stage I. Although the court's task is not to enforce the contract, the contract may provide the best evidence of the value of the claimant's performance when restitution is awarded.

Diagram 7D Claim for non-money performance: calculation of the 'just sum' in *BP v Hunt*

	BP = s 1(3) claimant	*Hunt*
Contractual obligation	To provide: • services in exploring and developing the oil field, 'farm-in' oil + • money	To give BP: • 50% of his concession • 50% of oil output and reimbursement oil to the value of $98 million (=125% of BP's 'farm-in' oil + money)
Benefit received prior to frustration	• 50% of H's concession (now replaced by compensation for confiscation) • oil to the value of **$63 million**	*Stage I: Identification and valuation of benefit received by Hunt* Half the value of: • oil reaped • compensation for confiscation (= the end product of the increased value of H's 50% concession adjusted by the frustrating event) = half of $170 million = **$85 million**

Stage II: 'just sum' to BP
= reasonable value of BP's work and expenses
= contractual value of performance due from Hunt ($98m) *minus* value of performance received from Hunt ($63m)
= **$35 million**

7.7 Hardship and contract modification: frustration, duress, and consideration

In practice, a supervening event that makes the contract impossible or more onerous for one party to perform may trigger renegotiation of the contract (usually to pay more or to accept less). Whether the parties are bound by the modified contract brings together questions of frustration, duress, and consideration.

(i) **Frustration**: if the original contract is frustrated then the modified contract is enforceable because there is, strictly speaking, an entirely new contract so that the problems raised by one party paying more or accepting less than under the original contract are sidestepped: the *consideration* doctrine presents no obstacle (3.1.5.3 and 3.1.5.4), and neither does *duress* since a threat not to make a new contract is generally legitimate (8.6.1). However, a party may escape the modified contract by pleading mistake of law (ie she only renegotiated because she thought the original contract was still binding).

(ii) **No frustration, just hardship**: if the supervening event does not frustrate the contract but merely results in hardship to one of the parties, the enforceability of the renegotiation depends on: (a) whether it is supported by *consideration*; and (b) whether *duress* vitiates the renegotiation. The problems raised by *Williams v Roffey Brothers* (1989) on these issues are discussed at 3.1.5.3.

Pause for reflection

This is not the only solution to the problem of exceptional hardship.

1. The contract may include a force majeure clause expressly providing for price or other adjustments in specified circumstances of hardship, and may require good faith renegotiation or submission to arbitration (7.4.1).

2. In the absence of express provision, the law could require the parties to renegotiate, backed up by judicial modification if renegotiations fail in defined circumstances of hardship. The UNIDROIT Principles of International Commercial Contracts stipulate (at Arts 6.2.1 and 6.2.2) that in such circumstances the parties are bound to enter into *negotiations* with a view to adapting the contract or terminating it. On failure to reach agreement within a reasonable time, either party can resort to the *court* to modify the contract, or to terminate the contract at a date and on terms fixed by the court.

THIS CHAPTER IN ESSENCE

The key areas and core topics in this chapter are summarised in an easy-to-use list, ideal for revision purposes, on the online resources at www.oup.com/uk/chenwishart6e/. Links to websites relevant to the topics covered and any updates to the chapter can also be found on the online resources.

QUESTIONS

1. 'The frustration doctrine is quite distinct from that of mistake; it deals with the ending of a contract and not its formation and its consequences are quite different from that of mistake.' To what extent is, and to what extent should, this be true?

2. 'A contract is only frustrated when its performance is impossible.' Discuss.

3. You have been asked to advise the Law Commission on the problem raised by *The Super Servant Two*. Should the law on self-induced frustration be reformed? If so, how?

4. What can the parties do about losses suffered in performance of a contract which is discharged for frustration?

5. In February, Paul books Queenie to perform at Paul's concert venue for two weeks in August. In early April, Rex books Queenie to perform for late August. Queenie suffers widely publicised bouts of ill health in March and, in mid-April, she is admitted to hospital with a poor chance of recovery. Paul and Rex book other acts instead.

(i) Can Paul and Rex get their £500 deposit back from Queenie?

(ii) What if Queenie had spent £400 on new costumes in preparation for her performances?

(iii) What if Queenie recovers completely by the end of July?

For hints on how to answer these questions, please see the online resources at www.oup.com/uk/chenwishart6e/

KEY FURTHER READING

Clark, P (1996), 'Frustration, Restitution and the Law Reform (Frustrated Contracts) Act 1943', *LMCLQ* 170.

McKendrick, E (1991), 'Frustration, Restitution and Loss Apportionment' in A Burrows (ed), *Essays on the Law of Restitution* (OUP) 147.

McKendrick, E (1995), 'Force Majeure and Frustration—Their Relationship and a Comparative Assessment' in E McKendrick (ed), *Force Majeure and Frustration in Contract* (2nd edn, LLP) 33.

Treitel, G (1994), *Frustration and Force Majeure* (Sweet & Maxwell).

8

Duress

'You pressured me'

Contract law has always put limits on the permissible means of persuading others to enter into contracts. Chapter 5 on misrepresentation discusses one such limit. This chapter examines another, namely duress.

If I force you to sign a contract by putting a gun to your head, the law will refuse to help me enforce that contract: you can call it off at your option, subject to the usual bars to rescission (5.2.2), including the requirement of 'substantial' restitution (*Halpern v Halpern* (2006)). There are four categories of actionable duress: whilst the law on duress to the *person* and to *property* is relatively settled, the precise contours of the newer categories of *economic* duress and *lawful act* duress are still unclear. In particular, the law on economic duress regulates the troublesome issue of when contract modifications should be enforced, and so overlaps to some extent with the law on consideration. The questions to be addressed are the following:

(i) What is the *justification* for the duress doctrine?

(ii) What *sorts* of pressures are regarded as illegitimate by the law?

(iii) How *much* pressure must the illegitimate threat exert on the other party?

(iv) Is the current law on duress *satisfactory?* If not, how might it be developed in the future?

8.1 **The justification for duress**

8.1.1 **Inadequacy of the overborne will theory**

Although duress was originally explained in terms of the victim's will being overborne and her consent vitiated,[1] this is now recognised as inadequate. **Atiyah** argues that contract law should follow criminal law's rejection of the 'overborne will' theory in *DPP v Lynch* (1975) because a victim of duress submits *knowingly* and *intentionally* ('Economic Duress and the Overborne Will' (1982) 98 *LQR* 197). If you tell me to 'hand over £100,000 or be horribly maimed', my decision to hand over the money is *very real* indeed. I *know* what I am agreeing to, I *intend* to agree and I very much *want* to agree. The real objection is not that I did not consent, but that you induced my consent by illegitimate pressure; the complaint is the nature and acceptability of the choices left to the victim. In *Lynch*, the House of Lords recognised that duress does not make the victim's actions involuntary, the victim's will is not 'overborne' or destroyed, merely deflected. Lord Simon said of the victim: 'There is still an intention on his part to contract in the apparently consensual terms . . . The contrast is with *non est factum* (where the victim does not know what she is signing, 6.1.3). The contract procured by duress is therefore not void: it is voidable.'

On the other hand, it is not duress just because consent was given under pressure, however strong. Valid consent does *not require freedom from pressures*. I may have 'no choice' but to agree to a lender's interest rate, or to the prices charged for food, shelter, or clothing, but such *ordinary pressures* will not excuse me from my contractual obligations. As Lord Wilberforce said in *Barton v Armstrong* (1976): 'in life . . . many acts are done under pressure, sometimes overwhelming pressure, so that one can say that the actor had no choice but to act. Absence of choice in this sense does not negate consent in law: for this the pressure must be one of the kind which the law does not regard as legitimate.' Thus, duress is not ruled out by knowing and willing consent, but neither is it indicated merely by the presence of (even overwhelming) pressure.

---

[1] *Occidental Worldwide Investment Corp v Skibs A/S Avanti (The Siboen and The Sibotre)* (1976); *North Ocean Shipping Co Ltd v Hyundai Construction Co Ltd (The Atlantic Baron)* (1979); *Pao On v Lau Yiu Long* (1980); *Barton v Armstrong* (1976); and see P Birks and N Chin, 'On the Nature of Undue Influence' in J Beatson and D Friedmann (eds), *Good Faith and Fault in Contract Law* (OUP, 1995) 55, 62, 88–9.

8.1.2 **Illegitimate pressure**

In *Universe Tankships Inc of Monrovia v International Transport Workers Federation* (1983), the House of Lords recognised that: 'The classic case of duress is . . . not the lack of will to submit but the victim's intentional submission arising from the realisation that there is no other practical choice open to him.' If I *distort* your decision-making process by introducing an *illegitimate pressure*, which presents you with *no practicable alternative* but to submit to my demands, the law will not expect you to take the normal responsibility for your apparent exercise of will; it will *deem* your consent to be vitiated. The illegitimate pressure view of duress explains why:

(i)   the enforcing party must be tainted in the sense that she has applied, or at least knows of, the pressure;

(ii) *duress* makes contracts *voidable* analogous to misrepresentation, and not void like mistake (which focuses on the complainant's lack of consent); and

(iii) the *standard of causation* for duress is less than might be expected on the overborne will theory; the illegitimate pressure need not be the overwhelming cause of the victim's consent to contract.

8.2 **What must be proved?**

In *Universe Tankships v International Transport Workers*,[2] the House of Lords held that the complainant must show the following:

(i)   The pressure applied by the enforcing party is **illegitimate**: this depends on the nature of the *threat* and of the *demand*:

- If the conduct threatened is independently *unlawful* (ie it would amount to a breach of duty by the enforcing party), the threat is generally regarded as *illegitimate*.

- Correspondingly, threats of *lawful* conduct are generally treated as *legitimate*, unless they are 'immoral or unconscionable' when coupled with an illegitimate demand; the more unfair the *demand*, the more likely that the threat used to back it up will be regarded as illegitimate.

(ii) The illegitimate pressure **induced** the complainant to enter the contract: The precise *degree* of causation required varies with the type of duress in question, with economic duress posing a particularly difficult category.

(iii) The complainant had **no practicable alternative** but to submit to the demand. This requirement only applies explicitly to claims of economic duress (8.4.3).

---

[2] See also *Dimskal Shipping Co SA v ITWF (The Evia Luck) (No 2)* (1992); *Huyton SA v Peter Cremer GmbH & Co Inc* (1999); *R v Her Majesty's Attorney-General for England and Wales* (2003).

8.3 **Duress to the person and to property**

8.3.1 **Illegitimate pressure**

If I do (or threaten to do) *violence* to you or to *detain* you (or someone in a close relationship with you) to induce your consent to contract, I have clearly applied illegitimate pressure (*Barton v Armstrong; Duke de Cadaval v Collins* (1836)). *Chitty* (at para 8-012) suggests that 'the threat against even a stranger should be enough if the claimant genuinely believed that submission is the only way to prevent the stranger from being injured or worse'. The same applies if I threaten to damage, take, or keep your *property* (*Astley v Reynolds* (1731); *Maskell v Horner* (1915)), or your *money* (*Crescendo Management Pty Ltd v Moral Westpac Banking Corp* (1988)).

8.3.2 **Causation**

Threats to the person, by analogy with misrepresentation, need only be *'a'* cause of the complainant's decision to contract. It is enough if the threat contributed *in any way* to her decision to contract (*Barton v Armstrong*). The complainant need not show that it was *'the'*, the *'clinching'*, the *'predominant'*, or the *'overwhelming'* cause for the contract, or that *'but for'* the threat they would not have entered the contract. It is insufficient for the enforcing party to show that the complainant might, or would, have consented for other reasons, even without the threat: to enforce the contract, she must show that the illegitimate pressure had *no effect whatsoever* on the complainant's decision. Any one strand in the hangman's rope is *'a'* reason for the victim's ultimate demise, although the same result would have ensued without that one strand.[3] In *Barton v Armstrong*, the parties, both major shareholders in a company, were locked in a bitter power struggle for its control. B claimed that he was coerced to buy out A's interests on very generous terms, by A's threats to murder him and his family. The trial judge accepted that A made the threats but denied relief because B's main reason for buying out A was to ensure the company's survival. The Privy Council disagreed, holding that B could succeed if A's threats were merely *a* reason for his decision to enter the contract, and even if he might have done so without the threats. It was up to A to show that the threat had *no influence* on B at all.

In **duress to goods** cases, the complainant must show that the threat was a *'significant cause'* (*Dimskal Shipping Co SA v ITWF* (1992)) of her consent to the contract. In practice, this causation requirement is easily met. In *Astley v Reynolds* (1731), R told A that he could not redeem his plate (pawned to R) unless he paid more than twice the legal interest rate. A paid but then successfully recovered the excess payment for duress. The court was prepared to *assume* that A 'might have such an immediate want of his property that [an alternative course of action, eg a tort action for wrongful interference with goods] would not do'. A did not need to actually prove it. **Diagram 8A** summarises the law on duress to the person and to property.

---

[3] I am indebted to Professor Robert Stevens for this analogy.

Pause for reflection

Duress to the person and to property are such clear contraventions of fair dealing that they are sufficient *in themselves* to justify legal sanction: there is no explicit requirement that the accompanying demand be unfair or improper, although it invariably will be. Indeed, the unfairness of the demand in *Barton v Armstrong* was treated as *evidence of the causation requirement*; that is, that the threat to kill must have had *some* effect on the complainant's decision to agree.

Diagram 8A Summary of duress to the person and to property

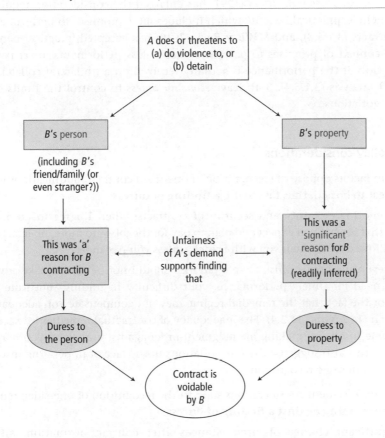

8.4 **Economic duress: threats to breach a contract**

Since *The Siboen and The Sibotre* (1976), the courts have accepted that economic duress may be as coercive and worthy of relief as duress to the person or to property (*The Atlantic Baron* (1979); *Pao On v Lau Yiu Long* (1979)). The most important practical application of economic duress is in the area of **one-sided contract modifications**, where one party threatens to breach an existing contract unless the other agrees to: (i) *pay more* for the original performance; or (ii) *accept less* performance than was originally due. When, if ever, should such renegotiations be enforced?

- Traditionally, the *doctrine of consideration* (especially the pre-existing duty rule, 3.1.4) gave a negative answer, since no additional consideration supports the promise to pay more or accept less.

- However, the promissory estoppel doctrine can enforce promises of 'less for the same' in limited circumstances (3.1.5.4 and 3.2.2.1), but not if the promisee had applied illegitimate pressure since it would not then be inequitable for the promisor to renege on the promise;

- *Williams v Roffey Brothers* (1991) has enlarged the consideration requirement to include 'practical benefit', which includes mere promises to perform existing contracts (3.1.5.3); and *MWB v Rock* (2016) has accepted 'practical benefit' in the context of promises to pay the same for less performance (part payment) but only if the performance is actually received on a unilateral collateral contract analysis (3.1.5.4). Both leave *economic duress* to control the limits of such renegotiations.

8.4.1 **Policy considerations**

Two main factors oppose the recognition of one-sided contract modifications induced by a threat to breach, thus **favouring a finding of duress**:

(i) Promoting certainty and security of contracts: when I agree to do a job for £2,000, that is what you expect and plan to pay for the job—no more, no less. I should not be allowed to threaten you with breach unless you pay more.

(ii) Preventing opportunistic exploitation: I should not be able to take advantage of your need for timely performance, your difficulty in finding substitute performance, or the fact that the remedial regime may not compensate you adequately for my breach (14.2.3 and 14.2.4). The inadequacy of contractual remedies is exacerbated if I become insolvent, making me judgment-proof against any claim you may have. Ironically, this also suggests why renegotiations in the face of impending insolvency *should* warrant some recognition.

Four pro-enforcement considerations support the recognition of one-sided renegotiations, thus **leaning** against a finding of duress:

(i) Significant change of circumstances after contract formation, although insufficient to frustrate the contract (Chapter 7), may make performance so difficult for one party that she must seek some adjustment if she is to complete performance, eg a party facing impending insolvency has no incentive to perform if this would merely exacerbate her indebtedness. Thus, Beatson[4] draws a distinction between:

    ✗ *'threats'*, which should be illegitimate: where the threatening party has a *choice* whether to carry out the threat; and

    ✓ *'warnings'*, which are not illegitimate: where the warning party is simply giving notice of her *inevitable* non-performance without renegotiation.

(ii) If performance is not viable without renegotiation then, ironically, the concern to protect the victim (the recipient of performance) would support renegotiation. Since a party in difficulty may be better off breaching a contract to cut her losses (recognised in *Williams v Roffey Brothers*), she has no incentive to perform if the law refuses to enforce such renegotiations or the victim can recover any extra made; the victim could not pay more to ensure performance, however much more she is prepared to pay for it.

(iii) Reasonable renegotiations to facilitate the completion of contractual performance may be economically efficient. Birks points out that it may 'minimise the waste and inconvenience between parties already embarked on a project', and 'bring projects safely to a conclusion without interruptions and unnecessary ill-will' ('The Travails of Duress' [1990] *LMCLQ* 342). It may be cheaper overall to pay more to get the job done than to have the whole thing unravel with its consequential waste and hassle. On the other hand, Birks warns against giving contract parties the incentive of bidding low for a job in the expectation of renegotiating up later.

(iv) The values of cooperation, mutual accommodation, and good faith also support contract renegotiations when one party gets into difficulty. This rests on a relational view of contract as an essentially cooperative enterprise in the nature of joint ventures (1.3.6).

The courts *have* upheld some renegotiations induced by threats to breach, but they have done so without explicitly weighing these competing policies, and via different approaches: one based on causation and one on illegitimate pressure.

8.4.2 The causation-led approach

A threat to breach an existing contract is a threat of unlawful action since it would breach a legal duty and has generally been regarded as illegitimate pressure, 'particularly where the defendant must know that it would be in breach if the threat were implemented' (*Kolmar Group AG v Traxpo Enterprises Pty Ltd* (2010)). This means that any renegotiations induced by a threat to breach an existing contract would amount to duress, unless the causation requirement is raised to block a finding of economic duress. In *Huyton v Cremer* (1999), Mance J justified the stronger causal connection required for economic duress on the basis that economic duress is *less serious* than duress to the person or to property. His honour explains that:

    ✓ the minimum basic test should be the *'but for'* test: 'The illegitimate pressure must have . . . actually caused the making of the agreement, in the sense that it would

---

⁴ J Beatson, *The Use and Abuse of Unjust Enrichment* (Clarendon Press, 1991) 118–20.

not otherwise have been made either at all or, at least, in the terms in which it was made. In that sense, the pressure must have been decisive or clinching.'

✓ Moreover, the complainant should also show that she had *no practicable alternative* but to submit to the demand, although this is not 'an inflexible third essential ingredient' (8.4.3).

In *Pao On v Lau Yiu Long* (1980), Lord Scarman said that, in deciding whether sufficient causation was present, the court should ask whether the complainant:

(i)   protested;

(ii) had a practicable alternative open to her, such as an adequate legal remedy;

(iii) was independently advised; and

(iv) acted promptly to avoid the renegotiation.

However, these factors are inconclusive. The victim may not protest because she sees no point in it or she may not wish to antagonise the coercing party whose performance she needs. Knowing that the threat is unlawful does not necessarily increase the victim's realistic options. Any delay in complaining after the renegotiation does not negate the causative effect of the illegitimate pressure *at the time* of formation, although it may bar rescission for affirmation (5.2.2.3).

The degree of pressure facing the victims does not explain why economic duress has been found in some cases but not others:

✓ In *Atlas Express v Kafco (Importers and Distributors) Ltd* (1989), A, a carrier company, mistakenly under-quoted (by half) the price for carrying K's goods to Woolworth's in time for the Christmas sales. On realising its mistake, A refused to make the delivery unless K agreed to double its payment. K agreed, since it was unlikely to find alternative carriers at such short notice and, if no delivery were made, K would have lost its lucrative contract on which the viability of its small business depended.

✓ In *The Atlantic Baron* (1979), H agreed to build a ship for N at a fixed price payable in US dollars. The value of the US currency dropped by 10% and H threatened not to deliver unless N agreed to a 10% increase in the price.

✓ In *B & S Contracts and Design Ltd v Victor Green Publications Ltd* (1984), B agreed to build exhibition stands for V but its workforce, which had been notified of impending redundancies, refused to work unless they received £9,000 in severance pay. V offered £4,500 as advance payment to help B to meet its workers' demand, but B made clear that performance would not proceed unless an *extra* £4,500 was paid. There was no express threat to breach, but the court found an *implied* threat. V agreed because non-performance would have damaged its reputation and exposed it to heavy claims from exhibitors.

✓ In *Adam Opel v Mitras Automotive (UK) Ltd* (2007), AO, a manufacturer of vans, informed M in February that it would stop buying parts from M in August. In response, M demanded certain 'compensation' and increased the price of parts it was already obliged to supply. AO unsuccessfully sought an *ex parte* injunction (without giving M notice) against M. AO continued to negotiate until it had only 24 hours' worth of supplies remaining. AO agreed to M's demands when M threatened to cut off supplies, because cessation of production would result in severe financial losses and have other adverse knock-on effects. The agreement was set aside for economic duress.

In contrast, economic duress was rejected in the following cases, although, arguably, the victims faced no less pressure to submit:

✗ In *The Siboen and The Sibotre* (1976), charterers of a ship told the ship-owners that they would go into liquidation unless the charter price was reduced significantly. The owners agreed because they were unlikely to find alternative charterers in the poor state of the market and any rights they had against the charterer would be rendered worthless by its insolvency. The court found no duress, only 'commercial pressure'.

✗ In *Pao On v Lau Yiu Long*, the parties exchanged shares in their companies. In addition, P agreed to delay selling 60% of the shares it received for at least a year to avoid triggering a fall in their value and L agreed to *buy back* those shares at a fixed price at or before the end of the year. When P realised that it would be disadvantaged if the shares rose *above* the fixed price, he refused to proceed with the contract unless L replaced the buy-back agreement with a *guarantee by way of indemnity* (ie L would only indemnify P if the shares fell *below* the fixed price). L agreed in order to avoid the delay and loss of public confidence that legal action against P would attract at a critical time in the company's restructuring. Moreover, L believed that the risk entailed in the modification was 'more apparent than real'. When the share price plummeted, L would neither buy back the shares at the fixed price (alleging this arrangement was ended by the modification) nor indemnify P (alleging the modification was voidable for duress). The court found no duress, only 'commercial pressure', and upheld the agreement to indemnify.

8.4.3 **The role of 'no practicable alternative'**

The requirement that the victim should have had no practicable alternative but to submit to the threat should be regarded as an *independent and additional requirement* of duress since it goes to the very essence of the jurisdiction.

- The House of Lords describes the classic case of duress as 'the victim's intentional submission arising from the realisation that there is no other practicable choice open to him' (*Universe Tankships v International Transport Workers*).

- The US Second Restatement of Contracts describes duress as an improper threat which leaves no reasonable alternative (§ 175(1)).

- In *Huyton v Cremer*, Mance J said that the 'but for' test 'could lead too readily to relief being granted. It would not, for example, cater for the obvious possibility that, although the innocent party would never have acted as he did, but for the illegitimate pressure, he nevertheless had a real choice and could, if he had wished, equally well have resisted the pressure and, for example, pursued alternative legal redress.'

✓ In *Adam Opel v Mitras Automotive*, the court rejected M's argument that AO *had* a practical alternative. AO's new supplier was not ready to begin production and AO could not have obtained supplies elsewhere. While it had a strong case for an injunction, the court recognised that AO:

> had to take a rapid decision in circumstances where the threat had already become reality. Capitulation would ensure with certainty the restoration of supplies and at a price which, though seen . . . as extortionate, would be a fraction of the loss which would otherwise be suffered. By contrast, there were serious imponderables about the injunction route . . . [AO were] entitled to consider that the outcome would not inevitably be in their favour . . . [T]he court's attitude to the grant of a mandatory interim injunction to supply an indeterminate number of units on an indeterminate timetable could not . . . have been assumed.

✗ In *DSND Subsea v Petroleum Geo-Services* (2000), Dyson J recognised 'no practicable alternative' as a separate requirement of duress but found that P *did* have the practicable alternative of terminating the contract and finding alternative vessels for the job. However, what was arguably most determinative was Dyson J's finding that D's conduct (part-suspension of the job pending resolution of its concern about P's provision of insurance and indemnities), even if it amounted to breach which coerced P, was 'reasonable behaviour by a contractor acting *bona fide* in a very difficult situation'.

8.4.4 **Alternative approaches based on illegitimate pressure**

Instead of the problematic causation-led approach to economic duress cases, the focus of the inquiry should switch to the illegitimacy of the pressure applied, with the causation requirement stabilised at the *'but for'* standard. Three variants have been suggested.

First, the legitimacy of the threat to breach can be made to depend on the presence or absence of good faith of the party making the threat.[5] This accords with the idea that contract variations negotiated in bad faith (ie having no honest belief in the reasons advanced for the demand) are unenforceable as a bad-faith compromise and lack consideration (3.1.3.6). However, the concept of *good faith* is notoriously unstable (see further Chapter 15). Burrows suggests that[6] a threatened breach of contract should be regarded as illegitimate if aimed at exploiting the claimant's weakness rather than solving financial or other problems of the defendant, but not 'if the threat is a reaction to circumstances that almost constitute frustration . . . [or] if it merely corrects what was always clearly a bad bargain'.

---

[5] See P Birks, *An Introduction to the Law of Restitution* (Clarendon Press, 1989) 183; *DSND Subsea Ltd v Petroleum Geo-Services ASA*.

[6] A Burrows, *The Law of Restitution* (3rd edn, OUP, 2010) 233.

Counterpoint

1. Judicial scepticism: despite its application in *DSND Subsea v Petroleum Geo-Services* (8.4.3), Mance J in *Huyton v Cremer* describes the good faith approach as 'by no means uncontentious', adding that it does not rule out relief for duress just because a party believes *bona fide* in his case. Indeed, Judge Wilkie QC concluded that an *honest but mistaken demand* amounted to economic duress in *Cantor Index Ltd v Shortall* (2002).

2. Inconsistent with cases where duress was found although good faith was present because the coercing party:

   • badly miscalculated and so underpriced the contract by a half (*Atlas v Kafco*);

   • lost on the real value of the contract price due to currency devaluation (*The Atlantic Baron*);

   • found the cost of performance substantially increased due to industrial action (*B & S Contracts v Victor Green*); or

   • was not paid by a third party while still being obliged to perform (*Vantage Navigation Corp v Suhail & Saud Bahwan Building Materials LLC (The Alev)* (1989)).

3. Inconsistent with competing policies: the good faith approach suppresses some important policies, such as responsibility in contract formation and preserving the security and certainty of contracts. A party who deliberately, recklessly, or even mistakenly tenders low to win a job should not necessarily be able to renegotiate a better deal by threatening breach just because it is 'clearly bad' for her or has become much more difficult to perform. Short of frustration, contractual obligations are absolute and not discharged by change of circumstances which makes performance less profitable or more costly (but see 7.7). The future is inherently uncertain and allocating the risks for such uncertainties (so that parties know where they stand) is the reason why most contracts (not simultaneously performed) are made in the first place.

The second approach, advocated by McKendrick, is to treat *all* **threats to breach as illegitimate pressure**, which would only have to be **'a' reason** for the complainant's consent ('The Further Travails of Duress' in A Burrows and A Rodger (eds), *Mapping the Law: Essays in Memory of Peter Birks* (OUP, 2006) 180). McKendrick reasons that: (i) courts should uphold the integrity of the original contract; and (ii) English law does not distinguish between good faith and bad faith threats to breach. This accords with Coleman J's dicta in *South Caribbean Trading Ltd v Trafigura Beheer BV* (2005) that the promisee who threatens to breach an existing duty cannot rely on 'practical benefit' as consideration for any extra payment because the threat is 'analogous to economic duress' (3.1.5.3(v)).

Pause for reflection

Whilst the good faith approach is under-inclusive (it avoids too few renegotiations for duress), McKendrick's approach is over-inclusive and avoids too many renegotiations.

→

Where the difficulties *threaten the performing party's economic survival so that performance is practically impossible without some renegotiation*, it is appropriate to uphold a reasonable and consensual modification. This suggests a **third 'no practicable alternative' approach**: A party should be able to renegotiate to her advantage if she has *no practicable alternative* if she is to complete contractual performance. A party's difficulties in performing must be *severe* (most usually because of the risk of insolvency) before she can seek renegotiation by intimating the likelihood of breach; only then does she have 'no practicable alternative' but to seek negotiation. This approach strikes the right balance between the relevant **competing policies**:

(i) It minimises the threat to the sanctity of the original contract and the risk of exploitation by narrowly confining the scope of permissible renegotiations.

(ii) It protects the victim's interest in receiving performance when her substitute right to sue an insolvent party for breach would be worthless.

(iii) It avoids the economic waste entailed by breach or insolvency by encouraging cooperation and compromise between parties faced with difficult circumstances.

(iv) It explains the cases. Economic duress was rejected in *The Siboen and The Sibotre* where charterers said that they would go into liquidation unless the charter price was reduced. The court found only commercial pressure and so no duress. But the real reason may lie in Kerr LJ's observation that renegotiations in such circumstances are common and sensible in the charter market. Similarly, in *Williams v Roffey Brothers*, W's financial difficulty, exacerbated by the initial underpricing of the contract, made timely performance practically impossible. The court upheld R's promise to pay more, observing that 'a main contractor who agrees too low a price with a subcontractor is acting contrary to their own interests. He will never get the job finished without paying more money'. In contrast, the threatening parties in *Atlas v Kafco, The Atlantic Baron, B & S Contracts v Victor Green*, and *The Alev* were able to perform without demanding more.

If a party *can* perform without modification, any non-performance would be 'self-induced' (analogous to frustration), and any modification induced by threats to breach would amount to duress.

8.4.5 The demand

Recall Lord Scarman's statement (in *Universe Tankships v International Transport Workers*) that the legitimacy of the pressure depends on the nature of the threat *and* the nature of the *demand*. Similarly, § 176(2) of the US Second Restatement of Contracts asks whether it was commercially reasonable to seek renegotiation *and* whether the *renegotiated terms are fair and equitable*. Thus, contrary to the orthodox view that duress is concerned solely with *procedural* unfairness, it is impossible to exclude the *substantive* fairness of the *renegotiated contract* from the assessment.

Pause for reflection

1. Fairness of the renegotiated contract: even where the threatening party has no practicable alternative to renegotiation, she should only be allowed to seek such *reasonable* modification as is necessary to give her the incentive to complete her contractual performance. If more is demanded, then she *does* have a practicable alternative, namely, to ask less; her threat is illegitimate.

2. The fairness of the *original contract* may also be relevant; the underprice in the original contract contributed to the courts' assessment in *Williams v Roffey Brothers* that there was no question of duress. But *Atlas v Kafco* shows that correcting substantive unfairness *alone* will not legitimise a threat to breach. Substantive concerns were also influential in *Pao On v Lau Yiu Long*, where duress was denied in order to avoid the unfairness of leaving P without the protection that the parties originally intended.

3. Beatson suggests that, where it is not commercially practicable for a party to continue performance unless the contract is renegotiated, it should not inevitably be viewed as a threat to point that out. Some monitoring of the substantive fairness of the bargain may be inevitable ('Duress, Restitution and Contract Modification' in *The Use and Abuse of Unjust Enrichment* (Clarendon Press, 1990) 95).

8.5 **Other forms of economic duress**

The court will take into account the statutory background in determining whether any threat to the victim's economic interests is illegitimate:

✗ Thus, the House of Lords held that a trade union's threat to 'black' a ship (withdraw labour) *could* taint any contract induced by the threat with duress (*Universe Tankships v International Transport Workers*). However, the presence of statutes protecting trade unions from claims for the tort of intimidation may persuade courts not to find duress.

✓ In *Progress Bulk Carriers Ltd v Tube City IMS LLC* (2012), P chartered its vessel to T. P committed a repudiatory breach when it fixed the vessel to another charterer without informing T. T did not accept that breach as terminating the contract and P undertook to provide a substitute and pay full compensation, but ultimately only offered T an alternative vessel at a discount on condition that T waived all claims for loss. T had no option but to accept the settlement agreement to avoid further loss, although it did so under protest. Cooke J held that it was illegitimate for P to produce the 'take-it-or leave-it' offer, having made T vulnerable by its original breach and subsequent conduct. Illegitimate pressure 'can be constituted by conduct which was not in itself unlawful, although it would be an unusual case where that was so, particularly in the commercial context.' A past unlawful act, as well as a threat of a future unlawful act, could, in appropriate circumstances, amount to 'illegitimate pressure'.

✓ In *Akai Holding Ltd (Liquidators) v James Ting* (2010), T, the former chairman of Akai Holdings, failed to assist the liquidators in their investigation of Akai's affairs through 'a long process of evasion and prevarication'. T also resorted to forgery and the provision of false evidence to defeat the liquidator's proposed scheme to raise money to investigate T's misdeeds. T only agreed to withdraw his opposition to the scheme in exchange for the liquidator's agreement not to pursue any claims against him in relation to the company. The Privy Council held that:

(i)   economic duress can include unconscionable although lawful action for improper motive;

(ii) T's opposition 'was not made in good faith, but for an improper motive', and was 'unconscionable'; and

(iii) the liquidators had no reasonable or practical alternative but to make a deal with T, who had them over a barrel.

Thus, it would offend justice to allow T to rely on the settlement to prevent the liquidators from suing him, or to bar rescission because the parties could not be restored to the position created by T's illegitimate pressure. The settlement was set aside.

8.6 **Lawful act duress**

Courts have accepted that the categories of duress are not closed and that even a lawful threat may be illegitimate (eg *CTN Cash and Carry v Gallaher Ltd* (1994)), although it must 'at least be *immoral or unconscionable*' (*Alf Vaughan & Co Ltd v Royscot Trust plc* (1999)). The threat may be to the victim's economic interests, reputation, or her concern to protect a loved one. The first step in mapping the uncertain scope of lawful act duress is to put aside the lawful threats that are generally permitted.

8.6.1 **Lawful pressure that is legitimate**

The following lawful threats are generally regarded as **legitimate**:

(i) Since the **threat not to contract** is implicit in all contractual negotiations, it is difficult to see how that can be objectionable in the absence of a doctrine of inequality of bargaining power or substantive unfairness. Duress was rejected in *Smith v Charlick Ltd* (1923), where the Wheat Board (with a monopoly on selling wheat) threatened to stop trading with S unless S agreed to pay more for the grain that S was already contractually entitled to.

(ii) A party can **refuse to waive** an existing contractual obligation (*Alec Lobb Garages Ltd v Total Oil Ltd* (1983)). Duress was denied in *Alf Vaughan v Royscot Trust*, where A bought cars from R but went into receivership with £34,000 owing under the hire-purchase agreement. R lawfully terminated the contract and threatened to recover the cars (which it was entitled to do) unless £82,000 was paid. A's receivers paid because the cars were necessary for the business to be sold as a going concern.

(iii) A party's **exercise of a right for legitimate purposes** does not amount to duress. In *R v Her Majesty's Attorney-General for England and Wales* (2003), an SAS soldier of the celebrated Bravo Two Zero patrol breached a confidentiality agreement by attempting to publish an account of his experiences. He argued that the confidentiality agreement was voidable for duress since the Crown threatened to return him from the elite regiment to his regular unit unless he signed it. The Privy Council rejected his claim because the Crown's threat was not only *lawful*, being within its discretion to transfer soldiers, it was also *reasonable*, being legitimately concerned to prevent unauthorised disclosures which may threaten the security of its operations and personnel. The threat was lawful and the demand reasonable.

(iv) The law on compromise of claims legitimises advantages obtained from threats to sue to enforce an honest, even if mistaken, claim, particularly in a commercial context (3.1.3.6). In *CTN Cash and Carry v Gallaher* (1994), G delivered C's order of £17,000 worth of cigarettes to the wrong warehouse. The cigarettes were subsequently stolen before the mistake was rectified. G nevertheless demanded payment from C, honestly but mistakenly believing that they were entitled to do so. G threatened to withdraw C's future credit facility if C did not pay. The Court of Appeal found no duress because G acted in good faith and were entitled to vary the terms of future contracts with C. The court stressed that lawful act duress would not be lightly found in arm's-length commercial dealings where certainty is paramount.

 Pause for reflection

1. In the *commercial* context, the lawfulness of the threat correlates very strongly with the legitimacy of the threat, overriding even clear bad faith as in *Smith v Charlick* and *Alf Vaughan v Royscot Trust*. However, the extraction of a sum that was, in truth, not due in *CTN Cash and Carry* prompted Sir Donald Nicholls VC to comment that the outcome seemed unconscionable and to amount to unjust enrichment.

2. The legitimacy of the demand should be relevant to the legitimacy of the pressure since, as Lord Scarman stated (in *Universe Tankships v International Transport Workers*), duress can exist 'even if the threat is one of lawful action: whether it does so depends upon the nature of the demand'.

3. Beatson[7] argues that, if the objectionable conduct or threat goes beyond the 'wrongful' to encompass the 'illegitimate' (which involves no breach of legal duty), then it is hard not to see economic duress as part of a general doctrine of inequality of bargaining power.

8.6.2 Lawful pressure that is illegitimate

In addition to *Akai Holdings v Ting* discussed earlier, three categories of cases can be interpreted as varieties of lawful act duress:

(i) Lord Scarman said in *Universe Tankships v International Transport Workers* that: 'Blackmail is often a demand supported by a threat to do what is lawful', eg to report criminal conduct to the police. In many cases, therefore, 'What [one] has to justify is not the threat, but the demand'. Blackmail is made unlawful by the Theft Act 1968 (s 2(1)).

---

[7] 'Duress, Restitution and Contract Modification' in *The Use and Abuse of Unjust Enrichment* (Clarendon Press, 1990) 95.

(ii) Relief in salvage cases (involving threats not to rescue life or property on ships in distress unless extortionate terms are agreed) may be considered another long-standing example of lawful act duress. In *The Port Caledonia* (1903), two large laden vessels were sheltering from a storm in a harbour when one was dragged dangerously close to the other. The master of a rescue tug demanded '£1,000 or no rope'. This sum was set aside as extortionate and agreed under compulsion; £200 was substituted for the rescue services rendered.

(iii) Cases involving threats to harm the victim or their loved ones (by **threatening prosecution** (*Williams v Bayley* (1866)) or **publication of information** (*Norreys v Zeffert* (1939))) were historically decided as cases of **actual undue influence**. They belong more naturally in the category of lawful act duress. In *Mutual Finance Ltd v John Wetton & Sons Ltd* (1937), Joseph Wetton forged the signatures of his brother Percy and father John, directors of the defendant company, guaranteeing his friend's hire purchase to M. On the friend's default, M threatened to prosecute Joseph unless Percy agreed to pay. The court set aside this agreement for actual undue influence because M knew that Percy only did so for fear that his father's life would be endangered by the shock of his brother's prosecution.

In a non-commercial context, the question of whether the lawful threat has been used to further a proper purpose is a useful starting point in deciding whether it is illegitimate in the context of duress. However, since the pursuit of profit is prima facie a legitimate purpose in a capitalist society,[8] intervention in commercial contracts induced by lawful threats is difficult to justify. Thus, lawful act duress is unlikely to have significant scope beyond relationships which are deemed by the law to warrant special protection, such as those in need of rescue and those who are dependent on, or otherwise vulnerable to, exploitation by the other party. The doctrines which more directly meet these concerns are examined in Chapter 9.

 Pause for reflection

The crime of blackmail and the public law concept of improper purpose suggest that the pathology in cases where relief has been granted lies in the *mismatch between* the *means* used (the threatened action) and the *ends* sought (the demand made). For example, whilst it is legitimate to publish information, inform the police, or threaten to do these, in support of proper purposes (eg freedom of information or the proper administration of justice), it is improper and so illegitimate to use them to make an unwarranted demand. The threatening party's conduct may be objectionable because she has:

1. no legitimate basis for the demand (as with blackmail);

2. a legitimate demand but directed against the wrong party (ie who does not owe it, as in *Williams v Bayley*, where B threatened to prosecute W's son if W did not pay on his son's forged promissory note); or

➜

---

[8] Consistently, the tort of conspiracy to injure does not require unlawful means but regards increasing profit, market share, or wages as legitimate.

→

3. used inappropriate means in support of a legitimate demand; this has been expressed as using 'leverage' which rightly belongs to another, for example, that of:

- the state in cases of threats to prosecute as in **Williams v Bayley**; and
- the recipient of the information in cases of threats to inform.

Diagram 8B Overview of duress: requirements and policies

	Duress to the PERSON	Duress to PROPERTY	ECONOMIC duress	LAWFUL ACT duress
1. Illegitimate pressure	Unlawful threat		Unlawful threat to breach contract *Should it always be illegitimate?*	Immoral or unconscionable threat
– Demand	Generally unwarranted			
– Lack of Good faith	No mention but likely		Relevant but inconclusive	
2. Causation	'A' cause	'Significant' cause, readily inferred	At least 'but for' cause; clinching or decisive cause *Inconsistently applied*	No mention but necessarily implicit to high degree
3. No practicable alternative	No mention		Formal requirement	No mention but necessarily implicit
Policy considerations	• *Protection of physical integrity* • *Wrongdoers should not profit from own wrong*	• *Protection of property rights* • *Wrongdoers should not profit from own wrong*	• *Promote sanctity of contract* • *Prevent exploitation* ***BUT** modification may be desirable because:* • *Change of circumstances has made performance impossible without it* • *The victim cannot obtain actual performance without it* • *It is economically efficient* • *It encourages cooperation and accommodation in contracts*	• *Prevents lawful but unconscionable conduct* • *Prevents abuse of rights* ***BUT** uncertainty in drawing the line*

8.6.3 Causation

Whilst the cases recognise the possibility of lawful act duress, there is a notable absence of discussion of the causation element. Nevertheless, a high level of causation is implicit in the cases identified as likely candidates for lawful act duress (blackmail, salvage, and actual undue influence by threats to prosecute or inform). The applicable test here should be the usual one in the law of obligations, the '*but for*' test to be proved by the complainant.

Diagram 8B gives a summary of duress.

8.7 **Aggressive commercial practices against consumers**

See the discussion in Chapter 5 (5.5.1).

| **THIS CHAPTER IN ESSENCE**

The key areas and core topics in this chapter are summarised in an easy-to-use list, ideal for revision purposes, on the online resources at www.oup.com/uk/chenwishart6e/. Links to websites relevant to the topics covered and any updates to the chapter can also be found on the online resources.

| **QUESTIONS**

1 In February, Samson agrees to make crucial deliveries of Tara's speciality candles for the pre-Christmas trade for £1,000. Samson fails to make a number of deliveries and explains that this is because he had a small heart attack (from which he has recovered but, under doctor's orders, must take it easier) and because petrol prices had increased by 300% because of international events. He tells Tara that unless she agrees to increase the price to £3,000 and reduce the number of deliveries by 40%, the deliveries will not be made. He adds: 'What we agreed just can't be done. I'll go bust or keel over and that's no use to you.' Tara reluctantly agrees as she feels she has no other choice at this late stage. Samson makes the deliveries. Advise Tara.

2 How do the doctrines of economic duress, consideration, promissory estoppel, and frustration apply in the context of one-sided contract modifications?

3 'The current law on economic duress is a mess. It is unclear what pressure and how much pressure is required.' Do you agree?

4 Giving examples, how is the line, and how should it be, drawn between threats of lawful action which are legitimate and those which are illegitimate?

For hints on how to answer these questions, please see the online resources at www.oup.com/uk/chenwishart6e/

| **KEY FURTHER READING**

Atiyah, P S (1982), 'Economic Duress and the Overborne Will', 98 *LQR* 197.

Beatson, J (1990), 'Duress, Restitution and Contract Modification' in *The Use and Abuse of Unjust Enrichment* (Clarendon Press) 95.

Birks, P (1990), 'The Travails of Duress', *LMCLQ* 342.

Enonchong, N (2005), *Duress, Undue Influence and Unconscionable Bargains* (Sweet & Maxwell).

Tiplady, D (1983), 'Concepts of Duress', 99 *LQR* 188.

9

Unfairness: undue influence, non-commercial guarantees, unconscionable bargains

'You took advantage of me'

9.1 **Introduction**

In contrast to continental civil systems, English law recognises no general principle controlling unfairness in contracting. Instead, it has developed *piecemeal solutions* to particular problems of unfairness (per Bingham LJ, *Interfoto Picture Library Ltd v Stiletto Visual Programmes Ltd* (1988)). We have seen that contracts may be vitiated by doctrines that focus on the blameworthy conduct of the party seeking to enforce the contract ('the defendant'), thus:

- *misrepresentation* deals with fraud and induced mistakes (Chapter 5); and
- *duress* deals with illegitimate pressure (Chapter 8).

Other vitiating doctrines focus on the complainant's defective consent:

- *mistake* deals with un-induced mistakes (Chapter 6);
- *frustration* deals with radical change of circumstances which fundamentally alters the significance of the contract made (Chapter 7); and
- *incapacity* deals with the most obvious causes of defective consent: youth, mental infirmity, alcohol, or drugs. Incapacity is summarised at the end of this chapter and discussed in more detail in Additional Chapter 1 which is available on the online resources.

In this chapter, we examine the less obvious cases of impairment and blameworthy inducement to contract that may vitiate contracts:

- undue influence, which deals with the abuse of relationships of trust and confidence;
- a doctrine protecting non-commercial guarantors of another's debts; and
- unconscionable bargains, which deal with the exploitation of bargaining weaknesses.

It is difficult to pinpoint the pathology (unfairness) that these doctrines seek to remedy. Here, the complainant's *bargaining impairment* may qualify her for relief, although it is not attributable to a present or future mistake, not as clear-cut as minority, or as severe as mental incapacity. Likewise, the defendant may be denied enforcement although she has *not acted unlawfully* in procuring the contract, but merely 'against conscience'.

Two conflicting ideas wrestle for dominance here: the *fiction of equality* in respect of all adults of sound mind, and the *reality of inequality* which, to some degree, marks every contractual negotiation (1.3.3). Neither idea can be fully recognised by the law. To require exact equality of bargaining power would leave no contract standing. But the law is not blind to weaknesses short of recognised incapacities that impair the ability of parties to negotiate reasonable deals in their own self-interests. Such parties are easier *targets for exploitation* by contracting, without the need for any independently unlawful conduct such as misrepresentation, duress, breach of fiduciary obligations, or the like.

The traditional justification for the doctrines discussed in this chapter is firmly anchored in procedural unfairness; ie the doctrines focus on the process of contract formation and are 'content-independent' reasons of invalidity. Namely:

(i)   the *defective consent* of the 'weaker' complainant; or

(ii) the *reprehensible conduct* of the 'stronger' defendant.

On the other hand, **substantive unfairness** (unfairness in the resulting transaction; this is 'content-dependent') will often be the most conspicuous feature of the contracts avoided by these doctrines. This suggests a third justification for invalidity, namely:

(iii) *relief from improvident transactions.*

These justifications overlap. It is often said that 'equity will relieve a party from a contract which he has been induced to make as a result of victimisation. Equity will not relieve a party from a contract on the ground only that there is contractual imbalance not amounting to unconscionable dealing' (*Hart v O'Connor* (1985)). However, while it will often be very difficult to pinpoint the procedural unfairness being targeted, the improvidence of the transaction to the complainant is usually glaring where relief is granted. The questions to be addressed are the following:

(i) What is the *justification* for these doctrines? This can inform any uncertainty about the application of the doctrines.

(ii) What is the *burden of proof* for undue influence, unfair non-commercial guarantees, and unconscionable bargains?

(iii) *In practice*, how is each element of the respective burdens of proof satisfied?

(iv) Is the law *satisfactory*? If not, how might it be developed in the future?

(v) Should English law adopt a *general principle against unfair contracting*?

9.2 **Undue influence**

Undue influence concerns the exploitation of a relationship of influence to obtain an undue advantage (*R v Attorney-General for England and Wales* (2003)). In *Tate v Williamson* (1866), Lord Chelmsford LC said:

Wherever two persons stand in such a relation that, while it continues, confidence is necessarily reposed by one, and the influence which naturally grows out of that confidence is possessed by the other, and this confidence is abused, or the influence is exerted to obtain an advantage at the expense of the confiding party, the person so availing himself of his position will not be permitted to retain the advantage, although the transaction could not have been impeached if no such confidential relation had existed.

9.2.1 **Basis of the doctrine**

9.2.1.1 Unconscientious conduct

The dominant view, found in many recent leading cases,[1] including *Royal Bank of Scotland plc v Etridge (No 2)* (2001), is that undue influence targets the defendant's reprehensible conduct in inducing the complainant's agreement to the transaction.

---

[1] Eg *R v Attorney-General for England and Wales* (2003) and *National Commercial Bank (Jamaica) Ltd v Hew* (2003).

Lord Nicholls' leading judgment, with which the other Lordships agreed, explains that the doctrine seeks to:

> ensure that the influence of one person over another is not abused. In everyday life people constantly seek to… persuade those with whom they are dealing to enter into transactions, whether great or small. The law has set limits to the means properly employable for this purpose… If the intention was produced by an unacceptable means, the law will not permit the transaction to stand. The means used is regarded as an exercise of improper or 'undue' influence, and hence unacceptable, whenever the consent thus procured ought not fairly to be treated as the expression of a person's free will.

 Counterpoint

1. Uncertain: it is seldom clear what the defendant has done wrong.

2. Unnecessary: it is unnecessary to find any unconscientious behaviour at all. In *Jennings v Cairns* (2003), Arden LJ said: 'the fact that the conduct of the person exercising influence is unimpeachable is not by itself an answer to a claim in undue influence.' This suggests that the real objection lies elsewhere.

3. Contrary to authority: the classic case of *Allcard v Skinner* (1887) is inconsistent with an unconscientious conduct rationale.

In *Allcard v Skinner* (1887), a young novice nun took a vow of poverty, chastity, and obedience, and gave all her worldly possessions to the Mother Superior of the convent. The rules imposed the most absolute submission by the sisters to the Mother Superior who was to be regarded as the 'voice of God': they could not seek advice outside the sisterhood without her permission. The novice eventually left the sisterhood and sought the return of what remained of her gifts. The undue influence doctrine applies equally to gifts and contracts; the court held that the gift here was voidable for presumed undue influence, although the court acquitted the Mother Superior of any active exploitation. She did not act selfishly, preferring her own interests. Indeed, she must have regarded it as in the novice's own best interest to be divested of her worldly goods. Nevertheless, *objectively*, by the standards of equity, the parties' relationship and the resulting improvidence of the transaction to the novice, the Mother Superior *failed to do all that she should have to protect the novice's interests* (9.2.1.3).

At the same time, it was clear that the complainant's consent was not defective. Lindley LJ said that everything she did was 'referable to her own willing submission to the vows she took and to the rules which she approved, and to her own enthusiastic devotion to the life and work of the sisterhood', and that nothing justified 'the inference that she was unable to take care of herself or to manage her own affairs'. Bowen LJ continued that even 'persons who are under the most complete influence of religious feeling are perfectly free to act upon it in the disposition of their property, and not the less free because they are enthusiasts. Persons of this kind are not dead in law'. This gives a lie to the following justification.

9.2.1.2 Defective consent

Birks and Chin argue that undue influence is concerned with the complainant's defective consent, in the sense of her 'excessive' or 'morbid dependency'. She 'lacks the capacity for self-management'; her judgment is 'markedly substandard' or 'impaired to an exceptional degree' ('On the Nature of Undue Influence' in J Beatson and D Friedmann (eds), *Good Faith and Fault in Contract Law* (Clarendon Press, 1995)).

➡️⬅️ Counterpoint

1. Uncertain and contrary to authority: it is impossible to draw the line between appropriate and inappropriate levels of dependency. Although Birks and Chin suggest that 'the law relieves only an extreme loss of autonomy', something beyond the 99th percentile, the cases do not draw the line so restrictively. *A relationship of influence* is a broad notion and potentially encompasses anyone you love, like, respect, work with, or can be said to have common cause with. It is only when your transaction with that person is disastrously imbalanced against you that the question of undue influence arises.

2. Unrealistic: it is unrealistic to say that the novice in *Allcard v Skinner* lacked autonomy or that her consent was 'impaired'. As Lord Nicholls said in *Etridge*, the victim's consent is only *deemed* to be defective.

3. Trusting is not pathological: undue influence complainants (like the former nun) may be naive, romantic or idealistic, trusting and even altruistic, but they should not be regarded as thereby 'subnormal'. When the nun gave away her worldly possessions, she did not lack autonomy—she *exercised* it. There is nothing intrinsically wrong with the existence or use of influence. As Kekewich J said in *Allcard v Skinner*: 'The law ... recognises influence as natural and right. Few, if any, men are gifted with characters enabling them to act, or even think, with complete independence of others, which could not largely exist without destroying the foundations of society. But the law requires that influence, however natural and however right, shall not be unduly exercised.'

4. I explain in more detail why undue influence cannot be explained solely by reference to either the complainant's impaired consent or the defendant's role in distorting consent ('Undue Influence: *Beyond* Impaired Consent and Wrong-Doing, Towards a Relational Analysis' in A Burrows and A Rodger (eds), *Mapping the Law, Essays in Memory of Peter Birks* (OUP, 2006)).

9.2.1.3 Failure to protect

Allcard v Skinner describes the undue influence doctrine as 'a fetter placed upon the conscience of the [trusted party], and one which arises out of public policy and fair play'. In *Etridge*, undue influence was described in terms of the defendant 'preferring his own interests' and 'failing to protect the claimant's interests'. Here, the language of advantage-taking and victimisation designates an *omission*: a failure by the defendant to protect the complainant's interests as the parties' relationship requires.

Pause for reflection

In 'Undue Influence: Vindicating Relationships of Influence' (2006) 59 *CLP* 231, I set out a **relational theory of undue influence**. Relationships are vital to our quality of life. Close relationships such as marriage, romance, family, care, and friendship trigger implicit *relational norms* about how people in such relationships treat each other. They determine the appropriate range of *behaviour* and *outcomes* that are constitutive of (define) the relationship and are implicit in the distinction between 'due' and 'undue' influence. Undue influence targets:

- the defendant's violation of the implicit *procedural* norm of the parties' relationship by applying pressure on the complainant to agree, although much less is required than for duress because of the relationship;

- but, given that influence is not bad in itself, it is impossible to tell whether its exercise/effect was 'due' or 'undue' without reference to the fairness of the outcome. Moreover, an unfair outcome can be seen as procured by the defendant's violation of the implicit *substantive* norm of the parties' relationship of influence when the defendant accepts a benefit which glaringly disadvantages the complainant. An unfair outcome is the 'bad thing' against which the complainant is protected. If the defendant violates these norms, the transaction cannot stand even if she has not acted illegitimately to procure the complainant's consent and even if she acts in good faith.

9.2.2 **Overview and burden of proof**

9.2.2.1 The *traditional* categories of undue influence

Allcard v Skinner sets out two categories of undue influence which, despite the refinements by *Etridge*, remain substantially intact.

(i) **Class 1 Actual undue influence:** where the complainant can prove the defendant's positive application of pressure inducing her consent to the contract.

(ii) **Class 2 Presumed undue influence:** from the complainant's proof that:

(a) she was in a 'relationship of trust and confidence' with the defendant:

- **Class 2A** covers specified relationships where the influence is automatically presumed;

- **Class 2B** describes other relationships where the existence of influence must be *proved*; and

(b) the resulting transaction is manifestly disadvantageous to the complainant.

This raises a *presumption* of undue influence, which can be rebutted by the defendant's proof that the complainant nevertheless entered the transaction freely (usually by evidence of the presence of independent advice).

9.2.2.2 The restatement by *Etridge*

In *Etridge*, the House of Lords said that too much should not be made of the distinctions between the traditional categories of undue influence, particularly Class 2B.

Doing so was apt to lead to error and confusion. The old categories did not reflect different bases for intervention, but are merely different ways of proving *one* category of undue influence. The burden of proof lies on the complainant throughout. Lord Clyde said:

> At the end of the day, after trial, there will either be proof of undue influence or that proof will fail and it will be found that there was no undue influence. In the former case, whatever the relationship of the parties and however the influence was exerted, there will be found to have been an actual case of undue influence. In the latter there will be none.

The complainant proves undue influence, either actually or with the benefit of an evidential inference (a presumption), which remained unrebutted.

9.2.3 Failure to protect by *overt pressure* (old actual undue influence)

9.2.3.1 Relational pressure

Once we move the cases dealing with threats to prosecute and to disclose into the category of lawful act duress (8.6.2), we are left with cases involving the defendant's overt exploitation of the complainant's relational motivation for consenting. The overt exploitation can take different forms:

(i)   **Threats to abandon**

   ✓ In *Langton v Langton* (1995), the son and daughter-in-law of the complainant moved in with him after his release from prison for murdering his wife. They knew he feared further institutionalisation and threatened to stop caring for him as his health deteriorated if he did not transfer his property to them.

   ✓ In *Bank of Scotland v Bennett* (1997), the husband used wounding and insulting language to accuse his wife of disloyalty in contrast to the loyalty of his relatives. He said she would be a 'waste of rations' if she refused to guarantee his business debt and would be splitting up the family. The judge found 'moral blackmail amounting to coercion and victimisation'.

(ii) **Excessive control, secrecy, and exclusion of others**

   ✓ In *Morley v Loughan* (1893), M became a member of the 'Exclusive Brethren' and went to live with L in practical seclusion for the last seven years of his life. M was physically frail and L controlled every aspect of his life including his diet and medicines. M placed his entire fortune of £140,000 at L's disposal.

   ✓ In *Re Killick v Pountney and another* (2000), K had been P's lodger for 40 years. As K's health failed and he entered a nursing home, P took over his possessions and papers. P banned K from contact with his relatives on threat of not allowing him to come home after hospital, which terrified him. K's will provided very generously for P.

(iii) **Bullying, confrontation, and harassment**

   ✓ In *Clarke v Prus* (1995), after the elderly C's wife died, he was befriended by the younger P. C gave P gifts totalling £1.9 million over some 20 years. The court held that 'what started out as Mr Clarke's folly... finished up as

Mrs Prus' victimisation at the end of his life' when her requests turned into increasingly vehement demands made by verbal onslaughts and oppressive harassment.

✓ In *Drew v Daniel* (2005), Daniel coerced his aged aunt to confer a significant benefit on him at the expense of her own son in a distressing and lengthy conversation, coupled by his threat to sue her. He concealed his dealings from her son and her solicitor. Ward LJ found Daniel's conduct 'unacceptable' in view of Drew's vulnerability, naivety in business, and fear of confrontation.

✓ In *Re Craig* (1971), the court *inferred* overt coercion from past dealings. An 84-year-old man hired a companion after his wife's death. Over the next six years, he transferred three-quarters of his wealth to her. The court found no direct evidence of pressure but found actual undue influence given: 'the amount of the gifts, the circumstances in which they were made, the vulnerability of Mr Craig to pressure by Mrs Middleton [the companion], the evidence of the direct exercise of that pressure on other occasions and for other purposes, the knowledge of Mr Craig and Mrs Middleton of his utter dependence on her, and the whole history of the relationship'.

9.2.3.2 Relationship of influence and manifest disadvantage

Proof of actual undue influence is traditionally thought to *dispense* with the need for two elements necessary for the inference (presumption) of undue influence:

(i) the existence of a **relationship of influence** between the parties (because proof of undue pressure is enough, see *Chitty* at para 8-063); and

(ii) **manifest disadvantage** of the transaction to the complainant; it was held in *CIBC Mortgages v Pitt* (1993) that: 'actual undue influence is a species of fraud... A man guilty of fraud is no more entitled to argue that the transaction was beneficial to the person defrauded than is a man who has procured a transaction by misrepresentation' (see *Chitty* at paras 8-058, 8-062-3).

 Counterpoint

Both these exclusions are questionable:

1. It is the relationship of influence that makes the, otherwise low-level, coercion (harassment, emotional blackmail, or bullying, which would not register on the radar of the duress doctrine), legally relevant.

2. There is a world of difference between a mother pressuring her children to do their homework and her pressuring them to hand over their savings. The outcome colours the determination of whether the pressure applied is 'due' or 'undue'. In *Etridge,* Lord Nicholls said that an allegation of undue influence 'is likely to arise only when, in some respect, the transaction was disadvantageous'. Moreover, an unfair outcome is evidence that the pressure, and not something else, induced the complainant's agreement.

9.2.4 **Failure to protect by *omission* (old presumed undue influence)**

9.2.4.1 The burden of proof

This category maps on to the old Class 2 (presumed undue influence). In *Etridge*, Lord Nicholls said:

> Proof that the complainant placed trust and confidence in the other party in relation to the management of the complainant's financial affairs, coupled with a transaction which calls for explanation, will normally be sufficient, failing satisfactory evidence to the contrary, to discharge the burden of proof. On proof of these two matters the stage is set for the Court to infer that, in the absence of a satisfactory explanation, the transaction can only have been procured by undue influence. In other words, proof of these two facts is *prima facie* evidence that the defendant abused the influence he acquired in the parties' relationship. He preferred his own interests. He did not behave fairly to the other. So the evidential burden then shifts to him. It is for him to produce evidence to counter the inference which otherwise should be drawn.

The key point is that the presumption raised is:

✗ not *legal*; this *would* reverse the burden of proof or make the presumption irrebuttable.

✓ Rather, the presumption is *evidential*; it merely allows an inference to be drawn, analogous in operation to the doctrine of *res ipsa loquitur* ('the facts speak for themselves'). Talk of 'rebuttal of the presumption' merely refers to a shift of the evidential onus to the defendant to *displace* the **evidential inference** raised by the complainant in the first place; the burden of proof is not reversed. What is needed to counter the inference will depend on the *weight* of the inference; it may prove very difficult, even impossible, to shift on the facts.

The inference is *not* that the defendant has exerted undue pressure on the complainant, but that she has preferred her own interests and failed to safeguard the complainant's. '[T]he question is whether one party has reposed sufficient trust and confidence in the other' such that the latter owes the former 'an obligation of candour and protection' which she has failed to observe. The answer depends on the nature of the parties' relationship and the fairness of their transaction.

9.2.4.2 Relationship of influence: automatic presumption (old Class 2A)

In *Etridge*, Lord Nicholls explains that: 'The law has adopted a sternly protective attitude towards certain types of relationship in which one party acquires influence over another who is vulnerable and dependent and where, moreover, substantial gifts by the influenced or vulnerable person are not normally to be expected.' Well-known examples falling within this category are:

- doctor and patient;
- solicitor and client;
- parent and child;
- guardian and ward;

- trustee and beneficiary;
- religious adviser and disciple; and
- more controversially, a man and his fiancée (*Leeder v Stevens* (2005)), although not a husband and wife.

These relationships trigger an irrebuttable (*legal*) presumption of the existence of a relationship of influence. This must be distinguished sharply from the *evidential* presumption of undue influence that operates in the old class 2B from a relationship of influence, coupled with a transaction calling for an explanation.

 Pause for reflection

1. Enonchong observes that this 'leaves the law in a curious position. For, the law would be saying that couples who are engaged to be married repose sufficient trust and confidence in one another but that the trust and confidence somehow evaporate as soon as they are married' ('The Irrebuttable Presumption of Influence and the Relationship between Fiancé and Fiancée' (2005) 121 *LQR* 567).

2. Even in these cases, it should be possible to rebut the presumption of undue influence by specific evidence that *this particular* relationship was *not* one of influence. People are not as obedient and compliant in status relationships as they were when this category was developed. Thus, Lord Clyde's view that Class 2A should simply raise a very strong but *rebuttable* evidential presumption is preferable.

9.2.4.3 Proved relationship of influence (old Class 2B)

Relationships of influence 'tend to arise where someone relies on the guidance or advice of another, where the other is aware of that reliance and where the person upon whom reliance is placed obtains, or may well obtain, a benefit from the transaction or has some other interest in it being concluded' (*Lloyds Bank v Bundy* (1975)). The following points can be distilled from the case law:

(i) **There is often an element of exclusivity in the relevant relationship.**

- Its essence from the complainant's side is an expectation that the defendant will give conscientious advice in the complainant's interest. Therefore, the complainant lets down her guard and may not consciously self-protect or seek outside advice.

- The defendant knows of, and has participated in, the relationship (eg has encouraged or acquiesced in the complainant's reliance and trust), thereby raising an obligation to restrain her self-interest and have regard to the complainant's interest in transacting with her.

(ii) **It is unnecessary to prove 'blind, unquestioning trust' or a 'dominating influence'** (*Tufton v Sperni* (1952)). It is enough that, in past dealings, the complainant generally reposed trust and confidence in the defendant. Typical examples include:

- a wife and her husband (*BCCI v Aboody* (1990));

- parents and their adult child (*Avon Finance v Bridger* (1985));

- a great-uncle and great-nephew (*Cheese v Thomas* (1994));

- an elderly man and his housekeeper-companion (*Re Craig*);

- a customer and a bank (*Lloyds Bank v Bundy*);

- a pop singer and his manager (*O'Sullivan v Management Agency and Music Ltd* (1985));

- an elderly farmer and his farm manager (*Goldsworthy v Brikell* (1987)); and

- a junior employee and her employer (*Crédit Lyonnais v Burch* (1997)).

(iii) **Reliance may be exacerbated by the complainant's illness or frailty, incompetence or inexperience** (eg *Re Craig, Goldsworthy v Brikell, Tufton v Sperni*; here, there is an overlap with the unconscionable bargains doctrine, 9.4).

(iv) **A relationship of influence may even arise in a one-off dealing.** In *Tufton v Sperni*, S (a Muslim with business expertise) sold T (a convert with no business experience) a house to set up a centre for Muslim culture; S charged twice the market value and reserved numerous privileges, including a right to substitute other premises at his complete discretion. The transaction was set aside.

(v) **The unfairness of the transaction** provides strong evidence of a relationship of influence. Alternatively, substantive unfairness can be seen as narrowing the potential width of 'relationships of influence'. For example, in *Crédit Lyonnais v Burch* (1997), a young junior employee gave a personal guarantee and an unlimited charge on her flat to secure her employer's existing debt to the bank and slightly extend his overdraft facility. Direct evidence of a potentially exploitative relationship of influence with her employer was flimsy: she had worked for him for ten years and sometimes babysat and visited his family in London and Italy. Millett LJ explains that:

> [T]he mere fact that a transaction is improvident or manifestly disadvantageous to one party is not sufficient by itself to give rise to a presumption that it has been obtained by the exercise of undue influence; but where it is obtained by a party between whom and the complainant there is a relationship like that of employer and junior employee which is easily capable of developing into a relationship of trust and confidence, the nature of the transaction may be sufficient to justify the inference that such a development has taken place; and where the transaction is so extravagantly improvident that it is virtually inexplicable on any other basis, the inference will be readily drawn.

Conversely, no inference will be drawn if an apparently disadvantageous transaction *is* explicable. In *Re Brocklehurst's Estate* (1978), an elderly aristocrat, without independent advice, gave a garage proprietor a 99-year lease of the shooting rights over his estate. This heavily reduced the value of the estate. The court's conclusion that no relationship of trust and confidence existed between the parties coincided with its finding that the gift was a 'spontaneous and independent act' explicable in terms of the friendship between the parties and the donor's desire to deliberately reduce the estate's value before it was inherited by a detested nephew.

9.2.4.4 A transaction calling for explanation

Coupled with a relationship of influence, the unfairness of the transaction operates to raise the inference (or presumption) that the relationship of influence has been exploited, in the sense that the defendant has failed to safeguard the complainant's interests (*Etridge*). Conversely, in *R v Attorney-General for England and Wales*, while the Privy Council conceded that the Army had considerable influence over R, the *reasonableness of R's agreement* not to divulge his activities as a member of the SAS gave rise to no inference that it was obtained by an unfair exploitation of that relationship, even though R lacked independent advice.

The requirement, formerly called 'manifest disadvantage', was:

- confirmed in the modern law by *National Westminster Bank plc v Morgan* (1985);
- dispensed with in cases of actual undue influence (*CIBC Mortgages v Pitt*); and
- relabelled 'transaction calling for an explanation' by the House of Lords in *Etridge*. Their Lordships criticised the expression 'manifest disadvantage' as inappropriate in the *husband and wife situation* where, typically, the wife agrees to guarantee or provide security to support a bank's loan to her husband but later claims undue influence or misrepresentation (9.3). It is an error to treat such guarantees as *always* bad for the wife (because she undertakes an onerous financial obligation while personally receiving nothing in return), or as *never* bad for her (because her fortunes are bound up with her husband's). Rather, the inference of undue influence arises when the transaction is 'not readily explicable by the parties' relationship'. Lord Nicholls, relying on Lindley LJ's judgment in *Allcard v Skinner*, justifies the substantive requirement as:

> a necessary limitation upon the width of the first prerequisite [the relationship of influence]. It would be absurd for the law to presume that every gift by a child to a parent, or every transaction between a client and their solicitor or between a patient and their doctor, was brought about by undue influence unless the contrary is affirmatively proved. Such a presumption would be too far-reaching... The law would be rightly open to ridicule, for transactions such as these are unexceptionable. They do not suggest that something may be amiss. So something more is needed before the law reverses the burden of proof, something which calls for an explanation. When that something more is present, the greater the disadvantage to the vulnerable person, the more cogent must be the explanation before the presumption will be regarded as rebutted.

When does a transaction 'call for explanation'? It must entail a disadvantage that would 'have been obvious as such to any independent and reasonable person who considered the transaction at the time with knowledge of all the relevant facts', and not only emerges 'after a fine and close evaluation of its various beneficial and detrimental features' (*BCCI v Aboody* (1990)). Four relevant considerations can be deduced from the case law:

(i) Impact on the complainant's future autonomy

Transactions involving an extreme degree of improvidence that threaten the complainant's future autonomy will 'call for an explanation'. This is why most undue influence cases involve the loss of the complainant's home or the vast proportion of the complainant's wealth.

✓ This was arguably the real problem in *Allcard v Skinner*. Describing the novice's gift to the church as 'calling for explanation' is misleading (because it is perfectly explicable by her devotion); it is shorthand for saying that it is *objectively inappropriate*. The gift substantially undermined her future autonomy because it failed to provide for the contingency that she might later choose to leave and need some resources. Even if it was unobjectionable for the Mother Superior to accept the original gift, her refusal to return what was left of the gift violated the implicit norms of the relationship.

✓ In *Hammond v Osborn* (2002), H (an elderly and frail man), was befriended by his neighbour, O, who helped him as he became increasingly infirm over 18 months. O claimed that H told her to cash in all his investments (some £300,000 worth) and to keep the proceeds. In finding undue influence, the court emphasised that the sum represented 92% of his liquid assets, while making him liable for capital gains tax of £50,000; H would be unable to meet the costs of his care as he became more infirm.

(ii) **Consistency with the nature of the parties' relationship**

A relationship of influence does not bar transactions between the parties to it; 'something more is needed before the law reverses the burden of proof... the greater the disadvantage to the vulnerable person, the more cogent must be the explanation before the presumption will be regarded as rebutted' (*Etridge*). A transaction that is disproportionate to the gratitude, love, or affection evinced by the evolution of the party's relationship will 'call for an explanation'.

✗ *Portman Building Society v Dusangh* (2000) shows that guarantees by parents to support loans to their children, while improvident for the parents, are regarded as unexceptional and 'capable of reasonable explanation on the basis of parental affection'.

✓ In contrast, in finding undue influence in *Crédit Lyonnais v Burch*, Swinton Thomas LJ observed that: '[I]t would cause a bank manager to raise his eyebrows more than a little when he was engaged in entering into a contract with a young employee which involved guaranteeing her employer's indebtedness in the sum of £270,000, and mortgaging her home to the bank.'

✓ Recall *Hammond v Osborn*. Ward LJ commented that the gift was: '[W]holly out of proportion to the kindness shown to him. Looking at the matter objectively, it was an irrational decision, not a good one. The very scale of the gift with the disadvantageous consequences that ensued serves only, in my judgment, to heighten the anxiety which founds this presumption, namely that pressure was operating on his mind.'

(iii) **Consistency with the complainant's relationship with others**

✓ In *Randall v Randall* (2004), the court set aside gifts of land made by an elderly woman to her nephew because, inter alia, they were inconsistent with her desire to protect her beloved donkeys living on part of the land, and they effectively disinherited other close relatives, including the nephew's own mother who lived on part of the land; they also divested her of all the property in the twilight of her life when she would need extra care.

✓ In *Humphreys v Humphreys* (2005), a mother's improvident transfer of her home to her son when she had six other children called for an explanation.

✓ Similarly, in *Pesticcio v Huet* (2004), a man's transfer of his home to his sister was suspicious since it would leave his beloved mother without a home.

(iv) The *explicability* of any apparent improvidence

Transactions that appear very improvident may not be so on closer examination, or may otherwise be satisfactorily explained:

✗ Recall that undue influence was denied in *Re Brocklehurst's Estate* where the complainant's gift of a 99-year lease of the shooting rights over his estate was explicable by his desire to reduce its value to his detested nephew who would inherit it.

✗ Likewise, recall *Portman Building Society v Dusangh*.

✗ Similarly, no undue influence was found in *Campbell v Campbell* (1996), where the complainant gave her house to one of her children whom she believed had been unjustly imprisoned.

9.2.4.5 Rebutting the presumption

To rebut the evidential presumption of undue influence raised by the complainant's proof of a relationship of influence and a transaction calling for explanation, the defendant must show that the complainant's consent to the transaction was 'full, free and informed' (*Zamet v Hyman* (1961)), usually by showing that the complainant received adequate independent advice, although this is unnecessary if it can be otherwise proved (*Inche Noriah v Omar* (1929)). The complainant's understanding of the transaction is necessary, but not sufficient. As Lord Nicholls (*Etridge*) explains:

> [A] person may understand fully the implications of a proposed transaction... and yet still be acting under the undue influence of another. Proof of outside advice does *not, of itself*, necessarily show that the subsequent completion of the transaction was *free from the exercise of undue influence*. Whether it will be proper to infer that outside advice had an *emancipating effect*, so that the transaction was not brought about by the exercise of undue influence, is a question of fact to be decided having regard to all the evidence in the case (emphasis added).

A weighty piece of evidence in determining whether the inference is rebutted is the extent of unfairness ('inexplicability') in the transaction. If the degree of disadvantage to the claimant is serious enough, the court may infer that:

(i) The complainant's refusal to get or follow independent advice indicates the continuing impact of undue influence: in *Bank of Montreal v Stuart* (1911), the court said of the wife, who was 'absolutely cleaned out' by acting as surety for her husband: 'She says she acted of her own free will... and that she would have scorned to consult anyone... Her declarations shew how deeprooted and how lasting the influence of her husband was.'

(ii) Any advice received by the complainant was inadequate: it failed to emancipate her from the defendant's undue influence. In **Inche Noriah v Omar**, the complainant's gift of land to her nephew was set aside despite her receipt of independent advice, because it failed to meet the requirements of *adequacy*. Namely, that it should be: independent; given with knowledge of the complainant's vulnerability and the material aspects of the negotiation; effectively communicated to the complainant; and competent, in only supporting transactions that can sensibly be entered into by a party free of influence.

In *Crédit Lyonnais v Burch* (9.2.4.3), the junior employee refused two suggestions from the bank to obtain independent advice. However, Millett LJ said that the transaction was voidable *even if she had received advice*, because while a party is 'normally entitled to assume that the solicitor has discharged his duty and that the complainant has followed his advice... he cannot make any such assumption if he knows or ought to know that it is false'. The latter was so here because, in the light of the staggering burden she was assuming, the lender 'must have known that no competent solicitor could advise her to enter into a guarantee in the terms she did'.

(iii) The complainant did not adequately understand the transaction: in *Hammond v Osborn*, the Court of Appeal described H's gift as 'an act of generosity wholly out of proportion to the kindness shown to him'. Ward LJ thought it 'inconceivable... that the deceased, who was prudently investing for his future, would have saddled himself with a debt he could not pay'.

 Pause for reflection

The function of the rebuttal is to determine whether the defendant had *successfully shifted* her obligation to protect the complainant's welfare to a third party (the independent adviser). If so, the paradigm will have changed from a relational to an arm's-length one, leaving the defendant free to deal self-interestedly with the complainant. This makes sense of the requirement of 'adequacy' of the independent advice. *Comprehension* of the transaction is necessary, but not sufficient. The question is whether the advice *emancipated* the complainant from the defendant's influence arising from their relationship. The greater the disadvantage to the vulnerable person, the more she needs help, the more cogent must be the explanation, evoking 'a stronger application of the safeguard' (*Allcard v Skinner*).

9.2.5 Rescission for undue influence

9.2.5.1 The bars to rescission

Contracts and gifts tainted by undue influence are voidable and may be rescinded at the complainant's option. The operation of rescission, including its bars, is the same as that applicable for misrepresentation (5.2.2). Thus, rescission may be barred by:

✓ the complainant's *affirmation* of the contract;

✓ *lapse of time* after the cessation of the influence (known as *laches* or acquiescence);

✓ if a *third party* acquires an interest in the subject matter of the contract as a good faith purchaser; and

✓ if it is impossible to effect *mutual restoration of benefits received* under the transaction.

In *O'Sullivan v Management Agency and Music Ltd* (1985), a *fully performed* contract to manage an inexperienced pop musician was rescinded for presumed undue influence. The manager was required to return the musician's copyright in songs and account for the profit it had made. The manager's services, which had brought fame and fortune to the musician, could not be 'returned' but were recognised by allowing deduction of a sum from the liability to account for profit. The logic of this approach is to abolish the bar of proprietary mutual restitution. If conversion into money is allowed then, subject to quantification difficulties, *mutual restitution is never impossible*.

9.2.5.2 The defence of change of position

In *Etridge*, Lord Scott said that, where undue influence or misrepresentation is established, 'the victim, is entitled, subject to the usual defences of change of position, affirmation, delay etc, to avoid the contract'. The change of position defence, recognised in the law of unjust enrichment, *reduces the claimant's recovery* to protect a good faith defendant's expenditure in reliance on the security of their receipt. *Cheese v Thomas* (1994) is an arguable example.[2] C (an 88-year-old man) contributed £43,000 and his great-nephew contributed £40,000 towards the purchase of a home for C to live in for life, but in the nephew's name. The transaction was voidable for undue influence. When the nephew failed to keep up the mortgage payments, the lender forced a mortgagee's sale which realised less than the parties had paid. The court ordered this loss to be borne by both parties in proportion to their contributions. The great-uncle only got back *what was left* of his share. The court exercised its equitable discretion to achieve 'practical justice' because the transaction was in the nature of a *joint venture*, and because the great-nephew was *not morally reprehensible*, having acted with good faith to provide his great-uncle with a home.

This is consistent with dicta in *Allcard v Skinner* in that, had the nun not been barred by her delay, the court held that she would have recovered only so much as had not already been spent on the charitable purposes of the convent in which she participated.

9.2.5.3 No partial rescission

In *Glanville v Glanville* (2003), Park J sets out the law: 'relief for undue influence is an all or nothing matter... either the [transaction] stands as it is, or it is set aside in its entirety. The judge cannot vary what the complainant did and substitute something else for it.' Partial rescission is further discussed at 9.3.3.

---

[2] M Chen-Wishart, 'Loss Sharing, Undue Influence and Manifest Disadvantage' (1994) 110 *LQR* 173.

9.3 Non-commercial guarantees

9.3.1 The problem and the policies

Where a wife is induced to guarantee the debts of her husband (or his company) by the husband's undue influence, misrepresentation, or pressure, can the lender enforce the guarantee against the wife? The question has vexed the courts because the policies for and against enforcement of such guarantees are so finely balanced. The arguments supporting enforcement include that:

✓ the wife should take responsibility for her apparent agreement to the guarantee;

✓ she may stand to benefit from the loan to her husband, particularly if she is financially dependent on him;

✓ it is the husband and not the lender who has behaved reprehensibly; and

✓ such lending is socially and economically useful by unlocking the wealth tied up in the family home for commercial purposes; lenders will be *reluctant to lend* if they lack confidence in the enforceability of their securities; Lord Nicholls points out that 95% of all businesses in the UK are small businesses responsible for about one-third of all employment and their most important source of finance is bank loans raised by second mortgages on the domestic home.

On the other hand, there are arguments against enforcement:

✗ the marriage relationship provides scope for abuse when one party (usually the husband), desperate for finance, may use unconscientious means to induce his or her spouse to guarantee their loan (*Etridge*);

✗ the guarantor is usually peripheral to the loan negotiations, often brought in only at the last moment, and so is in no real position to assess the wisdom of her guarantee;

✗ the lender is, or ought to be, aware of the risk of abuse here;

✗ the guarantor's economic interests is not identical with the primary debtor's, although it will be linked; and

✗ homelessness, with its attendant social problems for adults and especially children, should be avoided.

9.3.2 The legal response

In *Royal Bank of Scotland v Etridge* (2001), the House of Lords clarified the steps laid down in the seminal case of *Barclays Bank v O'Brien* (1994). In this important area, located at the border between the private and commercial spheres, their Lordships tilted the balance towards commercial certainty in favour of the banks. They sought to lay down 'clear, simple and practically operable' minimum requirements which, if followed in the ordinary case without abnormal features, would ensure the enforceability of the guarantee. An overview is given in **Diagram 9A**. Accordingly, **a guarantee is unenforceable if:**

(i) some vitiating factor affects the dealing between the guarantor and debtor;

(ii) the lender knows that the guarantor is not acting commercially (ie for consideration) and the transaction is for the benefit of the primary debtor; and

(iii) the lender has not taken *reasonable steps* to ensure that the guarantor was properly advised.

9.3.2.1 Vitiation by the primary debtor

The complainant must first show that the guarantee was vitiated by the debtor's misrepresentation, undue influence, or other legal or equitable wrongdoing. However, *Etridge* said that courts should not be too ready to find this in *husband and wife cases*:

> Statements or conduct by a husband which do not pass beyond the bounds of what
> may be expected of a reasonable husband in the circumstances should not, without

Diagram 9A Non-commercial guarantees: the test of enforceability

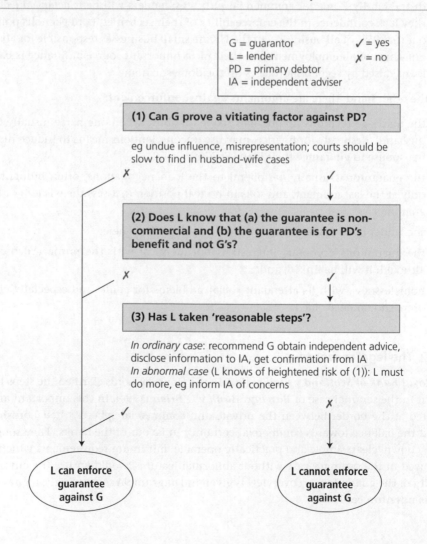

G = guarantor   ✓ = yes
L = lender   ✗ = no
PD = primary debtor
IA = independent adviser

(1) Can G prove a vitiating factor against PD?

eg undue influence, misrepresentation; courts should be
slow to find in husband-wife cases

(2) Does L know that (a) the guarantee is non-commercial and (b) the guarantee is for PD's benefit and not G's?

(3) Has L taken 'reasonable steps'?

In ordinary case: recommend G obtain independent advice,
disclose information to IA, get confirmation from IA
In abnormal case (L knows of heightened risk of (1)): L must
do more, eg inform IA of concerns

L can enforce guarantee against G

L cannot enforce guarantee against G

more, be castigated as undue influence. Similarly, when a husband is forecasting the future of his business, and expressing his hopes or fears, a degree of hyperbole may be only natural. Courts should not too readily treat such exaggerations as misstatements.

Their Lordships said that undue influence is not especially indicated by a wife guaranteeing her husband's debt; it is 'possible but relatively unlikely'. Rather, her support is the 'natural and admirable consequence of the relationship of a mutually loyal married couple'; it is readily explicable in terms of her normal trust and confidence in her husband. However, this is precisely why the law is especially vigilant over transactions between those in a relationship of influence. Thus, it is arguable that, in seeking to protect lenders, the courts have failed to give proper protection commensurate with the gist of undue influence.

Lord Nicholls concedes that, exceptionally, such a transaction may 'call for explanation', but he does not say *when* courts will be prepared to infer that a husband has preferred his own interest and thereby failed to discharge his obligation of candour and fairness to his wife.

9.3.2.2 Lender's 'notice'

Barclays Bank v O'Brien had referred to the lender's constructive notice (or being 'put on inquiry') of the debtor's wrongful inducement of the guarantor where it knows that: (i) the debtor–guarantor *relationship* is of a 'sexual or emotional' nature; and (ii) the loan is *for the debtor's benefit*. However, *Etridge* recognises that talk of constructive notice, while convenient in this context, is 'a misnomer'. *Etridge* has established the following:

(i) Since **relationships** of influence are infinitely various and lenders cannot be expected to probe into or evaluate the emotional relationship between debtor and guarantor, 'the only practical way forward' is to require the bank to take reasonable steps 'in every case where the relationship between the surety and the debtor is non-commercial'.

(ii) The lender has notice that the **transaction is for the debtor's benefit** if the guarantee relates to his debts or the debts of his company. This applies even if the guarantor is nominally a shareholder, director, or secretary of the company, since these are not reliable indicators of her real involvement in the conduct of the business. The loan will only be for joint purposes if the guarantor 'is an active participant in managing the company's affairs and is rewarded by remuneration for her work', such that her 'interest and/or involvement is substantive rather than titular'. But, not if the negotiations are conducted by the primary debtor and the guarantor plays no part (*Mahon v FBN Bank* (2011)).

Knowledge of these two factors alerts the lender to initiate an *administrative procedure* ('reasonable steps') that does not require difficult and sensitive judgment calls.

9.3.2.3 Lender's failure to take reasonable steps

Etridge held that, **in the ordinary case**, with no abnormal features, the lender should take 'reasonable steps' to satisfy itself that the guarantor *understands the nature and* *effect of the transaction.* Lenders have generally refused to provide this information themselves for fear of exposing themselves to allegations of misrepresentation, undue influence, or negligence. The House of Lords accepts that it is enough for lenders to:

(i) communicate directly with the guarantor that the lender will require a confirmation from a solicitor to the effect that she has been duly advised in order to prevent her from later challenging the guarantee. The solicitor may also act for her husband, or even the lender;

(ii) disclose the necessary financial information to the guarantor's solicitor: ordinarily this includes information about the purpose of the loan, the debtor's current indebtedness and overdraft facility, and the terms of the new loan;

(iii) obtain a confirmation from the guarantor's solicitor to the effect that the guarantor has been advised about the nature and effect of the transaction, in the absence of the primary debtor and, for a sufficient duration to:

    (a) explain the *nature and effect of the guarantee* in a meaningful way;

    (b) emphasise the *seriousness of the risk* of her being made bankrupt or losing her home;

    (c) discuss her financial means, the value of the property being charged and the availability of other assets to meet the repayment; and

    (d) state clearly that she has a *choice* whether to proceed and ask whether she wishes to renegotiate particular terms (eg to lower her liability or vary the order of call between various securities).

Failure to obtain this confirmation may render the guarantee unenforceable (*First National Bank plc v Achampong and Owusu* (2003)). However:

- the lender *need not even observe the steps* laid out 'if the surety already knew the details or if the creditor had reason to believe that the surety already knew' (*Etridge*).

- The lender is 'safe' as long as it has a solicitor's confirmation.

- If the *solicitor* giving the confirmation has acted unprofessionally or incompetently, the matter is between the guarantor and the solicitor.

- The lender is protected even if the *solicitor* has a *conflict of interest* by also acting for the debtor or the lender in the guarantee, or has been instructed by the lender to advise the guarantor. Any knowledge acquired by the solicitor, which may raise suspicions, is not generally imputed to the lender.

The **solicitor** 'does not have a duty to satisfy himself of the absence of undue influence' (*Etridge*). If he believes that the transaction is not in the guarantor's best interest, he should give advice to that effect but *need not veto it* (by refusing to provide the confirmation certificate), unless it is 'glaringly obvious that the wife is being grievously wronged', when the solicitor should decline to act (which *would* effectively veto the transaction).

Pause for reflection

This shifts the balance in favour of lenders and against guarantors. The advice is aimed at *informing* the guarantor *rather than emancipating her from undue influence.* Lord Hobhouse observes that the solicitor's advice is often a 'formality or merely served to reinforce the husband's wishes and undermine any scope for the wife to exercise an independent judgment whether to comply…. The law has, in order to accommodate the commercial lenders, adopted a fiction which nullifies the equitable principle and deprives vulnerable members of the public of the protection which equity gives them.' Gardner's comment is apposite here:[3]

> The clarity… of this message is good news for banks, of course… [and] even better news for solicitors, one imagines. One might pause, however, over the question whether it truly empowers guarantors… If the debtor asserts that he needs the loan for his business, and a guarantee is required for which there seems to be no other source than his wife or other emotional dependent, it may avail her very little to have it spelled out to her that, if the worst comes to the worst, she may for example lose her home; knowing this may create for her very little or nothing by way of additional choice in the matter.

Etridge recognises the possibility of the **abnormal or exceptional case**, when the lender may have to take further steps. The lender may know facts that indicate a *heightened risk* of undue influence, duress, or misrepresentation by the debtor, from: the lender's past dealings with and knowledge of the parties; the guarantor's conduct that reveals a misunderstanding of the transaction; the debtor's refusal to disclose financial information to the guarantor; or the lender's knowledge or suspicion that the guarantor has not received proper advice. In these exceptional cases, the court will determine whether the lender has taken reasonable steps in response to its heightened suspicion. *Appropriate extra steps might include*:

- insisting on legal advice which is genuinely independent of the debtor or the lender; and
- informing the debtor's solicitor of any facts giving rise to the lender's heightened suspicion that the guarantor's consent may be improperly obtained.

9.3.3 **The remedy**

The primary relief available to guarantors is **rescission** of the guarantee. The remedy is subject to the usual bars already discussed (5.2.2 and 9.2.5.1). Two issues warrant particular mention.

In his summary in *Etridge*, Lord Scott said that the restitutionary defence of change of position, along with other bars, will operate to qualify the complainant's right to rescission. Since bad faith parties are disqualified from the defence, it should only be available (if at all) in 'ordinary' cases when the lender knows no facts that suggest a

---

[3] S Gardner, 'Wives' Guarantees of their Husbands' Debts' (1999) 115 *LQR* 1, 7–8.

heightened risk that the guarantor's consent was improperly obtained. More impor-tantly, since the defence operates *by* reducing the complainant's restitution by the amount of the defendant's change of position, it could logically allow lenders to retain a charge for the sum lent to debtors in reliance on the enforceability of the guarantees. This would substantially undermine the little protection remaining to guarantors. The defence was not mentioned in *O'Brien* itself and has not been applied.

The courts have no power to award partial rescission. In *TSB Bank plc v Camfield* (1995), a woman was induced by her husband's innocent misrepresentation (that her maximum liability would be £15,000 when it was unlimited) to charge her interest in their home to secure his debts. The charge was voidable because the bank failed to take 'reasonable steps' in the circumstances. At first instance, the charge was partially rescinded to leave a charge of £15,000 because the wife was 'quite prepared to risk' that sum; but the Court of Appeal set aside the charge completely saying that rescis-sion 'is an all or nothing process' and the right 'of the representee, not that of the court', so that a court cannot grant 'equitable relief to which terms may be attached'.

 Counterpoint

The Court of Appeal's inflexible position is open to question. If it is clear that the guarantor would have been prepared to contract on the basis represented, then partial rescission of the charge to uphold her understanding is a logical response to the problem. Her consent to the lower sum is not vitiated. In *Vadasz v Pioneer Concrete (SA) Pty Ltd* (1995),[4] the Australian High Court allowed partial rescission on similar facts. Partial rescission is also recognised in the UNIDROIT Principles of International Commercial Law (Art 3.16), and the European Draft Common Frame of Reference (Art II.-7:213).

9.4 Unconscionable bargains

9.4.1 General principles

The equitable doctrine of unconscionable bargains is distinguishable:

- from *duress* in not requiring the application of illegitimate pressure; and
- from *undue influence* in not requiring a relationship of influence between the parties.

This colourful doctrine plays out in an array of cases where the sick, the mentally or physically infirm, the drunk, the illiterate, the uneducated, and the incompetent walk on and off stage. It is said to arise 'from the circumstances or conditions of the parties contracting—weakness on one side, usury on the other, or extortion or advan-tage taken of that weakness... it means an unconscientious use of the power arising out of these circumstances and conditions' (*Chesterfield v Janssen* (1751)). This fairly

---

[4] See also *Commercial Bank of Australia v Amadio* (1983) where partial rescission was considered but rejected on the facts, and *Scales Trading Ltd v Far Eastern Shipping Co Public Ltd* (1999).

loose and potentially 'run-away' jurisdiction to grant relief is restrained by the stated requirements for relief in the leading modern cases of *Boustany v Pigott* (1993) and *Alec Lobb (Garages) v Total Oil* (1985).

(i) The complainant must be under an operative *bargaining impairment,* placing her at a serious disadvantage vis-à-vis the other party.

(ii) The defendant must have *exploited* the complainant's weakness in a morally culpable manner.

(iii) The resulting transaction is *manifestly improvident* to the complainant.

(iv) The complainant lacked adequate independent advice.

For example, contracts were set aside as unconscionable where:

✓ a poor man, entitled to a share of an estate worth £1,700, sold it for 200 guineas (about £210) cash (*Evans v Llewellin* (1787));

✓ two brothers (a plumber's assistant and a laundryman), advised by an inexperienced solicitor also acting for the defendant, sold their reversionary interests at significantly below market value (*Fry v Lane* (1889));

✓ an elderly man, ill and 'intellectually not gifted', sold his property for an inadequate consideration in undue haste and without independent advice (*Clark v Malpas* (1862));

✓ a wife, in the process of divorce, transferred her share in the matrimonial home to her husband without independent advice and for inadequate consideration (*Cresswell v Potter* (1978); *Backhouse v Backhouse* (1978)); and

✓ an 84-year-old widow with senile dementia sold paintings worth £6,000–7,000 for £40 to a young bric-a-brac dealer (*Ayres v Hazelgrove* (1984)).

 Pause for reflection

The meaning of 'unconscionable' and its variants can be confusing because it can be used in different senses in different areas of private law. In 'Unconscionability as a Vitiating Factor' [1995] *LMCLQ* 538, Bamforth helpfully distinguishes between unconscionability as:

1. a vitiating factor (as discussed in this section);

2. a descriptive label for conduct or transactions which other distinct vitiating factors exist to prevent and as the general policy justification for their existence; and

3. an element of another legal rule.

9.4.2 **Basis of the doctrine**

The older cases emphasise the *impaired consent* of the 'poor and ignorant' (*Fry v Lane* (1888)), making the defendant's unconscionable conduct superfluous. The prevailing view now is that **prevention of unconscionable conduct** is the true basis of the jurisdiction. In *Boustany v Pigott*, Lord Templeman explains that:

Unequal bargaining power or objectively unreasonable terms provide no basis for equitable interference in the absence of unconscientious or extortionate abuse of power... equity will not provide relief unless the beneficiary is guilty of unconscionable conduct... namely that unconscientious advantage has been taken of his disabling condition or circumstances.

In *Alec Lobb v Total Oil*, Dillon LJ said that: 'The courts would only interfere in exceptional cases where as a matter of common fairness it was not right that the strong should be allowed to push the weak to the wall. The concepts of unconscionable conduct and of the exercise by the stronger of coercive power are thus brought in.'

 Counterpoint

The concern to protect vulnerable non-commercial parties from manifest substantive unfairness provides the best explanation for the relief granted.[5] Three arguments support this view:

1. Substantive unfairness is a *necessary condition for relief*; no relief is available without it, even if the procedural unfairness is clear (ie weakness and lack of adequate advice on one side and unconscionable conduct on the other).

2. Substantive unfairness is the *best predictor of unconscionability*; like undue influence, direct evidence of procedural unfairness is usually ambiguous at best, and absent at worst. But it becomes legally significant in the presence of manifest substantive unfairness, which allows courts to infer that:

   • the complainant *must have* been sufficiently impaired in his or her bargaining ability;

   • the impairment *must have* been known or suspected by the defendant; and

   • the complainant *could not have been adequately* protected by any advice received.

3. Substantive unfairness determines our conception of *procedural unfairness*. It is practically impossible to *define* what impairment, adequate advice, and unconscionable conduct mean or, indeed, why we even *care* about them, if we do not think that a bad deal is a bad thing. It is odd to say that we do *not* care about the reasonableness of a deal but we do care about someone's *ability to make* a reasonable deal. It may not be too much of an exaggeration to say that 'inadequate' advice is advice which fails to save the complainant from a disastrous deal, and unconscionable advantage-taking comprises little more than procuring or accepting the benefit of an extremely one-sided contract at the expense of the complainant. Getting an *obscenely* good deal from such a person, like taking candy from a baby, is hardly a glowing character reference.

9.4.3 **What must be proved?**

9.4.3.1 Improvident transaction

Where unconscionability has been concluded, it is often difficult to put your finger on precisely what the defendant has done wrong and why the complainant warrants

---

[5] See further M Chen-Wishart, *Unconscionable Bargains* (Butterworths, 1989).

special protection. But the extreme unfairness of the transaction will usually be clear. Mere undervalue is insufficient; it must be overreaching and oppressive or entail such substantial undervalue that it 'shocks the conscience of the court' (*Alec Lobb (Garages) Ltd v Total Oil (Great Britain) Ltd* (1983)).

9.4.3.2 Bargaining impairment

Short of mental incapacity (see Additional Chapter 1, available on the online resources), what types of bargaining disability qualify for the protection of the unconscionability doctrine? The jurisdiction originated in the perceived need to protect expectant heirs who traded their uncertain future expectancies for more certain and immediate gains, often at considerable undervalue (*Earl of Aylesford v Morris* (1873)). From this, protection was extended to those designated as 'poor and ignorant' (*Fry v Lane*), although the category has been stretched to encompass members 'of the lower income group' and the 'less highly educated' (*Cresswell v Potter*), granting relief to:

- ✓ a telephonist 'in the context of property transactions' (*Cresswell v Potter*);
- ✓ a woman of substantial means who was anxious to 'get a steady and regular income' (*Boustany v Pigott; Ayres v Hazelgrove*); and
- ✓ an intelligent businesswoman of some ability but 'in circumstances of great emotional strain' during a marriage break up (*Backhouse v Backhouse* (1978)).

Pause for reflection

The 'poor and ignorant' formulation is outmoded in a modern welfare state with universal compulsory education. It is time to openly recognise, as in other Commonwealth jurisdictions,[6] and as the English cases accept in practice, that all types of personal and circumstantial weaknesses may adversely affect a party's bargaining power: '[a]mong them are poverty or need of any kind, sickness, age... infirmity of body or mind, drunkenness, illiteracy or lack of education, lack of assistance or explanation where... [this] is necessary' (*Blomley v Ryan* (1956), an Australian decision). This emphasis on *personal weakness* excludes the sorts of commercial and economic pressures dealt with by the duress doctrine and goes beyond the relational vulnerabilities addressed by undue influence.

However, 'personal weakness' is ubiquitous. It lies legally dormant until activated by serious substantive unfairness. Substantive unfairness is relevant: 'firstly as supporting the inference that a position of disadvantage existed, and secondly as tending to show that an unfair use was made of the occasion... It will almost always... [be] "an important ingredient in considering whether a person did exercise any degree of judgement in making a contract, or whether there is a degree of unfairness in accepting the contract"' (*Blomley v Ryan*).

---

[6] Australia: *Commercial Bank of Australia v Amadio* (1983). Canada: *Paris v Machnik* (1973). New Zealand: *Nichols v Jessup* (1986). US: Uniform Commercial Code, § 2–302.

9.4.3.3 Unconscionable conduct

Unconscionable conduct is a necessary condition of relief and is the formal justification *for* relief. What is required is that 'one of the parties to [the contract] has imposed the objectionable terms in a morally reprehensible manner... in a way which affects his conscience' (*Boustany v Pigott*). However, despite the colourful language often used, actual fraud is unnecessary; *constructive* fraud is enough. The conduct proscribed is that which 'falls below the standards demanded by equity... it is victimisation which can consist either of the active extortion of a benefit or the passive acceptance of a benefit in unconscionable circumstances' (Lord Selborne in *Earl of Aylesford v Morris*). The cases have identified a wide range of negotiating conduct as unconscientious; much of it is common and, absent a grossly unfair outcome, inconclusive as to immorality.

- Active victimisation[7] includes: taking the initiative in the transaction, haste in concluding it, contributing to a misapprehension without creating it and low-level pressure on the complainant to agree.

- *Passive victimisation* describes the acceptance of a highly advantageous bargain at the expense of a complainant known to be impaired, without 'bring[ing] to the notice of that other party the true nature of the transaction and the need for advice' (*Cresswell v Potter*). Knowledge of impairment may be *constructive*, as where the facts known to the defendant must have indicated the complainant's impairment or put her on inquiry (*Ayres v Hazelgrove*).

In *Boustany v Pigott* (1993), P (an elderly woman, described as 'quite slow') leased premises to B for less than one-sixth of the market value (fixed for ten years and with an option to renew at the same price for another ten years). Unconscionable conduct was found on the basis that B, knowing P's affairs were being managed by her cousin G, invited P to a tea party whilst G was away and then 'lavished attention and flattery upon [her]' to secure P's agreement to the lease. B gave P a ride to a solicitor where the transaction was concluded with undue haste and against the solicitor's advice. It seems clear that the harshness of the transaction (rather than just the invitation to tea, the flattery, and the ride) convinced the court of B's moral culpability.

9.4.3.4 Absence of adequate advice

As in undue influence, the absence of adequate independent advice shows that the complainant was not protected by anyone else equal to the task, and that the defendant failed to take adequate steps to meet the complainant's known weakness. Like undue influence, the transaction is not saved simply because:

- the defendant has recommended independent advice if the complainant's refusal to obtain advice is interpreted by the court as evidence of the seriousness of her impairment (eg *Bank of Montreal v Stuart*);

- the complainant has received independent advice if the court concludes (usually from the harshness of the transaction) that the advice was inadequate (eg *Fry v Lane*), or that the severity of the complainant's impairment rendered her incapable of benefiting from it (eg *Boustany v Pigott*).

---

[7] See M Chen-Wishart, *Unconscionable Bargains* (Butterworths, 1989).

Crédit Lyonnais v Burch (facts at 9.2.4.3) shows the relationship between a grossly unfair outcome and independent advice.[8] Although the bank's solicitor wrote to B twice, stressing the unlimited nature of the proposed mortgage and advising her to seek independent advice, the contract was set aside when B proceeded with the transaction without advice. The court held that it is not enough simply to take reasonable steps to meet the suspicion that the complainant may have been impaired, 'the *result* of the steps which it took must be such as *would* reasonably allay any such suspicion' (emphasis added). The bank should have disclosed the extent of B's potential liability and *insisted*, not merely recommended, that she obtain independent legal advice. Even then the transaction would not stand, for, although it can normally be assumed that the advisers have advised competently and that those advised have understood the advice, this could not be assumed here because C must have known 'that no competent solicitor could advise her to enter into a guarantee in the terms she did' or must have suspected that her impairment has 'cause[d] her to disregard any advice not to do so'.

9.5 **Aggressive commercial practices against consumers**

See the discussion in Chapter 5 at 5.5.1.

9.6 **Incapacity: a brief summary**

The complainant's incapacity to make the contract in question provides a basis for invalidating it. However, the *need to protect* those whose self-protective abilities are impaired to an unacceptable degree must be balanced against the interests of those who have dealt fairly and in good faith with the incapacitated party. Thus, although an incapacitated person is logically *incapable* of giving valid consent (rendering the contract void and of no effect), the legal consequences of incapacity often vary. Recognised categories of personal incapacity are infancy, mental incapacity, and those so affected by drink or drugs as not to know what they are doing. In addition to personal incapacity, certain non-natural persons such as companies and public authorities may have limited capacity; the concern here is to protect the groups on behalf of which they act. What follows is a brief summary; see the more detailed discussion in Additional Chapter 1 on the online resources.

(i) Children: the law adopts a strongly protective attitude to minors. In general, they can enforce their contracts (although not by specific performance), but are not bound by them unless they ratify them after reaching 18 years of age. Exceptions have been created to protect those who deal fairly and in good faith with the child and to allow children to enter beneficial contracts:

   (a) *contracts for 'necessaries'* are, on the whole, binding if they are beneficial to the child, but not if the terms are harsh or onerous; 'necessaries' is given a wide meaning;

[8] See M Chen-Wishart, 'The *O'Brien* Principle and Substantive Unfairness' (1997) 56 *CLJ* 60.

(b) *contracts beneficial to the child* overall are binding; eg, contracts to obtain education, training, employment, medical care, and legal advice;

(c) *contracts involving land, company shares, and partnerships* bind the minor unless she repudiates the contract before or within a reasonable time of attaining majority.

A contract not binding on the child may still generate *non-contractual obligations* such as that requiring the child to make restitution of benefits received under section 3(1) of the Minors' Contracts Act 1987.

(ii) **Mental incapacity, drink, and drugs**:

(a) a person lacking capacity under the *Mental Incapacity Act 2005* cannot make a valid contract although she remains liable to pay a reasonable price for 'necessaries';

(b) *incapacity due to mental infirmity, drink, and drugs* renders a contract voidable if the complainant can show that her incapacity was known to the other party; and

(c) *lesser impairments* (short of incapacity) by those who appear sane are subject to the doctrine of unconscionable bargains.

(iii) **Companies and public authorities**: limiting the capacity of such *non-natural persons* is necessary to protect those on whose behalf they act (eg shareholders, lenders, taxpayers):

(a) a *company*'s capacity to contract is limited by its *objects* contained in the memorandum of association. Acts outside its objects are ultra vires (beyond its powers or capacity) and thus void. However, the Companies Act 1985 abolished the ultra vires rule as regards parties who deal in good faith with the company and the Companies Act 2006 prevents the validity of an act done by a company from being called into question on the ground of lack of capacity by reason of anything in the company's constitution;

(b) *public authorities'* powers are confined by the functions for which they were created, although there is now a statutory presumption under the Localism Act 2011 that a local authority has unlimited powers except where there is a specific restriction on it in a statute. Ultra vires contracts are void. Possible hardship is mitigated by allowing recovery of money paid and property transferred under void contracts unless this would amount to indirect enforcement of the contract.

▎THIS CHAPTER IN ESSENCE

 The key areas and core topics in this chapter are summarised in an easy-to-use list, ideal for revision purposes, on the online resources at www.oup.com/uk/chenwishart6e/. Links to websites relevant to the topics covered and any updates to the chapter can also be found on the online resources.

QUESTIONS

1 'Undue influence, the doctrine in *Etridge* and unconscionable bargains address quite different problems; it is impossible and pointless to find one justification for them all.' Discuss.

2 '*RBS v Etridge* (2001) has clarified the role of independent advice, manifest disadvantage and notice in the law on undue influence and non-commercial guarantees.' Discuss.

3 'If a contract is stigmatised as "unfair" it may be unfair in one of two ways. It may be unfair by reason of the unfair manner in which it was brought into existence; a contract induced by undue influence is unfair in this sense. It will be convenient to call this "procedural unfairness". It may also, in some contexts, be described (accurately or inaccurately) as "unfair" by reason of the fact that the terms of the contract are more favourable to one party than to the other... it will be convenient to call [this] "contractual imbalance". The two concepts may overlap' (*Hart v O'Connor* (1985)).

How far *does* and how far *should* contract law give relief against either sort of unfairness?

4 Advise the Law Commission on: (i) whether English law should recognise a general doctrine of unfairness in contract formation, and (ii) what such a general doctrine might comprise.

5 Uriah, a retired businessman with a reputation for toughness and independence, dies after a brief but crippling illness. Viv, Uriah's executor, discovers that, in the year before his death, Uriah had become friendly with his new gardener Wayne and invited him to move into Uriah's house. Uriah had given Wayne lavish gifts totalling £30,000 and guaranteed a loan of £500,000 to Wayne from Xerxes Bank for an unlimited duration. When Xerxes Bank advised Uriah to get independent advice, Uriah refused saying, 'It's a waste of money, I trust Wayne totally. Anyway, it's only for 6 months.' On Xerxes' insistence, Uriah saw Zak, a solicitor who stressed the disadvantageous nature of the guarantee, but Uriah was quite obviously dozing off. Wayne has defaulted on the loan and Xerxes Bank seeks to enforce Uriah's guarantee. Advise Viv.

 For hints on how to answer these questions, please see the online resources at www.oup.com/uk/chenwishart6e/

KEY FURTHER READING

Atiyah, P S (1986), 'Contract and Fair Exchange' in P S Atiyah, *Essays on Contract* (Clarendon Press).

Bamforth, N (1995), 'Unconscionability as a Vitiating Factor', *LMCLQ* 538.

Birks, P, and Chin, N (1995), 'On the Nature of Undue Influence' in J Beatson and D Friedmann (eds), *Good Faith and Fault in Contract Law* (Clarendon Press) 57.

Brownsword, R (2000), *Contract Law: Themes for the Twenty-First Century* (Butterworths) paras 5.3–5.25.

Capper, D (1998), 'Undue Influence and Unconscionability: A Rationalization', 114 *LQR* 479.

Chen-Wishart, M (1997), 'The *O'Brien* Principle and Substantive Unfairness', 56 *CLJ* 60.

Chen-Wishart, M (2006), 'Undue Influence: *Beyond* Impaired Consent and Wrong-Doing, Towards a Relational Analysis' in A Burrows and A Rodger (eds), *Mapping the Law: Essays in Memory of Peter Birks* (OUP) 201.

Chen-Wishart, M (2006), 'Undue Influence: Vindicating Relationships of Influence' 59 *CLP* 231.

Collins, H (2003), *The Law of Contract* (4th edn, LexisNexis) ch 11.

Waddams, S (1976), 'Unconscionability in Contracts', 39 *MLR* 369.

PART V

The contents of contracts

'Precisely what do we owe each other under the contract?'

INTRODUCTION

Once the existence of a contract is established by the test of *formation* (Part II) and its validity is untainted by the *vitiating factors* (Part IV), the question arises as to the precise *content* of the parties' respective rights and obligations under the contract. Part V examines how the law responds when the parties are in dispute over the enforceability of alleged obligations—'I say you are bound by *X* and you say you are not'. The traditional answer is that courts identify and interpret contractual terms *according to the parties' intentions* at formation, no matter how apparently unfair or unreasonable, unless specific countervailing common law rules or legislation apply. Determining whether an alleged obligation is enforceable is a five-step process (set out in the Introductory Diagram):

(1) **Identification of express terms:** is the alleged obligation a term of the contract or a 'mere' representation?

(2) **Incorporation:** if it is a written term, has the other party had sufficient notice of it to be bound by it?

(3) **Interpretation:** if bound, does the term apply to the circumstances of the case?

(4) **Implied terms:** if the alleged term is not express, can it be implied into the contract?

(5) **Invalidity:** if the alleged term exists and applies to the event, is it nevertheless invalidated or subject to variation by statute or common law rules?

The ostensible basis for answering questions (1)–(5) is the parties' intentions, since courts do not rewrite bargains. However, contrary to this orthodoxy, numerous techniques give the courts considerable latitude in controlling the contents of contracts. These techniques are part of the common law's piecemeal solutions to specific problems of unfairness. Courts justify them by reference to upholding the parties' 'presumed intentions' or their 'reasonable expectations', but this can be taken too far. For, in truth, the parties' intentions and expectations are often *unclear*, *contradictory*, or *non-existent*. Moreover, in general, disputes only reach the courts if *both* parties genuinely believe their respective interpretations are 'reasonable'. Ultimately, it is for the *courts* to say:

(i)   what, amongst the parties' assurances, are intended to be *inside* the contract and what *outside* (and so determine the term–representation distinction and the incorporation question);

(ii) what the terms actually *mean* (by the process of interpretation);

(iii) what may be *added* to the express terms (by finding collateral and implied terms); and

(iv) what can be *subtracted* (by eg invalidity under the Unfair Contract Terms Act 1977 (UCTA) or the Consumer Rights Act 2015 (CRA) or the penalty rule).

 The picture of the legal control of the *contents* of contracts is incomplete without at least a passing reference to the existence of the doctrine that invalidates **contracts which are illegal or contrary to public policy**. The subject is summarised at 11.9 and more fully discussed in Additional Chapter 2 which is available on the online resources.

Part V Introductory Diagram Overview of the legal control of the contents of contracts

10

Identifying and interpreting contractual terms

'Which assurances are terms inside the contract?'

10.1 **The problem of standard form contracts**

In order to understand the law in this area, we must be mindful of the policies in play:

- On the one hand, the traditional concerns to promote freedom and certainty of contract call for the enforcement of the terms ostensibly agreed.

- On the other hand, concern to curb the worst excesses of unfairness and exploitation resulting from significant inequality of bargaining power may call for enforcement to be denied, or for terms to be added or subtracted to mitigate the unfairness.

Whilst the vitiating factors discussed in Part IV can meet some instances of substantive unfairness, they are usually ineffective against unfair standard form contracts. The increasing use of such contracts in the last hundred years has put enormous pressure on traditional contract rules which are premised on the model of individual negotiation between notionally equal parties. In contrast, standard form contracts do not involve 'bargain', 'negotiation', or 'consent' in any meaningful sense (1.3.4). They are generally:

- ✔ printed documents containing terms of the contract/clearly purporting to be the contract;

- ✔ put forward by a commercial (the presenting) party who makes many contracts of the same type;

- ✔ presented to the other (the adhering) party explicitly or implicitly on a take-it-or-leave-it basis (the model is closer to an imposition of one party's will than a mutually agreed arrangement, hence it has been described as 'private legislation' or 'contracts of adhesion'); and

- ✔ signed or accepted by the adhering party who enters few such contracts.

The *advantages* of standard form contracting are clearly weighted in favour of the presenting party:

(i)   It reduces the presenting party's *transaction costs* in making repeat transactions and increases its profits; in theory, this saving may be passed on to the adhering party in the form of reduced prices.

(ii) It allows the senior management in large operations to *maintain control* over the contractual arrangements made by subordinate sales staff.

(iii) It allows the presenting party to *set terms advantageous to itself* by putting in the 'fine print' terms that:

- shrink its own obligations;
- inflate the adhering party's obligations;
- strengthen and facilitate its remedies against the adhering party; and
- exclude or limit its own liability.

The danger of exploitation varies with the status of the adhering party. In *Schroeder v Macaulay* (1974), Lord Diplock observes that standard form contracts widely used in commercial transactions have generally resulted from extensive prior negotiations and are adopted because they 'facilitate the conduct of trade' (eg bills of lading, charterparties, insurance policies, and contracts of sale in the commodity market). These contracts will generally be binding because they are used by parties 'whose bargaining power is fairly matched'. But this is not necessarily so even among commercial parties. Thus, eg, UCTA protects non-consumers contracting on another's standard form from unreasonable *exemption clauses* (11.3.2.1).

Where the adhering party is a consumer, the risk of serious unfairness is magnified. Lord Diplock regarded such contracts as 'a classic instance of superior bargaining power' which requires special vigilance on the court's part to see that it has not been abused to drive an unconscionable bargain (*Schroeder v Macaulay*). Absent a lawyer at their elbow, consumers may not even know of the existence of the fine print, and if they do know, reading will be deterred by the density and length of the fine print, the complicated and unintelligible language, the confusing layout and the strong social pressure not to appear awkward or confrontational. One study found that, even in an environment conducive to reading (the comfort of one's home or office), only one in every 1,000 retail software shoppers clicks on the licence agreement for more than one second. And, those few spent an average of 47.7 seconds[1] on agreements that 'were an average of 74,000-plus words, which is basically the length of the first Harry Potter book'.[2] Lord Reid paints a familiar picture (*Suisse Atlantique Société d'Armement Maritime SA v NV Rotterdamsche Kolen Centrale* (1967)):

> In the ordinary way the customer has no time to read them, and if he did read them he would probably not understand them. And if he did understand and object to any of them, he would generally be told he could take-it-or-leave-it. And if he then went to another supplier the result would be the same. Freedom of contract must surely imply some choice or room for bargaining. At the other extreme is the case where parties are bargaining on terms of equality and a stringent exemption clause is accepted for a *quid pro quo* or other good reason.

Thus, the **dangers of standard form contracts** include:

(i) lack of comprehension ('unfair surprise'): reading and comprehension is deterred by the context in which the contract is made, the small print (eg tiny grey font on light grey paper in a hurried transaction, or the dense software agreement which must be 'agreed' before your computer can run it), the unintelligible language, the confusing layout, and the strong social pressure not to 'fuss';

(ii) lack of negotiability due to the inequality of bargaining power; or

---

[1] This tracked 45,091 households with respect to 66 online software companies. Y Bakos, F Marotta-Wurgler, and D Trossen, 'Does Anyone Read the Fine Print? Testing a Law and Economics Approach to Standard Form Contracts', CELS 4th Annual Conference on Empirical Legal Studies Paper, 2009.

[2] See A Tugend, 'Those Wordy Contracts We All So Quickly Accept', *The New York Times*, 12 July 2013, http://www.nytimes.com/2013/07/13/your-money/novel-length-contracts-online-and-what-they-say.html?pagewanted=1&src=me&_r=1&, accessed 3 March 2014.

(iii) substantive unfairness in the parties' rights and obligations to the detriment of the adhering party.

These concerns are magnified in respect of 'exemption clauses' (terms that exclude or limit the presenting party's liability for breach). They can leave the adhering party with no effective remedy when her reasonable expectations arising from the contract are defeated.

We will see that **courts can counter substantive unfairness by finding**:

(i)   a *collateral* or *implied term* in favour of the adhering party that is not contained in the standard form contract;

(ii) that insufficient notice has been given of an *onerous* or *unusual standard term* in an unsigned document to bind the adhering party;

(iii) that the unfair term, *properly interpreted*, is less disadvantageous to the adhering party than first appears; or

(iv) that the unfair term is *unenforceable* under a common law or statutory rule.

These techniques are most commonly applied against *standard form exemption clauses* and many texts discuss them under that heading. However, (i)–(iii) are, in principle, of *general application* and will be so treated here; (iv) is discussed in Chapter 11.

10.2 **What are terms?**

We have seen that, where one party's expectation from a contract is disappointed, the law's response to that disappointment depends on the *status* accorded to the other party's words or conduct inducing those expectations, whether: (i) a term (sometimes called a 'warranty'); (ii) a representation; or (iii) a 'mere puff'. The remedial significance of the distinction between terms and representations is set out in **Diagram 10A** and discussed at 5.1.1.1. In any dispute, each party will argue for the status that yields the best remedial result. The first task in examining the content of contracts is to identify what are terms of the contract.

10.3 **Express terms**

Contractual terms may be express or implied. *Express terms* are those set out in the contract. *Implied terms* are those which are read into (added to) the contract (10.6). Express terms can be in writing or oral or both.

- Where the contract is entirely oral or partly oral and partly written (and the latter is not in a document purporting to have contractual effect), the enforceability of statements made between the parties depends on the term–representation distinction (5.1.1.2).

- Where a document purports to contain the terms of the contract, one question is whether its content can be added to or subtracted from by reference to extrinsic evidence.

Diagram 10A The remedial significance of the terms–representations distinction

✓ = Remedy available
✗ = Remedy unavailable

	Damages (getting money)	**Ending the contract** (getting out)	**Specific enforcement** (getting performance)
Representation which is false	✓ **Reliance** damages on fraud measure under Misrepresentation Act 1967 *unless* speaker can prove honesty and reasonable basis (see diag 5E) ✓ Restitution on rescission	✓ **Rescission** for any misrepresentation subject to common law and statutory bars	✗ not for misrepresentation
Contractual term (express, collateral, or implied) which is breached	✓ **Expectation damages** for any breach, ✓ reliance damages not exceeding speculative expectation, ✓ restitution if total failure of consideration, ✓ account of profits or *Wrotham Park* damages in 'exceptional' cases	**Termination** narrowly available: ✓ breach of a 'condition' ✗ breach of a 'warranty' ✓ breach of an 'innominate' term if consequences serious	✓ **Specific performance** narrowly available

10.3.1 **The parol evidence rule**

Contract parties are generally barred from adducing extrinsic (or 'parol') evidence to add to, vary or contradict a document that purports to record the parties' agreement (*Jacobs v Batavia & General Plantations Trust Ltd* (1924)). Contract law accords almost sacred status to such documents; they are regarded as *exclusively* embodying the 'four corners of the contract'. The parol evidence rule ostensibly promotes certainty and predictability and avoids evidential difficulties. However, the long list of *exceptions* to the rule necessitated by the demands of justice and respect for the parties' intentions undermines the claims of certainty and predictability. Thus, extrinsic evidence can be adduced when it is claimed that the contract:

- is vitiated;
- includes terms *additional* to those contained in the contractual document, whether express (ie 'collateral', 10.3.2) or implied (see 10.6); or
- should be *rectified* (6.1.2).

The collective width of the exceptions calls the rule into question since, in practice, it will rarely prevent a party from adducing the sort of evidence that the rule theoretically prohibits. The rule is better understood as an easily rebuttable presumption that a document purporting to be the contract contains the whole contract.

Pause for reflection

1. The reasoning supporting the exceptions to the parol evidence rule (set out in *Allen v Pink* (1838)) is circular. It says that the document is presumed to contain the whole contract, unless the parties did not so intend (such intention requiring extrinsic evidence to prove); ie the rule applies, unless it does not apply. This is a 'self-evident tautology' which deprives the rule of most of its effect.

2. In *Shogun Finance Ltd v Hudson* (2003), the House of Lords held that the parol evidence rule bars extrinsic evidence in a claim of mistaken identity (6.2.4). The case undoubtedly strengthens the parol evidence rule, although its reasoning is open to question. The rule that the contents of the contract must be determined by the contractual document does not seem applicable when the question is *whether* there is a valid contract in the first place.

10.3.2 Collateral terms and collateral contracts

A term (or a contract) may be *collateral* to the main terms (or contract). The existence of collateral terms or contracts is, again, said to depend on the parties' intentions. The test is analogous to that between terms and representations (5.1.1.2). However, for the defendant's assurance to amount to a collateral term, the claimant must show that the assurance was so important that she would not have entered the contract *but for* the assurance. It is not enough that the statement was *a* cause of the claimant entering the contract (as is the test for misrepresentation). This stronger causal link is understandable since: (i) stronger rights are conferred by collateral terms than by representations, and (ii) collateral terms may potentially override inconsistent express terms in the contractual document. Phillimore LJ provides the justification for collateral terms (*Mendelssohn v Normand Ltd* (1970)):

> [W]hen a man has made, by word of mouth, a promise or a representation of fact, on which the other party acts by entering into the contract... the man is not allowed to repudiate his representation by reference to a printed condition... nor is he allowed to go back on his promise by reliance on a written clause... The reason is because the oral promise or representation has a decisive influence on the transaction—it is the very thing which induces the other to contract—and it would be most unjust to allow the maker to go back on it. The printed condition is rejected because it is repugnant to the express oral promise or representation... Whether you regard that promise as... a collateral term of the contract, or whether you regard the contract as being partly oral and partly in writing... it seems to me it can make no real difference.

It used to be insisted that a collateral *term* could only add to, but not vary or contradict, the written document.[3] The courts sidestepped this problem by simply finding a whole

---

[3] *Mann v Nunn* (1874); *Angell v Duke* (1875); *Henderson v Arthur* (1907).

other collateral *contract* instead (ie a second (unilateral) contract containing the promise, in consideration of the promisee entering the main contract). It is now accepted that collateral terms and collateral contracts perform the same functions. Namely:

(i) Conferring the **remedial advantages** of an action for breach over that for misrepresentation. Prior to the Misrepresentation Act 1967, the collateral device mitigated the unavailability of damages for non-fraudulent misrepresentations. Even after the MA (widening the availability of such damages), the collateral device is still useful if the claimant prefers the protection of her expectation, rather than reliance, interest.

(ii) **Overriding the privity rule**: in *Shanklin Pier Ltd v Detel Products Ltd* (1951), D told S that its paint was suitable for painting S's pier and would last seven to ten years. S then instructed its contractor to buy and use D's paint, which turned out to be less durable than stated. Although S did not contract with D directly, S successfully sued D on the basis of a collateral unilateral contract whereby D's promise in relation to the paint was exchanged for S's consideration in directing its contractor to buy D's paint.

(iii) **Overriding inconsistent terms in the main written contract**: circumventing the parol evidence rule and so *adding to, varying, or contradicting a contractual document*, eg:

✔ In *City and Westminster Properties (1934) Ltd v Mudd* (1959), a tenant was induced to sign a new lease (which limited use of the premises to business purposes) by the landlord's oral assurance that the tenant could continue to live on the premises. The landlord was prevented from forfeiting the lease against the tenant for doing so.

✔ In *Harling v Eddy* (1951), a heifer was sold at auction on standard printed conditions that it was 'without warranty'. The seller had enticed a bid by saying that he would guarantee the heifer in every respect. The buyer could claim for breach when the heifer died of tuberculosis three months later.

✔ In *Mendelssohn v Normand Ltd* (1970), M parked in N's garage on terms that N would 'accept no liability for any loss or damage sustained by the vehicle its accessories or contents howsoever caused'. M left the car unlocked on the insistence of N's employee who undertook to lock it for him. M successfully sued for valuables stolen from the car.

✔ In *Curtis v Chemical Cleaning & Dyeing Co Ltd* (1951), C took a wedding dress to CCD for cleaning and was asked to sign a 'receipt' exempting CCD from liability for 'any damage howsoever arising'; C signed after being assured that the exemption only related to beads or sequins on the dress. When the dress was returned badly stained, CCD could not rely on the wide exclusion clause beyond the limited extent stated.

✔ In *J Evans & Sons (Portsmouth) Ltd v Andrea Merzario Ltd* (1976), the carrier assured the owner of goods that their goods would be shipped *under* deck; the goods were shipped *on* deck and lost overboard. The carrier's oral assurance was treated as a collateral term which had been breached, *overriding* the contractual document (which gave the carrier complete discretion over the placement of cargo and excluded liability for all but wilful neglect or default).

Entire agreement clauses (also called 'integration' or 'merger' clauses) seek to replicate the parol evidence rule by the parties' express agreement and are enforceable. They state 'that the full contractual terms are to be found in the document containing the clause and not elsewhere, and that, accordingly, any promises or assurances made in the course of the negotiations (which might otherwise have effect as a collateral warranty) shall have no contractual force' (*Inntrepreneur v East Crown Ltd* (2000)). Such clauses thus exclude the finding of collateral terms (*SERE Holdings Ltd v Volkswagen Group UK Ltd* (2004)), but may not exclude liability for misrepresentations (5.4).

10.3.3 The incorporation of terms

One party may attempt to enforce a term in a document purporting to be the contract that is *unknown and very prejudicial* to the other party. The legal question is *not* whether the statement is a term (the nature of the document in which it is contained assumes that it is); rather, it is one of 'incorporation', ie whether the term forms part of the contract and so binds the parties. A written term can be 'incorporated' into the contract by:

(i)   signature;

(ii) reasonable notice; or

(iii) previous dealing or custom.

Only if the term is binding do the subsequent questions of interpretation (10.4) and possible invalidity (Chapter 11) arise.

10.3.3.1 Signed documents

English law attaches overwhelming significance to signatures. The general rule is that a person is bound by the contents of a contractual document that she signs whether or not she has read or understood it, and even if she does not know the language in which the contract is expressed (*Parker v South Eastern Railway Co* (1876); *The Luna* (1919)). The potential harshness of this rule is shown by *L'Estrange v Graucob Ltd* (1934). E bought an automatic cigarette vending machine from G which stopped working after a few days. G denied E's claim for breach of an implied term as to fitness for purpose because E had signed an order form which excluded liability for all express and implied terms and statements. Although the exemption clause was in 'regrettably small print', printed on brown paper, and in an unexpected place, the Court of Appeal held E bound by her signature.

The signature rule is subject to **very narrow exceptions**:

(i)   *non est factum* (6.1.3);

(ii) misrepresentation (Chapter 5);

(iii) other vitiating factors such as mistake, undue influence, unconscionability, duress, and incapacity (Part IV); and

(iv) the non-contractual nature of the signed document: in *Grogan v Robin Meredith Plant Hire* (1996), an oral contract was made for the hire of machinery. The Court of Appeal held that the 'time sheets' signed after the contract commenced could not incorporate the additional terms contained therein. Auld LJ said that it was 'too mechanistic' to treat a signature as invariably binding the signer to its contents irrespective of its nature and the parties' understanding of its purpose and effect. A signature will not bind if the document is only *administrative* in the sense of merely allowing the parties to *implement* their prior agreement.

 Pause for reflection

The signature rule can be criticised:

1. It is unrealistic. Lord Devlin concedes that the rule is premised on a 'world of make-believe which the law has created'. A standard form contract 'is not meant to be read, still less to be understood. Its signature is in truth about as significant as a handshake that marks the formal conclusion of a bargain' (*McCutcheon v David MacBrayne Ltd* (1964)).

2. Spencer argues that a person should not be bound by a signed document if the other party knew of or was responsible for her mistake ('Signature, Consent, and the Rule in *L'Estrange v Graucob*' (1973) 32 *CLJ* 104). Waddams agrees. He writes (at [319]):

   One who signs a written document cannot complain if the other party reasonably relies on the signature as a manifestation of assent to the contents, or ascribes to the words he used their reasonable meaning. But the other side of the same coin is that only a reasonable expectation will be protected. If the party seeking to enforce the document knew or had reason to know of the other's mistake the document should not be enforced.

This approach was adopted in *Tilden Rent-a-Car Co v Clendenning* (1978). The Ontario Court of Appeal held that a signor is only bound when it is *reasonable* for the enforcing party to believe that the signature manifests assent to the onerous term sought to be enforced. The court distinguished:

✓ ordinary *commercial* practice, where a signature can reasonably be taken to manifest assent, from

✗ the *hurried, informal, or consumer transaction* with finely printed, unexpected and harsh clauses 'where the signature by itself does not truly represent an acquiescence to unusual and onerous terms which are inconsistent with the true object of the contract'. Here, 'the party seeking to rely on such terms should not be able to do so in the absence of first having taken reasonable measures to draw such terms to the attention of the other party'. On the facts, the hirer was not bound by a clause making him liable for damage to the car in a wide range of circumstances far beyond his reasonable expectation because: (i) he had paid extra for 'additional' insurance cover; (ii) it was plain that he did not read nor was expected to read the fine print; and (iii) the speed in completing the transaction was one of the attractions of the service being offered.

Consistently, the European Draft Common Frame of Reference provides that standard form 'terms are not sufficiently brought to the other party's attention by a mere reference to them in a contract document, *even if that party signs the document*' (Art II.-9:103). 'Reasonable steps' must be taken to give notice of standard terms even if they are contained in signed writing.

→

> ➡
> The signature rule is justifiable on the basis of *certainty, efficiency, administrative convenience* and, ultimately, even the parties' *autonomy*. In reality, the obstacles to giving informed consent to every term in a standard form contract of any complexity are simply insurmountable. A person today who refused to contract without being adequately apprised of the fine print would deny themselves most means of living in a modern society, or would lead a rather boring or unproductive life. The fine print is for all intents and purposes invisible, and meaningful consent to it is simply impossible. Given that the parties clearly consent to the main subject matter of the contract, the law treats the signature as a proxy for consent in order to make the contract enforceable. Any unfairness can be mitigated by legal techniques in determining the contents and meaning of the contract (discussed in the following sections), and by rules invalidating unfair terms (Chapter 11).

10.3.3.2 Unsigned documents

In the course of negotiations, a document containing terms may have simply be *delivered* by one party to the other, *displayed* in a notice, or *incorporated by reference* (eg an order form stated to be 'subject to our usual terms'). The presenting party must have given the other party *adequate notice* of the terms to bind her to them. The rationale is that *notice* serves to warn the other party what she is letting herself in for and gives her the opportunity to renegotiate or withdraw. The notice must be:

(i) given *at or before* contract formation;

(ii) in a document intended to have *contractual effect*; and

(iii) *reasonable* (ie commensurate with the harshness or unexpectedness of the terms).

In applying these requirements, courts balance the practical convenience and certainty of standard form contracts against the risk that they may contain grossly unfair and unconsented to terms.

(i) **Timing of notice:** the relevant notice must have been given *at or before contract formation*. Notice given thereafter is an impermissible unilateral variation of the contract *after* formation. Thus:

  ✗ An unfair term was not incorporated in *Olley v Marlborough Court Ltd* (1949). O registered and paid at the reception of M hotel. He only saw the notice exempting M from liability for lost or stolen articles when he went up to his room. M was held to be liable when O's property was stolen because the negligence of M's staff allowed a thief to enter O's room. Notice exempting M from liability came too late.

  ✗ In *Thornton v Shoe Lane Parking Ltd* (1971), T drove his car into S's multistorey car park, put money into an automatic machine and was issued with a ticket stated to be 'subject to the conditions of issue as displayed on the premises'; these excluded liability for damage and for personal injury. When T was injured partly due to S's negligence, the court held S liable. S made the offer by holding out the machine as ready to receive money; the customer accepted when he inserted the money. From that point, the customer is 'committed beyond recall'. The notice inside the premises and even *the notice on the ticket* came too late.

(ii) **Contractual document or 'mere receipt'?** If a party does not, and cannot reasonably be expected to, know that the document she receives contains contractual terms, she is not bound by its contents.

✗ In *Chapelton v Barry UDC* (1940), B's sign indicated the hire charges for deckchairs. On picking up a deckchair, C received a ticket from the attendant, which C put in his pocket unread. When C fell through the defective deckchair and was injured, the court prevented B from relying on the exclusion clause printed on the back of the ticket because it was contained in a 'mere receipt', which could not reasonably be expected to contain contractual terms. Section 2 of UCTA 1977 now automatically voids exemptions of liability for personal injury caused by negligence (11.5.1).

✗ Other examples of non-contractual documents that cannot incorporate terms contained therein are a cheque book cover (*Burnett v Westminster Bank Ltd* (1966)) and a ticket for a public bath house (*Taylor v Glasgow Corp* (1952)).

✔ However, commercial or consumer practices may indicate the contractual nature of the document in question. In *Alexander v Railway Executive* (1951), the court noted that 'most people nowadays know that railway companies have conditions subject to which they take articles into their cloakrooms'.

(iii) **Reasonable notice:**

✔ In *Parker v SE Railway Co*, P deposited a bag in the station cloakroom. P received a ticket, which said 'See back'. On the back were printed conditions including a clause limiting liability to £10 per item. P saw the writing on the ticket, but neither read it nor thought it contained terms. P claimed £24 10s for his lost bag. The Court of Appeal held that the recipient of a ticket is bound if she has reasonable notice that the document *contains terms*, even if she remains ignorant of the terms. Mellish LJ said:

> The railway company... must be entitled to make some assumptions respecting the person who deposits luggage with them... [, that] he can read, and that he understands the English language, and that he pays such attention to what he is about as may be reasonably expected from a person in such a transaction... [if the railway company's action] was sufficient to inform people in general that the ticket contains conditions, I think that a particular plaintiff ought not to be in a better position than other persons on account of his exceptional ignorance or stupidity or carelessness.

✔ *Thompson v LM & S Railway Co* (1930) shows how little notice may suffice. T bought a railway ticket (for 2 shillings 7 pennies) which stated in 'quite big print and quite legible print', 'for conditions see back'. On the back, passengers were referred to the railway timetable for the conditions (which cost 6 pennies). T was illiterate, but L successfully relied on an exclusion clause appearing on page 552 of the timetable as having been validly incorporated when L's negligence caused T's personal injury.

✗ However, if a party *knows* or should have known that the recipient of the notice cannot read the notice, more would need to be done to satisfy the notice requirement (*Geier v Kujawa, Weston and Warne Bros (Transport)* (1970)), and such knowledge may also trigger the unconscionability doctrine (9.4).

There was insufficient notice to incorporate a document where:

✗ a ticket made no reference to the existence of conditions on the back (*Henderson v Stevenson* (1875));

✗ a ticket was folded over and the conditions partially obscured by a red ink stamp (*Richardson, Spence & Co Ltd v Rowntree* (1894));

✗ the relevant clause was obscured by a date stamp (*Sugar v London, Midland and Scotland Railway* (1941)); and

✗ reference was made to terms 'on the back' of a faxed document, but the back page was inadvertently not sent (*Poseidon Freight Forwarding Co Ltd v Davies Turner Southern Ltd* (1996)).

Where a party seeks to enforce **onerous** or **unusual** terms, it is not enough just to give notice of their *existence*. She must show that she took such *additional* steps as were reasonable to bring their *significance* to the other party's notice. In *Spurling Ltd v Bradshaw* (1956), Denning LJ said that 'the more unreasonable a clause is, the greater the notice which must be given of it'. He instanced the exclusion clause in **Thornton v Shoe Lane Parking** as being 'so wide and so destructive of rights that the court should not hold any man bound by it unless it is drawn to his attention in the most explicit way... In order to give sufficient notice, it would need to be printed in red ink with a red hand pointing to it—or something equally startling'.

✗ This '**red hand**' *rule* has struck down terms *beyond* exemptions of liability. In **Interfoto Picture Library Ltd v Stiletto Visual Programmes Ltd** (1989), S ordered photographic transparencies from Interfoto; 47 transparencies were sent with a delivery note stipulating a 'holding fee' of £5 per day per transparency retained past the stipulated period. S was invoiced for £3,783.50 when they returned the transparencies two weeks late. The Court of Appeal found the term onerous and unusual (the charge was 'high and exorbitant' and 'many times greater than was usual or heard of'); it was unenforceable because Interfoto 'did not do what was necessary to draw this unreasonable and extortionate clause fairly to [S's] attention'. The court substituted a *quantum meruit* award of £3.50 per transparency *per week*, representing their reasonable (market) value.

The orthodox **justification** for the higher level of notice required to incorporate onerous and unusual terms is based on the presumed intention of the party being bound. In *Parker v SE Railway Co*, Bramwell LJ thought there was 'an implied understanding that there is no condition unreasonable to the knowledge of the party tendering the document and not insisting on its being read'. Similarly, in *Interfoto Picture Library*, Dillon LJ observed that the recipient who knows that the document contains terms will 'generally still tend to assume that such conditions are only concerned with ancillary matters of form and are not of importance'.

 Pause for reflection

The increased notice required to incorporate harsh terms allows courts to control unfair terms without appearing to do so directly. In theory, a party can incorporate any term, however onerous or unusual, so long as adequate notice of it is given. In practice, the courts' power to determine: (i) whether terms are 'onerous or unusual', and (ii) what amounts to reasonable notice, allows them to invalidate onerous and unusual terms (the print may not be sufficiently large, bold, clear, red or framed by flashing neon signs). For example, the term was not enforced in *Interfoto* when there seems little procedural unfairness but significant substantive unfairness. The borrower of the transparencies was a business party and commercial practice would generally impute to the recipient of a delivery note notice of the terms contained therein. Macdonald concludes that it is impossible to regard the whole of the 'red hand' rule as a logical extension of *Parker* ('The Duty to Give Notice of Unusual Contract Terms' [1988] *JBL* 375). In *Interfoto v Stiletto*, Bingham LJ said of the cases on notice and incorporation:

> At one level they are concerned with a question of pure contractual analysis, whether one party has done enough to give the other notice of the incorporation of the term in the contract. *At another level they are concerned with a somewhat different question, whether it would in all the circumstances be fair (or reasonable) to hold a party bound by any conditions or by a particular condition of an unusual and stringent nature....* [This is] a concept of fair dealing that has very little to do with a conventional analysis of offer and acceptance (emphasis added).

The law's concern with substantive unfairness can be dealt with directly under UCTA and CRA (Chapter 11). Nevertheless, the 'red hand' rule still plays an important role when the unfair term falls outside statutory control (eg a penalty clause disguised as an extra charge in a business contract, as in *Interfoto*).

10.3.3.3 Previous dealing and custom

In the absence of signature or adequate notice, a term in a printed document may be incorporated by a consistent course of previous dealing between the parties or by the custom of the relevant trade, eg the challenged term was incorporated in:

✔ *Henry Kendall Ltd & Sons v William Lillico & Sons Ltd* (1969); after the parties made an oral contract over the telephone, a document was dispatched containing the challenged exemption which had been consistently used in over 100 transactions between the parties over three years;

✔ *British Crane Hire Corp Ltd v Ipswich Plant Hire Ltd* (1975); B hired a crane urgently from Ipswich. Ipswich subsequently sent out a printed form. Although the parties had only contracted twice previously on these forms, the document was incorporated because: the parties were of equal bargaining power; both were in the crane hire business; and the terms relied upon were habitually used *in the trade*, including by B itself when hiring out;

✔ *Motours Ltd v Euroball (West Kent) Ltd* (2003); M's standard conditions were incorporated by a course of dealing because E's director had previously signed 14 order forms containing M's standard terms over 18 months, although E never read them, they were 'very difficult to read' and not in plain language, and they were never discussed or negotiated between the parties. However, the challenged term was struck down under UCTA.

In contrast, the challenged terms were *not* incorporated in:

✗ *McCutcheon v David MacBrayne*; McC's car was lost when McB's ferry sank due to the latter's negligence. McB sought to exclude liability by reference to a risk note, which McC had only signed four times previously when using McB's services, and did not know of its specific contents. This was held not to be sufficiently *regular* or *consistent* to incorporate the exemption of liability when McC had not signed on this occasion;

✗ *Hollier v Rambler Motors (AMC) Ltd* (1972); H (a consumer) had signed forms exempting R (a garage) from liability three or four times over five years but had, on this occasion, contracted over the telephone without mentioning the exemption. H's car was damaged by fire due to R's negligence.

10.4 **Interpretation of terms**

Once courts have identified the express terms of the contract, the next question is what those terms *mean*; in particular, ie, whether and, if so, how they apply to the dispute before the court. Lord Goff said: 'the staple diet of the Commercial Court can be summed up in one word—"Construction".'[4] Given the large number of contractual disputes involving the interpretation of contract terms, the general principles of interpretation assume great practical importance. While the *parties* are masters of their contracts, it is for the *courts* to determine the meaning of contractual terms. As with other areas of contract law, the usual **policies** operate in this area, namely:

- giving effect to the parties' intentions;
- ensuring certainty and administrability; and
- avoiding unfair results.

In-so-far as these policies push in different directions, and judges may weigh them differently from time to time, we can detect the **swing of the legal pendulum**:

- between the literal and the contextual ends of the spectrum; and
- between elucidating the meaning of words and modifying or contradicting the words of the agreement.

---

[4] R Goff, 'Commercial Contracts and the Commercial Court' [1984] 1 *LMCLQ* 382, 385.

Since the meaning of a term depends on the precise words used in the particular context in which the specific contract was made, precedents are of limited value ('a decision on a different clause in a different context is seldom of much help on a question of construction'; *Surrey Heath BC v Lovell Construction Ltd* (1990)). However, some broad principles can be stated.

10.4.1 Towards contextual interpretation

The parol evidence rule (10.3.1) points towards a literal stance towards documents embodying the contract (*Lovell and Christmas Ltd v Wall* (1912)). Accordingly, a contract's meaning is to be discovered within the '**four corners**' of the document without reference to extrinsic evidence. This approach is said to increase certainty and administrative efficiency; it assumes that words have a 'plain', 'simple', 'ordinary', immutable, or absolute meaning, independent of their context. In reality, words usually take their meaning from their *context*. Multiple meanings can be attached to even the simplest of words, as a cursory glance at a dictionary shows, eg an academic who employs a student research assistant for the 'summer' will mean a different period of time from a farmer or an astronomer using the same words. Thus, courts often have to *choose* between different *reasonable* meanings based on factors that go beyond purely linguistic ones.

Prenn v Simmonds (1971) represents a more contextual approach. Lord Wilberforce stated that agreements should *not* be seen in isolation 'from the matrix of facts in which they were set and interpreted purely on internal linguistic considerations'. Rather, courts must 'inquire beyond the language and see what the circumstances were with reference to which the words were used, and the object, appearing from the circumstances, which the persons using them had in view'. In *Reardon Smith Line Ltd v Yngvar Hansen-Tangen* (1976), he continued:

> No contracts are made in a vacuum: there is always a setting in which they have to be placed. The nature of what is legitimate to have regard to is usually described as 'the surrounding circumstances' but this phrase is imprecise: it can be illustrated but hardly defined. In a commercial contract it is certainly right that the Court should know the commercial purpose of the contract and this in turn presupposes knowledge of the genesis of the transaction, the background, the context, the market in which the parties are operating... what the Court must do must be to place itself in thought in the same factual matrix as that in which the parties were.

Lord Hoffmann famously restated the contextual approach in *Investors Compensation Scheme v West Bromwich* (*ICS*), with the professed aim of assimilating 'the way in which such documents are interpreted by judges to the common sense principles by which any serious utterance would be interpreted in ordinary life'. His Lordship set out five general principles on interpretation. First, the overall aim of interpretation is the 'ascertainment of the meaning which the document would convey to a reasonable person having all the background knowledge which would reasonably have been available to the parties in the situation in which they were at the time of the contract'. This background can be considered even if there is no ambiguity or other problem in the language.

How much contextual information is admissible in interpreting contractual words? Lord Hoffmann's controversial second principle states that 'subject to the requirement that it should have been reasonably available to the parties and to the exception to be mentioned..., it includes absolutely anything which would have affected the way in which the language of the document would have been understood by a reasonable man'. Lord Hoffmann's view that 'there is no conceptual limit to what can be regarded as background' seems incontrovertible. It should be a question of the *weight* attached to the evidence rather than artificially restricting the scope of admissible evidence. In *BCCI v Ali* (2001), Lord Hoffmann explains that he was not 'encouraging a trawl through 'background' which could not have made a reasonable person think that the parties must have departed from conventional usage', but only 'anything which a reasonable man would have regarded as *relevant'*.

The contextual approach remains the law (*Globe Motors v TRW Lucas Varity Electric Steering Limited* (2016), *Wood v Capita Insurance Services Ltd* (2017)).

 Pause for reflection

Staughton warns that admitting a larger volume of relevant information ('How Do the Courts Interpret Commercial Contracts?' (1999) 58 *CLJ* 303):

1. will *increase costs* and prolong litigation;

2. can generate *uncertainty* since multiple and contradictory, but all reasonable, meanings may emerge;

3. may smack of *judicial rewriting of contracts*; and

4. moreover, can result in the contract meaning one thing to the parties aware of the factual matrix, and another to *third parties* who can only rely on the wording of the contract.

However, Arden LJ observed that '[T]he powers of case management in the Civil Procedure Rules could obviously be used to keep evidence within its proper bounds' (*Static Control Components (Europe) Ltd v Egan* (2004)).

10.4.2 Something must have gone wrong with the language: context used to modify or contradict the words

Lord Hoffmann's **third** principle is discussed at 10.4.4. His fourth and fifth principle emphasise that the aim is to ascertain the meaning of the *person* using the words:

[4] The meaning of words is a matter of dictionaries and grammars; the meaning of the document is what the parties using those words against the relevant background would reasonably have been understood to mean. The background may not merely enable the reasonable man to choose between the possible meanings of words which are ambiguous but even (as occasionally happens in ordinary life) to conclude that the parties must, for whatever reason, have *used the wrong words or syntax* . . .

(5)... if one would nevertheless conclude from the background that *something must have gone wrong* with the language, the law does not require judges to attribute to the parties an intention which they plainly could not have had.... [As Lord Diplock said in *The Antaios* (1984)] 'if detailed semantic and syntactical analysis of words in a commercial contract is going to lead to a conclusion that flouts business common-sense, it must be made to yield to business commonsense' (emphasis added).

Furthermore, in *Chartbrook Ltd v Persimmon Homes Ltd* (2009), Lord Hoffmann stated that, if it is clear that something has gone wrong with the language *and* it is clear what a reasonable person would have understood the parties to have meant, then there is no 'limit to the amount of "red ink" or verbal rearrangement or correction which the court is allowed'.

When will courts conclude that 'something has gone wrong with the language' and depart from the meaning of the words used? They can do so where that meaning:

(i)   is inconsistent with the parties' intention as evinced by the context (*Chartbrook Ltd v Persimmon Homes*);

(ii) would not accord with business common sense. In *Rainy Sky SA v Kookmin Bank* (2011), Lord Clarke said that, where a term is open to more than one interpretation, it is generally appropriate to adopt that which is most consistent with business common sense. In *Napier Park European Credit Opportunities Fund Ltd v Harbourmaster Pro-Rata and others* (2014), Lewison LJ said that, where possible, courts should test any interpretation against the commercial consequences as part of the iterative exercise of interpretation, and not merely as a safety valve in cases of absurdity;

(iii) would lead to very unfair results. Lord Hoffmann restates what Staughton describes as 'the most important'[5] principle of interpretation; namely, the *presumption against unreasonable results*. Staughton cites Lord Reid in *L Schuler AG v Wickman Machine Tool Sales Ltd* (12.2.3.2):

'The more unreasonable the result the more unlikely it is that the parties can have intended it, and if they do intend it the more necessary it is that they should make that intention abundantly clear.' When speaking to students, I tell them that what Lord Reid said there is something which they should learn by heart.

 Pause for reflection

1. The potential for courts to attribute a different meaning from the natural meaning of clear and unambiguous language where the context requires, facilitates a more realistic, more accurate and fairer approach to ascertaining intentions. Kramer supports Lord Hoffmann's approach as being: based on the 'common sense principles of interpretation', 'the matrix of fact', and 'the parties' reasonable expectations'; versatile; having a sound theoretical basis; and reflected elsewhere in the existing law ('Common Sense Principles of Contract Interpretation (and how we've been using them all along)' (2003) 23 *OJLS* 173).

2. **Lord Sumption** has strongly criticised the Hoffmann contextual approach.[6] He argues extrajudicially:

   • *The importance of words*: '[T]he language of the parties' agreement, read as a whole, is the only direct evidence of their intentions which is admissible.... Language

   ➡

---

[5] C Staughton, 'How Do the Courts Interpret Commercial Contracts?' (1999) 58 *CLJ* 303, 308.
[6] 'A Question of Taste: The Supreme Court and the Interpretation of Contracts', Farquharson Lecture, Keble College, Oxford, 8 May 2017.

→

is a mode of communication. Its efficacy depends on the acceptance of a number of conventions that enable people to understand each other. Dictionaries and grammars are simply reference books which record these conventions. If we abandon them as the basic tools of construction, we are no longer discovering how the parties understood each other.'

- *The rigorous exclusion of pre-contractual negotiations* as evidence of intention is inconsistent with the use of context to modify the effect of language (10.4.4).

- *Judges are not necessarily well-placed to assess commercial common sense* since the parties will usually have conflicting purposes and 'can be most unfair and entirely unreasonable' at the time of formation, whereas courts approach with hindsight, with notions of common sense moulded by ideas of fairness.

- *Inconsistent with the law on implied terms* (10.6) *and rectification* (6.1.2), which the Supreme Court in *Wood v Capita* (2017) has subsequently recognised as resting on a distinct basis and requiring higher thresholds.

10.4.3 Latest Supreme Court pronouncements: continuity or change?

Here, we may be able to detect the swing of the legal pendulum:

- between the literal and the contextual ends of the spectrum;
- between elucidating the meaning of words and modifying or contradicting the words of the agreement; and
- between the language of the contract and the reasonableness of the result.

Diagram 10B sets out an overview of the approach to interpretation.

Lord Sumption observed that: 'Just as *ICS* changed the judicial mood about language and tended to encourage the view that it was basically unimportant, so the more recent cases may in due course be seen to have changed it back again, at least to some degree'.[7]

Lord Hodge has denied any such change judicially and extrajudicially.[8] Delivering the majority judgement in *Wood v Capita* (2017), with which Lord Sumption concurred, Lord Hodge declared the recent history of the law on interpretation to be one of *continuity* rather than change. Certainly, *ICS* and *Rainy Sky* have neither been overruled nor criticised. Moreover, recent Supreme Court decisions signalling a change of direction contain powerful dissents from those who felt that too much weight was given to the language of the contract and not enough to the unreasonableness of the result (eg Lord Carnwath's dissent in *Arnold v Britton* (2015)).

Recent Supreme Court decisions set out guidance on the approach to be adopted, which still contains a significant degree of flexibility (perhaps, more than Lord

---

[7] Ibid.
[8] 'Recent Developments in Contract Law in the Supreme Court', Guest Lecture, Law Faculty, Oxford University, 2 March 2017.

Diagram 10B Interpretation of contract

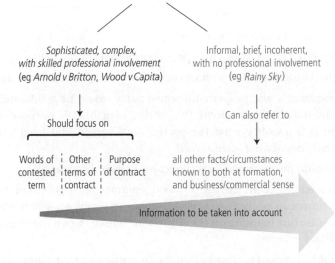

Interpretation of contract

Theory: (i) Objective approach to parties' intentions
(ii) Unitary and iterative exercise balancing text and context.
(iii) Distinct from implication of terms and rectification.

Practice: (i) Pendulum swing between the textual and contextual ends of spectrum.
(ii) Depends on particular case–
Where rival interpretations possible, must consider:
quality of drafting, legal professional involvement, complexity, formality
and coherence of the contract. Where the contract is

Sophisticated, complex,
with skilled professional involvement
(eg *Arnold v Britton, Wood v Capita*)

Informal, brief, incoherent,
with no professional involvement
(eg *Rainy Sky*)

Should focus on

Can also refer to

Cannot take
account of:
✗ pre-contractual
negotiation
✗ post-contractual
conduct
✗ hindsight
✗ court's view
of what should
have been agreed

Words of | Other | Purpose
contested | terms of | of contract
term | contract |

all other facts/circumstances
known to both at formation,
and business/commercial sense

Information to be taken into account

Sumption would consider desirable). The following can be regarded as the most recent **restatement** based on *Rainy Sky* (2011), *Arnold v Britton* (2015), and *Wood v Capita* (2017):

(i) The court's task is to ascertain the **objective meaning of the *language*** with which the parties expressed their agreement, rather than of the parties' intention. Thus, where neither party's interpretation was satisfactory, the Court of Appeal could reject both in favour of the objective interpretation of the disputed words (*Anglo Continental Education Group Ltd v Capital Homes (Southern) Ltd* (2009)).

(ii) It is a **unitary and iterative exercise** that entails examining and balancing both:

(a) **textualism**: the wording of the disputed term and other terms of the contract, and

(b) **contextualism**: including circumstances known to both parties at formation, the contractual purpose, and business common sense.

(iii) Where rival interpretations are possible, the following factors **guide the respective weight to be accorded to (a) and (b):**

✔ The *nature, formality, and quality of drafting of the contract*: where the agreement is sophisticated, complex, formal, and has been negotiated and prepared with the assistance of skilled professionals, principal weight must be given to (a) the textual analysis. In contrast, greater emphasis on (b) the factual matrix is in order where an agreement is informal, brief, or lacking skilled professional assistance.

✔ The *coherence* of the agreement: even professionally assisted agreements may lack coherence (eg due to: the parties' conflicting aims; failures of communication; differing drafting practices; inability to reach precise compromises; and lack of time). In such cases, more weight should be given to (b).

(iv) The court **cannot have regard to**:

✗ subjective declarations of intention;

✗ pre-contractual negotiations and post-contractual conduct (10.4.4);

✗ hindsight, being irrelevant to the context in which parties contracted; and

✗ what a reasonable and properly informed party would have intended, since this would illegitimately rewrite the parties' bargain. The purpose of interpretation is to identify what the parties have agreed, not what the court thinks that they should have agreed.

(v) The court should bear in mind that **'business common sense'**:

• may be unclear since 'in the tug o' war of commercial negotiation, business common sense can rarely assist the court in ascertaining on which side of the line the centre line marking on the tug o' war rope lay, when the negotiations ended' (*Wood v Capita*);

• should not be invoked to undervalue the importance of the language; and

• should not override what turned out to be a bad bargain for one of the parties.

Some examples illustrate how these principles are applied:

In *Rainy Sky v Kookmin Bank* (2011) the court was concerned with an obligation in a shipbuilder's refund guarantee. Here, the bank, in consideration of the buyer's payment of pre-delivery instalments for the ship, undertook to pay as primary obligor 'all such sums due to you under the contract'. A dispute arose when the builder became insolvent as to whether 'all such sums' referred:

✔ back to the pre-delivery instalments repayable on an insolvency event, as the buyer argued, or

✗ to the same instalments in a prior clause which were repayable only on termination of the contract or on the total loss of the vessel, as the builder and its guarantor contended.

Where the words were clearly open to two possible and credible constructions, the court had to ascertain what a reasonable person, with all the background knowledge reasonably available to the parties at the time of the contract, would have understood the parties to have meant. If two constructions were possible, the court should prefer the construction which was consistent with business common sense. Here, the buyer's construction was preferred because it conformed to the commercial purpose of the bonds which was to deal primarily with a builder's insolvency.

In *Arnold v Britton* (2015), 21 lessees held 99-year leases of chalets in a leisure park, granted between 1977 and 1991. Each lessee covenanted to pay a proportion of the cost of providing the services, expressed as £90 in the first year, rising by 10% every subsequent year. On its literal meaning, the tenants would be paying £1,025,004 annually by 2072. The Supreme Court:

✔ accepted the landlord's argument for the natural meaning of the term; and

✗ rejected the tenants' argument that the potentially catastrophic consequences meant that 'something has gone wrong with the language', and that the term should only require them to pay a fair proportion of the cost of the services '*up to*' the stipulated amount.

Notably, the majority took account of the clear words used, but *also* the commercial sense of the term given:

- the high rates of price inflation when the leases were entered by comparison with the much lower rates more recently; and

- the utility of imposing a fixed contribution to avoid disputes over what would be a proportionate share.

In *Wood v Capita Insurance Services* (2017), the Supreme Court interpreted an indemnity clause in an agreement for the sale and purchase of shares in an insurance company to cover the buyer's loss caused by the seller's mis-selling:

✔ (i) *only* where such loss followed a claim *by a customer* to the Financial Services Authority (FSA) or other regulator, as the wording of the clause clearly stated; and

✗ (ii) not the loss from having to compensate customers after the *buyer referred itself* to the FSA pursuant to an employee's whistle-blowing, as happened in the case.

Again, in reaching this conclusion, the majority took account of the clear words of the clause, but also its commercial sense given:

- the existence of another warranty in the contract conferring wide-ranging but time-limited protection on the buyer which would have covered (ii);

- the buyer could have invoked the warranty if it had acted within the two-year time-limit; and

- while the buyer's business common sense points to it obtaining the broadest indemnity against the seller, the seller's business common sense points in the opposite direction.

10.4.4 Inadmissibility of pre-contractual negotiations and subsequent conduct

Lord Hoffmann's third principle in *ICS* sets out what *cannot* be taken into account in interpreting the contractual document, namely, evidence of the parties' pre-contractual negotiations. Lord Hoffmann recognises that this exclusion undermines the general aim of contextual interpretation, but explains that, since the parties are free to change their bargaining postures, and their positions are unstable until the contract is finalised by formal acceptance of the offer, '[a]ll a court can do is to decide what the final contract means' (*Canterbury Golf International Ltd v Yoshimoto* (2002)).

However, in *Chartbrook*, Lord Hoffmann conceded that the exclusionary rule did not apply to evidence of negotiations as evidence 'to establish a fact which may be relevant as *background* known to the parties, or to support a claim for rectification or estoppel. These are not exceptions to the rule. They operate outside it.' On the facts, although the contractual words in question made syntactical sense, this 'background' revealed a mistake that needed correction to achieve commercial sense. That this was done as an exercise in construction and not rectification is controversial. Baroness Hale agreed but added that she 'would not have found it quite so easy to reach this conclusion had we not been made aware of the agreement which the parties had reached on this aspect of their bargain during the negotiations which led up to the formal contract'. She saw 'attractions' in the arguments that the exclusionary rule should be reconsidered.

In *Oceanbulk Shipping and Trading SA v TMT Asia Ltd* (2010), the Supreme Court cast further doubt on the exclusionary rule. First, Lord Clarke noted that it may be very difficult to distinguish between material which forms part of the pre-contractual negotiations, which is part of the factual matrix and therefore admissible as an aid to interpretation, and that which is not, and so is inadmissible. Second, Lord Clarke noted that the width of the principles of construction now encompasses rectification (6.1.2), which *does* allow resort to pre-contractual negotiations. The issue at hand concerned the admissibility of evidence of what was said or written in the course of 'without prejudice' negotiations. The court concluded that it should in principle be admissible both when rectification is sought and 'when the court is considering a submission that the factual matrix relevant to the true construction of a settlement agreement includes evidence of an objective fact communicated in the course of such negotiations'.

Schuler AG v Wickman Machine Tool Sales (1973) held that evidence of conduct subsequent to contract formation is also inadmissible since, otherwise, the meaning of the contract could change over time.

 Counterpoint

The exclusionary rules are difficult to justify. McMeel rejects both exclusions and argues that the matter should be one of the weight, and not the admissibility, of the evidence ('Prior Negotiations and Subsequent Conduct—The Next Step Forward for Contractual Interpretation' (2003) 119 *LQR* 272).

Lord Nicholls, writing extrajudicially, sets out the reasons against the exclusions ('My Kingdom for a Horse: The Meaning of Words' (2005) 101 *LQR* 577):

1. Injustice: 'Whenever a court is disabled from considering evidence which would assist, the court is to that extent less able to decide how the language of the contract ought fairly to

→

→

be interpreted'. It allows 'one party to contend for a meaning he knows was not intended'. It seems that Lord Hoffmann regards the injustice in the occasional case as outweighed by the certainty and predictability to be derived from the exclusionary rules.

2. Best evidence: it would be 'perverse' to 'be barred from having regard to what may be the best evidence of all'. Evidence of pre-contract negotiations should be 'admissible if they would have influenced the notional reasonable person in his understanding of the meaning the parties intended to convey by the words they used'. A reasonable person with knowledge of the background circumstances minus the negotiations will usually have an incomplete picture of the background to the contract.

3. There are already many 'exceptions': evidence of **previous negotiations** is admissible to resolve:

   • questions about the formation of contracts not reduced to a formal contract but made through a course of dealings;

   • claims for misrepresentation or rectification;

   • a plea of estoppel or to show that the contract has been varied;

   • questions on the nature and object of the contract; and

   • ambiguity in written documents.

   Judges have noted the difficulty in distinguishing such *admissible* evidence from *inadmissible* evidence of the parties' previous negotiating positions.

   Conduct subsequent to contract formation is already admissible to establish:

   • estoppel or variation of the contract (*James Miller & Partners Ltd v Whitworth Street Estates (Manchester) Ltd* (1970));

   • the content of an *oral* contract (*Maggs t/a BM Builders (A Firm) v Marsh* (2006)). Smith LJ said: 'The accuracy of those recollections may be tested and elucidated by things said and done by the parties or witnesses after the agreement has been concluded.'

4. Transparency: since evidence of the parties' actual intentions often does become known by, and so influences, judges on disputes about interpretation, that should be recognised openly. Lord Nicholls adds: 'As with pre-contract negotiations... I suspect that in practice judges from time to time do have regard to post-contract conduct when interpreting contracts... Judges are well able to identify, and disregard, self-serving subsequent conduct.'

5. Concern about certainty and increased costs can be managed: Lord Nicholls sees the solution lying 'in case management and appropriately tight judicial control over the evidence sought to be adduced'.

6. Comparative law: the exclusions are inconsistent with most other legal systems and international restatements of contract law such as:

   • the Vienna Convention on Sale of Goods;

   • the UNIDROIT Principles of International and Commercial Contracts;

   • the European Draft Common Frame of Reference; and

   • the Principles of European Contract Law, which state that '[I]n interpreting a contract, regard shall be had, in particular, to:

→

→

> (a) the circumstances in which it was concluded, including the preliminary negotiations;
>
> (b) the conduct of the parties, even subsequent to the conclusion of the contract;
>
> (c) the nature and purpose of the contract;
>
> (d) the interpretation which has already been given to similar clauses by the parties and the practices they have established between themselves;
>
> (e) the meaning commonly given to terms and expressions in the branch of activity concerned and the interpretation similar clauses may already have received;
>
> (f) usages; and
>
> (g) good faith and fair dealing.'
>
> The Scottish Law Commission has comprehensively criticised the exclusionary rule (*Discussion Paper on Interpretation of Contract* (No 147, 2011))

10.5 **Interpretation of exemption clauses**

10.5.1 **Then and now**

Terms that limit or exclude liability for breach of contract ('exemption clauses') can undermine or totally defeat the innocent party's contractual expectations by depriving her of compensation for loss caused by the other party's breach. Just as the courts can manipulate the standard of notice required to make onerous or unusual terms (that are often exemptions of liability) unenforceable for lack of incorporation (10.3.3.2), they have evolved special rules of interpretation to restrict the coverage of exemption clauses, even if they have been properly incorporated. 'Judicial creativity, bordering on judicial legislation' has sought to prevent contract-breakers from escaping the normal consequences of breach under the 'cover' of exemption clauses (*BCCI v Ali* (2001)).

However, the pendulum is swinging the other way due to two developments. First, legislation such as UCTA and CRA (Chapter 11) have reduced the need 'to go through all kinds of gymnastic contortions to get round' unfair exemption clauses (*Photo Production Ltd v Securicor Transport Ltd* (1980)). There, Lord Diplock said that:

> any need for this kind of judicial distortion of the English language has been banished... In commercial contracts negotiated between businessmen capable of looking after their own interests and of deciding how risks inherent in the performance of various kinds of contract can be most economically borne (generally by insurance), it is... wrong to place a strained construction upon words in an exclusion clause which are clear and fairly susceptible of one meaning only....

Second, in *Investors Compensation Scheme*, Lord Hoffmann declares that '[a]lmost all the old intellectual baggage of 'legal' interpretation has been discarded', including the 'artificial rules' relating to the construction of exemption clauses (*BCCI v Ali* (2001)). The Court of Appeal has confirmed that, in interpreting an exemption clause, 'artificial approaches to the construction of commercial contracts are to be avoided in favour of giving the words used by the parties their ordinary and natural meaning' (*Transocean Drilling U.K. Ltd v Providence Resources Plc* (2016)).

Nevertheless, courts have continued to reason along traditional lines, albeit incrementally moving towards the modern position, in respect of clauses that:

(i)   totally exclude liability;

(ii)   merely limit liability;

(iii) exclude or limit liability for negligence; and

(iv)   exclude or limit liability for indirect or consequential loss.

These rules show how the common law has sought to respond to perceived problems of unfairness. The law is summarised in **Diagram 10C**.

10.5.2 Fundamental breach and inconsistency with the main purpose of the contract

In essence, parties were *barred* from relying on clauses which excluded liability for a breach that is fundamental in the sense that it 'goes to the very root' of the contract.

✔ Lord Denning advocated it as a rule of law to be applied *irrespective of the parties' intentions*; that is, liability for fundamental breach *cannot* be excluded no matter how widely or clearly it is drawn.[9] This approach was rejected (*Suisse Atlantique Société d'Armement Maritime SA v NV Rotterdamsche Kolen Centrale* (1966)).

✔ The fundamental breach doctrine is now regarded simply as a rule of construction based on the assumption that, the *more* unreasonable the result, the *less* likely it is that the parties could have intended it.

Thus, *very* clear words will be necessary to exclude liability for:

• breach of terms that go to the root/essential character/purpose of the contract (*Karsales (Harrow) Ltd v Wallis* (1956)); or

• a deliberate repudiation of the contract (*Chartbrook Ltd v Persimmon Homes Ltd*).

However, such exclusions are effective if they are clearly set out and fairly susceptible to that interpretation, eg in *Photo Production v Securicor Transport* (1980) P engaged S to make periodic security patrols of its factory. During one such visit, S's employee started a fire to keep warm and burnt the factory down. S relied on an exclusion clause which stated that 'under no circumstances' were they to 'be responsible for any injurious act or default by any employee... unless [this]... could have been foreseen and avoided by the exercise of due diligence'. The House of Lords held the clause effective to shield S from liability because: no due diligence would have revealed the employee's predilection; P only paid a small sum for S's service; the service offered was limited; and P could have insured more cheaply than S.

---

[9] *Karsales (Harrow) Ltd v Wallis* (1956); *Harbutt's Plasticine Ltd v Wayne Tank Pump Co Ltd* (1971).

Diagram 10C Control of exemption clauses via interpretation

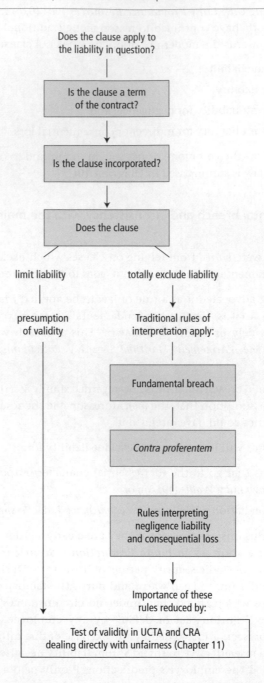

In *Kudos Catering (UK) Ltd v Manchester Central Convention Complex Ltd* (2013), the Court of Appeal construed an exclusion clause as covering only defective performance of the contract and not a refusal to perform it or be bound by it, otherwise the contract would be 'effectively devoid of contractual content since there is no sanction for non-performance.... It is inherently unlikely that the parties intended the clause to have this effect.' This construction gives effect to 'the presumption that parties do not lightly abandon a remedy for breach of contract afforded them by the general law'.

10.5.3 *Contra proferentem*

The doctrine of fundamental breach as a rule of construction is merely an extreme version of *contra proferentem* interpretation. The latter requires any *ambiguity* in a contractual term to be construed against the party who introduced it. It receives legislative recognition in CRA (section 69(1)) in relation to consumers.

However, in relation to **commercial contracts** negotiated between parties of equal bargaining power, the *contra proferentem* rule now has a very limited role, applying only where there is ambiguity. The Court of Appeal held that: 'It has no part to play... when the meaning of the words is clear... nor... in relation to a clause which favours both parties equally' (***Transocean Drilling UK Ltd v Providence Resources Plc*** (2016)). There is 'no need to approach them with horror or a mindset designed to cut them down' (*Persimmon Homes Ltd v Ove Arup and Partners Ltd* (2017)). The Court of Appeal in *Nobahar-Cookson v Hut Group Ltd* (2016) explains that:

> Commercial parties are entitled to allocate between them the risks of something going wrong in their contractual relationship in any way they choose. Nor is [*contra proferentem*] to be mechanistically applied wherever an ambiguity is identified in an exclusion clause. The court must still use all its tools of linguistic, purposive and common-sense analysis to discern what the clause really means.

The following illustrate the applicability of *contra proferentem* interpretation:

✔ In *BCCI v Ali* (2001), a clause stated that A's settlement of claim against B was 'in full and final settlement of all or any claims whether under statute, common law or in equity of whatsoever nature that exist or may exist and, in particular, all or any claims rights or applications of whatsoever nature that the applicant has or may have or has made or could make in or to the industrial tribunal'. This clause was held not to exclude a claim that *neither party could have been aware of* at the time of the settlement. Lord Nicholls said that courts should be slow to infer that parties have surrendered unknown rights and claims in the absence of clear language. However, since the natural wording seems abundantly clear, Lord Hoffmann's observation is apposite: 'When judges say that 'in the absence of clear words' they would be unwilling to construe a document to mean something, they generally mean... that the effect of the document is unfair.'

✔ In *Nobahar-Cookson v Hut* (2016), a commercial contract provided that the sellers of a company would not be liable for any claim unless the buyer served notice of it within 20 business days 'after becoming aware of the matter'. Given the commercial purpose of the term was to prevent the buyer from keeping claims of which it was aware 'up its sleeve', the court interpreted the phrase to mean awareness of a claim and not merely an awareness of facts which could give rise to a claim.

✗ In ***Transocean Drilling UK Ltd v Providence Resources*** (2016), a contract to hire an oil-drilling rig contained mutual undertakings by the owner and the hirer to indemnify each other against their own consequential losses. The question was whether the hirer was entitled to recover consequential losses for delay caused by the owner's failure to provide the rig in good working order. The court rejected the applicability of *contra proferentem* interpretation since the meaning of the clause was clear, it favoured both parties equally, and they were of equal bargaining power.

✗ In *Persimmon Homes Ltd v Ove Arup and Partners Ltd* (2017), consultant engineers claimed to be exempted from 'liability for any claim in relation to asbestos' under the contract in relation to unexpected quantities of asbestos found on a development site. The Court of Appeal refused to accept the developers' argument that the wording was limited to 'liability for causing the presence of asbestos' (as opposed to failing to identify it) because of: the clear language used by the parties, business common sense, and the equality of bargaining power in this major construction project.

10.5.4 **The limitation–exclusion distinction**

The courts have declared themselves less hostile towards clauses which *limit* rather than totally *exclude* liability for breach on the basis that parties are more likely to agree to limit rather than exclude liability altogether and because limitation clauses play a legitimate role in risk allocation (***Ailsa Craig Fishing Co Ltd v Malvern Fishing Co Ltd*** (1983)). **Limitation clauses are therefore presumptively valid.**

◆◀ Counterpoint

1. The distinction is artificial since exclusion clauses may represent legitimate risk allocation (as in *Photo Production v Securicor Transport*, 10.5.2) while limitation clauses may be so severe as to amount, in substance, to a total exclusion (eg limiting liability to £1).

2. UCTA and CRA do not distinguish between their controls of these terms.

3. In *Darlington Futures Ltd v Delco Australia Pty Ltd* (1986), the High Court of Australia rejected the distinction.

10.5.5 **Exemptions of negligence liability**

Courts have maintained their hostility towards exclusions of liability for *negligence* because it is said to be 'inherently improbable' that the innocent party would have agreed to them, and that parties should not be allowed to hide unfair exemptions behind general words when they are 'shy' of making it explicit for fear of alerting the other party (*EE Caledonia Ltd v Orbit Valve Co Europe plc* (1994)). UCTA and CRA both severely limit the effectiveness of exemptions for negligence (11.5.1

and 11.6). But these statutes only apply if the relevant exemption is, *first*, inter-preted as exempting negligence liability. The relevant clause will only do so when it can mean nothing else, according to Lord Morton's three rules set out in *Canada Steamship Lines Ltd v The King* (1952) (summarised in **Diagram 10D**). These are com-plex, and it is important to bear in mind that *Investors Compensation Scheme* and subsequent cases have **downgraded the importance** of these rules but not entirely overruled them.

10.5.5.1 Where express exemption for negligence

An exemption clause will only cover negligence liability if it *expressly* exempts such liability; use of words synonymous with negligence may be effective (*Smith v South Wales Switchgear Co Ltd* (1978)), but even exempting liability for 'loss whatsoever or howsoever occasioned' may *not* be sufficiently express (*Shell Chemicals UK Ltd v P&O Roadtanks Ltd* (1995)).

10.5.5.2 Where no express exemption for negligence

Absent express words exempting negligence liability, the question is whether the words used are *wide enough* in their ordinary meaning to cover negligence liabil-ity (any doubt being resolved against the party relying on the clause, the *proferens*). Examples of such words are: 'will not be liable for any accident howsoever caused' (*White v Blackmore* (1972)), 'shall not be liable under any circumstances whatsoever

Diagram 10D Exemptions from liability in negligence: the *Canada Steamship* rules

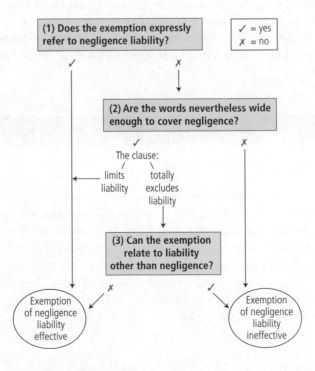

for theft' (*L Harris (Harella) Ltd v Continental Express Ltd & Burn Transit Ltd* (1961)), and excluding liability 'arising from any cause whatsoever' (*Farr (AE) Ltd v Admiralty* (1953)).

- If *not*, the exemption will not cover negligence liability.

- If so, *and* the clause only *limits* rather than excludes liability, the term is effective (*Ailsa Craig Fishing v Malvern Fishing*; *George Mitchell v Finley Lock Seeds*).

- If a clause which is apparently wide enough to cover negligence totally *excludes* liability, another question arises.

10.5.5.3 Can the exemption cover liability other than negligence?

- If *not*, and the contract-breaker's *only* possible liability is for negligence, then the exemption is effective. In *Alderslade v Hendon Laundry Ltd* (1945), H negligently lost A's handkerchiefs sent in for cleaning. H could only have been liable for negligent loss and was permitted to rely on a clause limiting liability to 20 times the cleaning charge.

- If the clause *can* apply to liability other than negligence (eg it can also cover strict liability for breach of contract or for breach of statutory duty), it will *only* exempt from the non-negligence liability and *not the negligence liability*. Steyn LJ (in *EE Caledonia Ltd v Orbit Valve Co Europe*) said that the potential for non-negligence liability should not be so 'fanciful or remote' that the *proferens* cannot be supposed to desire protection from it. However, 'fanciful' aptly describes *Hollier v Rambler Motors* (1972). R contracted to fix H's car. A term totally excluding liability 'for damage caused by fire to customers' cars' was held not to cover R's negligent damage to H's car by fire because the car could also be so damaged without R's negligence. Since R could not have been liable without negligence, it *does* seem 'fanciful' (because redundant) for R to exclude liability for it. Such a construction deprives the term of any effect although it avoided an unfair result pre-UCTA.

▶◀ Counterpoint

The *Canada Steamship* rules are open to criticism:

1. They may *contradict the parties' intentions*.

2. The test applicable where negligence is *not* expressly exempted makes contradictory demands, simultaneously requiring the exemption to be drafted *widely* enough to cover negligence but *narrowly* enough to exclude all other possible liability.

3. *Caledonia* supported the rules on the basis that commercial parties are legally advised. However, those unaware of the rules cannot negotiate or draft around them. They were rejected by the Supreme Court of Victoria in *Schenker & Co (Aust) Pty Ltd v Maplas Equipment and Services Pty Ltd* (1990).

While affirming the 'general authority' of the *Canada Steamship* rules, the House of Lords in *HIH Casualty and General Insurance v Chase Manhattan Bank* (2003) said that the court's primary task was to give effect to the intention of the parties. In *Mir Steel UK Ltd v Morris* (2012), the Court of Appeal held that the *Canada Steamship* principles 'should not be applied mechanistically and ought to be regarded as no more than guidelines'. In particular, they do not provide an 'automatic solution' to a particular case. In *Persimmon Homes Ltd v Ove Arup and Partners Ltd* (2017), the Court of Appeal stated that 'in commercial contracts, the *Canada Steamships* guidelines (in so far as they survive) are now more relevant to indemnity clauses', ie stipulating that 'B must compensate A for the consequences of A's own negligence'.

The *Canada Steamship* rules were not applied in recent cases:

✗ In *Mir Steel*, the court held that there was no justification for reading the words 'any claim' narrowly to exclude negligence claims.

✗ In *National Westminster Bank plc v Utrecht-America Finance Co* (2001), a term excluding liability for negligent *and* even fraudulent non-disclosure was upheld. The contract was between large banks dealing at arm's length and advised by commercial lawyers, and the term was not unfair since it operated both ways.

✗ In *Greenwich Millennium Village Ltd v Essex Services Group plc and others* (2014), the Court of Appeal upheld an indemnity clause although the indemnitee should have detected the defects on inspection (ie was negligent). In the context of construction contracts, a failure by the indemnitee to spot defects perpetrated by its contractor should not ordinarily defeat the operation of an indemnity clause, even if that clause failed expressly to encompass damage caused by the negligence of the indemnitee.

✗ In *Persimmon Homes Ltd v Ove Arup*, the court upheld an exemption of liability in respect of a consultant's negligent failure to identify and report on quantities of asbestos later found on a development site.

10.5.6 Exemptions for 'indirect and consequential loss'

Clauses that exclude liability for 'indirect and consequential loss' may also be strictly interpreted. Such exemptions are often used in commercial contracts to confine potential liability for pure economic loss (ie of profit). They will not cover loss that flows directly and naturally in the ordinary course of events from the breach, but only less direct or more remote loss, eg in *Hotel Services Ltd v Hilton International Hotels (UK) Ltd* (2000), a hotel owner claimed £127,000 for defective 'Robobars', an automated minibar, comprising of the cost of removing and storing them, and of loss of profits. The suppliers were unable to rely on a clause excluding liability for 'any indirect or consequential loss... arising from any defect in or failure of the System' because all the losses were held to be 'direct' and outside the scope of the exclusion. Relying on the remoteness test set out in *Hadley v Baxendale* (13.2.5.1), the court interpreted 'direct' loss as that arising *naturally* from the breach and 'indirect' or consequential loss as that which was reasonably contemplated in view of *special known facts*. Sedley

LJ said that, if the equipment 'turns out to be unusable and possibly dangerous, it requires no special mutually known fact to establish the immediacy both of the consequent cost of putting it where it can do no harm and—if when in use it was showing a direct profit—of the consequent loss of profit. Such losses are not embraced by the exclusion clause.'

 Pause for reflection

This interpretation seems to be inconsistent with the ordinary meaning of 'consequential loss'. All loss of profit is loss *consequential on breach*. Rather than distorting this natural meaning, it would be preferable to control unfairness through UCTA or CRA.

10.6 **Implied terms**

In addition to express terms (incorporated by signature, notice, or previous dealing (10.3)), a contract may also contain implied terms. Terms may be implied:

(i)   in *fact* (from the circumstances of the particular contract); or

(ii) in *law* (by statute, common law, or custom).

The justifications for implied terms and the test for each type of implication are summarised in **Diagram 10E**. Lord Bingham MR explains that, since 'the implication of terms is so potentially intrusive', contract law 'imposes strict constraints on the exercise of this extraordinary power' (*Phillips Electronique Grand Public SA v B Sky B Ltd* (1995)).

10.6.1 **Implication in fact**

Terms may be implied into contracts from the *factual context* to give effect to the parties' *unexpressed intention*. The reasoning is that, whether through forgetfulness, lack of time, or bad drafting, the parties have failed to include a term which *they would have done*, had they thought about it or had the time to draft properly.

10.6.1.1 The traditional tests for implication in fact

Two overlapping tests have been put forward, each emphasising the high threshold for implying terms in fact by reference to the requirement of 'necessity':

(i) Business efficacy: *The Moorcock* (1889) stipulated that the term sought to be implied must be *necessary* to give the transaction *business efficacy*. Here, the claimant ship-owner contracted to unload the ship at the defendant's jetty. The ship was damaged when it settled on a hard ridge at low tide. The court implied a term requiring the defendant to take reasonable care to ascertain the safety of the berth, since this was necessary for business efficacy in such transactions; the defendant was liable for its breach.

Diagram 10E Overview of implied terms

	Implication in **FACT**	Implication by **LAW** (common law, statute or custom)
Applies to	*Any* specific contract.	Contracts of certain *types* (eg employment, tenancy, sale of goods or services), in particular *trades* or *locality.*
Test for implication of term	✓ Is it necessary for business efficacy; ✓ Would it satisfy the officious bystander test (reasonableness not enough); or ✗ Is it the meaning which the contract would convey to a reasonable person having all the background knowledge reasonably available to the parties?	Is it: ✓ provided for in statute; *or* ✓ established in precedents; *or* ✓ certain, notorious, accepted as binding, and reasonable; ✓ otherwise reasonably 'necessary' in contracts of that type?
Contra-indications for implication	✗ If inconsistent with express term, unknown to one party, too vague, complicated or novel, or if it is unclear whether the parties would have agreed.	✗ Inconsistent with express term, but NB some implications cannot be excluded in certain situations.
Justifications for implying terms	• presumed intention of the parties; • efficiency of providing default rules; • protection of reasonable expectations; • reasonable and fair risk allocation; and • correcting contractual imbalance.	

(ii) **'Officious bystander'**: *Shirlaw v Southern Foundries (1926) Ltd* (1939) held that a term implied in fact 'is something so obvious that it goes without saying; so that, if, while the parties were making their bargain, an officious bystander were to suggest some express provision for it in the agreement, they would testily suppress them with a common "*Oh, of course!*"'.

A term will **not be implied** if:

✗ one of the parties is ignorant of the content of the alleged term (*Spring v NASDS* (1956));

✗ it is unclear whether both parties would have agreed to the term (*Luxor (Eastbourne) Ltd v Cooper* (1941));

✗ the parties have entered into a carefully drafted written contract containing detailed terms, raising a strong presumption that this constitutes the complete agreement (*Shell UK Ltd v Lostock Garages Ltd* (1976));

✗ the alleged term is too complicated (*Ashmore v Corp of Lloyd's (No 2)* (1992)), or too vague (eg good faith negotiation in *Walford v Miles* (1992); operating commercial aircraft in *Durham Tees Valley Airport Ltd v BMI Baby Ltd* (2009));

✗ the contract is a novel or risky one (*Phillips Electronique v BSkyB*); or

✗ it is inconsistent with an express term (*Duke of Westminster v Guild* (1985)).

The rule that a term implied in fact **cannot contradict an express term** is subject to the contextual interpretation of the express term itself to avoid defeating the overriding purpose of the term, eg in *Attorney-General of Belize v Belize Telecom Ltd* (2009), the articles of association of BT stipulated the election of directors according to particular types and quantity of shareholding. Although they provided that these directors could only be removed on grounds such as lunacy and bankruptcy, the Privy Council implied a term that a director could also be removed when the shareholder with the required shareholding to support his appointment ceased to exist. This was necessary to avoid defeating the overriding purpose of the machinery for appointing directors—to ensure that the board of directors reflected the type and degree of shareholder interests.

10.6.1.2 Implied in fact terms different from construction

Here the pendulum has swung back and forth quickly. The traditional position that implying terms is different from interpreting terms was called into question by Lord Hoffmann in *Attorney-General of Belize v Belize Telecom Ltd* (2009). His Lordship stated that:

(i) Implying terms in fact is an exercise in the construction of the instrument as a whole. The test was 'whether such a provision would spell out in express words what the instrument, read against the relevant background, would reasonably be understood to mean'.

(ii) The different stated tests are not different or cumulative tests. They are 'best regarded... as a collection of different ways in which judges have tried to express the central idea that the proposed implied term must spell out what the contract actually means'. They are not 'freestanding' tests that must be satisfied (*Crema v Cenkos Securities plc* (2010)).

Lord Hoffmann's view that the process of construction and implying terms in fact are the same has been approved (eg *Jackson v Dear* (2013); *Yam Sen Pte Corp v International Trade Corp* (2013)). In *Stena Line Ltd v Merchant Navy Ratings Pension Fund Trustees Ltd* (2011), Arden LJ welcomed the development for promoting 'the internal coherence of the law'.

◆◀ Counterpoint

1. There is a significant difference between:

- interpreting the words that the parties have expressly agreed by reference to the view of a reasonable person in the parties' position; and

- implying *new* words into a contract to fill a gap in the agreement; it is logically impossible to do this by a process of interpreting something that is, by definition, not there.

Collins[10] rejects 'the imperialism of the interpretivists'. He argues that, while interpretation deals with a lack of specificity or precision in the words of the contract, implication in fact

➡

---

[10] In 'Implied Terms: The Foundation in Good Faith and Fair Dealing' (2014) *CLP* 1, 17.

→

concerns a reallocation of risk to counter unconscionability (in the sense of taking advantage of an omission to protect against risk in circumstances where this advantage had not been bargained for as part of the consideration).

2. Lord Hoffmann's judgment changes the test for implied-in-fact terms from necessity to reasonableness: it is enough that the term implied-in-fact is commercially reasonable and must therefore have been intended. This was in fact Lord Denning's position, decisively rejected by the House of Lords in *Liverpool City Council v Irwin* (1977).

3. The Singapore Court of Appeal[11] has expressly rejected the *Belize* reasoning.

The **business efficacy test was reasserted** by a unanimous Supreme Court in *Marks & Spencer Plc v BNP Paribas Securities Services Trust Co* (2016). Lord Neuberger said that Lord Hoffman's observations in *Belize* should be treated as 'a characteristically inspired discussion rather than authoritative guidance on the law of implied terms'. The applicable law is that:

(i)   'a term can only be implied if, without the term, the contract would lack commercial or practical efficacy'. His lordship warned against any suggestion that the strict test for implying terms had been relaxed; **the test is still necessity.**

(ii) **Interpretation is different from implication**; interpretation involves construing the words the parties use in their contract and *precedes* any question of implication.

(iii) A term should not be implied into a detailed commercial contract merely because it appears fair or because the parties would have agreed if it had been suggested to them; **fairness and reasonableness are necessary but not sufficient.**

(iv) **The business necessity and obviousness tests** could be alternatives, in the sense that only one of them needs to be satisfied:

  • if the officious bystander test is used, the question to be posed by him must be formulated with the utmost care;

  • necessity for business efficacy requires a value judgment of whether, without the implied term, the contract would lack commercial or practical coherence; 'absolute necessity' is unnecessary.

✗   In the *Marks and Spencer* case, M&S rented retail premises under a detailed commercial lease. It relied on a term that allowed the tenant to terminate the lease early and sought to imply a term that the landlord was obliged to refund two months of the advance rent paid. While the claim was reasonable, the Supreme Court refused to imply the term given that:

---

[11] *Foo Jong Peng v Phua Kiah Mai* [2012] 4 SLR 1267.

- The lease was a detailed document prepared by professional lawyers.

- The common law did not allow for the apportionment of rent, and statute (Apportionment Act 1870, s 2) only provided for the apportionment of rent payable in arrears but not rent paid in advance.

- The claim that the landlord should repay 'sat uneasily' with the requirement that the tenant pay both advance rent and also a substantial premium as conditions of early termination.

- A further provision, requiring the landlord to pay the tenant if the tenant did *not* terminate the lease early, suggested that the parties had carefully considered the financial consequences of early termination.

✗ Another example of a strict necessity approach is *Mediterranean Salvage & Towage Ltd v Seamar Trading & Commerce Inc, The Reborn* (2009), which is reminiscent of the *Moorcock* but came, in its particular circumstances, to the conclusion that the charterer had no implied obligation to nominate a safe berth and was not liable for the damage to the owner's ship when the berth nominated turned out to be unsafe. Applying the necessity test for implying terms, the court considered relevant:

- the fact that the safety of the berth was apparently unascertainable by either party;

- the fact that there was no express warranty that the port was safe; and

- the owner had given certain warranties which meant that it had agreed that it would either investigate the berths or take the risk of getting to whatever berth was nominated. The implied term was not necessary to make the contract work.

10.6.1.3 Implied limits on the exercise of discretionary power

An agreement may leave a particular matter to be determined by one of the contracting parties. This contractual discretion over the rights or liabilities of the other party may be conferred in an *unqualified* way, using terms such as 'satisfied', 'approved', 'as he thinks fit', or 'in his sole discretion'. Whilst the exercise of discretionary powers by public authorities is constrained by public law concepts, the logic of freedom of contract may suggest that such powers agreed by private parties are unrestricted. However, Leggatt LJ said that: 'where A and B contract with each other to confer a discretion on A, that does not render B subject to A's uninhibited whim' (*Abu Dhabi National Tanker Co v Product Star Shipping Ltd (The Product Star)* (1993)).

Legislation controls such terms in particular circumstances, eg (Chapter 11):

- in consumer contracts, certain terms that confer broad discretionary powers on traders are presumptively unfair (CRA, Sch 2 Part 1, paras 7, 11–16); and

- terms purporting to allow a business the discretion of giving *no, only partial* or *substantially different* performance from that reasonably expected by the other party are invalid if they are unreasonable where a business contracts on the other's standard terms (UCTA, s 3(2)(b)).

Judicial control, setting out minimum standards by which even absolute discretionary contractual power must be *exercised*, is long-standing. In *Braganza v BP Shipping Ltd* (2015), Lady Hale explains that:

> Contractual terms in which one party to the contract is given the power to exercise a discretion, or to form an opinion as to relevant facts, are extremely common.... [T]he party who is charged with making decisions which affect the rights of both parties to the contract has a clear conflict of interest. That conflict is heightened where there is a significant imbalance of power between the contracting parties.... The courts have therefore sought to ensure that such contractual powers are not abused. They have done so by implying a term as to the manner in which such powers may be exercised, a term which may vary according to the terms of the contract and the context in which the decision-making power is given.... [T]he authorities show that not only must the discretion be exercised honestly and in good faith, but, having regard to the provisions of the contract by which it is conferred, it must not be exercised arbitrarily, capriciously or unreasonably.

Unreasonableness must be understood in the *Wednesbury* sense of prohibiting irrationality (*Socimer International Bank Ltd v Standard Bank London Ltd* (2008)). What is required is 'that there should be some logical connection between the evidence and the ostensible reasons for the decision, and... an absence of arbitrariness, of capriciousness or of reasoning so outrageous in its defiance of logic as to be perverse' (*Hayes v Willoughby* (2013)). It has two limbs:

- the first focuses on the decision-making process—whether the right matters have been taken into account; and

- the second focuses upon its outcome—whether the result is so outrageous that no reasonable decision-maker could have reached it.

The overall approach essentially mirrors that employed in the public law context of judicial review of administrative actions, although its application will vary with the **different context and purpose** for which the contractual power is conferred,[12] eg:

- In *consumer credit* contracts—the lender usually insists on having unilateral power to vary the interest rate in its absolute discretion, subject to notice to the debtor (*Lombard Tricity Finance Ltd v Paton* (1989)). In *Paragon Finance plc v Nash* (2001), the Court of Appeal implied the term that the rate of interest should not be set dishonestly, for an improper purpose, capriciously, or arbitrarily, or in a way in which no reasonable lender, acting reasonably, would do.

- In *employment cases*—in *Braganza v BP Shipping Ltd* (2015), the Supreme Court held that a higher standard of rationality is required of an employer in exercising a discretionary contractual power in the employment context since it must be exercised in accordance with the implied obligation of trust and confidence. There, an employer decided that an employee had committed suicide after

---

[12] H Collins, 'Discretionary Powers in Contracts' in D Campbell, H Collins, and J Wightman (eds), *Implicit Dimensions of Contracts* (Hart Publishing, 2003) 219; T Daintith, 'Contractual Discretion and Administrative Discretion: A Unified Analysis' (2005) 68 *MLR* 554.

disappearing from a ship, thereby depriving his family of a death-in-service payment. The Supreme Court held the decision to be irrational since there were no positive indications of suicide.

- The *commercial* context demands a far wider margin of tolerance. In *Paragon Finance plc v Plender* (2005), Parker LJ said: 'a commercial lender is... free to conduct its business in what it genuinely believes to be... its best commercial interest'. Even a discretion that is to be exercised in a 'commercially reasonable' manner permits the party exercising it to do so in its own interest in preference to the other party's interest (*Barclays Bank plc v Unicredit Bank AG* (2014)). Longmore LJ reasoned that it was impossible to see how a requirement to have regard to the other party's interests could work in practice. It is hard to see how it would assess what those interests were, let alone weigh those interests in comparison to its own interests. The obligation to act in a commercially reasonable manner would only be breached if it demanded a price way above what could reasonably be anticipated as a reasonable return from the contract.

However, a more stringent standard was applied in *Watson, Hersov and Moore v Watchfunder.co.uk Ltd* (2017). There, the claimants introduced prospective customers and investors to the defendant in exchange for, inter alia, a share option which, however, could only be exercised with the consent of the defendant's board of directors. Relying on *Braganza*, the judge held that this did not give the defendant the right of unconditional veto since that would render the option meaningless, while it was always intended to be part of the overall contractual package. Rather, the veto could not be exercised unreasonably, capriciously, or arbitrarily. This required the defendant to take into account relevant and disregard irrelevant considerations, and reach an outcome that was not unreasonable. On the facts, this meant asking whether the claimants had made a real or significant contribution to the defendant's progress or growth. Since the answer was 'yes', the court must proceed as if consent had been given and awarded the claimants specific performance of the Option Agreement. This result follows as a matter of construction or of implication of terms, since it was clearly necessary for business efficacy, obvious, and reasonable.

10.6.1.4 Implied duty of good faith in contract performance?

We saw in *Walford v Miles* that English law recognises no duty to negotiate contracts in good faith (2.6.2.5). Does English law recognise an implied duty of good faith in the *performance* of contracts? In *Yam Seng v International Trade Corp* (2013), Leggatt J said that: 'there is nothing novel or foreign in doing so'. There, ITC granted YS the exclusive right to distribute Manchester United fragrances in parts of the Middle East, Asia, Africa, and Australasia. YS terminated the contract alleging misrepresentation and various breaches of contract by ITC, including failing to ship orders promptly, refusing to supply some products after YS had marketed them, undercutting agreed prices, and attempting to claw back certain distribution rights. Leggatt J found misrepresentation and repudiatory breaches of the contract justifying YS's termination and awarded reliance damages. He also held that a duty of good faith could be implied in fact, on the basis of the presumed intention of the parties and the relevant background against which the contract was made, consistent with the *Belize* and *ICS* cases (but note that courts have retreated from these decisions by Lord Hoffmann). Relevant background 'includes not only facts known to the parties, but also shared values and norms of behaviour', often taken as read at the time of entering into a contract. '[F]idelity to the parties' bargain' is one of many generally accepted standards of commercial dealing that are central to good faith; contracts cannot expressly provide for every possible event, so their language must be given a reasonable construction which promotes the values and purposes expressed or implicit in the contract. Whilst agreeing with this, the appeal courts express a much more cautious approach to finding an implied term of good faith (*Globe Motors, Inc v TRW Lucas Varity Electric Steering Limited, TRW Limited* (2016)), and what even an express good faith duty might require (*Mid Essex Hospital Services NHS Trust v Compass Group UK and Ireland Ltd (t/a Medirest)* (2013)). The question of the role of good faith in English contract law is explored in Chapter 15.

10.6.2 Implication in law

In contrast to terms implied in *fact*, which are necessary to a particular contract, terms implied in *law* set out the default terms of a definable category of contractual relationship on the basis of wider considerations that will serve to regulate this market transaction (*Scally v Southern Health & Social Services Board* (1992); *Equitable Life Equitable Life Assurance Society v Hyman* (2000)).

Contracts that fall into certain commonly occurring types attract their own set of obligations as terms implied in law unless the parties contract out of (ie exclude) them, if permissible. Terms may be implied in law by statute, custom, or common law.

10.6.2.1 Terms implied in law by statute

The main example here is the **Sale of Goods Act 1979**, which implies into sale of goods contracts in commercial contracts that:

✔ the seller has title to sell the goods (s 12(1));

✔ goods sold are free from charges or encumbrances, and the buyer will enjoy quiet possession of the goods subject to the disclosed or known rights of others before contract formation (ss 12(2), (4), and (5));

✔ goods sold by description correspond with their description (s 13(1)) or their sample (s 15(2));

✔ goods sold in the course of business are of satisfactory quality, unless the buyer's attention has been drawn to, or the buyer's examination ought to reveal, any defect (s 14(2) and (2C)); and

✔ goods sold in the course of business are reasonably fit for the purpose that the buyer has made known to the seller (s 14(3)).

Similar terms are implied into **hire-purchase** contracts by the Supply of Goods (Implied Terms) Act 1973, and into contracts for the **supply of goods and services** by the Supply of Goods and Services Act 1982.

In contracts between a **consumer** and a trader, Part I of CRA sets out terms that are 'to be treated as included', including that:

✔ goods are to be of satisfactory quality (s 9);

✔ goods are to be fit for particular purpose (s 10);

✔ goods are to be as described (s 11);

✔ other pre-contract information provided is part of the contract (s 12);

✔ goods are to match a sample (s 13);

✔ goods are to match a model seen or examined (s 14);

✔ installation is part of conformity of the goods with the contract (s 15);

✔ items that include digital content must conform to the contract (s 16);

✔ services should be performed with reasonable care and skill (s 49);

✔ information provided about the trader or the service is to be binding (s 50); and

✔ services should be performed within a reasonable time (s 52).

These are **mandatory** terms since:
'A term of a contract to supply goods is not binding on the consumer to the extent that it would exclude or restrict the trader's liability arising under any of these provisions' (ss 31, 57).

The remedies for the breach of these terms are discussed later in this book:

• the right to reject (12.4);

• price reduction (13.6); and

• repair and replacement, and repeat performance (14.4).

10.6.2.2 Terms implied in law by custom

We saw that custom can incorporate terms in unsigned documents (10.3.3.2). Equally, terms may be implied by the custom of the market, trade or locality in which the contract is made. Such terms must be: certain, notorious, recognised as binding, reasonable, and consistent with the express terms or nature of the contract (*Cunliffe-Owen v Teather & Greenwood* (1967)). A term may be implied by custom even if it is *unknown* to one or even both parties at contract formation. Collins argues[13] that, more often, custom is 'a point of reference for understanding the meaning of the contract'; ie it aids interpretation. He cites a local custom in Suffolk in 1832 that a promise to sell 1,000 rabbits really meant 1,200 rabbits (*Smith v Wilson* (1832)).

10.6.2.3 Terms implied in law by the courts

It is implied in **employment** contracts that:

✔ the employee will serve diligently, loyally, and with reasonable competence (*Lister v Romford Ice & Cold Storage Co Ltd* (1957));

✔ the employer will not require the employee to act unlawfully (*Gregory v Ford* (1951));

---

[13] 'Implied Terms: The Foundation in Good Faith and Fair Dealing' (2014) 67 CLP 297, 303,

✔ the employer will provide safe premises (*Matthews v Kuwait Bechtel Corp* (1959); Employers' Liability (Defective Equipment) Act 1969), and take reasonable care not to endanger the employee's health (*Johnstone v Bloomsbury Health Authority* (1992)); and

✔ the parties owe each other a duty of trust and confidence (*Malik v Bank of Credit and Commerce Intl* (1997)).

It is implied into **building** contracts that:

✔ the work will be done in a good and workmanlike manner, the builder will use good and proper materials and the building, once completed, will be reasonably fit for human habitation (*Miller v Cannon Hill Estates Ltd* (1913)).

10.6.2.4 The test for terms implied in law

The courts have said that the test for implication by law is also 'necessity' rather than 'reasonableness' (*Liverpool CC v Irwin* (1977); *Scally v Southern Health and Social Services Board* (1992)). However, it is clear that the standard of 'necessity' here is *less stringent* than that required for implication in fact. In *Liverpool CC v Irwin* (1977), the House of Lords found that, in tenancy agreements, landlords had an implied-in-law obligation to their tenants (in this instance, living on the 9th and 10th floors of L's tower block) to take reasonable care to maintain the common parts of tower blocks they controlled such as the lifts, staircases, lights, and rubbish chutes. However, L had fulfilled this obligation, since it spent more on the repairs than it received in rents. Lord Denning's reasonableness approach was firmly rejected by the House of Lords in favour of the necessity test. Nevertheless, all their Lordships arrived at the same result. Atiyah (at 207) observes that:

> the difference between the judges on this point seems somewhat unreal.... It is not *necessary* to have lifts in blocks of flats ten storeys high [indeed high-rise buildings predate the invention of lifts], though it would no doubt be exceedingly inconvenient not to have them. So 'necessary' really seems to mean 'reasonably necessary', and that must mean, 'reasonably necessary having regard to the context and the price'. So in the end there does not seem to be much difference between what is necessary and what is reasonable.

Lord Denning MR returned to this theme in *Shell UK v Lostock Garages* (1976):

> These obligations are not founded on the intention of the parties, actual or presumed, but on more general considerations... the problem is not to be solved by asking what did the parties intend?... [but] by asking: has the law already defined the obligation or the extent of it? If so, let it be followed. If not, look to see what would be reasonable in the general run of such cases... and then say what the obligation shall be... the obligation is a legal incident of the relationship which is attached by the law.

Consistently, Dyson LJ said in *Crossley v Faithful & Gould Holdings Ltd* (2004) that:

> rather than focus on the elusive concept of necessity, it is better to recognise that, to some extent at least, the existence and scope of standardised implied terms

raise questions of reasonableness, fairness and the balancing of competing policy considerations.

The Court of Appeal also approved the policy considerations outlined by **Peden** in 'Policy Concerns Behind Implications of Terms in Law' (2001) 117 *LQR* 459, namely, that the courts consider:

✔ whether the proposed term is consistent with the existing law;

✔ how it would affect the parties; and

✔ wider issues of fairness in society.

Peden urges courts to recognise that the underlying idea in all types of implied terms is to maximise the social utility of the relationship; that is, to ensure cooperation between the parties and compliance with society's standards.

 Pause for reflection

Collins argues that 'such an open-ended examination of policy considerations is neither appropriate nor necessary'. He posits a two-stage inquiry. First, a court should try to discover a default rule that achieves an efficient allocation of risks as between the parties, since this reduces transaction costs and is likely to have been agreed by the parties had they considered it. Second, the rule should conform to the reasonable expectations of the parties (informed by normal commercial practices, customs, usages, and an understanding of an appropriate commercial balance of obligations); this would avoid the potential risk of granting one or the other an unexpected advantage ('Implied Terms: The Foundation in Good Faith and Fair Dealing' (2014) 67 *CLP* 297).

The *imposed* **nature of terms implied by law** is consistent with the following features of terms implied in law:

(i) Courts often rely exclusively on *precedents* rather than examining the intentions of the parties to the particular contract (*Yeoman Credit Ltd v Apps* (1962)).

(ii) Terms implied in law may be very *complex* and so unlikely to have been overlooked because they 'go without saying' (see *Scally v Southern Health and Social Services Board*).

(iii) The parties *cannot agree to exclude* some terms implied by law, eg:

• the employer and employee's implied obligation of mutual trust and confidence;

• the employer's duty to take reasonable care of the health and safety of its employees; and

• the terms 'treated as included' in consumer contracts under CRA.

Pause for reflection

The effect of implied terms in sale of goods contracts, especially the mandatory (non-excluda-ble) terms in consumer contracts, is to reverse the presumption of *caveat emptor* ('let the buyer beware'). Instead of leaving the buyer unprotected except for any specific undertakings extracted from the trader, sale of goods implied terms assure the buyer of a 'minimum kit' of rights in respect of the goods purchased. The argument that they are necessary to express the parties' pre-sumed intention is unrealistic. Here is the clearest example of the implication of terms to protect *reasonable expectations* (specifically those of buyers) and to counter unequal bargaining power.

The court's power to imply terms by law is limited: The proposed implication can only be made into a contract that fits the generality of contracts of that type and not only particular instances of it (*Reid v Rush & Tompkins Group plc* (1990)). However, courts have considerable latitude in the *level of detail* that they deploy in prescrib-ing the relevant class of contracts. In *Scally v Southern Health and Social Services Board* (1992), a term was implied into a very *narrow subcategory of employment con-tracts* when some doctors lost out on additional pension entitlements under their employment contracts because they did not know to take certain action. The House of Lords implied a term requiring the employer to take reasonable steps to inform their employees of this right in cases where: (a) a particular term makes a valuable right available to an employee contingent on her taking action; (b) the term results from collective bargaining; and (c) the employee cannot reasonably be expected to know of the term without being notified. Freedland observes that: 'There are few if any other situations where this would occur in an employment context' ('Individual Contracts of Employment and the Common Law Courts' (1992) 21 *ILJ* 135).

Pause for reflection

1. If the class of contracts into which terms can be implied in law can be subdivided into more detailed and numerous categories, so that the terms implied necessarily have *less general application*, this reduces the distinction between: terms implied *in fact* into *specific* con-tracts, and terms implied *by law* into contracts of a *recognised type*. It becomes arguable that, in respect of *all* contracts, the implication of terms is based on the appropriateness of doing so in all the circumstances including: the express agreement; the nature of the contract; the presumed intentions of the parties; the price; the fair and efficient allocation of rights and obligations; and the reasonable expectations of the parties. It is a matter of *degree; policy* considerations once again take centre stage.

2. The overlap between terms implied in law and in fact is well recognised. Cooke P said that implied terms are 'categories or shades in a continuous spectrum', so that 'it may be doubted whether tabulated legalism will ever produce an exhaustive or rigidly discrete

→

→

classification' (*Vickery v Waitaki Intl Ltd* (1992)). McMeel warns against exaggerating the differences: 'Historically it is likely that all today's implied terms in law commenced as incidents of particular transactions, and then migrated to the sub-category of terms implied in law (once the existence of that classification was made explicit). Today similar journeys are being made' (*The Construction of Contracts* (2nd edn, OUP, 2011) 320).

3. The traditional justification that courts imply terms in order to fill gaps left by the parties, to reduce the parties' transaction costs and to give effect to their presumed intentions is often unrealistic. The function of contracts is to allocate risks between the parties, so that any 'gap' left by the contract implicitly allocates the risk to the party who suffers the loss which 'lies where it falls'. The language of 'gap-filling' merely serves to hide the court's reallocation of the contractual risk away from the party who would otherwise bear the loss. Implied terms often *temper one-sided standard form contracts* by adding to the burdens or reducing the benefits of one party. Terms implied by the courts as a matter of law rest on the court's view of the *fair and practical allocation of risks* in particular types of contract. This draws from the same well as duties of care in the tort of negligence and allows courts 'to equalise the obligations of the parties, even in the teeth of express terms of standard form contracts, and so pursue ideas of fairness' (Collins at 246). Lord Steyn saw scope for further development of implication by law and said 'it is tolerably clear that the court may take into account considerations of reasonableness... this function of the court is essential in providing a reasonable and fair framework for contracting' ('Contract Law: Fulfilling the Reasonable Expectations of Honest Men' (1997) 113 *LQR* 433).

THIS CHAPTER IN ESSENCE

The key areas and core topics in this chapter are summarised in an easy-to-use list, ideal for revision purposes, on the online resources at www.oup.com/uk/chenwishart6e/. Links to websites relevant to the topics covered and any updates to the chapter can also be found on the online resources.

QUESTIONS

1 To what extent has the law responded to the problems raised by standard form contracts?

2 'The law on implied terms is very difficult to state; the test for implication is unclear and the categories shade into each other.' Discuss.

3 Adam's advertisement for his airport car hire service states that 'You'll be off in minutes'. Consider the following situations:

(a) Bella is late for a business meeting and she quickly signs Adam's standard form without reading it after Adam tells Bella 'It's all standard stuff.' The car breaks down almost immediately. Bella incurs £150 to get to her meeting. Adam claims £250 for the hire period and £200 for his costs in towing the car back to Adam's premises, as stipulated in the contract. Advise Bella.

(b) As Don is about to drive off, Adam rushes up and hands him the standard form contract but he forgets to ask Don to sign. The brakes in the car fail, causing Don to crash; Don's valuable painting is damaged but Adam states that he has excluded all liability in the contract. Advise Don.

(c) Erik is a regular business customer. On this occasion, he is not asked to sign Adam's newly revised standard form contract. He returns the car five minutes late. He is told that, as per the contract, he is now liable to a £300 surcharge for late return. Advise Erik.

4 'Rule one is that the task of the judge when interpreting a written contract is to find the intention of the parties.' Discuss the principles which guide the judge in interpreting contract terms, including exemptions of liability.

5 What evidence is, and what evidence should be, admissible when courts interpret contractual documents?

 For hints on how to answer these questions, please see the online resources at www.oup.com/uk/chenwishart6e/

KEY FURTHER READING

Buxton, R (2010), 'Construction' and Rectification after *Chartbrook*', 69 *CLJ* 253.

Clarke, P (1976), 'Notice of Contractual Terms', 35 *CLJ* 51.

Collins, H (2014), 'Implied Terms: The Foundation in Good Faith and Fair Dealing', 27 *CLP* 1.

Gee, S (2001), 'Constructing Contracts with Mistakes in Them', *LMCLQ* 214.

Gee, S (2001), 'The Interpretation of Commercial Contracts', 117 *LQR* 358.

Kramer, K (2003), 'Common Sense Principles of Contract Interpretation (and how we've been using them all along)', 23 *OJLS* 173.

Leggatt, G (2015), 'Making Sense of Contracts: the Rational Choice Theory' 131 *LQR* 454.

McCaughran, J (2011), 'Implied Terms: The Journey of the Man on the Clapham Omnibus', 70 *CLJ* 607.

Macdonald, E (1988), 'The Duty to Give Notice of Unusual Contract Terms', *JBL* 375.

McLaughlin, D (2016), 'A Better Way of Making Sense of Contracts?' 132 *LQR* 577.

McMeel, G (1998), 'The Rise of Commercial Construction in Contract Law', *LMCLQ* 382.

McMeel, G (2003), 'Prior Negotiations and Subsequent Conduct—The Next Step Forward for Contractual Interpretation', 119 *LQR* 272.

Lord Nicholls (2005), 'My Kingdom for a Horse: The Meaning of Words', 121 *LQR* 577.

Peden, E (2001), 'Policy Concerns Behind Implications of Terms in Law', 117 *LQR* 459.

Spencer, J (1973), 'Signature, Consent, and the Rule in *L'Estrange v Graucob*', 104 *CLJ* 104.

Staughton, C (1999), 'How Do the Courts Interpret Commercial Contracts?', 58 *CLJ* 303.

11

Direct control over terms

'Can the law refuse to enforce an agreed term?'

11.1 **Introduction**

In Chapter 10, we examined how contractual terms are identified and interpreted. In doing so, courts can exercise some *indirect* control over the contents of contracts. This chapter examines the *direct* controls over the contents of contracts, with particular emphasis on the Unfair Contract Terms Act 1977 (UCTA) and the Consumer Rights Act 2015 (CRA). Put most broadly:

- UCTA controls exemption clauses (excluding or limiting liability for breach) in favour of **businesses** by, in specified circumstances:
  - voiding some outright; and
  - subjecting others to a test of reasonableness.
- *CRA* only operates in favour of *consumers* by, in specified circumstances:
  - *voiding* certain exemptions of liability outright; and
  - subjecting all other *non-core terms* (terms not relating to the main subject matter or adequacy of price) to a test of *fairness*.

11.1.1 **Procedural or substantive unfairness?**

Logically, before we even get to the question of the validity of the challenged term, it must already be determined that the contested statement:

(i)   is a term of the contract (5.1.1, 10.2, 10.3, 10.6);

(ii) is incorporated (10.3.3); and

(iii) covers the events in question on its proper interpretation (10.4).

An unfair term can be knocked out by (i) and (ii) or neutralised by (iii). The availability of the direct statutory controls discussed in this chapter has reduced the need to manipulate these prior steps in order to avoid unfairness, but they are not redundant. If a term is not incorporated or not wide enough to cover the events in question, it does not apply, irrespective of its reasonableness or fairness. These prior questions appear to focus on procedural concerns, ie on flaws in the way the contract was made, or on ascertaining and giving effect to the presumed intention of the parties. Substantive unfairness is said to function merely as evidence of procedural unfairness. However, the effect of substantive unfairness can be decisive (recall the 'red hand' rule (10.3.3.2): the more onerous or unusual the term, the more notice is required to bind the other party to it).

It is also possible to explain the statutory intervention contained in UCTA and CRA in procedural terms. The ostensible concerns with 'inequality of bargaining power' leading to 'unfair surprise' (unusual or onerous terms in fine print) and 'lack of negotiability' ('take-it-or-leave-it') can explain the special vigilance shown by the law over standard or non-negotiated terms, especially in consumer contracts. This is reinforced by *economic efficiency* arguments (1.4.3):[1] namely that the incomprehensibility of standard form contracts can leave customers simply shopping for the lowest price, resulting in 'low-cost, harsh terms' contracts. This is inefficient because some customers would prefer 'higher-cost, better terms' contracts. Thus, the statutory controls *correct market imperfections* and encourage businesses to *offer more choice* and so *enhance freedom of contract*.

 Counterpoint

UCTA and CRA reveal a direct concern with substantive unfairness, albeit shrouded in the language of protecting the parties' 'reasonable expectations'[2] and 'legitimate interests'[3] or by general references to fair dealing. Any power to invalidate particular terms (or to imply others) *alters the balance* of the parties' rights and obligations expressly agreed:

- To strike out an exemption clause makes compulsory obligations that would otherwise have been excluded.

- To strike out an unfair term relieves a party from observing or being liable for it.

The law seeks to balance its concern to *avoid unfairness* (both procedural and substantive) with the competing demands of *certainty* and *respect for the parties' intentions*. Where the balance is struck bears directly on the relevance and workability of the main distinctions made in this area, namely, between:

- business-to-business (B2B) contracts and business-to-consumer (B2C) contracts;

- negotiated contracts and standard form contracts; and

- exemption of liability clauses and other clauses.

---

[1] V P Goldberg, 'Institutional Change and the Quasi-invisible Hand' (1974) 17 *J Law & Economics* 461, 483–4.

[2] J Steyn, 'Contract Law: Fulfilling the Reasonable Expectations of Honest Men' (1997) 113 *LQR* 433.

[3] Council Directive (EC) 13/1993 on unfair terms in consumer contracts [2003] OJ L95/29 [16].

11.2 **The patterns of control**

UCTA and CRA differ in their history, conception, and structure, but deal with similar concerns:

UCTA is national in origin; it evolved from piecemeal legislative control of particular exemption clauses and a Law Commission report.[4] Its name (the Unfair Contract Terms Act) is misleading since it confers *no general power* to regulate unfair contractual terms:

- It applies to many B2B contracts, particularly standard form ones (its former protection of consumers and those 'dealing as a consumer' is now transferred to the CRA).

- It only deals with exemption clauses and related clauses:

  (i)   by making some of these absolutely invalid; and

  (ii) subjecting others to a test of reasonableness.

CRA is mixed in origin. The EU Directive on Unfair Terms in Consumer Contracts[5] was originally implemented[6] in the UK by the Unfair Terms in Consumer Contracts Regulations (UTCCR) 1994 and then by UTCCR 1999. These largely copied out the Directive without attempting to dovetail it with UCTA. This resulted in a regime with two overlapping pieces of legislation (UCTA and UTCCR) that differed in their scope, in the concepts, definitions, and terminology employed and in the way they operated. This 'nightmarish complexity'[7] was replaced by the CRA, which creates a dedicated regime to review consumer contracts by:

- invalidating outright clauses that exempt liability for breach of terms stipulated 'as included' in consumer contracts;

- imposing a requirement of transparency; and

- imposing a test of unfairness for all non-'core' terms in consumer contracts and consumer notices, and 'core' terms that are not transparent and prominent (most of this replicating UTCCR).

In contrast to UCTA, under which only the party seeking to invalidate the term can sue, CRA also empowers the Competition and Markets Authority (CMA) and other 'regulators' to seek an injunction to prevent the future use of unfair terms.

Diagram 11A summarises the main differences between UCTA and CRA.

Diagram 11B gives a more detailed overview of the patterns of control. It provides a *map* for the rest of the chapter and should be a helpful tool for *revision*. In determining whether and how UCTA and CRA apply to any particular situation, the **first column of Diagram 11B** sets out the key questions, namely:

A.   Against whom is the statutory control exercised?

B.   In favour of whom?

C.   What type of terms are controlled?

---

[4] Law Commissions (joint report), 'Exemption Clauses: Second Report' (Law Com No 69, Scot Law Com No 39, (1975)) (hereafter 'Report 69').

[5] Council Directive (EC) 13/1993 of 5 April 1993 on unfair terms in consumer contracts.

[6] Under the European Communities Act 1972, s 2(2).

[7] F M B Reynolds, 'Unfair Contract Terms' (1994) 110 *LQR* 1.

Diagram 11A Summary of the main *differences* between UCTA and CRA

	UCTA	CRA
1. Type of dealing	B2B contracts.	B2C contracts.
2. Consumers covered?	No.	Yes.
3. Standard form or negotiated	Some only applies to standard terms, others apply to both.	Applies to all.
4. Types of terms affected	Only to exemption clauses, but scope of this expanded.	Any term other than 'core' terms.
5. 'Blacklist'/ 'grey list'	Small 'blacklist' of terms which are absolutely invalid.	Larger 'blacklist' and very large 'grey list' of terms which may be regarded as unfair.
6. Review mechanism	Absolute invalidity, or 'reasonableness' test.	Absolute invalidity, or 'fairness' test.
7. Guidelines	Guidelines for applying the reasonableness test.	Few guidelines for judging fairness.
8. Burden of proof	On the party seeking to rely on the challenged term to show its reasonableness.	'neutral' assessment by Court.
9. Duty of Court to consider	No duty to consider reasonablenes.	Duty to consider fairness even if not raised by the parties.
10. Enforcement mechanism and effect	Enforced by the party seeking to escape the challenged term; the outcome only affects the immediate parties.	Enforcement by the party seeking to escape the challenged term *or* by 'regulator' to prevent the future use of unfair terms.

D. What is the control mechanism?

E. Who can challenge the term?

We will take each row in turn and conclude with an overview of the illegality doctrine and other statutory and direct common law controls over the substance or contents of contracts.

11.3 **The parties affected and excluded contracts**

11.3.1 **Against whom?**

11.3.1.1 'Business liability' under UCTA

In general, the 'active' sections which subject particular terms to review (sections 2–7) only apply to *business liability*, leaving private sales outside the control of UCTA

Diagram 11B Overview of UCTA and CRA: the patterns of control

	UCTA			CRA	
A. Against whom?	'Business liability' s 1(3)			'Trader' s 2(2)	
B. In favour of?	Non-consumer			'Consumer' s 2(3)	
C. Reviewable Terms:	1. Exemptions of liability for negligence (s 2 UCTA)	2. Exemptions of liability for breach of specific statutory implied terms in sale and supply contracts (ss 6,7 UCTA)	3. Exemptions of liability for breach of any other contract term (s 3 UCTA)	4. Exemptions of liability for breach of terms 'treated as included' in contracts for goods, services, and digital content (Part 1 CRA)	5. Any 'non-core' term; 'core' term only reviewable if not transparent and prominent (Part 2 CRA)
D. Control mechanism	Invalid *outright* or only valid if *reasonable*		Valid if *reasonable*	Invalid *outright*	- Any ambiguity subject to adverse construction - Invalid if *unfair*. NB: Schedule 2 list of indicatively unfair terms.
E. Enforcement by:	Contract party			Contract party or 'regulator'	

(see row B, **Diagram 11B**). Section 1(3) provides that UCTA can only operate against a party incurring liability from:

- conduct in the course of a business, or
- the occupation of premises used for business purposes (this relates to 'occupier's liability', generally covered in the tort law syllabus).
  - ✗ The occupier is *not* liable if the other party suffered loss whilst using the premises for '*recreational or educational*' *purposes*,
    - *unless* it is within the occupier's business purposes to provide access for recreational or educational purposes.

  This excludes landowners who allow ramblers across their land, but not the 'for-profit' leisure centre.

- 'Business' also includes (i) a profession and (ii) the activities of any government department or local or public authority (s 14). Thus, the local council operating a school or a leisure centre comes under UCTA's control, although not operating for profit.

11.3.1.2 'Traders' under CRA

CRA applies to 'an agreement between a trader and a consumer for the trader to supply goods, digital content or services, if the agreement is a contract' (s 1(1)). Section 2(2) defines 'trader' as:

> a person acting for purposes relating to that person's trade, business, craft or profession, whether acting personally or through another person acting in the trader's name or on the trader's behalf.

This definition reflects EU directives; the European Court of Justice has adopted a broad interpretation of 'trader'. Thus, it is unnecessary that the consumer contract forms an integral part of the trader's business or is concluded with any degree of regularity by the trader. The definition is wide enough to include not-for-profit organisations, such as charities, mutuals, and cooperatives, where they carry on a business.

Section 2(7) states that '"Business" includes the activities of any government department or local or public authority.' There is no need for the trader to act for profit. In *R (Khatun and others) v Newham LBC* (2005) (pre-CRA), the Court of Appeal held that UTCCR applied to contracts made by local authorities pursuant to their statutory duty to house homeless persons (by offering leased accommodation in the private sector). The local authority was a 'seller or supplier' within regulation 3 and homeless persons were 'consumers'.

11.3.2 **In favour of whom?**

11.3.2.1 Non-consumers under UCTA

The active sections of UCTA are sections 2–3, 6–7 (regulating exemptions of liability for: negligence, breach of particular statutory implied terms in contracts for goods or services, and breach of contract where the business deals on 'the other's written standard terms of business'). All explicitly state that they do *not* apply to terms in consumer contracts or to consumer notices (covered by CRA). The rationale is that there is a limit to the advantages that can be extracted by superior bargaining power even in the commercial arena.

11.3.2.2 Consumers under CRA

The old UCTA operated in favour of a claimant *'dealing as a consumer'* even where it was not a natural person (ie was a company), if the contract related to goods *ordinarily supplied for private use or consumption* and only incidental to and outside of the claimant's regular business activity; eg a freight forwarding company buying a car for its director's personal and business use (*R & B Customs Brokers Co Ltd v United Dominions Trust Ltd* (1988)). CRA has deleted the concept of 'dealing as a consumer'. This narrows the scope of protection. Consumers can now only look to CRA.

Under CRA, a 'consumer' is defined as an 'individual acting for purposes that are wholly or *mainly* outside that individual's trade, business, craft or profession' (emphasis added, s 2(3)). The emphasised part was added in response to a concern that many consumers occasionally use products such as mobile phones or home computers for work purposes. It is for the trader who claims that an individual is *not* a 'consumer' to prove it (s 2(4)).

11.3.3 Excluded contracts

Schedule 1 of UCTA excludes the following types of contract from its control, although these contracts are themselves subject to significant controls:

✗ contracts of insurance;

✗ contracts creating, transferring, or terminating interests in land;

✗ contracts creating or transferring securities or any right or interest in securities;

✗ in employment contracts, section 2 of UCTA (referring to the exemptions of negligence liability) does not apply in favour of employers;

✗ contracts relating to intellectual property rights (patents, trade marks, copyright, and designs);

✗ the formation or dissolution of a company or its constitution; and

✗ charterparties and carriage of goods by sea.

Also excluded are terms authorised or required by statute or international conventions.

CRA applies to *all consumer contracts* and *notices*, including contracts of insurance, supply of financial services, sale of land, contracts with builders or land developers, consumer mortgages, and leases between business landlords and consumer tenants. **Excluded** from review are:

✗ Terms that reflect 'mandatory statutory provisions' under the law of any EU Member State, or in EU legislation having effect in the UK without further enactment (s 73). This is particularly important in the provision of public services where many terms are set by legislation.

✗ Terms that reflect 'the provisions or principles of international conventions to which the Member States or the EU are party' (s 73). This excludes terms aimed at complying with conventions in the transport area, notably the Warsaw Convention on International Carriage by Air (1929).

✗ Contracts of employment or apprenticeship (s 61(1)).

11.4 **Types of terms controlled and control mechanisms: overview**

Terms that are controlled under UCTA and CRA are shown in **Diagram 11B** row C. **Diagram 11C** provides another representation, with the shaded part being terms subject to statutory control:

• The **left side = B2C contracts** (ie one party deals as a consumer whilst the other acts in the course of business). Here, *all* 'non-core' terms are subject to control whether negotiated or not. **1*** denotes that even 'core' terms are reviewable if they are not transparent and prominent.

Diagram 11C Terms controlled under UCTA and CRA

- The **right side = B2B** (both parties act in the course of business). Here, the terms subject to control are exemptions of liability for: (a) negligence, (b) certain statutory implied terms, and (c) breach of contract where the term is on written standard form. The **broken lines** signify the uncertain scope of reviewable terms in the relevant category due to extensions of the definition of 'exemption clauses' (11.5.4).

11.5 Types of terms controlled by UCTA and control mechanisms

11.5.1 Exemptions of liability for negligence under UCTA

Where contractual terms or non-contractual notices exempt business liability for *negligence* against other businesses:

- section 2(1) makes an exemption for business liability in respect of **personal injury or death** absolutely invalid;[8] the term is blacklisted, and the negligent party is liable as if the term did not exist; and

---

[8] With certain exceptions, eg contracts for insurance or transfers of interests in land.

- section 2(2) subjects to a test of reasonableness any exemption for business liability in respect of other loss or damage (other than personal injury or death).

Other provisions and cases refine the *scope* of the jurisdiction to control exemptions for negligence:

- UCTA's operation extends to notices exempting negligence liability even absent any contract between the parties (s 1(1)), although not to notices exempting occupiers' liability to *trespassers*.

- UCTA's control cannot be evaded by a business appealing to the defence of *volenti non fit injuria* (ie that the other party voluntarily consented to the risk of injury or loss), simply because the other party agreed to the term or was aware of the notice (s 2(3)).

- Only terms which 'exclude or restrict' negligence liability to the *victim of the negligence* are reviewable; terms that merely *transfer* liability to a business claimant fall outside section 2 (11.5.4.3).

11.5.2 **Exemptions of specific statutory implied terms under UCTA**

Section 6 controls exemptions of liability for breach of statutory implied terms in sale of goods and hire purchase contracts.

Section 7 controls exemptions of liability for breach of statutory implied terms in other contracts under which the possession or ownership of goods passes, eg hire, barter, or contracts for works and materials such as building contracts.

In respect of these, exemptions of liability:

- for breach of implied terms as to **title** to the goods are totally invalid (ss 6(1), 7(3A));

- for breach of implied terms relating to the **conformity of the goods** with the description or sample, satisfactory quality and fitness for purpose are only valid if they are reasonable (ss 6(3), 7(3)); and

- in respect of contracts passing **ownership or possession of goods** are only valid if they are reasonable (s 7(4)).

11.5.3 **Exemptions of liability in contract under UCTA**

Section 3 of UCTA imposes more general control over exemptions of *contractual* liability where a business party deals on the other's **written standard terms** of business. It applies to *any* contract (unless exempted by Schedule 1), and to any exemption clauses *not* caught by sections 2 (negligence) and 6–7 (specific statutory implied terms). This covers a very significant number of B2B contracts made by reference to signed or unsigned standard terms printed in order forms, confirmations, catalogues, or price lists.

(i) Here, UCTA does not apply to contracts that are oral or partly written and partly oral.

(ii) It is for the claimant to prove that the challenged exemption clause is part of the defendant's standard terms of business, although the terms could be negotiated (ie not standard terms) even if the exemption clause itself was not negotiated (*African Export-Import Bank, Diamond Bank Plc, Skye Bank Plc v Shebah Exploration & Product ion Co Ltd, Allenne Ltd, Ambrose Bryant Chukwueloka Orjiako* (2017)).

(iii) Whether written terms are standard is a matter of 'fact and degree'. Stannard J observes that it would 'emasculate' UCTA if it could be evaded simply because it could be shown that the term was occasionally varied or not used. He said (in *Chester Grosvenor Hotel Co Ltd v Alfred McAlpine Management Ltd* (1991), and see the *African Export-Import Bank* case (2017)) that the terms:

> should be so regarded by the party which advances them... [who] should habitually contract in those terms. If it contracts also on other terms, it must be determined... whether this has occurred so frequently that the terms in question cannot be regarded as standard, and if on any occasion a party has substantially modified its prepared terms, it is a question of fact whether those terms have been so altered that they must be regarded as not having been employed on that occasion.

In *St Albans City & DC v International Computers Ltd* (1996), the Court of Appeal held that a party still 'deals on the other's standard terms' if ostensible negotiations result in *no alteration* to those terms. Nourse LJ said: '"deals" means "make a deal", irrespective of any negotiations that may have preceded it'. Parties cannot evade control by going through sham negotiations or regularly changing their standard forms in minor ways.

(iv) Where the parties deal on model contracts drafted by a trade or professional association, it is a matter of evidence whether 'the Model Form is invariably or at least usually used by the party in question. It must be shown that either by practice or by express statement a contracting party has adopted a Model Form as his standard terms of business' (*British Fermentation Products Ltd v Compair Reavell* (1999)).

Section 3(2)(a) prevents a party from enforcing a term which exempts its business liability for breach of contract unless it satisfies the requirement of reasonableness.

11.5.4 The jurisdictional question: what counts as reviewable 'exemption clauses' under UCTA?

11.5.4.1 Defensive or duty-defining?

- The terminology in UCTA assumes that the function of exemption clauses is defensive; they only come into effect *after* liability for breach of the primary obligations is established and operate to exclude or limit the contract-breaker's liability for breach.
- The rival view is that exemption clauses are **duty-defining**; they cut back the *extent* of the primary obligations owed in the first place so that no breach may arise.

Diagram 11D The function of exemption clauses: defensive or duty-defining?

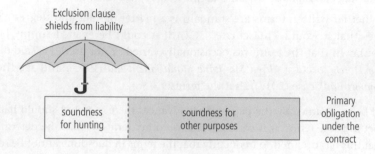

(1) Defensive: this is assumed by UCTA. Eg 'Horse promised to be sound *but exclusion of liability for unsoundness in hunting'*

Exclusion clause
shields from liability

| soundness for hunting | soundness for other purposes | Primary obligation under the contract |

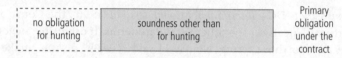

(2) Duty defining: Coote's preferred approach. Eg 'Horse promised to be sound *except for hunting'*

| no obligation for hunting | soundness other than for hunting | Primary obligation under the contract |

Both approaches can produce the same outcome. **Diagram 11D** illustrates the example given by **Coote** in *Exception Clauses* (Sweet & Maxwell, 1964) 9.

In a contract to sell a horse promised to be 'sound', a term:

(1) appears defensive if it stipulates that 'the seller shall not be liable if the horse is not sound for hunting'; and

(2) appears duty-defining if the seller promises that it is 'sound, except for hunting'.

In (1), the seller who does not provide a horse which is sound for hunting is in breach of her contract to provide such a horse, but her liability is excluded in the contract. In (2), the seller never contracts to provide a horse sound for hunting in the first place, so there can be no breach of contract if the horse is not sound for hunting.

In short, excluding liability for X amounts to the same thing as not having an obligation to do X at all.

Coote supports the duty-defining view. He says:

the true juristic function and effect of exception clauses are quite different from those currently ascribed to them by the courts. Instead of being mere shields to claims based on breach of accrued rights, exception clauses substantively delimit the rights themselves. . . It may seem feasible that the parties should have intended a contractual duty to remain when they excluded liability for its breach, but this is in reality a juristic impossibility. A duty of sorts there may be, but it will be a duty of honour, not a contractual one. It would follow, then, that the current approach to exception clauses is based on a fallacy.

> **Pause for reflection**
>
> Presenting UCTA as only applying to terms 'excluding or restricting' specified types of liability (and not duty-defining terms) allows the law to preserve the appearance of upholding freedom of contract, intervening only in exceptional and clearly prescribed circumstances as an aspect of the court's legitimate authority to determine the appropriate *remedies for breach*. To openly acknowledge that exemption clauses are merely 'disguised duty-defining clauses' would directly challenge the oft-stated position that the law does not control the substantive fairness of contracts.

The fact remains that exemptions of liability and duty-defining terms may be functionally indistinguishable and the former may be redrafted into the latter. Thus, UCTA counters attempts to evade its control by **expanding the definition of what counts as 'exemption clauses'**.

In **Diagram 11E**:

(1) The three shaded boxes in the centre represent the exemption clauses *expressly* controlled by UCTA (those for negligence, breach of statutory implied terms, and breach of contract). These are extended in three ways.

(2) All three exemptions are extended to include terms that make claims more difficult to prove (11.5.4.2).

Diagram 11E Expanding the definition of 'exemption clause'

ok on
online
ources
iew this
ire as a
erPoint®
entation

(3) Exemptions of liability for negligence and breach of statutory implied terms are extended to include duty-defining clauses (11.5.4.3).

(4) Exemptions of liability for breach of contract are extended to include certain duty-defining clauses by section 3(2)(b) (11.5.4.4).

11.5.4.2 Terms that make claims more difficult to prove

Section 13(1) UCTA brings within the definition of exemption clauses, terms which make it more difficult for the claimant to prove her case by:

(a) making the liability or its enforcement subject to restrictive or onerous conditions (eg requiring claims to be made within a short timeframe or in a specified form);

(b) excluding or restricting any right or remedy (eg the right to rescind or terminate the contract), or subjecting the claimant to prejudicial consequence, if she claims any right or remedy (eg withholding payment to her); and

(c) excluding or restricting general rules of evidence or procedure (eg reversing the burden of proof or stating that a customer's signature is conclusive proof that no breach has occurred).

11.5.4.3 Expanding exemptions for negligence and breach of statutory implied terms subject to sections 2, 6–7

The last two lines of **section 13(1) UCTA** state that: '... sections 2, 6 and 7 also prevent excluding or restricting liability by reference to terms and notices which exclude or restrict the relevant obligation or duty'. This recognises that any exemption clause (limiting *liability* for breach) can be drafted in duty-defining terms (limiting the *obligation* owed to reduce the possibility of breach in the first place), and it extends UCTA's control to the latter. In *Johnstone v Bloomsbury Health Authority* (1992), J (a junior doctor employed by B) was expressly required to work for 40 hours a week and be 'on call' for up to 48 more hours. The court held this term to be a clause falling within the final part of section 13(1) (and so an exemption clause) and invalid under section 2(1).

The jurisdictional problem at the heart of UCTA comes to the fore when deciding whether certain indemnities are *really exemptions* of negligence liability (by virtue of section 13(1)) and so subject to section 2. The short answer is that:

✔ it is an exemption clause and subject to section 2 if the term shifts liability to the *victim* of negligence,

✗ it is not an exemption clause, and so not subject to section 2, if it merely shifts liability to *someone other than the victim* of negligence.

The former is illustrated by *Phillips Products v Hyland* (1987). P hired a JCB excavator and driver from H, but condition 8 of the contract made the driver *P's employee* and made P responsible for all claims arising from the driver's operation of the excavator. The driver negligently crashed the excavator into P's factory wall and P claimed damages. H relied on condition 8 and argued that it was outside the control of section 2(2) of UCTA because it did not exempt liability for breach of duty. It merely restricted H's duty (by shifting it to P) so that H committed no breach (ie negligence) in the first place. The Court of Appeal rejected this argument by reference to section 13(1) and the 'but for' test. Slade LJ said that, in considering whether there was negligence liability, the court must *ignore* the clause being relied on to defeat the negligence claim (ie would H be liable 'but for' the challenged term?). This liability cannot be transferred to P (the injured party) if it effectively excludes liability to P.

In contrast, in *Thompson v Lohan (Plant Hire)* (1987), an identical clause shielded the defendant from his negligence liability because it was held to be outside the scope of section 13(1) and so *outside* the control of section 2. The facts were identical to *Phillips Products*, except that the driver's negligence caused loss to a third party (it killed Mr Thompson). The hirer had paid compensation to Thompson's widow and then sought to recover that payment from Lohan which had hired out the JCB excavator and the driver. The court said that the question is not whether the *party relying on the clause* was seeking to exempt liability (this was plainly so in both the *Phillips Products* and the *Thompson* cases), but whether the exemption excluded liability against the *victim* of the negligence ('yes' in *Phillips Products*, but 'no' in *Thompson*). Section 2 only controls clauses which exclude liability to the *victims* of negligence by transferring liability to them. It does not apply to terms that transfer liability to someone other than the victim of negligence. Thus, the clause was valid and not subject to section 2.

The contrast between *Phillips Products v Hyland* and *Thompson v Lohan (Plant Hire)* is summarised in **Diagram 11F**.

Diagram 11F Contrasting *Phillips* and *Thompson*

		C = claimant D = defendant
	Phillips	**Thompson**
Contract	D hires excavator and driver to C	
Term	C is responsible for all claims arising in connection with the driver's operation of the excavator	
Victim	C	Another party already compensated by C
Does s 13(1) bring term under control of s 2?	✓ Clause seeks to exclude D's liability to the victim (C) for negligence; D *cannot* transfer liability to C unless reasonable	✗ Since clause does not seek to exclude D's liability to the victim for negligence, s 2 is inapplicable, hence applicability of s 13(1) does not even arise; D can transfer liability to C even if unreasonable.

Pause for reflection

These cases can be criticised:

1. From the point of view of the *businesses* using the clause, the outcomes are inconsistent.

2. The result in *Thompson* requires *implying words into section 13(1)* so that it only covers attempts to exempt negligence liability 'to the victims of negligence'.

On the other hand, the very point of section 13(1) is that UCTA's control should rest on the substance (or effect) of a term, and not just its form.

Unless all duty-defining terms are thereby brought under UCTA's control, a **distinction must be made between reviewable and unreviewable duty-defining clauses**. There is no obvious way to draw the line, eg, are the following *really* exemptions of liability dressed up as duty-defining clauses?

- A clause stating that the kitchen utensils sold are unsuitable for non-stick pans?
- A clause stating that a survey only relates to valuation and not structural soundness?
- A clause denying or restricting the authority of an agent to give undertakings?
- A clause entitling one party to terminate the contract in certain circumstances?

A **'but for' test** is supported by *Smith v Eric Bush* (1989) and *Phillips Products v Hyland* (1987). Accordingly, the question is: would liability arise 'but for' the challenged term? This was qualified by Newey J in *Avrora Fine Arts Investment Ltd v Christie, Manson & Woods Ltd* (2012); the question is: does the challenged term attempt to retrospectively alter the character of what has gone before, to rewrite history or part company with reality? F purchased a painting falsely represented and warranted to be by a famous Russian artist. C's conditions of sale provided that each item is sold 'as is'; and that, subject to a limited warranty, no representation, warranty, or guarantee is given on attribution or authenticity. The court found that this term did not shield the transaction from UCTA's reasonableness requirement since it *did* part company with reality.

Counterpoint

The 'but for' test is *uncertain* and *too* wide:

1. Taken literally, the 'but for' test could swallow up virtually all duty-defining clauses, since *all* definitions of the primary duties (whether positive or negative) imply what there will *not* be liability for. The test assumes that it is possible to determine the parties' *normative* rights and obligations so that, when the challenged term purports to cut back those rights or obligations, it amounts to an 'exemption clause' and comes under UCTA's control.

➡

2. The distinction between 'main subject matter and adequacy of price' terms and other terms now in CRA (11.6.3) may be helpful. Accordingly, a consumer's attention is generally focused on the core bargain or price; other terms will rarely figure. Thus, only non-core terms fall under CRA's prohibition of unfairness because they are unlikely to have come to the consumer's notice and unlikely to have been meaningfully consented to. The same idea could guide our answer to the scope of UCTA, so that only core terms (relating to the price or main subject matter of the contract) fall outside its control.

11.5.4.4 Exemptions for breach of contract

Section 3(2)(a) invalidates unreasonable exclusions or restrictions of liability for breach of contract. This too can be evaded by repackaging exemptions for breach of contract as duty-defining terms. This is countered by **section 3(2)(b)**, which extends the reasonableness requirement to terms purporting to reserve to one party the discretion to give no, only partial, or substantially different performance from that reasonably expected by the other party. If such a term is set aside as unreasonable under section 3(2)(a), then a party's non-, partial, or substantially different performance is not a lawful exercise of discretionary power conferred by the contract, but a breach of contract, eg a holiday contract which allows the provider to substantially vary the accommodation or destination of the holiday, or to cancel the holiday in whole or in part.[9]

As with section 13, section 3(2)(b) assumes that there is a *normative* standard of reasonable expectations which is ascertainable, independent of the *expectations* defined in the contractual document itself.

 Pause for reflection

1. There is a problem of circularity. It is arguable that the parties' expectations are only 'reasonable' if they are contained *in* the contractual document. To the extent that the two differ, why should the claimant's expectations ever take precedence over what the contract says? Why should the law ignore the challenged clause in determining the claimant's reasonable expectations? Why should only the burdensome terms be ignored when all the terms (whether burdensome or advantageous) make up the whole contract?

2. Section 3(2)(b)(ii) refers to non-performance of part or the whole of a party's *contractual* obligation. This makes sense if that party's discretion to perform is *partial*. However, if his discretion is *total* (ie it is entirely up to that party whether to perform), there is effectively no contractual *obligation* to perform at all; there is arguably no contract since that party's consideration is illusory.

3. Again, the distinction between reviewable main subject matter and adequacy of price terms and other terms now in CRA (11.6.3) can guide our answer to the scope of s 3(2)(b) UCTA.

---

[9] *Anglo-Continental Holidays v Typaldos* (London) Ltd (1967) and see Package Travel, Package Holidays and Package Tours Regulations 1992 (SI 1992/3288): regulation 12 requires the organisers to allow consumers to withdraw from the contract if an essential term is altered significantly.

Timeload Ltd v British Telecommunications plc (1995) illustrates the potential width of section 3(2)(b). BT's contract to supply services gave BT the right 'at any time' to terminate on one month's notice. T argued that the clause was an exemption clause under section 3(2)(b); BT answered that T could not expect that which the contract never offered (ie enjoyment of services for an indefinite period). Sir Thomas Bingham MR disagreed. Given that BT was a public telecommunications operator:

> If a customer reasonably expects a service to continue until BT has substantial reason to terminate it, it seems to me at least arguable that a clause purporting to authorise BT to terminate it without reason purports to permit partial or different performance from that which the customer expected.

 Pause for reflection

1. The outcome in *Timeload* is questionable since the right to terminate was mutual. Moreover, it is unclear that there was a 'substantial' deviation from what is reasonably expected (as required by s 3(2)(b)(i)). On the other hand, as a quasi-monopoly at that time, BT needed customers less than customers needed BT's services.

2. Section 3(2)(b) reinforces Coote's argument that promising much, but then disclaiming liability for not keeping the promise, is the same as promising very little to begin with. This explains why UCTA *must deem* certain duty-defining terms as *statutory* exclusion clauses.

3. The *substance* of UCTA's control rests on the assumption that a certain *minimum duty* should be owed by reference to the nature and circumstances of the transaction, quite independent of the specific terms ostensibly agreed. In this sense, the reasoning is analogous to terms implied by law (10.6.2). UCTA maintains this minimal duty by invalidating terms that purport to allow a significant deviation from it.

4. The major difficulty is jurisdictional. It arises from the fallacy that UCTA can achieve its aims by confining control to what are *in essence* exemption clauses and that these are distinguishable from duty-defining clauses. Analogous difficulties arise in distinguishing between 'main subject matter and adequacy of price terms' and other terms under CRA (11.6.3) and between penalty and liquidated damages clauses under the penalty rule (14.3.2).

11.5.5 **Control mechanisms under UCTA**

11.5.5.1 Outright invalidity

We have seen that UCTA contains a '**blacklist**' of terms that are invalid outright. Namely, terms that attempt to exclude or restrict:

(i) business liability for death or personal injury caused by *negligence* (s 2(1)); and

(ii) business liability for breach of *implied terms as to title* in contracts for sale, hire purchase, or other transfers of property in goods (ss 6(1), 7(3A)).

All other terms caught by UCTA are subject to the requirement of *reasonableness*.

11.5.5.2 Review for reasonableness

Section 11 UCTA states that: 'the term shall have been a fair and reasonable one to be included having regard to the circumstances which were or ought reasonably to have been, known to or in the contemplation of the parties when the contract was made.'

(i) The time of assessment

The test should be assessed 'when the contract was made'. Facts arising subsequently, such as the seriousness of the loss or damage actually sustained, are irrelevant, except insofar as they were foreseeable at formation. Further, circumstances known only to the party seeking to allege that the term is reasonable, eg that the product supplied is experimental, are irrelevant if they are not known, and could not reasonably have been known, to the other party at the time the contract was made (*Singer Co v Tees and Hartlepool Port Authority* (1988)). The justification rests on *certainty* and *predictability*: at the time of contract formation, parties should be able to assess whether the term will survive the law's review.

(ii) The potential width of the exemption

It follows from **(i)** that the assessment of reasonableness or fairness must be made about the potential width of the term and not the actual use made of it (the former may be unreasonable or unfair even if the latter is reasonable and fair). The court has no power to rewrite the term to make it more reasonable. Thus, the *wider* the term, the more likely it is to be judged *unreasonable*. A term will be unreasonable if it is susceptible of both reasonable and unreasonable application since, at formation, it is impossible to know which use will be made of it. A court *will not sever the unreasonable part* of a term and leave the rest intact; the *whole* clause is invalidated (*Stewart Gill Ltd v Horatio Myer & Co Ltd* (1992)). Thus, in drafting such clauses, several narrow exemptions would seem preferable to a single all-embracing one so that, if unreasonableness or unfairness is found, it will not taint the entire attempt to evade liability.

(iii) The onus of proof

Most notably, UCTA puts the onus of proving reasonableness on the business seeking to rely on the term: 'it is for those claiming that a contractual term or notice satisfies the requirement of reasonableness to show that it does' (s 11(5)). This amounts to *a presumption of unreasonableness* unless the contrary is proved; this takes on 'great significance' when evidence as to the reasonableness of the term or notice is obscure or absent (*Phillips Products v Hyland*).

(iv) The reasonableness test under UCTA

The nature of the reasonableness test will be discussed by reference to:

- the statutory guidelines;
- its discretionary character; and
- illustrations of its application.

The statutory guidelines: Strictly speaking, three slightly different tests of reasonableness appear in UCTA:

- the general test (s 11(1));
- the test applicable to statutory implied terms falling within sections 6–7 (Sch 2); and
- the test applicable to terms which limit rather than exclude liability (s 11(4)).

However, the courts have made clear that all the factors mentioned in the various guidelines are applicable to *all* cases in which they appear relevant. Moreover, these factors are neither exhaustive nor determinative; the court may take into account any other relevant circumstances (*Rees Hough Ltd v Redland Reinforced Plastics Ltd* (1984); *Stewart Gill v Horatio Myer* (1992)). In practice, therefore, there is *a single test of reasonableness*. Collectively, the statutory guidelines require consideration of:

(i)   The parties' respective bargaining power, taking into account any alternative means of meeting the customer's requirements—eg, in *Air Transworld Ltd v Bombardier Inc* (2012), the court enforced the exclusion of liability where the parties were of equal bargaining power, the terms were set out in capital letters, and the terms of the warranty were specifically drawn to the purchaser's lawyer's attention.

(ii) Whether the customer received any inducement to accept the term or could have contracted with others without the exemption clause.

(iii) Whether the customer knew or ought reasonably to have known of the existence and extent of the term, having regard, amongst other things, to any custom of the trade and any previous course of dealing between the parties. In *Stag Line Ltd v Tyne Ship Repair Group Ltd (The Zinnia)* (1984), Staughton J said that he was inclined to find the exemption clause unreasonable because the print was so small as to be barely legible and 'the draughtsmanship was so convoluted and prolix that one almost need[ed] an LLB to understand them'.

(iv) The reasonableness of any conditions imposed on making claims. A term is unreasonable if a breach may not be detectable within the time allowed for making claims (eg in *RW Green v Cade Bros Farms* (1978), three days with respect to the sale of seed potatoes), or if it makes the remedying of defects subject to the customer's return of the product (eg a ship in *Stag Line* (1984)).

(v)   Whether the goods were manufactured, processed, or adapted to the customer's special order. If so, this may entail particular risks that make it reasonable for the seller to exempt liability.

(vi) The defendant's resources to meet claims. If the defendant is unable to meet claims, or if the magnitude of the claim is vast in relation to the contract price, the exemption is more likely to be reasonable. However, any limitation of the claim to a particular sum requires justification (*Salvage Association v CAP Financial Services Ltd* (1995)). This is related to the next factor.

(vii) The availability, affordability, and efficiency of insurance. The *actual* insurance position of the parties is strictly irrelevant (*Singer Co (UK) Ltd v Tees and Hartlepool Port Authority* (1988) and *The Flamar Pride* (1990)). The question is whether the exemption of liability is reasonable in view of the *potential availability* of insurance to *either* party, and of its relative *cost*. This guideline aims to protect small businesses that might have inadequate resources to meet or be unable to obtain insurance cover against potential liability. Conversely, it is more likely to be unreasonable for large companies with considerable assets to exempt liability where insurance is available and *affordable*. Thus, in *St Albans City & DC v International Computers* (1995), it was unreasonable for a multinational company with insurance cover of £50 million to limit liability to £100,000. The *efficiency* of insurance is also relevant. In *Photo Production Ltd v Securicor Ltd* (1980), the House of Lords held that the challenged clause excluding liability for a fire which destroyed P's factory would have been reasonable since the claimant would already have to insure against fire and the defendant might not have been able to obtain the appropriate insurance, in any case, not without passing its cost on to the claimant in higher charges for its security service.

The discretionary character of the reasonableness test: Although the statutory guidelines inform the courts' assessment of reasonableness, there is still a large discretionary element in the assessment since judges may differ in the *weight* they attach to particular factors. Courts must take account of a wide 'range of considerations, put them in the scales on one side or the other, and decide at the end of the day on which side the balance comes down' (*George Mitchell (Chesterhall) Ltd v Finlay Lock Seeds Ltd* (1983)). Nevertheless, the decision of a first instance judge should be treated 'with the utmost respect'; appellate courts should 'refrain from interference with it unless satisfied that it proceeded upon some erroneous principle or was plainly and obviously wrong', eg *Watford Electronics Ltd v Sanderson CFL Ltd* (2001), where the first instance judge adopted an incorrect interpretation of the exemption clause and failed to take account of relevant considerations.[10]

Illustrations of the reasonableness test: Precedents are of limited value since the precise circumstances of each case will vary (eg the relative position of the parties and the precise wording of the clause in question). Moreover, earlier cases relating to consumers or parties dealing as a consumer now fall under CRA. Nevertheless, some illustrations will show how courts weigh the factors (for an extensive list of further examples, see *Chitty*, paras 15-104 to 15-111).

✗ In *George Mitchell (Chesterhall) Ltd v Finlay Lock Seeds Ltd*, G (farmers) bought *winter* cabbage seeds from F but received *autumn* cabbage seeds that produced inferior plants and were useless for G's purposes. G sought to recover losses of £61,000 but an exemption clause limited damages to the cost of the seeds (£200). The House of Lords invalidated the clause as unreasonable. The main factors were:

(a) the availability and affordability of insurance to the seller;

(b) the seller's breach was due to its negligence; and

(c) the seller's past practice of settling claims in excess of the limit imposed if it regarded the claims as 'genuine'; this shows that even F regarded the clause as often inappropriate and unreasonable.

---

[10] E Peel, 'Reasonable Exemption Clause' (2001) 117 *LQR* 545.

Pause for reflection

In respect of factor (c), clauses that exclude or severely restrict liability allow the contract-breaker to decide whether to invoke the exemption or not, depending on its commercial interest (eg it may not invoke the exemption against profitable business customers to preserve good will and future business opportunity); this may operate unfairly against smaller customers. The exemption in *George Mitchell* was objectionable for conferring an *unreasonable remedial discretion* on the contract-breaker, raising the spectre of favouritism. This may also explain why having the power to elect is regarded as self-induced frustration, barring relief in cases of radical change of circumstances after contract formation (7.5.3).

✗ Recall *Phillips Products v Hyland*, where a term required P (the party hiring a JCB excavator and a driver from H) to indemnify H for liabilities arising from the driver's operation of the excavator. The effect of the clause was to exclude H's liability to P when the driver's negligence damaged P's buildings (11.5.4.3). The term was struck out as unreasonable under s 2(2) UCTA because:

(a) H was in the business of hiring out, while P only hired such equipment occasionally;

(b) the hire was for a very short period of time, arranged at short notice, on H's standard form and not negotiated;

(c) P had little opportunity to arrange insurance cover and would have had to make a special arrangement to insure against an employee's damage to its own property; and

(d) P had no choice over the driver and no realistic control over how he did the job.

✗ In *Motours Ltd v Euroball (West Kent) Ltd* (2003), telephone services provided by E to M (a travel agency) were partially defective. E sought to exclude liability for all consequential loss howsoever arising. Although it was a commercial bargain between businessmen, the judge found the term unreasonable because:

(a) the exclusion included that for negligence (which could not have been within M's contemplation);

(b) exclusion clauses were common in the industry so M had little choice;

(c) the term was not negotiated (the appearance and language of the contract suggests that customers were not expected or encouraged to read it); and

(d) E had much greater financial strength and bargaining power and could present its terms on a 'take-it-or-leave-it' basis; M was in no position to negotiate.

✔ In *Regus (UK) Ltd v Epcot Solutions Ltd* (2008), E hired serviced office accommodation from R. E sought substantial damages for loss of business due to the faulty air-conditioning. A standard term in the contract excluded any liability for loss of business, profits, anticipated savings, third party claims, or any consequential loss, and loss of or damage to data. The Court of Appeal found this to be *reasonable* under UCTA because:

(a)   E could still sue for the defective air-conditioning by reference to the diminution in value of the services promised.

(b)   The exclusion did not cover fraud or wilful, reckless, or malicious damage, which would be unreasonable.

(c)   R reasonably limited its liability to the higher of 125% of the fees or £50,000.

(d)   There was no inequality of bargaining power.

(e)   R advised its customers to protect themselves by insurance for business losses since this was cheaper than R obtaining liability insurance.

 Pause for reflection

1. Adams and Brownsword reviewed the operation of UCTA 10 years after it came into operation ('The Unfair Contract Terms Act: A Decade of Discretion' (1988) 104 *LQR* 94). They concluded that:

   • uncertainty has resulted from appellate courts' view that the first instance judges' determinations on the issue of reasonableness should not be disturbed;

   • there was inconsistency in the courts' attitudes towards the appropriate level of intervention in commercial contracts; Lord Wilberforce signalled a 'hands-off' approach in *Photo Production*, but this was not heeded in the *George Mitchell* case; and

   • the more interventionist approach threatened commercial certainty.

2. Macdonald (in 'Unfair Contract Terms Act—Thirty Years On' in A Burrows and E Peel (eds), *Contract Terms* (OUP, 2007), 153):

   • detects more certainty in the factors taken into account in determining the reasonableness of exemption clauses;

   • supports the continuing need for UCTA in commercial contracts;

   • but argues that courts have not made enough use of the extended definition of exemption clauses in section 3(2)(b)(i).

3. While some of the statutory guidelines relate to procedural unfairness (the *way* the contract came about, eg notice and bargaining power), courts can find a term unreasonable under UCTA *solely* because of its substantive unfairness (ie its adverse impact on the adhering party). Courts can conclude that an exemption of liability is unreasonable, even if the business has given reasonable notice of it without objection from the other party. Unreasonableness under UCTA may comprise both procedural and substantive unfairness, only procedural or only substantive unfairness, to the extent that these are separable. The same can be said of the fairness test under CRA, to which we now turn.

11.6 **Types of terms controlled by CRA and control mechanisms**

The CRA has three mechanisms of control:

(i)   Blacklisting certain exemptions of liability.

(ii) Subjecting terms that are not transparent to *contra proferentem* interpretation.

(iii) Subjecting non-'core' terms and 'core' terms that are not transparent and prominent to a test of unfairness.

11.6.1 **Blacklisting exemptions for breach of 'terms treated as included'**

Part 1 of CRA stipulates that, in consumer contracts for the supply of goods, services, or digital content, certain terms are to be 'treated as included' (eg as to title, satisfactory quality, and fitness for purpose, 10.6.2.1). Terms that attempt to exclude or restrict the trader's liability arising out of these terms are **not binding** on the consumer (ss 31, 47, and 57). Mirroring UCTA, s 31(2) and (3) of CRA expand the scope of such exemptions of liability to include terms that attempt to:

(a)   exclude or restrict a right or remedy in respect of such liability;

(b)   make such a right or remedy or its enforcement subject to a restrictive or onerous condition;

(c)   allow a trader to put a person at a disadvantage as a result of pursuing such a right or remedy;

(d)   exclude or restrict rules of evidence or procedure; or

(e)   prevent an obligation or duty arising or limit its extent.

Exemptions of liability for negligently caused personal injury or death are also blacklisted (CRA, s 65), mirroring s 2(1) of UCTA.

11.6.2 **Terms that are not transparent**

Three provisions are relevant here.

(i)   Section 68 of CRA imposes the requirement of transparency:

(1)   A trader must ensure that a written term of a consumer contract, or a consumer notice in writing, is transparent.

(2)   A consumer notice is transparent... if it is expressed in plain and intelligible language and it is legible.

In *The Office of Fair Trading v Abbey National* (2008), Andrew Smith J lays down some markers:

- Relevant considerations include the complexity and legibility of the language, the opportunity to understand it prior to contract formation, the parties' previous contractual dealings, and any non-contractual leaflets and brochures given to consumers at or before contract formation.

- The standard required is high. Absence of ambiguity is not enough, nor that the challenged term is expressed as clearly as is reasonably possible.

Even plain, intelligible language may be ambiguous (eg an unfair term that is accompanied by the familiar phrase 'your statutory rights are not affected' is 'plain and intelligible' but may mislead consumers into believing that they cannot complain). What is required is that the typical consumer should be able to understand 'the actual words used... [and] how the terms affect the parties' rights and obligations'.

In *Kásler v OTP Jelzalogbank Zrt* (2014), the European Court of Justice was even more demanding:

- The requirement is not limited to clarity and intelligibility from a purely structural and grammatical point of view.

- The court should determine whether the average consumer would not only be aware of the existence of the particular term, but also be in a position to evaluate, on the basis of clear, intelligible criteria, the economic consequences for her of the term in question.

- The reasons for the trader using the term and its relationship with other contractual terms should be clear and intelligible.

Where terms could have different meanings, 'the meaning that is most favourable to the consumer is to prevail' (s 69(1)). This duplicates the common law *contra proferentem* approach to the interpretation of ambiguous terms (10.5.3).

(ii) Terms that relate to the main subject matter or adequacy of price of the contract ('core' terms) cannot be reviewed for fairness (11.6.3), but only if they are 'transparent and prominent' (s64(2)); ie if a 'core' term is *not* transparent and prominent, it *can* be reviewed for fairness.

- A term is 'transparent' if it is expressed in plain and intelligible language, and (if written) is legible (11.5.2).

- A term is 'prominent' if it is brought to the consumer's attention in such a way that an average consumer would be aware of the term.

- 'Average consumer' means a consumer who is reasonably well-informed, observant, and circumspect. The test is objective but can vary according to context. If a business targets particularly vulnerable consumers, then the 'average consumer' standard should be appropriately lowered; but if a business targets sophisticated high-income individuals (who may be independently advised), then the standard of 'average consumer' should be appropriately raised (*Chitty*, para 38-240).

11.6.3 The jurisdictional question: what are main subject matter or adequacy of price terms?

Section 64(1) CRA states:

A term of a consumer contract may not be assessed for fairness under section 62 to the extent that:

(a) it specifies the **main subject matter** of the contract; or

(b) the assessment is of the **appropriateness of the price** payable under the contract by comparison with the goods, digital content, or services supplied under it.

And, the term is both:

- 'transparent and prominent' (s 64(2)), and
- *not* on the list of indicatively **unfair terms** in Schedule 2 Part 1 (s 64(6)).

The wider the scope of the exemption from CRA's control, the less consumer protection is afforded. The approach of the **European Court of Justice** is embodied in *Kásler v OTP Jelzalogbank Zrt* (2014) and *Matei v SC Volksbank Romania SA* (2015):

(i) The exemption from review requires an autonomous and uniform interpretation throughout the EU, taking into account its context and the purpose of the legislation.

(ii) The exemption must be strictly interpreted as it provides an exception to consumers' protection against unfairness. Terms relating to the **main subject matter** are those laying down the essential obligations of the contract and, as such, characterise it. Courts must take a broad contextual approach in their identification. Once identified, these terms are not reviewable for unfairness *at all*.

(iii) Terms relating to the **adequacy of the price** are more limited in scope:

    ✗ They *do not cover* terms that stipulate the consideration from the consumer; or have an impact on the *actual* price to be paid by the consumer,

    ✔ *except* where they go to whether the amount of consideration or price are *adequate* as compared with what the trader is supplying in exchange.

The following illustrate the ECJ's restrictive approach to the exemption:

✗ *Kásler* involved a mortgage loan denominated in a foreign currency. The repayment provision set the exchange rate as the creditor bank's 'selling rate' in one term, but the bank's 'buying rate' in another. The claimants challenged the former as unfair since it applied a different exchange rate to that used for the advancement of the loan. The ECJ held that this term could not be excluded from review; since the lender did not actually provide any foreign exchange service, the financial costs resulting from the difference between the buying and selling rates of exchange could not be regarded as remuneration due as consideration for a service.

✗ In *Matei v SC Volksbank Romania SA* (2015), the ECJ held that the following terms were not exempted from unfairness review:

- An interest rate variation clause in the event of significant changes in the market: (a) this is on the list of presumptively unfair terms; (b) it looks 'ancillary' as it adjusts the interest rate which is part of the main subject matter of the contract; and (c) it is concerned with when the lender can vary the rate and so is not concerned with the limited issue of the *adequacy* of the varied rate for what was supplied in exchange.

- The 'risk charge', which is aimed at ensuring the consumer's repayment of the loan and is an important part of the lender's income; however, the consumer protection objective makes this in principle irrelevant to determining whether the term concerns the adequacy of the amount as compared with the service provided, since the lender does not provide anything for it; the lender's risk is already guaranteed by a mortgage.

✗ *Van Hove v CNP Assurances SA* (2015) concerned an insurance contract which guaranteed cover of all loan repayments in respect of two loans in the event of death, permanent and absolute invalidity, or 75% of such in the event of total incapacity for work; the insured is deemed totally incapacitated if, after a waiting period, he is unable to take up any activity, paid or otherwise. The insured suffered permanent partial incapacity assessed at 72% but was medically advised that he could carry out appropriate part-time employment. The ECJ held that the relevant terms *did* come within the scope of the main subject matter of an insurance contract since they set out the conditions for the insurer's risk. Nevertheless, they were *not excluded from review* since they were insufficiently transparent; they were 'extremely broad and vague', could be understood in various ways and, being related to the two loans, the consumer could not be expected to exercise the same level of vigilance as if the insurance contract had been concluded separately.

The following **English law examples** on the exemption from review were decided on the equivalent provisions under UTCCR.

In *DGFT v First National Bank plc* (2001), FNB (the largest independent provider of consumer finance in the UK) used a standard form loan agreement which included a term requiring borrowers who defaulted on the repayment to continue paying interest at the contractual rate until the whole debt was discharged. Thus, even if the court gave extra time to repay, the borrower was liable for all interest accruing during that extended period, *over and above* the payments due under the judgment. The House of Lords held that the exclusionary regulation must be interpreted restrictively so as not to undermine the consumer protection objective of the UTCCR. The relevant term deals with what happens if the contract is breached. It is *not exempt* from review because it does not define the main subject matter or the price of the contract. It would not have appeared 'core' to the consumer.

OFT v Ashbourne (2011) concerned a series of contracts for gym memberships that imposed a minimum membership period on the gym user. Kitchin J held that the scope of exclusion from review:

✔ relates to 'the meaning or description of the length of the minimum period, the facilities to which the member gains access or the monthly subscription which he has to pay… [or] the adequacy of the price as against the facilities provided'; but

✗ not 'the obligation upon members to pay monthly subscriptions for the minimum period when they have overestimated the use they will make of their memberships and failed to appreciate that unforeseen circumstances may make their continued use of a gym impractical or their memberships unaffordable. Put another way, it relates to the consequences to members of early termination in light of the minimum membership period'.

✔ The most controversial decision on the scope of exclusion from review is the Supreme Court case of *Office of Fair Trading v Abbey National plc and others* (2009). Reversing the decisions in the High Court and the Court of Appeal, the Supreme Court held that terms imposing charges (amounting to £billions) on UK personal current account customers who went into unauthorised overdraft were exempt from review for unfairness as price terms. This was very surprising, given the Supreme Court's acknowledgement that the exclusionary regulation should be interpreted restrictively given UTCCR's aim of consumer protection. The court's main reasons were that:

(a) The exemption from review was of 'the adequacy of the price or remuneration, as against the goods or services supplied in exchange'. This should be given its natural meaning. There is no reason to narrow this by requiring that the price relates to the *main* subject matter of the contract. Thus, there is no distinction between main price or ancillary price.

(b) The customers contracted on the basis that they received a free-if-in-credit account in exchange for paying the charges if the account is overdrawn. These charges *are* part of the essential bargain because they form over 30% of the banks' revenue stream.

 Counterpoint

The Supreme Court's interpretation of the scope of exemption from unfairness review is too broad and insufficiently protective of the consumers:[11]

1. On the ECJ approach, *Abbey* must be regarded as wrongly decided:

   (a) In truth, the 'price' paid by most customers for 'free-in-credit' banking, is the bank's use of the customers' money for very little interest payment; the overdraft charges are ancillary to that and not a payment in exchange but a charge levied in particular circumstances. It is difficult to argue that the bank charges constituted an 'essential element' of the bank customer's contract, since their contingent nature means that they would not apply to all customers.

   (b) The fact that the charges generated a significant part of the bank's revenue stream should have been irrelevant, just as the same factor in relation to the 'risk charges' were discounted in *Kásler*.

2. Transparency is not enough: In *Abbey*, Lord Mance said that: 'The consumer's protection . . . is the requirement of transparency. . . . That being present, the consumer is to be assumed to be capable of reading the relevant terms and identifying whatever is objectively the price and remuneration under the contract.' However, the chief feature of CRA is that it goes *beyond* requiring transparency to requiring fairness. The question is: 'of which terms?'

3. The problem for consumers is not so much lack of comprehension as the high transaction cost of comprehension. The reason why section 64 only exempts transparent main subject matter and adequacy of price terms (and not *all* terms) is that consumers are presumed to know and consent to these 'headline' terms. Only *these* are justifiably exempted from review for unfairness in the name of freedom of contract. In contrast, there is 'no market in non-core contractual terms'[12] and consumers need protection where these are unfair.

---

[11] See Chen-Wishart 'Transparency and Fairness in Bank Charges' (2010) 126 *LQR*, 157–62; S Whittaker 'Unfair Contract Terms, Unfair Prices and Bank Charges' (2010) 73 MLR 106.

[12] S Bright 'Winning the Battle Against Unfair Terms' (2000) 20 *LS* 331,352.

11.6.4 **Review for unfairness**

Section 62(4) CRA states that: 'A term is unfair if, contrary to the requirement of good faith, it causes a significant imbalance in the parties' rights and obligations under the contract to the detriment of the consumer.' Given the essentially identical wording to UTCCR, decisions as to fairness in relation to UTCCR are applicable to the fairness test under CRA.

11.6.4.1 The time of assessment

The test of unfairness under CRA, like that of reasonableness under UCTA, should be assessed 'at the time of conclusion of the contract' (s 62(5)), so that circumstances occurring after contract formation should be excluded from the assessment.
However:

- The judicial concern is with the potential unfairness of the challenged term and the use that might be made of it after formation, and it is unclear how courts should approach the issue where 'new' terms are introduced after the conclusion of the original contract (eg bank accounts, iTunes).
- Moreover, the CRA permits the CMA or a 'regulator' to bring preventive proceedings for an injunction against the use, proposed use or recommended use of an unfair term (11.7.2). These:
  - ✗ do not concern the terms of an individual contract, thus individual circumstances are irrelevant in determining unfairness;
  - ✔ concern the terms applicable to contracts of a particular type or types made by a particular business, or recommended for use by a trade association; the court must assess fairness by reference to the *likely future* circumstances of contract formation.

11.6.4.2 The onus of proof

Unlike UCTA, CRA says nothing explicit about which party has the burden of proving or disproving unfairness. *Chitty* (para 38-309) takes the view that the ECJ is most likely to opt for a 'neutral assessment' of the challenged term. The European Commission said: 'the unfair nature of a clause is not a matter of facts to be substantiated by the parties concerned, but a matter of law which the court must independently decide upon according to the rules of law'.

11.6.4.3 The court's duty

Additionally, section 71 of CRA imposes a duty on courts to consider the issue of fairness of their own motion, even if neither party raises the issue, but only 'if the court considers that it has before it sufficient legal and factual material to enable it to consider the fairness of the term'.

11.6.4.4 The test of unfairness: overview

The ECJ has held that it is for national courts to determine the fairness of a term (in *Freiburger Kommunalbauten GmbH Baugesellschaft v Hofstetter* (2003)). The ECJ will only declare a term unfair where it would be unfair on any possible appropriate application of the fairness test (*Oceano Grupo Editorial SA v Murciano Quuitero* (2000)). The unfairness test is defined in terms of 'contravention of "good faith" and significant imbalance'. These are unfamiliar in English contract law and must be understood by reference to:

(i)   the statutory guidelines (s 62(5));

(ii) the general test of unfairness (s 62(4)) as interpreted by the ECJ and by English courts;

(iii) the judicial applications of the test;

(iv) the list of indicatively unfair terms (Sch 2 Part 1); and

(v)   the enforcement mechanism.

11.6.4.5 The statutory guidelines

- **Section 62(5) of CRA** directs the courts to assess unfairness by '(a) taking into account the nature of the subject matter of the contract and (b) by reference to all the circumstances existing when the term was agreed and to all the other terms of the contract or of any other contract on which it is dependent.'

- **Recital 16** of the originating European Directive requires courts to take into account similar factors as those relevant to the assessment of reasonableness under UCTA, including the public interest (*Chitty*, para 38-245).

- In addition, recital 16 directs courts to consider whether the trader dealt 'fairly and equitably with the other party whose legitimate interests he has to take into account'.

Whilst the factors referred to in assessing reasonableness under UCTA and fairness under CRA are not identical, there is a high degree of similarity. Moreover, neither list is exhaustive. Any differences between the two tests will not be due to the different language of 'fairness' and 'reasonableness'. Rather, it will come down to differences in the scope of the two pieces of legislation: the different parties affected, and principally, the different types of terms being tested.

11.6.4.6 The general test of unfairness under section 62(4)

In *Aziz v Caixa d'Estalvis de Catalunya, Tarragona i Manresa* (2013), the ECJ advised that, in determining the question of 'significant imbalance', the court must ask:

> what rules of national law would apply in the absence of an agreement by the parties in that regard. Such a comparative analysis will enable the national court to evaluate whether and, as the case may be, to what extent, the contract places the consumer in a legal situation less favourable than that provided for by the national law in force.

Likewise, *Constructora Principado SA v Menéndez Álvarez* (2014) requires courts to compare the parties' rights and obligations under the challenged term and under the national law rules which would apply absent any such term. A *significant* imbalance can only result from a sufficiently serious impairment of the consumer's legal situation because the challenged term restricts the consumer's default rights, constrains the exercise of those rights or imposes additional obligations not envisaged by the national rules.

The **European** cases above explain that the question in respect of 'good faith' is whether, hypothetically, the trader 'dealing fairly and equitably with the consumer, could reasonably assume that the consumer would have agreed to such a term in individual contract negotiations'. Unlike the European Directive, **CRA** applies even to *individually negotiated* terms, and, in such cases, it is arguable that the consumer *did* agree to the term in question. However, Lord Mance considered this test relevant (although not conclusive) in the assessment of good faith (*ParkingEye Ltd v Beavis* (2015)). This tallies with the view of the CMA[13] that the 'requirement of good faith ... allows for proper account to be taken of the significance of any real negotiation that has actually taken place', but considers that 'individual consumers rarely in practice have the required knowledge and bargaining power to ensure that contractual negotiations involving them are effectively conducted on equal terms.'

While English courts have put forward inconsistent tests of significant imbalance and contravention of good faith in the past and generally required procedural unfairness (eg in *First National Bank, West v Ian Finlay & Associates* (2014)), the Supreme Court finally aligned itself with *Aziz* in *ParkingEye Ltd v Bevis* (2015) and took it as authority for the following propositions:

(i) The test of 'significant imbalance' and 'good faith' merely defines in a general way the factors that render a contractual term unfair. A significant element of judgment is left to the national court to exercise in the light of the circumstances of each case.

(ii) The question whether there is a **'significant imbalance in the parties' rights'** depends mainly on whether the consumer is being deprived of an advantage which she would enjoy under national law in the absence of the contractual provision, ie, does the challenged provision derogate from the consumer's default legal position under national law?

(iii) However, such a provision will not necessarily be treated as unfair. The imbalance must arise 'contrary to the requirements of **good faith**'. That will depend on whether the trader, 'dealing fairly and equitably with the consumer, could reasonably assume that the consumer would have agreed to such a term in individual contract negotiations'.

(iv) The court is required to take account of, among other things, the nature of the goods or services supplied under the contract. This includes the significance, purpose, and practical effect of the term in question, and whether the challenged term is 'appropriate for securing the attainment of the objectives pursued by it ... and does not go beyond what is necessary to achieve them'.

11.6.4.7 Judicial applications of the unfairness test

Recall that, in *OFT v Abbey*, the Supreme Court held that the overdraft charges levied by the banks were exempted from review for unfairness (11.6.3). Nevertheless, Lord Phillips went on to say that the charges could be challenged for unfairness 'according to other criteria', in particular, 'whether it is fair to subsidise some customers by levies

---

[13] *Unfair contract terms guidance, Guidance on the unfair terms provisions in the Consumer Rights Act 2015* (CMA37, July 2015), para 2.30.

on others who experience contingencies that they did not foresee when entering into their contracts'. The Supreme Court noted that 20% of current account customers incur the relevant charges, and they generate 30% of the banks' total revenue from current account customers. The remaining 80% of in-credit customers only generated 50% of the total revenue (from the banks' use of their funds).

- Lord Mance commented that the banks 'were engaged in a sort of "reverse Robin Hood exercise"'.
- Lord Walker said that 'Ministers and Parliament may wish to consider the matter further'.
- However, Lady Hale thought the banks' charging structure was not 'necessarily unfair when viewed as a whole'.

 Pause for reflection

1. A complete answer to Lady Hale is that s 62(4) is concerned with the fairness of the challenged term between a particular trader and a particular consumer and not with whether the trader treated consumers fairly *as a group*. Thus, good faith and significant imbalance 'to the detriment of the consumer' must be judged on the micro-level of the individual; fairness at the macro-level, in the sense that banks may not be over-profiting overall, is irrelevant.

2. Although section 64 prevents a direct assessment of substantive unfairness, by exempting the price and main subject matter, section 62(4) inevitably requires some assessment of substantive fairness:

   - The fairness of non-exempt terms is assessed against *the background of the whole contract* (Recital 19 of the Council Directive (EC) 13/1993).

   - The exclusion of 'core' terms from review can be seen as evidence against legal control of substantive unfairness. But, there is another perspective. Since an unfair term under section 62(4) is knocked out, and the rest of the contract only binding 'so far as practicable' (s 67), the exemption of 'core' terms from review preserves the continuation of the contract. Substantive unfairness is better remedied by cutting out the offending terms than by striking down the whole contract and depriving consumers of the subject matter of the contract.

✔ In *OFT v Ashbourne*, Kitchin J granted an injunction to prevent the use of terms in standard form agreements for membership of gym and health clubs specifying minimum membership periods of 24 to 36 months. Such terms were unfair, since they were designed and calculated to take advantage of the naivety and inexperience of the average consumer who overestimates the use that she would make of such facilities.

✗ In *West v Finlay & Associates* (2014), W employed F to renovate W's house. The contract limited F's liability 'to the amount that it was reasonable for it to pay having regard to "the contractual responsibilities of other consultants, contractors and specialists appointed by [W]"'. The Court of Appeal concluded that the term was not unfair because:

- while the term was imbalanced against W, was not drawn W's attention and was expressed in a way that concealed its dangers, the imbalance was not significant because: (a) the term is prevalent in the industry standard forms, (b) the clause would be not be regarded as unusual in a commercial contract, and (c) W had the final decision on the choice of the other contractors.

- Even if there was significant imbalance, it was not contrary to the requirement of good faith because: (a) the term was clearly and openly presented to W, (b) F did not set out to exploit W, and (c) the parties had reasonably equal bargaining power.

✗ In *ParkingEye Ltd v Bevis* (2015), the court considered a sign at the entrance of a car park close to retailers, which stated that a consumer could park for free for up to two hours, but would incur an £85 charge for breaking stated rules, such as overstaying this permitted period. A consumer overstayed by over an hour. The Supreme Court decided that:

- The charge was not the price for use of the car park and so was not excluded from review for unfairness.

- In determining significant imbalance, and consistent with *Aziz*, the court took account of the trader's legitimate interest in organising their legal relationship in ways that may even derogate from the default rules that would otherwise apply. Here, while the term did create the relevant significant imbalance, the management company and the owners of the car park had a legitimate interest in imposing a liability on consumers in excess of any damages recoverable to induce them to observe the two-hour time limit. The term was 'objectively reasonable' since the consumer was given valuable parking in exchange for a charge for overstaying which was not disproportionately high.

- In determining good faith, the Supreme Court applied the *Aziz* test and concluded that a reasonable consumer would have agreed to such a term in individual negotiations; the test being an objective one.

- Lord Toulson's dissenting view is persuasive. He saw the charge as significantly imbalanced against the consumer since it far exceeded anything that was likely to be recovered as damages. On good faith, the starting point is that the consumer needs special protection, and it is for the trader to show that a non-core term, which is significantly disadvantageous to the consumer, is one that the trader can fairly assume that the consumer would have agreed in individual negotiations on level terms. His Lordship did not think the consumer would have agreed; compared with the basic state pension of £115 per week, £85 is a substantial sum. Moreover, the charge makes no allowance for situations where the consumer may unintentionally overstay by a short period and provides no room for adjustment.

11.6.4.8 The indicative list of unfair terms

Schedule 2 Part 1 CRA:

- substantially replicates the 17 examples of indicatively unfair terms from UTCCR;
- adds three new examples; and
- provides for amendment of the list by the Secretary of State.

The indicatively unfair terms 'convincingly demonstrate[s]' that good faith may be breached by substantive unfairness alone (Lord Steyn in *First National Bank*). Since significant imbalance is clearly aimed at substantive unfairness, it seems, therefore, that a term may be unfair under CRA if it is substantively unfair without any procedural unfairness. Only one of these terms focuses directly on *procedural* unfairness (para 10: the consumer's real opportunity to know of the term). It is arguable that even this has an implicit substantive dimension; analogous to unsigned documents, the more unusual or onerous the term, the more notice may be required. Such a term is unobjectionable if it causes no significant imbalance to the consumer.

This list of 20 terms not only covers the type of terms regulated by UCTA, but goes well beyond them. They can be grouped into three main types, being:

(i) **Terms that defeat consumers' reasonable expectations, eg:**
  - binding consumers to hidden terms (para 10);
  - allowing only the trader to cancel contract (para 7);
  - having the power to vary the contract (para 11);
  - the right to change what is supplied (paras 12, 13); and
  - the right of final decision on the meaning of terms, including whether the trader's own performance complies with the contract (para 16).

(ii) **Terms that reduce the consumer's redress on the trader's breach, eg:**
  - exclusion or restriction of liability for death or injury (para 1), beyond that prohibited in respect of negligence liability by section 65;
  - exclusion or restriction of liability for breaches of contract (para 2);
  - binding consumers although the trader defaults (para 18); and restricting the consumer's access to legal rights or remedies (para 20).

(iii) **Terms that impose unreasonable burdens on consumers in performance or on breach, eg:**
  - allowing the trader to fix the price at the time of delivery or to increase the price (paras 14, 15);
  - letting the trader keep the consumer's payments where the consumer does not proceed with or cancels the contract (para 4);
  - requiring a disproportionate penalty on the consumer's breach (paras 5, 6); and
  - automatic extension of the contract if the consumer does not refuse (para 9).

11.6.4.9 The availability of pre-emptive challenge

Under CRA, the CMA and other 'regulators' can apply to courts for injunctions against the *future use* of specific unfair terms (11.7.2). Logically, this must be done *without* reference to any procedural unfairness that has occurred or might occur in any particular case. As Lord Steyn explains, 'inevitably, the primary focus of such a pre-emptive challenge is on issues of substantive unfairness' (*First National Bank*). Moreover, once an injunction is granted against a particular unfair term (including terms with like effect), its use is prohibited no matter what transparency, notice, or other procedural safeguards surround it.

11.7 **The enforcement mechanism**

11.7.1 **UCTA**

Only a party directly affected can claim under UCTA. Such challenges will rarely be worth the cost in money, time, and general aggravation to small businesses. Even if terms are invalidated under UCTA, nothing prevents their future use.

11.7.2 **CRA**

In contrast to UCTA, CRA lays down a *dual system* of individual challenges and pre-emptive challenges by appropriate bodies. The first is an individual challenge like that under UCTA.

This enforcement mechanism suffers from the same problems as UCTA: consumers will rarely find it worthwhile to go to court and the impact of any success will not extend beyond the individual consumer.

The effect of a successful challenge is to make the offending term not binding on the consumer, but 'the contract continues, so far as practicable, to have effect in every other respect' (s 67). The consumer can rely on the term if she so chooses (s 62(3)).

The ECJ added an important nuance in *Kásler v OTP Jelzalogbank Zrt* (2014): if the deletion of an unfair term would render the contract unenforceable, the court could substitute the invalidated term with a supplementary provision of the law to further the aims of consumer protection by rebalancing the contract while preserving, as far as possible, the validity of the contract. This made sense in the context of the case involving a loan where the invalidity of one of the repayment terms would otherwise mean that the whole of the outstanding sum would become due. Since this was likely to exceed the consumer's financial capacities, it would penalise the consumer rather than the lender.

CRA also authorises pre-emptive challenges by the CMA and other 'regulators' (detailed in Schedule 3 para 8, including a variety of industry regulators, all weights and measures departments, the Consumers' Association, and now, the Financial Conduct Authority). In particular, regulators can:

✔ apply for injunctions against the use, proposed use, or recommended use of:
  - an unfair consumer *term* or consumer *notice*;
  - a term or notice that breaches the requirement of *transparency*; or

- a term *exempting liability for breach of terms 'treated as included'* in contracts to supply goods, services or digital content, which are invalidated under Part 1 of CRA.

✔ consider complaints and accept undertakings from traders to the effect that the trader 'will comply with the conditions that are agreed... [with] the regulator about the use of terms or notices...'.

The CMA and other 'regulators' have responsibility, amongst other things, for:

- investigating complaints; 'regulators' have wide powers to investigate (s 75, Sch 5). If a regulator decides not to apply for an injunction, it must give reasons to the complainant (Sch 3 para 2(3));
- bringing actions, coordinating actions with other regulators, and monitoring actions;
- responding to requests about what terms or notices (or ones of a similar kind or with similar effect) have been the subject of an injunction or undertaking;
- disseminating information about the operation of CRA; and
- monitoring compliance generally.

Pause for reflection

In 'Winning the Battle Against Unfair Contract Terms' (2000) 20 *LS* 331, Bright reports on the effectiveness of the Unfair Contract Terms Unit ('UCTU', the predecessor of the CMA) in getting traders to change or discontinue the use of unfair terms and contracting practices. This is overwhelmingly achieved by negotiation and requiring traders to give informal undertakings. The trader has many incentives to cooperate with the UCTU: to give an undertaking and perhaps accept a reduced profit margin will often be less costly than defending a court action; cooperation also avoids bad publicity, is good for its public image, and cultivates a good working relationship with regulators. The success of this administrative model of enforcement is partly attributable to its *pro-active approach* and the implicit threat of court action if matters are not satisfactorily resolved. The UCTU (and now the CMA) will not only investigate the term complained of, but also assess the contract as a whole. It has initiated investigations of whole sectors and liaised with relevant trade associations such as the home improvement, vehicle rental, and package holidays industries, and considered conditions of airline use, achieving notable success in securing the amendment of terms in mobile phone contracts. Actual court action is regarded as the *last resort*. Bright warns that the success of such measures will be threatened if courts adopt a less consumer-orientated interpretation of the legislation.

11.8 **Other statutory and common law control of terms**

Other statutes and common law rules control the *contents* of contracts. A course on general contract law cannot examine these in detail (they are the subject of specialist texts and courses, eg on consumer, employment, or tenancy law). Suffice it to note that their existence and emphasis on avoiding domination and unfairness necessitates an adjustment in the fundamental assumptions of classical contract law, especially that it does not respond to unfairness in the substance of contracts (1.3.5).

11.8.1 Statutory control of terms

Aside from UCTA and CRA, many other statutes regulate the content of *particular types* of contract. The approach is piecemeal; the trouble hotspots identified affect *most* contracts which ordinary consumers make, eg:

* Consumer Credit Act 2006;
* Financial Services and Markets Act 2000;
* Sale of Goods Act 1979;
* Supply of Goods and Services Act 1982;
* Landlord and Tenant Act 1985;
* Employment Rights Act 1996;
* Equality Act 2010;
* Consumer Protection Act 1987;
* Defective Premises Act 1972;
* Package Travel, Package Holidays and Package Tours (Amendment) Regulations 1992 (SI 1998/1208); and
* Consumer Contracts (Information, Cancellation and Additional Charges) Regulations 2013 (SI 2013/3134).

They counter unfairness by, eg:

(i)   invalidating whole or parts of contracts;

(ii) implying terms (and often prohibiting the parties from contracting out, effectively making them mandatory terms);

(iii) prohibiting certain terms;

(iv) imposing notice or a 'cooling off' period (a period when consumers can cancel the contract without penalty) requirements; and even

(v)   modifying unfair terms (eg Consumer Credit Act 1974, s 140).

11.8.2 Common law control of terms

These can be divided into three categories:

(i) **Indirect controls** can be imposed over the contents of contracts by instrumental applications of other rules to reach just results (ie 'backward reasoning' (1.2.3, 2.5.1.3)). Some notable examples are the *identification*, *incorporation*, and *interpretation* of terms, whether express, implied, or collateral (Chapter 10).

(ii) **Direct control:** Courts are directly empowered to invalidate certain terms, including:

* exemptions of liability where the presenting party misrepresents its effect (*Curtis v Chemical Cleaning and Dyeing Co* (1951));

- penalty clauses (exorbitant payments on breach, 14.3.2);
- unreasonable deposits and forfeitures (forfeiture of money already paid on breach, 14.3.3);
- exclusion of liability for fraud (5.4); and
- unreasonable restraints of trade (restricting a party's liberty to carry on his trade in the future, W2.1.2.9 (in the online rsources).
- The entire contract can be rendered unenforceable for being illegal or contrary to public policy, although this doctrine is narrowly applied. Discussion of the illegality doctrine (including an examination of restraint of trade) can be found in W2 (in the online resources).

(iii) **Varying a term:** the following may be seen as such:

- The 'discount' on the contract price available to consumers where the trader has engaged in prohibited (misleading or aggressive) practices, in steps of 25%, 50%, 75%, and 100% depending on the seriousness of the prohibited practice, assessed by reference to: the behaviour of the trader, the impact of the practice on the consumer, and the time that has elapsed since the prohibited practice took place (Consumer Protection (Amendment) Regulations 2015 reg 27I).
- Section 2(2) Misrepresentation Act 1969 allows courts to award damages in lieu of rescission broadly in circumstances where it would be fair to do so; the damages effectively rewrite the contract by treating the misrepresentation as if it were a term which has been breached (5.2.3).
- In equitable common mistake cases (6.3.6), the complainant has been granted *rescission on terms* that he gives the other party the option of contracting on fairer terms.
- Courts can rectify the contract to reflect the parties' true agreement (6.1.2).

11.9 **Illegality: a brief summary**

One doctrine that overtly controls the contents of contracts, and yet is left off the syllabus of most contract law courses, is the so-called 'illegality' doctrine. For reasons of space, a brief summary is offered here. A more detailed discussion is offered in Web Chapter 2 on the online resources.

This represents the most open and direct interference with contract parties' freedom to determine the *substance* of their contracts. It is justified in terms of the law's refusal to support immoral or reprehensible contracts. Before the recent Supreme Court judgment in *Patel v Mirza* (2016), courts would generally neither *enforce* an illegal contract nor allow restitution of any money or property transferred under it, subject to limited exceptions. Following the majority's reasoning in that case, the enquiry is a more nuanced one, with the courts' assistance likely to depend on balancing relevant policy factors and the proportionality of denying assistance.

What contracts are illegal or contrary to public policy? Statutes may prohibit the *formation, purpose, or performance* of certain contracts. Examples include prohibitions on the trade of certain weapons and body parts. The categories of **common law illegality** reflect changing social and moral values. They include contracts which:

- commit or further a criminal or civil wrong;
- interfere with the administration of justice;
- oust the jurisdiction of the court, although parties can agree to arbitrate before resorting to the courts;
- prejudice the state, such as trading with the enemy in wartime, and contracts which corrupt public life, like the buying of 'honours';
- prejudice family life, such as contracts to transfer parental rights and duties;
- unduly restrict personal liberty, such as contracts of slavery and 'servile' employment contracts;
- further sexually immoral purposes, such as prostitution; however, changes in societal attitudes mean that courts are unlikely to hold with the past refusal to enforce contracts such as to pay rent on premises known to accommodate the promisor's mistress or contracts between unmarried cohabiting couples; or
- are in **restraint of trade** (in practice, the most important head of illegality), whereby one party agrees to restrict her freedom to trade or conduct her profession or business in a particular locality for a specified time. The doctrine applies principally to employment, sales of businesses, and exclusive dealing agreements. Such restraints are invalid to the extent that they are more than is reasonably necessary to protect the legitimate interests of the party imposing the restraint.

What is the effect of illegality? The relevant statute may stipulate the consequence of the illegality (eg impose a penalty or bar enforcement by either or both parties). If not, the court must decide the consequences on the same general principles as apply to common law illegality. These principles have changed following the majority's approach in *Patel v Mirza*, although the precise implications of that decision are not yet clear. It is clear, following *Patel v Mirza*, that **restitution** of the benefits which one party conferred on the other under an illegal contract is likely to be more widely available, not simply in the exceptional circumstances previously recognised, which included where the claimant:

- was less blameworthy than the defendant (eg was a member of the protected class);
- had *withdrawn* from the transaction in time; or
- could establish a legal or equitable *proprietary right* to the property independent of the illegal contract.

Instead of the **rules-based** approach that was advocated prior to *Patel v Mirza*, the majority in that case supported a more flexible, **policy-based** approach. In order to determine whether to allow recovery in respect of benefits conferred under an illegal contract, the court should consider (i) 'the underlying purpose of the prohibition that had been transgressed' and (ii) 'other relevant public policies which may be rendered ineffective or less effective by denial of the claim'; it should also keep in mind 'the possibility of overkill unless the law is applied with a due sense of proportionality'

(Lord Toulson). Various **factors** might be relevant to this enquiry; Lord Toulson declined to set out a 'prescriptive or definitive list' but suggested potentially relevant factors included 'the seriousness of the conduct, its centrality to the contract, whether it was intentional and whether there was marked disparity in the parties' respective culpability'.

What about **enforcement** of an illegal contract? The rule of thumb prior to *Patel v Mirza* was that courts would **not enforce** contracts expressly or impliedly prohibited by statute or contrary to public policy, irrespective of the claimant's good faith, subject to some exceptions, eg:

- A *collateral contract* not tainted by illegality could be enforced.

- An innocent claimant could claim damages for *fraudulent misrepresentation*.

- Even a bad faith claimant could enforce the contract if: (a) the purpose of the illegality was to protect a class of persons to which the claimant belongs; (b) the illegality was too remote from the contract; or (c) the claimant was seeking to enforce a statutory entitlement (eg against unfair dismissal) attaching to the contract.

- A good faith claimant ignorant of the illegal manner in which the other party is performing a legal contract could enforce the contract. Even the offender could enforce the contract if the purpose of the illegality was merely to impose a penalty on the offender rather than to prohibit the contract.

- A contract was enforceable if its illegal part could be severed.

In all these cases, the rule was that enforcement must *not subvert the policies underlying the illegality.* This is still likely to be the case and enforcement is still likely to be permitted in these circumstances following *Patel v Mirza*; however, it may be that it is now permitted in a wider range of circumstances. Although the case concerned restitution, the policy-based approach suggested by the majority was not confined to restitutionary remedies but appears to apply more generally to enforcement as well.

11.10 **Control of substantive unfairness**

11.10.1 **To what extent does the law control the substance of contracts?**

This question is *descriptive* and can be answered by collecting together the instances of indirect and direct judicial control of substantive unfairness (in the sense of a significant imbalance of the rights and obligations under the contract). Although reasonable observers may disagree on the *extent* of control, there is clearly scope on the doctrinal level and evidence on the practical level for arguing that the law *can* and *does* exercise control over the substantive unfairness of contracts. Thus, we have seen that rules have developed to control:

- particular fact situations or relationships that entail a heightened risk of substantive unfairness (eg undue influence, non-commercial guarantees, salvage, consumer contracts, and standard form contracts);

- particular conduct likely to induce agreement to unfair terms (eg misrepresentation, duress, and unconscionable conduct);
- particular terms likely to contain substantive unfairness (eg clauses exempting liability for breach or stipulating payments or forfeitures on breach); and
- contracts of certain types that have attracted a high incidence of substantive unfairness (eg consumer, employment, tenancy, and package holidays).

11.10.2 **Justifications for controlling the substance of contracts**

Three justifications can be advanced.

The traditional justification is that substantive unfairness plays an evidentiary role. It is merely indirect or corroborative evidence of procedural unfairness (ie one side's defective consent and the other's reprehensible conduct). On such a view, the concern about substantive unfairness is consistent with supporting freedom to contract. However, we have seen that such reasoning can wear thin. It results in the 'finding' of bargaining disabilities and unconscionable conduct in commonplace and unremarkable situations which do not stand out from the norm (see generally Chapter 9) and which only become legally significant when accompanied by glaring substantive unfairness.

A bolder justification is based on the idea that freedom of contract is not the only value in contract law and must be balanced against the value of fairness. It may be necessary to restrain contractual power to *uphold the practice of contracting itself,*[14] *and to shape it according to widely held conceptions of social justice* (1.4.6). It is perfectly reasonable for the law to inject community standards of fairness into *both* the procedural rules governing how the 'game' of contract should be played *and* the *substantive* limits on what can be gained or lost by playing it. The argument that judges, not being sophisticated economists, may not know what is substantively unfair[15] is exaggerated in the context of the manifest unfairness involved in the mainly *non-commercial* cases where relief has been given. Moreover, courts will sensibly give a wide margin of tolerance to *commercial* cases where operative bargaining disability is unlikely to be legally relevant. Given the vagueness of statutory standards like 'reasonableness' and 'fairness' and judicial appeals to the 'standards of equity', there is no particular reason to think that courts are more qualified in laying down procedural limits than substantive ones. In any case, the two overlap significantly; the standard of procedural unfairness required cannot be fixed without reference to the substantive outcome likely to be produced.

The boldest justification follows on the view that contractual enforcement amounts to 'state subsidisation'. If we see contract law's control of substantive unfairness in the conventional language of legal 'interference', 'paternalism', 'rewriting the contract for the parties', or 'saving parties from foolish bargains', we insert a bias into the inquiry. It assumes the starting point that parties are free and so entitled to the

---

[14] J Raz, 'Promises in Morality and Law' (1982) 95 *Harvard L Rev* 916.

[15] M Trebilcock, 'The Doctrine of Inequality of Bargaining Power: Post-Benthamite Economics in the House of Lords' (1976) 26 *University of Toronto LJ* 359; S Thal, 'The Inequality of Bargaining Power Doctrine: The Problem of Defining Contractual Unfairness' (1988) 8 *OJLS* 17, 25.

enforcement of *all* contracts they make, any restrictions would amount to interference with this right/freedom which must be justified. But we can adopt the *different starting point* that sees contract law as a form of *state subsidisation* of a valuable activity; that of enhancing individual autonomy. The institution of contract is a social creation through which the community provides support for the agreements of its members by facilitating them and giving them greater security. That the state is justified in enforcing contracts does not require it to do so in an unqualified way (*always* and in *absolute* terms). Since resources are limited, priorities for action justifiably rest on the worthiness of the project being supported.

From this perspective, the law's refusal to help in enforcing substantively unfair contracts or terms can be understood as the state's refusal to support an unworthy activity.[16] In the same vein, Shiffrin[17] speaks of the law's avoidance of complicity with exploitation; Dalton[18] refers to the restraint on self-interest necessitated by the norms of *decency* and *equality*; Smith[19] argues that contracts at non-normal prices disrupt individuals' planning and ability to lead self-directed, autonomous lives.

Problems of uncertainty are bound to arise at the level of application. The most obvious examples come from the class of illegal contracts and contracts against public policy (see Web Chapter 2). But more work is needed to elaborate the collective values by which the worthiness of contracts should be measured in a market system which inevitably accepts some level of exploitation of inequality.

This general explanation provides a helpful context for understanding the direct and indirect legal control of substantive unfairness manifested in many, if not most, rules of contract law, whether at the level of doctrine or application. It also provides a starting point for understanding the law's reluctance to enforce certain transactions involving controversial subject matter such as the trading in babies, child labour, body parts, reproductive services, sex, weapons, and addictive drugs. There is something unsavoury about these, even if there is no procedural unfairness in the way the contracts were created.

THIS CHAPTER IN ESSENCE

The key areas and core topics in this chapter are summarised in an easy-to-use list of essential points that can be accessed on the online resources which accompany this book at www.oup.com/uk/chenwishart6e/

---

[16] J Raz, *The Morality of Freedom* (Clarendon Press, 1988) ch 14.

[17] S Shiffrin, 'Paternalism, Unconscionability, and Accommodation' (2000) 29 *Philosophy and Public Affairs* 203.

[18] C Dalton, 'An Essay in the Deconstruction of Contract Doctrine' (1985) 94 *Yale LJ* 997, 1024–38.

[19] S Smith, 'In Defence of Substantive Unfairness' (1996) 112 *LQR* 138.

QUESTIONS

1 'First appearances suggest that the Unfair Contract Terms Act 1977 only applies to terms that limit or exclude liability, but the reality is far messier.' Discuss.

2 'The picture of legislative control of unfair terms is bewildering. Some terms are 'blacklisted', some are 'grey listed', some must be reasonable and some must not be unfair, some controls apply to consumer contracts and some to business contracts.' Discuss.

3 'To avoid frustrating the purpose of Part 2 of the Consumer Rights Act 2015, the scope of unreviewable contractual terms, sometimes called core terms, must be narrowly construed.' Discuss.

4 What amounts to 'unfairness' under the Consumer Rights Act 2015?

5 Finn, a business customer, and Gigi, a consumer, each purchase computers, the price payable by six monthly instalments, from Herman, a retailer. Finn and Gigi are handed a document. They do not notice the following terms in very small and faint print:

(i) All implied terms are excluded.

(ii) Herman's liability is limited to £200 per customer.

(iii) Customers must notify Herman of any complaints within 48 hours of purchase and cannot withhold any monthly payments for whatever reason.

Advise Finn and Gigi, who find out a week later that the computers are seriously defective and practically useless.

 For hints on how to answer these questions, please see the online resources at www.oup.com/uk/chenwishart6e/

KEY FURTHER READING

Adams, J, and Brownsword, R (1988), 'The Unfair Contract Terms Act: A Decade of Discretion', 104 *LQR* 94.

Bright, S (2000), 'Winning the Battle Against Unfair Contract Terms' 20 *LS* 331.

Chen-Wishart, M (2010) 'Transparency and Fairness in Bank Charges', 126 *LQR* 157.

Chen-Wishart, M (2015) 'Controlling Unfair Terms: Protecting the Institution of Contract', in L Gullifer and S Vogenaur(eds), *English and European Perspectives on Contract and Commercial Law* (Hart) 105.

Collins, H (1994), 'Good Faith in European Contract Law', 14 *OJLS* 229.

MacDonald, E (2007), 'Unfair Contract Terms Act—Thirty Years On' in A Burrows and E Peel(eds), *Contract Terms* (OUP) 153.

Whittaker, S (2011), 'Unfair Contract Terms, Unfair Prices and Bank Charges', 74 *MLR* 106.

For updates to this chapter and links to websites relevant to the topics covered, please see the online resources at www.oup.com/uk/chenwishart6e/

Breach and remedies for breach

'What can I get if you break the contract?'

INTRODUCTION

In Part VI, we examine the end of the life of a contract. A contract may be lawfully brought to an end by:

(i) full performance: the overwhelming majority of contracts are discharged by due performance, ie they are 'spent'; the lawyer's role is confined to drafting the initial contract;

(ii) agreement: to modify the original contract. This must normally be supported by consideration (3.1.5). If neither party has started or finished performance, consideration is provided by each party giving up her rights against the other;

(iii) operation of a term in the contract: which stipulates:

- that the contract will come to an end on the happening of an event (not amounting to breach); or

- that one party can serve notice to cancel or terminate the contract under certain conditions (12.2.3.2);

(iv) operation of the law: as where contracts are frustrated (Chapter 7);

(v) termination for breach of contract: the scope of an aggrieved party's right to terminate the contract for the other party's breach is discussed in this chapter.

Introductory **Diagram A** gives a brief overview of how contracts may be brought to an end. Contract parties are entitled to performance in accordance with the terms of the contract. Contracts that are made and performed simultaneously (eg buying a bus ticket) require little support from contract law, while those involving a time lag between contract formation and performance (eg a building contract) are vitally dependent on contract law's remedial regime should one party defect from the contract. The parties may have specifically agreed the remedies for breach. These are enforceable, subject to significant controls by the law (14.3). In the absence of agreed remedies or where the courts invalidate them, contract law provides a *menu of default remedies* to the aggrieved party who meets the qualifying conditions. Introductory **Diagram B** gives an overview of these remedies. The aggrieved party may claim:

- termination: call the contract off (Chapter 12);
- damages: monetary compensation for loss (Chapter 13);
- specific performance: compel the contract-breaker to do what she undertook in the contract (Chapter 14).

These remedies may be claimed in any combination, except that termination and specific performance cannot be claimed together, being mutually exclusive. The relationship between these remedies can be confusing. Introductory **Diagram C** offers a flow diagram that suggests a sequential approach to problems in determining the appropriate remedies for breach of contract.

Part VI Introductory Diagram A: Overview of the end of a contract

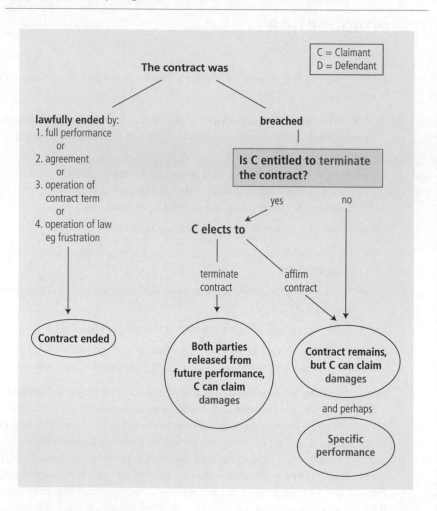

Part VI Introductory Diagram B: Overview of remedies for breach of contract

✓ = Yes
✗ = no

CB = contract-breaker
IP = innocent party

Remedy	Effect	Availability
IP wants to get out of the contract **Termination (ch 12)**	**Termination** discharges both parties from further performance of the primary obligations (IP can claim damages or restitution (see below)).	IP has not completed performance, and can show: ✓ Renunciation, ✓ Impossibility of performance, or ✓ Actual breach of *'condition'* or serious breach of 'innominate term' by CB.
	IP may, instead, elect to **affirm** the contract (12.3) in order to sue for the *agreed price* (14.1).	✗ Not if IP's performance requires CB's co-operation or IP has no 'legitimate interest' in affirming
IP wants to claim money **Damages (ch 13)**	**Expectation** measure	✓ All breaches but subject to limits, eg mitigation and remoteness
	Reliance measure	✓ Where expectation damages is speculative and CB cannot prove that IP made a bad bargain.
	Restitution measure	If contract terminated, IP can recover ✓ money paid if total failure of consideration (CB can also make this claim), and ✓ value of non-money performance (*quantum meruit /quantum valebat*).
	Negotiating damages	If IP would otherwise be inadequately protected, can claim: ✓ compensation for loss of hypothetical bargain, or ✓ account of profits if IP has special interest in preventing CB from profiting by the breach.
IP wants CB to perform the contract **Specific remedies (ch 14)**	**Performance** of primary obligations: (a) to pay money- agreed price (b) to confer non-monetary performance- specific performance, or (c) not to do something- injunction	✓ (a) as debt action, few limits ✓ (b) but subject to extensive bars, eg adequacy of damages, constant supervision, personal services, and unfairness. ✓ (c) but no indirect specific performance
	Agreed remedies - performance of secondary (remedial) terms, eg exemption clauses, damages clauses, forfeiture clauses, termination clauses, agreed specific performance clauses	Subject to strict controls, eg UCTA 1977, CRA 2015, penalty rule, forfeitures rules.

Part VI Introductory Diagram C: How to tackle a problem question on remedies

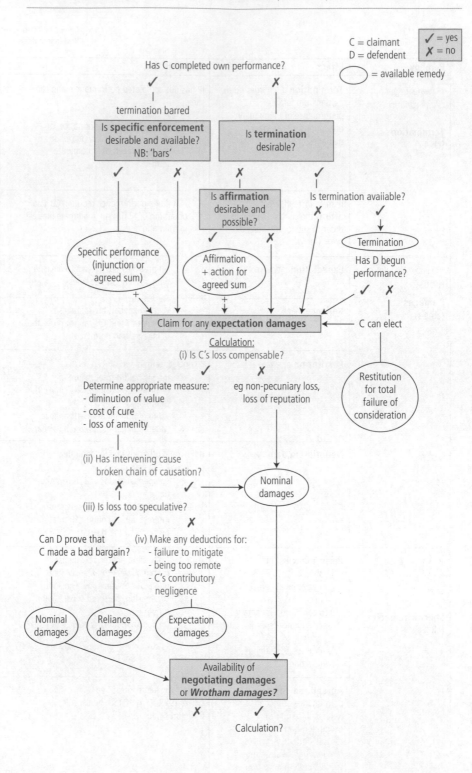

12

Breach of contract and termination

'You have breached the contract and I want out'

When a contract is breached, the aggrieved party must first decide whether to:

- continue with (affirm) the contract and sue for money and/or specific performance; or

- stop performing (terminate) the contract and sue for money.

The amount of money she can claim will depend on whether she has terminated or affirmed the contract after the other's breach.

The questions addressed in this chapter are:

(i) *What* is breach of contract and *when* does it occur?

(ii) When will breach entitle the innocent party to end (terminate) the contract?

(iii) What is the effect of termination?

(iv) When can the claimant insist on continuing with her own performance when the defendant no longer wants it?

12.1 **Breach of contract**

A party breaches a contract when, *without lawful excuse*, she fails to perform any of her contractual obligations. The burden of proof is on the claimant alleging breach. The question is whether the claimant has received *exact and precise performance* of the contract from the defendant. In *Re Moore & Co Ltd and Landauer & Co* (1921), a contract to sell 3,000 tins of fruit to be packed in cases of 30 tins was breached when some of the consignment contained cases of 24 tins. This entitled the buyer to reject the whole consignment, and get out of the contract even though the performance was no less valuable than that promised.

Most contractual obligations are strict liability; that is, the promisor guarantees to achieve *a particular state of affairs* (eg to paint a house, to sell goods of satisfactory quality). The contract is breached when performance falls short of this, even if the defendant has done her best. However, contracts can stipulate a lesser standard of performance, requiring only the exercise of reasonable care, without guaranteeing any particular end result.[1] Contractual liability for professional services such as that of a lawyer or doctor will usually be fault-based (*Thake v Maurice* (1986)) and can trigger a concurrent tort duty to take reasonable care (1.6.2).

The defendant's breach may be:

- anticipatory: by (i) renunciation (expressly or impliedly refusing to perform), or (ii) impossibility (being unable to perform) *before* performance is due; or

- actual: by (iii) failure to perform *when* performance is due.

The *timing* matters because, where breach is anticipatory, the claimant can *immediately* sue for remedies, even before the time due for performance.

'Renunciation', 'impossibility', and 'failure of performance' can overlap, although each has its own distinctive characteristics (12.1.1–12.1.3). They are often called 'grounds of termination' and are collectively known as 'repudiatory breaches'. However, while they always give rise to claims for damages, they only entitle the claimant to terminate the contract when they cross a 'seriousness' threshold (12.2.2.2).

12.1.1 **Renunciation ('repudiation')**

Renunciation (also called repudiation) occurs when one party by *words or conduct* evinces an *intention not to perform* part, or all, of the contract. Absent an express refusal, the question is whether the defendant's acts or omissions would lead a reasonable person to conclude that she no longer intends to perform her contractual obligations (*Universal Cargo Carriers Corp v Citati* (1957)). Renunciation *at* or *after* the time of performance amounts to *actual* breach.

(i) **Timing**: renunciation before the time fixed for performance is often referred to as 'anticipatory breach', suggesting erroneously that breach is 'to come'. In fact,

---

[1] Under the Supply of Goods and Services Act 1982, s 13, a person who supplies a service in the course of a business impliedly undertakes to 'carry out the service with reasonable care and skill'.

renunciation is itself a breach and, if sufficiently 'serious' (12.2.2.2), entitles the claimant to terminate the contract *immediately* and claim damages for the loss of the contract. In *Hochster v De la Tour* (1853), DlT employed H to commence work for three months from 1 June but repudiated the contract on 11 May. H could claim damages *immediately* (before 1 June). As Cockburn CJ explains in *Frost v Knight* (1872): 'The promisee has an inchoate right to the performance of the bargain, which becomes complete when the time for performance has arrived. In the meantime he has a right to have the contract kept open as a subsisting and effective contract. Its unimpaired and unimpeached efficacy must be essential to his interests.'

 Pause for reflection

Awarding damages on termination for breach *before performance* is due may seem objectionable, especially where there is a long interval between termination and the time of performance. It accelerates the defendant's obligations and increases the potential for errors in quantifying damages since that normally rests on the market value of the lost performance *at the time of performance*. However, this rule encourages the speedy resolution of broken-down contracts and minimises the claimant's losses by encouraging her to terminate the contract immediately and make substitute arrangements, instead of keeping herself ready to perform a contract that will inevitably be breached. In long-term contracts with periodic performances, the rule avoids the inefficiency of requiring the claimant to sue as each performance falls due.

(ii) **The extent of renunciation**: where the defendant refuses to perform *all* of her contractual obligations, the claimant can undoubtedly terminate the contract. Otherwise, the court must decide whether any *partial* renunciation is sufficiently 'serious' to justify termination (12.2.2.2).

(iii) **The relevance of the defendant's mistake or good faith**: a party's words or conduct can amount to renunciation even when they result from an *honest but mistaken view* of her contractual rights and obligations. Where you and I make a contract, the question is whether my conduct objectively signals to you:

✓ an intention not to perform the objective interpretation of the contract, which constitutes renunciation by me; or

✗ a genuine *dispute about the proper construction of the contract*, when the courts will find no renunciation by me.

Where you purport to terminate the contract for my alleged renunciation but get it wrong (ie the court concludes that I did not renounce the contract), your unjustified termination will itself amount to a wrongful repudiation entitling me to terminate (your termination 'gun' turns back on yourself). This means that, instead of you being able to claim damages from me, you become liable to me for damages. The distinction can be a fine one and the cases are not entirely consistent. No renunciation was found in the following cases:

✗ *Woodar Investment Development Ltd v Wimpey Construction UK Ltd* (1980): the buyer of land honestly but mistakenly purported to exercise a contractual right to terminate the contract; the seller then claimed termination for repudiatory breach and sued for damages. The House of Lords denied the seller's claim for, 'far from repudiating the contract, [the buyer was] relying on it and invoking one of its provisions'. Moreover, the seller's letter showed that he knew the buyer was willing to perform the contract if his purported termination was found to have been invalid.

✗ *Eminence Property v Heaney* (2010): sellers of land purported to terminate the contract on a mistaken basis. The buyer then purported to terminate for the seller's wrongful termination. The Court of Appeal rejected this because the seller's mistake would have been clear to a reasonable buyer, as would the seller's desire that conveyance be completed by the actual date. Thus, the seller had not 'clearly shown an intention to abandon and altogether refuse to perform the contract'.

✓ Renunciation was found in *Federal Commerce and Navigation Co Ltd v Molena Alpha Inc (The Nanfri)* (1978) where the owner disputed the charterer's deductions from the hire payments. On legal advice, the owner threatened not to issue freight prepaid bills of lading, which would have very serious consequences for the charterer. The House of Lords held that this amounted to a repudiatory breach by the owner entitling the charterer to terminate the contract, although the owner had wanted to maintain the profitable charterparty.

Come the time for performance, a party whose performance deviates from the objectively correct interpretation of the contract will have actually breached the contract irrespective of her good faith.

12.1.2 **Impossibility of performance**

A party whose act or omission has disabled her from performance commits a breach of contract. This is usually more difficult to prove than renunciation:

- Renunciation only requires the defendant's conduct to lead a *reasonable person* to believe that she was *intending not to perform*.

- Impossibility requires the claimant to show, on the balance of probabilities, that the defendant's performance was *impossible in fact* (*Alfred C Toepfer Intl GmbH v Itex Hagrani Export SA* (1993)).

The answer may be clear, eg:

✓ Where the defendant sells the subject matter of the contract to a third party (*Bowdell v Parsons* (1808)).

✓ In *Universal Cargo Carriers Corp v Citati* (1957), U chartered a ship to C who agreed to provide the cargo and nominate a berth and a shipper before a certain date.

C wanted to perform but had done nothing three days before the due date. This left it so late that performance would inevitably be delayed and this would frustrate the commercial purpose of the contract. The court held that C had not renounced the contract, but its inability to perform entitled U to terminate and find another charterer.

However, impossibility is not made out just because the defendant:

✗ declares its intention to perform in a way that seems impossible if it can also choose to perform by a possible means (*The Vladimir Ilich* (1975)); or

✗ enters into inconsistent obligations (*Alfred C Toepfer v Itex Hagran* (1993)); it *may* find an alternative way of successfully performing.

(i) **Timing**: impossibility occurring *before* performance is due amounts to anticipatory breach; the contract can be terminated from this point and damages claimed. Impossibility occurring *after* performance is due constitutes actual breach.

(ii) **The extent of impossibility**: as with renunciation, a party is only entitled to terminate the contract if the part that is impossible to perform would amount to a sufficiently 'serious' breach of contract (12.2.2.2). Although the test has been compared with that for frustration (*Trade and Transport Inc v Iino Kaiun Kaisha Ltd* (1973)), the analogy is really to *self-induced frustration* since the impossibility of performance does not excuse the defendant.

(iii) **The contract-breaker's good faith is irrelevant**: she is liable for the breach that is bound to happen whether due to her own acts or omissions, or from circumstances for which she bears the risk (*Universal Cargo v Citati*). If neither party bears the risk for the occurrence of circumstances making performance impossible, the issue becomes one of frustration (Chapter 7).

12.1.3 Failure of performance

Failure of performance when performance becomes due amounts to actual breach. Failure can take the form of non-, late, or defective performance: all entitle the claimant to sue for damages and, if sufficiently serious, to terminate the contract.

12.2 Termination for breach

Unnecessary confusion can result from the inconsistent use of terminology in this area of law:

• Contracts that are terminated for breach may be referred to in judgments and academic writings as: 'repudiated', 'rescinded', 'brought to an end', 'discharged', or 'rejected' (in sale of goods). They can all mean the same thing.

• Where termination is described as 'rescission for breach', this sets aside the contract prospectively (*de futuro*), and gives the claimant the right to expectation remedies (*Johnson v Agnew* (1980)).

- This must be distinguished from 'rescission for vitiating factors' (eg misrepresentation and duress), which sets aside a contract both *retrospectively and prospectively* (5.2), requires mutual restitution and, of course, gives no expectation remedies.
- Where termination is expressed as '*discharge by breach*', note that a serious breach merely entitles the claimant to *elect* to terminate.
- In contrast, *discharge* by frustration occurs *automatically*.

12.2.1 **The effect of termination**

(i) Termination discharges *both* parties from further performance of their primary obligations under the contract. Neither party needs to accept and neither can demand performance from the other. But the contract-breaker's unperformed primary obligation is replaced by 'a *secondary* (remedial) obligation to pay monetary compensation' to the claimant for her loss (*Photo Production Ltd v Securicor Transport Ltd* (1980)). The claimant can also claim damages for loss from the breach up to the time of termination.

(ii) **Accrued and other continuing obligations remain enforceable**: since the contract only discharges the parties from future obligations (ie due after termination), 'rights are not divested or discharged which have been unconditionally acquired' (*The Dominique* (1989)), eg a reasonable deposit paid cannot be recovered. Terms in the terminated contract that specifically relate to the post-termination situation (eg agreed damages (14.3)) or restriction of otherwise available remedies for breach (eg requiring arbitration or exempting liability) continue to apply.

(iii) **Claims for restitution**: subject to the bar on double recovery, the **claimant** may (instead of expectation damages), elect to sue for:

> ✓ restitution of any money paid under the contract if there has been a *total failure of consideration* from the defendant (13.4); or
>
> ✓ a *quantum meruit* or *quantum valebat* for the reasonable value of goods or services supplied but not yet paid for under the contract (*Planché v Colburn* (1831)).

These restitutionary claims are preferable if the claimant has made a bad bargain. If instead, the claimant elects for **expectation damages**, any benefits received from the defendant are brought into the calculation of the claimant's expectation damages. Thus, the claimant may elect to do nothing, keep such benefits received and wait for the defendant to sue in respect of them.

On termination, **the contract-breaker** can only:

✓ recover part-payments for goods or land for total failure of consideration (*Dies v British and Intl Mining & Finance Corp Ltd* (1939));

✓ claim the contract price in respect of the divisible part of the contract earned by performance if the contract is divisible (rather than entire, 12.2.2.1 III), but subject to the claimant's counterclaim; or

✓ obtain relief from forfeiture (*Workers Trust & Merchant Bank Ltd v Dojap Investments Ltd* (1993) and 14.3.3).

The contract-breaker cannot claim:

✗ the deposit paid (14.3); or

✗ the contract price for part performance if the contract is entire (12.2.2.1 III).

 Pause for reflection

The European Draft Common Frame of Reference:

1. does not take an all-or-nothing approach: termination may be in whole or only in part (Art III.-3:506);

2. takes a more even-handed approach to restitution: *mutual* restitution is required except 'to the extent that conforming-performance by one party is met by conforming-performance by the other' (Arts III.-3:510 and III.-3:511). If precise restitution cannot be made, then restitution can be made in money's worth (Art III.-3:312); and

3. allows the claimant who *accepts* non-conforming performance to claim a price reduction (Art III.-3:601).

The **advantages of termination for the claimant** are the following.

(i) Termination is a self-help remedy: the claimant can end the contract quickly without the inconvenience and cost of going to court, leaving it to the contract-breaker to challenge the termination in court.

(ii) Faced with a serious breach, it is often preferable for the claimant to discontinue her own performance than to continue (eg by paying money), only to claim unsecured damages later (she will lose out if the defendant becomes insolvent).

(iii) Termination can save the claimant from a bad bargain: she might be better off not performing and recovering her payment than claiming expectation damages for breach (eg where she pays or has promised to pay £10,000 for goods which, by the time of performance, are only worth £6,000).

However, termination may be very **disadvantageous to the contract-breaker:**

(i) she may have incurred *expenses* in performance, which will now be wasted;

(ii) her part-performance may have conferred *benefits* on the claimant, who may not be liable to make restitution (13.4.2);

(iii) she may *lose the benefit of a good bargain*, which would amount to a penalty entirely disproportionate to the harm caused by the breach.

12.2.2 **When is termination allowed?**

Where breach or anticipatory breach is **total**, the claimant can clearly terminate the contract; where it is **partial**, difficult technical questions arise. The answer ostensibly depends on the *status* of the term breached. The rule of thumb is that the defendant's:

✓ breaches of '*conditions*' allow the claimant to terminate; but

✗ her breaches of mere '*warranties*' do not.

However, balancing the parties' conflicting interests necessitates a **consequentialist approach**:

✓ if the breach has seriously prejudiced the claimant's position, she should be able to call the contract off; but,

✗ if the defendant has largely performed what was bargained for, substantial justice is done if the contract remains on foot and damages are paid to compensate the claimant for the breach.

We will see that the law has moved some way in that direction by recognising the category of '*innominate terms*'. However, the concern to promote certainty (important for a self-help remedy not requiring resort to the courts) while also avoiding harshness to the defendant has resulted in considerable complexity.

12.2.2.1 Clearing the ground

Treitel examines the many senses in which the expression 'condition' is used when determining whether a claimant can withhold her own performance. ('"Conditions" and "Conditions Precedent"' (1990) 106 *LQR* 185). An overview is provided by **Diagram 12A**.

- **Levels I–III** concern the order of performance: the claimant may be able to withhold her own performance simply because it is 'not her turn yet'.

- **Level IV** concerns the conformity of any performance with the contractual obligations: here, lack of conformity amounts to breach and the claimant's withholding of her own performance, if she is entitled, amounts to termination.

Level I: Contingent or promissory obligation?
At the highest level of generality, 'conditions' may be either contingent or promissory.

- A *contingent* condition is one for which neither party is responsible, but upon which both parties' obligations to perform or keep performing depend. It may be a *condition precedent* (as where performance depends on one party obtaining a licence or planning permission: *Pym v Campbell* (1865)), or a *condition subsequent* (as where continuing performance depends on continued funding from a specified source: *Brown v Knowsley BC* (1986)). There is no question of breach (and thus, of termination for breach) if the condition precedent fails or the condition subsequent occurs: the obligation to perform the contract simply does not arise or is discharged. Recall that the mistake doctrine has been interpreted as an instance of an implied condition precedent (6.3.7.1), and the frustration doctrine, an instance of an implied condition subsequent (7.2.1).

- A *promissory* condition refers to something which one party has an *obligation* to bring about. But whether breach of this condition entitles the claimant to terminate the contract depends on whether the promissory condition is 'dependent' or 'independent'.

Level II: Dependent or independent obligation?

- Where the promissory condition undertaken by *A* is independent of *B*'s performance, *A* cannot terminate the contract on *B*'s breach, however serious (*A* must

Diagram 12A Overview of the claimant's right to withhold performance

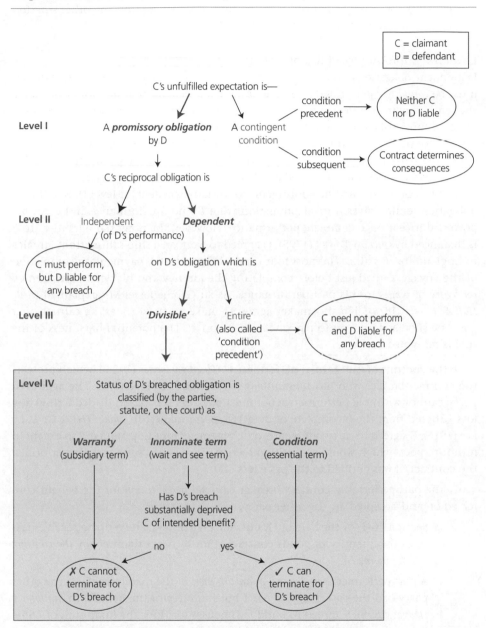

Look on the online resources to view this figure as a PowerPoint® presentation

still perform), eg a tenant's covenant to pay rent is independent of the landlord's covenant to repair: the tenant cannot withhold payment even if the landlord fails to repair (*Taylor v Webb* (1937)). Since this may leave *A* inadequately protected from *B*'s non-performance, courts are slow to designate an obligation as being 'independent' unless the contract makes this very clear.

- Contractual obligations are normally regarded as being **dependent** (or *interde-pendent*): each party's obligation to perform is dependent on the other's perfor-mance or readiness and willingness to perform.[2]

Level III: 'Entire' or 'divisible' obligation?

Dependent obligations may be 'entire' or 'divisible'. An obligation is 'entire' when it must be *completely* performed *before* the other party is obliged to perform (also called the 'entire contract' rule), eg where *A* engages *B* to build a conservatory for £40,000, payment on satisfactory completion of the whole (or part-payment for defined parts), *A* need not pay, and *B* cannot sue for part-payment, if *B* fails to complete the whole (or stipulated part). *B* has not fulfilled the condition triggering the payment. *B*'s perfor-mance here is sometimes described as a 'condition precedent' to *B*'s right to payment (not to be confused with the contingent 'condition precedent' at level I). Making an obligation 'entire' gives *A* great protection from *B*'s non-performance and gives *B* a powerful incentive to complete performance. However, the potential harshness to *B* is instanced by *Cutter v Powell* (1795). C agreed to work on a ship sailing from Jamaica to England for 30 guineas (almost four times the going rate), payment on completion of the voyage. C died just before completing the journey and his widow was denied recovery of wages for his part-performance. As Sir George Jessel MR explained in *Re Hall & Barker* (1878), 'if a shoemaker agrees to make a pair of shoes, he cannot offer you one shoe and ask you to pay you one half the price'. The potential harshness of the rule is mitigated by:

(i) the doctrine of 'substantial performance' (*Hoenig v Isaacs* (1952)), which protects the contract-breaker who has *substantially* performed her obligations. The aggrieved party cannot withhold performance but must pay after setting-off (ie deducting) any loss suffered from the incomplete or defective performance. In *Dakin (H) & Co Ltd v Lee* (1916), D agreed to carry out repairs on L's premises for £1,500 and did so except in minor respects which would cost £80 to rectify. Since D had substantially performed the contract, it was entitled to the price less £80;

(ii) the part-performing contract-breaker can claim *restitution* for the benefit con-ferred on and 'accepted' by the other party:

✓ Section 30(1) of the Sale of Goods Act 1979 allows a buyer who receives less than the quantity of goods contracted for to reject them *or pay the contract rate for them*.

✓ A part-performer can claim a *quantum meruit* (the market value) if the other party had the *opportunity to reject* but has *accepted* the benefit. In *Sumpter v Hedges* (1898), S agreed to build two houses for H for the lump sum of £565. When S informed H that he could not complete because he had run out of money, H completed the houses himself. S was denied a reasonable remu-neration for the work done since H had no option but to accept what was done on his land. However, S could recover the value of the *materials* left behind, which H had a choice to reject but chose to accept by using them.

---

[2] Eg the Sale of Goods Act 1979, s 28, regarding the delivery of the goods and payment of the price; the failure of one party discharges the other from performance.

Such acceptance counters a recipient's right to say that the part-performance received (one shoe as opposed to two) is worth *less* than the reasonable market value or *nothing at all* to them.

To avoid the potential unfairness associated with 'entire' obligations, courts lean towards finding obligations to be 'divisible'. Breach gives the aggrieved party an action for damages, but does not *necessarily* allow her to withhold her own performance by terminating the contract. Whether it does depends on the status of the term breached, to which we now turn.

12.2.2.2 The status of terms: conditions, warranties, and innominate terms

It was once assumed that *every* contractual term could be classified at the time of formation as:

- a condition: an essential term, the breach of which (a 'repudiatory breach') gives the claimant the right to terminate and claim damages for losses *up to* termination and *beyond* (ie for loss of the bargain); or
- a warranty: a non-essential or subsidiary term, the breach of which yields no right to termination; the claimant can only claim damages for losses *up to* the time of the action (but not for loss of the bargain since the contract continues).

In short, the claimant can terminate if the term breached is a condition, but not if it is a warranty, irrespective of the seriousness of the *actual consequences* of breach.

However, **if a term is not clearly classified** by the parties, by statute, or by binding precedent (12.2.3), it may be difficult to say *at the time of formation* how important the term is, because the consequences of its breach may vary wildly in seriousness, depending on the precise circumstances of the breach (*Bentsen v Taylor, Sons & Co* (1893)). The judicial solution was to recognise a new category of *'wait and see'* terms, called **'innominate'** (or 'intermediate') terms. Whether termination is available for breach of such terms depends on 'waiting and seeing' whether the actual *consequences* of breach are sufficiently grave for the claimant. Its effect is still all-or-nothing; the difference is simply in the *timing* of the decision (ie at breach). Diplock LJ explains in *Hong Kong Fir Shipping Co Ltd v Kawasaki Kisen Kaisha Ltd* (1962) that the legal consequences of the breach of innominate terms 'do not follow automatically from a prior classification of the undertaking, as a "condition" or a "warranty"'. It depends upon whether the breach has deprived or will deprive the claimant 'of substantially the whole benefit which it was intended he should obtain from the contract'. In that case, H chartered a ship to K for 24 months, but breached the term requiring the ship to be 'in every way fitted for ordinary cargo service' by failing to provide competent personnel to maintain the aged ship. The ship had many serious breakdowns and only spent two months at sea in the first seven months. The seaworthiness term was held to be an innominate term, the breach of which would only entitle the charterer to terminate if its consequence was so serious as to frustrate the commercial purpose of the venture. Upjohn LJ explains:

> It is for the simple reason that the seaworthiness clause is breached by the slightest failure to be fitted 'in every way' for service . . . If a nail is missing from one of the timbers of a wooden vessel or if proper medical supplies or two anchors are not on board

at the time of sailing, the owners are in breach of the seaworthiness stipulation. It is contrary to common sense to suppose that in such circumstances the parties contemplated that the charterer should at once be entitled to treat the contract as at an end for such trifling breaches.

The essence of innominate terms is that they can be breached in different ways, resulting in consequences of varying seriousness. On the facts, it was held that, in spite of the delays already occurring and likely to occur, the steps H had taken to remedy the failings and the length of the charter period remaining meant that K was *not* substantially deprived of the whole benefit of the contract. Thus, K's purported termination itself amounted to a repudiatory breach entitling H to damages for loss of profit. These were substantial since the market had dropped significantly: indeed, the real motive for K's attempted termination was to get a cheaper deal elsewhere.

The high threshold for termination has been expressed by saying that the breach:

✓ must go to 'the root of the contract' (*Cehave NV v Bremer Handelsgesellschaft (The Hansa Nord)* (1976));

✓ be 'fundamental' (*Suisse Atlantique Société d'Armement SA v NV Rotterdamsche Kolen Centrale* (1967));

✓ amount to 'a substantial failure to perform the contract at all' (*Wallis, Son & Wells v Pratt & Haynes* (1910)); or

✓ 'frustrate the commercial purpose of the venture' (*Trade and Transport Inc v Iino Kaiun Kaisha Ltd (The Angelia)* (1973)).

In determining whether breach of an innominate term entitles the claimant to terminate, the court must balance the position of the parties at the date of the purported termination. In *Telford Homes (Creekside) Ltd v Ampurius Nu Homes Holdings Ltd* (2013), Lewison LJ sets out the nature of the multi-factorial assessment:

[T]he starting point must be to consider what benefit the injured party was intended to obtain from performance of the contract. . . .

The next thing to consider is the effect of the breach on the injured party. What financial loss has it caused? How much of the intended benefit under the contract has the injured party already received? Can the injured party be adequately compensated by an award of damages? Is the breach likely to be repeated? Will the guilty party resume compliance with his obligations? Has the breach fundamentally changed the value of future performance of the guilty party's outstanding obligations?

Some examples illustrate the high threshold:

✗ In *Telford Homes*, the Court of Appeal held that a property company had not been entitled to terminate an agreement to take 999-year leases in four blocks on the ground of the construction company's delay in building two of the blocks.

✗ Likewise, the buyer of a 125-year lease was held not entitled to terminate because the delay of one month on the completion of the building could not possibly be said to have deprived the buyer of substantially the whole benefit of the contract (*Urban I (Blonk Street) Ltd v Ayres* (2013)).

In practice, this high threshold of seriousness required, the wide range of factors considered, their uncertain relative weight and the potentially disastrous consequences of an attempted termination which turns out to be wrongful will act as strong disincentives to elect termination in response to its breach.

12.2.3 **How are terms classified?**

Terms may be classified by: (i) statute; (ii) the parties' express agreement; or (iii) the court (applying binding precedents or finding the parties' implied intentions). Awareness of the relevant policies is important in understanding what is at stake in the distinctions. The ubiquitous tensions in contract law between certainty, fairness, and respect for the parties' intentions come into sharp focus here. Policies favouring *prior determination* (ie at formation) support the classifications of 'conditions' or 'warranties'; policies favouring *subsequent determination* (ie after breach) support the classification of 'innominate terms'.

(i) Commercial certainty: certainty supports prior determination because it enables commercial parties to know, immediately and unequivocally, how they are entitled to respond on the other party's breach. Certainty is particularly important (*Bunge Corp v Tradax Export SA* (1981)):

    (a) where the contract is one of a chain or 'string' of contracts because 'most members of the "string" will have many ongoing contracts simultaneously and they must be able to do business with confidence in the legal results of their actions', or

    (b) where it would be difficult for the claimant and the court to quantify the loss suffered.

(ii) Freedom of contract: this also supports prior determination; contract parties should be free to determine in advance which breaches will entitle the parties to terminate, irrespective of their consequences.

(iii) Avoiding bad faith terminations: this supports subsequent classification as an innominate term.

    ✓ The potential unfairness of termination for 'technical' or unmeritorious reasons is instanced by *Arcos Ltd v E A Ronaasen & Son* (1933). The parties contracted for the sale and purchase of timber staves cut to 8/16-inch thickness. The buyers were allowed to reject the goods for being 9/16-inch thick (ie terminate the contract), although their real reason was to escape what had turned into a bad bargain. A fall in timber prices meant that the buyers could now buy wood cheaper than under the contract.

    ✗ The courts have made use of the innominate term classification to counter such economic opportunism. In *Cehave v Bremer (The Hansa Nord)* (1976), the parties contracted for the sale of citrus pulp pellets for £100,000 to arrive 'in good condition'. Meanwhile, the market price for pellets dropped to about £86,000. The buyers rejected the goods on the ground that some of the pellets were damaged. The seller then sold the pellets to a third party who resold them to the original buyer for about £30,000; the buyer used them to manufacture cattle feed, as originally intended. The buyer's termination was held to be unlawful since the term breached was classified as innominate and the consequences were not sufficiently serious to allow the contract to be avoided 'according to the whims of market fluctuations and where there is a free choice between two possible constructions... the court should tend to prefer that construction which will ensure performance and not encourage avoidance of contractual obligations'.

(iv) Upholding bargains: dicta from *The Hansa Nord* suggest that courts should encourage the performance, rather than the termination, of contracts (unless the claimant has been substantially deprived of the benefit of the contract). This leans towards the innominate term classification. On the other hand, the converse is arguable since classifying a term as a condition would discourage breach in the first place for fear of its potentially drastic consequences.

The modern default position is to treat terms as innominate, unless a court is compelled to find otherwise by reference to statute, the parties' express provision or binding precedent. The question is not '*why* innominate term?' but '*why not?*' As Lord Scarman said in **Bunge Corp v Tradax**, 'unless the contract makes it clear, either by express provision or by necessary implication arising from its nature, purpose, and circumstances... that a particular stipulation is a condition or only a warranty, it is an innominate term'. This tendency is certainly detectable in classifications by the courts, but it is even detectable where terms are classified by *statute* and by the *parties'* ostensible agreement (12.2.3.1 and 12.2.3.2). An overview is provided by **Diagram 12B**. The

Diagram 12B Classification of terms

Has the term been classified by:

Statute?

✗ ✓ → Implements legislative policy → Condition

The parties?

✗ ✓ → Filtered through judicial interpretation and shaped by policies supporting—
• certainty
• freedom of contract
• flexibility
• fairness
• contractual performance and against—
• bad faith withdrawal
Note the trend towards the default category of innominate term

The courts?

by reference to
(a) binding precedent
or
(b) judgment in the individual case

(cannot have negative answer) ✓ →

Classification as:

or

Warranty

or

Innominate term

European Draft Common Frame of Reference treats all terms as innominate for the purposes of the remedy of termination (Art III.-3:502).

12.2.3.1 Classification by statute

Statute may classify terms as either conditions or warranties. Recall that the Sale of Goods Act 1979 (10.6.2.1) implies as **conditions** into sale of goods contracts terms guaranteeing that:

- the seller has *title* to sell the goods (s 12(1));
- goods sold by *description* correspond with their description (s 13(1));
- goods sold by *sample* correspond with the sample (s 15(2));
- goods sold in the course of business are of *satisfactory quality* unless the buyer's attention has been drawn to, or the buyer's examination ought to have revealed, any defect (s 14(2) and (2C)); and
- goods sold in the course of business are reasonably *fit for the purpose* that the buyer has made known to the seller (s 14(3)).

The Sale of Goods Act also implies as **warranties** terms guaranteeing that:

- goods sold are *free from charges or incumbrances* in favour of third parties not disclosed or known to the buyer before the contract, and that the buyer will enjoy *quiet possession* of the goods subject to the disclosed or known rights of others (s 2(2), (4)–(5)).

There are no examples of statutes classifying a term as **'innominate'**, but this is the effect of section 15A(1) of the Sale of Goods Act. While breach of any implied *condition* entitles the buyer to *reject* the goods (ie terminate the contract), this section requires a *non-consumer buyer* to treat the breach as one of *warranty* (ie no rejection allowed) where the breach is 'so slight that it would be unreasonable for him to reject them', unless the parties otherwise agree. This would counter the potential unfairness of cases like *Arcos v Ronaasen*.

However, section 15A(1) is *one-sided* in limiting the buyer's right to terminate, but not the seller's. Moreover, it is unclear when breaches will be regarded as *'slight'* (the difference between 8/16 and 9/16 of an inch may not be slight for certain uses).

12.2.3.2 Classification by the parties

In principle, it is always open to the parties to agree the status (and hence, consequences of breach) of particular terms (*Bunge Corp v Tradax*), although there are no examples of parties' classification as innominate terms. Even apparently trivial terms can be classified as 'conditions', allowing termination for their breach, eg in *Lombard North Central plc v Butterworth* (1987), B essentially agreed to buy on hire-purchase terms a computer from L, making quarterly payments for five years (totalling £11,680), time being 'of the essence' of the contract (ie a condition). When the payments were almost complete, B was late with some payments and L terminated the contract. The computer was repossessed and resold for only £173. The Court of Appeal upheld L's termination and allowed L's claim to recover arrears as damages *up to* termination *and* claim *future instalments* as damages for loss of the bargain consequent on termination.

Thus, classification by the parties has the clear potential for unfairness. The stronger party can insist that even minor obligations of the other party are conditions, or can include a 'termination clause' giving itself a wide power to end the contract. This power can be exercised opportunistically (even for a trivial breach) to escape a bad bargain and so deprive the contract-breaker of its bargain. Courts have developed a number of **techniques for controlling the unreasonable creation of conditions and termination clauses**, although careful drafting may still evade the court's control:

(i) **Courts may find that the parties used the labels 'condition' or 'warranty' in their non-technical sense** (ie simply meaning 'terms') and not in their technical sense of determining whether there is a right to termination on breach; this leaves the court free to classify the term as innominate. In *Schuler v Wickman* (1974), W had the sole right to sell S's goods in the UK for over four years. Clause 7 made it a 'condition' that W's two named representatives should visit particular manufacturers each week to promote S's goods; they failed to do so. The House of Lords denied that clause 7 was a condition in the termination-yielding sense, since this would turn even one missed visit (out of the 1,400 due over the period) into a repudiatory breach. Although Lord Reid accepted that the parties' use of the word 'condition' was a 'strong indication', the fact that 'a particular construction leads to a very *unreasonable result* must be a relevant consideration. The more unreasonable the result the more unlikely it is that the parties can have intended it, and if they do intend it the more necessary it is that they shall make that intention abundantly clear' (10.4.2).

(ii) **Courts may treat termination under an agreed 'termination clause' as less remedially potent than breach of a 'condition' proper**: this restricts the available damages. In *Financings Ltd v Baldock* (1963), B bought a van from F on hire purchase on payment of £100 and monthly instalments of £28 for two years. Clause 8 gave F the express right to terminate the contract if any instalment was more than ten days late. F terminated the contract when B failed to make the first two payments and sold the van for £140. The court confined F to the recovery of the two late instalments but denied its claim for loss of *future* instalments (ie loss of the bargain); the latter was only available when terminating for a *repudiatory breach*, while F merely exercised a power conferred by the contract on an event not amounting to such.

On the other hand, if the claimant can terminate both under a termination clause and under the common law, the court will be slow to find that the claimant has abandoned her valuable rights under the common law (*Stocznia Gdynia SA v Gearbulk Holdings Ltd* (2009)).

(iii) **Courts may read down agreed 'termination clauses' to restrict their scope of operation**: in *Rice (t/a Garden Guardian) v Great Yarmouth BC* (2000), an agreement by R to maintain and manage G's sports facilities, parks, gardens, and playgrounds allowed G to terminate the contract 'if the contractor commits a breach of any of its obligations'. G purported to terminate the contract after serving a number of default notices on R. This was held to be unlawful since it could only terminate for a *repudiatory breach* and this had not occurred. Analogous to *Schuler v Wickman*, the court rejected a literal interpretation of the words of the termination clause as offending 'commercial sense'; R's performance involved 'a myriad of obligations of differing importance and varying frequency' which could be broken in many different ways with varying consequences typical of innominate terms. Likewise, Kitchin J noted that: 'the courts have shown some reluctance to interpret a termination clause in a complex contract containing many innominate terms as providing a party with the right to terminate for any breach, however minor' as this 'flouts business common-sense' (*Dominion Corporate Trustees Ltd v Debenhams Properties Ltd* (2010)).

Pause for reflection

1. The decision renders the termination clause pointless since G could have terminated for a repudiatory breach anyway. A party seeking to rely on a wide termination clause is now well-advised to state expressly that it can terminate for 'any breach even if it does not amount to a repudiatory breach'.

2. The court's commendable aversion to interpretations that lead to very unreasonable results mirrors its *contra proferentem* construction of harsh exemption clauses (10.5.3) and *force majeure* clauses (7.4.1). It is motivated by the same concerns about inequality of bargaining power and the avoidance of harsh outcomes, which defeat parties' reasonable expectations.

3. In 'Termination Clauses' in A Burrows and E Peel (eds), *Contract Terms* (OUP, 2007) 253, Whittaker examines the ways in which such clauses are controlled, including by invalidation under the Unfair Terms in Consumer Contracts Regulations 1999 (now the Contracts Rights Act 2015).

12.2.3.3 Classification by the courts

Where a term is not classified by the parties or by statute, the courts must do so. Where a binding precedent has classified the term, certainty generally requires it to be followed, eg time clauses are often treated as conditions, as are stipulations in a time charterparty as to the date for payment (*Bowes v Shand* (1876–7)), or in voyage charterparties as to the time when the chartered vessel should be ready to load (*The Mihalis Angelos* (1971)). However, Lord Wilberforce describes some previous decisions as 'excessively technical' and warned that they were open to re-examination by the House of Lords (*Smith Line Ltd v Yngvar Hansen-Tangen* (1976)).

Where a term is previously unclassified, the default position is to treat it as an **innominate** term unless this is contra-indicated (*Bunge Corp v Tradax*). Nevertheless, Lord Wilberforce said that courts should not be reluctant to find a condition if the intentions of the parties so indicate, especially in the case of *time* clauses in *mercantile* (ie commercial) contracts.

In the last analysis, the court is making 'what is in effect a *value judgment* about the commercial significance of the term in question' (*State Trading Corp of India Ltd v M Golodetz* (1989)), and different courts may reach different conclusions. Classification as a condition is more likely if the term:

- involves a single performance with a clearly specified time limit and sequence of performance (eg a period within which events inhibiting performance are to be notified, an extension of time to be claimed, or the buyer is to have the option of cancelling the contract);

- can only be breached in one way;
- is vital to the contract; or
- is necessary for commercial certainty.

A term is more likely to be classified as **innominate** if:

- it can be breached in different ways with varying degrees of seriousness;
- performance is to take place over a long time and substantial performance has been given; or
- the obligation is loosely framed.

A condition was found in ***Bunge Corp v Tradax***. The buyer of soya bean meal was required to nominate the *time* for shipment, giving the seller 'at least 15 consecutive days' notice of probable readiness of vessel(s) and of the approximate quantity required to be loaded'. The seller would then nominate a port to load the goods (shipment being required by 30 June). The seller treated the buyer's late notice as a repudiatory breach. The House of Lords agreed that the term breached was a condition, although it did not deprive the seller of substantially the whole benefit under the contract, because:

- of the need for certainty in commercial transactions, particularly those involving a chain of sales, when timely performance is vital and parties need to know where they stand when faced with breach;
- the seller's (claimant's) obligation to nominate a port and be ready to load was dependent on the buyer (contract-breaker) giving the requisite notice;
- damages for breach would be very difficult to assess; and
- this was consistent with precedents on similar time terms and predominant commercial practice.

In contrast, an innominate term was found in *Bremer Handelsgesellschaft mbH v Vanden Avenne-Izegem PVBA* (1978). Here, a time term in another soya bean meal contract required the seller to advise the buyer 'without delay' of impossibility of shipment because of prohibition of export. However, it did *not stipulate any time limit* by which the advice was to be given.

Even precise time clauses may be construed as innominate terms depending on their 'commercial significance'. In *Ioannis Valilas v Valdet Januzaj* (2014), the Court of Appeal found that a dentist had not committed a repudiatory breach when he informed the practice owner that he would be making payments late because:

- the time of payment was not generally of the essence in a commercial contract unless the parties had agreed that it should be an innominate term;
- the effect of the dentist's past and threatened future breaches could not be said to deprive the practice owner of substantially the whole benefit of the contract. The owner had other sources of income and knew that he would obtain payment in the end. His only likely loss was the loss of the use of the money in the meantime.

12.2.4 **Electing termination**

A repudiatory breach does *not* automatically bring a contract to an end. It gives the claimant a right to *elect* whether to terminate or to affirm the contract (even in respect of employment contracts: *Geys v Société Générale, London Branch* (2012)). Five points should be noted about electing to terminate (also known as 'acceptance of the repudiation'):

(i) Termination must be **clear and unequivocal**: mere inactivity will not normally suffice. Election to terminate the contract must generally be communicated to the contract-breaker, but it 'requires no particular form... The aggrieved party need not personally, or by an agent, notify the repudiating party... It is sufficient that the fact of the election comes to the repudiating party's attention' (*Vitol SA v Norelf Ltd* (1996)).

(ii) Termination can only come **after repudiatory breach**: in *North Eastern Properties Ltd v Coleman & Quinn Conveyancing* (2009), C's notice to N, the vendor, saying that C would deem N in breach of contract and 'consider themselves discharged from the contract' if the properties were not ready for occupation within ten working days, was merely a statement of intention and not an effective termination since there was no right to make an election prior to the repudiatory breach.

(iii) The claimant is **not bound to elect at once**; she can wait for performance or negotiate in the hope of a settlement (*The Mihalios Xilas* (1978)). However, the claimant who does not accept the repudiation must herself remain ready and willing to perform. Further, as Rix LJ explains in *Stocznia Gdanska SA v Latvian Shipping Co (No 2)* (2002), the claimant runs a risk whilst making up her mind:

> If he does nothing for too long, there may come a time when the law will treat him as having affirmed . . . [Anyway, as] long as the contract remains alive, the innocent party runs the risk that a merely anticipatory repudiatory breach, a thing 'writ in water' until acceptance, can be overtaken by another event which prejudices the innocent party's rights under the contract—such as frustration or even his own breach. He also runs the risk . . . that the party in repudiation will resume performance of the contract and thus end any continuing right in the innocent party to elect to accept the former repudiation as terminating the contract.

The length of time that a claimant may wait whilst making up her mind will depend upon the facts of each case: some cases 'may well be more or less complex and call for more or less urgency' (*Force India v Etihad Airways* (2010)).

(iv) The claimant's termination is valid if she is legally entitled to terminate even if her real motive is to escape what has become a bad bargain because of market fluctuations, and even if the **reason she puts forward** is:

- invalid (eg being mistaken);
- dishonest (eg *Arcos v Ronaasen*); or
- she gives no reason, because she was unaware of the good reason at the time of termination (eg **The Mihalis Angelos** (1971)).

In these senses, the phrases 'election' and 'acceptance of the repudiation' may be misleading since there is no need for any causal relationship between the repudiatory breach and the claimant's decision to terminate. Such 'bad faith' terminations are criticised for allowing parties to 'blow hot and cold'.[3] On the other hand:

- it may be very difficult to determine a party's *real* motivation for terminating;
- it is not clear that a claimant should lose her right to terminate simply because she was unaware of her right to do so when she offered a bad reason for terminating; and
- *both* parties may have acted in bad faith (as in *The Mihalis Angelos* (1971)).

Article III.-1:103 of the European Draft Common Frame of Reference imposes a non-excludable 'duty to act in accordance with good faith and fair dealing'. This duty will bar termination for invalid or dishonest reasons.

(v) The choice, once made, is irrevocable.

12.2.5 Loss of the right to terminate

The claimant's right to terminate a contract may be lost by:

(i) **The claimant's conduct**, eg in affirming the contract (12.3); by operation of 'waiver by estoppel' (3.2.2.1); or by her own subsequent breach making her liable for damages (*Fercometal SARL v Mediterranean Shipping Co SA (The Simona)* (1989)).

(ii) **The defendant's performance** when it becomes due, in the case of renunciation or anticipatory breach. However, once there has been an *actual* repudiatory breach, the claimant's right to terminate is *not* lost by the defendant's cure of the breach. In *Buckland v Bournemouth University* (2010), the Court of Appeal held that the university's action in having the claimant professor's marking of examination scripts re-marked by someone else, behind the claimant's back, amounted to a breach of its implied duty of trust and confidence, entitling the claimant to terminate the contract. This right of termination was not lost although the university had effectively cured the breach by establishing a formal inquiry into the matter, which exonerated the claimant.

(iii) **The operation of a rule of law**, eg supervening frustration (*Avery v Bowden* (1856)), or section 11(4) of the Sale of Goods Act 1979, which deprives the buyer of her right to reject the goods if she has 'accepted' the goods even if she was ignorant of the breach. Section 35 states that the buyer is deemed to have accepted the goods: (a) when she so communicates to the seller; (b) when her conduct in relation to the goods delivered is inconsistent with the seller's ownership; or (c) by lapse of time.

12.3 **Affirmation**

Rather than terminate the contract for the defendant's breach, the claimant may elect to affirm (continue with) the contract. It had been hotly contested whether employment contracts are *automatically* terminated on a repudiatory breach, because specific

---

[3] R Brownsword, 'Retrieving Reasons, Retrieving Rationality? A New Look at the Right to Withdraw Breach of Contract' (1992) 5 *JCL* 83, 92–3.

performance is generally denied in such contracts (14.2.1.3). In *Geys v Société Générale, London Branch* (2012), the Supreme Court:

✗ rejected the automatic termination approach; and

✓ affirmed the general election approach.

There, the employee elected to affirm the contract on the employer's unfair dismissal. The effect was that the contract of employment was deemed to have remained in being until it was eventually validly terminated; this extended the period of service upon which the employee's bonus entitlement was based, increasing the employee's bonus entitlement by several million pounds.

(i) **Electing affirmation:** the claimant must evince an unequivocal intention (expressly or impliedly) to continue with the contract, *with knowledge* of the facts giving rise to the breach, and her legal right to elect (*Peyman v Lanjani* (1985)). The claimant does not generally affirm the contract by mere inactivity (*Perry v Davis* (1858)) or by simply calling for the defendant's performance: 'the law does not require an injured party to snatch at repudiation and he does not automatically lose his right to treat the contract as discharged merely by calling on the other to reconsider his position and recognise his obligation' (*Yukong Line Ltd of Korea v Rendsberg Investments Corp of Liberia* (1996)). However, she *will* have affirmed the contract if she continues to press for, or accepts, performance (*Davenport v R* (1877)). Thus, in *Tele2 International Card Co SA v KUB 2 Technology Ltd* (2009), the Court of Appeal held that Post Office Ltd (PO) could not terminate for T's breach of a term because PO's delay of almost a year in giving notice of termination and continued performance during that time constituted affirmation of the agreement by election. PO's attempted termination was therefore a repudiatory breach.

The **existence** of a 'waiver clause' providing that delay or failure to enforce a provision should not prevent later enforcement, cannot negate an election to affirm (it is doubtful that any clause can). It only emphasises that an election to abandon a right to terminate requires a clear and unequivocal communication of an election.

(ii) **Irrevocability:** once the claimant has communicated her affirmation to the contract-breaker, it is irrevocable, even without *reliance* by or detriment to the contract-breaker (*Peyman v Lanjani*). Lord Wilberforce said in *Johnson v Agnew* (1980) on termination that 'the contract has gone—what is dead is dead' (at least, its primary obligations). But, if the contract-breaker *persists* with her non-performance or commits a fresh breach, the claimant can rely on this to terminate the contract.

(iii) **The effect of affirmation:** both parties remain bound to perform their primary obligations ('an unaccepted repudiation is a thing writ in water', *Howard v Pickford Tool Co Ltd* (1951)), but the claimant is entitled to damages for any loss flowing from the delay (although logically not for loss of bargain). The claimant may also seek specific performance come the time for performance.

(iv) **Restrictions on the right to affirm:** faced with an *anticipatory repudiatory* breach, the claimant will prefer to affirm a contract, complete her own performance, and claim the contract price (ie the '**agreed price**'; 14.1) where:

- she has incurred substantial expenses that would be difficult to recover as damages;
- her expectation damages would be nominal (eg due to the mitigation requirement (13.2.5.2)) or too remote (13.2.5.1);

- termination would damage her *reputation*, for which damages are rarely available and difficult to assess (13.2.4.3);
- termination would put her in breach of contracts with third parties; or
- the contract-breaker has repudiated in bad faith (eg because of a personal dispute with the claimant) and not because the claimant's performance was unwanted.

However, the claimant cannot always affirm. In *White & Carter (Councils) Ltd v McGregor* (1962), M contracted for his garage business to be advertised on rubbish bins that W&C supplied to the local council for three years. On the same day, M tried to cancel the contract but W&C refused. The latter continued with the advertisement and sued M for the agreed price. The House of Lords by a 3:2 majority upheld W&C's claim, but Lord Reid set out two limits on the claimant's ability to affirm the contract (neither applied in this case):[4]

(i) Need for the contract-breaker's cooperation: in practice, the claimant faced with a repudiatory breach will often have no choice but to terminate the contract because she cannot complete her own performance without the contract-breaker's cooperation.

(ii) 'No legitimate interest': the claimant cannot affirm if she has 'no legitimate interest, financial or otherwise, in performing the contract rather than claiming damages'. However, the threshold is a very high one (*The Oldenfield* (1978)). Simon J said (*Ocean Marine Navigation Ltd v Koch Carbon Inc (The Dynamic)* (2003)) that:

(a) the burden of proof is on the *contract-breaker* to show that the claimant has no legitimate interest in performing the contract;

(b) it is not enough to show that the benefit of affirmation to the claimant is small in comparison with the loss to the contract-breaker;

(c) the exception to the general rule applies only in extreme cases where damages would be adequate and where an election to keep the contract alive would be wholly unreasonable.

 Pause for reflection

White & Carter v McGregor is much **criticised**.[5]

1. The court must impliedly have found that W&C had a legitimate interest in performing the unwanted services, although damages would seem an adequate remedy and allowing W&C to perform unwanted services seems unreasonable.

2. The decision encourages wasteful performance, contrary to the claimant's duty to mitigate her loss in damages claims (13.2.5.2). In contrast, no mitigation is required for affirmation.

3. The decision allows the claimant to increase the contract-breaker's liability by conferring unwanted goods or services. →

---

[4] See also *Hounslow LBC v Twickenham Garden Developments Ltd* (1971).

[5] P Nienaber, 'The Effect of Anticipatory Repudiation: Principle and Policy' (1962) 20 *CLJ* 213; M Furmston, 'The Case of the Insistent Performer' (1962) 25 *MLR* 364; W Goodhart, 'Measure of Damages when a Contract is Repudiated' (1962) 78 *LQR* 263.

➡

4. Article III.-3:301(2) of the European Draft Common Frame of Reference would reverse *White & Carter v McGregor*. It bars affirmation if:

(a) the claimant could have made a reasonable substitute transaction without significant effort or expense; or

(b) performance would be unreasonable in the circumstances.

On the other hand, *White & Carter v McGregor* can be **supported** on the following basis:

1. Contract law would fail to protect the aggrieved party's performance interest if it denies her right to affirm and perform the contract.

2. English law does not require the claimant to act reasonably in selecting her remedies (*White & Carter v McGregor*).

Subsequent cases illustrate **the operation of the 'legitimate interest' factor.** The question is whether, on the facts, the wastefulness of the claimant's continuing performance is completely *disproportionate* to its performance interest in earning the contract price. The scale is easily tipped in the claimant's favour.

✓ In *The Oldenfield*, the claimant owners under a time charter were permitted to affirm the contract because it would be difficult to find other employment for the ship, termination would put them in breach of other contracts, and damages would be hard to assess.

✓ Likewise, in *Reichmann v Gauntlett* (2006), a landlord was allowed to affirm and sue for unpaid rent where the tenants, a firm of solicitors shut down by the Law Society, vacated the premises. The landlord had a legitimate interest in affirming the contract since he foresaw difficulties in re-letting the property and could not be sure of obtaining damages for loss of future rent.

✓ In *The Isabella Shipowner Ltd v Shagang Shipping Co Ltd (The Aquafaith)* (2012), a vessel was chartered by IS to SS for a minimum period of 59 months. When SS attempted to return the ship three months early, IS was held to be entitled to refuse redelivery and to retain the prepaid hire. IS did not require SS's cooperation to continue with performance of the contract. Nor could IS's conduct in continuing with performance be described as 'perverse' or beyond all reason, or wholly unreasonable.

✗ In contrast, affirmation was denied in *The Puerto Buitrago* (1976). The charterer had returned the ship to the owner damaged and almost a year before the end of the hire period. Since repairs would have cost £2 million and the ship's value fully repaired was only £1 million, the owner could *not* insist on repairing the ship and charging hire for the charter period because the obligation to repair was not a condition precedent to the right to redeliver. The court added that the charterer could not continue without the charterer's cooperation and that the owner had no legitimate interest in affirming the contract, although these statements do not clearly form part of the *ratio*.

✗ Likewise, in *The Alaskan Trader* (1984), the owner chartered a ship to the charterer for 24 months but the charterer returned it after 12 months as it required extensive repairs which would take several months to complete. The owner refused to accept the charterer's repudiation, repaired the ship and kept it fully crewed and ready for the charterer's use for the remaining hire period. The arbitrator found this to be 'wholly unreasonable' and allowed the charterer to recover the hire for the period after the ship's return. While accepting the importance of commercial certainty and the difficulty of distinguishing between affirmation which is '*merely* unreasonable' (and permissible) and that which is '*wholly* unreasonable' (and impermissible), Lloyd J upheld the arbitrator's conclusion that the owner had effectively no legitimate interest in affirming the contract; the assessment of damages was not thought to present special difficulty even if the owner's prospects of re-letting the ship were poor.

12.4 **The position of consumers**

The Consumer Rights Act 2015 treats certain terms as included in consumer contracts for goods, services, and digital content (see 10.6.2.1). Where certain of these are breached, eg as to goods contracts,[6] the CRA provides **additional special remedies** that include (ss 19–24):

✓ the short-term right to reject within 30 days from receipt; or

✓ after a trader's failed attempt to repair or replace within a reasonable time, the right to a price reduction *or* the final right to reject.

These rights are detailed and complex, but in general:

• These rights to rejection entitle the consumer to 'reject the goods and treat the contract as at an end'.

• The right is exercised 'if the consumer indicates to the trader that the consumer is rejecting the goods and treating the contract as at an end' by words or conduct.

• The trader has a duty to refund the consumer within 14 days and the consumer has a duty to return or make the goods available for collection by the trader, subject to agreement.

Where the consumer exercises:

✗ the short-term right to reject, the trader cannot make any deduction from the sum refunded for the consumer's use of the goods returned; or

✗ the final right to reject, the trader *can* make deductions for the consumer's use with some exceptions.

---

[6] Eg, sections 9 (Goods to be of satisfactory quality), 10 (Goods to be fit for particular purpose), 11 (Goods to be as described), 13 (Goods to match a sample), 14 (Goods to match a model seen or examined), and 16 (Goods not conforming to contract if digital content does not conform).

THIS CHAPTER IN ESSENCE

The key areas and core topics in this chapter are summarised in an easy-to-use list, ideal for revision purposes, on the online resources at www.oup.com/uk/chenwishart6e/. Links to websites relevant to the topics covered and any updates to the chapter can also be found on the online resources.

QUESTIONS

1 'Identifying when a party can terminate a contract for breach raises difficult technical and policy questions.' Discuss.

2 Should all terms be treated as innominate terms?

3 Ida, a gizmo manufacturer, hires Jack to deliver her gizmos to her customers in London for one year. The contract states that: 'It is a condition that gizmos should be collected before 6 pm each day and delivered by 8.30 am the next morning.' Jack is late in two collections and three deliveries in the second week. Ida's customers have not complained. Meanwhile, Ida discovers a much cheaper way of making the deliveries. On Monday morning of the third week, Jack shouts sexist abuse at one of Ida's employees and Ida terminates the contract because of Jack's sexist views. Advise Jack.

4 Explain and distinguish each of the following, giving examples.
   (a) Termination, breach of an entire obligations clause, rescission, and discharge.
   (b) Breach, anticipatory breach, and repudiatory breach.

5 'The sanctity of contract requires, at the very least, that the innocent party be permitted to continue with the contract even if the other party commits a repudiatory breach.' Discuss.

For hints on how to answer these questions, please see the online resources at www.oup.com/uk/chenwishart6e/

KEY FURTHER READING

Liu, Q (2011), 'The *White & Carter* Principle: A Restatement', 74 *MLR* 171.

Smith, J (1997), 'Anticipatory Breach of Contract' in E Lomnicka and C Morse (eds), *Contemporary Issues in Commercial Law: Essays in Honour of A G Guest* (Sweet & Maxwell) 175.

Treitel, G (1990), '"Conditions" and "Conditions Precedent"', 106 *LQR* 185.

Whittaker, S (2007), 'Termination Clauses' in A Burrows and E Peel (eds), *Contract Terms* (OUP) 253.

13

Damages

'I want you to pay me money for my loss due to your breach'

13.1 **Introduction**

13.1.1 **Judicial remedies**

The vast majority of contractual disputes are settled out of court. Parties have every incentive to reach a compromise, if at all possible, to avoid the significant time, money, general aggravation, and uncertainties inherent in litigation. Going to court is the 'nuclear option'. However, parties bargain in the shadow of the law. On breach, well-advised parties will negotiate settlements by reference to the remedy that the aggrieved party (the claimant) is likely to be awarded, with deductions for the risk of the claim not being proved and for avoiding the trouble and expense of going to court. If the contract-breaker (the defendant) is facing insolvency, the claimant will be forced to accept a much-reduced settlement, rather than risk getting less or even nothing at all as an unsecured creditor.

Where the parties have not agreed on the consequences of breach or any agreed remedies are judged to be unenforceable (Chapter 11 and 14.3), the law supplies *default rules* to determine the available remedies. The claimant's *self-help* remedy of termination, discussed in Chapter 12, is supplemented by various *judicial* remedies for breach.

(i) **Damages** are available as of right to compensate the claimant's loss of *expectation* for every breach of contract. Exceptionally, in qualifying circumstances, the claimant may be awarded the following *instead* of her expectation:

- her reliance loss as a proxy for her expectation (13.3);
- restitution of the benefit conferred on the defendant (13.4); or
- the defendant's gains from the breach (see 13.5).

The distinctive feature of the contract action, its unique claim, is that it purports to fulfil the expectations created by binding contracts. In contrast:

- tort actions prevent foreseeable harm to the claimant; and
- unjust enrichment actions reverse the defendant's unjust enrichment at the expense of the claimant.

(ii) In *limited* cases, the court may order **compulsory compliance** with the contract's primary obligations by: an award of the agreed sum; an order for specific performance; or an order for an injunction. The court must also determine whether any agreed remedies in the contract are enforceable (Chapter 14).

The very fact that compulsory performance is the *secondary* remedy, while damages are the primary remedy, shows that contract law is:

- not fully committed to the protection of the claimant's *performance* interest (in receiving the defendant's actual performance);
- as opposed to the claimant's *expectation* interest (in having the money's-worth of the defendant's performance).

The questions for consideration in this chapter are:

(i) What *types* of loss are recognised and so compensable for breach of contract? What types of loss are not, or are imperfectly, recognised, and why?

(ii) How is loss *calculated* since some methods will yield more than others?

(iii) Why is the prima facie measure of loss subject to deductions (eg for remoteness or mitigation) which will result in the claimant not being as well off as if the contract was performed?

(iv) When and why might contract law allow departures from the expectation measure and allow awards based on *reliance, restitution, account of profits, or loss of opportunity to bargain*?

(v) What policy considerations are at work in determining the compensation awarded to the aggrieved party?

13.1.2 **Policy considerations**

Contract law's commitment to the protection of an innocent party's interest in the performance of the contract is the starting point when considering the remedies for breach. However, it is not the only important value. Recognition of other concerns in this area helps us to understand the court's selection of the appropriate remedy. They group around three clusters:

(i) The aggrieved claimant:

   • protecting her expectation of performance and of what the performance was *for*; in other words, acknowledging her losses from breach;

   • protecting her from unfairness (eg by controlling exemption clauses, Chapter 11); and

   • encouraging her to act and react sensibly in relation to the contract (eg by requiring mitigation of loss).

(ii) The defendant contract-breaker:

   • avoiding unnecessary interference with her freedom (eg by not compelling specific performance if the claimant can otherwise be adequately protected);

   • protecting her from the claimant's unforeseeable and preventable losses (eg remoteness and mitigation); and

   • signalling disapproval of the breach even where the claimant's loss is unclear (eg nominal damages, and resorting to measures of loss other than expectation).

(iii) Administration of law:

   • responding to evidential and quantification difficulties, and the potential for fraudulent claims (eg reluctance to give damages for pain and suffering);

   • avoiding indeterminate liability and opening the floodgate to claims (eg again in respect of pain and suffering); and

   • preventing waste (eg mitigation).

13.1.3 **Damages: expectation, reliance, and restitution**

In the celebrated article by Fuller and Perdue, 'The Reliance Interest in Contract Damages' (1937) 46 *Yale LJ* 52, the authors introduced the different possible measures of damages by reference to the terminology of 'expectation', 'reliance', and 'restitution'.

The following illustrates their different effect, although it should be emphasised that only the expectation measure is available as of right for breach. The availability of other measures is discussed in this chapter.

A buys a picture for £50,000 which B, a dealer, sells as the work of C, a famous painter. In fact, it is a forgery worth only £200.

(i) Where **A makes a** *good bargain* (ie had the picture been genuine as B promised, it **would have been worth at least £70,000**):

- If A *keeps* the picture, A's **expectation** interest, aimed at putting A in the position she would have been in if the contract had been performed, is:

Expected value (£70,000) – the value received (£200) = £69,800

- A's **reliance** interest, aimed at putting A in the position she would have been in if *no* contract had been made,[1] is:

Amount paid (£50,000) – the value received (£200) = £49,800

- A's **restitution** interest if she *returns* the picture is aimed at preventing B's unjust enrichment at A's expense. B should return A's payment of £50,000.

(ii) If the contract was a *good bargain,* A's expectation interest will generally cover both her reliance and restitution interests; A would be reimbursed for the amount paid and other costs incurred, and would have made a profit.

(iii) If **A had made a bad bargain** (ie the picture was only worth £10,000 even if genuine), then:

- A's **expectation** interest is:

Expected value (£10,000) – the actual value received (£200) = £9,800

- A's **reliance** interest is:

Amount A paid (£50,000) – the value received (£200) = £49,800

- A's **restitution** interest if she *returns* the picture is:

The amount A paid = £50,000

A is clearly better off claiming reliance or restitution *if either is available.*

If B makes a profit from breaching the contract, say, by lending the picture to an exhibitor for £5,000, A may now be able to claim **damages for loss of opportunity to negotiate for B's breach.**

13.1.4 **The contract interest: performance, expectation, or both**

While Fuller and Perdue argue that damages should, and often are, aimed at the protection of reliance, this is powerfully criticised by Friedmann, in 'The Performance Interest in Contract Damages' (1995) 111 *LQR* 628, who defends the primacy of the expectation interest in contract damages, preferring the terminology of 'performance interest'. However, as has already been noted, claimants are rarely awarded actual performance, having generally to settle for damages, which are, moreover, subject to various deductions that can leave them inadequately compensated.

---

[1] But, reliance damages which compensate for the loss of opportunity to make an alternative bargain can mimic the expectation measure (5.3.1 (iii) 4).

Pause for reflection

There is a certain ambiguity about the purpose of contract remedies—whether it is to secure the claimant's right to performance, or only to secure the claimant's economic end result of performance (her 'expectation'). In 'Performance and Compensation: An Analysis of Contract Damages and Contractual Obligation' (2006) 26 *OJLS* 41, Webb notes that the word 'remedy' conceals which interest is being protected. There are two distinct contractual interests: in receiving performance (the 'performance interest'), and in being compensated for losses caused by non-performance (the 'compensation interest'). The compensation interest is not an alternative way of enforcing the performance interest. Webb suggests that the claimant should be able to claim *both* so long as there is no double recovery. Even if a claimant has suffered no loss *from* non-performance, she has still lost the performance due to her.

13.2 Expectation damages

13.2.1 The compensatory aim

The normal measure of damages in a contract action is the *expectation* measure. The general rule stated by Parke B in *Robinson v Harman* (1848) is: 'that where a party sustains loss by reason of a breach of contract, he is, so far as money can do it, to be placed in the same situation, with respect to damages, *as if the contract had been performed*' (emphasis added). The relevant 'loss' is the claimant's *expectation* from the contract, which is lost by the breach. Whilst damages in tort may protect *pre-existing* expectations (eg of earning capacity or of business profits) impaired or destroyed by the tort, the distinctive feature of a contractual action is that it protects expectations *created by the contract*. In this sense, it is 'forward-looking', while reliance and restitutionary damages, which aim to make the claimant no 'worse off', are 'backward-looking'.

Four points follow from the compensatory aim of contract damages, although each is subject to significant qualification:

(i) **Only nominal damages if no loss**: if the claimant has suffered no recognised loss from the breach, she will receive no substantial damages, but only nominal damages (usually £5) to acknowledge the breach and attach costs. Common examples are where:

- goods are not delivered, but the claimant has not yet paid and can buy substitute goods for the same price or less;
- the defendant's defective performance is worth no less on the market than the performance due (ie there is no diminution of value); or
- the performance was intended for a third party so that the claimant suffers no loss.

(ii) **No protection from bad bargains**: the claimant cannot claim her reliance in order to circumvent a *bad bargain* (13.3).

(iii) **No claim to the contract-breaker's gains from breach**: traditionally, damages are not measured by the defendant's gains from breach of contract (*Teacher v Calder*

(1899)) or her savings (*Tito v Waddell (No 2)* (1977)). However, the House of Lords decision in *Attorney-General v Blake* (2000) now permits exceptional claims to an account of profits from breach (see 13.5).

(iv) **No punishment of the contract-breaker**: *Addis v Gramophone Co Ltd* (1909) bars punitive or exemplary damages (to punish the contract-breaker) in a purely *contractual* action, even where the breach is deliberate and calculated to increase the contract-breaker's profits by performing for someone else instead (*Cassell & Co Ltd v Broome* (1972)). However:

- As we will see, punitive considerations cannot be entirely excluded from the increasing recognition of non-pecuniary loss (13.2.4) or of exceptional account of profits and 'hypothetical bargain' or negotiating damages (13.5).

- In tort actions, the House of Lords held (in *Kuddus v Chief Constable of Leicestershire Constabulary* (2001)) that punitive damages should be freed from the narrow circumstances in which they were available prior to *Rookes v Barnard* (1964). Rather, the question should be whether the case involves: (a) oppressive, arbitrary, and unconstitutional action by public officials, or (b) the defendant calculating that her wrongful conduct will make profits exceeding any compensation payable to the claimant. There may be a similar development in contractual actions. As Lord Nicholls predicted: 'Never say never' (*A v Bottrill* (2003)). The current position will push claimants towards actions where punitive damages are available.

- The Supreme Court of Canada has affirmed the exceptional availability of restrained punitive damages to 'address the purposes of retribution, deterrence and denunciation' where appropriate, eg $100,000 was awarded in *Royal Bank of Canada v W Got & Associates Electric Ltd* (2000), where the bank's conduct was a serious affront to the administration of justice and caused grave and irrevocable consequences to its client's business.

13.2.2 **Basis of calculation: loss of expectation minus gains**

The basic measure of the claimant's expectation damages is loss of expectation minus any 'gains' made under the contract. The question is: 'How well off would he have *been* if the contract had been performed? How well off is he *now*? The difference is the measure of damages'.[2] An overview is given by Diagram 13A.

The *'plus'* **side** is the claimant's expectation loss from breach. A contract can give rise to two quite separate expectations:

A. that of receiving the promised performance, and

B. that of being able to put it to some particular use.

These losses, consequential on not getting the due performance, may comprise losses from *not being made better off* as expected under the contract, and losses from *being made worse off* than expected under the contract.

---

[2] J Smith, *The Law of Contract* (4th edn, Sweet & Maxwell, 2002) 217.

Diagram 13A Expectation losses: the pluses and minuses

✓ = Recoverable ? = Uncertainty over recoverability		IP = innocent party CB = contract-breaker

Compensatable loss: the 'plus' side ✚	**Restrictions and deductions:** the 'minus' side ▬

A. Loss of the performance
✓ if conventionally measurable by diminution of value, or cost of cure
 	
? otherwise, recovery under *Panatown* 'broad' ground?
 	
B. Consequential loss (loss of what the performance was *for*, failure to achieve the *purpose* of performance)
This may take the forms of:
  not being better off:
  ✓ physically (eg health not improved),
  ✓ financially (eg loss of profits), or
  ? satisfaction-wise (eg enjoyment or amenity);
and/or
  being worse off:
  ✓ physically (eg building destroyed by breach),
  ✓ financially (eg wasted expenses, reasonable costs of mitigation, liability to third parties),
  ? satisfaction-wise (eg pain and suffering, physical inconvenience, damage to reputation).
	1. **Costs saved** by IP from terminating performance
	
	2. **Benefits received** from CB's part-performance
	
	3. **Gains** from breach or **mitigation**
	
	4. Failure to **mitigate**
	
	5. Generally **loss measured at time of breach**
	
	6. IP's **contributory negligence**
	
	7. Loss from **intervening causes**
	
	8. Loss **too** speculative
	
	9. Loss **too** remote

In *Parsons (Livestock) Ltd v Uttley Ingham & Co Ltd* (1978), P (a pig farmer) bought a food storage hopper from U (a manufacturer) to store pignuts. The hopper was installed defectively so that the pignuts became mouldy and many of the pigs died of a rare intestinal infection. On the 'plus' side, P's claim comprised of:

- not getting a hopper fit for the purpose (the promised performance);
- the dead pigs (consequential loss in being made worse off);
- the profits which would have been made on the sale of the pigs (consequential loss in not being made better off).

The **'*minus*' side**, which can reduce the expectation measure, includes the items in column 2 of **Diagram 13A** (discussed 13.2.5).

13.2.3 **What losses are recognised and how are they measured?**

Compensation for financial or physical loss is the predominant domain of contract law. *Parsons (Livestock) v Uttley Ingham* shows that the claimant can recover for loss of: the performance itself, not being able to put that performance to its intended use, and any additional costs wasted or incurred consequential on breach. Things get more difficult when at least part of the claimant's motivation for contracting is non-financial, so that her loss from breach is not readily measured in money (eg if some of the dead pigs had been much loved family pets). Contract law is much less prepared to recognise and compensate for such non-pecuniary loss. When this is combined with the other 'minus' side factors, which drive down the expectation measure (see 13.2.5), the result is a significant deviation from contract law's stated commitment to the protection of the claimant's performance, or even expectation, interest.

13.2.3.1 Minimum obligation undertaken

The courts will only enforce the minimum obligation undertaken by the defendant. In the first type of case, the contract requires the defendant to do X and the claimant has a reasonable expectation (but no contractual right) that the defendant will do Y. In this case, the court should assess damages on the basis that the defendant would only have done what was minimally required, eg, in *Lavarack v Woods of Colchester Ltd* (1967). L was employed by W, 'at the rate of not less than £4000 per annum... and such bonus (if any) as the directors... shall from time to time determine'. When L was wrongfully dismissed, the Court of Appeal denied L's claim for damages in respect of the lost bonus, because W had no contractual obligation to provide it.

In the second category of cases, the contract requires the defendant to do X but allows her discretion as to how she performs it. In this case, the court should assess damages according to how the defendant would in fact have exercised the discretion (on the balance of probabilities approach), eg in *Durham Tees Valley Airport v BMI Baby* (2010), BMI contracted to operate flights from D's airport. In breach of contract, BMI withdrew from the airport but argued that, since the contract did not require them to operate a minimum number of flights, they were not liable for damages. The Court of Appeal rejected this, holding that the contract-breaker must be assumed to act 'in his own interests having regard to the relevant factors prevailing at the time'. The court 'is not required to make assumptions that the defaulting party would have acted uncommercially merely in order to spite the claimant'.

13.2.3.2 Diminution of value, cost of cure, or loss of amenity?

The claimant's loss of the expected performance can be measured by:

- **'diminution of value'**: the *market value* of the performance that the defendant promised, minus that *actually* given;
- **'cost of cure'**: the cost of buying *substitute* performance from another party, including undoing any defective performance; or
- **'loss of amenity'**: the non-pecuniary loss to the claimant.

Diminution of value and the cost of cure may produce the *same* amount, eg, under section 51(3) of the Sale of Goods Act 1979, a buyer who has not received goods (worth

£5,000) to which she is entitled, but who has yet to pay the contract price (£4,000), can claim the difference between the market price of the goods and the contract price (ie £1,000). This can be described *either* as the cost of cure (the buyer can add this sum to the unpaid price and buy from elsewhere) *or* as the diminution in the value between the buyer's entitlement (£5,000) and what she received (£0), taking account of what she would have paid under the contract (£4,000).

However, in some cases, the two measures will yield very **different** **amounts**. In *Tito v Waddell (No 2)* (1977), a company obtained a licence to mine phosphate on Ocean Island, promising to restore the island afterwards by replanting 'coconuts and other food-bearing trees'. The company failed to do this and the islanders claimed the cost of cure ($A73,140 per acre). The court denied this because, by the time of the action, all the islanders had resettled some 1,500 miles away after their small Pacific island was devastated by the events of World War II. They were only entitled to the diminution of value ($A75 per acre), although there can hardly be a market for 'worked out plots of land in Ocean Island'.

(i) How is the applicable measure decided?

Statute may prescribe which measure is applicable, eg a tenant's covenant to repair is assessed on a diminution of value basis (Landlord and Tenant Act 1927, s 18). Or, the law may adopt *conventions* or presumptions, which can be displaced in particular cases, eg, diminution of value is applied to *defective surveys* and the supply of *defective goods* (Sale of Goods Act 1979, s 53(3)), although it is arguable that, if an attempt is made to cure the defects at a *reasonable cost*, this should be recoverable, and even if the cure ultimately fails (*Harling v Eddy* (1951)).

The conventional starting point for assessing damages for breach of a **building con-tract** is the cost of curing the defect or completing the work (*Mertens v Home Freeholds* (1921)), even if this exceeds the enhancement of the claimant's financial position (ie the diminution of value). However, this is subject to the requirement of *reasonableness* as the next case shows.

(ii) *Ruxley Electronics and Construction Ltd v Forsyth*

R agreed to build a swimming pool for F for £17,797. The pool actually built was shal-lower than the specified depth but it was still safe for diving and F's property was no less valuable for the breach. F claimed £21,560 as the cost of cure, to demolish and rebuild the pool to the specified depth. The Court of Appeal allowed this on the rea-soning that F was contractually entitled to his *exact* preference on the pool's depth. However, the House of Lords held that the cost of cure was *unreasonable* and irrecover-able by taking into account:

(a) the claimant's *purpose(s)* in contracting;

(b) whether the claimant has cured or *intends to cure* the breach; and

(c) the *proportionality* between the cost of cure, the contract price, the benefit already received by the claimant, and the benefit he would receive from cure.

Applied to the particular facts of the case:

(a) The claimant's purpose(s) in contracting: the extra depth stipulated constituted a loss of pleasure or amenity since F wanted the comfort of a deep pool. The *cost of cure* is the appropriate starting point where the claimant's purpose for a building contract is not purely financial, eg, a contract for alterations to make a house 'more comfortable, more convenient' to the owner's individual preference, or a contract for expensive redecoration of a house in good decorative order to the owner's eccentric taste, even if it would *lower* the market value of the house (an ugly fountain, gaudy wallpaper, yellow and pink tiles and fittings throughout).

(b) Cure or intention to cure: on the facts, the cost of cure exceeded the *extent* of F's loss because the court found that F had no genuine intention to cure the defect. While courts are normally unconcerned about what claimants actually do with their damages award, their intention to cure is *evidence* of the *extent* of their non-pecuniary loss flowing from the breach. If the claimant does not care enough to cure, awarding him the cost of cure while he keeps the existing pool would over-compensate him. The court noted: that R, the builder, had already rebuilt the pool once to rectify other defects and had reduced the price by £10,000 to compensate F for that disturbance; that, thereafter, F still refused to pay, alleging various minor deficiencies; and that F's statements of defence and counterclaim made no mention of the pool's depth until five years later. The House of Lords refused to allow F's promise to cure 'to create a loss, which does not exist, in order to punish the defendants'.

(c) Proportionality: given the benefit F *had* received, the House of Lords thought the cost of cure wholly disproportionate to the disadvantage F suffered from having a pool 9–18 inches shallower than he wanted. F still had a useable and safe pool which enhanced the value of his property no less for its shallowness. As Lord Jauncey said: '[a] failure to achieve the precise contractual objective does not necessarily result in the loss which is occasioned by a total failure' warranting the cost of total rebuilding.

In contrast, the cost of cure was awarded in *Radford v de Froberville* (1977) where dF failed to build a boundary wall on adjoining land she purchased from R. Although the wall would not increase the value of R's property, it represented R's 'genuine loss' from dF's breach, in terms of R's (in fact, R's tenants) desire for privacy. However, if the claimant had intended to sell his property, then his interest in the property would be purely financial and the diminution of value measure would have sufficed (*Birse Construction Ltd v Eastern Telegraph Co Ltd* (2004)).

In *Ruxley*, the House of Lords:

✗ rejected the cost of cure measure as over-compensating the claimant;

✗ rejected the diminution of value measure as under-compensating him (it would render the personal preference 'part of the promise illusory, and unbalance the bargain'); and

✓ endorsed a third measure: damages for loss of amenity 'where the value of the promise to the promisee exceeds the financial enhancement of his position which full performance will secure'. Such an award 'is incapable of precise valuation in terms of money, exactly because it represents a personal, subjective and non-monetary gain' (at 360–1). The trial judges' assessment of F's loss at £2,500 was not challenged in the House of Lords.

Pause for reflection

1. To modern eyes, the refusal to award the cost of cure in *Tito v Waddell (No 2)* gives insufficient recognition to the islanders' non-pecuniary interests in the restoration of their ancestral homeland. The court's conclusion that the islanders had no real intention to cure would not now be determinative: it merely shows that the claimant's loss may be *less* than the full cost of cure. Today, with better understanding of and sympathy for environmental issues and the spiritual value that indigenous peoples place on their land, a similar case may well be decided differently.

2. Substantial damages are not awarded for the fact of breach *itself* (for which only nominal damages are available), but for *loss* flowing from the breach measured in money's worth. Hence, 'loss of amenity', 'cost of cure', and 'diminution of value' can be seen as merely different ways of achieving the same aim, namely, to compensate the claimant for the *extent* to which her purposes were left unfulfilled by the breach, even if it may not enable her to obtain the exact performance.

3. *Ruxley* extends the category of contracts for enjoyment (for which, exceptionally, the law allows damages for non-pecuniary loss, 13.2.4.1), by reference to the concept of the 'consumer surplus', which is triggered whenever 'the value of the promise to the promisee exceeds the financial enhancement of his position which full performance will secure'.

4. Some dicta supports the availability of damages for loss of performance itself. In *Farley v Skinner* (2001), Lord Scott said that the claimant in *Ruxley* suffered *no* vexation, anxiety, or other species of mental distress. He simply did not get the depth of pool he contracted for. Likewise, Lord Millett said, in *Alfred McAlpine v Panatown* (2001), that 'viewed objectively, there was no loss of amenity' in *Ruxley*; the loss suffered 'could equally well, and perhaps more accurately, be described as a defeated expectation'. But *Ruxley v Forsyth*:

   ✗ should not be interpreted as awarding damages for the claimant's loss of her right to performance itself; but rather

   ✓ her loss from not getting performance that has non-pecuniary value to her.

The claimant who does not receive due performance may be judged to have suffered no loss at all, whether pecuniary or non-pecuniary. In the famous US case, *Jacob & Young v Kent* (1921), contractors building a large house used a different brand of pipes from those specified in the contract. The owner of the house claimed the cost of demolishing and rebuilding the house with the correct pipes, but the New York Court of Appeals awarded only nominal damages since the pipes used were functionally identical with those stipulated and did not reduce the value of the house. Presumably, the claimant had no particular reason for insisting on the pipes stipulated in the contract.

13.2.4 The problem of non-pecuniary loss

Breach of contract may cause non-pecuniary loss to the claimant, whether *positively* (ie the failure to obtain satisfaction and enjoyment), or *negatively* (ie the claimant's annoyance, anger, frustration, disappointment, distress, and loss of reputation from breach). In 'Contract Remedies and the Consumer Surplus' (1979) 95 *LQR* 581, Harris, Ogus, and Phillips urge courts, in calculating damages, to take more account of the subjective value of the contract's subject matter to the recipient, over and above its market value; this is what economists call the 'consumer surplus' or 'personal preference'. To the extent that contract law traditionally does not recognise or undervalues claims for non-pecuniary loss caused by breach, the claimant's *expectation interest* is unprotected.

13.2.4.1 The general approach

In the leading case on damages for non-pecuniary loss of *Farley v Skinner*, Lord Steyn said: '[t]he general principle is that compensation is only awarded for financial losses resulting from the breach... [Citing *Watts v Morrow* (1991)] as a matter of legal policy "a contract-breaker is not in general liable for any distress, frustration, anxiety, displeasure, vexation, tension or aggravation which his breach of contract may cause to the innocent party"' even if they are the foreseeable consequences of breach. Such loss can only be compensated if it falls within an **established exception**, namely, where breach:

✓ is of a contract for enjoyment or alleviation of distress; or

✓ causes mental distress consequent on physical injury or inconvenience.

 Pause for reflection

Canada and Australia take a more permissive approach, eg in *Fidler v Sun Life Assurance* (2006), the Supreme Court of Canada viewed the 'remedial ostracisation' of mental distress as unwarranted. It contradicts the general principle of recovery for loss of reasonable expectations, rests on flimsy policy grounds, and is not followed by the High Court of Australia (*Baltic Shipping v Dillon* (1993)). The European Draft Common Frame of Reference on contract law expressly recognises that recoverable loss includes non-economic loss, which 'includes pain and suffering and impairment of the quality of life' (Art III.-3:701(3)).

13.2.4.2 The policies in play

A number of concerns explain the law's caution towards claims for non-pecuniary loss:

(i) Problems of proof and quantification: claimants may fake or exaggerate their mental distress. Moreover, as the Law Commission points out, there is 'no standard measure of assessment by reference to which the harm can be converted into monetary form... This incommensurability gives rise to real danger of indeterminacy and of inconsistent awards'.[3] *However*, this should not bar recovery for losses which are proven, well recognised, and awarded in other areas of the law such as in personal

---

[3] Law Commission, *Aggravated, Exemplary and Restitutionary Damages* (Law Com Consultation Paper 132, 1993) para 2.12.

injuries actions. Nevertheless, non-pecuniary loss for breach of contract will be more varied, and less likely to generate the sort of notional tariffs applicable in personal injuries cases.

(ii) 'Floodgates' and avoidance of hardship to the defendant: since mental distress is all too foreseeable and a common consequence of breach, if damages were to be available for it, claims would multiply. Staughton LJ expressed his alarm at the prospect of every ship-owner in the Commercial Court, having successfully claimed for unpaid freight, adding a claim for her mental suffering whilst waiting for her money (*Hayes v James & Charles Dodd* (1990)); Lord Steyn warned against the 'creation of a society bent on litigation' (*Farley v Skinner*). The legal response has been to confine recovery to exceptional categories ('pockets') and only extend recovery by analogy to them. *However*, contractual liability for non-pecuniary loss can only be owed to one's contract partner, who must prove damage, causation, mitigation, and remoteness.

(iii) Protection of the claimant's non-pecuniary motive for contracting: Lord Mustill (*Ruxley*) notes that the principle of *pacta sunt servanda* (agreements must be kept) would be eroded if the law did not recognise that consumers often make contracts that, although not of economic value, have value to them and for which they may have paid extra. The promisor should not be allowed to 'please himself whether or not to comply with the wishes of the promisee which, as embodied in the contract, formed part of the consideration for the price'. Most contracts made by most people (not acting in the course of business) are aimed wholly, or partly, at satisfying *individual preferences* or improving quality of life (eg contracts made in respect of one's food, accommodation, clothing, employment, recreation, or provision for one's family and friends). The same considerations apply to contracts made from altruism to improve the *environment* or for other *good causes*. In all these cases, failure to protect the claimant's non-pecuniary interest in the performance of the contract *contravenes the compensatory principle* and allows the defendant to 'get away' with the breach.

13.2.4.3 Contracts for enjoyment or alleviation of distress

One recognised exception to the general rule against damages for non-pecuniary loss is where the *purpose* of the contract or of an important term is to provide enjoyment, peace of mind, or freedom from distress.

(i) Illustrations

✓ In *Jarvis v Swan Tours* (1973), J (a solicitor) bought a package holiday with S. S's brochures promised a 'house party' with a variety of activities and entertainment (including a yodeller evening). In fact, there were only 13 people at the hotel in the first week, and only J in the second week. The Court of Appeal took account of the value of what he received (effectively nothing) and awarded J the sum he paid for the holiday; he was also compensated for 'disappointment, distress, upset and frustration'.

Damages for mental distress were also awarded where:

✓ a solicitor failed to take effective legal steps to protect the claimant from being harassed (*Heywood v Wellers* (1976));

✓ a solicitor's negligence resulted in the claimant's twins being kidnapped by their father and taken to Tunisia where he was awarded their custody (*Hamilton Jones v David & Snape (a firm)* (2003));

✓ a photographer failed to turn up for the claimant's wedding day (*Diesen v Sampson* (1971));

✓ a touring holiday was spoiled by a car purchased for the purpose from a seller who knew that it was not of merchantable quality (*Jackson v Chrysler Acceptances Ltd* (1978));

✓ an undertaker failed to inter a corpse properly (*Lamm v Shingleton* (1949)); and

✓ a cemetery owner failed to grant the claimants burial plots adjacent to their parents (*Reed v Madon* (1989)).

(ii) The non-pecuniary purpose

Originally, the non-pecuniary purpose (enjoyment, peace of mind, or alleviation of distress) had to be the 'sole' object of the contract (*Watts v Morrow* (1991)). In *Farley v Skinner*, the House of Lords relied on *Ruxley* to dilute the requirement; it is now enough if the non-pecuniary purpose represents 'a distinct and important obligation' of the contract. This meets the injustice of *Knott v Bolton* (1995) (now overruled), where a couple were denied compensation for an architect's breach in designing their 'dream home' because the contract *also* had an economic purpose. The House of Lords in *Farley v Skinner* recognised that this made an important part of the couple's expectations unenforceable. This injustice is reinforced when their non-pecuniary purpose would have been enforceable if it had been contained in a *separate* contract. In **Farley v Skinner**, F employed S to survey a property he intended to buy for quiet and peaceful weekends, expressly asking S to report on the likelihood of disturbance from aircraft noise. S reported that it was 'unlikely that the property will suffer greatly from such noise'. F bought the house and spent more than £100,000 improving it. In fact, the house suffered from substantial disturbance during busy periods such as the weekends. The breach caused no diminution of value, since F did not pay more than the property was actually worth. However, the House of Lords upheld the trial judge's award of £10,000 for the loss of enjoyment caused by the noise.

Farley v Skinner was applied in *Hamilton Jones v David & Snape* (2003), where the defendant solicitors' negligence resulted in the claimant's twins being kidnapped by their father and taken to Tunisia where he obtained custody of them. Neuberger J held that both parties 'would have had in mind that a significant reason for the claimant instructing the defendants was with a view to ensuring, so far as possible, that the claimant retained custody of her children for her own pleasure and peace of mind'. Neuberger J awarded £25,000 for her *financial* loss and £20,000 for mental distress. The latter figure was arrived at by taking into account her grief, anxiety, and hurt, the fact that the Fatal Accidents Act 1976 provides for statutory damages of £10,000 for negligence resulting in death of a child, and the fact that she still had some access to the twins.

When is the provision of enjoyment, peace of mind, or alleviation of distress a 'distinct and important obligation' under the contract?

✓ These are obvious in holidays, weddings, funerals, custody of children, and the like.

✗ In contrast, *Farley* approved the view in *Watts v Morrow* that a house survey would normally not qualify.

Less clear-cut are *Ruxley* (which rests on a distinction between a contract to build a swimming pool and to build one *which brings pleasurable amenity in its depth*) and *Farley* (which necessitates a distinction between an *ordinary* survey and one which ensures, inter alia, the prospective owner's quiet enjoyment). *Ruxley* and *Farley* give considerable scope for arguing that some aspect of the contract incorporates a significant non-pecuniary purpose. The problem is acute since all non-commercial contracts (indeed, in a sense, even commercial contracts) confer peace of mind which breach reduces or destroys. The courts will have considerable latitude in determining whether terms have an important non-pecuniary purpose. It is a question of degree and judgment. In *Farley*, Lord Hutton stressed the need for a clear test to prevent damages being generally available for anxiety and aggravation caused by breach and 'to prevent the exception expanding to swallow up, or to diminish unjustifiably, the principle itself.'

Five factors restrict the scope of recovery for non-pecuniary loss:

(i) In general, commercial claimants are excluded. Lord Cooke notes that '[c]ontract breaking is treated as an incident of commercial life which players in the game are expected to meet with mental fortitude' (*Johnson v Gore Wood & Co (a firm)* (2001); also *Farley v Skinner* and *Hamilton Jones v David & Snape*).

(ii) Lord Hutton (*Farley v Skinner*) said that the non-pecuniary purpose must be: important to the claimant, made a specific term of the contract, and clearly communicated to the defendant.

(iii) The loss must have been caused by, and not be too *remote* a consequence of, the breach. In practice, this requires that the defendant knows the importance of the claimant's non-pecuniary purpose and so foresees the loss from breach. Damages were denied in *Johnson v Gore Wood* (2001), since it was not foreseeable at formation that business losses would result in the claimant's mental distress and anxiety. Likewise, damages were denied in *Wiseman v Virgin Atlantic Airways Ltd* (2006), because 'it would not have been in the contemplation of the parties that the mere fact of not permitting a passenger to board the aircraft for his return flight would lead to a breakdown in health'.

(iv) The awards should be kept low; £10,000 was regarded as being at the top end in *Farley v Skinner*, but note that £20,000 was awarded in *Hamilton Jones v David & Snape*. In *Milner v Carnival plc (trading as Cunard)* (2010), the Court of Appeal awarded the claimants £12,000 in respect of their unhappy time on a cruise. They had paid some £60,000 and their legitimate expectations were 'sky high': they had been promised luxury, glamour, 'star treatment', and the 'experience of a life time'. Unfortunately, they were unable to sleep due to vibrations and noise in their cabin and they disembarked 28 days into the 78-day cruise. In relation to the claim for damages for physical inconvenience, discomfort, and mental distress, the Court of Appeal sought to ensure a measure of consistency by having regard to damages awarded for bereavement and for an affront to feelings in cases of sex and race discrimination. The court noted the modest nature of these awards. Even allowing for the exceptional nature of the present case, the disappointment, distress, annoyance, and frustration in the present case was a less serious kind and did not equate with bereavement. In practice, the small awards will make non-pecuniary loss not worth pursuing in view of the potential costs and risks of litigation.

(v) Other measures must be inappropriate or yield no substantial damages, eg, in *Farley*, cure was impossible and there was no diminution of value and, in *Ruxley*, there was no diminution of value and the cost of cure was inappropriate. Lord Scott said that to allow damages for both discomfort and diminution of value 'would allow double recovery for the same item'.

 Counterpoint

Damages for both pecuniary and non-pecuniary loss were awarded in *Hamilton Jones*. If the facts in *Farley* remain the same except that F also suffers a diminution of value, why should *both* types of loss not be recoverable? If your failure to lay the precise colour of tiles I order causes me *both* a diminution of value (because my house now lacks a matching colour scheme) *and* loss of satisfaction (in not living with my favourite colour), I should be able to claim for both.

13.2.4.4 Mental distress consequent on physical injury or inconvenience

The second exception to the general rule against damages for non-pecuniary loss is where breach has caused personal injury (eg *Godly v Perry* (1960)), physical inconvenience, or discomfort.

(i) Illustrations

Modest damages were recovered where:

- ✓ a railway company took a family to the wrong station, leaving them to walk four or five miles home on a rainy night (*Hobbs v L & SW Railway Co* (1875));
- ✓ a man, his wife, and child were forced to live with his wife's parents for two years when a solicitor failed to obtain possession of a house (*Bailey v Bullock* (1950));
- ✓ the claimant bought a house in reliance on a negligent survey that failed to mention a leaking roof and an offensive-smelling septic tank. Damages were awarded for the distress and discomfort of living there and for the claimant's anxiety as to when repairs would be made since he could not afford them himself (*Perry v Sydney Phillips & Son* (1982)).

(ii) The scope of physical injury or inconvenience

Farley v Skinner extends this category insofar as disturbance by aircraft noise was classed as physical inconvenience: this was the secondary ground for the £10,000 awarded by four of their Lordships and the primary ground for Lord Clyde.

What amounts to *physical* inconvenience or discomfort?

- Lord Scott explains that the issue is not the types of inconvenience suffered, but rather how they were *caused*. Mere disappointment does not sound in damages even if it has led to a complete mental breakdown. 'But, if the cause of the inconvenience or discomfort is a sensory (sight, touch, hearing, etc) experience, damages can, subject to the remoteness rules, be recovered.'

- Lord Steyn draws an analogy with causes which could constitute nuisance in tort.
- Lord Clyde thought it unnecessary to give a detailed analysis or definition beyond excluding 'purely sentimental' matters and mere 'disappointment'. The other Law Lords were also content to assess inconvenience on the facts of the particular case.

Farley v Skinner seems a very borderline case; Lord Scott notes the 'evidence that many, perhaps most, of the residents in the area were not troubled by the noise'. Acceptance of physical inconvenience in the case must therefore be based on the claimant's *subjective experience* of 'real discomfort' and interference with his preference for 'a quiet reflective breakfast, a morning stroll in the garden' and pre-dinner drinks on the terrace. This increases the *potential scope* of this exception. Lord Cooke, dissenting in *Johnson v Gore Wood*, was prepared to extend this further by treating the claimant's *extreme financial* embarrassment as physical inconvenience and discomfort (the defendant's breach reduced him from a prosperous state to subsistence on social security benefit and led to the significant deterioration of his relationship with his wife and son). Lord Cooke said: 'the common law would be defective and stray too far from reality, humanity and justice if it remorselessly shut out even a restrained award under these heads'.

13.2.4.5 Loss of reputation and breach of employment contracts

Some cases previously regarded as exceptional can now be seen as examples of a third exception to the non-recoverability of non-pecuniary loss; namely, where *loss of reputation* causes *financial* loss to the claimant.

(i) Illustrations
Damages were awarded where:

- ✓ a bank wrongly dishonoured a cheque, causing damage to the customer's reputation and credit rating (*Kpohraror v Woolwich Building Society* (1996)); and
- ✓ breach of a contract to employ an actor caused loss of anticipated publicity (*Clayton & Waller v Oliver* (1930)).

(ii) Employment contracts
Addis v Gramophone has long been regarded as authority for the rule that, where an employee is wrongly dismissed, no damages are available for the employee's:

- ✗ mental distress; *or*
- ✗ damage to reputation due to the harsh and humiliating manner of her dismissal.
- ✓ However, it is now the case that, where the damage to reputation causes foreseeable pecuniary loss, the claimant may recover damages for the financial loss.

In *Malik v Bank of Credit & Commerce Intl SA* (1998), M and other senior employees made redundant following BCCI's insolvency claimed damages for being unable to obtain similar employment because of the stigma of being former employees of a bank widely known to have engaged in corrupt and dishonest practices, in breach of its implied duty of trust and confidence to its employees.

This general position has been cut back so that, in practice, employees will rarely recover damages for the unfair manner of dismissal:

(i) It will be very difficult to prove causation of loss. The claimants in *Malik* failed to prove that the stigma had caused actual financial loss given the employer's general discretion in selecting employees. *Addis* has been explained in terms of lack of causation. Lord Steyn said in *Malik*: '[L]oss which an employee would have suffered even if the dismissal had been after due notice is irrecoverable, because such loss does not derive from the wrongful element in the dismissal. Further, it is difficult to see how the mere fact of wrongful dismissal, rather than dismissal after due notice, could of itself handicap an employee in the labour market.'

(ii) In *Johnson v Unisys*, the House of Lords held that, given the statutory scheme providing compensation for unfair dismissal (under which the claimant had already obtained the statutory maximum of £11,000), the common law should not provide additional compensation for the unfair manner of dismissal.

(iii) *Johnson v Unisys* has also been explained by a later House of Lords decision (in *Eastwood v Magnox Electric plc* (2004)) on the basis that the implied duty of trust and confidence is not breached by the unfair manner of *dismissal* (independent of any failure to give notice) because the duty only exists where employment is *continuing* and when there has not been a dismissal; in the case of dismissal the employer no longer has any trust or confidence in the employee.

(iv) In *Dunnachie v Kingston upon Hull CC* (2004), the House of Lords held that, on unfair dismissal, an employee cannot claim for non-pecuniary loss.

◆◆ Counterpoint

1. Damages should be available for non-pecuniary loss from unfair dismissal since 'a person's employment is usually one of the most important things in his or her life. It gives not only a livelihood but an occupation, an identity and a sense of self-esteem' (*Johnson v Unisys*).

2. The implied duty of trust and confidence *should* apply when employment is being terminated, since the obligation was originally developed in the context of constructive dismissal claims.

3. The current position can produce the *perverse result* that an employer is better off dismissing than suspending an employee, because the statutory claim for unfair dismissal is capped whilst the common law claim for unfair suspension (by breach of the implied duty of trust and confidence) is not.

4. A separate common law remedy would not amount to double recovery, because the statutory regime:

   • does not allow recovery for non-pecuniary loss;

   • does not cover financial loss from psychiatric injury; and

   • is capped so severely that it can only deal with 'cases at the lower end of seriousness'.

13.2.4.6 Loss of performance to a third party

A parent may make a contract to obtain music lessons for her child. Companies in a group may decide for reasons of convenience and profitability that one of them will contract for work to be done for another in the group. Where *A* contracts for *B*'s performance to be directed towards a third party *C* (hereafter 'third party contracts'), *C* may now have a claim under the Contracts (Rights of Third Parties) Act 1999 (4.1.3), but what damages can *A* claim on *B*'s breach? Since *A* will generally have suffered no direct *pecuniary* loss, the answer to this question informs the larger question of the extent to which contract law recognises a claimant's *performance interest* beyond her expectation of *financial* gain.

The traditional rule is that a party can only claim compensation for her *own* losses, not for loss to third party beneficiaries (*McAlpine v Panatown* (2001), 4.1.6.2). This is subject to the *promisee*'s *claim* under the '*Albazero* exception' (*Albacruz v Albazero* (1977), 4.1.6.2) to recover damages for the third party's loss, *held in trust for* the third party. The assumption here is that the loss belongs to the *third party*, on behalf of whom the promisee sues.

In *Linden Gardens v Lenesta Sludge* (1994), substantial damages were awarded under the *Albazero* exception, but Lord Griffiths decided the case on the ground of protecting the promisee's performance interest. Where a husband makes a contract to procure roof repair for his wife's house, and the builder fails to perform properly:

> the husband has suffered loss because he did not receive the bargain for which he had contracted with the first builder and the measure of damages is the cost of securing the performance of that bargain by completing the roof repairs properly by the second builder.

 Pause for reflection

The recognition that the loss belongs meaningfully to the promisee is persuasive. A mother who pays for treatment for her drug-addicted son would be astonished to be told, if no proper treatment is given, that the law regards her as suffering no loss. She made the contract to confer this benefit on her son; awarding *her* substantial damages would allow her to achieve this bargained-for result from someone else. Directing the damages to her son translates her gift into money, which is not what she wanted to give. Moreover, in the nature of addiction, this money is unlikely to be put to the original purpose.

In *McAlpine v Panatown*, the promisee engaged the promisor to construct a new building on the third party's land. The majority of the House of Lords (Lords Clyde, Jauncey, and Browne-Wilkinson) held the applicable law to be the *Albazero* exception, this is the **'narrow ground'**, but declined to award damages on the facts because the third party had rights against the promisor under a duty of care deed, hence there was no 'legal blackhole' (4.1.6.2).

Our interest is in the court's pronouncement on the **'broad ground'**. Lords Goff and Millett held that substantial *damages should be awarded* to compensate the *promisee* for the loss of its performance interest. Lord Browne-Wilkinson held that the promisee's claim would fail even if he 'assume[s] that the broader ground is sound in law' because the duty of care deed exhausts the promisee's performance interest. It is arguable that Lord Browne-Wilkinson's, albeit lukewarm, support for the broad ground combines with the judgments of Lords Goff and Millett to constitute *another 'majority'* on the applicable law, namely that the promisee's compensable performance interest may *in principle* go beyond his or her narrow pecuniary expectation.

(i) How would the promisee's damages be measured on the 'broad' ground in third party contracts?
This can be measured by the promisee's:

  (i) pecuniary loss;

  (ii) non-pecuniary loss; or

  (iii) loss of the literal *performance* itself.

Taking each in turn:

  (i) **Pecuniary loss**: in third party contracts, the promisee will generally suffer no *direct* pecuniary loss from breach since she expected no improvement of her own financial position from the defendant's performance. Where she *does* suffer direct pecuniary loss, this is recoverable (eg where breach leaves the promisee's obligation to the third party undischarged (*Price v Easton* (1833)) or makes her liable to the third party).

In *Panatown*, Lords Clyde and Jauncey first appear to adopt a narrow 'balance sheet' approach recognising only pecuniary loss. However, they both accept that the claimant may claim the cost of cure *where she has or intends to cure,* subject to a reasonableness qualification. Thus, the intention to cure *creates* a recoverable *financial* loss. Moreover, their Lordships accept that damages *are* properly available for non-pecuniary losses. For example, in *Radford v de Froberville*, the landlord obtained the cost of the cure to provide his tenants with the benefit of having a boundary wall.

  (ii) **Non-pecuniary loss**: This may exist in third party contracts.

  ✓ Lord Griffiths instances a husband who contracts for repairs to the roof of the matrimonial home owned by his wife (*Linden Gardens v Lenesta Sludge*).

  ✓ Lord Goff refers to the wealthy philanthropist who contracts for repairs, renovation, or reconstruction of the village hall belonging to the parish council or trustees (*McAlpine v Panatown*).

  ✓ In *Jackson v Horizon Holidays Ltd* (1975), J obtained substantial damages for the grossly substandard holiday that he and his family endured: the case is interpreted in *Woodar Investment v Wimpey Construction* as recovery for J's *own* mental distress (which includes his distress at his family's distress), or as a case calling for 'special treatment' (eg contracts for family holidays, restaurant meals for a party, or a taxi for a group).

In these cases, the promisee's loss comprises loss of satisfaction (enjoyment, peace of mind, or freedom from distress) consequential on the benefit not being conferred on the third party. Recovery for this is broadly analogous to that awarded in contracts of enjoyment (see 13.2.4.1).

(iii) **Loss of performance itself** even absent pecuniary or non-pecuniary loss: Lords Goff and Millett's judgments in *McAlpine v Panatown* emphasise that the prima facie measure is the cost of cure. They cite in support:

- ✓ Lord Griffiths' example of the husband's loss of bargain when a builder fails to repair the roof of his wife's house (*Linden Gardens*);

- ✓ Oliver J, who said 'if that which is contracted for is not supplied by the other contracting party I do not see why, in principle, he should not be compensated by being provided with the cost of supplying it through someone else or in a different way' (*Radford v de Froberville*);

- ✓ Wetmore J, who said that the promisee in a building contract is 'entitled to recover such damages as will put him in a position to have the building he contracted for' (*Allen v Pierce* (1895));

- ✓ Lord Millett who interpreted the compensation in *Ruxley v Forsyth* as for simply not getting the depth of pool contracted for; the 'loss could equally well, and perhaps more accurately, be described as defeated expectation'.

However, elsewhere, Lords Goff and Millett also accept limitations on the cost of cure by reference to:

- the reasonableness qualification in *Ruxley v Forsyth*;

- the requirement of the promisee's intention to cure for a cost of cure claim;

- the famous article 'Contract Remedies and the Consumer Surplus' (1979) 95 *LQR* 58, 58, in which Harris, Ogus, and Phillips state that the proper protection of the performance interest would make a significant difference only in a minority of cases; this would impliedly reject an automatic cost of cure award, since that would make a radical difference.

Lord Browne-Wilkinson's judgment is consistent with this; he explains that:

[t]he essential feature of the broader ground is that the contracting party A, although not himself suffering the physical or pecuniary damage . . . has suffered his own damage being the loss of his performance interest, ie the failure to provide C with the benefit that B had contracted for C to receive . . . it follows that the critical factor is to determine what interest A had in the provision of the service for the third party C.

Moreover, awarding an automatic cost of cure would be inconsistent with the basic principle that a 'breach of contract may cause a loss, but is not in itself a loss in any meaningful sense' (*McAlpine v Panatown*).

 Pause for reflection

All the judgments in *McAlpine v Panatown* are broadly consistent with the availability of recovery for pecuniary and non-pecuniary losses. The real differences are ones of *emphasis* rather than of kind.

→

> →
> - Lords Clyde and Jauncey who overtly support the narrow 'balance sheet' approach nevertheless concede that damages are properly available for non-pecuniary losses based on actual or intention to cure, which is subject to a reasonableness qualification.
>
> - From the other end, Lords Goff and Millett's starting point on the right to performance is not taken to its logical conclusion of an *automatic* cost of cure award. Again, the award is made to depend on the promisee's actual or intention to cure and the reasonableness of curing.
>
> - The convergence makes non-pecuniary loss an appropriate mechanism for conceptualising the promisee's remedy for loss of performance to third parties.

13.2.4.7 The future scope of recoverable non-pecuniary loss

Ruxley v Forsyth and *Farley v Skinner* significantly extend the previous law. Even if we resist an automatic cost of cure award to a promisee for breach (wholly appropriate in *McAlpine v Panatown*, where the commercial promisee neither paid for the original performance nor would pay for the repairs), we may be sympathetic to a more liberal approach to non-pecuniary loss than is hitherto recognised. Lord Millett said (*McAlpine v Panatown*, citing Lord Scarman in *Woodar Investment v Wimpey Construction*): 'that a contracting party has required services to be supplied at his own cost to a third party is at least *prima facie* evidence of the value of those services to the party who placed the order.' To the extent that the law is more willing to award damages for non-pecuniary loss, it better protects the claimant's performance interest.

13.2.5 Factors limiting the protection of the expectation interest

Aside from restrictions on the *types* and *measure* of loss already mentioned, other rules further restrict contract law's commitment to the protection of the claimant's performance interest. The result is that the stated aim of putting an innocent party in the same money position 'as if the contract had been performed' (*Robinson v Harman* (1848)) is merely the *starting point*. Ultimately, the claimant can only recover such of her losses as are readily *foreseeable*, are *unavoidable*, and are *provably caused*, by the defendant. These restrictions are discussed by reference to:

1. the doctrine of remoteness of loss;
2. the requirement of mitigation of loss;
3. the time at which loss is measured;
4. the speculativeness of the loss;
5. intervening causes;
6. the claimant's contributory negligence; and
7. time limits on contract claims.

13.2.5.1 Remoteness of loss

The expectation measure would suggest that claimants should be compensated for *all* provable losses flowing from the breach of contract, including physical injury, large-scale property damage, and anticipated profits from other transactions now disrupted by the breach (ie *all* the dominoes that fall, triggered by the initial breach). However, the law departs from this position (and so from the full protection of the innocent party's expectation interest) by relieving the defendant of liability for losses that are too 'remote' (only some of the falling dominoes 'count'). This means that losses genuinely sustained may be unrecoverable.

(i) The justifications for the remoteness limit

(i)   The *internal* point of view would justify the remoteness limit in terms of it expressing what the parties have undertaken responsibility for; what they impliedly intended.

(ii) The *external* point of view regards the remoteness limit as aimed at alleviating the potential harshness of liability on a defendant if it is imposed irrespective of the foreseeability of the loss, the disproportion between the contract price and the size of the liability, and the defendant's ability to bear or bargain around it. Wiles J illustrates such an unfair case: 'where a man going to be married to an heiress, his horse having cast a shoe on the journey, employed a blacksmith to replace it, who did the work so unskilfully that the horse was lamed, and, the rider not arriving in time, the lady married another; and the blacksmith was held liable for the loss of the marriage' (*The British Columbia & Vancouver Island Spar, Lumber and Saw Mill Co v Nettleship* (1868)).

(iii) The remoteness rule encourages efficient risk allocation: if the claimant must disclose remote risks, the defendant has the opportunity to exclude or restrict liability for them or vary the contract price, and the claimant can insure appropriately.

(ii) The rule/s of remoteness
Baron Alderson sets out the tests for remoteness in *Hadley v Baxendale* (1854). The defendant need not actively accept the risk of liability for particular losses; it is enough that she *knows* it is liable to result from their breach. Recoverable loss is divided into two limbs:

(i)   those 'arising naturally, that is, according to the *usual* course of things, from such breach of contract itself': knowledge of these losses is *imputed* to the defendant as a reasonable person even if she does not actually know it; and

(ii) 'such [loss] as may reasonably be supposed to have been in the contemplation of both parties, at the time they made the contract, as the probable result of the breach of it': the claimant must prove the defendant's *actual* knowledge of the special circumstances aggravating the claimant's loss.

These two rules are overlapping and not mutually exclusive, since what occurs naturally will almost always be in the contemplation of the parties. In *Victoria Laundry (Windsor) Ltd v Newman Industries Ltd* (1949), Asquith LJ said that they express *the single principle* that the claimant can only recover such losses as were *reasonably contemplated* by the defendant, at the time of contracting, as liable to flow from the breach.

The Heron II (1969) clarified the following:

- **What must be foreseen?** The defendant is liable if, at the time of contracting, she 'contemplated as a serious possibility the type of consequence, not necessarily the specific consequence that ensued upon breach' (*Parsons (Livestock) v Uttley Ingham*); that is, she is liable if she foresees the general *type*, even if she does not foresee the *extent*, of the loss.

- **How foreseeable must the loss be?** The required degree of foreseeability of the type of loss claimed is *higher in contract actions* (it must be a '*serious possibility*', a 'real danger', or a 'very substantial' probability) than in *tort actions* (a '*slight possibility*' is enough) (*The Wagon Mound* (1961)). The same loss may be too remote in contract, but not in tort (see (iv) in this section).

In sum, loss is recoverable in contract if the defendant contemplated that *type* of loss as a *serious possibility* at the time of contracting, or *ought* reasonably to have done so.

(iii) Judicial discretion in applying the remoteness tests

Knowledge of the formal tests of remoteness (the verbal formulae) is only the starting point. Students must get a 'feel' for the way the test is *applied*. In particular, for the courts' considerable latitude in determining:

(i) which type of loss is *ordinarily* foreseeable to a *high degree* (under the first limb); and

(ii) which type of loss is only foreseeable with *special knowledge* or disclosure to a high degree (under the second limb).

The remoteness limit can be reconciled with protection of the claimant's expectation interest by the reasoning that the claimant had no *real* expectation that the contract would protect her against such remote losses (the *internal* perspective). However, this simply begs the question 'why not?' Contract parties rarely contemplate breach, let alone the nature and extent of losses caused by breach. It is for the *court* to say what a *reasonable person* with the defendant's knowledge *should* have contemplated. In this way, the standard of the reasonable person may represent no more than the *court*'s conception of justice (*Davis Contractors Ltd v Fareham UDC* (1956)). Thus, a finding that the loss was or was not reasonably foreseeable is really a statement of the *conclusion* reached, and *not* the *reason* for the conclusion: the real reason must be sought elsewhere. The cases show that these **reasons** include:

- whether the defendant was aware of the claimant's intended use for the subject matter of the contract;

- the defendant's opportunity and ability to negotiate around the risk (eg by increasing the price or restricting liability);

- the parties' relative abilities to estimate the extent of the risk and to provide for it;

- the defendant's expertise in the subject matter of the contract.

(iv) Loss 'in the ordinary course of things': the first limb

✓ In *Victoria Laundry v Newman*, V purchased a boiler from N. N knew that V needed it for *immediate use* in V's laundry business. The boiler was delivered five months late. N was liable for V's loss of profits that it would *ordinarily* have made in this period, in view of the business relationship between the parties and N's expertise as qualified engineers.

✗ However, N was *not* liable for the loss of some *exceptionally profitable* government contracts due to N's delay because N knew nothing of them and could not be expected to foresee this loss, which belongs under the second limb.

✓ *Brown v KMR Services Ltd* (1995) approves the distinction made by *Victoria Laundry* between: (i) *ordinary* loss of profits and (ii) *exceptional* loss of profits (from particularly lucrative contracts) as different 'types' of loss, although it is arguable that they are loss of the same type albeit to a greater extent in the case of (ii). However, the case also illustrates the difficulty in making the distinction between (i) and (ii). B sought damages for K's negligence in failing to advise on the risks of joining high-risk syndicates. K argued that the loss claimed was too remote because the run of major catastrophes was unprecedented and unforeseeable. This was rejected because the claim was only in respect of one *type* of loss, namely underwriting loss: this was entirely foreseeable and recoverable, although its *extent* was far greater than foreseen. Thus, courts can broaden the scope of recovery under the first limb by emphasising that only the *broad type* of the loss suffered needs to be foreseen, and not the specific nature or extent of the loss or the exact way it arose.

✓ In *The Heron II* (1969), the claimant contracted for its sugar to be carried to Basrah for immediate sale on arrival. The sugar arrived nine days late, and the claimant was awarded damages resulting from the fall in the market during the delay. Although the carrier did not know the claimant's intention to sell the sugar, in view of its *past dealings* with the claimant, and its knowledge that there was a market for sugar at Basrah, 'if he had thought about the matter, he must have realised that at least it was not unlikely that the sugar would be sold in the market at market price on arrival'.

✓ In *Parsons (Livestock) v Uttley Ingham*, U supplied P with a defective hopper for storing pig food, the food became mouldy and 254 pigs died from a rare intestinal disease. The trial judge found that U could not have reasonably contemplated the serious possibility of mouldy pignuts causing such serious illness in pigs. Nevertheless, the Court of Appeal allowed recovery because it was enough that U must have appreciated 'that food affected by bad storage conditions might well cause illness in the pigs fed upon it'. The claimant also recovered loss of profits on the dead pigs but not loss of future sales from rearing additional animals.

✓ In *Jackson v Royal Bank of Scotland* (2005), J imported dog biscuits from Thailand and sold them on to EB at great profit. RBS, in breach of its duty of confidence to J, disclosed the extent of J's mark-up to EB, whereupon, EB switched to buying directly from the Thai suppliers. J sought damages for the loss of repeat business from EB as loss arising from the normal course of things. The House of Lords held that 'loss of the chance or opportunity of repeat business should in principle be available, and that the issue in this case was for how long it was or should have been in the reasonable contemplation of the parties that the trading relationship would continue' at the time of formation. Lord Walker quantified the loss at four further years at decreasing profit margins. Lord Hope stated that 'there is no arbitrary limit that can be set to the amount of damages once the test of remoteness according to one or other of the rules in *Hadley v Baxendale* has been satisfied'.

The courts can also *narrow* the scope of recoverable loss under the first limb by finding that the loss suffered was unforeseeable by the defendant, especially when her expertise and ability to meet potential liabilities is low.

✗ In *Hadley v Baxendale*, H's claim for loss of profits was denied where H sent a broken shaft from his mill with B, a carrier, to Greenwich to enable a new one to be copied. B's breach resulted in several days' stoppage in the mill. Although B knew what was being carried, that H were millers, and that the mill was stopped, the court found the loss to be *unforeseeable* under the first limb, since B was not specifically informed of the 'special circumstance' that he was carrying an article on which the operation of the entire mill depended (see also *Victoria Laundry v Newman*), and B might reasonably think that H had a spare shaft, or was able to get one, or that other defects with the mill were stopping its current operation. Had he been so informed, B would have been able to limit his liability. It seems crucial to the denial of liability that (unlike the defendants in *The Heron II* and in *Victoria Laundry v Newman*) B was only a *general* carrier and so less able to foresee the effects of delay.

✗ The claim also failed in *Balfour Beatty Construction (Scotland) Ltd v Scottish Power plc* (1994) where disruptions in S's supply of electricity to BB at a critical moment in BB's construction process meant that a significant part of the construction had to be demolished and rebuilt. Lord Jauncey explains that remoteness depends on what the defendant can be taken to reasonably know of the other's activity:

> However, when the activity of A involves complicated construction or manufacturing techniques, I can see no reason why B who supplies a commodity that A intends to use in the course of those techniques should be assumed, and merely because of the order for the commodity, to be aware of the details of all the techniques undertaken by A and the effect thereupon of any failure of or deficiency in that commodity.

(v) Exceptional loss: the second limb
The defendant who *knows* of *special circumstances*, which may increase the claimant's loss, is liable for it. The court can increase the scope of recoverable loss under the second limb by being more willing to *infer* the relevant knowledge from the circumstances.

✓ In *Simpson v London and North Western Railway* (1876), N transported S's sample of cattle food from the Bedford agricultural show to Newcastle for its agricultural show. The goods were marked 'must be at Newcastle by Monday certain', but did not arrive until the show was over. S was awarded the loss of profit that he would have made from the Newcastle show. Although S did not expressly refer to the show, the court was prepared to *infer* N's knowledge of this special circumstance because the contract was made with N's agent at the Bedford Showground, sent there specifically to attract such customers.

Conversely, the court may **narrow liability** under the second limb by increasing the specificity of the loss which must be foreseeable and finding such knowledge absent in the circumstances.

✗ In *Horne v Midland Railway Co* (1872), H had an urgent contract to deliver military shoes to London for the French army at an unusually high price. H sent them with M, giving notice that the shoes were 'under contract' and the date by which they had to arrive. The shoes arrived a day late and were rejected by the intending buyer; H resold them at a much lower price because demand had fallen due to the cessation of the war. H was denied the loss of profits from the lucrative contract ostensibly because H did not sufficiently disclose it. However, the dissenting view that there *was* adequate notice under the second limb seems compelling: 'It is said that the defendants would not contemplate so large a loss from the notice that they received. If this notice be not sufficient it must be necessary in such a case to communicate the exact details of the contract. I cannot think this is so.'

 Pause for reflection

The real reasons for denying the claim can be found in the court's reference to: the defendant being a railway (ie a general carrier), the concern that it may be exposed to a flood of claims from customers, and the unfairness arising from the disproportion between the contract price and the potential contract liability. The US Second Restatement of Contracts, § 351(3), empowers courts to limit damages for foreseeable loss if justice so requires to avoid disproportionate compensation (ie an extreme disproportion between the price and the loss). The majority in *Horne v Midland Railway* achieved the same result by increasing the level of notice required of onerous or unusual potential liability. The same technique is used by courts to avoid binding a party to onerous and unusual terms contained in unsigned documents purporting to have contractual effect (ie by finding that the other party failed to satisfy the heightened requirement of notice, 10.3.3.2).

The final example of the flexible application of the rules to achieve a just result is *Cory v Thames Ironworks & Shipbuilding Co Ltd* (1867) where TIS delivered the hull of a boat late. If it had been used as coal storage, as TIS believed, C would have sustained £420 of loss. However, it was intended for use in an innovative way, unknown to TIS, and C's actual loss was £4,000. This was held to be too remote, but the court awarded C £420, explaining that 'there can be no hardship or injustice in making the seller liable to compensate him in damages so far as the seller understood and believed that the article would be applied to the ordinary purposes to which it was capable of being applied'.

(vi) The test of remoteness where concurrent contract and tort actions exist
The Heron II requires:

- a *higher* degree of foreseeability for recoverable loss *in contract actions* (the defendant must contemplate the type of loss as a *serious* possibility at the time of contracting), and

- a lower degree of foreseeability in *tort actions* (only requiring contemplation of the type of loss as a *slight* possibility).

Lord Reid justifies this on the basis that a claimant in the contractual context can protect herself by disclosure of unusual risks before contract formation (the defendant has the option of restricting liability for it and the claimant can take out insurance), whilst the claimant in tort has no such opportunity. *However*, this distinction is inapt where the tortious duty arises in the context of the parties' contractual relationship, ie there is concurrent liability in contract and tort (see Scarman LJ in *Parsons (Livestock) v Uttley Ingham*). In *Brown v KMR* (1995), the court held that where the parties are in a contractual relationship, the *contract test applies* (requiring higher foreseeability or a stricter remoteness test) even where the claim is brought in tort. But recent cases have given contradictory answers, although *Yapp* may be confined to its own facts:

- In *Yapp v Foreign and Commonwealth Office* (2014), the Court of Appeal held that whether *psychiatric injury* was too remote a consequence of a breach of the *employer's common law duty of care* was to be determined by the test applicable in tort.

- In *Wellesley Partners LLP v Withers LLP* (2015), the Court of Appeal accepted the view that in cases of concurrent liability, the contract test should apply to a tort claim for economic loss for which, anyway, the claimant would have to prove the defendant's assumption of responsibility.

 Pause for reflection

1. In 'Remoteness of Damages in Contract and Tort Law: A Reconsideration' (1996) 55 *CLJ* 488, Cartwright explains that the foreseeability standard varies with the reason for imposing the duty or liability in the first place. Thus, where the duty is contractual or based on an 'assumption of responsibility' in tort, the question is the scope of the risks assumed by the defendant. In respect of tortious liability for physical injury, it is inappropriate to ask what liability the defendant has assumed, and compensating the claimant takes on more prominence. See also A Burrows, 'Limitations on Compensation' in Burrows and Peel, *Commercial Remedies* (2003) 27.

2. The European Draft Common Frame of Reference shifts the inquiry to the *quality of the defendant's breach*. The foreseeability test limits recoverable loss 'unless the non-performance was intentional, reckless or grossly negligent' (Art III-3:703). This focus on *fault* can be justified. To the extent that the remoteness qualification aims to avoid harsh outcomes to the contract-breaker, it is much less compelling where the contract-breaker causes the loss deliberately or with gross negligence.

(vii) *The Achilleas* modification: assumption of responsibility
The House of Lords has ruled that:

- even where loss is foreseeable under the *Hadley v Baxendale* foreseeability test of remoteness, the claimant will not recover if the defendant has not assumed responsibility for losses of the kind suffered.

- Conversely, even where loss is unforeseeable under *Hadley v Baxendale*, the defendant who has assumed responsibility for the loss suffered will be liable for that loss.

In *Transfield Shipping Inc v Mercator Shipping Inc (The Achilleas)* (2008), the charterers returned a vessel late in breach of contract, causing the owners to lose the profits on a lucrative follow-on charter. The owners were denied this loss of profits, although the arbitrators and the courts below found that the loss was clearly foreseeable under the first limb in *Hadley v Baxendale*. Lords Hoffmann and Hope (with the concurrence of Lord Walker) reasoned that it was too crude to rely solely on the foreseeability of the loss in question. The real question is what liability the defendant had assumed the risk for, ie, the contracting parties' *common intention* in respect of loss occasioned by relatively short delay in redelivery.

✓ Given the understanding in the shipping industry and the uniform dicta over many years in which judges said or assumed that the damages for late delivery were the difference between the charter rate and the market rate, this is the appropriate measure.

✗ The charterer could not reasonably be regarded as having assumed the risk of the owner's loss of much greater profit on the follow-on charter.

Lord Rodger and Lady Hale also denied the owner's claim, but on the alternative basis that the loss was not foreseeable. This contradicts the lower courts' finding that it *was* foreseeable.

In *Supershield Ltd v Siemens Building Technologies FE Ltd* (2010) Toulson LJ recognises that *The Achilleas* may not only result in narrower liability than the foreseeability test (as in *The Achilleas* itself), it may also yield wider liability (as in *Supershield* itself where the contract-breaker was held liable for a type of unforeseeable loss). Thus, 'the question of remoteness cannot be isolated from consideration of the purpose of the contract and the scope of the contractual obligation'.

 Pause for reflection

1. In *The Achilleas*, Lord Hoffmann sought to transplant the approach in *South Australia Asset Management Corp v York Montague Ltd* (*SAAMCO*) (1997). There the House of Lords decided that valuers were not liable for all the foreseeable consequences of their breach, but only for the consequences that they had assumed responsibility for. Thus, recoverable loss was limited to the difference between the amount lent based on the negligent valuation and the amount that would have been lent if the correct value had been provided to the lender. The valuers were not liable for the loss occasioned by a subsequent fall in property prices.

2. Lord Hoffmann criticises the foreseeability approach for being highly indeterminate and open to manipulation.

3. However, the 'assumption of responsibility' approach can also be criticised for being: (i) too uncertain—there will usually be no direct evidence of the parties' intention as to liability and courts will inevitably have to rely on other criteria; (ii) unnecessary—this already happens under the rubric of foreseeability.

In *Sylvia Shipping Co Ltd v Progress Bulk Carriers Ltd* (2010), Hamblen J did not see *The Achilleas* as heralding a new substitute test of remoteness. The orthodox approach remains the standard rule. In most cases it will not be necessary for the court to consider the assumption of responsibility test because 'the fact that the type of loss arises in the ordinary course of things or out of special known circumstances will carry with it the necessary assumption of responsibility'. It is only in relatively rare and unusual cases that consideration of assumption of responsibility will be required. Namely, cases where the foreseeability test:

- leads or may lead to an unquantifiable, unpredictable, uncontrollable, or disproportionate liability; or

- would be contrary to market understanding and expectations.

In ***John Grimes Partnership Ltd v Gubbins*** (2013), Sir David Keene affirmed the emerging consensus that:

(i) Lord Hoffmann was not departing from the foreseeability test of remoteness, but merely rationalising it on the basis of the parties' imputed intention in the ordinary case; and

(ii) the foreseeability test would only be inapplicable where the circumstances showed that the parties could not have contracted on that basis.

In other words: there is normally an implied term accepting responsibility for the types of losses which can reasonably be foreseen at the time of contracting to be not unlikely to result if the contract is broken. But if that implied assumption of responsibility for a type of loss in a particular case is inappropriate because of the nature of the contract, the commercial background, or other relevant special circumstances, then the contract-breaker escapes liability. Such was the case in *The Achilleas*.

13.2.5.2 Mitigation

(i) The mitigation rule
The mitigation rule requires the claimant to act reasonably to limit or reduce her loss caused by the defendant's breach (***British Westinghouse Electric & Manufacturing Co v Underground Electric Rly Co*** (1912)). Although this is often expressed as a claimant's 'duty' to mitigate, it is not a duty that attracts liability on its breach; it merely reduces or negates the damages otherwise recoverable by the claimant. No duty to mitigate traditionally attaches to an aggrieved party's election to affirm the contract or to claim specific performance. Nevertheless, the desirability of mitigation explains why a claimant cannot affirm if she has no *legitimate interest* in doing so (because it would be very wasteful and grossly unreasonable, see 12.3).

(ii) The standard of reasonable mitigation
The burden is on the defendant contract-breaker to show that the claimant has failed to mitigate. The standard of mitigation required from the claimant is not high for it lies ill in the defendant's mouth to criticise the claimant's actions when these have been necessitated by the defendant's own breach. The claimant need not 'take any step which a reasonable and prudent man would not ordinarily take in the course of his business' (*British Westinghouse*), eg, the claimant need *not* take steps:

✗ which would entail substantial financial risks or involve complicated litigation (*Pilkington v Wood* (1953));

✗ which would require it to risk its commercial reputation (*James Finlay & Co Ltd v Kwik Hoo Tong Handelsmaatschappij* (1929));

✗ which it cannot afford; thus, impecuniosity, including inability to borrow, may excuse a failure to mitigate (*Clippens Oil Co Ltd v Edinburgh & District Water Trustees* (1907)); or

✗ while an action for specific performance is being determined (*Radford v de Froberville*).

(iii) The requirement of positive action

The first limb of mitigation requires the claimant to take *positive* action to minimise the loss flowing from the breach. What is required is fact-specific; however, in general:

✓ a claimant who does not receive the *goods or services* contracted for must make reasonable efforts to buy substitute performance (*Kaines (UK) v Osterreichische Warrenhandelsgesellschaft Austrowaren GmbH* (1993)); this will require prompt action in a volatile market (*Coastal (Bermuda) Petroleum Ltd v VTT Vulcan Petroleum (No 2)* (1994));

✓ a wrongly dismissed *employee* must make reasonable efforts to obtain suitable alternative employment (*Yetton v Eastwoods Froy Ltd* (1967));

✓ a claimant who sustains *property damage* from the breach should accept help to prevent further damage (*Anderson v Hoen, The Flying Fish* (1865)); and

✓ a claimant who sustains *physical injury* from the breach may be expected to undergo an operation to reduce or eliminate the injury unless the operation entails the risk of complications (*Selvanayagam v University of the West Indies* (1983)).

More controversially, mitigation may even require the claimant to renegotiate the contract with the contract-breaker:

- *Brace v Calder* (1895) held that a wrongly dismissed *employee* may be required to accept re-employment from his former employer unless their relationship has been damaged, the new job would involve a loss of status, or alternative employment is more permanent (*Yetton v Eastwoods Froy* (1967)).

- In *Payzu Ltd v Saunders* (1919), S (suppliers of silk) wrongly insisted on cash payment on delivery, whereupon P sued for the difference between the contract price and the greater market price. This was denied because P's rejection of S's offer to supply the silk on cash terms amounted to a failure to mitigate its loss. The court held that, in *commercial* cases,[4] a party can be expected to consider and accept a reasonable offer made by the contract-breaker. The claimant may even be expected to initiate the renegotiation.

- In *The Soholt* (1983), the buyers of a ship who lawfully terminated the contract for late delivery were denied the difference between the contract price ($5 million) and the market price ($5.5 million) because they should have offered to buy the ship for the contract price adjusted to reflect the costs of delay to them.

---

[4] No such requirement attaches to contracts for personal services, *Clayton-Greene v de Courville* (1920).

Counterpoint

The law can produce perverse results. Where the claimant fails to mitigate *in a rising market* by renegotiating with the contract-breaker, the latter gets to keep the benefit from the increase in the market price of the goods contracted for but not delivered. Thus, in *The Soholt*, the sellers who should have delivered a ship to the claimant, but sold it to another party for $300,000 more than the contract price, did not have to compensate the claimant, who had to pay more to replace the ship in the same rising market.

(iv) Refraining from unreasonable action

The second limb of mitigation bars any claim arising from *incurring unreasonable expenses* in mitigation. Again, what is reasonable is fact-specific, but examples of *reasonable* expenses include:

✓ advertising costs to mitigate the claimant's loss of business (*Holden Ltd v Bostock & Co Ltd* (1902));

✓ hire charges to replace an asset damaged or not delivered (*Bacon v Cooper (Metals) Ltd* (1982));

✓ the cost of printing new bank notes and of exchanging all old notes for new ones when printers wrongly delivered the old bank notes to criminals who put them into circulation (*Banco de Portugal v Waterlow & Sons Ltd* (1932));

✓ expenses in attempted mitigation even if it fails (*Esso Petroleum v Mardon* (1976));

✗ but, it was *unreasonable* to take a loan at very high interest rates to release a ship, which had been wrongly detained (*Compania Financiera Soleada SA v Hamoor Tanker Corp Inc* (1981)).

(v) Gains from mitigation

Gains flowing *directly* from a claimant's mitigation are deducted from the claimant's damages. But no deductions will be made if the gains are indirect, merely collateral, or accrue from acts that are independent of, or too remote from, the act of mitigation.

✗ In *Globalia Business Travel SAU of Spain v Fulton Shipping (The New Flamenco)* (2017), the Supreme Court said that: 'The essential question is whether there is a sufficiently close link between the two…. The benefit to be brought into account had to have been caused either by the breach of the charterparty or by a successful act of mitigation.' There, a charterer returned the ship two years early; the ship-owner sold its ship and sued the charterer for two years' loss of profits. The charterer argued that its liability should be reduced by $16.7million since this was the amount that the owner gained from selling the ship early. The Supreme Court disagreed for the following reasons:

   • The owners' interest in the ship's capital value had nothing to do with its interest in the income stream injured by the charterers' repudiation of the charterparty.

- The premature termination of the charterparty did not cause the sale, either at all or at any particular time. The ship could have been sold during the term of the charterparty, any sale had nothing to do with the repudiation of the charterparty.
- The market price at the end of the charterparty is irrelevant since a sale was not inevitable then or on premature termination.
- The ship-owners could not have claimed for any *rise* in the value of the ship between its sale and the end of the charterparty, any more than the charterer can bring into account any *fall* in that value, as occurred.

Other examples:

✓ damages were reduced by the savings achieved when a defective turbine was replaced by a more efficient one that used less coal (*British Westinghouse*);

✗ proceeds of an insurance policy will not reduce the claimant's damages since the insurance contract is made before the breach (*Lavarack v Woods of Colchester Ltd* (1967));

✗ *where supply exceeds demand*, the seller's damages for loss of profits are not reduced although he subsequently sells the car to another party at the contract price because, but for the breach, the seller would have made two sales and two profits (*Thompson Ltd v Robinson (Gunmakers) Ltd* (1955)).

In *Lavarack v Woods of Colchester Ltd* (1967), the employer's breach released the employee from a clause prohibiting his involvement in other businesses:

✓ the court reduced the employee's damages by the remuneration he received from his new employer (a salary and half-share in a company);

✗ but no reduction was made for his profits from investing in another company, since this was too indirectly related to the employer's breach.

✗ Where *A* delivers defective goods to *B*, which *B* had previously contracted to (and does) sell on to *C* for more than their actual value (preventing *B*'s loss from *A*'s breach), *Slater v Hoyle & Smith* (1920) nevertheless permits *B* to claim the difference between the expected value and the actual value of the goods; it is 'immaterial that by some good fortune with which the [sellers] have nothing to do [the buyer] has been able to recoup himself what he paid for those goods'.

(vi) The justification for the mitigation requirement

Atiyah famously notes that the mitigation requirement 'makes a large dent' in the theory that the claimant is entitled to damages representing her lost expectations. If I refuse to perform my contract with you, but you can get substitute performance at the same price, your compensable expectation will be nil. Atiyah concludes: 'the reality is that the bindingness of executory contracts protects not the expectation of performance, but the expectation of profit; and even that is only protected so long as the promisee cannot secure it elsewhere'.[5]

What then is the justification for the mitigation rule?

---

[5] P S Atiyah, *The Rise and Fall of Freedom of Contract* (Clarendon Press, 1979) 430.

(i) Fulfilment of expectations: Burrows explains the requirement of mitigation as adding 'a supplementary policy to those policies justifying protection of the expectation interest... [Namely] that the promisee should not leave it simply to the courts to ensure fulfilment of his expectations, but should rather take it upon himself to adopt other reasonable means to ensure the fulfilment of his expectations.'[6] With respect, this seems to contradict (rather than supplement) the policies supporting the protection of the claimant's expectation interest. A party makes a contract *so that* the other party (backed up by the law), and *not they themselves*, will fulfil their contractual expectation.

(ii) *Altruism*: Fried explains mitigation as a 'kind of altruistic duty, towards one's contractual partner'.[7] But why should an altruistic duty be raised in favour of the promise-*breaker* if, as Fried believes, promise-*keeping* is the essence of contractual liability?

(iii) *Efficiency*: mitigation is aimed at minimising wasteful conduct and encouraging efficient conduct. The concern to avoid waste is reflected in other restrictions on the measure of damages. Efficiency theories (1.4.3) reconcile this with the promisee's *right* to her expectation on the basis that mitigation leaves her no worse off: it is therefore said to be a 'cost-free' duty.[8] However, mitigation costs the promisee the effort of making a substitute contract and this will often not be trivial. Moreover, the rule bites precisely where the promisee is judged to have *failed* to mitigate and is denied some or all of her *provable* losses flowing from the breach: this clearly 'costs' the claimant.

(iv) Good faith: the claimant must act with due regard for the minimal interest of the other party in not being liable for easily avoidable loss.

13.2.5.3 The time for measuring loss

Where the market for the subject matter of the contract fluctuates, the amount of compensation will depend on *when* damages are assessed. In a rising market (ie prices are increasing), the *earlier* the time fixed for assessment, the *less* will be awarded. Courts normally measure the loss at the earliest date that the claimant can be expected to mitigate (find substitute performance or take remedial action). She cannot sit back in the hope of claiming a greater loss at the date of the trial. Hence, loss is normally assessed at the *date of breach*. On termination for anticipatory breach, the claimant comes under a duty to mitigate at the date of termination even if this is *before* the date of performance (*Bunge SSA v Nidera* (2015)). Damages may also be measured *after* the date of breach if that is more appropriate (*Johnson v Agnew* (1980)), eg, if:

(i) The claimant could not with reasonable diligence have discovered the breach at the time (*The Hansa Nord* (1976)).

(ii) The claimant reasonably waits to see whether the defendant will remedy the breach, or pending an action for specific performance (*Radford v de Froberville* and *Wroth v Tyler* (1974)).

---

[6] A Burrows, 'Contract, Tort and Restitution—A Satisfactory Division or Not?' (1983) 99 *LQR* 217, 266.

[7] C Fried, *Contract As Promise* (Harvard University Press, 1981) 131.

[8] C J Goetz and R E Scott, 'The Mitigation Principle: Toward a General Theory of Contractual Obligation' (1983) 69 *Virginia L Rev* 967.

(iii) The claimant cannot afford to take remedial action because of his or her own impecuniosity or inability to obtain credit (*Wroth v Tyler*).

Even if these factors are present, damages may still be reduced if the claimant unreasonably drags her heels through the courts (*Malhotra v Choudhury* (1980)).

13.2.5.4 Speculative loss

The claimant must prove the *extent* of her loss. But the fact that damages are hard to quantify does not bar the claimant if she has suffered substantial loss; the court will do its best on the available evidence. Particular problems arise when the law must quantify the claimant's loss of opportunity to make gains or avoid losses due to the breach.

(i) When is loss of a chance compensable?

✗ Loss of chance damages are not available where the causation of loss rests on the hypothetical actions of the claimant, eg *McWilliams v Sir William Arroll & Co Ltd* (1962), where the question was whether, had the employer provided the safety equipment, the claimant would have used it and avoided his loss. In these cases, loss must be determined on the *balance of probabilities*, and all-or-nothing damages awarded accordingly. However, such cases are better dealt with by proportional reduction for contributory negligence rather than wholesale denial (13.2.5.6).

✓ *Allied Maples Group v Simmons & Simmons* (1995) confines damages for loss of a chance to cases where the causation of loss rests on the hypothetical actions of a third party. If there is a *substantial chance* (not merely a speculative one) that the third party would have acted to confer a benefit on or avoid a loss to the claimant, then the court can award a sum for the claimant's loss of a chance. Here, a solicitor's failure to warn his client about the potential liabilities of a company the client was acquiring meant that the latter did not try to negotiate a better deal with the seller. The court held that, if the client could show that: (i) on the balance of probabilities, she *would* have sought renegotiation with the third party; *and* (ii) she had a *substantial chance* of negotiating (it is unnecessary to prove that she *would* on the balance of probabilities have negotiated) a better deal from the third party, then the court should quantify and award compensation for her loss of chance of doing so.

✓ In *Chaplin v Hicks* (1911), the defendant's breach of contract prevented the claimant from taking part in the final stage of a beauty contest where 12 of the 50 finalists (from 6,000 original entrants) would win places in a chorus line. The claimant was awarded damages for her loss of a chance, assessed at 25% of winning the competition.

  ✓ Where the claimant's loss depends on a contingency that might occur (not involving the hypothetical actions of the claimant or a third party), damages are assessed by reference to the chance of the contingency occurring, eg outbreak of war entitling the defendant to cancel the contract.

  ✓ Where the contingency has occurred by the time of trial, damages should be assessed by reference to the known facts. In *The Golden Victory* (2007) (*Golden Strait Corp v Nippon Yusen Kubishiki Kaisha*), the charterer breached by returning the ship four years before the charterparty expired. Fourteen months later, the Gulf War broke out which would have entitled either party to terminate the charterparty. The House of Lords restricted damages to 14 months rather than four years of hire because contract damages should put the claimant in the position it would have been in had the contract been performed. The court should not shut its eyes to subsequent events that reduce the claimant's loss, even if this may reduce certainty and give defendants an incentive to delay settling cases.

✓ In *Bunge SSA v Nidera* (2015), the buyer terminated the contract for the seller's repudiation but the seller would have been entitled to cancel the contract four days later when an export ban came into effect. Although the contract contained a damages clause providing a scheme for establishing damages on default by either party, the Supreme Court awarded only nominal damages because: (a) account had to be taken of what would have happened had the defendant not repudiated, and since the export ban remained in force throughout the contractual period, the claimant had suffered no loss; and (b) the damages clause did not deal with the effect of subsequent events which would have resulted in the original contract not being performed.

(ii) How is loss of a chance quantified?

Quantification of the lost chance is necessarily speculative; it depends on the *value* of the expected benefit and the *likelihood* of the claimant actually getting it; 'the more the contingencies, the lower the value of the chance' (*Hall v Meyrick* (1957)). The rigour with which the quantification issue is approached varies. In *Chaplin v Hicks*, the court seemed to proceed on the claimant's *statistical* chance of winning (as if she were a lottery player), perhaps to avoid assessing the claimant's 'merits' against any particular criteria of beauty. However, a claim will be excluded if it depends on very *remote* and hypothetical possibilities, eg *McRae v Commonwealth Disposals Commission* (1950), where a salvor wasted money fruitlessly searching for the non-existent wreck of an oil tanker. His claim for the loss of profits expected from a successful salvage was dismissed as far too speculative (but damages were awarded for wasted expenses, 13.3).

13.2.5.5 Intervening causes

The claimant cannot recover more than nominal damages if no loss was caused by the defendant's breach. Neither can she claim for loss incurred but not as a result of the breach. In *Levicom International Holdings BV v Linklaters* (2009), solicitors were in breach of contract by not giving clear and proper advice but were liable only for nominal damages because the court found that, even given the proper advice, the claimant would not have acted differently. Thus, the solicitors' breach did not cause any loss.

The causal link may also be broken by the occurrence of unforeseeable events overwhelming the breach:

(i) **Acts of independent third parties** will negate the claim unless the defendant was contracted to guard against that very occurrence (*London Joint Stock Bank Ltd v Macmillan & Arthur* (1918)). A house painter who leaves the house where he is working unlocked is liable to the owner for the value of goods stolen from it by a third party thief (*Stansbie v Troman* (1948)).

(ii) **Acts of God,** in the sense of natural or other unforeseeable external events, may negate the causal effect of the defendant's breach. A party supplying an unseaworthy ship in breach of contract is liable for any losses caused by foreseeable difficulties at sea (*Smith, Hogg & Co Ltd v Black Sea and Baltic General Insurance Co Ltd* (1940)), but *not* if delay caused by its breach caused the ship to run into a typhoon; the delay is not of equal causal potency to the typhoon in causing the loss (*Monarch Steamship Co v Karlshamns Oljefabriker* (1949)).

(iii) **Unreasonable acts of the claimant**: in *Lambert v Lewis* (1982), the claimant continued to use a trailer coupling after it broke. This severed the chain of causation between the defendant's breach (in supplying the defective coupling) and the loss claimed (for liability to persons injured when the coupling gave way). Damages were also denied in *Quinn v Burch Bros (Builders) Ltd* (1966), where the defendant employer's failure to supply a stepladder was held to be (a) merely the 'occasion', and *not* (b) the effective cause, of the loss occasioned by the defendant's breach (ie the employee's personal injury when the employee used and fell from an unstable unfooted trestle). Glidewell LJ said that the distinction between (a) and (b) depends on:

- the *likelihood* of the intervening cause;
- the *reasonableness* of the claimant's actions (*Galoo Ltd v Bright Grahame Murray* (1994)); and
- 'the application of the court's common sense'.

This uncertain formula blurs the issue of *intervening cause* with the issues of *contributory negligence* and *remoteness* of loss, to which we turn.

13.2.5.6 Contributory negligence

At common law, a claimant whose negligence contributes to her own loss but does not break the chain of causation cannot have her damages reduced (*Quinn v Burch Bros*). But can her damages be reduced under the Law Reform (Contributory Negligence) Act 1945? The answer, stated in *Vesta v Butcher* (1989), depends on the **nature of the contractual duty breached**:

✓ Where a **contractual duty of care coexists with a tortious duty of care** (so-called category 3 in the Law Commission's *Contributory Negligence as a Defence in Contract* (Law Com No 219, 1993)) damages *are* reducible for contributory negligence where the claimant's action is: (i) for the tort of negligence (the 1945 Act explicitly permits this); or (ii) for breach of a concurrent contractual duty of care, eg in *Trebor Bassett Holdings Ltd and the Cadbury UK Partnership v ADT Fire and Security plc* (2012), ADT supplied a tailor-made fire suppression system for TB's confectionery factory. ADT's breach caused a fire in the popcorn production area, which spread and destroyed the whole factory. The Court of Appeal upheld the finding that TB was contributorily liable for 75% of the loss because: it had negligently failed to segregate the production area from the rest of the building, failed to install sprinklers and encouraged the spread of the fire upon its discovery by ejecting the entire load of burning popcorn and trying to stamp out the fire (this was held to be entirely predictable and did not completely break the chain of causation). ADT undertook to exercise reasonable skill and care in the design of the system; it did not guarantee the system's success.

✗ Where any **duty of care is purely contractual** (with no coexisting tortious duty of care; so-called category 2), damages cannot be reduced for the claimant's contributory negligence. A rare example is *Raflatac Ltd v Eade* (1999), where the acts of the defendant's subcontractor amounted to breach of the defendant's *contractual* duty of care, but the defendant was not vicariously liable for the subcontractor's negligence. The Law Commission recommends extending contributory negligence to category 2 cases by analogy to category 3 cases, but this would make little practical difference given the rarity of category 2 cases.

✗ Where the **contractual obligation is strict** (so-called category 1), damages cannot be reduced for the claimant's contributory negligence. Most contractual obligations are strict: the defendant warrants the truth of something or guarantees a particular result, irrespective of fault. In *Barclays Bank plc v Fairclough Building Ltd* (1994), a claim for £4 million damages for breach of a contract to remove asbestos from buildings was *not* reduced for the claimant's contributory negligence: the defendant had a strict duty to comply with the contract and not simply to take reasonable care. The Law Commission recommends *no change* here because:

- the parties' allocation of risk should be respected; and

- allowing loss apportionment in all three categories would transform currently straightforward cases into complex disputes about comparative blame, introducing intolerable uncertainty and hampering out-of-court settlements.

▶◀ Counterpoint

1. Burrows supports a more radical extension of loss apportionment on the basis that the proportionate approach of contributory negligence is preferable to an 'all or nothing' approach,[9] eg in *Quinn v Burch Bros*, a fairer result would have been to reduce the claimant's damages for his foolish use of unsafe equipment, rather than deny his claim altogether and shield the employer from all responsibility for its failure to provide safe equipment. The same may be concluded of a claimant who ruins expensive clothes by using a new iron on them, although the iron is clearly missing its heat dial and noticeably defective in other respects.[10]

2. The availability of contributory negligence has not prevented settlements in negligence cases.

3. Uncertainty can be alleviated if the courts make clear that any reduction would be in 'steps', eg in multiples of 25% rather than a complete spectrum between 0% and 100%.[11]

4. Although the concern not to undermine the parties' risk allocation in agreeing a strict contractual duty remains, it is arguably already undermined by the rules on mitigation and intervening causes.

5. The European Draft Common Frame of Reference stipulates that: '[t]he debtor is not liable for loss suffered by the creditor to the extent that the creditor contributed to the non-performance or its effects' (Art III.-3:704).

---

[9] A Burrows, 'Contributory Negligence in Contract: Ammunition for the Law Commission' (1993) 109 *LQR* 175.

[10] Law Commission, *Contributory Negligence as a Defence in Contract* (Working Paper No 114, 1990) para 2.9.

[11] A Burrows, 'Limitations on Compensation' in A Burrows and E Peel (eds), *Commercial Remedies* (OUP, 2003) 27, 43.

13.2.5.7 Time limit

The law discourages stale claims, because, as time passes, it becomes increasingly difficult for a defendant to produce the evidence to defend herself. The law draws a line beyond which a claimant cannot seek a remedy from the courts.

Sections 5 and 8 of the Limitation Act 1980 provide that an action founded on:

- a simple contract must be brought within six years, and
- a deed within 12 years

from the date the cause of action accrued. The cause of action accrues in contract *when the breach occurs*, or when the claimant elects to terminate the contract for an anticipatory breach. In contrast, the cause of action accrues in tort when the damage is suffered, and in unjust enrichment when the defendant is unjustly enriched. Time runs even if the claimant was unaware or could not have been aware of the existence of her cause of action until after the time limit has expired. But where the claimant's action is based on *fraud* or *mistake*, or where the defendant has deliberately *concealed* facts relevant to the claimant's right of action, time only starts to run when the claimant *discovers* the fraud, concealment, or mistake, or could have done so with reasonable diligence (Limitation Act 1980, s 32). However, this cannot prejudice the rights of third parties taking bona fide and for value.

Claims in equity or for equitable remedies to which the Limitation Act does not apply are subject to the doctrine of laches (*Lindsay Petroleum Co v Hurd* (1874)). Thus, delay may bar equitable remedies such as rescission, rectification, specific performance, or injunction. The delay necessary to make it unjust to allow a claim to be brought must be judged against the particular circumstances of the case. This may be shorter or longer than the statutory limitation of six years (5.2.2.3).

13.3 **The role of the reliance measure**

It has been said that a claimant suing for breach of contract can choose between her expectation and her 'reliance' loss (*CCC Films (London) Ltd v Impact Quadrant Films Ltd* (1985)). This is misleading. The aim of compensatory damages for breach of contract is *always* to put the claimant in the same position *as if the contract had been performed* (*Robinson v Harman* (1848)).

13.3.1 **Not an alternative measure of damages**

The only circumstance in which a claimant would *prefer* a reliance claim is where she has made a bad bargain (eg she paid more than her expected profits from the defendant's performance). But this is the very circumstance when the law bars the claimant from claiming reliance to get around the fact that she would have suffered loss even if the contract had been duly performed (ie circumvent a bad bargain; *C & P Haulage v Middleton* (1983)). That is, the claimant cannot be put in a better position than if the contract had been performed. She is confined to the expectation measure which will yield nominal damages only.

The High Court of Australia, in *Commonwealth of Australia v Amman Aviation* (1991), rejected as inappropriate, 'the language of *election* or the notion that *alternative* ways are open to a plaintiff in which to frame a claim for relief'. In truth, 'damages for loss of profits and damages for expenditure reasonably incurred are simply two manifestations of the general principle enunciated in *Robinson v Harman*'. Likewise, in *Omak Maritime v Mamola Challenger Shipping (The Mamola Challenger)* (2010), Teare J held that 'reliance losses are a species of expectation losses and that they are neither... "fundamentally different" nor awarded on a different "juridical basis of claim"'. How does this work?

13.3.2 The assumption that expectation would at least equal expenditure

It will sometimes be very difficult for the claimant to prove what position she would have been in had the contract been properly performed. One way around this evidential difficulty is to assume that the claimant's profits under the contract (ie her expectation interest) would *at least* have equalled her expenditure in reliance on the contract (ie her reliance interest) (*Yam Seng Pte Ltd v International Trade Corp Ltd* (2013)). This includes expenditure incurred *before* contract formation, based on the unlikelihood of a claimant spending more on performing a contract than she is likely to gain from it, eg:

✓ In *Anglia Television Ltd v Reed* (1972), R contracted to star in A's film but repudiated the contract at the last moment. A, unable to find a replacement, abandoned the project. It was impossible to assess how profitable the film would have been if R had performed. But A was awarded its expenses, although these were incurred *before* the contract was made, since it was foreseeable that they could be wasted on breach.

✓ In *McRae v Commonwealth Disposals Commission* (1951), CDC sold M a sunken oil tanker which turned out not to exist, although CDC had promised that it did. The value of the non-existent ship and its contents was held to be too speculative for the purpose of measuring M's expectation interest. The court awarded M's reliance loss, being: (i) the price paid to CDC, and (ii) the wasted expenditure in attempting to find and salvage it.

✓ In *Yam Seng v ITC* (10.6.1.4), ITC's breach deprived YS of more sales. It was impossible to quantify this and ITC had not proved that YS would have made a loss. Therefore, YS was entitled to its reliance loss, including its expenditure on marketing and promoting the product.

13.3.3 Burden of proof

It is the defendant's breach that has caused the claimant's evidential difficulty, hence it is for the *defendant* to prove that the claimant has made a bad bargain and so is barred from a reliance claim (*Parker v SJ Berwin & Co* (2008); *Yam Seng* (2013)).

13.4 Restitution of benefits conferred

The claimant will prefer to recover the benefit she conferred on the defendant in performance of the contract where:

• her expectation and reliance losses are *too speculative* to quantify;

- the *benefit* conferred is substantially the claimant's whole *loss*; or
- she has made a *bad bargain*.

However, restitution is only available for **total failure of consideration**. This occurs when the defendant has performed nothing of her contractual obligation (consideration), eg where you pay me £200 for a bicycle worth only £100 but I fail to deliver, you are better off getting your money back than seeking expectation damages (£100).

13.4.1 The contract must be terminated

In general, restitution is only available if the contract has been terminated for breach (*Kwei Tek Chao v British Traders and Shippers Ltd* (1954)). The defendant's enrichment is justified by the contract until the contract ceases to govern the parties' rights and remedies; only then does the enrichment become 'unjust' and liable for return.

 Pause for reflection

Three related reasons can be suggested for allowing an innocent party to 'go backwards' by claiming restitution (and perhaps avoiding a bad bargain) once a contract is terminated, when the contractual response characteristically projects the parties 'forwards':

1. The contract reason: a contract is *two-sided*, the purpose of each party is to get the other party's reciprocal performance. Each party's undertaking is generally *conditional* on the other's *substantial* performance ('I will if you will'). Where one party does not substantially perform, the other party should be able to choose whether to go 'forwards' (claiming expectation damages) or 'backwards' (claiming restitution). In particular, the innocent party should not be forced to go forwards if it requires her to pay for performance that she does not get. The defendant should not be enriched by her own breach. The idea that 'you can't get something for nothing' is a contractual principle.

2. The unjust enrichment reason: failure of consideration is an *independent* cause of action in the law of unjust enrichment. However, a claimant's payment cannot both be justified by a valid contract *and* liable to be returned as an unjust enrichment. The contractual regime takes priority because the parties' autonomy should be respected. Thus, contracts must generally be set aside (terminated, rescinded, discharged, or rendered unenforceable) before restitution can be claimed.

3. The pragmatic reason: it is less objectionable to ignore the contractual allocation of risk and permit escape from bad bargains if the defendant has not even commenced performance. Moreover, restitution for *total* failure of consideration avoids quantification difficulties.

13.4.2 Total failure of consideration in money claims

Traditionally, a claimant can only recover *money* if there has been a *total* failure of consideration in the sense that she has received *nothing of* the performance she contracted for. Receipt of benefit does not bar recovery if it is not 'what was contracted for' on a proper construction of the contract (*Rowland v Divall* (1923)).

Counterpoint

The requirement that the failure of consideration must be **total** is:

1. Unfair: a defendant may also be unjustly enriched where failure of consideration is only partial.

2. Unnecessary: if the real concern is that it is unfair to require the defendant to give back everything when she has conferred some benefit on the claimant, a set-off can be allowed.

3. Subject to exceptions, eg:

   • the Law Reform (Frustrated Contracts) Act 1943 (7.6) allows recovery (for money or non-money performance) even if the claimant has received some counter-performance before the frustrating event, although allowance must be made for this in calculating the restitution;

   • the Consumer Rights Act 2015 provides for *price reduction* in respect of non-conforming goods in consumer contracts (13.6);

   • where mutual performances consist of money payments, recovery is allowed because these can easily be set-off against each other (*Goss v Chilcott* (1996));

   • claims for non-money performance (13.4.3), analysed as failure of consideration, have never required the failure to be total; and

   • in *Attorney-General v Blake* (2000), Lord Nicholls suggests 'a part refund' for cases of partial failure of consideration. Where 'the defendant fails to provide the full extent of services he has contracted to provide, he should be liable to pay back the amount of expenditure he saved by the breach'.

4. On termination, the European Draft Common Frame of Reference requires mutual restitution of the benefits received, either in specie or in money's worth, **except** to the extent that 'conforming performance by one party has been met by conforming performance by the other' (Arts III.-3:510 and III.-3:511).

13.4.3 **The aggrieved party's claim for restitution of *non-monetary* benefits**

A party who has *completed* her non-monetary performance can sue for her expectation of payment, the 'agreed price'. If she has only *partially* performed before terminating the contract for breach, she cannot claim the contract price; rather, she can claim (*de Bernardy v Harding* (1853)):

• a *quantum valebat* (the reasonable value of the goods supplied); or

• a *quantum meruit* (the reasonable charge for the services supplied).

• In *Planché v Colburn* (1831), P agreed to write a book for a series published by C, for £100. After P had done much work, C abandoned the project. P was awarded a £50 *quantum meruit*, although he never handed over any of his work and could not be said to have conferred any meaningful benefit on the defendant.

13.4.4 **The *contract-breaker*'s restitutionary claim**

In principle, the contract-breaker should also be able to claim for failure of consideration to recover *money* paid under the contract once it is terminated (subject to the other party's expectation loss, if any). *Dies v British and Intl Mining and Finance Co Ltd* (1939) can be interpreted in this way, although it did not adopt this reasoning. D made an advance part-payment for ammunition, but breached by refusing to accept delivery. D was allowed to recover his payment subject to B's damages claim.

It is arguable that the contract-breaker should also be able to recover *non-money* benefits for failure of consideration. However, courts have denied contract-breakers' *quantum meruit* or *quantum valebat* claims (see *Sumpter v Hedges* (1898), 12.2.2.1 III). Support for restitution of non-money benefits to contract-breakers has been given by the Law Commission (*Pecuniary Restitution on Breach of Contract* (Law Com No 121, 1983)) and by dicta in House of Lords cases, eg, in *Hain SS Co Ltd v Tate and Lyle Ltd* (1936), Lord Wright said that a court should award a reasonable remuneration if a 'steamer carrying a cargo of frozen meat from Australia to England deviates by calling at a port outside the usual or permitted route' but the cargo is duly delivered with only a trifling delay, even if the contract can be and is terminated (and see *Miles v Wakefield Metropolitan DC* (1987)).

13.4.5 **How much can be claimed?**

Restitution can be claimed alongside reliance if it does not amount to double recovery. However, restitution cannot be combined with a claim for expectation damages since this *would* amount to double recovery (*Rogers v Parish (Scarborough) Ltd* (1987)); you cannot claim both your expectation and what you 'paid' to buy it.

Claims for restitution on total failure of consideration *can* allow claimants to escape from bad bargains.

- In *Bush v Canfield* (1818), B paid a $5,000 deposit on an agreement to buy wheat at $7 a barrel. When C failed to deliver, B was allowed to recover his deposit although the market price had fallen to $5.50 a barrel.

- Claimants seeking the restitution of *non-money performance* can even claim more than would have been due under the contract. In *Boomer v Muir* (1933), M's breach entitled B to quit his work and recover $250,000 as the reasonable value of his work, although only $20,000 was due under the contract.

 Counterpoint

Allowing the claimant to circumvent a bad bargain by making the contract-breaker *return* the claimant's *payment* is arguably quite different from making the contract-breaker *pay for* the claimant's non-money performance where the market value exceeds the contract rate originally agreed. Money *is* the measure of value conferred on the defendant, but the value of non-money performance *to the defendant* is the *contract* valuation agreed. Contract damages are determined by reference to the valuation contained in the contract even if the contract is terminated. Hence, the contract valuation should also act as a *ceiling* limiting any restitutionary claim. Consistently, Goff J supports a *pro rata contract rate* approach in the context of non-money claims on frustration (*BP v Hunt (No 2)* (1979), 7.6.4.2).

13.5 **Account of profits and loss of bargain**

13.5.1 **The general rule and two exceptions**

The orthodox position is that damages for breach of contract *cannot* be measured by:

✓ the defendant's *gains* (eg by making a larger profit from transferring her performance to a third party, see *Teacher v Calder* (1899)); or

✓ the defendant's *savings* (eg by incomplete or defective performance, see *Tito v Waddell (No 2)* (1977)).

This is subject to two exceptions:

(i) Where a breach of contract *also* involves a breach of confidence or of fiduciary duty, the defendant must account for *all of her profits* to the claimant, eg a defendant who accepts a bribe in breach of his contract of employment must hand over the bribe to his employer (*Reading v Attorney-General* (1951)), and a defendant who sells land he has already sold to the claimant must hand over his proceeds to the claimant (*Lake v Bayliss* (1974)).

(ii) Where breach of contract *also* involves the use of or interference with the claimant's proprietary rights, whether by trespass (*Penarth Dock Engineering Co Ltd v Pounds* (1963)), wrongful detention of goods (*Strand Electric and Engineering Co Ltd v Brisford Entertainments Ltd* (1952)), or breach of a restrictive covenant attaching to land (*Wrotham Park Estate Co Ltd v Parkside Homes Ltd* (1974)), the defendant is required to pay a *reasonable fee* for the use of, or interference with, the claimant's proprietary right, even if no loss is caused to the claimant's property. In **Wrotham Park Estate**, W sold land to P, developers who made additional profits by building in excess of the restrictive covenant contained in the contract. W's application for an injunction to undo the breach was denied for social and economic reasons, but damages were awarded in lieu assessed at 5% of P's estimated profits.

However, in *Attorney-General v Blake* (2000), the House of Lords awarded an account of profits for a simple breach of contract (not involving (i) or (ii) in the list).

13.5.2 *Attorney-General v Blake*: account of profits

In *Attorney-General v Blake*, a double secret agent made profits from publishing his autobiography in breach of his contract of secrecy with the British Crown and in breach of the criminal law. The House of Lords awarded the Crown an account of profits for breach of contract to meet the demands of 'practical justice' in the 'exceptional circumstances' of the case.

Their Lordships said that settled expectations in the commercial or consumer world would be undisturbed and that the majority of cases would remain unaffected. It is not enough for the claimant to show:

✓ that the defendant's breach was cynical or deliberate; or

✓ that the breach enabled the defendant to enter into a more profitable contract.

However, the blameworthiness of the breach is relevant to the overall assessment (*Experience Hendrix LLC v PPX Enterprises* (2003)).

Their Lordships emphasised the *exceptional* nature of this award, adding that it should only be available when:

✓ the ordinary remedies for breach of contract are 'inadequate';

✓ the claimant has 'a legitimate interest in preventing the defendant's profit-making activity and, hence, in depriving him of his profit'; and

✓ the award is consonant with the demands of 'practical justice'.

Courts must take a *'case by case'* approach, having 'regard to all the circumstances, including the subject matter of the contract, the purpose of the contractual provision which has been breached, the circumstances in which the breach occurred, the consequences of the breach and the circumstances in which relief is being sought'.

On the unusual facts of *Blake*, it was held that the Crown had a *legitimate interest* (in preventing its security and intelligence employees from profiting by disclosing information that they would not have obtained except by undertaking secrecy) to protect the operation of the secret services. The double agent had to account for the full profits he made to the Crown.

Experience Hendrix recognised that a full account of profit could be awarded in commercial cases. This has happened only in *Esso Petroleum Co Ltd v Niad Ltd* (2001), although its facts do not appear exceptional. N breached its agreement with E not to sell E's petrol above a set price. E was unable to show what loss was caused, but it was held that E had a strong interest in performance and was entitled to N's full profits from breach.

13.5.3 *Wrotham Park* damages

Blake relied on the authority of *Wrotham Park* as a 'shining beacon'. The problem is that *Wrotham Park* only awarded 5% of the profit made and was clearly not a case of disgorgement of the whole profit as in *Blake*. It is explained as 'hypothetical bargain' damages, representing what the claimant could have negotiated for allowing the defendant to breach the contract.

- This was originally explained as restitutionary in that it strips the defendant of its profit from breach (*Experience Hendrix* (2003)).

- But it was later held to be a form of compensatory damages (*WWF-World Wide Fund for Nature v World Wrestling Federation Entertainment Inc* (2007)).

In *Pell Frischmann Engineering Ltd v Bow Valley and PT Bakrie Interinvestindo* (2009), P had 'pre-qualified' status to bid for a contract with N, an oil company, to develop an oil field. BV later entered into confidentiality agreements to work exclusively with P in a consortium to undertake the project. In breach of contract, BV entered a contract with N without P's consent. The Privy Council awarded P $US2.5 million as *Wrotham Park* damages, although the defendants' actual profit was much *less* (between $1 million and $1.8 million) because the parties' negotiations prior to its breakdown showed that they had expected the contract with N to be much more profitable than it turned out to be. This case shows that *Wrotham Park* damages are compensatory rather than restitutionary, since the compensatory award exceeded the profits made from breach.

Lord Walker explained that *Wrotham Park* damages (called 'negotiating damages' by Neuberger LJ in *Lunn Poly Ltd v Liverpool & Lancashire Properties Ltd* [2006]) represent such a sum of money as might reasonably have been demanded by the claimant from the defendant as a quid pro quo for permitting the continuation of the breach of covenant or other invasion of right.

13.5.4 The relationship between account of profits and *Wrotham Park* damages

In *WWF*, Chadwick LJ said that, while the account of profits and *Wrotham Park* damages 'may differ in degree', they have the same underlying feature; namely, as flexible responses to circumstances where the claimant cannot demonstrate identifiable financial loss.

In *Vercoe v Rutland Fund Management Ltd* (2010), Sales J also appears to regard the two measures as distinct from the other measures. He explains that, where the claimant's rights are of a 'particularly powerful kind and his interest in full performance is recognised as being particularly strong', the claimant may well be 'entitled to a choice of remedy' as between damages, an account of profits and a notional reasonable agreement to buy release from his rights. Further, '[t]he law will control the choice between these remedies, having regard to the need to strike a fair balance between the interests of the parties at the remedial stage, rather than leaving it to the discretion of the claimant':

- An account of profits may be more appropriate 'where the right in question is of a kind where it would never be reasonable to expect that it could be bought out for some reasonable fee, so that it is accordingly deserving of a particularly high level of protection'.

- A reasonable buy-out fee will be more appropriate where 'one is not dealing with infringement of a right which is clearly proprietary in nature', such as intellectual property, and 'there is nothing exceptional to indicate that the defendant should never have been entitled to adopt a commercial approach in deciding how to behave in relation to that right'.

13.5.5 When will *Wrotham Park* damages be awarded?

Many cases have involved infringements of intellectual property rights or breach of confidence. Without these, *Wrotham Park* damages will only be available in *special circumstances* (although they need not be exceptional in the way that an account of profits would require). In **Experience Hendrix LLC v PPX Enterprises** (2003), PPX repeatedly and deliberately breached a settlement agreement on the royalties payable for the use of licensed material belonging to Jimi Hendrix's estate. The court ordered PPX to pay a *sum* assessed by reference to what the claimant could reasonably have demanded for use of the material (in addition to an injunction against future infringements). In doing so, the court took into account:

(i)   the impossibility of quantifying the claimant's financial loss from the breach; and

(ii) the defendant's 'flagrant contravention' of its obligations in deliberately doing what it knew it had contracted not to do.

In addition, in *One Step (Support) Ltd v Morris-Garner* (2016), the Court of Appeal held that a relevant factor supporting the award of *Wrotham Park* damages in a case involving a non-competition clause is:

(iii) that it is doubtful that interim relief could be obtained.

However, the Court of Appeal held that the damages need not be impossible to quantify, but it is enough if damages would be very difficult to prove; the question is whether the award would be a just response.

13.5.6 Assessing *Wrotham Park* damages

In *Pell Frischmann*, Lord Walker said that both parties must be assumed to act reasonably: 'It is a negotiation between a willing buyer (the contract-breaker) and a willing seller (the party claiming damages)... The fact that one or both parties would in practice have refused to make a deal is therefore to be ignored.'

In *Vercoe v Rutland*, Sales J lists three relevant factors in determining the price of release:

✓ the likely parameters given by ordinary commercial considerations bearing on each of the parties;

✓ any additional factors particularly affecting the just balance between the competing interests of the parties; and

✓ the court's overriding obligation to ensure that the award does not provide relief out of proportion to the real extent of the claimant's interest in proper performance, judged on an objective basis.

In *Lane v O'Brien Homes Ltd* (2004), Clarke J said that the calculation 'is not a precise mathematical process'; 'at the end of the day the deal has to feel right... the sort of damages questions involved in cases like the present are matters of judgment which are incapable of strict rational and logical exposition from beginning to end'.

13.5.7 Why an account of profits?

The uncertainties about:

* when it is appropriate to award a full account of profits and when *Wrotham Park* damages; and

* the quantification of *Wrotham Park* damages,

reflect the instability in the juristic basis of these awards. The main justification for awarding account of profits for breach of contract, stated in *Blake*, is the inadequacy of traditional remedies to deter or punish the defendant's breach. This was identified by Lord Hobhouse, dissenting, as the primary motivation behind the majority's decision in *Blake*: 'the policy which is being enforced is that which requires Blake to be punished by depriving him of any benefit from anything connected with his past deplorable criminal conduct'. The public would be outraged if Blake were to receive his money.

Counterpoint

A deterrence justification is problematic.

1. It contradicts the traditional rejection of punishment as a proper aim of contract law (hence, no punitive damages are available). But, if punishment is the real motivation, then we should recognise the availability of punitive damages.

2. It is unclear what degree of moral blameworthiness is required for each type of award if the mere fact of the defendant's breach being cynical or deliberate is not enough.

The second justification for allowing an account of profits for breach of contract is the **inadequacy of contract remedies** to protect claimants' performance interest. In *WWF (Nature) v WWF (Entertainment)*, the Court of Appeal referred to Lord Nicholls' statement in *Blake* that 'the plaintiff's interest in performance may make it just and equitable that the defendant should retain no benefit from his breach of contract'.

Counterpoint

1. *Blake* is a questionable example of an inadequate remedy. The Crown had a perfectly effective remedy: it knew about the breach and could have applied for an injunction to restrain publication. It merely failed to act until it realised the extent of Blake's potential profit. Moreover, it is hard to see what loss the Crown suffered from disclosures that were no longer secret.

2. The case creates an irrational picture of quite *distinct* measures of money awards aimed at the *same* goal of protecting the claimant's expectation interest.

3. The logical response to the inadequacy of contract remedies is to make them adequate (eg by increasing the availability of recovery for non-pecuniary losses, specific enforcement and cost of cure awards).

4. A full account of profits bears no correlation to the claimant's interest and it is only available *if* gains are actually made from breach.

5. Paradoxically, *Wrotham Park* damages protect the claimant's performance interest by enforcing a sale of the claimant's right.

13.5.8 **Protection of the performance interest**

In 'Damages for Breach of Contract: Compensation, Restitution and Vindication' (2008) 28 *OJLS* 73, Pearce and Halson argue that the purpose of contract damages is not only to indemnify loss caused by the breach, but also to 'vindicate' the claimant's contractual right over and above her right to her provable losses. This has been put forward as the justification for *Ruxley* damages and the broad ground in *Panatown*. *Wrotham Park* joins the list in awarding damages where the claimant may otherwise be unable to prove loss. The clearest case, however, is the account of profits award. In *Blake*, Lord Nicholls sought to equate contract rights with property rights, which traditionally allow gains-based remedies. He adopts Smith's argument[12] that contractual rights should be protected as strongly against expropriation by the defendant, but he does not take this to its logical conclusion of allowing gain-based awards for every breach: they are only available for very *exceptional* breaches, while *Wrotham Park* damages are only available in *special* circumstances.

 Pause for reflection

1. As a matter of policy, contract law has simply not valued contract rights as highly as proprietary rights. The choice is reflected in and reinforced by many features of contract law that are inconsistent with the protection of the claimant's performance interest, eg:

    (i)   no *punitive damages*;

    (ii) severe limits on the availability of *specific performance* (14.2.1);

    (iii) *limits on the expectation measure* of damages, notably mitigation (13.2.5);

    (iv) *restrictions on the right to affirm the* contract on anticipatory breach (12.3); and

    (v)   control of agreed damages clauses by the penalty rule (14.3.2).

2. These restrictions manifest the *balance* that contract law has struck between its commitment to the protection of the performance interest and other concerns, such as:

    (i)   not to *deter contracting* by allowing remedies which are 'unnecessarily' oppressive to the contract-breaker;

    (ii) to *avoid waste*; and

    (iii) not to stifle wealth-creating economic activity.

13.6 Consumer's right to price reduction

In 10.6.2, we mentioned some terms that are 'regarded as included' in consumer contracts for goods by virtue of the Consumer Rights Act 2015. The additional remedies available to the consumer for her breach include price reduction.

Where the consumer's claim for repair or replacement of **goods** (14.2.1.2(iv)) fails because (s 24(5)):

- after one attempt, the goods still do not conform to the contract;
- it is impossible (s 23(3)); or
- the trader fails to do so within a reasonable time and without significant inconvenience to the consumer,

the consumer can elect between price reduction or the final right to reject (12.4).

---

[12] L Smith, 'Disgorgement of Profits of Contract: Property, Contract and 'Efficient Breach' (1995) 24 *Can BLJ* 121.

Price reduction requires the trader to reduce the price appropriately, even to the point of extinguishing the price (s 24(2)).

Breach of certain terms 'regarded as included' in contracts of services (ss 49–50, 52) also allows the consumer to claim price reduction where (s 56(3)):

- the consumer cannot require repeat performance; or
- the consumer has required repeat performance, but the trader fails to do it within a reasonable time and without significant inconvenience to the consumer.

Section 58 confers **wide powers on courts**; if the consumer applies for price reduction, but the court determines that 'the exercise of another right is appropriate' then 'the court may proceed as if the consumer had exercised that other right'. Thus, eg, where the court decides that the consumer's claims for repair or replacement, or repeat performance, would be disproportionate or even cause severe hardship to the defendant, the court can instead award a price reduction. The court may make an order under this section unconditionally or on such terms and conditions as to damages, payment of the price, and otherwise as it thinks just.

THIS CHAPTER IN ESSENCE

The key areas and core topics in this chapter are summarised in an easy-to-use list, ideal for revision purposes, on the online resources at www.oup.com/uk/chenwishart6e/. Links to websites relevant to the topics covered and any updates to the chapter can also be found on the online resources.

QUESTIONS

1 Where contract law awards reliance damages, restitution, or account of profits for breach of contract, to what extent, if any, is the protection of the performance interest undermined?

2 'Monetary awards for breach of contract should do no more, and no less, than compensate the innocent party for her loss.' To what extent is this true? To what extent should it be true? What other considerations, if any, affect the selection of remedies for breach?

3 'Contract law recognises non-pecuniary loss reluctantly and only within narrow confines.' Discuss.

4 Ken employed Lou to install a new kitchen and add an extension to the living room: he paid Lou £30,000 on completion. Advise Ken on the following facts:

(a) Ken is very annoyed to find that the plasterwork in the extension has been painted a slightly different shade from that stipulated. Ken has rejected Lou's offer to redo the plasterwork for an extra £3,000, and hired Milo to redo the plasterwork for £6,000.

(b) Completion is delayed, necessitating Ken and his family staying an extra month with Ken's in-laws in very cramped accommodation which causes great discomfort and distress all around. Moreover, the delay meant that Ken had to pay £500 for an alternative venue for his friend's wedding, which Ken had offered to hold at his house.

(c) After a few weeks, Lou's faulty wiring in the kitchen caused small sparks which ignited a gas leak that Ken had been meaning to fix for some time. The ensuing fire resulted in £15,000 worth of damage to the kitchen.

(d) What difference would it make if Ken has not yet paid?

5 Bugbusters won a major contract to clean 40 hospitals, undertaking to meet ten specified targets. Bugbusters instructed its workers to meet only six of the targets, saving £30,000 over six months. The hospitals are outraged when they learn of the breach, but it is impossible to prove whether any additional infections have resulted. Advise the hospitals.

 For hints on how to answer these questions, please see the online resources at www.oup.com/uk/chenwishart6e/

KEY FURTHER READING

See generally, Burrows, A (2004), *Remedies for Torts and Breach of Contract* (3rd edn, OUP).

Bridge, M (1989), 'Mitigation of Damages in Contract and the Meaning of Avoidable Loss', 105 *LQR* 398.

Burrows, A (2003), 'Limitations on Compensation' in A Burrows and E Peel (eds), *Commercial Remedies* (OUP) 27–43.

Coote, B (1997), 'Contract Damages, *Ruxley* and the Performance Interest', 56 *CLJ* 537.

Coote, B (2001), 'The Performance Interest, *Panatown*, and the Problem of Loss', 117 *LQR* 81.

Friedmann, D (1995), 'The Performance Interest in Contract Damages', 111 *LQR* 628.

Fuller, L, and Perdue, W (1937), 'The Reliance Interest in Contract Damages', 46 *Yale LJ* 52.

Lord Hoffmann (2010), '*The Achilleas*: Custom and Practice or Foreseeability?', 14 *Edinburgh LR* 47.

Law Commission (1997), *Aggravated, Exemplary and Restitutionary Damages* (Law Com No 247, HC 346).

McKendrick, E (2003), 'Breach of Contract, Restitution for Wrongs and Punishment' in A Burrows and E Peel (eds), *Commercial Remedies* (OUP) 93.

Pearce, D, and Halson, R (2008), 'Damages for Breach of Contract: Compensation, Restitution and Vindication', 28 *OJLS* 73.

Rowan, S (2010), 'Reflections on the Introduction of Punitive Damages for Breach of Contract', 30 *OJLS* 495.

Webb, C (2006), 'Performance and Compensation: An Analysis of Contract Damages and Contractual Obligation', 26 *OJLS* 41.

Wee, P C K (2010), 'Contractual Interpretation and Remoteness', *LMCLQ* 150.

14

Specific and agreed remedies

'I want you to do what you undertook in the contract'

Protection of an innocent party's ('the claimant') performance interest is evident in awards of expectation damages, or so it is often assumed. But the most obvious way of protecting a claimant's expectation of performance (her performance interest) is to make the defendant perform her contractual obligations (although this will usually be later than originally specified). Specific performance, where it is still wanted, is the most effective way of avoiding the risk of under-compensation due to the operation of doctrines such as remoteness and mitigation that limit the award of damages.

- The performance promised may be to pay money, or to do (or not do) something other than paying money; these are primary obligations under the contract.

- In addition, the parties may also have expressly agreed on how any breach should be remedied (eg to pay a stipulated sum or to forfeit money already paid). These are secondary obligations; they are the agreed *remedies* for breach of the primary obligations.

This terminology of primary and secondary obligations is used in *Photo Production Ltd v Securicor Transport Ltd* (1980).

We will see that:

- courts are very willing to award orders compelling the defendant to pay the agreed price.

- In contrast, orders compelling non-monetary performance (for specific performance or injunctions) are rarely given; many 'bars' obstruct such awards. In this sense, they are regarded as 'secondary' or 'supplementary' remedies granted at the court's *discretion*, while damages, being available as of right, are the 'primary' remedy.

- In addition, courts exercise significant control over the parties' agreed remedies (secondary obligations).

The questions to be considered are the following:

(i)   To what extent does (and should) the law grant specific enforcement of contract?

(ii) When and why will claims for specific performance or injunction be barred? How can this be reconciled with the protection of the aggrieved party's performance interest?

(iii) To what extent does (and should) the law permit the parties to agree on the remedies for breach?

(iv) Are there any areas that need reform? If so, how?

14.1 **The agreed sum**

A contract may require the defendant to pay a specific sum: on the defendant's breach; on the occurrence of a specified event or condition that does not constitute breach; or as a deposit, pre-payment, or instalment. We will discuss these situations at 14.3 on agreed remedies. In this section, we will discuss the claim for the agreed sum (or agreed price) on full performance by the claimant. This form of specific performance is the most common claim for breach of contract. It is distinguishable from a claim for damages because the claimant need not prove any loss caused by the defendant's breach, merely that she has *earned* the sum by due performance. Moreover, her claim cannot be reduced for being too *remote* or for her failure to *mitigate* loss (*Jervis v Harris* (1996)) and is not subject to the penalty rule (14.3.2.1). It is treated as a claim for the payment of a *debt*, which has many **advantages for the claimant**:

(i) Availability of summary judgment: the claimant can take advantage of a quick and truncated legal process with procedural advantages.

(ii) Additional availability of damages: the claimant can also sue for loss flowing from the defendant's failure to pay on time (*Overstone Ltd v Shipway* (1962)).

On the other hand, **the defendant's interests are protected by**:

(i) Strict interpretation of the pre-condition for payment: while courts have mitigated the 'entire obligations' rule by the doctrine of 'substantial performance' (12.2.2.1III), the claimant must still give 'substantial' performance to trigger the defendant's obligation to pay, eg full payment was *not* due in a contract to install central heating for £560 when defects amounted to 31% of the total price (*Bolton v Mahadeva* (1972)). But, full payment *was* due, subject to deductions, where the defects amounted to less than 10% of the value of the contract (*Hoenig v Isaacs* (1952)). The Consumer Rights Act 2015 (CRA) specifies as indicatively unfair (and invalid) any term 'obliging the consumer to fulfil all of the consumer's obligations [usually that is to pay money] where the trader does not perform the trader's obligations' (Sch 2 Part 1 para 18).

(ii) Allowing the defendant's set-off: the defendant can deduct what the claimant owes her from the sum to be paid, if it would be unjust not to allow it (*Federal Commerce & Navigation Co Ltd v Molena Alpha Inc* (1978)). A clause that bars this right of set-off was held to be unreasonable (and so unenforceable) under the Unfair Contract Terms Act 1977 (UCTA) in *Stewart Gill Ltd v Horatio Myer & Co Ltd* (1992). Likewise, the CRA identifies as 'indicatively unfair' terms that prevent the consumer from exercising, or exclude or hinder the consumer's right to exercise, any legal remedy (Sch 2 Part 1 para 20).

(iii) Restricting the claimant's right to affirm: where the contract is repudiated, the claimant will be barred from rendering the performance no longer wanted by the defendant (and earning her right to the agreed sum) if she needs the defendant's cooperation to complete her performance or if she has no legitimate interest in wholly unreasonable and wasteful completion (12.3).

 Pause for reflection

Whilst the action for the agreed sum can be held up as the shining example of full protection of the claimant's performance interest, it is also at odds with contract law's restrictions on that protection manifest in: the calculation of damages; the restrictions on the specific enforcement of *non-monetary* obligations; and the controls on agreed remedies. In *The Puerto Buitrago* (1976), Lord Denning MR noted the similarities between the action for the agreed sum and specific performance; on the facts, he denied the claim for the agreed sum since damages were perfectly adequate. Burrows also takes the view that the law here should to be brought in line with that relating to specific performance, chiefly in support of the mitigation requirement.[1]

14.2 **Specific enforcement**

A claim to compel the defendant to perform her primary obligation may be:

- for specific performance (of the defendant's *positive* undertaking to do something); or

[1] A S Burrows, *Remedies for Torts and Breach of Contract* (3rd edn, OUP, 2004) 440.

- for an injunction (of the defendant's *negative* undertaking to *refrain* from doing something).

Monetary awards such as damages and the action for the agreed sum are *common law* remedies and available *as of right*. In contrast, non-monetary specific enforcement is historically available only in the courts of *equity* and still regarded as an exceptional and discretionary remedy.

14.2.1 Specific performance

In *Beswick v Beswick* (1968), the House of Lords held that specific performance should be ordered if it would 'do more perfect and complete justice' than an award of damages. The courts have developed settled principles, which are followed in all but exceptional circumstances. Ultimately, it is a matter for the court's discretion.

14.2.1.1 Overview of limits on the availability of specific performance

A claim for specific performance is best understood by reference to the factors that weigh *against* the remedy. These 'bars' to specific performance are identified, instanced, and then discussed as follows:

- *14.2.1.2 Claimant-sided considerations*:

    (i) adequacy of damages; (ii) lack of clean hands; and (iii) delay.

- *14.2.1.3 Defendant-sided considerations*:

    (iv) the contract is for personal services or to carry on an activity; (v) impossibility and hardship; and (vi) want of mutuality.

- *14.2.1.4 Administrative considerations*:

    (vii) uncertainty; (viii) the need for constant supervision; and (ix) avoidance of waste.

The overlapping operation of these factors is illustrated by the leading modern case on specific performance, *Cooperative Insurance Society Ltd v Argyll Stores (Holdings) Ltd* (1998). C leased out the largest ('anchor') unit in its shopping centre to AS to operate a supermarket. AS covenanted that it would, for 35 years, 'keep the demised premises open for retail trade during the usual hours of business in the locality and the display windows properly dressed in a suitable manner in keeping with a good class parade of shops'. The supermarket started to run at a loss with 19 years of the lease still to run; AS stopped trading and stripped out the fittings. Since the supermarket was the main attraction in the shopping centre, its closure would undoubtedly impact adversely on surrounding shops and on C as the lessor of those premises. C's claim for specific performance was denied at first instance, granted by the Court of Appeal, and denied again by the House of Lords.

Supporting specific performance, the *Court of Appeal* emphasised:

- the inadequacy of damages in compensating C, who faced enormous obstacles in proving what loss was caused by AS's breach; and

- the deliberate and cynical nature of AS's breach.

Against specific performance, the *House of Lords* played down these factors since both parties were large sophisticated commercial organisations who entered the contract for purely financial reasons, knowing that the remedy for breach of the covenant was likely to be limited to damages. Rather, emphasis was placed on:

- the settled practice against specific performance when this would require a defendant to carry on an activity, as opposed to achieving a result by performing a single well-defined act;

- the oppressiveness of requiring AS to run a business under the heavy-handed threat of proceedings for contempt of court for which one may be imprisoned;

- the need for constant supervision (ie the likelihood of repeated and costly litigation over compliance), which is wasteful of the resources of the parties and of the court, oppressive for AS, and perpetuates a continuing hostile relationship; this is exacerbated by:

    - the uncertainty in the contract, which makes it impossible to draw up the terms of any order with sufficient precision (eg as to the kind and level of trade) to enable AS to know exactly what it must do; and

    - the enormous losses AS would suffer from compulsory performance (in refitting the shop at the cost of over £1 million and carrying on a loss-making business for the next 19 years).

The decision can be criticised for tilting the balance too far in favour of the contract-breaker. However, the risk of under-compensating the claimant must be weighed against the enormous scale of the loss that the contract-breaker is likely to suffer if forced to perform and the potential for continuing conflicts between the parties which require judicial and parties' resources to settle. As Lord Hoffmann said, the principles of equity have 'a strong ethical content', the application of which is influenced by moral values. The balance to be weighed will often be a fine one.

14.2.1.2 Claimant-sided considerations

(i) The 'adequacy' of damages

Historically, the basis of the equitable jurisdiction to order specific performance of a contract is that the claimant cannot obtain a sufficient remedy by the common law judgment for damages (*Harnett v Yielding* (1805)). Hence specific performance is normally barred where damages would provide an adequate remedy. The fact that the claimant can buy substitute performance in the market is the single most important bar to specific performance. However, damages are regarded as 'adequate' even if the established limits (eg mitigation and remoteness) reduce the damages awarded to the claimant. Damages have been regarded as *inadequate* in the following situations:

(i) **Uniqueness:** the subject matter of the contract is physically unique if it has strong sentimental value or significance for the claimant and so is irreplaceable in the market. It is not enough to point to difficulty in quantifying the claimant's loss, since courts are very willing to overcome quantification difficulties (13.2.5.4).

- For sale of **goods**, damages will almost always be considered adequate. Heirlooms, great works of art, and rare antiques were commonly regarded as 'unique', but this category is sparingly used (*Falcke v Gray* (1859)).

- Section 52 of the Sale of Goods Act 1979 gives courts the discretion to award specific performance for the delivery of 'specific or ascertained' (as opposed to generic) goods, although they may not be unique.

Most notably, the adequacy of damages bar does *not* apply in contracts to transfer interests in **land**, where specific performance is *routinely* ordered, even if the *buyer* attaches no particular significance to, or has no special need for, the land, as where it is only traded for investment, so that damages would be adequate. Even the *vendor* can obtain specific performance (and so 'thrust the property down the purchaser's throat', *Hope v Walker* (1900)) although the land is readily resaleable. The automatic availability of specific performance in land contracts has been explained in terms of: the court *deeming* interests in land to be unique; the rule that land contracts confer an immediate equitable *proprietary interest* on buyers; and the *mutuality* of granting the seller the same remedy as the buyer is entitled to.

 Counterpoint

The automatic availability of specific performance in land contracts should be *reconsidered*. The assumption that land is inherently and indisputably unique, and so warrants automatic specific performance, has been rejected or questioned in Canada (*Semelhago v Paramadevan* (1996)), New Zealand (*Landco Albany Ltd v Fu Hao Construction Ltd* (2006)), and Singapore (*E C Investment Holding Pte Ltd v Ridout Estate Pte Ltd* (2011)).

Specific performance may also be available if the subject matter of the contract, while not physically unique, is 'commercially unique'. The difficulty of obtaining a substitute may mean that the claimant's business will be gravely disrupted without specific performance:

✓ In *Sky Petroleum Ltd v VIP Petroleum Ltd* (1974), an interim injunction amounting to specific performance was granted to compel V to continue supplying petrol to S garage during the petrol shortage of 1973, when V was, in effect, S's 'sole means of keeping their business going' and S would otherwise be 'forced out of business' (see also *Howard E Perry & Co Ltd v British Railways Board* (1980) and *Thames Valley Power Ltd v Total Gas and Power Ltd* (2006)).

✓ Although damages are normally adequate in respect of *shares*, where substitution is not readily available (as where breach deprives the claimant of the controlling interest), damages may be regarded as inadequate and specific performance ordered (*Harvela Investments Ltd v Royal Trust Co of Canada Ltd* (1986)). This is consistent with the US Uniform Commercial Code, which requires uniqueness to be judged in the total situation (§ 2-716(1)).

(ii) **No other substantial remedy available**: in *Beswick v Beswick*, an elderly and ailing coal merchant sold his business to his nephew in return for various undertakings, including a promise to pay his widow £5 a week after his death. When the nephew failed to pay, the widow, acting as the administratrix of his estate, claimed specific performance of the contract. The case raised the classic 'legal black hole' problem, since the payments were to be made to the widow (a third party) who could not sue in her own right (the case predates the Contracts (Rights of Third Parties) Act 1999), and the husband's estate, which *could* sue as a party to the contract, had lost nothing by the breach. The House of Lords ordered specific performance to achieve a 'just result' (4.1.6.1).

Adequacy of damages is the main restriction on the availability of specific performance. But, even if damages are *inadequate*, other restrictions may 'bar' specific performance.

(iii) **Damages limited or excluded by the contract**: in *AB v CD* (2014), Underhill LJ explains that: 'The primary obligation of a party was to perform the contract. The requirement to pay damages in the event of breach was a secondary obligation, and an agreement to restrict the recoverability of damages in the event of breach could not be treated as an agreement to excuse performance of the primary obligation.' Where the only losses suffered were excluded by the contract, it would be unjust if specific performance were barred, even for the most gross and cynical breach of contract. The bar of adequacy of damages should be applied in a way that reflects the substantial justice of the situation. The parties' commercial expectations were not undermined; their expectation was that the contract would be performed. The expectations created by an exclusion or limitation clause were about something different, namely, what damages would be recoverable in the event of breach.

(ii) The claimant's 'lack of clean hands'
The maxim that 'he who comes to Equity must come with clean hands' translates into a denial of specific performance where the claimant has induced the contract by unfair means even if this has not rendered the contract void or voidable. Thus, specific performance has been denied where the claimant:

- ✗ unfairly hurried the defendant into granting a mining lease in ignorance of the value of the property (*Walters v Morgan* (1861));

- ✗ took advantage of the defendant's drunkenness (*Malins v Freeman* (1837)) or the defendant's mistake (*Webster v Cecil* (1861));

- ✗ during a petrol price war, subsidised all garages to which it supplied petrol in the area except the defendant, who was forced to sell petrol at a loss; the defendant switched to a cheaper supplier in breach of contract with the claimant (*Shell UK Ltd v Lostock Garages Ltd* (1976));

- ✗ artificially increased the sale price of his car and portable telephone business (calculated on the number of customers at completion date) by giving away free telephones to inflate the number of customers (*Quadrant Visual Communications Ltd v Hutchison Telephone (UK) Ltd* (1993)); and

✗ sought an injunction amounting to specific performance, but was unwilling to assure the defendants of its own counter-performance. The claimant must not only come with 'clean hands' but 'he who seeks equity must do equity' (*Chappell v Times Newspapers Ltd* (1975)).

✗ While *inadequacy of consideration* is no ground for setting aside a contract, it will bar specific performance if the court finds any *trace of procedural unfairness* (*Griffith v Spratley* (1787)), bearing in mind that procedural unfairness itself is often inferable from serious substantive unfairness (9.4.3).

✗ Moreover, since 'equity will not assist a volunteer', specific performance is not available to enforce *gratuitous deeds* (*Cannon v Hartley* (1949)), or contracts for nominal consideration (*Jeffreys v Jeffreys* (1841)).

(iii) Delay, acquiescence, and termination

• Although the six-year limitation period generally applicable to contract actions does not apply to claims for specific performance (13.2.5.7), delay can bar specific performance on the particular facts. Traditionally, a claimant must show herself 'ready, desirous, prompt and eager' to perform (*Milward v Earl of Thanet* (1801)). Where the contract involves property of fluctuating value or where the defendant would be prejudiced, delay of more than a few months has barred specific performance (*Glasbrook v Richardson* (1874)), but a delay of over two years did not bar the remedy in *Lazard Bros & Co v Fairfield Properties Co (Mayfair) Ltd* (1977) since 'it was just that the plaintiff should obtain the remedy'.

• Acquiescence occurs when the claimant leads the defendant to believe that she will not object to the defendant's breach. This will bar specific performance, particularly if the defendant has detrimentally relied on this belief.

• The claimant's termination of the contract will bar a claim for specific performance (since the two are mutually contradictory), even in the absence of the defendant's detrimental reliance (*Johnson v Agnew* (1980)).

(iv) Non-conforming goods supplied to consumers
The CRA treats certain terms as included in consumer contracts for goods, services, and digital content (10.6.2.1). Where these are breached, the CRA provides *additional* **special remedies** that includes:

(i) the right to repair or replacement in respect of goods (s 19(3)(b)) or digital content (ss 42(2)(a) and 43): the consumer cannot require the trader to repair or replace the goods or digital content if 'that remedy' is (a) 'impossible', or (b) 'disproportionate compared to the other of those remedies', ie if it 'imposes costs on the trader which, compared to those imposed by the other, are unreasonable' (ss 23(3) and 43(3)).

(ii) the right to require repeat performance in respect of services, within a reasonable time and without significant inconvenience to the consumer (ss 54(3)(a) and 55): repeat performance cannot be required where completing performance would be impossible.

However, section 58 confers wide powers on courts; if it determines that 'the exercise of another right is appropriate', then 'the court may proceed as if the consumer had exercised that other right', and these include price reduction. Thus, where ordering either repair or replacement or repeat performance would be disproportionate or even cause severe hardship to the defendant, the court can instead award a price reduction.

14.2.1.3 Defendant-sided considerations

The blameworthiness of the defendant's breach may *encourage* courts to order specific performance (eg Lord Hoffmann's example of 'cases of gross breach of personal faith, or attempts to use the threat of non-performances as blackmail' (*Cooperative Insurance v Argyll Stores*)). However, defendant-sided considerations generally operate *against* specific performance, revealing a concern for the contract-breaker.

(iv) Contracts for personal services or to carry on an activity

✗ *Cooperative Insurance v Argyll Stores* shows that courts will generally deny specific enforcement of contracts to carry on an activity because of the potential for continuing conflicts over compliance which will require court resources to resolve, and the oppressiveness of compelling the defendant to carry on the activity 'under a sword of Damocles which may descend if [he]... does not conform to the terms of the order'. The law is concerned to avoid undue interference with the contract-breaker's *personal* liberty if the claimant can be adequately compensated. This explains the long-established denial of specific performance in contracts of *personal services* lest they are turned into 'contracts of slavery' (*de Francesco v Barnum* (1890)).

✗ Consistently, legislation prohibits orders compelling an *employee* to perform a contract of employment (Trade Union and Labour Relations (Consolidation) Act 1992, s 236). However, *employers* may be compelled to reinstate the employee (Employment Rights Act 1996, ss 113–17), although these provisions are relatively little used (perhaps as low as 3%; *Johnson v Unisys* (2001)), since employees usually prefer compensation and a new start elsewhere once relations have soured, and employers may resist reinstatement by paying enhanced compensation. Courts will not prevent employers from dismissing employees where *trust and confidence has broken down* and conflict would be created or perpetuated. Specific performance is only appropriate where the employer–employee relationship has not broken down (*Hill v CA Parsons & Co Ltd* (1972) and *Powell v Brent London BC* (1998)). But, even if it has, specific performance may be granted to enable proper disputes or disciplinary procedures to be complied with, but *on terms* that the employee may not turn up for, and the employer need not provide, work (*Irani v Southampton and SW Hampshire Health Authority* (1985) and *Robb v Hammersmith & Fulham LBC* (1991)). As Megarry J explains in *Giles & Co Ltd v Morris* (1972), the courts' reluctance to specifically enforce personal services contracts relates not only to the concern about constant supervision, but is:

> more complex and more firmly bottomed on human nature. If a singer contracts to sing, there could no doubt be proceedings for committal if, ordered to sing, the singer remained obstinately dumb. But if instead the singer sang

flat, or sharp, or too fast, or too slowly, or too loudly, or too quietly, or resorted to a dozen of the manifestations of temperament traditionally associated with some singers, the threat of committal would reveal itself as a most unsatisfactory weapon: for who could say whether the imperfections of performance were natural or self induced? . . . However, not all contracts of personal service or for the continuous performance of services are as dependent as this on matters of opinion and judgment, nor do all such contracts involve the same degree of the daily impact of person upon person. In general, no doubt, the inconvenience and mischief of decreeing specific performance of most of such contracts will greatly outweigh the advantages and specific performance will be refused. But . . . it should [not] be assumed that as soon as any element of personal service or continuous service can be discerned in a contract the court will, without more, refuse specific performance.

✓ This bar is limited to services that are *personal* in nature. Thus, specific performance has been ordered in *building contracts* and *repairing covenants* where: (i) the work is capable of sufficiently precise definition; (ii) damages will be inadequate to compensate the claimant; and (iii) the defendant has possession of the land on which work is to be done so that the claimant cannot employ someone else to do it (*Wolverhampton Corp v Emmons* (1901); *Jeune v Queens Cross Properties Ltd* (1974)).

(v) Impossibility and hardship

✗ Specific enforcement will be denied where performance is physically or legally impossible, as where: the defendant contracts to sells land which she does not own and cannot obtain (*Castle v Wilkinson* (1870)); the defendant assigns a lease without the necessary consent of the landlord (*Wilmot v Barber* (1880)); or the defendant agrees to sublet to the claimant, when his head lease prohibits subletting (*Warmington v Miller* (1973)).

✗ Specific enforcement may also be denied where it would cause the defendant severe hardship, far exceeding any uncompensable loss suffered by the claimant. In *Patel v Ali* (1984), the claimant sought specific performance four years after the defendant contracted to sell her home. By then, the defendant had: suffered cancer necessitating the amputation of her right leg at the hip joint, borne two more children (three in all), and her husband was adjudged a bankrupt and imprisoned. Moreover, her poor English made her highly dependent on the support of friends and relatives living close by, so that compelling her to move would cause a 'hardship amounting to injustice'. Goulding J emphasised that 'mere pecuniary difficulties' are insufficient:

> [O]nly in extraordinary and persuasive circumstances can hardship supply an excuse for resisting performance of a contract for the sale of immovable property. A person of full capacity who sells or buys a house takes the risk of hardship to himself and his dependants, whether arising from existing facts or unexpectedly supervening in the interval before completion . . . [but] equitable relief may . . . be refused because of an unforeseen change of circumstances not amounting to legal frustration.

On the facts, great emphasis was put on the claimant's *delay*, which reinforced the injustice of compelling the defendant to perform after her change of circumstances over four years.

✗ However, hardship can operate *alone*. In *Denne v Light* (1857), the court refused specific performance against a buyer who had mistakenly bought landlocked farmland.

✗ In *Wroth v Tyler* (1974), specific performance of a contract to sell land was denied because it would have required the defendant to take legal action to evict his wife and daughter from the matrimonial home.

✗ In *Cooperative Insurance v Argyll Stores*, the House of Lords denied specific performance partly because it would cause loss to the defendant which would be 'enormous, unquantifiable and unlimited, as well as being out of all proportion to any uncompensable loss' suffered by the claimant. Lord Hoffmann observed that the availability of specific performance would, in practice, simply *strengthen the claimant's bargaining power in settling the case*. That is, the claimant can charge a sum for *releasing* the defendant from performance that far exceeds the *value* of actual performance to the claimant.

(vi) Want of mutuality

A claimant is barred from claiming specific performance if the defendant, who is compelled to perform, might be inadequately protected *should the claimant subsequently breach* (eg if the defendant cannot get specific performance *or* adequate damages against the claimant). This bar seems too pro-defendant. As Burrows notes,[2] it will already have been concluded that damages will not adequately compensate the claimant, yet the court is prepared to deny her an admittedly more appropriate and just remedy because of the mere *risk* that the *contract-breaker* may not be adequately compensated *if* the claimant subsequently breaches. The bar is more understandable if the defendant's potential hardship (ie difficulty of proof and scale of loss) greatly exceeds the claimant's.[3]

14.2.1.4 Impracticality and unsuitability

(vii) Uncertainty

Specific performance will be an unsuitable remedy if the performance cannot be defined with sufficient precision, even though there was sufficient certainty for contract formation. Contracts regarded as too uncertain to specifically enforce include those:

✗ to publish an 'article on jade' (*Joseph v National Magazine Co Ltd* (1959));

✗ to build 'a railway station' (*Wilson v Northampton and Banbury Railway Co* (1874));

✗ to 'layout £1,000 in building' (*Moseley v Virgin* (1796)); and

✗ to 'run a supermarket' (*Cooperative Insurance v Argyll Stores*).

---

[2] A Burrows, *Remedies for Torts and Breach of Contract* (3rd edn, OUP, 2004) 493.
[3] E Durfee, 'Mutuality in Specific Performance' (1921) 20 *Mich L Rev*, 289.

As Lord Hoffmann said (*Cooperative Insurance v Argyll Stores*), 'the less precise the order, the fewer the signposts to the forensic minefield which he has to traverse', the more the 'oppression caused by the defendant having to do things under threat of proceedings for contempt'. Uncertainty also increases the likelihood of further litigation.

(viii) Constant supervision

It was once thought that specific performance would be denied if it involves a continuous act. But this was read down in *Posner v Scott-Lewis* (1987), where a covenant to employ a resident porter was specifically enforced since the contract stated the required performance with *sufficient precision*. In *Cooperative Insurance v Argyll Stores*, Lord Hoffmann explains that the 'constant supervision' bar refers to the likelihood of repeated and costly litigation over compliance; this is greatest where uncertainty surrounds what must be done. The general public interest in the *finality* of dispute resolution may require the claimant to settle for damages, although it does less perfect justice than specific performance.

(ix) Avoidance of waste

Specific enforcement may be denied where it would involve a significant waste of resources (ie when the cost of performance far exceeds the benefit to the claimant; the cost of cure is also denied for this reason, 13.2.3.2). This rationale is sometimes obscured by talk of constant supervision or finding that the claimant has suffered no or little loss. In *Tito v Waddell (No 2)* (1977), the court declined to compel the defendant to incur enormous costs to restore and replant the island it had ravaged by mining because the islanders had resettled elsewhere. In *Cooperative Insurance v Argyll Stores*, the court would not compel a party to continue running a loss-making supermarket for 19 more years. The concern to prevent waste overlaps with the concern to avoid hardship to the defendant.

14.2.2 Injunctions

- A mandatory injunction compels the defendant to *undo* the effects of breaching a negative undertaking.

- A prohibitory injunction specifically enforces a contractual obligation *not to do something*.

Both are equitable remedies given at the court's discretion.

(i) Mandatory injunction

Courts are reluctant to compel *positive* action by mandatory injunctions. A court will generally deny a mandatory injunction and award damages in lieu unless the defendant has 'trodden roughshod over the plaintiff's rights' (*Luganda v Service Hotels Ltd* (1969)) or the claimant would otherwise suffer extreme or serious prejudice (*Durrell v Pritchard* (1865)). Mandatory injunctions are subject to the 'balance of convenience' test, and may accordingly be refused if the prejudice suffered by the defendant in having to restore the original position heavily outweighs the advantage that will be derived from such restoration by the claimant (*Shepherd Homes Ltd v Sandham* (1971)).

✗ In *Wrotham Park Estate Co v Parkside Homes Ltd* (1974), the court declined to order the destruction of 14 homes to enforce a restrictive covenant because it would be 'an unpardonable waste of much-needed houses'.

✗ In *Sharp v Harrison* (1922), the court refused to order the removal of a window built in breach of contract overlooking the claimant's property because no damage was occasioned; the defendant undertook to prevent any future damage by the continuing breach; and an order would inflict damage on the defendant out of all proportion to the relief derived by the claimant.

✓ In *Wakeham v Wood* (1982), a mandatory injunction was awarded where the defendant had, in breach of a restrictive covenant, deliberately erected a building so as to block the claimant's sea view and damages would not have been an adequate remedy.

(ii) Prohibitory injunction

A prohibitory injunction is the main remedy to restrain threatened or future breaches of negative undertakings. As Lord Cairns LC said, in *Dolman v Allman* (1878), it will be granted *as a matter of course* and is not 'a question of the balance of convenience or inconvenience, or the amount of damage or of injury'. A prohibitory injunction may be granted to prevent the defendant from doing what she has *negatively* undertaken (eg not to sing for someone else, *Lumley v Wagner* (1852)), even though the court would not order specific performance in respect of what she has positively undertaken to do in the same contract (to sing for the claimant). This is because granting a prohibitory injunction (rather than compelling positive action):

- seems less restrictive of the defendant's individual liberty;
- is less likely to run up against the claimant's duty to mitigate and the problem of constant supervision; and
- avoids the difficulty of assessing loss from breach of a negative undertaking.

For example, in *Araci v Fallon* (2011), F, a famous jockey, contracted with A to ride A's racehorse (and no one else's) at the Epsom Derby. The Court of Appeal granted a prohibitory injunction to prevent F from riding a rival horse because: even if the adequacy of damages were relevant, which it was not, damages were not adequate because it would be exceptionally difficult to calculate the loss that would result if the rival horse beat the claimant's horse, and nothing could compensate the claimant for losing the prestige that would flow from one of its horses winning the Derby.

However, the courts have refused prohibitory injunctions on similar grounds as would bar specific performance, such as the claimant's delay (*HP Bulmer Ltd v J Bollinger SA* (1977)), acquiescence (*Shaw v Applegate* (1977)), lack of clean hands (*Grobbelaar v News Group Newspapers Ltd* (2002)), or the trivial nature of the claimant's loss (*Harrison v Good* (1871)).

(iii) No indirect specific performance

The main reason against granting a prohibitory injunction is that it will amount to indirect specific performance of a contract for personal services (which would not have been specifically enforced). Thus, injunctions are denied that seek to enforce undertakings not to accept any other employment *at all*, as where *X* promises to work for *Y* for ten years and not to 'engage himself in any other business' during that time (*Ehrman v Bartholomew* (1898)). Granting the injunction will, in practice, compel *X* to choose between working for *Y* and starvation. However, injunctions to enforce undertakings to refrain from only *particular activities* will be granted if they will not *in practice* compel the defendant to perform her positive obligations. Thus:

✗ in *Mortimer v Beckett* (1920), an injunction to enforce a boxer's implied undertaking not to box for anyone else for seven years was denied because it would amount to indirect specific enforcement of a personal services contract;

✓ an injunction was *granted* in **Lumley v Wagner** (1852) to restrain W from singing for anyone else during the three months she had agreed to sing at L's theatre, although the court would not compel her to sing for L. The period was short and there was no risk of W's skills atrophying if she refused to perform;

✓ an injunction was *granted* in the questionable decision in *Warner Brothers Pictures Inc v Nelson* (1937). The court's view that to restrain Nelson ('Bette Davis') from working as an actress elsewhere for three years was not indirect specific performance because she could, at the height of her career, stop acting and do something else albeit less well paid, has since been described as 'extraordinarily unrealistic' (*Warren v Mendy* (1989)). Recent cases take a more realistic approach:

✗ an injunction was denied in *Page One Records Ltd v Britton* (1968), where a pop group, The Troggs, breached a contract to be managed by and make records solely for the claimant for five years;

✗ an injunction was denied in *Warren v Mendy*, where the boxer Nigel Benn breached a contract to be managed by the claimant for three years. Nourse LJ said that 'an injunction lasting for two years or more... may practically compel performance of the contract';

✓ an injunction was granted in *Lauritzen Cool AB v Lady Navigation Inc* (2005) to prevent ship-owners from using their vessels inconsistently with the contract, although its practical effect was to specifically enforce the contract. This is justified when, exceptionally, the subject matter of the contract is of particular value to the claimant and damages would be inadequate.

14.2.3 Damages in lieu of specific performance or an injunction

Under section 50 of the Senior Courts Act 1981, the High Court has the *discretion* to award the claimant damages:

• in *addition* to an injunction or specific performance (eg for losses suffered from delayed performance; *Ford-Hunt v Raghbir Singh* (1973)); or

• in *lieu* of them where the discretion is exercised against granting them.

Damages in lieu of specific performance or an injunction are said to 'constitute a true substitute for specific performance' (*Wroth v Tyler*) and to be assessed on the *same* basis and subject to the same limits as common law damages for breach of contract

(*Johnson v Agnew* (1980)). Both have the stated aim of putting the claimant 'in the same position... as if the contract had been performed' (*Robinson v Harman* (1848)), but neither is followed through to its logical conclusion. Damages in lieu of specific performance or an injunction may be reduced by reference to remoteness and mitigation. Where breach causes no financial loss to the claimant, courts have awarded, as damages in lieu of specific enforcement, a 'reasonable payment' representing 'the sum which [the claimant] could have extracted from the defendant as the price of his consent [to the breach]' (13.5). This seems sensible for, if specific enforcement is denied to avoid undue waste and harshness to the defendant, it hardly makes sense to compel the defendant to pay the monetary equivalent of specific performance. Analogous reasoning applies to the measure of damages in lieu of rescission in section 2(2) of the Misrepresentation Act 1967 (5.2.3.2).

14.2.4 Should specific enforcement be more widely available?

The case for a wider availability of specific enforcement centres around four factors.

14.2.4.1 Inadequacy of damages

In 'The Case for Specific Performance' (1979) 89 *Yale LJ* 271, Schwartz argues that if the law is committed to putting disappointed claimants in as good a position as they would have been in had the contract been performed, specific performance should be available as a matter of course. He reasons that:

- damages under-compensate in many cases where specific performance is currently unavailable;

- since claimants would prefer to sue for damages if they are likely to be fully compensated as 'a breaching promisor is reluctant to perform and may be hostile', they should be able to have specific performance if they choose it;

- claimants have better information than courts as to the adequacy of damages and the difficulties of coercing performance.

►◄ Counterpoint

1. The current level of damages awarded is the outcome of balancing the various policies identified in Chapter 13. If we accept the validity of policies such as the avoidance of waste and undue harshness to defendants, and the desirability of mitigation of loss by the claimant, then under-compensation to that extent is inevitable. Such policies should not be evaded by simply choosing specific performance.

2. On one view, automatic specific enforcement may amount to 'over-compensation', because it allows the claimant to sell the right to specific performance for *more than* the *true* value of the performance to him or her (Lord Hoffmann in *Cooperative Insurance v Argyll Stores*).

14.2.4.2 Protection of the claimant's performance interest

In 'The Performance Interest in Contract Damages' (1995) 111 *LQR* 628, Friedmann argues that 'the essence of contract is performance. Contracts are made in order to be performed.' Since factors such as prevention of hardship or economic waste do not prevent the formation of contracts, neither should they bar specific performance. Otherwise, it is questionable that the claimant has acquired a *right* to contractual performance.

In 'Disgorgement of Profits of Contract: Property, Contract and "Efficient Breach"' (1995) 24 *Can BLJ* 121, Smith argues that the right to performance should be elevated to that of a *proprietary right*, entitling the claimant to the defendant's profits from breach on the proprietary reasoning that the defendant's performance (and hence its fruits) is already the claimant's property (1.4.5 and 13.5).

 Counterpoint

1. As a matter of policy, English law has not valued contractual rights so highly as to coerce literal observance as a matter of course. Indeed, the original rule against penalties substantially undermined the claimant's performance interest by refusing to enforce secondary terms designed to deter breach of the contract's primary obligations (*Dunlop v Pneumatic Tyres* (1915)). Although this test has been abrogated in *Cavendish v Makdessi* (2015), the claimant seeking to enforce such a term must still show that she has a legitimate interest in deterring the breach, and that the clause is not extravagant or unconscionable in proportion to that interest (14.3.3).

2. Valuable autonomy is dynamic; it includes not only the right to bind oneself, but also some accommodation of one's **change of mind**. Changes in our assumptions, knowledge, attitudes, values, priorities, or passions might entail the rejection of previous beliefs, commitments, projects, or goals that are now no longer authentically ours. Being forced to keep a regretted undertaking may unduly compromise one's integrity, authenticity, and self-respect. There should be a 'general presumption in favour of liberty'. In essence, the adequacy of damages bar allows the defendant to change her mind, while still vindicating the claimant's right to performance. That is, the defendant's change of mind is *not cost free*; she must pay damages to protect the claimant's interests. But, that cost is reduced by rules limiting the amount of damages payable.

3. The claimant's performance interest must also be weighed against other legitimate policies when remedies are determined, eg the social interest in the *finality* of dispute resolution, and the related interests in avoiding waste of judicial resources and ending hostile relationships which may generate further litigation.

14.2.4.3 Efficient breach

In 'Specific Performance' (1978) 45 *U Chi L Rev* 35, Kronman argues that the current pattern of protection by specific performance where the subject matter is 'unique', but otherwise by damages, is economically efficient. The theory of *'efficient breach'* supports a restrictive approach to specific enforcement. The basic idea is that contract law should aim at maximising overall wealth and this is facilitated if the law permits 'efficient' breaches of contract. Breaches may be efficient because the defendant has made a mistake or because a third party has offered more for the defendant's performance. Thus, if I agree to supply a widget to you for £10,000, but Jack is prepared to offer me £20,000 for it, I will increase overall wealth by selling the widget to Jack and paying you damages for not supplying the widget, as long as that is less than £20,000. Jack and I are better off without you being any worse off. But I will have no incentive to breach if damages to you would equal or exceed £20,000.

 Counterpoint

1. Schwartz argues[4] that the routine availability of specific performance would be more efficient because it would minimise the inefficiencies of under-compensation, reduce the need for liquidated damage clauses, minimise strategic behaviour, and save the cost of litigating complex damage issues.

2. The efficient breach argument for current restrictions on the remedy of specific performance is difficult to assess (1.4.3). On the previous example, it is arguable that the widget would still move to Jack even if specific performance were the primary remedy. If Jack values the widget more highly than you, you would agree to release me from specific performance for *a share of my* gains and this is a fairer outcome. But the relative efficiency of this outcome must take into account the transaction costs of negotiating my release and making the new contract with Jack, which may reduce or negate any overall gain. In the end, which remedy is more efficient 'depends entirely upon the relative transaction costs... [which can] only be determined inductively from empirical evidence'.[5] The matter remains inconclusive.

14.2.4.4 Comparative law

Other jurisdictions such as Scotland and continental civilian systems treat specific performance as the primary remedy. But, in spite of this apparent difference, there is significant convergence in the circumstances when specific performance will be denied. Article III.-3:302 of the European Draft Common Frame of Reference recognises a general entitlement to specific performance *unless*:

- performance would be unlawful or impossible, unreasonably burdensome or expensive, of such a personal character that it would be unreasonable to enforce it;
- the claimant has unduly delayed in seeking the remedy; or
- the claimant 'could have made a reasonable substitute transaction without significant effort or expense'.

Courts of all systems must engage in the same delicate balancing of competing policies on the facts of particular cases.

---

[4] 'The Case for Specific Performance' (1979) 89 *Yale LJ* 271, 277.
[5] I Macneil, 'Efficient Breach of Contract: Circles in the Sky' (1982) 68 *Virginia L Rev* 947, 957.

Different courts may reach different conclusions, as the progression of *Cooperative Insurance v Argyll Stores* up the levels of courts shows (specific performance denied at first instance, granted in the Court of Appeal, and denied in the House of Lords). Moreover, it may make a practical difference whether the *presumption* is for or against specific performance, since it determines which party has the effective burden of proving otherwise. In the Scottish equivalent of *Cooperative Insurance v Argyll Stores*, specific performance was allowed to enforce a covenant to keep retail trading premises open (*Highland and Universal Properties Ltd v Safeway Properties Ltd* (2000)). The period of time (11 years) was shorter than in *Cooperative Insurance v Argyll Stores* (19 years), but the different starting point may also have been significant in a finely balanced case.

14.2.5 Can parties agree to specific performance or an injunction?

Parties can determine the remedies for breach by agreeing, eg:

✓ exemption clauses;

✓ payments on breach; or

✓ termination clauses.

However, these agreed remedies are subject to controls since courts have always jealously guarded their jurisdiction over contract remedies to prevent one party from exploiting the other's bargaining weakness or abusing their rights.[6] Enforcing agreed specific enforcement clauses would oust the court's jurisdiction to determine whether specific enforcement is appropriate *at the time it was claimed*. In *Quadrant Visual v Hutchison Telephone* (1993), the Court of Appeal held that the discretion over whether to grant specific performance belongs to the courts and cannot be usurped by the parties. The court cannot be reduced to a 'rubber stamp'; 'its discretion cannot be fettered'. Injunctions are granted more liberally, and clauses stipulating prohibitory injunctions are persuasive although not determinative (*Warner Brothers v Nelson*).

Where the parties' agreement purports to give one party the discretion to perform, and thus effectively to veto specific performance, the court may interpret the discretion to be subject to implied limits rather than as unconditional (10.6.1.3). In *Watson v Watchfunder.co.uk Ltd* (2017), the contract stipulated that the share option conferred on the claimants could only be exercised with the consent of the defendant's board of directors, which was denied. Relying on *Braganza v BP Shipping Ltd* (2015), the judge held that the veto could not be exercised unreasonably, capriciously, or arbitrarily. This required the defendant to take into account relevant, and disregard irrelevant, considerations, and reach an outcome that was not unreasonable. On the facts, this meant asking whether the claimants had made a real or significant contribution to the defendant's progress or growth. Since the answer was 'yes', the court proceeded as if consent had been given and awarded specific performance of the share option.

---

[6] See generally D Friedmann, 'Good Faith and Remedies for Breach of Contract' in J Beatson and D Friedmann, Good Faith and Fault in Contract Law (Clarendon Press, 1995) 399.

Pause for reflection

1. In *Quadrant Visual*, the refusal to enforce the specific performance clause was reinforced by the claimant's lack of 'clean hands' (14.2.1.2(ii)). Analogously, other policies against the award of specific enforcement also weigh against the enforcement of an agreed specific enforcement clause.

2. If the only bars are adequacy of damages or 'want of mutuality', it is arguable that the courts should give greater weight to a specific performance clause. A specific performance clause could be treated as a persuasive indicator of the claimant's loss, as long as the contract was not procedurally or substantively unfair at formation. At least, any doubts on these issues should be resolved in favour of the claimant when a specific performance clause is present.

The presence of an agreed damages clause may be thought to impliedly oust the court's jurisdiction to grant specific enforcement, since the clause: (i) gives the defendant the *option* to perform or pay the agreed damages; or (ii) indicates that the agreed damages are adequate. However, courts are eager to preserve their jurisdiction over specific remedies and have interpreted agreed damages clauses as only indicating the *quantum* of damages recoverable *if* the claimant sues for damages; the claimant is *not*, by virtue of an agreed damages clause, barred from claiming specific performance (*Howard v Hopkins* (1742)) or an injunction (*Jones v Heavens* (1877)).

14.3 **Agreed remedies**

14.3.1 **Introduction**

Where contract parties are silent on what should happen in the event of breach, contract law provides default rules to fill in that gap, namely, specific enforcement or damages. However, a 'majority' of standard form contracts will 'seek to augment, structure and confine the claims available to each party in relation to the breach of contract. In short, the normal remedy for breach of contract is that provided in the contract itself' (Collins, at 365). Where the parties *have* expressly agreed on the consequences of breach (aside from specific enforcement, 14.2.5), to what extent *are*, and *should*, they be enforceable?

14.3.1.1 Reasons for enforcing agreed remedies clauses

These mirror the reasons supporting the enforcement of standard form contracts (10.1):

- ✓ freedom of contract;
- ✓ certainty (parties know where they stand);
- ✓ avoiding the costs (to the parties and the judiciary) of resolving disputes through the courts;
- ✓ avoiding under-compensation by the courts, and ensuring adequate compensation;

✓ facilitating certain transactions (eg lenders will be reluctant to lend without some guarantee of repayment, and risky performance may not be rendered without limitations on potential liability); and

✓ deterring breach or ensuring performance.

The dangers of agreed remedies clauses that weigh against their enforcement are:

✗ harshness to the claimant (eg exemption clauses);

✗ undue harshness to contract-breakers (eg penalty clauses); and

✗ over-compensation to the claimant (eg penalty clauses),

especially where there is inequality of bargaining power.

14.3.1.2 Types of agreed remedies

The main types of agreed remedial obligations are clauses relating to money payments; these may stipulate:

(i)   an upper limit on the compensation payable on breach (ie exemption clauses, 10.5, Chapter 11);

(ii)   a particular sum payable on breach (agreed damages);

(iii)   a prepaid sum to be forfeited on breach (deposit); and

(iv)   instalments to be forfeited on breach (forfeiture).

This section focuses on (ii)–(iv).

Examples of other main types of agreed remedies are:

• *specific enforcement* clauses (14.2.5);

• *termination* clauses (specifying when a party can end the contract, 12.2.3.2);

• clauses that alter *property rights* on breach (eg failure to pay timely instalments, or give the seller title to the goods purchased or to the debtor's other property, or both);

• subsidiary provisions for *third party guarantees* of the contract party's performance (9.3); and

• stipulations that any disputes arising should be resolved by arbitration in a particular *forum alternative to the courts.*

14.3.1.3 Primary terms with remedial consequences

We have already discussed some *primary* terms that have clear *remedial* consequences, eg:

• an *entire obligations* clause means that a party need not pay until, at least substantial, performance by the other party (12.2.2.1III);

• designating a term as a *condition* may enable the claimant to terminate the contract for its breach (12.2.3.2);

- a *force majeure clause* that discharges the contract on certain events prevents any liability in respect of failure to perform (7.4.1).

A party may retain or create *property rights* as security against the other's breach, eg under hire-purchase contracts, the finance company retains ownership of the goods, leaving the debtor with only the possessory right which may be lost on breach; at the end of the hire period, the debtor can purchase the goods for a nominal sum. Another common example is *home loans* that grant the creditor an equitable charge over the debtor's property. If the debtor defaults, the creditor can possess and sell the property to satisfy the debt.

Diagram 14A gives an overview of the different techniques used to determine the enforceability of different types of terms with remedial consequences.

Diagram 14A Overview of primary terms with remedial consequences and secondary (remedial) terms

C = Claimant
D = Defendant
✓ = Enforceable
✗ = Unenforceable

C wants:	1. Monetary performance from D	2. Non-monetary performance from D	3. To withhold own performance
A. Enforceability of PRIMARY terms with remedial consequences	Action for the '*agreed sum*': ✓ on C's full performance (14.1), ✓ on other event not amounting to breach (14.3.1.3)	✓ *Specific performance* or *injunction* but restrictions on availability (14.2)	✓ *Termination* if D breaches a term agreed to be (a) a 'condition' or (b) an 'innominate' term which substantially deprives IP of intended benefits (12.2.2.2) ✓ IP need not perform if D breaches 'entire' obligation (12.2.2.1) ✓ Under *force majeure* clause (7.4.1)
B. Enforceability of SECONDARY terms agreed to apply on D's breach	✓ *Liquidated damages* clauses, ✗ *penalty* clauses (14.3.2.1) ✓ *forfeitures* clauses but subject to restrictions (14.3.3), ✓ *exemption* clauses but subject to restrictions (chs 10-11)	✗ Cannot fetter court's discretion by specific performance clause (14.2.5)	✓ 'Termination clause' but subject to strict construction and may not allow damages claim (12.2.3.2)

14.3.2 **Payments on breach: liquidated damages and penalties**

14.3.2.1 The penalty rule

The parties may agree on the sum to be paid by the defendant on her breach. This is:

✗ *unenforceable* if it amounts to a '**penalty**'; the court will then award damages on the usual principles; but

✓ *enforceable* otherwise as **liquidated damages**, even if it is greater or lesser than the claimant's actual loss.

This secondary (remedial) *agreed damages* clause is distinguishable from:

- an action for *damages*, which is the default money remedy (Chapter 13); and
- an action for the *agreed sum*, which enforces the defendant's primary obligation (14.1).

The law on this subject has been rewritten by the Supreme Court decisions (heard together) in *Cavendish Square v Makdessi*, and *Parkingeye Ltd v Beavis* (2015) (*Makdessi*), which widened the traditional understanding of *Dunlop Pneumatic Tyre Co Ltd v New Garage & Motor Co Ltd* (1915). Two preliminary points should be made. First, the penalty rule is often seen as anomalous because it contradicts the parties' agreement, even where they are experienced and have relatively equal bargaining power. Thus, courts lean against invalidating a term as a penalty. Second, on the other hand, the Supreme Court in *Makdessi* firmly rejected the argument that the penalty rule should be abolished. While consumers are protected by the CRA and its test of unfair terms, businesses may also need the protection of the rule. Moreover, its abolition would be inconsistent with other common law and civil law jurisdictions.

Dunlop v New Garage has been understood to hold that an agreed payment on breach is:

✓ *enforceable* if it amounts to '**liquidated damages**', ie a *genuine pre-estimate* of the loss likely to be caused by the breach; and

✗ *unenforceable* if it amounts to a '**penalty**', ie:

- not a genuine pre-estimate of loss, because 'the sum stipulated for is extravagant and unconscionable in amount in comparison with the greatest loss that could conceivably be proved to have followed from the breach'; and
- if it is aimed at deterring breach, ie 'in terrorem' of the defendant.

The following points elucidated this distinction:

(i)   The parties' own labels of 'liquidated damages' or 'penalty', while relevant, are not conclusive; neither does the test 'turn on the genuineness or honesty of the party or parties who made the pre-estimate. The test is primarily an objective one' (*Alfred McAlpine Capital Projects Ltd v Tilebox Ltd* (2005)).

(ii)   The question is one of construction, which means that it must be applied at the date of contract formation and not after breach (*Cavendish v Makdessi*).

(iii) Agreed damages do not become a penalty just because they exceed the actual loss; 'The parties are allowed a generous margin' (*Murray v Leisureplay* (2005)).

A clause is more likely to be penal if it lacks proportionality between the sum payable and the seriousness of the breach, eg requiring a builder to pay £1 million on breach of a contract for building work worth £50 (*Dunlop v New Garage*).

(iv) The baseline against which 'genuine pre-estimate of loss' is measured is that of common law damages (Chapter 13). This means that it can take into account the limits on expectation damages such as that based on the claimant's duty to mitigate. However, since the point of agreed damages may be to avoid under-compensation, it should also include:

✓ loss that may otherwise be too remote;

✓ loss of amenity or distress;

✓ *Wrotham Park* negotiating or hypothetical bargain damages; and

✓ losses that are difficult to assess.

Cavendish v Makdessi (2015) broadened the interpretation of *Dunlop v New Garages*. Accordingly, even if an agreed damages clause:

• does *not* represent a genuine pre-estimate of the loss, and

• *is* aimed at deterring a party from breaking the contract,

the clause may be *valid*, provided that:

• the claimant can show a **legitimate interest in deterring the breach** rather than simply being entitled to damages, and

• the clause is **not extravagant or unconscionable in proportion to that interest**.

This approach is consistent with *Dunlop v New Garage*, since their Lordships in *Makdessi* accept that: '[i]n the case of a straightforward damages clause, that interest will rarely extend beyond compensation for the breach', so that the traditional *Dunlop* test 'would usually be perfectly adequate to determine its validity'; it is only when the claimant has a 'legitimate interest' beyond compensation that the agreed payment on breach need not be a genuine pre-estimate of loss and can aim to deter breach, so long as it is not extravagant or unconscionable in proportion to that interest. *Makdessi* can also be reconciled with the more recent cases suggesting that an agreed payment on breach may be enforceable even if it was not, strictly speaking, a pre-estimate of the likely loss, if it was 'commercially justifiable' (eg the Court of Appeal in *Makdessi*, and *Murray v Leisureplay* (2005)); it is strongly arguable that 'commercial justifications' would satisfy the 'legitimate interest' required by the Supreme Court. However, *Makdessi* has reversed the law insofar as an agreed payment on breach is not necessarily a penalty just because it is aimed at deterring breach.

It is arguable that the claimant will have a **'legitimate interest'** (in obtaining performance rather than damages) which justifies an agreed damages clause that is intended to deter breach, rather than as a pre-estimate of loss where:

✓ the claimant would face serious difficulties in proving its loss from the breach;

✓ the claimant would face serious difficulties in detecting whether there has been a breach;

✓ the claimant would not be able to obtain substitute goods, property, or services, making damages an inadequate remedy;

✓ loss will be suffered by a third party instead of, or in addition to, the claimant (*Parkingeye v Beavis*);

✓ the claimant risks insolvency if she has to wait for damages from the defendant (*Thames Valley Power Ltd v Total Gas and Power Ltd* (2006));

✓ the claimant has an exceptional interest in ensuring that the defendant performs such that the court would award an account of profits, as in *AG v Blake* (1999); or

✓ more generally, if deterrence is an essential element of a lawful scheme (*Parkingeye v Beavis*).

In contrast, the claimant has *no* **legitimate interest** in:

✗ simply punishing the defendant;

✗ avoiding the time and expense in arranging a substitute transaction (ie mitigation);

✗ simply getting performance over damages; and

✗ claiming the defendant's profits from breach if damages would otherwise be adequate.

A claimant with a 'legitimate interest' must still show that the agreed damages sought to be enforced (while not a pre-estimate of loss or perhaps aimed at deterring breach) are **not extravagant or unconscionable** compared to the legitimate interest. The term will not be invalidated unless it is *very* substantially more than is necessary to deter the breach, judged at the time of formation. The parties have a generous margin of error; the more equal the parties' bargaining power, the greater the leeway given (*Makdessi*). Applying the *Makdessi* test to the facts:

✓ In *Dunlop v New Garages*, the defendants bought tyres from the claimant manufacturers and breached their undertaking, inter alia, not to sell them or allow them to be sold below the manufacturer's list price. The contract provided for £5 to be payable for every tyre sold or offered in breach of the undertaking:

• On the traditional test, the House of Lords upheld this sum as liquidated damages, since the loss likely to result from any breach was difficult to assess and £5 represented a genuine attempt to value it.

• The case would also satisfy the *Makdessi* test; Lord Mance said in *Makdessi* that the manufacturer had a legitimate interest in protecting its price maintenance system 'by imposing an undertaking on all its counterparties to respect the system, coupled with a provision requiring payment of an agreed sum in the event of any breach of such undertaking'. Moreover, the term was not extravagant, unconscionable or incommensurate.

✓ In *Parkingeye v Beavis*, the claimants operated a car park at a retail park on behalf of the owners. Motorists were allowed to park free for up to two hours; a charge of £85 would be imposed for 'failure to comply' and leave thereafter.

• On the traditional test, the term would have been a penalty since it was not a pre-estimate of the claimant's loss (which was nil), and was designed to deter breach.

- However, on the *Makdessi* test, the claimant had a legitimate interest in ensuring limited free parking for the benefit of the retailers and customers; the charges were an essential part of a lawful scheme. Moreover, they were not manifestly excessive, having regard to the level of charges imposed by local authorities and others for overstaying in public car parks.

✓ In *Makdessi*, M had sold shares in his advertising and marketing business to another company, with C ultimately substituted for the original purchaser. The contract stated that, if M breached the non-competition clauses, C could require M to transfer his remaining shares at a much lower price than the option price:

- On the traditional test, the term was a penalty since M stood to lose $40 million and the amount was out of all proportion to the loss attributable to the breach and acted to deter breach.

- However, on the *Makdessi* test, C had a legitimate interest in preserving the good will for which it was paying a large amount (the company purchased would be of little value to C if M was not loyal), thus a sum designed to deter M from breach is not penal. However, it seems odd that a price reduction of $40 million was not regarded as extravagant for M's relatively minor breaches. It may be that, as the seller's loyalty was regarded as critical and indivisible, the question is what is extravagant on the worst-case scenario.

14.3.2.2 The types of clauses covered by the penalty rule

In *Makdessi*, the Supreme Court held that the penalty rule applies to:

✓ agreed payments on breach;

✓ provisions that would prevent a contract-breaker from receiving a sum to which it would otherwise be entitled;

✓ provisions that require a contract-breaker to transfer property to the claimant at a reduced value (*Jobson v Johnson* (1989));

✓ deposit clauses (14.3.3.1);

✓ forfeiture of payment clauses; and

✓ 'disguised penalties' (*Interfoto Picture Library Ltd v Stiletto Visual Prorammes Ltd* (1987), where a term required a hirer to pay a much higher charge if the slides hired were not returned within the fixed period).

The penalty rule has no application:

✗ where an agreed sum is payable on an event other than breach (see *Alder v Moore* (1961), where a professional footballer received £500 from an insurance company on terms that he would repay the amount if he resumed playing. The majority enforced the agreement to repay when the footballer resumed playing four months later.)

Pause for reflection

The penalty rule is another instance of English law's piecemeal approach to problems of unfairness, and throws up some familiar problems:

1. The restriction of the penalty jurisdiction to secondary terms is artificial, since primary terms can perform an identical function and yet remain largely uncontrolled, as **Diagram 14B** shows. Penalties can be redrafted into primary terms (ie making the event that triggers payment *not* a breach) to evade the penalty rule. This mirrors the problem with the distinction between terms that exempt liability for breach and terms that are duty-defining (11.5.4).

2. The penalty rule can be reformed to cover clauses stipulating payment on *events closely allied to breach*, wherever 'the object of the disputed contractual obligation is to secure the act or result which is the true purpose of the contract' (Law Commission, *Penalty Clauses and Forfeiture of Money Paid* (Law Com Consultation Paper 61, 1975) at para 26). In *OFT v Abbey* (11.6.3), the Supreme Court held that fees charged by the bank to its customers for exceeding their overdraft were *not* penalties because they were not charged upon breach. In contrast, the High Court of Australia, in *Andrews v Australia and New Zealand Banking Group Ltd* (2012), held that it is the *substance* of the clause that matters, not the *form*. Such charges *may* amount to penalties; the question is whether the stipulation is 'collateral' or 'secondary' to the primary obligation owed to the innocent party, and whether it imposes an 'additional detriment' on the contract-breaker. *Makdessi* has rejected this approach for being uncertain and unworkable.

Diagram 14B Payment clauses and their tests of validity

C = Claimant
D = Defendant

Type of term:	Test of enforceability:
Agreed sum (D's payment for C's performance)	• Requirement of 'substantial' performance by C
Limitation of damages (D to pay less or nothing for C's loss)	• Incorporation • Interpretation • UCTA or CRA
Payments on breach (D to pay the agreed damages)	• The penalty rule • CRA (Sch 2 part 1, Para 5)
Payments on other events (no breach but specified party must pay on the occurrence of specified event)	• CRA
Forfeiture (D forfeits sums already paid to C)	• The penalty rule • CRA (Sch 2 Part 1, paras 4 and 7)

14.3.3 **Forfeitures of payments**

An agreed damages clause requires the claimant to extract the sum *after* the defendant's breach. A better option is to obtain money *in advance* and refuse to return it (forfeit it) on breach by the defendant. In *Cavendish v Makdessi* (2015), the Supreme Court said that both deposits and forfeiture clauses are subject to the penalty rules.

14.3.3.1 Deposits and part-payments

In general, an advance payment is:

- ✗ *not recoverable* if it is a **deposit**, that is, a sum paid as 'a guarantee that the contract shall be performed' (*Howe v Smith* (1884)); but

- ✓ *recoverable* if it is a **part-payment** of the contract price, subject to the contract-breaker's liability to pay damages (*Dies v British and International Mining and Finance Co* (1939), 13.4.4).

The true nature of a payment is a matter of construction of the contract.

The Law of Property Act 1925 confers a statutory discretion empowering courts to return a deposit 'if it thinks fit' (s 49(2); this cannot be excluded by the parties). In practice, the case must be exceptional for the discretion to be exercised for the return of a standard 10% deposit, ie the payee can generally keep the deposit, provided that it does not exceed the customary amount (eg 10% of the purchase price of land); the payee need not show that it is a genuine pre-estimate of the loss.

In *Workers Trust & Merchant Bank Ltd v Dojap Investments Ltd* (1993),[7] the Privy Council applied the penalty rule to strike down an unfair deposit. There, a contract for the sale of land stipulated an unusually large deposit of 25% of the purchase price (almost $3 million). The balance was to be paid within 14 days, time being of the essence (ie a condition). The purchasers tendered the balance plus interest a week late, and the vendors terminated the contract, claiming to forfeit the deposit. The Privy Council advised that a payment is only a valid deposit if the 'sum is reasonable as earnest money'. Since there were no 'special circumstances' justifying its retention, the vendors were ordered to repay the deposit after deducting its provable losses from the breach, which turned out to be less than 10% of the contract price.

In *Union Eagle Ltd v Golden Achievement Ltd* (1997), forfeiture of a 10% deposit for the sale of a flat in Hong Kong was upheld when the buyer was *10 minutes* late in tendering the balance of the purchase price (amounting to $HK10 million). The Privy Council allowed the seller to terminate the contract because of the importance of certainty in commercial transactions (a seller needs to know immediately whether she is free to deal with someone else).

---

[7] The decision mirrors the Law of Property Act 1925, s 49(2), and the Consumer Credit Act 1974, ss 90, 132, and 136.

Pause for reflection

Although *Makdessi* says that the penalty rule applies to forfeiture clauses (including of deposits), there seems to be some differences, eg:

1. Land is treated differently insofar as a 10% deposit payment may be forfeited even if the payee suffered no loss (eg because the land can be quickly resold). This may be because the automatic availability of specific performance suggests that damages are inadequate and the seller has a legitimate interest in deterring breach. This reasoning does not apply to deposits paid in respect of goods where they can only be retained if they are a genuine pre-estimate of loss.

2. A vendor who validly terminates the contract because of a breach by the purchaser may *both* forfeit the deposit *and recover damages*, giving due allowance for the deposit (*Lock v Bell* (1931)). In contrast, no damages can be claimed in addition to an enforceable payment on breach.

3. In *Makdessi*, Lord Mance said that, even if a provision is *valid* under the penalty rule, the court may still grant relief against forfeiture.

14.3.3.2 Instalments

A contract may allow the price to be paid in instalments and stipulate the forfeiture of all the payments if the defendant defaults on any one instalment. Traditionally, the courts were willing to grant relief against two types of forfeiture clauses:

- ✓ forfeiture of a lease where a tenant fails to pay any instalment of rent; and
- ✓ forfeiture of the purchased land where the buyer fails to make instalment payments.

More recently, relief has been granted more widely:

- Where the contract is for **services** rendered over time in return for periodic payments, the sums paid are not recoverable on the payee's breach if they 'represent the agreed rate of hire for services already rendered, and not a penny more' (*The Scaptrade* (1983)). The result may be different if the payments are clearly 'front-loaded'.

- Where a contract for the sale of **property** is terminated for the buyer's breach and the subject matter remains the property of, or is returned to, the seller, forfeiture of instalment payments presents a clear danger of unfairness to the buyer. Denning LJ compares the situation where the buyer defaults after paying 5% of the price, where forfeiture is not unfair, with the situation where the buyer's default comes after paying 90% of the purchase price, where forfeiture is patently unfair (*Stockloser v Johnson* (1954)).

(i) Where the buyer is *ready and willing* to resume performance, the court can relieve against forfeiture by granting extra time for payment (*Re Dagenham (Thames) Dock Co* (1873)).

(ii) Where the buyer is *not ready and willing* to perform, the majority of the Court of Appeal in *Stockloser v Johnson* held that at least some of the instalments are still recoverable if retention would be oppressive and unconscionable (although Romer LJ limited recoverability to cases of *procedural* unfairness). This position was confined (in *Workers Trust v Dojap* and *The Scaptrade*) to cases of proprietary or possessory rights. But it has since been applied beyond that to give relief in a case regarding shares (*Jobson v Johnson* and *Cukurova Finance International Ltd v Alfa Telecom Turkey Ltd* (2013)), and a lease of chattels (*On Demand Information v Michael Gerson (Finance)* (2002)).

14.4 **Protection for consumers**

The Consumer Rights Act 2015 (CRA) provides that an unfair term in a consumer contract is not binding on the consumer.

✓ Among the illustrations of terms that may be regarded as unfair (Sch 2 Part 1) is a term 'requiring any consumer who fails to fulfil his obligations under the contract to pay a disproportionately high sum in compensation' (para 6).

✓ It has been held that a term may be unfair even though, on the facts, it did not amount to a penalty at common law (*Munkenbeck & Marshall v Harold* (2005)).

✓ It also seems clear that, in appropriate cases, the CRA can invalidate for unfairness a term specifying: a deposit, a forfeiture, and a payment on an event other than breach (Chapter 11).

THIS CHAPTER IN ESSENCE

The key areas and core topics in this chapter are summarised in an easy-to-use list, ideal for revision purposes, on the online resources at www.oup.com/uk/chenwishart6e/. Links to websites relevant to the topics covered and any updates to the chapter can also be found on the online resources.

QUESTIONS

1 '*Cooperative Insurance Society Ltd v Argyll Stores (Holdings) Ltd* (1998) has tipped the balance too far in favour of the contract-breaker.' When are specific performance and injunctions available, and when should they be?

2 'Contract parties enter contracts to get performance and not damages for non-performance. Therefore, specific performance, and not damages, should be the main remedy for breach.' Discuss.

3 Explain and distinguish each of the following, giving examples:

(a) An exemption clause and a penalty clause.

(b) A penalty clause and a liquidated damages clause.

(c) A deposit and a part-payment.

What is the test of enforceability in each case?

4 Should parties have greater freedom to agree on the consequences of breach?

5 Are the following terms in a contract between Nick and Olga enforceable? What further facts do you need to know?

(a) A term stipulating that 'if Olga breaches clause 8 then Nick can specifically enforce the term *or* is entitled to the sum of £50,000 as Nick chooses'.

(b) A term stipulating that 'On the occurrence of circumstances specified in clause 8 Olga must pay Nick £50,000.'

6 What protection do consumers have against unfair agreed remedies clauses?

 For hints on how to answer these questions, please see the online resources at www.oup.com/uk/chenwishart6e/

KEY FURTHER READING

See generally, Burrows, A (2004), *Remedies for Torts and Breach of Contract* (3rd edn, OUP).

Friedmann, D (1995), 'Good Faith and Remedies for Breach of Contract' in J Beatson and D Friedmann (eds), *Good Faith and Fault in Contract Law* (Clarendon Press) 399.

Goetz, C, and Scott, R (1977), 'Liquidated Damages, Penalties and Just Compensation', 77 *Col L Rev* 554.

Kronman, A (1978), 'Specific Performance', 45 *U Chi L Rev* 35.

Rowan, S (2010), 'For the Recognition of Remedial Terms Agreed Inter Partes' 126 *LQR* 448.

Schwartz, A (1979), 'The Case for Specific Performance', 89 *Yale LJ* 271.

Smith, S A (1997), 'Performance, Punishment and the Nature of Contractual Obligation', 60 *MLR* 360.

PART VII

Good faith

It is true that English contract law recognises no general duty of good faith[1] by that name. However, this only tells part of the story, for it ignores the diverse range of doctrines and principles deployed by the courts to deal with what may legitimately be regarded as contraventions of good faith, at all stages of the life of a contract. As Bingham LJ famously observed in *Interfoto Picture Library Ltd v Stiletto Visual Programmes Ltd* (1989):

> In many civil law systems, and perhaps in most legal systems outside the common law world, the law of obligations recognises and enforces an overriding principle that in making and carrying out contracts parties should act in good faith. This does not simply mean that they should not deceive each other, a principle which any legal system must recognise; its effect is perhaps most aptly conveyed by such metaphorical colloquialisms as 'playing fair', 'coming clean' or 'putting one's cards face upwards on the table'. It is in essence a principle of fair and open dealing.... English law has, characteristically, committed itself to no such overriding principle but has developed piecemeal solutions in response to demonstrated problems of unfairness.... Many examples could be given.... [These] may yield a result not very different from the civil law principle of good faith.

More recently, there has been an increasing challenge to English law's refusal to recognise a general good faith duty. In *Yam Seng PTE Ltd v International Trade Corporation Ltd* (2013), Leggatt J observed that English law is 'swimming against the tide', and that the traditional English hostility to good faith in the performance of contracts is 'misplaced'. It is useful to remember that the issue of good faith has been raised over the years in different iterations. Thus, for example, in *Lloyds Bank v Bundy* (1977), Lord Denning said, after surveying a number of vitiating factors:

> Gathering all together, I would suggest that through all these instances there runs a single thread. They rest on 'inequality of bargaining power'. By virtue of it, the English law gives relief to one who, without independent advice, enters into a contract upon terms which are very unfair or transfers property for a consideration which is grossly inadequate, when his or her bargaining power is grievously impaired by reason of his or her own needs or desires, or by his or her own ignorance or infirmity, coupled with undue influences or pressures brought to bear on them by or for the benefit of the other. When I use the word 'undue' I do not mean to suggest that the principle depends on proof of any wrongdoing.

---

[1] *Mid Essex Hospital Services NHS Trust v Compass Group UK and Ireland* (2013).

Likewise, the concept of 'unconscionability' has been mooted (Capper 'Undue Influence and Unconscionability: A Rationalization' (1998) 114 *LQR* 479). This distinctively common law concept has found fertile soil outside the UK (eg in the US Uniform Commercial Code, Australia, Canada and New Zealand). The open-textured elements of the unconscionable bargains doctrine can provide a unifying concept for a number of distinct rules dealt with under different headings. This chapter could equally well have been called 'unfairness' and the question posed is whether the common law should recognise a general doctrine against it. As we will see, the issues are complex and the answer may not be a simple choice of 'yes' or 'no'.

The questions to be considered are:

1. What does 'good faith' *mean*? What does good faith *require*? *When*? With what *consequences* for breach?

2. To what extent can the common law be said to *already* manifest a commitment to good faith? *Should* the common law openly recognise a good faith obligation?

3. What difference would it make if good faith were openly recognised?

15

Good faith

'You must act in good faith.'

While much has been said about good faith, most has been at a high level of generality that is difficult to pin down. There is no clear consensus on what it means. The aim of this chapter is to explore the meaning of good faith, identify its demands, map its variables, and assess the desirability of open recognition of a general doctrine of good faith.

15.1 The meaning of 'good faith'

As Lord Bingham noted, even jurisdictions openly recognising the duty 'have no common concept of fairness or good faith' (*DGFT v First National Bank* (2001)).

At its narrowest, it is simply synonymous with the **absence of bad faith**. Thus, in *Manifest Shipping Co Ltd v Uni-Polaris Shipping Co Ltd* (2001), Lord Scott stated in the insurance context, that: 'Unless the assured has acted in bad faith, he cannot ... be in breach of a duty of good faith, utmost or otherwise'. Insofar as 'bad faith' designates conduct that is already specifically regulated, this formulation simply begs the question of why certain conduct is regulated. It is conclusory rather than explanatory.

To give good faith minimum independent content, the starting point must be the recognition that good faith is a demand of interpersonal dealing that, in the contractual context, translates into **some limit on self-interested conduct, and, logically, some regard for the interests of the other party**. This is supported by or entirely consistent with the following:

- Commonly accepted legal standards at common law such as 'reasonableness', 'unconscionability', 'fairness', 'equity', and 'justice' are synonymous with good faith. Steyn LJ said (*First Energy (UK) Ltd v Hungarian International Bank Ltd* (1993)):

  > A theme that runs through our law of contract is that the reasonable expectations of honest men must be protected. It is not a rule or a principle of law. It is the objective which has been and still is the principal moulding force of our law of contract. It affords no licence to a judge to depart from binding precedent. On the other hand, if the *prima facie* solution to a problem runs counter to the reasonable expectations of honest men, this criterion sometimes requires a rigorous re-examination of the problem to ascertain whether the law does indeed compel demonstrable unfairness.

  This supports the point made above that the issues are identical with those which would be raised by the question of whether the common law should recognise a general principle of inequality of bargaining power, or against unfairness, or unconscionability.

- Section 62(4) of the Consumer Rights Act 2015 (CRA) invalidates unfair non-core term in the sense, inter alia, of contravention of good faith. CRA gives effect to the EC Directive on Unfair Terms in Consumer Contracts (93/13/EEC), and Recital 16 there refers to dealing 'fairly and equitably' with the consumer 'whose *legitimate interests* [the trader] has to take into account'.

- Good faith is said to require: '"playing fair", "coming clean", or "putting one's cards face upwards on the table". It is in essence a principle of fair open dealing' (*Interfoto Picture Library Ltd v Stiletto Visual Programmes Ltd* (1989)); it looks to 'good standards of commercial morality and practice' (*Director General of Fair Trading v First National Bank Plc* (2001)).

- The American Uniform Commercial Code defines good faith as 'honesty in fact and the observance of reasonable commercial standards of fair dealing'.

- The Supreme Court of Canada held that good faith requires parties to perform their contracts 'honestly and reasonably and not capriciously or arbitrarily'; this requires them to give appropriate consideration to the legitimate interests of the other party (*Bhasin v Hrynew* (2014)).

- Consistently, Finn argues that good faith, while 'permitting a party to act self-interestedly, nonetheless qualifies this by requiring that party, in his decision and action, to have regard to the other party's legitimate interests therein of the other party' ('The Fiduciary Principle', in T G Youdan (ed), *Equity, Fiduciaries and Trusts* (Toronto, Calgary, Vancouver, 1989) 1, 4).

Of course, the concept of good faith as a restraint on self-interest and regard for the counterparty's interests requires further definition. It begs the questions of:

- *What* interests of the counterparty must be taken into account?
- *What* good faith actually requires and so what remedies are available for contraventions of good faith?
- How *much* account must be taken of the counterparty's interest?
- *When* (ie in what circumstances)?

If Bingham LJ is right that the common law has responded to problems of unfairness by 'piecemeal solutions' that amount to much the same thing as a duty of good faith, and I think he is, then the answer to these questions must be contained within current English contract law doctrines. It is to these that we now turn, to be followed by an analysis of how they inform the nature of good faith.

15.2 Good faith in current contract law doctrines

Many specific legal principles, rules, and doctrines can be seen as activated by the principle of good faith. These 'piecemeal solutions' to problems of unfairness are discussed in greater detail elsewhere in this text. What follows are brief lists that illustrate the wide extent to which English contract law may be thought to manifest good faith in the sense proposed. As Lord Bingham observes: 'At one level they are concerned with a question of pure contractual analysis.... . At another level they are concerned with a somewhat different question, [what] it would in all the circumstances be fair (or reasonable) to' require (*Interfoto v Stilleto*). In the latter sense, it will be clear that the common law is animated by good faith through and through.

15.2.1 Good faith at contract formation

The examples are numerous, and include:

(i) The objective test of intentions which protects the counterparty's reasonable reliance on one's own conduct, subject to the honesty and fair dealing of the counterparty (2.1).

(ii) No acceptance by silence since one should not exploit the counterparty's inertia or 'set traps' for them (2.3.3.2).

(iii) A party's reasonable reliance (eg by performance) can be protected by many doctrines, eg:

- the bar on revocation of unilateral offers in appropriate circumstances (2.3.6.2);

- imposing collateral or ancillary contracts or terms to ensure that parties are held to the reasonable expectations they engender, eg duty to consider (10.3.2);

- curing uncertainty and incompleteness (2.6);

- waiving compliance with conditions such as formal execution of a contractual document;

- promissory estoppel (3.2);

- proprietary estoppel and estoppel by convention (3.2);

- constructive trust (3.3.4); and

- unjust enrichment claims where benefits have been conferred in anticipation of a contract that did not eventuate (1.6).

15.2.2 Good faith in contract vitiation

Even if the formal elements of a contract are present, the contract may be unenforceable at the election of one of the parties where the other party has not sufficiently restrained her self-interest and had regard to the other's interests. Clear examples here include:

(i) Misrepresentation, whether fraudulent, negligent, or even innocent (Chapter 5). It is unfair to hold the counterparty to a contract made on a mistaken basis, where the mistake is induced by one's own action.

(ii) Mistaken assumptions (6.3). It is unfair to hold the counterparty to a contract made on a mistaken basis that is shared and fundamental since one's own expectations are unreasonable.

(iii) Duties of disclosure imposed on certain classes of contracts, where the information is important and known or accessible to only one party (eg insurance) or where the parties' relationship demands it (eg partnership, fiduciary relationships) (5.1.3.1).

(iv) Duress, which prevents one party from using illegitimate pressure to induce the counterparty to enter into contracts (Chapter 8).

(v) Undue influence, which prevents one party's abuse of its relationships of trust and confidence by failure to show appropriate regard for the counterparty's legitimate interests (9.2).

(vi) Non-commercial guarantees, which require lenders to take reasonable steps to ensure that potentially vulnerable guarantors are properly advised (9.3).

(vii) Unconscionable bargains to the manifest disadvantage of a non-commercial party who operates under an operative impairment, which can be set aside against the other party who exploits that impairment (9.4).

15.2.3 **Good faith in the contents of contracts**

Here, English law vociferously denies tampering with the parties' strict agreement, and yet many techniques exist to allow courts to restrain a party's self-interest and require regard for the counterparty's interests. Again, the examples are numerous and include:

(i) The terms–representations distinction, which determines what remedy is available to the disappointed party, and which is made on the basis of whether it is fair in all the circumstances (eg relative expertise and importance of the subject matter) for the maker of a statement to be liable for the accuracy of the statement (5.1.1, 10.2).

(ii) The incorporation rules for onerous and unusual terms in unsigned documents, which require reasonable notice to the other party; the more onerous or unusual, the more notice is required (10.3.3.2). It is in this context that Lord Bingham said (*Interfoto v Stiletto*):

> At one level they are concerned with a question of pure contractual analysis, whether one party has done enough to give the other notice of the incorporation of a term in the contract. At another level they are concerned with a somewhat different question, whether it would in all the circumstances be fair (or reasonable) to hold a party bound by any conditions or by a particular condition of an unusual and stringent nature.

(iii) Implying terms in law and in fact where it is 'necessary', 'goes without saying', or would be consistent with social fairness for contracts of a particular type (10.6), eg the implied term of 'trust and confidence' as an incidence of the relational contract of employment (10.6.2.3). Ideas of good faith and fair dealing are central to the implication of terms (Collins, 'Implied Terms: The Foundation in Good Faith and Fair Dealing' (2014) 27 *CLP* 1).

(iv) *Contra proferentem* construction of ambiguous terms (10.5.3).

(v) Restrictions on the exercise of agreed discretionary powers requiring that one not act arbitrarily, capriciously, or irrationally against the counterparty's interests (10.6.1.3).

(vi) Rectification for unilateral mistake in favour of one party where the counterparty is tainted by unconscionability (6.1.2.3).

(vii) Frustration of contracts where unforeseen events, subsequent to contract formation, make performance illegal, impossible, or radically different for one or both parties (Chapter 7).

(viii) Legislation, some of EU origin, requires English courts to consider good faith in particular contexts, eg:

- section 62(4) of CRA invalidates an unfair term where: 'contrary to the requirement of good faith, it causes a significant imbalance in the parties' rights and obligations under the contract' (11.6.4).
- The Commercial Agents Directive 1986 requires agents to 'act dutifully and in good faith' towards their principals.

- Unreasonable terms purporting to allow a business the discretion of giving *no, only partial*, or *substantially different* performance from that reasonably expected by a business contracting on the other's standard terms are invalid under section 3(2)(b) of the Unfair Contract Terms Act 1977 (UCTA), (11.5.4.4).

15.2.4 Good faith in the selection of remedies for breach

The current law is replete with good faith limitations on the stated aim of remedies for breach of contract, namely, to put the aggrieved party in as good a position as if the contract had been performed.

(i)   Bars to specific performance, which reflect considerations of good faith that include (14.2.1):

✓ Taking account of the contract-breaker's (CB):

- welfare interests (eg the bars of impossibility, avoidance of hardship, uncertainty, and avoidance of waste); and

- autonomy interests (eg the bars of personal services, adequacy of damages, and continuing activity).

✓ Taking account of the claimant's conduct (eg the bars of lack of clean hands and delay).

(ii) Limits on affirmation by the claimant if she needs the CB's cooperation or has no legitimate interest in insisting on performance in the sense that it would be grossly unreasonable and so enormously wasteful to require the CB to pay for it (12.3).

(iii) Limits on termination of contract. Where termination has drastic consequences for the CB, courts can adopt a number of techniques to avoid such harshness, including:

- classifying a term as 'innominate' although the parties have designated it a 'condition' (12.2.2.2);

- making 'innominate' term the default designation where the parties and precedent are silent (12.2.3); and

- making the threshold for termination of innominate terms extremely high (12.2.2.2).

(iv) Limits on the award of expectation damages. The operation of many rules results in damages falling short of the stated aim of placing the claimant in the position, in money terms, that she would be in had the contract been performed. Most of these rules reflect good faith concerns to restrain self-interest and to take account of the counterparty's interests; they include:

- the switch to the diminution or amenity measure where the cost of cure would be unreasonable (13.2.3.2);

- the general bar on claims for non-pecuniary loss due to the potential harshness to the defendant, but subject to exceptions that take account of the claimant's legitimate interests (13.2.4);

- the reduction of the claimant's damages where she fails to mitigate, has been contributorily negligent, or where her losses are too remote (13.2.5.2, 13.2.5.6, and 13.2.5.1);

- where the claimant's losses are too speculative, she has a 'backstop' claim to reliance damages so long as this does not circumvent a bad bargain (13.3);

- where the claimant has received nothing from her contract, she can claim restitution of money paid even if this would allow her to circumvent a bad bargain since the defendant should not get something for nothing (13.4).

- in exceptional circumstances, where justice requires, the claimant, whose damages claim would otherwise be nominal or very difficult to prove, may be allowed to claim (13.5):

  ✓ negotiating damages; or

  ✓ even more exceptionally, an account of profits.

(v) Limits on the enforcement of agreed remedies, eg:

- the penalty rule invalidates agreed sums payable on breach that are unconscionable and disproportionate to the loss caused (14.3.2). Similar rules apply to the forfeiture of deposits and other sums (14.3.3);

- agreed specific performance clauses are unenforceable (14.2.5); and

- agreed termination clauses can be read down to dilute their effect (14.3).

15.3 **The nature of good faith**

If good faith means the restraint of self-interest and regard for the interests of one's contractual partner, what can we glean from this very brief review of contract law doctrines through the lens of good faith?

- What is the role of good faith?
- Is it intended by the parties or imposed by the law?
- What are the interests at stake?
- How does the duty translate into specific requirements?
- What are the consequences of a breach of good faith?
- What is the strength of the good faith requirement?

15.3.1 **Good faith has an explanatory, legitimising, *and* creative role**

Consistent with Bingham LJ's famous observation, good faith gives rise to no independent cause of action, as for example happens in German law. The latter approach should be rejected for being contrary to the English law tradition of cautious incrementalism, and for eschewing grand over-arching principles and for attracting, in their sharpest form, the concerns of uncertainty, judicial interference, and contravention of the parties' intention. Rather, good faith is manifested in English law in 'piecemeal solutions' in response to demonstrated problems of unfairness. The Canadian

Supreme Court expresses this role well; it recognised that good faith was a general organising principle of Canadian contract law which 'states in general terms a requirement of justice from which more specific legal doctrines may be derived'. Good faith is therefore 'not a freestanding rule, but rather a standard that underpins and is manifested in more specific legal doctrines and may be given different weight in different situations' (*Bhasin v Hrynew* (2014)).

Lord Hope of Craighead also emphasised the limited role of the good faith principle. In contrast to civilian systems where it is 'expressly recognised and acted upon…. The preferred approach in England is to avoid any commitment to overarching principle… Good faith in Scottish law, as in South African law, is generally an underlying principle of an explanatory and legitimating rather than an active or creative nature… It is not a source of obligation in itself.' (*R (European Roma Rights Centre) v Immigration Officer at Prague Airport* (2004)).

However, the 'active or creative nature' of good faith cannot be denied, even in English law:

- the doctrines mentioned in 15.2 were *developed* 'in response to demonstrated problems of unfairness';
- these sorts of developments are evident in current cases, eg *Yam Seng*; and
- the common law will *continue* its methodology of cautious incrementalism.

15.3.2 **Good faith is imposed by the law**

Good faith can be made 'safe' and uncontroversial by presenting it as merely based on the parties' implied intention. The view that good faith duties are agreed by the parties, the **'internal' approach**, has the great attraction of consistency with the orthodoxy that contract law merely enforces the parties' intentions. Thus, McKendrick notes that good faith has been perceived not as an external standard which is imposed by the law on the parties, but as reflecting the parties' intentions. ('Good Faith in the Performance of a Contract in English Law', in L DiMatteo and M Hogg (eds), *Comparative Contract Law: British and American Perspectives* (OUP, 2016) 196). Campbell sees a role for good faith so long as courts are merely interpreting contracts according to the intentions of the parties and the usual rules for implied terms rather than imposing external or 'exogeneous' standards ('Good Faith and the Ubiquity of the 'Relational' Contract' (2014) 77 *MLR* 475).

The internal approach to good faith is **unrealistic**:

1. While the parties' intentions must indeed be relevant, they will usually have no intention on the matter in any meaningful sense of the phrase; and if they do, the likelihood is that one party intends a duty of good faith, while the other does not.

2. The internal view masks the courts' role in imposing *objective* standards. Talk of 'implied terms' and 'reasonable expectations' often conceals the external imposition of good faith standards:

    - Leggatt J concedes that: 'the test of good faith is objective in the sense that it depends not on either party's perception of whether particular conduct is improper but on whether in the particular context the conduct would be regarded as commercially unacceptable by reasonable and honest people' (*Yam Seng*).

- Collins argues good faith in its broad sense is concerned with establishing efficient and balanced obligations under contracts with reference to the parties' reasonable expectations:

  > A party may still look primarily to his or her own interests, but in the performance of the contract and in the exercise of rights and powers conferred by the contract, that party must not defeat or undermine the reasonable expectations of the other. ('Implied Terms: The Foundation in Good Faith and Fair Dealing' (2014) 27 *CLP* 1))

3. Many rules that can be traced to good faith may not be evaded by agreement, eg, the rules on duress, and exemption of liability for fraud or negligently caused personal injury or death.

4. In jurisdictions that openly recognise good faith, it is certainly regarded as an externally imposed standard that cannot be evaded by agreement (eg Canada, New South Wales, and the USA; see also the Principles of European Contract Law (PECL, Article 1:102) and the UNIDROIT Principles of International Commercial Contracts (UPICC, clause 1.201 and Article 1.7 respectively)).

For these reasons, while courts undoubtedly take account of the parties' intentions, express and implied, the idea of good faith as the imposition of external standards paints a more realistic picture of what courts are doing. More importantly, it expresses the proper condition for the *legal* recognition and public enforcement of private arrangements (see 15.4.1).

15.3.3 **Good faith protects autonomy and welfare interests**

Here, it is useful to interrogate the common concepts of procedural and substantive unfairness in contract law:

- **Procedural unfairness** relates to content-independent factors such as the parties' capacities and conduct. Typically, its concern is the parties' autonomy interests, eg duress is procedurally unfair because it distorts the other party's intention to enter the contract; consequently, the contract is voidable at the option of the party prejudiced.

- In contrast, **substantive unfairness** describes content-dependent factors such as the fairness of the exchange, objectionable terms (eg penalties, exemptions of liability for fraud or negligently caused personal injury or death, statutory implied terms of satisfactory quality of goods sold). Substantive unfairness, therefore, concerns a party's welfare interests. Rules that invalidate contracts because of their unacceptable subject matter (eg babies and kidneys) can be rationalised in terms of procedural unfairness, albeit prophylactically, on the basis that invalidity guards against the risk of exploitation. Alternatively, they can be justified in terms of the interests of society; ours is just not the sort of society that trades in that sort of thing; to do so would undermine our conception of the good life or of human flourishing.

- Legal regulation of procedural unfairness is widely accepted as legitimate (since it ensures the genuineness of contractual intention), while

- legal regulation of substantive unfairness is widely rejected as:

  o *unnecessary* (because procedural fairness guarantees substantive fairness);

  o *undesirable* (as state paternalism); and

  o *impracticable* (because it imports excessive uncertainty and errors, may backfire in the long run, and redistribution should be left to the tax and welfare regime).

However, contract law is clearly more concerned about substantive unfairness (welfare interests) than it concedes:

- It is well recognised that procedural and substantive unfairness overlap to a significant degree (Atiyah, 'Contract and Fair Exchange' in *Essays on Contract* (Clarendon Press, 1986)). Since procedural unfairness precipitates substantive unfairness, it seems perverse to argue that the law is concerned with the former but not the latter. If there is no such thing as justice in the abstract, there is no such thing as a just procedure in the abstract. Once the law takes an interest in procedures, it must necessarily take an interest in substantive justice. Indeed, Kronman argues that it is impossible to generate a coherent theory of voluntariness that is not at the same time a theory of distributive justice in the sense of some specification of what advantages particular parties will be permitted to exploit vis-à-vis other parties with whom they contract. With coercion, we qualify the use of superior force. With fraud, we disallow the exploitation of a superior capacity for deception ('Contract Law and Distributive Justice' (1980) 89 *Yale Law Journal* 472).

- The overlap is reinforced by the expansion of our concept of valuable autonomy to include future autonomy. Individual autonomy is meaningful only if there is some minimum access to opportunities and resources. The law should not facilitate undertakings that threaten a party's means of living a minimally decent life. Moreover, since such contracts threaten a person's ability to care for herself and her family, leaving them to state welfare provisions, the state may be justified in adopting policies that redistribute private resources in accordance with some collective concept of distributive justice. There is a role for contract law in furtherance of this objective by attempting to constrain the gains from contracting. This is but an extension of the facility of bankruptcy, which effectively renders outstanding contracts unenforceable in order to give the bankrupt a fresh start rather than living a life of quasi-indentured servitude.

15.3.4 The specific requirements of good faith

Good faith can require that a party restrain her self-interest and take account of the counterparty's interests by:

(i) refraining from certain conduct (eg duress, fraud, not revoking unilateral offers, not revoking certain promises although they are unsupported by consideration, not abusing relationships of influence, not exploiting those with a known impairment in bargaining power);

(ii) refraining from seeking certain remedies (eg bars on specific performance, on cost of cure, on affirmation);

(iii) taking certain positive action (eg disclosure, giving notice, mitigating loss);

(iv) refraining from enforcing unfair terms (eg onerous and unusual terms, penalties, forfeitures, unreasonable standard form exemptions of liability, unfair consumer terms); or

(v) submitting to certain norms (eg objectivity, reasonableness standards, *contra proferentem* interpretation, discharge in frustrating circumstances).

15.3.5 The consequence of a breach of the duty of good faith

These are many and varied and include:

- setting aside the whole contract;
- setting aside terms within the contract;
- denial of the remedy claimed;
- imposition of additional obligations (eg implied and collateral terms or contracts);
- awarding damages (eg for misrepresentation or unjust enrichment);
- gap-filling (eg incomplete contracts);
- invalidating exercises of discretionary power;
- alteration of the contract (eg rectification for unilateral mistake, salvage, *contra proferentem* interpretation); and
- reduction of damages (eg for failure to mitigate).

15.3.6 The nature of the contract or relationship determines strength of good faith duty

The specific demands of the good faith duty will depend on the specifics of the case in question, namely:

- the terms of the contract;
- the nature and degree of the interests prejudiced;
- recognised inequality of bargaining power; and
- the nature of the contractual relationship.

As Leggatt J recognised, 'the content of the duty is heavily dependent on context and is established through a process of construction of the contract'. The failure to recognise this has generated great confusion in the discussion of good faith. The error is that good faith is assumed to be a static notion that sets down particular requirements, such as disclosure. Consequently, much of the opposition to good faith is, in truth, motivated by a rejection of the particular manifestation of good faith contended for by one of the parties in the particular circumstances of the case. It is not and indeed, given the ubiquity of manifestations of good faith instanced in 15.2, it cannot be a rejection of good faith per se. To do so would be inconsistent with the current law and entail a wholesale reform of the current law to an unimaginable shape. Rather, good faith is a matter of degree, not of kind. The question is not 'whither good faith?', but 'what does good faith demand *in the circumstances*?'.

- The analogy is to the 'neighbourhood principle' in the law of negligence set out in *Donoghue v Stevenson* (1932). The idea that people must take reasonable care not to injure others who could foreseeably be affected by their action or inaction is one of good faith. But its demands vary with the type of interests affected (eg, whether personal injury, property damage, nervous shock, or pure economic loss), and the relationship between the parties (hence, eg the categories of product liability, professional negligence, public authorities, and occupier's liability).

- Consider also the concept of 'fiduciary duty' which arises in 'fiduciary relationships', where one party is entitled to repose trust and confidence in the other party. Many different types of relationships are recognised as fiduciary, eg trustee and beneficiary, agent and principal, solicitor and client, as well as, more generally, relationships where the individual circumstances require it. However, the demands of fiduciary duties are not static, but depend on the precise nature of the parties' relationship. Millett LJ considered the core, 'distinguishing' obligation to be 'loyalty', whose 'core facets' include that a fiduciary 'must act in good faith'; this includes not profiting from his trust, not putting himself in a position where his duty and his interest may conflict, and not acting in his self-interest without the beneficiary's informed consent (*Bristol & West BS v Mothew* (1998)). Lord Browne-Wilkinson recognised the absence of a uniform concept of fiduciary duty in *Henderson v Merrett Syndicates Ltd* (1995): 'The phrase "fiduciary duties" is a dangerous one, giving rise to a mistaken assumption that all fiduciaries owe the same duties in all circumstances. That is not the case.'

Applied to good faith, we can see that its particular demands depend on:

- **the terms of the contract;** In *Mid Essex Hospital Services NHS Trust v Compass Group UK and Ireland Ltd (t/a Medirest)* (2013), an *express* term provided for good faith in respect of *some* aspects of performance, in a detailed contract for the supply of catering and cleaning services for a seven-year period. Beatson LJ observed: 'care must be taken not to construe a general and potentially open-ended obligation such as the obligation to "co-operate" or "to act in good faith" as covering the same ground as other, more specific provisions, lest it cut across those more specific provisions and any limitations in them.' He also refused to imply a duty of good faith in respect of *other* aspects of performance.

- **the seriousness of the autonomy and welfare interests affected** (hence, eg the requirements of duress depend on the seriousness of the interests prejudiced—whether to the person, to economic interest, or lawful act duress; exemptions of liability for personal injury or death are invalidated outright, while exemptions for other types of loss are only subject to the requirement of reasonableness; many causes of action or vitiating factors require very serious consequences framed in terms of 'manifest disadvantage', 'a transaction calling for an explanation', 'radical', 'fundamental', 'disproportionate', or 'unconscionable');

- **the inequality of bargaining power** (hence, eg the greater demands to have regard to the interests of consumers, employees, tenants, those dealing on the other's standard terms, those in pre-existing relationships of friendship or family that may expose them to exploitation, and ships in distress on the high seas); and

- **the nature of the contractual relationship.** In *Globe Motors, Inc v TRW Lucas Varity Electric Steering Limited, TRW Limited* (2016), Beatson LJ held that courts may be more willing to imply a duty to cooperate in contracts that involve a 'high degree of communication, co-operation and predictable performance based on mutual trust and confidence and expectations of loyalty... [which] are implicit in the parties' understanding and necessary to give business efficacy to the arrangements...the position will depend on the terms of the particular contract'. In *Yam Seng*, Leggatt J said: 'Traditionally, English law had drawn a sharp distinction between fiduciary relationships containing onerous disclosure obligations, and other contractual relationships where there was supposedly no duty of disclosure. That dichotomy was arguably too simplistic.' Thus, one can imagine a spectrum:

  - At one end are the commercial arm's-length dealings where the demands of good faith are low; subject to certain procedural safeguards (eg fraud and duress) the parties are relatively unconstrained in acting in their self-interest. Recent cases illustrate this:

    - In *Ilkerler Otomotiv Sanayai ve Ticaret Anonim v Perkins Engines Co Ltd* (2017), the Court of Appeal held that a principal was entitled to invoke a clause allowing it to terminate a distribution agreement with a distributor. The distributor's contention that the principal had breached specific good faith duties was rejected. The principal had no duty to provide the distributor with accurate appraisals of the continuing relationship, nor to provide warnings if it was considering termination so as to give the distributor an opportunity to alter its conduct or make representations. The principal was entitled to consider other distributors and there were sound commercial reasons for it not wishing to tell the existing distributor. The distributor had not been lulled into a false sense of security; the distributor's tenure was governed by the agreement. As Longmore LJ concluded, even if there is a general duty of good faith, it would not have been breached in this case.

    - In *Gold Group Properties Limited v BDW Trading Limited* (2010), the court held that the nature of the relationship (a landowner and land developer) meant that although the agreement contained an express requirement that the parties 'at all times act in good faith', this merely required the parties to act in a way that would allow both parties to enjoy the anticipated benefits of the contract and did 'not require either party to give up a freely negotiated financial advantage clearly embedded in the contract'.

o At the other end of the spectrum are parties in fiduciary relationships (eg client and lawyer, agent and principal) where the fiduciary is required to promote the beneficiary's interest at the expense of his own. The requirements here are both procedural and substantive and can be *extensive in scope*. But even here, the precise demands depend on the precise nature of the relationship and the interests affected, eg a trustee is subject to extensive fiduciary duties, whereas the fiduciary obligations of professionals such as accountants and surveyors tend to be more limited and context-dependent.

o In between these two ends is an entire range of contracts where good faith may demand more than for arm's-length contracts, but less than those in fiduciary relationships, eg:

• Leggatt J in *Yam Seng* opined that 'relational contracts', ie contracts involving a 'longer term relationship' and 'substantial commitment', may require 'a high degree of communication, cooperation and predictable performance based on mutual trust and confidence... and involve expectations of loyalty... implicit in the parties' understanding, and necessary to give business efficacy to the arrangements'. Examples of such 'relational contracts' included joint venture agreements, franchise agreements, and long-term distributorship agreements.

• Brownsword contrasts 'static market individualism' which is 'predicated upon adversarial dealings between short horizon contractors, each party seeking out his immediate advantage', and 'dynamic market individualism' where parties are driven by longer-term concerns, although they still act out of self-interest. Here, cooperative contractual relationships maximise commercial efficiency because deals are more likely where parties operate in a context of trust and confidence. ('Contract Law, Cooperation and Good Faith: The Movement from Static to Dynamic Market-Individualism' in S Deakin and J Michie (eds), *Contracts, Co-operation and Competition: Studies in Economics, Management, and Law* (OUP, 1997) 255).

• Collins rightly observes that the mere fact of a long-term contract is not sufficient; the context of the transaction 'may reveal that the long-term contract was intended to be rigid and binding'. He regards the 'crucial variable' as the point at which the contract falls on the spectrum between:

  o 'market' (where contract parties have antagonistic interests in a zero-sum game, with each seeking to gain at the other's expense); and

  o 'organisation' (where a network of contracts bind the parties together (eg employment contracts, share ownership, and directorships), and cooperation is required to maximise the joint profits to be distributed according to the contractual formula).

Implied duties of good faith 'should intensify as a contractual arrangement approaches the organizational end of the spectrum' where there is a shared expectation of performance that is not entirely self-interested, but entails loyalty, disclosure, and trustworthy behaviour. Collins describes the interdependence of the parties in such contracts as 'quasi-integrated production regimes' ('Implied Terms: The Foundation in Good Faith and Fair Dealing' (2014) 27 *CLP* 1).

Two examples illustrate this classification:

✓ A duty of good faith was implied in *Bristol Groundschool Ltd v IDC Ltd and others* (2014), in relation to a contract to develop computer-based pilot training materials. BG, in 'hacking' into IDC's computer and downloading material before it terminated the joint venture, showed a disregard for IDC's rights by acting in a way that would be regarded as 'commercially unacceptable' by reasonable and honest people in the particular context involved.

✓ In *D&G Cars Ltd v Essex Police Authority* (2015), the police authority granted a private contractor the right to dispose of cars in accordance with the police's instructions. Instead of crushing one car completely, as instructed, the contractor used the vehicle to demonstrate to staff how the chassis of vehicles could be exchanged without detection, whereupon, the police authority terminated the contract. The court described this as 'a relational contract par excellence', and stressed the need for the contractor to act with integrity and honesty in carrying out the instructions of the police authority, which was acting on behalf of the public. The court implied a term that the parties would act with honesty and integrity in operating the contract. Dove J explained:

> There may well be acts which breach the requirement of undertaking the contract with integrity which it would be difficult to characterise definitively as dishonest. Such acts would compromise the mutual trust and confidence between the parties in this long-term relationship without necessarily amounting to the telling of lies, stealing or other definitive examples of dishonest behaviour. They would amount to behaviour which the parties would, had they been asked, have identified as obvious acts which were inconsistent with the maintenance of their intended long-term relationship of fair and open dealing and therefore would amount to a breach of their contract.

15.4 *Should* English law recognise a general doctrine of good faith?

English contract law recognises no general good faith requirement. Should it?

15.4.1 **The arguments in favour of recognising good faith**

(i) *We already do it:* The discussion at 15.2 incontrovertibly illustrates the many and varied ways English contract law restrains a party's self-interest and requires regard to be paid to the legitimate interests of the counterparty. Like the character in Molière's play *Le Bourgeois gentilhomme* (Act II, sc. Iv), who was surprised and delighted to learn that he had 'been speaking prose without knowing it', the same can be said of English law in relation to good faith. The central question is not whether we should introduce it, for we already have it. Rather, it is what good faith should demand in particular circumstances.

(ii) *Transparency and coherent development:* Openly recognising good faith as the unifying principle underlying many specific contract rules and doctrines, currently dealt with under different headings, would improve the transparency of the law. It would also facilitate greater coherence and consistency in the law by identifying inconsistencies or gaps amongst the 'islands of intervention' calling for re-examination (eg *CTN Cash and Carry v Gallaher Ltd* (1994), 8.6.1(iv)) and facilitating the recognition of new rules and doctrines to address problems of unfairness present and future.

(iii) *Good faith recognised in other jurisdictions:* As Leggatt J concedes, in refusing to recognise good faith, English contract law is 'swimming against the tide'. Good faith is recognised by most systems of law—including those of:

- ✓ civil law systems such as Germany, France, and Italy;
- ✓ common law systems such as the US, Canada, and Australia;
- ✓ Scottish law;
- ✓ EU contract law directives, eg PECL, the European Draft Common Frame of Reference, and the Common European Sales Law (CESL);
- ✓ international instruments such as the Convention on International Sale of Goods (CISG) and UPICC.

(iv) *Consistent with the parties' intention:* The predominant view is that good faith duties merely give effect to the (usually presumed) intentions of the parties (*Yam Seng*). Consistently, good faith can be justified by reference to protection of the parties' 'reasonable expectations' (*First Energy (UK) Ltd v Hungarian International Bank Ltd* (1993)). As Leggatt J said in *Yam Seng*:

> [A]s the basis of the duty of good faith is the presumed intention of the parties and meaning of their contract, its recognition is not an illegitimate restriction on the freedom of the parties to pursue their own interests. The essence of contracting is that the parties bind themselves in order to co-operate to their mutual benefit. The obligations which they undertake include those which are implicit in their agreement as well as those which they have made explicit.

I have already argued at 15.3.2 that this line of reasoning is not entirely convincing.

(v) *The law should impose good faith duties:* Contracts require legal recognition and enforcement by courts. This can be justified for enhancing individual autonomy.

But, individual autonomy does not require the state to respect the parties' apparent intentions in an unqualified way (*always* and *absolutely*):

- First, the state must be equally concerned for the autonomy of all its citizens and so must insist on respectful dealing in contracting. Contract power needs to be restrained to preserve the maximum scope of freedom for all participants.
- But not all choices are worthy of support simply by virtue of being freely chosen, eg:
  - Significant inequality of bargaining power may raise concerns about the adverse results of playing the contract game for the weaker party. Contractual freedom in a capitalist system primarily means the opportunity to use property ownership in the market as a means of power over others.[2] The more powerful in the market can set the terms of the transaction in their favour. In such situations, the stronger party should not be allowed to 'push the weak to the wall' (*Lloyds Bank v Bundy* (1974)). Even boxing has weight classifications (14 in amateur and 18 in professional) to avoid unfair contests between wildly different sized participants and the predictable damage done to the smaller.
  - The state should also promote contracting in a way that is consistent with widely held notions of social justice. These can be expressed in terms of a duty to take account of the other party's legitimate interests. Accordingly, the imposition of good faith duties can be understood as the state's refusal to assist with unworthy (bad faith) conduct or choices. Shiffrin[3] speaks of the law's avoidance of complicity with exploitation; Dalton[4] refers to the restraint on self-interest necessitated by norms of *decency* and *equality*. These are external standards imposed by the courts to which the parties must adhere to when they play the contract 'game'.
  - The law should also ensure parties' minimal welfare in appropriate circumstances (hence, eg the avoidance of unconscionable bargains and the invalidity of exemptions of liability for negligently caused personal injury or death).

15.4.2 **The arguments against recognising good faith**

(i) *Interference with freedom of contract **and inconsistency with individualistic ethic:***
  - Moore-Bick LJ observed that: 'There is . . . a real danger that if a general principle of good faith were established it would be invoked as often to undermine as to support the terms in which the parties have reached agreement' (*MSC Mediterranean Shipping Co SA v Cottonex Anstalt* (2016)).

---

[2] M Weber in G Roth and C Wittich (eds), *Economy and Society* (Berkeley: University Of California Press, 1978) ii. 730. Collins, 225.

[3] S Shiffrin, 'Paternalism, Unconscionability, and Accommodation' (2000) 29 *Philosophy and Public Affairs* 203.

[4] C Dalton, 'An Essay in the Deconstruction of Contract Doctrine' (1985) 94 *Yale LJ* 997, 1024–38.

- Good faith in so far as it requires restraint on self-interest and regard for the interest of the other party 'cuts against the essentially individualistic ethic of English contract law' (R Brownsword, *Contract Law: Themes for the Twenty-First Century* (2nd edn, OUP, 2006) 114).

➡◀ Counterpoint

1. Freedom is already amply restrained: Limits on freedom of contract are so ubiquitous that we can fail to recognise it. In addition to those instanced at 15.2, there are large swathes of legislative protection afforded to the general public (eg health and safety, food safety, licensing of medical practitioners), and to specific groups (eg consumers, tenants, and employees) usually by prohibiting, controlling, or mandating certain terms and by imposing certain procedural safeguards (eg requiring advice prior to the contract or 'cooling off' periods during which parties can cancel the contract).

2. Moreover, by giving contracting parties greater security against the risk of opportunism and exploitation, imposing good faith duties may make parties **more** willing to embark on otherwise risky ventures, ie it could enhance, rather than restrict, freedom via contracting.

3. Freedom can be legitimately restrained (see 15.4.1, especially (v)).

4. The language of 'interference' with contractual freedom overlooks the fact that legal enforcement is itself a form of state 'interference'; it is a non-neutral stance in favour of one party and against the other. Indeed, it is impossible for the law to be neutral with respect to the distributive outcomes of private ordering.[5] The institution of contract is a social creation through which the community supports the agreements of its members by facilitating them and giving them greater security. These rules unavoidably operate in favour of some and against others.

5. The idea that good faith contradicts the individualistic ethic is flawed, being based on a questionable paradigm of the human actor. That person is a rugged individualist who is self-sufficient, self-knowing, and rationally self-interested. She is anonymous and atomistic; she exists without connection with others. Her diversity and complexity are pared away and she is reduced to an interchangeable sameness. Her stance towards other similarly constituted individuals is competitive: she has rights to protect her from their self-interested pursuits. This is a fiction. There is an abundance of evidence for human beings' essential irrationality (eg D Ariely, *Predictably Irrational: The Hidden Forces that Shape Our Decisions* (Harper Collins, 2009)). Moreover, it is simply delusional to view human beings as detached and self-sufficient (M Fineman, *The Autonomy Myth: A Theory of Dependency* (New Press, 2004)). Persons are embedded in society and only become persons in relations with others. Relationships are crucial to human survival and human flourishing; human beings behave relationally, their behaviour varying with the type of relationship involved. Good faith is entirely consistent with the character of human beings as social animals.

---

[5] Collins, 58.

(ii) *For Parliament, not the courts:* The concern here is one of legitimacy, that courts are going beyond their proper function through judicial law-making as unelected officials.[6] The argument is that Parliament has provided a certain degree of protection[7] for consumers, employees, and tenants amongst others; it is not the courts' place to go further.

 Counterpoint

Many urgent matters vie for parliamentary time (terrorism, crime, and so on); it is unsurprising that the details of contract law can take a low priority. But courts can take the lead given by Parliament:

- Lord Bingham MR said, in relation to UCTA that 'the common law could, if the letter of the statute does not apply, treat the clear intention of the legislature expressed in the statute as a platform for invalidating or restricting the operation of an oppressive clause' (*Timeload Ltd v British Telecommunications plc* (1995)).

- Likewise, Beatson observes that 'there are examples of statutory regimes which express a policy from which a principle can be derived being used analogically in developing the common law' ('The Role of Statute in the Development of Common Law Doctrine' (2001) 117 *LQR* 247, 299).

(iii) *Uncertainty:* Although good faith, at a minimum, includes honesty, its precise content is unclear.

 Counterpoint

Some uncertainty is unavoidable. English law regularly gives effect to other broad standards with a 'moral' flavour that can equally be said to be uncertain, eg 'fairness', 'reasonableness', 'unconscionability', 'substantial', 'radical', 'satisfactory', and 'foreseeable'. These open-textured standards, like 'good faith', are necessary for the legal system to nuance its response to the particular circumstances of transactions. As Priestly JA commented (in the Australian case of *Renard Construction (ME) Pty Ltd v Minister for Public Works* (1992)):

the ideas of unconscionability, unfairness and lack of good faith have a great deal in common. The result is that people generally, including judges and other lawyers, from all strands of the community, have grown used to the courts applying standards of fairness to contract which are wholly consistent with the existence in all contracts of a duty upon the parties of good faith and fair dealing in its performance.

---

[6] *National Westminster Bank plc v Morgan* (1985) 708; *Pao On v Lau Yiu Long* (1980) 634. Whittaker 'Good Faith, Implied Terms and Commercial Contracts' (2013) 129 *LQR* 463.

[7] Eg Consumer Rights Act 2015; Consumer Credit Act 1974; Rent Acts; Sex Discrimination Act 1975, s 6(1)(c); Disability Discrimination Act 1995, ss 4, 5, 12, 19.

(iv) *It would make the common law less attractive as the law governing contracts internationally:* Many choose English contract law to govern their contracts although neither party comes from the UK. In part, this is due to the perception that it is more certain, since it need not grapple with good faith.

 Counterpoint

If we otherwise accept the legitimacy of good faith duties, we have to question whether it should be rejected just because the (stronger) party who is in the position to choose the governing law would prefer English law because that party could then avoid its good faith duties to the other party.

(v) *Common law's preference for cautious incrementalism* of existing doctrines, over the recognition of a general broad principle.

 Pause for reflection

This is *not* so much an argument *against* good faith as an argument about the *way* in which good faith should be expressed. It is an important point. As discussed at 15.3.1, good faith currently has an explanatory and legitimising role, but it also has a *creative role* insofar as it will fuel future instances of cautious incrementalism. Moreover, as discussed at 15.3.6, this will continue whether or not good faith is overtly recognised:

• Even if good faith is overtly recognised, this would not dispense with the need to carefully identify its different manifestations and refine their particular features. Analogously, recognition of the 'neighbourhood principle' in negligence law does not dispense with the 'pockets' of intervention developed by the common law, although it may facilitate incremental extensions.

• Overt recognition of good faith is unlikely given the present judicial conservatism. This is based on the mistaken view that good faith will be extremely demanding in all circumstances. This is clearly not accurate; we have seen that its demands will depend on all the circumstances. The point here is that overt rejection of good faith will not prevent the continued development of the many and varied manifestations of good faith in existing doctrines. Moore-Bick LJ articulates the general judicial stance in *MSC Mediterranean Shipping Co SA v Cottonex Anstalt* (2016):

> The recognition of a general duty of good faith would be a significant step in the development of our law of contract with potentially far-reaching consequences... English law does not recognise any general duty of good faith in matters of contract. It has, in the words of Bingham L.J.... preferred to develop 'piecemeal solutions in response to demonstrated problems of unfairness', although it is well-recognised that broad concepts of fair dealing may be reflected in the court's response to questions of construction and the implication of terms. In my view the better course is for the law to develop along established lines.

→

- English contract law is seen as one of the UK's best exports (being the choice of law in international transactions even where parties have little or no connection to England), because of its perceived greater commitment to freedom of contract and minimal scope for the disruptive effect of good faith. Since the cases that come before the higher courts in England tend to involve valuable contracts between sophisticated parties, the demands of good faith would be minimal in any case. Refraining from overtly recognising a general principle of good faith would avoid 'scaring the horses', while doing little harm. Courts will take the same approach as they always have; one of cautious incrementalism in response to changing perceptions of what fair dealing requires in the particular context. The *extent* and speed of incrementalism, however, will be affected by the inherent cautiousness and current conservatism of the English judiciary.

15.5 What difference might a good faith doctrine make?

It is not suggested that any or all of the following possibilities are required by a good faith duty, but simply that, if the courts were to develop good faith via cautious incrementalism, the following *may* be appropriate in suitable circumstances (as they have been so found in other jurisdictions).

15.5.1 At formation

The recognition of a duty to negotiate in good faith. This is recognised under German law, French law, PECL, the European Draft Common Frame of Reference, and UNIDROIT principles. Some academics argue in favour of enforcing *express* agreements to negotiate in good faith since this upholds the parties' intentions,[8] but the law could go further and imply such a duty in appropriate circumstances. The content of such a duty may include:

- not revoking an offer before the expiry of the stipulated or an otherwise reasonable period of time;
- not entering into or continuing negotiations with no real intention of reaching an agreement with the other party; and
- not withdrawing from negotiations without giving a truthful reason, which should not be wholly unreasonable, and without giving the other party a reasonable chance to respond.

In *Knatchbull-Hugessen v SISU Capital Ltd* (2014), Leggatt J thought it open to the parties to make a collateral contract to regulate their negotiations of the main contract that would allow damages to be recovered for failed negotiations where one party acts unreasonably or concludes an agreement in secret with someone else.

---

[8] E McKendrick, 'Good Faith: A Matter of Principle?' in A Forte (ed), *Good Faith in Contract and Property Law* (Hart Publishing, 1999) 39), A Mills and R Loveridge, 'The Uncertain Future of *Walford v Miles*' [2011] *LMCLQ* 528; E Peel, 'Agreements to Negotiate in Good Faith' in A Burrows and E Peel (eds), *Contract Formation and Parties* (OUP, 2010) 37.

15.5.2 **On vitiation**

Alteration of the thresholds of qualifying invalidity or obligation (eg to disclose, or recommend independent advice). In *CTN Cash and Carry v Gallaher Ltd* (1994), the court was forced towards a conclusion that a payment pursuant to an agreement was not voidable for duress although it regarded the retention of the payment as 'at least unconscionable'. Such a case could be the occasion for development through cautious incrementalism in the future.

15.5.3 **On contents**

In appropriate circumstances, Leggatt J has suggested that what may be required of parties is:

- a high degree of communication, cooperation, and predictable performance based on mutual trust and confidence;
- duties of loyalty or fidelity to the bargain; and
- commercially acceptable conduct.

In the case of an unexpected change of circumstances that renders performance of the contract excessively onerous for a party who had not assumed such risk, good faith may require the other party to renegotiate the contract on pain of termination or alteration by the courts.

15.5.4 **On the selection of remedies**

- The threshold for barring affirmation may be lowered to avoid waste and harshness to the contract breaker.
- The remedy of price reduction can be awarded where the aggrieved party accepts non-conforming performance.
- Non-pecuniary damages may become more widely available.
- The risk of harshness to the contract-breaker can be reduced by the possibility of:
  - partial termination for 'divisible' contracts;
  - recognising the contract-breaker's right to restitution for benefits conferred post termination; and
  - treating all terms as 'innominate' terms so that termination is only allowed where the consequences of breach are drastic for the aggrieved party.

THIS CHAPTER IN ESSENCE

 The key areas and core topics in this chapter are summarised in an easy-to-use list, ideal for revision purposes, on the online resources at www.oup.com/uk/chenwishart6e/. Links to websites relevant to the topics covered and any updates to the chapter can also be found on the online resources.

QUESTIONS

1 'One of the main obstacles to the recognition of good faith is that there is no agreement as to what this means and what it would require.' Discuss.

2 To what extent can the common law be said to already manifest a commitment to good faith? *Should* the common law openly recognise a good faith obligation?

3 What *difference* would it make if good faith were openly recognised?

 For hints on how to answer these questions, please see the online resources at www.oup.com/uk/chenwishart6e/

KEY FURTHER READING

Arden, M (2013), 'Coming to Terms with Good Faith', 30 *JCL* 199.

Beatson, J and D Friedmann (1997), *Good Faith and Fault in Contract Law* (Clarendon Press).

Campbell, D (2014), 'Good Faith and the Ubiquity of the 'Relational' Contract', 77 *MLR* 475.

Collins, H (2014), 'Implied Terms: The Foundation in Good Faith and Fair Dealing', 27 *CLP* 1.

Friedmann, D (1995), 'Good Faith and Remedies for Breach of Contract' in J Beatson and D Friedmann (eds), *Good Faith and Fault in Contract Law* (Clarendon Press) 399.

McKendrick, E (1999), 'Good Faith: A Matter of Principle' in A Forte (ed), *Good Faith in Contract and Property Law* (Hart) 39.

McKendrick, E (2016), 'Good Faith in the Performance of a Contract in English Law', in L DiMatteo and M Hogg (eds), *Comparative Contract Law: British and American Perspectives* (OUP) 196.

Peel, E (2010), 'Agreements to Negotiate in Good Faith' in A Burrows and E Peel (eds), *Contract Formation and Parties* (OUP) 37.

Whittaker, S (2013), 'Good Faith, Implied Terms and Commercial Contracts', 129 *LQR* 463.

APPENDIX

ADDITIONAL CHAPTERS

Additional chapters accompanying this text can be found at
www.oup.com/uk/chenwishart6e/.

 Incapacity

This chapter examines a basis for invalidating an otherwise valid contract based on
the claimant's lack of capacity to make the contract in question. On the one hand,
the law should protect those whose self-protective abilities are impaired to an unacceptable degree. On the other hand, the law must also have regard to the interests
of those who have dealt fairly and in good faith with the incapacitated party. Thus,
although an incapacitated person is logically *incapable* of giving valid consent (rendering the contract void and of no effect), the legal consequences of incapacity often
vary. Recognised categories of personal incapacity are infancy, mental incapacity, and
significant impairment by drink or drugs. In addition to personal incapacity, certain non-natural persons such as companies and public authorities may have limited
capacity; the concern here is to protect the groups on behalf of which they act.

  (i) Children: the law adopts a strongly protective attitude to minors. In general,
they can enforce their contracts (although not by specific performance), but
are not bound by them unless they ratify them after reaching 18 years of age.
Exceptions have been created to protect those who deal fairly and in good faith
with the child and to allow children to enter beneficial contracts:

    (a) *contracts for 'necessaries'* are, on the whole, binding if they are beneficial to
the child, but not if the terms are harsh or onerous; 'necessaries' is given a
wide meaning;

    (b) *contracts beneficial to the child* overall are binding; eg, contracts to obtain
education, training, employment, medical care, and legal advice;

    (c) *contracts involving land, company shares, and partnerships* bind the minor
unless she repudiates the contract before or within a reasonable time of
attaining majority.

A contract not binding on the child may still generate *non-contractual obligations* such
as that requiring the child to make restitution of benefits received under section 3(1)
of the Minors' Contracts Act 1987.

  (ii) Mental incapacity, drink, and drugs:

(a) a person lacking capacity under the *Mental Incapacity Act 2005* cannot make a valid contract although she remains liable to pay a reasonable price for 'necessaries';

(b) *incapacity due to mental infirmity, drink, and drugs* renders a contract voidable if the complainant can show that her incapacity was known to the other party; and

(c) *lesser impairments* (short of incapacity) by those who appear sane are subject to the doctrine of unconscionable bargains.

(iii) Companies and public authorities: limiting the capacity of such *non-natural persons* is necessary to protect those on whose behalf they act (eg shareholders, lenders, taxpayers):

(a) a *company*'s capacity to contract is limited by its *objects* contained in the memorandum of association. Acts outside its objects are ultra vires (beyond its powers or capacity) and thus void. However, the Companies Act 1985 abolished the ultra vires rule as regards parties who deal in good faith with the company and the Companies Act 2006 prevents the validity of an act done by a company from being called into question on the ground of lack of capacity by reason of anything in the company's constitution;

(b) *public authorities'* powers are confined by the functions for which they were created, although there is now a statutory presumption under the Localism Act 2011 that a local authority has unlimited powers except where there is a specific restriction on it in a statute. Ultra vires contracts are void. Possible hardship is mitigated by allowing recovery of money paid and property transferred under void contracts unless this would amount to indirect enforcement of the contract.

Illegality and public policy

The so-called 'illegality' doctrine represents the most open and direct interference with contract parties' freedom to determine the *substance* of their contracts. The law may refuse to facilitate immoral or reprehensible contracts by refusing to *enforce* an illegal contract or order the restitution of any money or property transferred under it.

Statutes may prohibit the *formation, purpose, or performance* of certain contracts. Examples include prohibitions on the trade of certain weapons and body parts. The categories of common law illegality reflect changing social and moral values. They include contracts which:

- commit or further a criminal or civil wrong;
- interfere with the administration of justice;
- prejudice the state, such as trading with the enemy in wartime;
- prejudice family life;
- unduly restrict personal liberty, such as contracts of slavery;
- further sexually immoral purposes, such as prostitution;

- are in restraint of trade, whereby one party agrees to restrict its freedom to trade or conduct its profession or business in a particular locality for a specified time. Such restraints are invalid to the extent that they are unreasonable.

The effect of illegality varies. The relevant statute may stipulate the consequence of the illegality (eg impose a penalty or bar enforcement). Otherwise, the court must decide on the same general principles as apply to common law illegality.

Before the recent Supreme Court judgment in *Patel v Mirza*, courts would not generally order restitution of any money or property transferred under an illegal contract, except in exceptional circumstances including where the claimant:

- was less blameworthy than the defendant;
- had *withdrawn* from the transaction in time; or
- could establish a legal or equitable *proprietary right* to the property independent of the illegal contract.

Following the majority's reasoning in *Patel*, a more policy-based approach is likely to be taken which will balance relevant policy factors and the proportionality of denying assistance. Restitution is likely to be much more widely available. In determining whether to allow recovery, the court should consider (i) 'the underlying purpose of the prohibition that had been transgressed' and (ii) 'other relevant public policies which may be rendered ineffective or less effective by denial of the claim'; it should also keep in mind 'the possibility of overkill unless the law is applied with a due sense of proportionality' (Lord Toulson). Various **factors** might be relevant to this enquiry; Lord Toulson declined to set out a 'prescriptive or definitive list' but suggested potentially relevant factors included 'the seriousness of the conduct, its centrality to the contract, whether it was intentional and whether there was marked disparity in the parties' respective culpability'.

These principles would also now seem to apply to enforcement of an illegal contract. Before *Patel v Mirza*, the rule of thumb was that courts would not enforce contracts expressly or impliedly prohibited by statute or contrary to public policy, subject to exceptions including:

- where the purpose of the illegality was to protect a class of persons to which the claimant belongs;
- if its illegal part could be severed; and
- if the claimant was ignorant of the illegal manner in which the other party is performing an otherwise legal contract.

Following *Patel v Mirza*, it appears that enforcement may be allowed so long as it does not *subvert the policies underlying the illegality*, although the precise implications of the case are as yet unclear.

INDEX

In this index the following abbreviations are used:

C(RTP)A   Contracts (Rights of Third Parties) Act 1999
CRA   Consumer Rights Act 2015
LR(FC)A   Law Reform (Frustrated Contracts) Act 1943
UCTA   Unfair Contract Terms Act 1977
UTCCR   Unfair Terms in Consumer Contracts Regulations 1999